INTERMEDIATE ACCOUNTING

standard volume
7th ed.

Jay M. Smith, Jr., PhD, CPA
Professor of Accounting
Institute of Professional Accountancy
Graduate School of Management
Brigham Young University

K. Fred Skousen, PhD, CPA
Director, Institute of Professional Accountancy
Professor of Accounting
Graduate School of Management
Brigham Young University

Published by

A77 **SOUTH-WESTERN PUBLISHING CO.**

CINCINNATI   WEST CHICAGO, ILL.   DALLAS   PELHAM MANOR, N.Y.   PALO ALTO, CALIF.

Preface

Intermediate Accounting, Standard Volume, is a text for a second course in accounting to follow the introductory course in this subject. A companion volume *Intermediate Accounting*, Comprehensive Volume, has been prepared for those schools that can devote sufficient time to an expanded treatment of the intermediate study. Although differing in scope, each book seeks to serve the needs of two groups: (1) economics, business, or management students who do not plan to go beyond the intermediate course and (2) accounting students who expect to continue their study on an advanced level. Each group must be familiar with the objectives of accounting and the principles that have evolved in response to the objectives. They must also possess a full understanding of the nature of the basic accounting statements and the limitations involved in their preparation. With such a background, the student who does not specialize in accounting can properly interpret the statements and reports that emerge from the accounting process. Likewise, the accounting major can make important progress in the study of accounting and can look forward to achieving a full accounting competence and ultimate admission into the accounting profession.

The seventh edition of *Intermediate Accounting*, Standard Volume, is significantly changed from the sixth edition. Most accounting professors have become concerned with the explosion of accounting standards relating to financial accounting and the impact it has had on intermediate accounting courses and textbooks. More and more the textbooks have come to read like and resemble encyclopedias of accounting principles gleaned from the ever-growing number of official pronouncements.

As authors, we have wrestled with this problem, and have made a deliberate attempt to streamline the seventh edition of this well-established text. Some material that is less applicable in today's accounting environment has been condensed or eliminated. However, we have tried to be complete in our topical coverage. Major issues are identified and carefully explained, illustrated, and put into perspective by the authors, who have a total of over thirty-five years teaching experience in financial accounting topics. Given the expansion of accounting knowledge, the time allotted to teach intermediate accounting, and the varying levels of student interest and background, we feel it is essential to take this "selective approach."

A key objective of this revision is to make this edition to the most teachable intermediate text on the market. With this in mind, we have organized the twenty-one chapters into four logically related sections. Each chapter begins with a set of objectives explaining the chapter coverage. The chapter then follows a logical outline, with clearly identifed first, second, third, and in some cases, fourth-level headings. We have also added many illustrations and examples to clarify complex concepts. The exercises stress one, or perhaps two, concepts and may be used either as homework assignments or as illustrations in classroom presentations.

The seventh edition begins with a new chapter, "The Accounting Profession," which acquaints students with the field of accounting and the workings of the accounting profession. Other specific changes in the seventh edition include:

Completely revised chapters

1. Chapter 3, "The Conceptual Framework of Accounting," is completely rewritten to focus on the FASB Conceptual Framework Project. It highlights progress to date, incorporates the latest pronouncements, such as Statement of Concepts No. 1 and No. 2, and projects the direction in which the FASB seems to be heading.
2. Chapter 13, "Liabilities — Current and Contingent," includes a theoretical discussion of liabilities, and applies this discussion to many specific current and contingent liabilities. It also provides a sound, general basis for understanding specialized liability topics that are covered in separate chapters such as leases, pensions, bonds, and income taxes.
3. Chapter 18, "Nonoperating Income Components and Supplemental Disclosures," includes a discussion of "below-the-line" items (accounting changes, discontinued operations, and extraordinary items) as well as supplemental disclosures such as interim and segment reporting and forecasting.
4. Chapter 20, "Reporting the Impact of Changing Prices," covers both constant dollar and current cost accounting, focusing on the requirements of FASB Statement No. 33.

Other significant changes

1. The funds statement is introduced in Chapter 5 and covered extensively in Chapter 19. The presentation has been simplified to assist students in understanding this important statement.
2. Pedagogical aids have been added to the seventh edition; e.g., the chapter objectives mentioned earlier, shading for ease in reading and retention, and transparencies of all problems to assist in explaining solutions to problems.

We sincerely feel that this revision of *Intermediate Accounting*, Standard Volume, will have great appeal to the relatively wide spectrum of intermediate accounting professors.

These extensive changes are made in response to comments received in a survey of accounting educators and from in-depth evaluations made of the sixth edition by Professors R. Glen Berryman, University of Minnesota; Alan P. Johnson, California State University — Hayward; Donald A. Corbin, University of Hawaii; and Gorden E. Bell, Florida Atlantic University. We are especially appreciative of the careful suggestions made by these reviewers and other colleagues and know that this edition is greatly improved because of their contributions.

The authors wish to thank the Financial Accounting Standards Board, the American Institute of Certified Public Accountants, the Securities and Exchange Commission, and the American Accounting Association for permission to quote from their various publications and pronouncements.

Jay M. Smith, Jr.

K. Fred Skousen

ABOUT THE AUTHORS

Jay M. Smith, Jr., PhD, CPA, is Professor of Accounting at the Institute of Professional Accountancy, Brigham Young University. He holds a bachelor's and a master's degree from BYU and a PhD from Stanford University. He has twenty-three years of teaching experience at BYU, Stanford University, the University of Minnesota where he served as department chairman for four years, and at the University of Hawaii. He has received several awards and recognitions in accounting, including fellowships from the Danforth and Sloan Foundations, the Distinguished Faculty Award from the BYU School of Management, and several teaching excellence awards. Professor Smith has written extensively in accounting journals and has been involved in several research projects, including work done on grants from the Ford Foundation, Peat, Marwick, Mitchell & Co., and Arthur Andersen & Co. He served as editor of the Education Research Department of the Accounting Review from 1976 to 1978, as secretary to the Auditing Section of the American Accounting Association, and as a member of the editorial board for the Auditing Section's journal. He is a member of the American Institute of CPAs, the Utah Society of CPAs, and the American Accounting Association and has served on numerous committees of these organizations.

K. Fred Skousen, PhD, CPA, is Professor of Accounting and Director of the Institute of Professional Accountancy at Brigham Young University. He holds a bachelor's degree from BYU and the master's and PhD degrees from the University of Illinois. Professor Skousen has taught at the University of Illinois, the University of Minnesota, the University of California at Berkeley, and the University of Missouri. He received Distinguished Faculty Awards at the University of Minnesota and at BYU and was recognized as the National Beta Alpha Psi Academic Accountant of the Year in 1979. Professor Skousen is the author or co-author of numerous articles, research reports, and books. He served as Director of Research and a member of the Executive Committee of the American Accounting Association and is a member of the American Institute of CPAs, the Accounting Research Association, and the Utah Society of CPAs. He has also served as a consultant to the Controller General of the United States, the Federal Trade Commission, and the California Society of CPAs. He was a Faculty Resident on the staff of the Securities and Exchange Commission and a Faculty Fellow with Price Waterhouse and Co.

Contents

Part III Liabilities and Equities

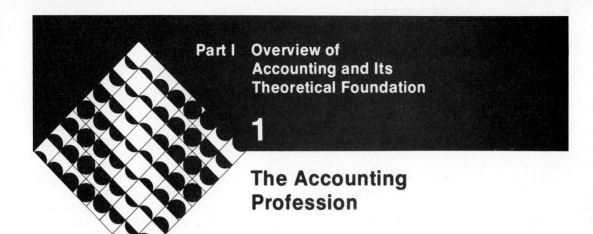

Part I Overview of
Accounting and Its
Theoretical Foundation

1

The Accounting Profession

CHAPTER OBJECTIVES

Describe the nature of accounting and the various opportunities available to students with an accounting background.

Identify the key historical events that have affected the growth and development of accounting.

Describe the public accounting profession and its entry requirements.

Identify and describe the organizations that exercise the greatest influence on the accounting profession.

Encourage students to prepare themselves for the many challenges facing accountants.

This text centers upon the accounting profession, one of society's youngest and most exciting professions. Traditionally, the term professional person has been used to designate a doctor, dentist, or lawyer — members of old and established professions. Increasingly, however, students are discovering the challenges and opportunities of accounting. To help students understand more fully the profession of accounting, this introductory chapter will focus upon (1) the different types of accountants and their attributes, (2) the historical development of the profession, and (3) the organizations which exercise considerable influence on members of the accounting profession.

1

WHAT IS ACCOUNTING?

As indicated in the following quotation, the objective of accounting is to provide information that can be used in making economic decisions.

> Accounting is a service activity. Its function is to provide quantitative information, primarily financial in nature, about economic entities that is intended to be useful in making economic decisions — in making reasoned choices among alternative courses of action.[1]

Several important concepts are included in this definition of accounting. Accounting is a **service activity**. It is intended to fulfill a **useful** function in our society by offering to provide service to various segments of the economic community involved directly or indirectly with business entities. It is primarily concerned with **quantitative financial information** describing the activities of a business, rather than qualitative, judgmental evaluations of those activities. The output of the accounting system is intended to serve as an aid to users who must make **economic decisions** between alternative actions available to them.

Economists and environmentalists remind us that we live in a world with limited resources. We must use our natural resources, our labor, and our financial wealth wisely so as to maximize their benefits to society. The better the accounting system that measures the cost of using these resources, the better the decisions that can be made for allocating them. To the extent that accounting information meets these needs, the accounting system is fulfilling its major purpose. As the needs of society and environmental conditions change, the techniques, concepts, and to some extent even the basic objectives of accounting must also change.

The profession of accounting is many faceted. To most people, accounting is equated with the designation **CPA (Certified Public Accountant)**. CPAs play a special role in the profession as independent experts in many accounting areas, especially in expressing an opinion on a firm's financial statements based on an audit of those statements. However, there are other areas open to a person trained in accounting. These include **managerial accounting**, with an emphasis on developing accounting information for use within a company; **internal auditing**, with an emphasis on the audit function within a firm; **systems analysis**, with an emphasis on combining accounting knowledge with knowledge of electronic data processing equipment to produce integrated information systems; and **tax planning and compliance**, with an emphasis on combining accounting knowledge with knowledge of federal, state, and local tax laws.

The fundamental objective of the accountant in each of these areas is to provide, or assist in providing, information useful in making a basic economic decision — how to allocate scarce resources such as capital, labor,

---

[1]*Statements of the Accounting Principles Board, No. 4*, "Basic Concepts and Accounting Principles Underlying Financial Statements of Business Enterprises" (New York: American Institute of Certified Public Accountants, 1970), par. 40.

land, and raw materials so as to achieve the goals of the particular entity involved. Internally, a major function of management is the allocation of resources among alternative projects. Do we make this product or another one? Do we open a new production plant or expand our old one? Do we increase prices or cut costs? Both management accountants and internal auditors wrestle with these and similar economic allocation problems. Systems analysts must study carefully the informational needs of an entity, and then select from alternative equipment and people configurations the one that is most efficient for the information needed. Tax specialists must determine the tax consequences associated with alternative projects.

Accounting data are essential to the making of these internal decisions. Without cost and benefit information dealing with alternative courses of action, management must make decisions in the dark based upon feelings rather than fact. Periodically, the results of these decisions must be measured and reported. This measurement and reporting activity, referred to as **financial accounting**, is the primary subject of this text. The main emphasis of this area of accounting is on the financial reporting necessary to provide information to those individuals who are interested in the financial activities of an entity, but who are not directly involved in its daily operations. These users of the reports must rely upon those managing the entity to provide a stewardship report of their activities. They are not in a position to obtain directly the information they desire. Most of these users are interested in more than one entity and need to compare entities in order to evaluate their relative efficiencies. They may wish to make choices among reporting entities to determine the extent of their economic involvement with them. Examples of these choices include investing decisions by stockholders, lending decisions by banks and other credit institutions, and employment decisions by employees. Essentially, these are all resource allocation decisions. In order to make comparisons, a consistent and comparable pattern must be followed in summarizing and reporting these activities to these varied users. The development of principles and procedures to promote uniformity, consistency, and quality in financial reporting is the subject matter of financial accounting.

Accounting is a discipline that is essential to the continued functioning of our entire economic community. The great demand for persons with backgrounds in accounting supports the theme of this introduction. This first chapter is designed to help students understand the overall profession of accounting. Regardless of the final direction an accounting student takes, intermediate accounting is basic to the development of the expertise required for any area within the profession.

HISTORICAL DEVELOPMENT OF ACCOUNTING

Accounting has been called "the language of business." Its development has closely paralleled the needs arising from reporting increasingly complex business and economic transactions. Among the earliest accounting records were those kept as part of the feudal system during the early middle ages. Lords of the manors collected taxes from their subjects, and used the proceeds to further the work of the estate and to meet their personal needs. A report of stewardship was prepared by the more conscientious of the lords for review by their subjects. Another activity about this time that involved the accountant's skills was the maintaining of voyage records for those involved with trade between countries. These records were usually maintained for a single voyage, at the end of which the records were closed, and the profit or loss was calculated. Banking institutions, which arose in the 11th and 12th centuries in the Italian states, often lent money to finance the voyages. These various business activities required a record of income and outgo, especially when the spoils were divided at the end of the voyage.

Because many of these business ventures originated in the European countries bordering on the Mediterranean Sea, such as Spain, Portugal, Italy, and Greece, it is not surprising that one of the earliest treatises in accounting was written by an Italian monk, Luca Paciolo. He was really a mathematician who used his analytical skills to describe the system of double-entry accounting which had been evolving for decades. The work was first published in 1494 and carried the title *Summa de Arithmetica Geometria Proportioni et Proportionalita.*

Accounting did not progress rapidly as a discipline until business began to grow in size, and until a need arose to distinguish more clearly between the ownership of the entity and its operation. The Industrial Revolution had its birth in England, and it was there that the increased need for accounting developed. In 1845, the first Companies Act was passed permitting a business to be organized as a company with the status of a legal entity. These companies could borrow money, issue stock, pay debts, and carry on activities in the same manner as an individual. This new organizational form permitted the pooling of capital by many individuals to acquire the economic resources necessary to produce the newly invented goods. But as many different individuals provided financial resources to carry out the business function, a need arose to account to them for the use of these resources. This accounting took the form of financial reports which summarized the increase or decrease in resources over a period of time, and the current status of the resources. In the United States, this concept of separate legal entities became popular as states such as New York, Vermont and Massachusetts passed corporation laws and created new entities with the same attributes as their English counterparts.

As the Industrial Revolution took hold in the United States, companies quickly grew in size. Large personal fortunes were invested in companies, marking the beginnings of Standard Oil, American Telephone and Telegraph, Ford Motor Company, and other twentieth-century industrial giants. Accounting systems became even more important following the adoption in 1913 of the Sixteenth Amendment to the U.S. Constitution giving the federal government the power to tax income. This placed added emphasis upon the concept of income to measure the ability of individuals and corporations to supply resources to the government for expanded social and defense needs.

A serious problem was emerging as the need for accounting increased. Because the discipline had grown so rapidly, and because business activities were changing at an ever-increasing pace, accounting procedures had to be developed without extended debate or discussion. Accountants developed methods that seemed to meet the needs of their respective companies, resulting in diverse procedures among companies in accounting for similar activities. The comparability of the resulting financial reports, therefore, often was very questionable. Management could manipulate the records and produce significantly different results depending upon the desired objective. During the 1920s, the differences led to financial statements that were often inflated in value. Market values of stocks rose higher than the underlying real values warranted until the entire structure collapsed in the Great Depression of the early 1930s. The government of the United States, under the leadership of President Franklin D. Roosevelt, vigorously attacked the depression, and among other things, created the Securities and Exchange Commission (SEC). The new agency was given a responsibility to protect the interests of stock investors by preventing a recurrence of the conditions that led to the stock market crash in 1929. In 1933, Congress passed the Securities Act and in 1934, the Securities Exchange Act. The broad power granted to the SEC by Congress will be more fully discussed in a separate section. The emergence of the SEC forced the accounting profession to unite and to become more diligent in developing accounting principles and ethics to govern the profession. The SEC required independent audits of companies that came under its jurisdiction. This was a great boost to the field of auditing, and has resulted in a tremendous increase in the number of certified public accountants who fill the role of independent auditor.

World War II brought a pause in the growth of the profession, but the prosperity that followed the war and the introduction of electronic data processing equipment into business systems created needs for increasingly sophisticated accounting systems. New high-technology industries such as television, aerospace, electronics, and synthetic fibers required systems that could organize vast amounts of accounting data into financial reports needed to meet varied users' needs. More responsibility was forced onto the professional accountants by the courts as class-action civil suits and even criminal suits were brought against accountants who were accused of being negligent in performing their functions.

Recently, Congressional committees have been studying the profession, and have proposed legislation to further control the profession and overcome perceived weaknesses in it. These include the Metcalf Committee, a Senate committee that published a mammoth report in 1977 called the *Accounting Establishment*, and the Moss Committee, a House of Representatives committee that drafted and introduced legislation to regulate the accounting profession. These committees are now led by other congressmen, but they are still conducting a surveillance of the profession. At the present time, control over the profession is still nominally held by the private sector. As a result of the profession's efforts to retain the right of self-regulation, the quality of audits is improving, and there appears to be a trend toward more accountability on the part of CPAs.

This brief review of accounting history demonstrates clearly how accounting in the United States has changed to keep pace with a rapidly changing economy. Similar changes have occurred in other countries, and more international co-operation in accounting is taking place each year. With the past as a guide, it can be assumed that there are many exciting challenges ahead for those who are part of the accounting profession. The organizations that will be instrumental in helping direct these changes are identified in the following sections.

PUBLIC ACCOUNTING

Members of certain professions — notably medicine and law — are charged with an especially high degree of public responsibility. Characteristics of such a profession include the licensing of members and a restriction on entry into the profession based upon such variables as education, experience, and the passing of a qualifying examination. Public accounting acquired these characteristics early in its development. England and its related countries in the British Empire identified its professionals as "Chartered Accountants" (CAs), and in the United States the designation became "Certified Public Accountant" (CPA).

The CPA Certificate

Public accounting developed rapidly in response to the need to add a degree of credibility to the financial statements being issued to investors and other users. The first CPA certificate was issued by the State of New York in 1896. It followed the pattern developed in England where the first CA certificate was issued in 1854. The establishment of laws providing for public accounting certification quickly spread to other states. By 1908 there were sixteen states issuing CPA certificates, and by 1925, all states and territories had provisions to control entry into public accounting. Requirements for certification varied, but typically included passing a written examination and obtaining experience in public accounting for a specified period of time.

Unlike the situation in England, the authority to regulate professions developed by states rather than by a central governmental agency. Upon meeting the certification requirements of a particular state, an individual could practice as a CPA only in that state. As the mobility of CPAs increased, and as CPA firms expanded from local offices to become regional, national, and international in scope, it became increasingly necessary to grant CPAs reciprocity across state lines without taking another written examination. This led to the states uniting with the profession to give a uniform CPA examination in all states and territories. The first uniform examination was given in 1917 in three states. This grew to 30 states by 1936, and in 1952, the last state adopted the uniform examination making it effective throughout the United States. This process differs from both the legal and medical professions that require separate examinations in each state.

The CPA examination is given over a 2½ day period the first week of May and the first week of November. It is given simultaneously in hundreds of locations throughout the country. Grading usually takes about three months, and is done uniformly under the direction of the American Institute of Certified Public Accountants (AICPA), the national professional body that has been given the authority to prepare and control the examinations. The examination contains four sections: (1) Accounting Practice, 2 parts, (2) Accounting Theory, (3) Auditing, and (4) Business Law. Some states add a fifth section dealing with ethics. The nationwide average pass rate on each section is about 30 percent, however, only about 10 percent pass the entire examination in one sitting. Most states permit a candidate to "conditionally pass" sections of the examination. This means that if the other sections are passed within a certain time period, the certificate will be granted without retaking the previously passed sections. Pass rates are affected greatly by the preparation of the students, including educational background and experience. For serious candidates, the pass rate is considerably higher than the above averages indicate.

The various states have still maintained the right to specify the experience and education requirements necessary for professional certification. These vary from no experience to three years' experience under the direction of a CPA, and from no specific education to a master's degree in accounting. After meeting a state's initial requirements for professional entry, annual dues must be paid to the state to maintain a valid certificate. Many states also require that CPAs meet certain continuing education requirements to retain the right to practice. Because each of these requirements is governed by state statutes, it is very difficult to bring them into uniformity. The AICPA has recommended that certain minimum guidelines for professional education be met, both for entry and for continuing education, but achieving the desired uniformity is a slow process.

As indicated in the table below, the number of professional accountants holding the CPA certificate has increased dramatically over the past ten

Year	Individuals Holding CPA Certificate (estimated)	Individuals Holding Membership in AICPA
1950	38,000	16,000
1960	70,000	38,000
1970	114,000	75,000
1973	146,000	95,000
1975	172,000	112,000
1977	200,000	130,000
1979	230,000	150,000

Sources: *Annual Report*. 1978–79, AICPA.
John L. Carey, *The Rise of the Accounting Profession*, (New York: American Institute of Certified Public Accountants, 1969), Vol. 1, p. 1.

years. Over 50,000 individuals sit for the examination each time it is offered. Although other accounting certificates have been introduced in the United States in the past ten years, namely the Certified Management Accountant (CMA) certificate and the Certified Internal Auditor (CIA) certificate, the CPA is still the most universally accepted evidence of professional accounting competence. Intermediate accounting is especially valuable in preparing candidates for the accounting practice and accounting theory sections of the examination.

The Relationship Between Accountants and Auditors

One of the frequently confused elements of the accounting profession is the distinction between accountants and auditors. **Accountants** have the responsibility for preparing the financial statements of an entity in accordance with generally accepted accounting principles. They may also design the system that accumulates the data for the statements and prepare the many government and industry reports required. Some accountants perform these services for only one entity as an employee of that enterprise. Other accountants provide these services for several companies and are thus **public accountants**. Some states require a person to be certified before using the words "public accountant." Noncertified accountants in these states must use other titles, such as "public bookkeeper." In other states, noncertified public accountants are licensed and controlled but do not have to take a qualifying examination or meet specific education or experience requirements. Many of these states enacted laws providing for registration of public accountants already practicing but made no provisions for new public accountants to enter the profession. This legislation is referred to as "dying class" legislation because in time, no public accountants will be left.

Auditors review the work done by accountants and, acting independently from management, issue opinions as to the fairness of the financial statements and their adherence to the generally accepted principles of accounting. Unlike lawyers, the auditor does not serve solely as an advocate for the client who pays for the services. An auditor should be protecting the interests of society as an independent expert. The relationship between a professional accountant, the client, and society is unique to the accounting profession. Auditors generally have many clients, thus they are also public. Some auditors, however, work for only one entity, and like certain accountants, are employees of that enterprise. These auditors are generally referred to as **internal auditors**, while the public auditors are known as **external auditors**. Much of the work done by CPAs, especially those in large CPA firms, relates to auditing rather than accounting. In addition to the required accounting skills, an auditor must possess skills in evaluating evidence that supports the amounts shown in the financial statements prepared by the accountant. This text relates only indirectly to auditing. Its major emphasis is upon the accounting principles that the accountant and the auditor must apply to elements in the financial statements.

Development of Large CPA Firms — The Big 8

Because of the importance of personal liability for professional conduct, professional firms are generally organized as either a proprietorship or a partnership. Only recently have state laws been changed to permit "professional corporations." These special corporations provide for many of the benefits of corporate structure, but still retain the personal liability of the professionals involved. As the accounting profession developed, the partnership form of organization became the most common. Over time, eight of these partnerships have become dominant in the United States. Each has spread its influence internationally, and all are now recognized as international organizations. The dominant role they play in relation to the United States economy is reflected in the following statistics. Approximately 85 percent of all companies listed on the New York Stock Exchange and the American Stock Exchange are clients of the Big 8 firms. Approximately 84 percent of all corporate profits in the United States are earned by clients of the Big 8 firms.[2] In 1977 the Big 8 firms audited 478 of the Fortune 500 companies.[3] Each of these firms has many offices, with offices in foreign countries often operated through a foreign national partner or affiliate firm.

Some of the Big 8 had their beginnings in England in the late 1800s and came to the United States as part of the shift in emphasis to the United States as the Industrial Revolution crossed the ocean. As business on this side of the Atlantic Ocean became prominent, these firms changed their headquarters to the United States and became recognized as primarily American firms with international affiliations. Other Big 8 firms originated in the United States and grew domestically first, then spread internationally. The chart below identifies these firms and includes some pertinent

Selected Data on Big 8 Accounting Firms

Name of Firm (Previous name)	Location of Home Office	Date Organized	1975[4] Number of U.S. Employees	Number of U.S. Partners	Number of U.S. Offices	Number of Offices Outside U.S.	1977[5] World-Wide Revenue (millions)	Number of Fortune 500 Clients
Arthur Andersen & Co.	Chicago	1913	8,554	638	48	58	471	72
Arthur Young & Company	New York	1894	4,800	414	64	150	390	52
Coopers & Lybrand (Lybrand, Ross Bros, and Montgomery)	New York	1898	6,189	521	81	242	490	50
Deloitte Haskins & Sells (Haskins & Sells)	New York	1895	4,798	443	93	137	410	53
Ernst & Whinney (Ernst & Ernst)	Cleveland	1903	5,795	484	112	146	385	61
Peat, Marwick, Mitchell & Co.....	New York	1897	8,297	791	100	199	516	67
Price Waterhouse & Co.	New York	1850	5,933	348	67	203	479	99
Touche, Ross & Co. (Touche, Niven, Bailey & Smart)	New York	1900	4,219	451	76	235	350	24

[2]U.S., Congress, Senate, Subcommittee on Reports, Accounting and Management of the Committee on Government Operations, *The Accounting Establishment: A Staff Study*, 94th Cong., 2d sess., 1976, p. 411.

[3]Peter W. Bernstein, "Competition Comes to Accounting," *Fortune* (July 17, 1978), p. 92.

[4]*The Accounting Establishment, loc. cit.*

[5]Bernstein, *loc. cit.*

data concerning them. Much of the data included in the figure were collected by the Metcalf Committee staff and were reported in *The Accounting Establishment*. Although each of the Big 8 has grown since the information was gathered, the data help to convey a feeling for the size of these firms.

Much of the criticism of the accounting profession by Congress and governmental bodies such as the Federal Trade Commission (FTC) has been directed to the monopoly position occupied by the Big 8 as reflected in the preceding data. However, members of these firms emphasize that among the Big 8, things are highly competitive. Different viewpoints on many issues are discussed openly, and there is no "single bloc" voting on issues such as accounting principles or accounting regulations. Big 8 firm members also correctly emphasize that many of their clients are very large multinational companies, and that only an accounting firm with similar size and scope of operations can provide the type of services needed by these entities.

Most large CPA firms are divided into three major areas: (1) Audit, (2) Tax, and (3) Management Advisory Services (MAS). Within each of these areas, a definite ordering of professionals has become traditional. New members of the firm are generally hired directly from college and begin as staff accountants. They progress through positions of senior staff, manager, and partner if they remain with the firm. In some firms, there are two supervisory levels between senior and partner. Responsibilities increase as the professional advances in the firm. Most partners reach their position within ten to fifteen years after being hired. Although salaries vary, it is not unusual for a partner to be earning well in excess of $100,000 per year.

Medium and Small Public Accounting Firms

There are several other firms with national, and a few with international, offices; however, they are significantly smaller than the Big 8. Among these firms, a merger movement seems to be accelerating which could lead to challenges to the Big 8 in the future. The "Second 7" was defined by the *Los Angeles Times* in September 1979 as follows:

Firm	Home Office
Alexander Grant & Co.	New York
Fox and Company	Denver
Pannell Kerr Forster	New York
Laventhol & Horwath	Philadelphia
McGladrey Hendrickson & Co.	Davenport, Iowa
Main Hurdman	New York
Seidman & Seidman	Houston

Many of the Second 7 began more recently as local and regional firms, and have expanded greatly through internal growth and mergers. Although their clients do not include as many of the corporate giants as the Big 8, they exercise considerable influence over medium and small corporations and governmental entities. It is interesting to note that while six of the Big 8 are headquartered in New York, only three of the next seven call New York their home.

The activities of the second tier of CPA firms are very similar in scope and variety to those of the Big 8. However, in the many smaller CPA firms which operate on a local or regional level, relatively more of the work is centered in the tax and systems planning areas, with some public accounting or recordkeeeping being performed. The role of the audit work becomes less important. A CPA in a small firm is expected to be something of an accounting generalist as opposed to the more specialized positions of CPAs in large regional and national firms. Not only do CPAs in these larger firms specialize in audit, tax, or MAS, they also tend to specialize in certain industries. A vital role is played by the medium and small CPA firms. Although their clients may not have as wide a variety of problems, they often have problems that are just as challenging as those faced by the clients of the Big 8 firms.

ORGANIZATIONS INFLUENCING AND REGULATING THE PROFESSION

An auditor's opinion on the financial statements is recognized as a label of credibility. In order to preserve this credibility, the profession has found it necessary to establish regulations for members within the profession, and to establish standards and principles to govern the work done by the professional people. Different organizations have in the past exercised influence over this regulation, and currently, some of these organizations are being examined carefully by Congress to see if they are adequately meeting the control objectives. The major organizations involved include the American Institute of Certified Public Accountants (AICPA), state boards and state societies of accountants, the Financial Accounting Standards Board (FASB), the Securities and Exchange Commission (SEC), and the American Accounting Association (AAA).

American Institute of Certified Public Accountants (AICPA)

The **American Institute of Certified Public Accountants** is the professional organization of practicing certified public accountants in the United States. The organization was formed in 1887 and was originally named the American Institute of Accountants. A monthly publication, the *Journal of Accountancy*, was first issued by the Institute in 1905, providing a means of communication concerning the problems of accounting and the challenges and responsibilities faced by the profession.

One of the major functions of the AICPA is to assist the states in the regulation of those entering the profession by administering and grading the Uniform CPA Examination. Other responsibilities include establishing and enforcing rules of professional conduct (professional ethics), establishing standards of auditing practice, representing and speaking for the members of the profession to government, education, and the business community, and, in the past, establishing generally accepted accounting principles. This latter responsibility has now been largely assumed by the Financial Accounting Standards Board (FASB), an entity organized separately from the AICPA. Only CPAs may belong to the Institute; membership, however, is voluntary. At the present time, about 65 percent of CPAs belong to the Institute (see page 7).

Although membership in the AICPA has been traditionally individual, the influence of the firm is often felt through the individual's participation in Institute activities. Because of this influence, and because the duties and responsibilities of members in large firms often differ from those in medium and small firms, the AICPA has instituted a firm membership in one of two sections: (1) the **SEC practice firms** section for firms that have clients subject to SEC registration and reporting requirements, and (2) the **private companies practice firms** section for those firms that do not have SEC clients. The SEC practice firms are subject to more stringent regulation than the private companies practice firms, although a high quality of performance is expected of all firms. The regulation of firms and establishment of these divisions was one of the actions taken by the AICPA to satisfy the governmental committees that were critical of the profession.

State Boards and State Societies

There are two groups within the states that assume responsibility for the professional activities of certified public accountants: (1) state boards and (2) state societies. The members of a **state board of accountancy** are normally appointed by the governor of the state. The state board is responsible for determining and regulating the admission requirements of new members into the profession. This responsibility includes administering the examination and evaluating the candidate's education and experience prior to the issuance of a certificate. Once a state board has approved issuance of a certificate, it must further determine that the appropriate regulations governing the use of the certificate are followed by those who are recognized as CPAs. These boards, therefore, have the power to issue and to revoke the CPA certificate.

The **state societies of certified public accountants** are responsible for meeting the professional organizational needs of the members in each state. State societies are presently independent organizations; however, they maintain close relationships with the staff of the AICPA. National committee assignments of the Institute, for example, are generally initiated by the state societies. Several state societies are also instituting continuing education requirements, often utilizing AICPA course offerings as one means of satisfying these requirements. While not all states have adopted mandatory continuing education requirements, there is a definite trend in that direction.

Neither the Institute nor the state societies can issue or revoke a certificate. They may admit and suspend members from their respective organizations based upon their own rules and regulations; however, they cannot prevent one from using the "CPA" designation.

Financial Accounting Standards Board (FASB)

In 1973, the **Financial Accounting Standards Board** was organized and given the private sector responsibility for establishing standards of financial accounting and reporting. The Board is an independent organization consisting of seven salaried, full-time members drawn from professional accounting and business. The headquarters of the Board is in Stamford, Connecticut. The Board has its own research staff and an annual budget in excess of 6 million dollars. Its major function is to study accounting issues and produce **Statements of Financial Accounting Standards** and **Statements of Financial Accounting Concepts**. Prior to issuing these statements, the Board typically appoints a task force of technical experts who study the existing literature and prepare and distribute a *Discussion Memorandum* that identifies the principal issues involved with a given accounting topic. The memorandum usually includes a discussion of the various points of view as to the resolution of the issues, but does not come to a specific conclusion. An extensive bibliography is usually included. Readers of the discussion memorandum are invited to comment either in writing or orally at a public hearing. Based upon the discussion memorandum and the input from interested readers, the Board issues an *exposure draft* of a Statement which includes specific recommendations for financial accounting and reporting. Reaction to the exposure draft is requested from the accounting and business community, and after this input is received and analyzed, the Board issues a final Statement.

Statements of *standards* are recognized by the profession as representing the generally accepted position of the profession, and must be followed unless circumstances warrant an exception to the standard. When exceptions to **generally accepted accounting principles (GAAP)** are necessary, the accountant must clearly disclose the nature of and reason for the deviation in the financial statements. Failure to include the disclosure is a violation of Rule 203 of the professional Code of Ethics issued by the AICPA. Statements of *concepts* do not establish accounting principles within the meaning of Rule 203, but "are intended to set forth objectives and fundamentals that will be the basis for development of financial accounting and reporting standards."[6]

The FASB is continually called upon to clarify and interpret its standards. In response to these requests, the Board issues interpretations of standards. *Interpretations* are reviewed and approved by the Board in the same manner as standards and have the same authority as standards. Thus, failure to follow an FASB Interpretation is a departure from GAAP. The FASB authorized its staff to issue *Technical Bulletins* to provide guidance on a timely basis concerning the application of accounting principles. They do not establish new financial accounting and reporting standards or amend existing standards.[7] Although the Board does not approve bulletins,

---

[6]*Statement of Financial Accounting Concepts No. 3,* "Elements of Financial Statements of Business Enterprises" (Stamford: Financial Accounting Standards Board, 1980), p. i.

[7]*Financial Accounting Standards Board Technical Bulletin No. 79-1,* (Stamford: Financial Accounting Standards Board, December 28, 1979), par 3.

members of the Board are kept informed of the matters proposed for bulletins and are given the opportunity to review proposed bulletins prior to issuance.

Prior to the formation of the FASB, accounting principles were established under the direction of the AICPA. From 1939–1959, principles were formed by the *Committee on Accounting Procedures (CAP)*. Their pronouncements were known as *Accounting Research Bulletins (ARBs)*. From 1959 to 1973, principles were formed by the *Accounting Principles Board (APB)* and issued as *Opinions*. Pronouncements of a conceptual nature were also issued by the APB. These *APB Statements*, like the FASB's Statements of Concepts, did not establish accounting principles. Dissatisfaction with the part-time nature of these boards, their failure to react quickly to some issues, and the lack of broad representation on the boards because of their direct relationship to the AICPA, led to the formation in 1972 of a special AICPA committee headed by a former commissioner of the SEC. This committee recommended the organization that became known as the Financial Accounting Standards Board.

The FASB is organized independently from the AICPA, although the AICPA does continue to have a major impact through its funding and involvement in the organizational structure. The Board is directly controlled by the Financial Accounting Foundation, composed of nine trustees appointed by the Board of Directors of the AICPA. The trustees are selected from nominees submitted from the six sponsoring institutions which are:

1. American Accounting Association (academe)
2. American Institute of Certified Public Accountants (public accounting)
3. Financial Analysts Federation (investors and investment advisors)
4. Financial Executives Institute (corporate executives)
5. National Association of Accountants (management accountants)
6. Securities Industry Associates (investment bankers)

In addition, there is a trustee-at-large who is endorsed by the principal national associations in the banking industry. The Foundation has the responsibility of appointing members of the FASB, of appointing a Financial Accounting Standards Advisory Council of at least twenty members (usually about thirty-five members have been appointed), of raising funds necessary to support the Board, and of periodically reviewing and revising the organizational structure. Approximately half of the funding comes from industry and the financial community; the other half from the public accounting profession. No single annual contribution of more than $50,000 can be accepted under the Foundation by-laws.

Securities and Exchange Commission (SEC)

The **Securities and Exchange Commission** was created by an act of Congress in 1934. Its primary role is to regulate the issuance and trading of securities by corporations to the general public. The Commission's intent is not to prevent the trading of speculative securities, but to insist that investors have adequate information. Thus, the SEC's objective is to insure *full and fair disclosure* of all material facts concerning securities offered for public investment. The SEC may use its statutory authority to prescribe accounting and reporting requirements for all companies falling under its jurisdiction. This includes most major companies in the United States.

The regulations of the SEC require independent audits of annual financial statements. The SEC reviews both the reports and the supporting verification to ascertain compliance with the law. The principal governing acts of the SEC are the Securities Act of 1933 and the Securities Exchange Act of 1934. Although the SEC has the power to issue regulations declaring how corporations should report financial affairs to shareholders, it has, for the most part, relied upon the accounting profession, through the AICPA and FASB, to perform this function.[8]

The pronouncements of the SEC are known as *Accounting Series Releases (ASRs)* and *SEC Staff Bulletins*. As of the beginning of the 1980s, over 260 ASRs had been issued by the SEC. Congress has urged the SEC to take a more active role in the regulation of the profession and requires an annual report from the SEC as to its evaluation of the profession. The first of these reports was issued in 1978. In the 1979 report, the SEC concluded:

> The Commission remains unconvinced that comprehensive direct governmental regulation of accounting or accountants would afford the public either increased protection or a more meaningful basis for confidence in the work of public accountants.[9]

American Accounting Association (AAA)

The **American Accounting Association** was known as the American Association of University Instructors in Accounting from 1918 until 1935, when its name was changed to its present designation. The AAA is primarily an organization for accounting educators, although others are admitted to membership. A quarterly journal, the *Accounting Review*, is sponsored by the AAA. Articles in the *Accounting Review* generally discuss matters of accounting theory as compared with articles in the *Journal of Accountancy* that are primarily concerned with matters of accounting practice. AAA committee reports and discussions of these reports are available to AAA members upon request. Selected research projects are published by the AAA in the accounting research monograph series.

Although the AAA has a permanent executive secretary, its officers and committees rotate each year among the members. The AAA does not claim to serve as a majority voice for accounting educators. Its major role is to serve as a forum within which individual educators can express their views either individually or in specially appointed committees. Another important objective is to encourage and support research activity designed to add new understanding in the field of accounting.

---

[8]For additional information on the nature and workings of the SEC, see K. Fred Skousen, *An Introduction to the SEC*, revised ed. (Cincinnati: South-Western Publishing Co., 1980).

[9]Report to Congress of the SEC on Accounting Regulation, 1979.

Recently, sections of interest have developed within the AAA. The largest of these is the auditing section, with over 1,000 members and with its own journal scheduled for the early 1980s. Other sections include tax, not-for-profit, historians, and management advisory services.

Other Organizations

Although the aforementioned groups have traditionally exercised the most direct influence upon the regulation of accountants and the establishment of accounting principles, the influence of other groups has also been felt. The **Financial Executives Institute (FEI)**, formerly the Controllers' Institute, is a national organization composed of financial executives employed by large corporations. The FEI membership includes treasurers, controllers, and financial vice-presidents. The FEI publishes a monthly journal, *The Financial Executive*, and has sponsored several research projects relating to financial reporting problems. These research projects have covered a variety of topics including the manner in which a company operating in a number of industries should report the financial progress attained by different company segments, the effect of price-level adjustments upon managerial decisions, the concept of materiality in financial reporting, and the accounting problems of multinational companies.

The **Cost Accounting Standards Board (CASB)** is another important standard-setting body. The CASB was established in 1970 by act of Congress and charged with the responsibility of setting cost accounting standards to be followed by contractors in negotiated defense contracts. The CASB has issued several standards; however, because of their restricted focus, these standards have had limited impact upon financial accounting in general.

Another influential group is the **National Association of Accountants (NAA)**. This organization is more concerned with the use of accounting information within the enterprise than with external reporting, and thus has directed its research primarily toward cost accounting and information systems. Its monthly publication, *Management Accounting*, has traditionally dealt mainly with problems involving information systems and the use of accounting data within the business organization. Because a firm's information system can provide information for both internal and external users, the NAA is concerned about the relationship of accounting principles for internal reporting to those for external reporting.

Several societies of financial analysts have been formed. The most prominent of these groups is the **Financial Analysts Federation**. Admittance to this group is based upon a qualifying examination. Because financial analysts are a major user of external accounting reports, they are very much concerned with the present status of financial reporting. Members of this group have often been critical of corporate financial reporting practices and have continued to request increased disclosure of pertinent financial data.

ATTRIBUTES OF PROFESSIONAL ACCOUNTANTS

A decision to pursue a particular career should be based on an understanding of the nature of the work involved. Accounting can be very rewarding, but at times very demanding. In addition to the requisite technical skills, a successful accountant or auditor must possess certain personal attributes and, perhaps most important of all, a genuine interest in performing the work.

Among the many important attributes a person who provides accounting services must have are the following: (1) an **analytical** mind, one that can look at many detailed parts and generalize to an evaluation of the whole; (2) an **orderly** mind, one that can organize many complex business transactions and summarize them into meaningful reports for the benefit of one or more users; and (3) a **quick** and **efficient** mind, one that can rapidly see the interrelationships of data.

In addition to these intellectual qualities, a successful accountant must relate well with people, and be able to communicate clearly, both orally and in writing. In many ways, an accountant must be a salesperson who can convince others of the importance of accounting reports. It is in this "people" area that many accountants fail to meet the needs of the profession. Students who possess a combination of these intellectual and social qualities are likely to find accounting very rewarding.

Accountants work under varying degrees of pressure. Deadlines are important, as financial decisions often must be made quickly and as accurately as possible. CPAs often must meet client deadlines for issuing new securities or satisfying demands of investors and creditors. Because of this pressure, hours are frequently long, especially as deadlines approach. Accountants are primarily selling their time and must develop the skill to work rapidly, but with accuracy.

CHALLENGES FOR THE PROFESSION

The profession of accounting is still experiencing growing pains. As the requirements for knowledge increase, students must be willing to stay longer in school preparing for professional entry, and be willing to continue the educational process throughout their careers. The larger public accounting firms have extensive training programs. It is not unusual for professionals in these firms to spend one or more months a year in formal training sessions.

Accountants do not work in a vacuum. Many currently unresolved issues, such as accounting for inflation, accounting for gas and oil producers, and accounting for foreign exchange rates have world-wide political and economic implications. As the economies of the world continue to become more interrelated and the international impact of business decisions becomes increasingly widespread, accountants must be willing to devote their talents to reporting events as they transpire in a clear and orderly fashion to facilitate the economic and political decision-making process.

QUESTIONS

1. What is the major function of accounting in our society?

2. Identify and describe briefly the different types of accountants within the accounting profession.

3. What is the nature of financial accounting?

4. How did the development of the corporate form of organization affect the need for accounting?

5. Why is comparability of financial statements among companies important?

6. The owner of a business is planning to sell and has requested a CPA to prepare statements for the information of prospective buyers. "Don't use your regular statements," the owner instructs the CPA, "because I want to get as much as I can. Make the business look as good as possible." Would it be proper for the CPA to prepare statements that are different from those ordinarily prepared for the client at the end of the year? If so, what form would they take?

7. What factors are present in our society that are tending toward public regulation of the accounting profession?

8. What are the requirements an accountant must meet to be a CPA?

9. Distinguish between an accountant and an auditor.

10. What factors have led to the development of large international CPA partnerships?

11. How does the mix of accounting work differ between the few large national and international CPA firms and the thousands of smaller regional and local firms?

12. What is the principal function of the AICPA, and how does the Institute relate to the state boards and state societies?

13. How is the FASB organized and supported?

14. How does the SEC influence the accounting profession?

15. What attributes are most critical to becoming a competent professional accountant?

16. Why is accounting considered an exacting profession?

EXERCISES

exercise 1-1

Three college students, Owen West, Ken Busbee and Cynthia Romans, are considering a career in accounting. They met at a careers day exhibit, and began discussing their perceptions of what an accounting career would be like. To Owen, accounting was a field in which he could use his great love for mathematics. "I have always done well in math classes, and see accounting as nothing more than applied mathematics. Anything to avoid taking more English." Ken saw the field differently. To him, an accountant has to be able to communicate clearly to others and in an organized way. "I really get a bang out of convincing people to see things my way. Accounting provides the facts that make presentations more persuasive." Cynthia thought that accounting offered many different opportunities and that the demand for accountants was so great that almost any combination of intellectual and social abilities would be successful. "I like the idea of being able to become an expert in some aspect of accounting, and thus name my price." After some discussion, they decided to meet with an accounting professor for more information. Professor Woodfield agreed to the meeting. As Professor Woodfield, how would you react to these points of view?

exercise 1-2

Beta Alpha Psi is the honorary society for students majoring in accounting. The various chapters on university campuses sponsor guest speakers who discuss timely and sometimes controversial topics. You have just accepted an invitation to join your local chapter, and receive notice that Representative Thompson of the United States House of Representatives is to be the speaker at the next chapter meeting. The topic is announced as ''The Need for Governmental Regulation of Professional Accountants.'' What do you think Representative Thompson's main arguments are going to be? What counter arguments would you make?

exercise 1-3

In 1979, Robert Parsons began a new business providing landscaping and yard maintenance services to businesses and individual homes. The business grew rapidly and several employees were hired. The additional employees required additional equipment and larger purchases of supplies and materials. To help finance the expansion, Parsons brought in a partner, John Sabin. Together they obtained a $50,000 loan from the bank to assist in their expansion needs. Neither Parsons nor Sabin has any business or accounting background. Their records consist of a check book with check stubs showing amounts but no explanations, and a receipts book used when customers pay for the services rendered. Usual terms are cash upon completion of the work, although credit is granted to some customers. No accounts receivable records are maintained; however, a daily log of jobs worked on by employees is kept for salary purposes.

The bank has called and requested a copy of the statements for the year 1980. In desperation, the partners look in the phone book and call Jane Bradford, a local CPA. They explain their problem and ask for help. Is this situation one in which a CPA can help? How can financial statements be prepared when records are as incomplete as those presented in this case?

2

Review of the Accounting Process

CHAPTER OBJECTIVES

Review the steps normally followed in accumulating and summarizing accounting data.

Describe and illustrate the use of a worksheet to facilitate the summarizing process.

Explain the nature of single-entry accounting systems and the preparation of financial statements from single-entry data.

Certain procedures must be established by every business unit to provide the data to be reported on the financial statements. These procedures are collectively referred to as the **accounting process** or the **accounting cycle**.

OVERVIEW OF THE ACCOUNTING PROCESS

The accounting process consists of two interrelated parts: (1) the **recording phase** and (2) the **summarizing phase**. During the fiscal period, transactions are recorded in the various books of record as they occur. At the end of the fiscal period, the recorded data are brought up to date through adjustments, are summarized, and the financial statements are prepared. There is an overlapping of the two phases since the recording of transactions is an ongoing activity which does not cease at the end of an accounting period, but continues uninterrupted while events of the preceding period are being summarized. The recording and summarizing phases of the accounting process are reviewed and illustrated in this chapter using data from the Jensen Corporation, a hypothetical manufacturing company. The underlying accounting concepts and principles, the form, and the content of the basic financial statements are discussed and illustrated in Chapters 3, 4, and 5.[1]

The accounting process, illustrated on page 22, generally includes the following steps in well-defined sequence:

Recording Phase
1. *Appropriate business documents are prepared or received.* This documentation provides the basis for making an initial record of each transaction.
2. *Transactions are recorded.* Based upon the supporting documents from Step 1, each transaction is recorded in chronological order in books of original entry (journals).
3. *Transactions are posted.* Each transaction, as classified and recorded in the journals, is posted to the appropriate accounts in the general and subsidiary ledgers.

Summarizing Phase
4. *A trial balance of the accounts in the general ledger is taken.* The trial balance, usually prepared on a work sheet, provides a summary of the information as classified in the ledger, as well as a general check on the accuracy of recording and posting.
5. *The data required to bring the accounts up to date are compiled.* Before financial statements can be prepared, all of the accountable information that has not been recorded must be determined. Often adjustments are first made on a work sheet, and may be formally recorded and posted at any time prior to closing (Step 7). If a work sheet is not used, the adjusting entries must be posted at this point so the accounts are current prior to the preparation of financial statements.
6. *Financial statements are prepared.* Statements summarizing operations and showing the financial position and changes in financial position are prepared from the information on the worksheet or directly from the adjusted accounts.
7. *Accounts are closed.* Balances in the *nominal (temporary) accounts* and, in the case of a periodic inventory system, balances in the inventory accounts are closed into appropriate summary accounts. As determined in summary accounts, the results of operations are transferred to the appropriate owners' equity accounts.
8. *A post-closing trial balance is taken.* A trial balance is taken to determine the equality of the debits and credits after posting the adjusting and closing entries.
9. *Accounts are reversed.* Accrued and prepaid balances that were established by adjusting entries are returned to the nominal accounts that are to be used in recording and summarizing activities involving these items in the new period. This last step is not required but is often desirable as a means of facilitating recording and adjusting routines in the succeeding period.

Recording Phase

Accurate statements can be prepared only if transactions have been properly recorded. A **transaction** is an event or action resulting in a change in

---

[1]Appendix B provides an illustrated set of financial statements from the 1979 annual report of General Mills, Inc.

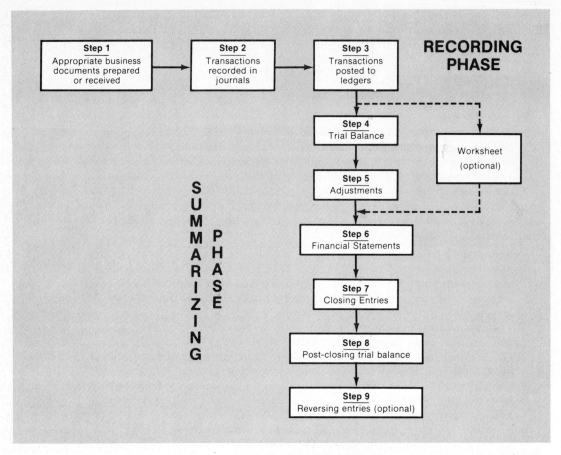

Step 1 Appropriate business documents prepared or received	**Step 2** Transactions recorded in journals	**Step 3** Transactions posted to ledgers	**RECORDING PHASE**

Step 4 Trial Balance

Worksheet (optional)

Step 5 Adjustments

SUMMARIZING PHASE

Step 6 Financial Statements

Step 7 Closing Entries

Step 8 Post-closing trial balance

Step 9 Reversing entries (optional)

The Accounting Process

the assets, the liabilities, and/or the owners' equity of a business. There are two general classes of transactions requiring accounting recognition: (1) *business transactions*, or transactions entered into with outsiders; and (2) *internal transactions*, or accountable transfers of costs within the business. For example, among the latter in manufacturing activities are the transfers of materials, labor, and manufacturing overhead costs to goods in process and transfers of goods in process to finished goods.

Accounting Records. The **accounting records** of a business consist of: (1) the original source materials evidencing the transactions, called *business* or *source documents*; (2) the records for classifying and recording the transactions, known as the *books of original entry* or *journals*; and (3) the records for summarizing the effects of transactions upon individual asset, liability, and owners' equity accounts, known as the *ledgers*.

The manner in which the accounting records are organized and employed within a business is referred to as its **accounting system**. The exact form the accounting records take depends on the complexity and degree of mechanization of the system. The various recording routines in each system are developed to meet the special needs of the business unit. Recording processes must be designed to provide accurate information on a timely and efficient basis, and at the same time they must serve as effective controls in preventing mistakes and guarding against dishonesty.

Business Documents. Normally a business document prepared or received is the first record of each transaction. Such a document offers detailed information concerning the transaction and also fixes responsibility by naming the parties involved. The business documents provide support for the data to be recorded in the books of original entry. Copies of *sales invoices* or *cash register tapes*, for example, are the evidence in support of the sales record; *purchase invoices* support the purchase or invoice record; *debit* and *credit memorandums* support adjustments in debtor and creditor balances; *check stubs* or *duplicate checks* provide data concerning cash disbursements; the corporation *minutes book* supports entries authorized by action of the board of directors; *journal vouchers* prepared and approved by appropriate officers are a source of data for adjustments or corrections that are to be reported in the accounts. Documents underlying each recorded transaction provide a means of verifying the accounting records and thus form a vital part of the information and control system.

Books of Original Entry. Transactions are analyzed from the information provided on business documents. They are then recorded in chronological order in the appropriate books of original entry, the **journals**. Transactions are analyzed in terms of accounts to be maintained for (1) assets, (2) liabilities, (3) owners' equity, (4) revenues, and (5) expenses. Classes (4) and (5) are nominal or temporary owners' equity accounts summarizing income data for the current period. The analysis is expressed in terms of **debit** and **credit**. Asset and expense accounts have left-hand or debit balances and are decreased by entries on the right-hand or credit side. Liabilities, owners' equity, and revenue accounts have credit balances and are decreased by entries on the debit side.

Although it would be possible to record every transaction in a single journal, this is rarely done. Whenever a number of transactions of the same character take place, special journals may be designed in which the transactions can be conveniently entered and summarized. Special journals eliminate much of the repetitive work involved in recording routine transactions. In addition, they permit the recording function to be divided among accounting personnel, each individual being responsible for a separate record. This specialization often results in greater efficiency as well as a higher degree of control.

Some examples of special journals are the *sales journal*, the *purchases journal*, the *cash receipts journal*, the *cash disbursements journal*, the *payroll register*, and the *voucher register*. Some of these journals are used by the Jensen Corporation and are illustrated later in this chapter. Regardless of the number and nature of special journals, certain transactions cannot appropriately be recorded in the special journals and are recorded in the *general journal*.

Sales on account are recorded in the sales journal. The subsequent collections on account, as well as other transactions involving the receipt of cash, are recorded in the cash receipts journal. Merchandise purchases on account are entered in the purchases journal. Subsequent payments on account, as well as other transactions involving the payment of cash, are recorded in the cash disbursements journal or in the *check register*. A *payroll record* may be employed to accumulate payroll information, including special payroll withholdings for taxes and other purposes.

Column headings in the various journals specify the accounts to be debited or credited; account titles and explanations may therefore be omitted in recording routine transactions. A Sundry column is usually provided for transactions that are relatively infrequent and account titles are specially designated in recording such transactions.

The use of special columns facilitates recording and also serves to summarize the effects of a number of transactions upon individual account balances. The subsequent transfer of information from the journals is thus simplified, as this process is performed with the aggregates of many transactions rather than with separate data for each transaction. Certain data must be transferred individually — data affecting individual accounts receivable and accounts payable and data reported in the Sundry columns — but the volume of transcription is substantially reduced.

Transactions not occurring frequently enough to justify a special journal are recorded in the general journal. The general journal provides debit and credit columns and space for designating account titles; thus, it can be used in recording any transaction. A particular business unit may not need certain special journals, but it must have a general journal.

The Voucher System. A relatively large organization ordinarily provides for the control of purchases and cash disbursements through adoption of some form of a **voucher system**. With the use of a voucher system, checks may be drawn only upon a written authorization in the form of a *voucher* approved by some responsible official.

A voucher is prepared, not only in support of each payment to be made for goods and services purchased on account, but also for all other transactions calling for payment by check, including cash purchases, retirement of debt, replenishment of petty cash funds, payrolls, and dividends. The voucher identifies the person authorizing the expenditure, explains the nature of the transaction, and names the accounts affected by the transaction. Vouchers related to purchase invoices should be compared with receiving reports. Upon verification, the voucher and the related business documents are submitted to the appropriate official for final approval. Upon approval, the voucher is numbered and recorded in a *voucher register*. The voucher register is a book of original entry and takes the place of a purchases journal. Charges on each voucher are classified and summarized in appropriate Debit columns and the amount to be paid is listed in an Accounts Payable or Vouchers Payable column. After a voucher is entered in the register, it is placed in an unpaid vouchers file together with its supporting documents.

Checks are written in payment of individual vouchers. The checks are recorded in a check register as debits to Accounts Payable or Vouchers Payable and credits to Cash. Charges to the various asset, liability, or expense accounts, having been recognized when the payable was recorded in the voucher register, need not be listed in the payments record. When a check is issued, payment of the voucher is reported in the voucher register by entering the check number and the payment date. Paid vouchers and invoices are removed from the unpaid vouchers file, marked "paid," and placed in a separate paid vouchers file. The balance of the payable account, after the credit for total vouchers issued and the debit for total vouchers paid, should be equal to the sum of the unpaid vouchers as reported in the voucher register and as found in the unpaid vouchers file. The voucher register, while representing a journal, also provides the detail in support of the accounts or vouchers payable total. Thus, the need for a separate record reporting the individual payable accounts is eliminated.

Posting to the Ledger Accounts. Information as reported on a business document and analyzed, classified, and summarized in terms of debits and credits in the journals is transferred to accounts in the ledger. This transfer is referred to as **posting**. The accounts then summarize the full effects of the transactions upon assets, liabilities, owners' equity, revenues, and expenses, and are used for preparing the financial statements.

Accounts are sometimes referred to as **real** (or permanent) accounts and **nominal** (or temporary) accounts. The balance sheet accounts are referred to as real accounts; the income statement accounts are referred to as nominal accounts. If during the course of the accounting period a balance sheet or an income statement account balance represents both real and nominal elements, it may be described as a **mixed account**. For example, the store supplies account before adjustment is composed of two elements: (1) the store supplies used, and (2) the store supplies still on hand. There is no need to analyze mixed accounts until financial statements are prepared. At this time the real and nominal portions of each mixed account must be determined.

When accounts are set up to record subtractions from related accounts reporting positive balances, such accounts are termed **offset** or **contra accounts**. Allowance for Doubtful Accounts is a contra account to Accounts Receivable. Sales Returns and Allowances is a contra account to Sales. Certain accounts relate to others but must be added rather than subtracted on the statements and are referred to as **adjunct accounts**. Examples of these are Freight In that is added to the Purchases balance and Paid-In Capital from Sale of Capital Stock at More Than Stated Value that is added to the Capital Stock balance.

The real and nominal accounts required by a business unit vary depending upon the nature of the business, its properties and activities, the information to be provided on the financial statements, and the controls to be employed in carrying out the accounting functions. The accounts to be maintained by a particular business are usually expressed in the form of a **chart of accounts**. This chart lists in systematic form the accounts with identifying numbers or symbols that are to form the framework for summarizing business operations.

It is often desirable to establish separate ledgers for detailed information in support of balance sheet or income statement items. The **general ledger** carries summaries of all of the accounts appearing on the financial statements, while separate **subsidiary ledgers** afford additional detail in support of general ledger balances. For example, a single accounts receivable account is usually carried in the general ledger, and individual customers' accounts are shown in a subsidiary *accounts receivable ledger*; the capital stock account in the general ledger is normally supported by individual stockholders' accounts in a subsidiary *stockholders ledger*; selling and general and administrative expenses may be summarized in a single general ledger account, individual expenses being carried in a subsidiary *expense ledger*. The general ledger account that summarizes the detailed information reported elsewhere is known as a **control account**. The accounts receivable account from a general ledger and excerpts from the corresponding accounts receivable subsidiary ledger are shown below.

GENERAL LEDGER

Account Accounts Receivable   **Account No.** 116

Date		Item	Post. Ref.	Debit	Credit	Balance	
						Debit	Credit
1981 Oct.	1	Balance	√			5,260	
	13		J18		25	5,235	
	28		J18		65	5,170	

ACCOUNTS RECEIVABLE LEDGER

Name   Allen Company
Address   436 Monroe St., Danville, California 94526

Date		Item	Post. Ref.	Debit	Credit	Balance
1981 Oct.	10		S35	750		750
	13		J18		25	725

Name   King & Co.
Address   48 Converse Rd., Los Angeles, California 90036

Date		Item	Post. Ref.	Debit	Credit	Balance
1981 Oct.	24		S35	1,502		1,502
	28		J18		65	1,437

Whenever possible, individual postings to subsidiary accounts are made directly from the business document evidencing the transaction. This practice saves time and avoids errors that might arise in summarizing and transferring this information. A business document also provides the basis for the journal entry authorizing the postings to the control account in the general ledger. In many instances business documents themselves are used to represent a book of original entry. When this is done, business documents are assembled and summarized, and the summaries are transferred directly to the appropriate control accounts as well as to the other accounts affected in the general ledger. Whatever the procedure may be, if postings to the subsidiary records and to the control accounts are made accurately, the sum of the detail in a subsidiary record will agree with the balance in the control account. A reconciliation of each subsidiary record with its related control account should be made periodically, and any discrepancies found should be investigated and corrected.

The use of subsidiary records results in a number of advantages: (1) the number of accounts in the general ledger is reduced, thus making the general ledger more useful as a basis for preparing reports; (2) errors in the general ledger are minimized because of fewer accounts and fewer postings; (3) the accuracy of the posting to a large number of subsidiary accounts may be tested by comparing the total of the balances of the accounts with the balance of one account in the general ledger; (4) totals relating to various items are readily obtained; (5) specialization of accounting duties and individual accounting responsibilities is made possible; and (6) daily posting is facilitated for accounts that must be kept up to date, such as customer and creditor accounts.

Illustration of Journals and Posting. The Jensen Corporation maintains the following books of original entry: sales journal, cash receipts journal, voucher register, cash disbursements journal, and general journal. The format of a particular journal must satisfy the needs of the individual business unit. Those presented for the Jensen Corporation are illustrative only.

Sales Journal. The sales journal as summarized at the end of the month appears as follows:

SALES JOURNAL					
Cash Sales Dr.	Accts. Rec. Dr.	Date	Description		Sales Cr.
	2,100	31	Sales on account for day...................		2,100
2,250		31	Cash sales for day.............................		2,250
9,800	40,150	31	Total		49,950
(√)	(116)				(41)

One entry is made to record the sales on account for each day. Accounts Receivable is debited; Sales is credited. Debits are posted to the individual customer's account in the accounts receivable ledger directly from the sales invoices.

One entry is also made for the cash sales for each day. Cash Sales is debited and Sales is credited. The Cash Sales column is used so that all sales transactions are included in the sales journal. An entry crediting Cash Sales is also made in the cash receipts journal.

The numbers in parentheses at the bottom of the journal refer to the accounts to which the totals are posted. The ($\checkmark$) under the Cash Sales column will be explained later in the chapter.

Cash Receipts Journal. The cash receipts journal appears as follows:

CASH RECEIPTS JOURNAL

Cash Dr.	Sales Disc. Dr.	Date	Description	Post. Ref.	Sundry Cr.	Cash Sales Cr.	Accts. Rec. Cr.
8,565		31	Notes Receivable...........	113	8,500		
			Interest Revenue	72	65		
1,960	40	31	Collection on accounts.	$\checkmark$			2,000
2,250		31	Cash Sales	$\checkmark$		2,250	
151,550	395	31	Total		106,245	9,800	35,900
(111)	(42)				($\checkmark$)	($\checkmark$)	(116)

One entry is made each day for the total amount collected on accounts receivable. In this entry Cash and Sales Discount are debited and Accounts Receivable is credited. Credits are posted to the individual customer's account in the accounts receivable subsidiary ledger from a separate list of receipts on account maintained by the cashier.

In order to maintain the cash receipts journal as a complete record of all cash received, an entry crediting Cash Sales is made each day. An entry debiting Cash Sales is also made in the sales journal as explained earlier. To avoid double posting of the transaction, the total of the Cash Sales Dr. column in the sales journal and the total of the Cash Sales Cr. column in the cash receipts journal are checked ($\checkmark$) and are not posted. As a result, the debit to Cash for cash sales is posted from the cash receipts journal as a part of the total of the Cash Dr. column, and the credit to Sales for cash sales is posted from the sales journal as a part of the total of the Sales Cr. column. A ($\checkmark$) under the Sundry column indicates that the amounts in this column are posted individually and not in total. In the illustration, $8,500 was posted to Notes Receivable (account number 113), and $65 was posted to Interest Revenue (account number 72).

Voucher Register. The voucher register takes the place of a purchase journal, providing a record of all authorized payments to be made by check. The voucher register appears on page 29. For illustrative purposes, separate debit columns are provided for two accounts — raw materials purchases and payroll. Other items are recorded in the Sundry Dr. column. Additional separate columns could be added for other items, such as advertising, if desired. The total amount of each column is posted to the corresponding account, with the exception of the Sundry Dr. and Cr. columns which are posted individually.

VOUCHER REGISTER

Date	Vou. No.	Payee	Paid Date	Paid Ck. No.	Accounts Payable Cr.	Raw Materials Purchases Dr.	Payroll Dr.	Sundry Account	Sundry Post. Ref.	Sundry Amount Dr.	Sundry Amount Cr.
31	7132	Security National Bank ...	12/31	3106	9,120			Notes Payable...............	211	9,120	
31	7133	Payroll.........................	12/31	3107	1,640		2,130	FICA Tax Payable............	215		90
								Income Tax Payable........	214		400
31	7134	Far Fabrications...............			3,290	3,290					
31	7135	Midland Mining...............			1,500	1,500					
31	7136	Nyland Supply Co...........			5,550	5,550					
31		Total................			55,375	24,930	2,130			33,645	5,330
					(213)	(51)	(620)			(√)	(√)

Cash Disbursements Journal. The cash disbursements journal is illustrated below. It accounts for all of the checks issued during the period. Checks are issued only in payment of properly approved vouchers. The payee is designated together with the number of the voucher authorizing the payment. The cash disbursements record when prepared in this form is frequently called a *check register*.

CASH DISBURSEMENTS JOURNAL

Date	Check No.	Account Debited	Vou. No.	Accounts Payable Dr.	Purchases Discount Cr.	Cash Cr.
31	3106	Security National Bank........	7132	9,120		9,120
31	3107	Payroll.................................	7133	1,640		1,640
31	3108	Pat Bunnell...........................	7005	1,500	30	1,470
31		Total		61,160	275	60,885
				(213)	(52)	(111)

General Journal. The general journal, with illustrative entries for the month of December, is given on page 30. This general journal is prepared in three-column form. A pair of columns is provided for the entries that are to be made to the general ledger accounts. A "detail" column is provided for the individual debits and credits to subsidiary records that accompany entries affecting general ledger control accounts.

From Manual Operations to Electronic Data Processing. As an organization grows in size and complexity, the recording and summarizing process becomes more involved, and means are sought for improving efficiency and reducing costs. Some enterprises may find that a system involving primarily manual operations is adequate in meeting their needs. Others may find that information processing needs can be handled effectively only through mechanical devices or electronic data processing (EDP) equipment.

JOURNAL

Date		Description	Post. Ref.	Detail	Debit	Credit
1981 Dec.	1	Notes Receivable................................	113		8,000	
		Accounts Receivable	116			8,000
		M. E. Scott	AR	8,000		
		Received note from customer.				
	13	Allowance for Doubtful Accounts	117		1,270	
		Accounts Receivable	116			1,270
		W. G. Haag.......................................	AR	1,270		
		To write off uncollectible account.				
	31	Payroll Taxes Expense	625		250	
		FICA Tax Payable	215			250
		To record employer's FICA tax for month.				

In a manual accounting system all operations are performed by hand. Original source materials — invoices, checks, and other business documents are written out, and the data they contain are transferred by hand to the journals, the ledgers, and eventually to the financial statements.

As the volume of record keeping expands, mechanical equipment may be added to the system. Machines to supplement manual operations often include posting machines, accounting machines, and billing machines. By using special papers, these machines are able to prepare original documents and journal and ledger records at one time, thus saving the work of transferring data. They also can perform a few routine arithmetic operations, such as adding journal columns and computing ledger balances.

Companies requiring great speed and accuracy in processing large amounts of accounting data may utilize an electronic computer system capable of storing and recalling data, performing many mathematical functions, and making certain routine decisions based on mathematical comparisons. These systems normally include various other machines that can "read" data from magnetic tapes or punched cards and print information in a variety of forms, all under the control of the computer.

Modern computer systems have great capabilities. The individual steps of recording, classifying, and summarizing may be combined into one process. The information traditionally recorded in journals and ledgers may be stored in memory banks or on computer discs and recalled as needed. On-line, real-time systems have the capability of continuous updating of all relevant files. This makes it possible for reports to be produced on a much more timely basis.

Despite their tremendous capabilities, electronic systems cannot replace skilled accountants. In fact, their presence places increased demands on the accountant in directing the operations of the system to assure the use of appropriate procedures. Although all arithmetical operations can be assumed to be done accurately by the computer, the validity of the output data depends upon the adequacy of the instructions given it. Unlike a human accountant, a computer cannot think for itself but must be given explicit instructions in performing each operation. This has certain advantages in that the accountant can be sure every direction will be carried out precisely. On the other hand, this places a great responsibility on the accountant to anticipate any unusual situations requiring special consideration or judgment. Particular techniques must also be developed for checking and verifying data recorded in electronic form.

The remainder of this chapter is concerned with the summarizing activities required in preparing periodic financial statements. The exact manner in which these activities are carried out will vary according to the degree of automation of the particular accounting system. Although the computer can be programmed to report information in any desired format, the input to and output from computer systems differs considerably in form from that of manual and machine systems. Despite such differences, all accounting systems are designed to serve the same information processing function.

Throughout this text, a manual accounting system is used to facilitate the illustration of concepts and procedures. In actual practice, most companies of any substantial size use some type of computer system. The advent of minicomputers has put EDP within the reach of many smaller companies which previously had to rely on manual or mechanized systems.

Summarizing Phase

The accounting routine at the close of the fiscal period is frequently referred to as the *periodic summary*. The steps in the process were outlined earlier, and they are described in more detail in the following sections.

Preparing a Trial Balance. After all transactions for the period have been posted to the ledger accounts, the balance for each account is determined. Every account will have either a debit, credit, or zero balance. A **trial balance** is a list of each account balance and it, therefore, indicates whether the debits equal the credits. Thus, a trial balance provides a check on the accuracy of the recording and posting.

Compiling Adjusting Data. Division of the life of a business into periods of arbitrary length creates many problems for the accountant who must summarize the financial operations for the designated period and report on the financial position at the end of that period. Transactions during the period have been recorded in *real* and *nominal* accounts. At the end of the period, accounts with mixed balances require adjustment. At this time, too, other financial data, not recognized currently, must be entered in the accounts to bring the books up to date. This is done by analyzing individual accounts and various source documents.

In order to illustrate this part of the accounting process, the adjusting data from Jensen Corporation are presented in the following sections. The data are classified according to the typical areas requiring updating at the end of a designated time period, in this case the year 1981. The adjusting data must be combined with the information on the trial balance in bringing the accounts up-to-date. The trial balance for Jensen Corporation appears in the first two amount columns of the work sheet on pages 36 and 37. The accounts listed in the trial balance do not reflect the following information:[2]

Asset Depreciation and Cost Amortization:
  (a) Buildings and equipment depreciation, 5% a year.
  (b) Office furniture and fixtures depreciation, 10% a year.
  (c) Patent amortization for the year, $2,900.

Doubtful Accounts:
  (d) The allowance for doubtful accounts is to be increased by $1,100.

Accrued Expenses:
  (e) Salaries and wages:
        Direct labor, $1,700.
        Indirect labor, $450.
  (f) Interest on bonds payable, $5,000.

Accrued Revenues:
  (g) Interest on notes receivable, $250.

Prepaid Expenses:
  (h) Prepaid insurance, $3,800.

Deferred Revenues:
  (i) Royalties received in advance, $475.

Provision for Income Tax:
  (j) Provision of $8,000 to be made for federal and state income taxes.

The expenses associated with buildings and equipment, insurance, and taxes (exclusive of income tax) are to be distributed 85% to manufacturing operations and 15% to general and administrative operations. Ending inventory balances are: raw materials, $22,350; goods in process, $26,500; and finished goods, $51,000.

Asset Depreciation and Cost Amortization. Charges to operations for the use of buildings and equipment and intangible assets must be recorded at the end of the period. In recording asset depreciation or amortization, operations are charged with a portion of the asset cost and the carrying value of the asset is reduced by that amount. A reduction in an asset for depreciation is usually recorded by a credit to a contra account. Adjustments at the end of the year for depreciation and amortization for Jensen Corporation are as follows:

(a) Depreciation Expense — Buildings and Equipment........................... 7,800
        Accumulated Depreciation — Buildings and Equipment   7,800
        To record depreciation on buildings and equipment.

(b) Depreciation Expense — Office Furniture and Fixtures.................... 1,900
        Accumulated Depreciation — Office Furniture and Fixtures   1,900
        To record depreciation on office furniture and fixtures.

(c) Amortization of Patents.. 2,900
        Patents...   2,900
        To record amortization of patents.

---

[2]The adjusting data are coded to correspond to the letters given on the work sheet on pages 36 and 37.

Doubtful Accounts. Provision is ordinarily made for the probable expense resulting from failure to collect receivables. In recognizing the probable expense arising from the policy of granting credit to customers, operations are charged with the estimated expense, and receivables are reduced by means of a contra account. When there is positive evidence that receivables are uncollectible, receivables are written off against the contra account. To illustrate, the adjustment for Jensen Corporation at the end of the year assumes the allowance account is to be increased by $1,100. The adjustment is as follows:

(d) Doubtful Accounts Expense..	1,100	
Allowance for Doubtful Accounts..		1,100
To provide for doubtful accounts.		

Accrued Expenses. During the period, certain expenses may have been incurred although payment is not to be made until a subsequent period. At the end of the period, it is necessary to determine and record the expenses not yet recognized. In recording an accrued expense, an expense account is debited and a liability account is credited. The adjusting entries to record accrued expenses for Jensen Corporation are:

(e) Direct Labor..	1,700	
Indirect Labor..	450	
Salaries and Wages Payable...		2,150
To record accrued salaries and wages.		
(f) Interest Expense..	5,000	
Interest Payable..		5,000
To record accrued interest on bonds.		

At the beginning of the new period, adjustments for accrued expenses may be reversed to make it possible to record expense payments during the new period in the usual manner. The nature of reversing entries is explained more fully later in the chapter.

Accrued Revenues. During the period, certain amounts may have been earned although collection is not to be made until a subsequent period. At the end of the period, it is necessary to determine and record the earnings not yet recognized. In recording accrued revenues, an asset account is debited and a revenue account is credited. The illustrative entry recognizing the accrued revenues for the year for Jensen Corporation is shown below:

(g) Interest Receivable...	250	
Interest Revenue...		250
To record accrued interest on notes receivable.		

Prepaid Expenses. During the period, charges may have been recorded on the books for commodities or services that are not to be received or used up currently. At the end of the period it is necessary to determine the portions of such charges that are applicable to subsequent periods and hence require recognition as assets.

The method of adjusting for prepaid expenses depends upon how the expenditures were originally entered in the accounts. The charges for the commodities or services may have been recorded as debits to (1) an expense account or (2) an asset account.

Original Debit to an Expense Account. If an expense account was originally debited, the adjusting entry requires that an asset account be debited for the expense applicable to the future period and the expense account be credited. The expense account then remains with a debit balance representing the amount applicable to the current period. The adjusting entry may be reversed at the beginning of the new period as is explained later in the chapter.

Original Debit to an Asset Account. If an asset account was originally debited, the adjusting entry requires that an expense account be debited for the amount applicable to the current period and the asset account be credited. The asset account remains with a debit balance that shows the amount applicable to future periods. In this instance, no reversing entry is needed. An adjusting entry for prepaid insurance for Jensen Corporation illustrates this situation as follows:

```
(h) Insurance Expense.............................................................  4,200
       Prepaid Insurance ..........................................................           4,200
            To record expired insurance ($8,000 − $3,800 = $4,200).
```

Since the asset account Prepaid Insurance was originally debited, the amount of the prepayment must be reduced to reflect only the $3,800 that remains unexpired.

Deferred Revenues. During the period, cash or other assets may have been received from customers in advance of fulfillment of the company's obligation to deliver goods or services. In recording these transactions, assets are debited and accounts reporting such receipts are credited. The latter balances must be analyzed at the end of the period to determine the portions that are applicable to future periods and hence require recognition as liabilities.

The method of adjusting for deferred revenues depends upon how the receipts for undelivered goods or services were originally entered in the accounts. The receipts may have been recorded as credits to (1) a revenue account or (2) a liability account.

Original Credit to a Revenue Account. If a revenue account was originally credited, this account is debited and a liability account is credited for the revenue applicable to a future period. The revenue account remains with a credit balance representing the earnings applicable to the current period. Again, this adjustment may be reversed as is explained later.

Assuming the credit was made originally to the revenue account, the entry to record royalties received in advance for Jensen Corporation is as follows:

```
(i) Royalty Revenue..............................................................  475
       Royalties Received in Advance .......................................           475
            To record royalties received in advance.
```

Original Credit to a Liability Account. If a liability account was originally credited, this account is debited and a revenue account is credited for the amount applicable to the current period. The liability account remains with a credit balance that shows the amount applicable to future periods. In this instance, no reversing entry is needed.

Provision for Income Tax. When a corporation reports earnings, provision must be made for federal and state income taxes. Income Tax is debited and Income Tax Payable is credited. The entry to record estimated tax payable for Jensen Corporation is as follows:

```
(j)  Income Tax ........................................................................  8,000
       Income Tax Payable ..........................................................              8,000
              To record estimated income tax payable.
```

Preparing a Work Sheet. The adjusting data must be combined with the information on the trial balance to bring the accounts up to date. This may be done and the financial statements developed through the preparation of a work sheet. In the construction of a **work sheet,** trial balance data are listed in the first two amount columns. The adjusting entries are listed in the second pair of columns. Sometimes a third pair of columns is included to show the trial balance after adjustment. Account balances as adjusted are carried to the appropriate statement columns. A work sheet for a manufacturing enterprise usually includes a pair of columns for (1) manufacturing schedule accounts, (2) income statement accounts, and (3) balance sheet accounts. Two columns for retained earnings may be placed between the Income Statement and Balance Sheet columns if sufficient transactions to this account warrant it. A similar work sheet form may be used for a merchandising enterprise except for the absence of Manufacturing Schedule columns. There are no columns for the statement of changes in financial position because this statement contains a rearrangement of information included in the balance sheet and income statement. A discussion of the preparation of the statement of changes in financial position is deferred to Chapter 19.

The work sheet for Jensen Corporation is shown on pages 36 and 37. All adjustments previously illustrated are included. The simple procedure for reporting the ending inventory balances should be noted. Beginning balances are transferred as debits to the Manufacturing Schedule or Income Statement columns, while ending balances are entered directly as credits in the Manufacturing Schedule or Income Statement columns and as debits in the Balance Sheet columns. An alternative procedure is to adjust the inventory balances in the Adjustments column by crediting the beginning balance and debiting the ending balance. Corresponding amounts are closed through Cost of Goods Sold or Income Summary to the Income Statement columns and the ending inventory balances transferred to the Balance Sheet.

It was indicated earlier that expenses associated with buildings and equipment, insurance, and taxes (exclusive of income tax) are allocated 85% to manufacturing activities and 15% to general and administrative activities. These percentages were developed by analyzing the expenses during the period. The percentages are then applied to the appropriate items on the work sheet.

	Account Title	Trial Balance Debit	Trial Balance Credit	Adjustments Debit	Adjustments Credit	
1	Cash	83,110				1
2	Notes Receivable	28,000				2
3	Accounts Receivable	106,500				3
4	Allowance for Doubtful Accounts		1,610		(d) 1,100	4
5	Finished Goods	45,000				5
6	Goods in Process	29,400				6
7	Raw Materials	21,350				7
8	Prepaid Insurance	8,000			(h) 4,200	8
9	Land	114,000				9
10	Buildings and Equipment	156,000				10
11	Accum. Depr. — Buildings and Equipment		19,300		(a) 7,800	11
12	Office Furniture and Fixtures	19,000				12
13	Accum. Depr. — Office Furniture and Fixtures		1,600		(b) 1,900	13
14	Patents	55,400			(c) 2,900	14
15	Accounts Payable		37,910			15
16	Payroll Taxes Payable		5,130			16
17	Dividends Payable		3,400			17
18	8% First-Mortgage Bonds		250,000			18
19	Common Stock, $20 par		150,000			19
20	Additional Paid-In Capital		50,000			20
21	Retained Earnings		113,610			21
22	Dividends	13,600				22
23	Sales		533,000			23
24	Sales Discount	3,500				24
25	Raw Materials Purchases	107,500				25
26	Purchases Discount		3,290			26
27	Freight In	5,100				27
28	Direct Labor	95,150		(e) 1,700		28
29	Indirect Labor	67,300		(e) 450		29
30	Factory Heat, Light, and Power	27,480				30
31	Payroll Taxes Expense	13,300				31
32	Miscellaneous Factory Overhead	12,610				32
33	Sales Salaries and Commissions	31,000				33
34	Advertising Expense	13,200				34
35	Administrative Salaries	87,300				35
36	Miscellaneous General Expense	14,700				36
37	Interest Revenue		1,100		(g) 250	37
38	Royalty Revenue		2,550	(i) 475		38
39	Interest Expense	15,000		(f) 5,000		39
40	Doubtful Accounts Expense			(d) 1,100		40
41	Depr. Exp. — Buildings and Equipment			(a) 7,800		41
42	Depr. Exp. — Office Furniture and Fixtures			(b) 1,900		42
43	Amortization of Patents			(c) 2,900		43
44	Salaries and Wages Payable				(e) 2,150	44
45	Interest Payable				(f) 5,000	45
46	Insurance Expense			(h) 4,200		46
47	Interest Receivable			(g) 250		47
48	Royalties Received in Advance				(i) 475	48
49	Income Tax			(j) 8,000		49
50	Income Tax Payable				(j) 8,000	50
51		1,172,500	1,172,500	33,775	33,775	51
52	Cost of Goods Manufactured					52
53						53
54	Net Income					54
55						55

Corporation
Sheet
December 31, 1981

#	Manufacturing Schedule Debit	Manufacturing Schedule Credit	Income Statement Debit	Income Statement Credit	Balance Sheet Debit	Balance Sheet Credit	#
1					83,110		1
2					28,000		2
3					106,500		3
4						2,710	4
5			45,000	51,000	51,000		5
6	29,400	26,500			26,500		6
7	21,350	22,350			22,350		7
8					3,800		8
9					114,000		9
10					156,000		10
11						27,100	11
12					19,000		12
13						3,500	13
14					52,500		14
15						37,910	15
16						5,130	16
17						3,400	17
18						250,000	18
19						150,000	19
20						50,000	20
21						113,610	21
22					13,600		22
23				533,000			23
24			3,500				24
25	107,500						25
26		3,290					26
27	5,100						27
28	96,850						28
29	67,750						29
30	27,480						30
31	11,305		1,995				31
32	12,610						32
33			31,000				33
34			13,200				34
35			87,300				35
36			14,700				36
37				1,350			37
38				2,075			38
39			20,000				39
40			1,100				40
41	6,630		1,170				41
42			1,900				42
43	2,900						43
44						2,150	44
45						5,000	45
46	3,570		630				46
47					250		47
48						475	48
49			8,000				49
50						8,000	50
51	392,445	52,140					51
52		340,305	340,305				52
53	392,445	392,445	569,800	587,425	676,610	658,985	53
54			17,625			17,625	54
55			587,425	587,425	676,610	676,610	55

Preparing Financial Statements. The **financial statements** are prepared using the work sheet as the basic source of data for the presentations. The basic financial statements are illustrated in Chapters 4 and 5. They include the balance sheet, the income statement, and the statement of changes in financial position.

Adjusting and Closing the Inventory Accounts. When perpetual or book inventory records are not maintained, physical inventories must be taken at the end of the period to determine the inventory to be reported on the balance sheet and the cost of goods sold to be reported on the income statement. When perpetual or book inventories are maintained, the ending inventory and the cost of goods sold balances appear in the ledger and an adjustment is not required. The closing procedures are described in the following paragraphs.

Physical Inventories — The Merchandising Enterprise. In a merchandising enterprise, the beginning inventory and the purchases account may be closed into the income summary account. The ending inventory is then recorded by a debit to the inventory account and a credit to the income summary account. The asset account now reports the inventory balance at the end of the period; the income summary account shows the cost of goods sold.

Physical Inventories — The Manufacturing Enterprise. In a manufacturing enterprise, three inventories are recognized: finished goods, goods in process, and raw materials. If cost of goods manufactured is to be summarized separately, beginning and ending raw materials and goods in process inventories are recorded in the manufacturing summary account, and beginning and ending finished goods inventories are recorded in the income summary account. To illustrate, assume the following data from Jensen Corporation:

> Inventories, January 1, 1981: Finished goods, $45,000; Goods in process, $29,400; Raw materials, $21,350.
> Charges incurred during 1981: Raw materials purchases, $107,500; Direct labor, $96,850; Factory overhead, $134,055.[3]
> Inventories, December 31, 1981: Finished goods, $51,000; Goods in process, $26,500; Raw materials, $22,350.

The entries to close the beginning inventories and to record the ending inventories follow:

To close the beginning inventories:	Manufacturing Summary.....................................	21,350	
	Raw Materials		21,350
	Manufacturing Summary.....................................	29,400	
	Goods in Process		29,400
	Income Summary	45,000	
	Finished Goods		45,000

---

[3]For purposes of this illustration, factory overhead includes all amounts shown on the Manufacturing Schedule of the Jensen Corporation work sheet, except net purchases and direct labor.

To record the ending inventories:	Raw Materials..	22,350	
	Manufacturing Summary		22,350
	Goods in Process...	26,500	
	Manufacturing Summary		26,500
	Finished Goods...	51,000	
	Income Summary		51,000

After manufacturing costs are closed into the manufacturing summary account, the balance in this account summarizes the cost of goods manufactured. The cost of goods manufactured is transferred to the income summary account and the latter then reports cost of goods sold. Inventory and summary accounts will appear as shown below.

Finished Goods

Beginning inventory	45,000	To Income Summary	45,000
Ending inventory	51,000		

Goods in Process

Beginning inventory	29,400	To Manufacturing Summary	29,400
Ending inventory	26,500		

Raw Materials

Beginning inventory	21,350	To Manufacturing Summary	21,350
Ending inventory	22,350		

Manufacturing Summary

Beginning goods in process inventory	29,400	Ending goods in process inventory	26,500
Beginning raw materials inventory	21,350	Ending raw materials inventory	22,350
Raw materials purchases	107,500	Cost of goods manufactured to Income Summary	340,305
Direct labor	96,850		
Factory overhead	134,055		
	389,155		389,155

Income Summary

Beginning finished goods inventory	45,000	Ending finished goods inventory	51,000
Cost of goods manufactured	340,305		

(Balance: Cost of goods sold, $334,305)

Perpetual Inventories — The Merchandising Enterprise. When a perpetual inventory is maintained, a separate purchases account is not used. The inventory account is charged whenever goods are acquired. When a sale takes place, two entries are required: (1) the sale is recorded in the usual manner, and (2) the merchandise sold is recorded by a debit to Cost of Goods Sold and a credit to the inventory account. Subsidiary records for inventory items are normally maintained. Detailed increases and decreases in the various inventory items are reported in the subsidiary accounts, and the costs of goods purchased and sold are summarized in the inventory control account. At the end of the period, the inventory account reflects the inventory on hand; the cost of goods sold account is closed into Income Summary.

Perpetual Inventories — The Manufacturing Enterprise. When perpetual inventories are maintained by a manufacturing enterprise, materials purchases are recorded by a debit to Raw Materials. Materials removed from stores for processing are recorded by debits to Goods in Process and credits to Raw Materials. Labor and factory overhead costs, also, are debited to Goods in Process. Finished Goods is debited and Goods in Process is credited for the cost of goods completed and transferred into the finished goods stock. The entry to record a sale is accompanied by an entry to record the cost of goods sold, Cost of Goods Sold being debited and Finished Goods being credited. At the end of the period, inventory accounts report the balance of goods on hand; Cost of Goods Sold is closed into Income Summary. Normally finished goods, goods in process, and raw materials inventory accounts are control accounts, individual changes in the various inventory items being reported in the respective subsidiary ledgers. Frequently such procedures are maintained as a part of a system designed to offer detailed information concerning costs.

Even if the perpetual inventory system is not used, a closing procedure similar to the foregoing may be preferred. The raw materials purchases account can be closed into the raw materials inventory account. The inventory account would then be reduced to the ending inventory balance, and Goods in Process would be debited. Direct labor and factory overhead accounts are closed into Goods in Process. Goods in process is then reduced to the ending inventory figure and Finished Goods is debited. Finished Goods is finally reduced to its ending balance and a cost of goods sold account is opened and debited for the inventory decrease. Cost of Goods Sold is closed into Income Summary.

Closing the Nominal Accounts. Upon completing the work sheet and statements, entries are made in the general journal to bring all accounts up to date and to close the accounts. The procedures for closing the inventory accounts were just described. Before closing the inventory and the nominal accounts, any correcting and adjusting entries are recorded. Although such entries usually have been prepared on the work sheet, these are now entered formally in the general journal. Closing entries may be conveniently prepared by using as a basis for the entries the balances as shown in the Manufacturing Schedule and Income Statement columns of the work sheet. The entries on page 41, including those needed to adjust and close inventories, are required for Jensen Corporation.

Preparing a Post-Closing Trial Balance. After the adjusting and closing entries are posted, a post-closing trial balance is prepared to verify the equality of the debits and credits. The post-closing trial balance for Jensen Corporation is given on page 42.

Closing Entries

1981
Dec. 31

Manufacturing Summary	340,305	
Goods in Process	26,500	
Raw Materials	22,350	
Purchases Discount	3,290	
Goods in Process		29,400
Raw Materials		21,350
Raw Materials Purchases		107,500
Freight In		5,100
Direct Labor		96,850
Indirect Labor		67,750
Factory Heat, Light, and Power		27,480
Payroll Taxes Expense		11,305
Miscellaneous Factory Overhead		12,610
Depreciation Expense — Buildings and Equipment		6,630
Amortization of Patents		2,900
Insurance Expense		3,570

      To close manufacturing accounts into Manufacturing Summary.

Sales	533,000	
Interest Revenue	1,350	
Royalty Revenue	2,075	
Income Summary		536,425

      To close revenue accounts into Income Summary.

Income Summary	518,800	
Finished Goods	51,000	
Finished Goods		45,000
Manufacturing Summary		340,305
Sales Discount		3,500
Payroll Taxes Expense		1,995
Sales Salaries and Commissions		31,000
Advertising Expense		13,200
Administrative Salaries		87,300
Miscellaneous General Expense		14,700
Interest Expense		20,000
Doubtful Accounts Expense		1,100
Depreciation Expense — Buildings and Equipment		1,170
Depreciation Expense — Office Furniture and Fixtures		1,900
Insurance Expense		630
Income Tax		8,000

      To close expense accounts into Income Summary.

Income Summary	17,625	
Retained Earnings		17,625

      To transfer the balance in Income Summary to Retained Earnings.

Retained Earnings	13,600	
Dividends		13,600

      To close Dividends into Retained Earnings.

Reversing the Accounts. At the beginning of a new period, the adjusting entries for accrued expenses, accrued revenues, prepaid expenses when the original debit was to an expense account, and deferred revenues when the original credit was to a revenue account may be reversed. **Reversing entries** are not necessary, but they make it possible to record the expense payments or revenue receipts in the new period in the usual manner. If a reversing entry is not made, for example, for accrued expenses, the expense payments would have to be analyzed as to (1) the amount representing payment of the

Jensen Corporation
Post-Closing Trial Balance
December 31, 1981

Cash..	83,110	
Notes Receivable...	28,000	
Accounts Receivable..	106,500	
Allowance for Doubtful Accounts..		2,710
Interest Receivable..	250	
Finished Goods..	51,000	
Goods in Process...	26,500	
Raw Materials..	22,350	
Prepaid Insurance..	3,800	
Land...	114,000	
Buildings and Equipment..	156,000	
Accumulated Depreciation — Buildings and Equipment......................		27,100
Office Furniture and Fixtures...	19,000	
Accumulated Depreciation — Office Furniture and Fixtures.................		3,500
Patents...	52,500	
Accounts Payable...		37,910
Income Tax Payable..		8,000
Payroll Taxes Payable...		5,130
Salaries and Wages Payable..		2,150
Interest Payable...		5,000
Dividends Payable..		3,400
8% First-Mortgage Bonds..		250,000
Royalties Received in Advance...		475
Common Stock, $20 par..		150,000
Additional Paid-In Capital..		50,000
Retained Earnings..		117,635
	663,010	663,010

accrued liability, and (2) the amount representing the expense of the current period. Alternatively, the accrued and deferred accounts could be left unadjusted until the close of the subsequent reporting period when they would be adjusted to their correct balances.

The adjustments establishing accrued and prepaid balances for Jensen Corporation were illustrated earlier in the chapter. The appropriate reversing entries are shown below.

Reversing Entries

1982			
Jan. 1	Salaries and Wages Payable...	2,150	
	Direct Labor..		1,700
	Indirect Labor..		450
	Interest Payable...	5,000	
	Interest Expense...		5,000
	Interest Revenue..	250	
	Interest Receivable...		250
	Royalties Received in Advance...	475	
	Royalty Revenue...		475

To illustrate accounting for an accrued expense when (1) reversing entries are made and (2) reversing entries are not made, assume that accrued salaries on December 31, 1981, are $350 and on December 31, 1982, are $500. Payment of salaries for the period ending January 4, 1982, is $1,000. Adjustments are made and the books are closed annually on December 31.

The possible entries are shown below:

	(1) Assuming Liability Account is Reversed	(2) Assuming Liability Account is Not Reversed	
		(a) Transaction in Next Period is Analyzed.	(b) Transaction in Next Period is Not Analyzed. Adjustment at Close of Next Reporting Period.
December 31, 1981 Adjusting entry to record accrued salaries.	Salaries........... 350 Salaries Payable 350	Salaries........... 350 Salaries Payable 350	Salaries........... 350 Salaries Payable 350
December 31, 1981 Closing entry to transfer expense to the income summary account.	Income Summary........ xxx Salaries xxx	Income Summary........ xxx Salaries xxx	Income Summary........ xxx Salaries xxx
January 1, 1982 Reversing entry to transfer balance to the account that will be charged when payment is made.	Salaries Payable........... 350 Salaries 350	No entry	No entry
January 4, 1982 Payment of salaries for period ending January 4, 1982.	Salaries........... 1,000 Cash 1,000	Salaries Payable........... 350 Salaries........... 650 Cash........... 1,000	Salaries........... 1,000 Cash........... 1,000
December 31, 1982 Adjusting entry to record accrued salaries.	Salaries........... 500 Salaries Payable 500	Salaries........... 500 Salaries Payable 500	Salaries........... 150 Salaries Payable 150

SINGLE-ENTRY SYSTEMS — A SPECIAL CASE

The procedures just described leading to the preparation of financial statements are those required in a **double-entry system**. This is the characteristic system employed in practice and requires the analysis of each transaction in terms of debits and credits. Any set of procedures that does not provide for the analysis of each transaction in terms of double entry is referred to as a **single-entry system**.

Single-entry systems differ widely depending upon the needs of the organization and the originality of the people maintaining the system. Records found in a single-entry system may vary from a narrative of transactions recorded in a single journal, called a *daybook*, to a relatively complete set of journals and a ledger providing accounts for all significant items.

Single-entry procedures are frequently found in organizations whose activities do not warrant the employment of a bookkeeper. Such organizations might include unincorporated retail businesses, professional and service units, and nonprofit organizations. Persons acting in a fiduciary capacity, such as estate executors and trust custodians, may also limit their record keeping to single-entry procedures. When double-entry records are not maintained, a professional accountant is normally engaged at different intervals to prepare financial statements, tax returns, and any other required reports on an accrual basis.

Records in Single-Entry Systems

All of the variations of a single-entry system encountered in practice cannot be described here. A characteristic single-entry system consists of the following records: (1) a daybook or general journal, (2) a cashbook, and (3) ledger accounts showing debtor and creditor balances.

Single-entry procedures commonly take the following form. A cashbook is maintained showing all of the transactions affecting cash. Instead of naming accounts to be debited or credited as a result of cash receipts and disbursements, a description of the transaction is offered and a column for the amount of cash is provided. Transactions not shown in the cashbook are recorded in a daybook in descriptive form. Whenever the account of a debtor, a creditor, or the owner is affected, attention is directed to the need for posting by indicating "dr" or "cr" before the amount. Offsetting debits or credits are not shown since accounts in the ledger are maintained only for customers, creditors, and the owner. At the end of the period, reports may be limited to summaries of customer and creditor balances. Of course, because it is single entry, there is no direct way to know if the balances are correct.

Preparation of Financial Statements from Single-Entry Records

When records do not offer a complete summary of transactions, the preparation of accurate financial statements raises a number of special problems. These are discussed in the following sections.

Preparation of the Balance Sheet. When the ledger consists of account balances for customers and creditors only, the preparation of the balance sheet calls for reference to a number of different sources. Cash is reported at the balance shown in the cashbook after this figure has been reconciled with the totals of cash on hand and on deposit with the bank. Receivables and payables are summarized from the accounts maintained with debtors and creditors. Merchandise and supplies balances are found by taking physical inventories. Past statements, cash records, and other documents are reviewed in determining the book values of depreciable assets. Other assets and liabilities, including accrued and prepaid items, are determined by a review of the records, including invoices, documents, and other available sources offering evidence or information concerning transactions of the past, present, and future. The owner's capital balance in a double-entry system represents an amount arrived at by combining beginning capital, additional investments and withdrawals, and revenue and expense account balances; in single-entry, capital is simply the difference between the total reported for assets less the total reported for liabilities.

Determination of the Net Income or Loss from Comparative Balance Sheet Data and Cash Summary. In the absence of revenue and expense accounts, net income may be calculated by the single-entry method. The owner's capital at the beginning of the period is subtracted from owner's capital at the end of the period. The difference is then increased for any withdrawals and decreased for any investments made by the owner during the period. Beginning and ending owner's capital balances are taken from the balance sheets prepared at the end of the previous period and at the end of the current period. Investments and withdrawals are ascertained from owner's capital and drawing accounts maintained in the ledger, or in the absence of these, from the cashbook and other memorandum records.

To illustrate the determination of the net income or loss, assume the owner's capital is reported on comparative balance sheets as follows: January 1, $20,000; December 31, $30,000. In the absence of investments or withdrawals by the owner, it must be concluded that the net income for the year was $10,000. However, assume the owner has invested $2,500 and has withdrawn $9,000 during the year. Net income is then computed as follows:

Owner's capital, December 31		$30,000
Owner's capital, January 1		20,000
Net increase in owner's capital		$10,000
Add excess of owner's withdrawals over investments:		
Withdrawals	$9,000	
Investments	2,500	6,500
Net income for the year		$16,500

Preparation of the Income Statement. A summary of the net income or loss calculated from comparative capital balances is generally inadequate. The owner needs a detailed statement of operations disclosing sales, cost of goods sold, operating expenses, and miscellaneous revenue and expense items to evaluate past success or failure and to plan future activities. Creditors may insist upon such statements. In addition, revenue and expense data must be itemized for income tax purposes.

An itemized income statement can be prepared by (1) rewriting transactions in double-entry form or (2) computing the individual revenue and expense balances by reference to cash receipts and disbursements and the changes in asset and liability balances. Obviously, little or nothing is saved by the adoption of a single-entry system if transactions are rewritten in double-entry form and posted to accounts. When the second procedure is followed, an analysis of all cash receipts and disbursements is required, unless this is already provided by special analysis columns in the cash journals. Cash receipts must be classified as: (1) receipts for goods sold for cash, (2) receipts of other revenue items, (3) collections on customers' accounts, (4) proceeds from the sale of assets other than merchandise, (5) amounts borrowed, and (6) investments by the owner. Cash payments must be classified as (1) payments for merchandise purchased for cash, (2) payments of other expense items, (3) payments on trade creditors' accounts, (4) payments for the purchase of assets other than merchandise, (5) loans paid off, and (6) withdrawals by the owner. These data, together with the data provided by the balance sheet, are used in the preparation of the income statement on an accrual basis. Obviously, the accuracy of the income statement will depend upon the accuracy of the information used in computing revenue and expense items. The procedures followed in computing revenue and expense balances on the accrual basis are illustrated in the following sections.

Sales. The amount to be reported for sales consists of the total of cash sales and sales on account. Sales are computed from the cash receipts analysis and comparative balance sheet data as follows:

Cash sales		$ 7,500
Sales on account:		
Notes and accounts receivable at the end of the period	$1,500	
Collections on notes and accounts receivable during the period	3,000	
	$4,500	
Deduct notes and accounts receivable at the beginning of the period	2,000	2,500
Sales for the period		$10,000

Notes and accounts receivable in the foregoing tabulation are limited to those arising from sales of merchandise.

The computation of gross sales is complicated if sales discounts and returns and allowances exist, or if accounts thought to be uncollectible are written off. For example, assume sales data as follows:

Data from cash records:	
Cash sales	$10,000
Collections on accounts receivable arising from sales	42,000
Data from balance sheets:	
Accounts receivable at the beginning of the period	$14,300
Accounts receivable at the end of the period	12,500
Supplementary data from special analysis of records:	
Accounts written off during the period	$ 600
Sales discounts allowed customers during the period	850
Sales returns and allowances during the period	300

The supplementary data indicate that uncollectible accounts of $600, sales discounts of $850, and sales returns and allowances of $300 are to be recognized. All of these amounts must be added to cash collections in arriving at gross sales, for there must have been sales equivalent to the reductions in accounts receivable from these sources. Gross sales for the period are computed as follows:

Cash sales		$10,000
Sales on account:		
Accounts receivable at the end of the period	$12,500	
Collections on accounts receivable	42,000	
Accounts receivable written off	600	
Accounts receivable reduced by discounts	850	
Accounts receivable reduced by sales returns and allowances	300	
	$56,250	
Deduct accounts receivable at the beginning of the period	14,300	41,950
Gross sales for the period		$51,950

Failure to recognize uncollectible accounts, sales discounts, and sales returns and allowances will be counterbalanced by an understatement in gross sales. Although the omissions will have no effect on the net income balance, revenue and expense balances will not be stated accurately.

Cost of Goods Sold. The inventory balance shown on the balance sheet prepared at the end of the preceding fiscal period is reported on the income statement as the beginning inventory.

The amount to be reported for purchases consists of the total of cash purchases and purchases on account. Purchases are computed from the cash payments analysis and comparative balance sheet data as follows:

Cash purchases		$1,500
Purchases on account:		
Notes and accounts payable at the end of the period	$2,500	
Payments on notes and accounts payable during the period..............	5,000	
	$7,500	
Deduct notes and accounts payable at the beginning of the period ..	3,500	4,000
Purchases for the period		$5,500

Notes and accounts payable in the foregoing tabulation are limited to those arising from purchases of merchandise.

The inventory balance shown on the balance sheet at the end of the current period is reported on the income statement as the ending inventory. In the first year complete statements are prepared, an estimate of the beginning inventory must be made.

When purchases discounts and purchases returns and allowances reduce accounts payable, the computation of purchases follows the same procedure as for gross sales. The purchases balance is increased by the total purchases discounts and purchases returns and allowances since there must have been purchases equivalent to the reductions in the accounts payable from these sources.

Expense Items. An expense balance is computed from the analysis of cash payments and comparative balance sheet data. The computation of an expense item is made as follows:

Cash payments representing expense..		$1,000
Add amounts not included in cash payments but to be charged to current period:		
Amount prepaid at the beginning of the period	$250	
Amount accrued at the end of the period	150	400
		$1,400
Deduct amounts included in payments but not to be charged to current period:		
Amount prepaid at the end of the period...	$200	
Amount accrued at the beginning of the period	100	300
Expense for the period..		$1,100

The charge for depreciation or amortization to be recognized on the income statement may be made by special analysis of balance sheet as well as cash data, if the balance sheet reflects depreciation in the asset balances. For example, assume no acquisition or disposal of property during the period and beginning and ending store furniture balances of $30,000 and $28,500 respectively. Depreciation is reported at $1,500, the net decrease in the asset account. Assume, however, the following information is assembled at the end of a fiscal period:

Data from cash records:
Payments for store furniture, including payments on notes arising from acquisition of store furniture .... $ 2,500
Data from balance sheets:
Store furniture at the beginning of the period $16,500
Store furniture at the end of the period.. 20,675
Installment notes payable arising from acquisition of store furniture 4,000

The charge for depreciation for the period is computed as follows:

Balance of store furniture at the beginning of the period $16,500
Add acquisitions of store furniture:
   Cash paid on acquisition of store furniture..................................... $2,500
   Amount owed at the end of the period on acquisition of store furniture 4,000   6,500

Balance of store furniture before depreciation................................. $23,000
Deduct balance of store furniture at the end of the period 20,675

Depreciation of store furniture for period .... $ 2,325

The charge for depreciation developed from the cash records and balance sheet data should be confirmed by computations based upon the individual property items held. The inability to confirm depreciation may indicate that property balances are not reported accurately on the balance sheet. The following analysis is made to support the charge calculated above.

Property	Date Acquired	Cost	Accumulated Depreciation — Prior Years	Remaining Cost	Estimated Life	Remaining Life from Beginning of Year	Depreciation Current Year
Store furniture ...	4/1/77	$24,000	$7,500	$16,500	12 yrs.	8¼ yrs.	$2,000
Store furniture ...	7/1/81	6,500	....	6,500	10 yrs.	....	325 (½ yr.)
		$30,500	$7,500	$23,000			$2,325

Other Revenue Items. Other revenue balances are computed from the analysis of cash receipts and comparative balance sheet data as follows:

Cash receipts representing revenue.. $ 800
Add amounts not included in cash receipts but to be credited to current period:
   Amount prepaid at the beginning of the period $300
   Amount accrued at the end of the period 50   350
          $1,150
Deduct amounts included in receipts but not to be credited to current period:
   Amount prepaid at the end of the period... $225
   Amount accrued at the beginning of the period 175   400

Other revenue for the period .... $ 750

In addition to the statements discussed in this chapter, a statement of changes in financial position could also be prepared. This statement is discussed in depth in Chapter 19.

Changing from Single Entry to Double Entry

The management of a business may find that single-entry procedures fail to meet its needs and may decide to change to double entry. Single-entry records may be converted to double entry by first drawing up a balance sheet as of the date of change. This statement is used as the basis for a journal entry establishing all of the asset, asset valuation, liability, and capital accounts. If additional accounts are to be added to a ledger already in use, accounts are opened and balances recorded for those items not included. If new books are to be used, accounts are opened and balances are recorded for all of the items reported in the opening journal entry.

Use of Single-Entry Systems

Single entry is described here because it represents a special type of system that accountants are likely to encounter when called upon to prepare financial statements, audit books and records, and prepare government informational reports and income tax returns, especially when dealing with small businesses.

Among the advantages of single-entry systems are the following:

1. Record keeping is simplified and the cost of maintaining records is minimal.
2. Individuals sometimes use formal financial statements only for tax returns and occasional borrowing. When needed for these purposes, financial statements can be prepared from the single-entry records as demonstrated in this chapter.

Among the disadvantages of single-entry procedures are the following factors:

1. A trial balance offering a check on the mathematical accuracy of posting is not available.
2. Preparation of the balance sheet from miscellaneous sources and memoranda may result in omissions and misstatements.
3. Detailed analysis of transactions is necessary in arriving at a summary of operations. Misstatements of assets and liabilities, particularly failures to report assets at properly depreciated or amortized balances, affect revenue and expense balances and may result in material misstatement of net income or loss.
4. There is failure to provide a centralized and coordinated accounting system subject to internal control and available for satisfactory and convenient audit by public accountants and Internal Revenue agents.

FROM TRANSACTION TO STATEMENTS

The usual procedures for recording transactions and the sequence of events leading to the preparation of financial statements have been briefly reviewed in this chapter. The treatment applied to these transactions and events was referred to as the accounting process.

The accounting process includes the entire field of analyzing, classifying, recording, summarizing, and reporting. It includes the successive steps that constitute the accounting cycle. It starts with the first written record of the transactions of an entity and concludes with the final summarized financial statements.

The significance of the accounting process in our economic society and its applicability to every business unit, regardless of size, must be appreciated. Although the procedures may be modified to meet special conditions, and may be effected through a variety of manual or computer systems, the process reviewed here is fundamental to the accounting for all enterprises.

QUESTIONS

1. Distinguish between the recording and summarizing phases of the accounting process.
2. List and describe the procedures in the accounting process. Why is each step necessary?
3. Distinguish between: (a) real and nominal accounts, (b) general journal and special journals, (c) general ledger and subsidiary ledgers.
4. What advantages are provided through the use of: (a) special journals, (b) subsidiary ledgers, and (c) the voucher system?
5. The Tantor Co. maintains a sales journal, a voucher register, a cash receipts journal, a cash disbursements journal, and a general journal. For each account listed below indicate the most common journal sources of debits and credits.

Cash	Capital Stock
Marketable Securities	Retained Earnings
Notes Receivable	Sales
Accounts Receivable	Sales Discount
Allowance for Doubtful Accounts	Purchases
Merchandise Inventory	Freight In
Land and Buildings	Purchases Returns and Allowances
Accumulated Depreciation	Purchases Discount
Notes Payable	Salaries
Vouchers Payable	Depreciation

6. As Beechnut Mining Company's independent certified public accountant, you find that the company accountant posts adjusting and closing entries directly to the ledger without formal entries in the general journal. How would you evaluate this procedure in your report to management?
7. Explain the nature and the purpose of (a) adjusting entries, (b) closing entries, and (c) reversing entries.
8. Give three common examples of contra accounts; explain why contra accounts are used.
9. What are the major advantages of electronic data processing as compared with manual processing of accounting data?
10. One of your clients overheard a computer manufacturer sales representative saying the computer will make the accountant obsolete. How would you respond to this comment?
11. What are the implications of electronic data processing for the accountant?
12. Payment of insurance in advance may be recorded in either (a) an expense account or (b) an asset account. Which method would you recommend? What periodic entries are required under each method?
13. Describe the nature and purpose of a work sheet.

14. What effect, if any, does the use of a work sheet have on the sequence of the summarizing phase of the accounting process?

15. Distinguish between the closing procedures followed by a merchandising enterprise using a physical inventory system and one using a perpetual inventory system.

16. The accountant for the S. A. Beckham Store after completing all adjustments except for the merchandise inventory, makes the entry reported below to close the beginning inventory, to set up the ending inventory, to close all nominal accounts, and to report the net result of operations in the capital account.

Merchandise Inventory (December 31, 1981)	22,500	
Sales	250,000	
Purchases Discount	2,500	
Merchandise Inventory (January 1, 1981)		25,000
Purchases		175,000
Selling Expense		25,000
General and Administrative Expense		18,750
Interest Expense		1,875
S. A. Beckham, Capital		29,375

(a) Would you regard this procedure as being acceptable? (b) What alternate procedure could you have followed in adjusting and closing the accounts?

17. Distinguish between single-entry and double-entry procedures.

18. What are the sources of information for balance sheet items when the single-entry plan is followed?

19. Distinguish between the manner in which the owner's capital balance is computed in a double-entry system as compared with a single-entry system.

20. State how each of the following items is computed in preparing an income statement when single-entry procedures are followed and the accrual basis is used in reporting net income:

(a) Merchandise sales
(b) Merchandise purchases
(c) Depreciation on equipment
(d) Sales salaries

(e) Insurance expense
(f) Interest revenue
(g) Rent revenue
(h) Taxes

21. In developing the sales balance, the owner of a business recognizes cash collections from customers and the change in the receivables balance but ignores the write-off of uncollectible accounts. Indicate the effects, if any, that such omissions will have on net income.

22. Greater accuracy is achieved in financial statements prepared from double-entry data as compared with single-entry data. Do you agree?

23. Describe the procedure to be followed in changing from a single-entry system to double entry.

EXERCISES

exercise 2-1

The Almond Paint Company, a manufacturer, engaged in the following transactions during April, 1981. Almond Paint Company records inventory on the perpetual system.

1981
April 1 Purchased a factory building and land for $50,000 in cash and a 30-year mortgage payable for $250,000. The land was appraised at $100,000 and the buildings at $300,000.

4 Sold finished goods to the Edmunds Corporation for $4,500; terms 2/10, n/30, FOB shipping point. Edmunds paid $75 freight on the goods. Finished goods cost $2,790.

5 Received raw materials worth $7,500; terms, n/30.

7 Received payment from Edmunds for goods shipped April 4.

15 The payroll for the first half of April was $8,000.

18 Traded in a truck that cost $3,000 with a net book value of $500 for a machine with a fair market value of $4,350. A trade-in allowance of $400 is allowed on the truck.

22 Declared a dividend at $.58 per share on the common stock. Common stock outstanding is 45,500 shares.

Record the above transactions in general journal form.

exercise 2-2

Using sales and cash receipts journals, as illustrated previously in the text, record the following transactions:

(a) A sale on account is made to J. A. Fairchild for $3,600.

(b) A check for $3,528 is received from Fairchild representing payment of the invoice less a sales discount of $72.

(c) Cash sales for the day are $5,260.

(d) Cash of $4,800 is received on a 60-day, 8% note for this amount issued to the bank.

(e) A dividend check for $320 is received on shares of stock owned.

exercise 2-3

In analyzing the accounts of John Ledbetter, the adjusting data listed below are determined on December 31, the end of an annual fiscal period.

(a) The prepaid insurance account shows a debit of $2,700 representing the cost of a 3-year fire insurance policy dated July 1.

(b) On October 1, Rental Revenue was credited for $3,600, representing revenue from sub-rental for a 4-month period beginning on that date.

(c) Purchase of advertising materials for $2,400 during the year was recorded in the advertising expense account. On December 31 advertising materials of $525 are on hand.

(d) On November 1, $2,250 was paid as rent for a 6-month period beginning on that date. The expense account, Rent, was debited.

(e) Miscellaneous Office Expense was debited for office supplies of $1,350 purchased during the year. On December 31 office supplies of $285 are on hand.

(f) Interest of $195 is accrued on notes payable.

(1) Give the adjusting entry for each item. (2) What reversing entries would be appropriate? (3) What sources would provide the information for each adjustment?

exercise 2-4

The following information is taken from the records of Tina's Tacos, Inc.:

	Balance January 1, 1981	Balance December 31, 1981	Transactions During 1981
Accruals:			
Interest receivable	$ 540	$ 650	
Wages payable	1,100	1,150	
Interest payable	800	950	
Cash receipts and payments:			
Interest on notes receivable			$ 1,240
Wages			64,000
Interest on notes payable			930

Compute the interest revenue, the wages expense, and the interest expense for the year.

exercise 2-5

Upon inspecting the books and records for Stanley Builders Supply Co. for the year ended December 31, 1981, you find the following data. What entries are required to bring the accounts up to date?

(a) A receivable of $225 from H. R. Thomas is determined to be uncollectible. The company maintains no allowance for such losses.

(b) A creditor, the Tanner Co., has just been awarded damages of $1,600 as a result of breach of contract during the current year by Stanley Builders Supply. Nothing appears on the books in connection with this matter.

(c) A fire destroyed part of a branch office. Furniture and fixtures that cost $8,500 and had a book value of $6,500 at the time of the fire were completely destroyed. The insurance company has agreed to pay $5,000 under the provision of the fire insurance policy. Ignore income tax consequences.

(d) Advances of $1,000 to salespersons have been recorded as sales salaries.

(e) Machinery at the end of the year shows a balance of $17,250. It is discovered that additions to this account during the year totaled $4,000, but of this amount $2,250 should have been recorded as repairs. Depreciation is to be recorded at 10% on machinery owned throughout the year, but at one half this rate on machinery purchased or sold during the year.

exercise 2-6

Accounts of Sunbay Heating Co. at the end of the first year of operations show the following balances:

Cash	$ 34,000	
Investments	40,000	
Land	80,000	
Factory buildings	160,000	
Machinery	100,000	
Accounts Payable		$ 60,000
Common Stock		400,000
Premium on Common Stock		80,000
Sales		600,000
Raw Materials Purchases	280,000	
Direct Labor	200,000	
Factory Overhead	145,000	
Operating Expenses	104,000	
Investment Revenue		3,000
	$1,143,000	$1,143,000

At the end of the year physical inventories are: finished goods, $60,000; goods in process, $60,000; raw materials, $80,000. Prepaid operating expenses are $3,000 and factory overhead payable is $1,000. Investment revenue receivable is $600. Depreciation for the year on buildings is $4,000, apportioned $3,000 to the factory and $1,000 to general operations. Depreciation of machinery is $5,000. Federal and state income taxes for the year are estimated at $20,000. Give the entries to adjust and close the books.

exercise 2-7

Account balances before and after adjustment on December 31 follow. Give the adjustment that was made for each account.

Account Title	Before Adjustment Debit	Before Adjustment Credit	After Adjustment Debit	After Adjustment Credit
(a) Merchandise Inventory	$67,000		$76,000	
(b) Allowance for Doubtful Accounts	3,500			$14,000
(c) Accumulated Depreciation		$36,000		43,000
(d) Sales Salaries	64,400		65,900	
(e) Income Tax	11,000		12,700	
(f) Royalty Revenue		18,000		23,000
(g) Interest Revenue		1,300		1,750

exercise 2-8

On May 16, 1981, Brenda Sycamore paid insurance for a three-year period beginning June 1. She recorded the payment as follows:

Prepaid Insurance	504	
Cash		504

(1) What adjustment is required on December 31? What reversing entry, if any, would you make?

(2) What nominal account could be debited instead of Prepaid Insurance? What adjustment would then be necessary? What reversing entry, if any, would you make?

exercise 2-9

The data listed below were obtained from an analysis of the accounts of Abbey Distributor Company as of March 31, 1981, in preparation of the annual report. Abbey records current transactions in nominal accounts and does not reverse adjusting entries. What are the appropriate adjusting entries?

(a) Prepaid Insurance has a balance of $14,100. Abbey has the following policies in force.

Policy	Date	Term	Cost	Coverage
A	1/1/81	2 years	$ 3,600	Shop equipment
B	12/1/80	6 months	1,800	Delivery equipment
C	7/1/80	3 years	12,000	Office and factory buildings

(b) Subscriptions Received in Advance has a balance of $56,250. The following subscriptions were included in the balance.

Inception	Amount	Term
July 1, 1980	$27,000	1 year
October 1, 1980	22,200	1 year
January 1, 1981	28,800	1 year
April 1, 1981	20,700	1 year

(c) Interest Payable has a balance of $825. Abbey owes an 8%, 90-day note for $45,000 dated March 1, 1981.

(d) Supplies has a balance of $2,190. An inventory of supplies revealed a total of $1,410.

(e) Salaries Payable has a balance of $9,750. The payroll for the 5-day workweek ended April 3, totaled $11,250.

exercise 2-10

Some of the account balances appearing in the ledger of the Elmer Equipment Co. on November 30, the end of a fiscal year, follow:

Raw Materials	$28,800	Sales	$432,000
Goods in Process	19,200	Operating Expense	72,000
Finished Goods	33,600		

(1) Prepare closing entries given the following information: physical inventories on November 30 are: finished goods, $18,000; goods in process, $16,000; raw materials, $28,000. Raw materials purchases are $136,000; direct labor is $62,400; and factory overhead is $48,000.

(2) Assuming that on a perpetual basis, cost of goods sold totals $266,000, close the accounts.

exercise 2-11

An accountant for Jolley, Inc., a manufacturing enterprise, has just finished posting all the year-end adjusting entries to the ledger accounts and now wishes to close the ledger balances in preparation for the new period.

For each of the accounts listed below indicate whether the year-end balance should be: (1) carried forward to the new period, (2) closed by debiting the account, or (3) closed by crediting the account. If the account is to be closed, identify into which summary account it will be closed.

(a) Cash	(k) Manufacturing Summary
(b) Sales	(l) Accounts Receivable
(c) Dividends	(m) Prepaid Insurance
(d) Finished Goods — Beginning Inventory	(n) Interest Receivable
(e) Selling Expense	(o) Raw Materials — Beginning Inventory
(f) Capital Stock	(p) Freight In
(g) Income Summary	(q) Interest Revenue
(h) Direct Labor	(r) Factory Supervision
(i) Dividends Payable	(s) Retained Earnings
(j) Raw Materials Purchases	(t) Accumulated Depreciation

exercise 2-12

The Lennon's Tannery shows a credit balance in the income summary account of $129,600 after the revenue and expense items have been transferred to this account at the end of a fiscal year. Give the remaining entries to close the books, assuming:

(a) The business is a sole proprietorship: the owner, D. H. Lennon, has made withdrawals of $36,000 during the year and this is reported in a drawing account.

(b) The business is a partnership: the owners, D. H. Lennon and B. L. Oster, share profits 5:3; they have made withdrawals of $48,000 and $38,400 respectively, and these amounts are reported in drawing accounts.

(c) The business is a corporation: the ledger reports additional paid-in capital, $800,000, and retained earnings, $200,000; dividends during the year of $56,000 were charged to a dividends account.

exercise 2-13

Service fee collections in 1981 are $43,500; service fee revenue reported on the income statement is $40,800. The balance sheet prepared at the beginning of the year reported service fees receivable, $1,800, and unearned service fees, $1,350; the balance sheet at the end of the year reported service fees receivable, $2,280. What is the amount of unearned service fees at the end of the year?

exercise 2-14

Sales salaries are reported on the income statement for 1981 at $19,260. Balance sheet data relating to sales salaries are as follows:

	January 1, 1981	December 31, 1981
Prepaid salaries (advances to sales agents)	$ 450	$ 180
Salaries payable	1,260	1,350

How much cash was paid during 1981 for sales salaries expense?

exercise 2-15

Total accounts receivable for the Bako Company were as follows: on January 1, $6,000; on January 31, $6,300. In January, $9,500 was collected on accounts, $600 was received for cash sales, accounts receivable of $700 were written off as uncollectible, and allowances on sales of $100 were made. What amount should be reported for gross sales on the income statement for January?

exercise 2-16

On November 1, the capital of D. T. Bonneville was $8,500 and on November 30 the capital was $12,187.50. During the month, Bonneville withdrew merchandise costing $500 and on November 25 paid a $4,000 note payable of the business with interest at 10% for three months with a check drawn on a personal checking account. What was Bonneville's net income or loss for the month of November?

exercise 2-17

An analysis of the records of J. L. Kane disclosed changes in account balances for 1981 and the supplementary data listed below. From these data, calculate the net income or loss for 1981.

Cash	$ 2,400 decrease
Accounts receivable	1,500 increase
Merchandise inventory	$15,500 increase
Accounts payable	2,100 increase

During the year, Kane borrowed $20,000 in notes from the bank and paid off notes of $15,000 and interest of $750. Interest of $250 is accrued as of December 31, 1981. There was no interest payable at the end of 1980.

In 1981, Kane also transferred certain marketable securities to the business and these were sold for $5,300 to finance the purchase of merchandise.

Kane made weekly withdrawals in 1981 of $250.

PROBLEMS

problem 2-1

Beesley Distributing, Inc., a fruit wholesaler, records business transactions in the following books of original entry: general journal (GJ); voucher register (VR); check register (CKR); sales journal (SJ); and cash receipts journal (CRJ). Beesley uses a voucher system. At the close of business on April 18, Beesley recorded and filed the following business documents:

(a) Sales invoices for sales on account totaling $4,600.
(b) The day's cash register tape showing receipts for cash sales at $700.
(c) A list of cash received on various customer accounts totaling $2,930. Sales discounts taken were $30.
(d) The telephone bill for $60 payable in one week.
(e) Vendor's invoices for $5,000 worth of fruit received.
(f) Check stub for payment of last week's purchases from All-Growers Farms, $5,940. Terms of 1/10, n/30 were taken.
(g) Check stub for repayment of a $10,000, 90-day note to Mercantile Bank, $10,200.
(h) A letter notifying Beesley that Littex Markets, a customer, has declared bankruptcy. All creditors will receive 10 cents on every dollar due. Littex owes Beesley $1,300.

Instructions:

(1) Indicate the books of original entry in which Beesley recorded each of the business documents. (Use the designated abbreviations.)
(2) Record the debits and credits for each entry as though only a general journal were used. Use account titles implied by the voucher system.

problem 2-2

A fire destroyed Fong Company's journals. However, the general ledger and accounts receivable subsidiary ledger were saved. An inspection of the ledgers reveals the information shown below.

General Ledger

Cash (11)				Sales (41)		
May 1 Bal.	7,500				May 31	8,925
31	7,165					

Sales Discount (42)			Accounts Receivable (12)			
May 3	25		May 1 Bal.	2,925	May 31	4,425
			31	6,160		

Accounts Receivable Ledger

A			B		
May 1 Bal.	275		May 1 Bal.	1,200	May 13	1,200
5	1,500		5	375		

C			D		
May 2	935		May 1 Bal.	1,450	May 11	725

E			
May 2	2,500	May 3	2,500	2,500
12	850		

Fong's credit policy is 1/10, n/30.

Instructions: Reconstruct the sales and cash receipts journals from the information given above. Assume a Cash Sales column is used in the journals.

problem 2-3

The trial balance of Kohler's Diamonds, shows, among other items, the following balances on December 31, 1981, the end of a fiscal year:

Accounts Receivable	225,000	
9% Century City Bonds	150,000	
Land	275,000	
Buildings	300,000	
Accumulated Depreciation — Buildings		86,625
8% First-Mortgage Bonds Payable		300,000
Rental Revenue		71,500
Office Expense	7,500	

The following facts are ascertained on this date upon inspection of the company's records.

    (a) It is estimated that approximately 2% of accounts receivable may prove uncollectible.

    (b) Interest is receivable semiannually on the Century City bonds on March 1 and September 1.

    (c) Buildings are depreciated at 2½% a year; however, there were building additions of $50,000 during the year. The company computes depreciation on asset acquisitions during the year at one half the annual rate.

    (d) Interest on the first-mortgage bonds is payable semiannually on February 1 and August 1.

    (e) Rental revenue includes $3,750 that was received on November 1, representing rent on part of the buildings for the period November 1, 1981, to October 31, 1982.

    (f) Office supplies of $2,000 are on hand on December 31. Purchases of office supplies were debited to the office expense account.

Instructions:

    (1) Prepare the journal entries to adjust the books on December 31, 1981.

    (2) Give the reversing entries that may appropriately be made at the beginning of 1982.

problem 2-4

The bookkeeper for the Sandie Corp. is preparing an income statement for the year ended December 31, 1981, reporting income from operations as $88,720. Accounts have not yet been closed, and a review of the books disclosed the need for the following adjustments:

    (a) The account, Office Expense, shows the cost of all purchases of office supplies for the year. At the end of 1981 there are supplies of $480 on hand.

    (b) The allowance for doubtful accounts shows a debit balance of $160. It is estimated that 3% of the accounts receivable as of December 31 will prove uncollectible. The accounts receivable balance on this date is $23,280.

    (c) The ledger shows a balance for accrued salaries and wages of $1,440 as of December 31, 1980, which was left unchanged during 1981. No recognition was made in the accounts at the end of 1981 for accrued salaries and wages which amounted to $1,560.

    (d) The ledger shows a balance for interest receivable of $300 as of December 31, 1980, which was left unchanged during 1981. No recognition was made in the accounts at the end of 1981 for accrued interest which amounted to $352.

    (e) The prepaid insurance account was debited during the year for amounts paid for insurance and shows a balance of $960 at the end of 1981. The unexpired portions of the policies on December 31, 1981, total $448.

    (f) A portion of a building was subleased for three months, November 1, 1981, to February 1, 1982. Unearned Rental Revenue was credited for $960 and no adjustment was made in this account at the end of 1981.

    (g) The interest expense account was debited for all interest charges incurred during the year and shows a balance of $1,500. However, of this amount, $400 represents a discount on a 60-day note payable due January 30, 1982.

    (h) Provision for income tax for 1981 is to be computed at a 45% rate.

Instructions: Give the entries that are required on December 31, 1981, to bring the books up to date. (In recording income tax, provide a schedule to show how the corrected income subject to tax was determined.)

problem 2-5

The accountant for Besner Plumbing made the following adjusting entries on December 31, 1981:

(a) Prepaid Rent	600	
Rent Expense		600
(b) Advertising Materials Inventory	1,000	
Advertising Expense		1,000
(c) Interest Revenue	250	
Unearned Revenue		250
(d) Office Supplies...	500	
Office Expense		500
(e) Prepaid Insurance..	525	
Insurance Expense..		525

Further information is provided as follows:

      (a) Rent is paid every October 1.
      (b) Advertising materials cost $2,400 each year.
      (c) Interest is received every March 1.
      (d) Office supplies are purchased every July 1 and used evenly throughout the year.
      (e) Yearly insurance cost is $900.

      Instructions: For each individual item above indicate the original transaction entry that was made.

problem 2-6

The bookkeeper for the Irwin Wholesale Electric Co. prepares no reversing entries and records all revenue and expense items in nominal accounts during the period. The following balances, among others, are listed on the trial balance at the end of the fiscal period, December 31, 1981, before accounts have been adjusted:

Accounts Receivable..	152,000
Allowance for Doubtful Accounts (credit balance)	1,000
Interest Receivable..	2,800
Discount on Notes Payable	300
Prepaid Real Estate and Personal Property Tax....................................	1,800
Salaries and Wages Payable	4,000
Discount on Notes Receivable	2,800
Unearned Rental Revenue..	1,500

Inspection of the company's records reveals the following as of December 31, 1981.

      (a) Uncollectible accounts are estimated at 3% of the accounts receivable balance.
      (b) The accrued interest on investments totals $2,400.
      (c) The company borrows cash by discounting its own notes at the bank. Discount on notes payable at the end of 1981 is $1,600.
      (d) Prepaid real estate and personal property taxes are $1,800, the same as at the end of 1980.
      (e) Accrued salaries and wages are $4,300.
      (f) The company accepts notes from the customers giving its customers credit for the face of the note less a charge for interest. At the end of each period any interest applicable to the succeeding period is reported as a discount. Discount on notes receivable at the end of 1981 is $1,500.
      (g) Part of the company's properties had been sublet on September 15, 1980, at a rental of $3,000 per month. The arrangement was terminated at the end of one year.

      Instructions: Give the adjusting entries required to bring the books up to date.

problem 2-7

Account balances taken from the ledger of the Farley Development Company on December 31, 1981, are listed below and at the top of page 59:

Accounts Payable...........................	$ 36,000	Capital Stock, $10 par...................	$180,000
Accounts Receivable.....................	67,200	Cash..	24,000
Advertising Expense	4,800	Dividends	14,400
Accumulated Depreciation —		Freight In...................................	3,600
Buildings	19,800	Insurance Expense........................	1,440
Allowance for Doubtful Accounts	1,380	Interest Expense...........................	2,640
Buildings..	72,000	Interest Revenue..........................	660

Inventory, Dec. 31, 1980	$ 64,800	Retained Earnings, Dec. 31, 1980	$ 14,040
Land	69,600	Sales	246,000
Long-Term Investments	12,600	Sales Discount	5,400
Mortgage Payable	48,000	Sales Returns	3,360
Notes Payable — Short Term	15,000	Selling Expense	49,440
Office Expense	16,080	Supplies Expense	4,200
Purchases	138,480	Taxes — Real Estate, Payroll,	
Purchases Discount	1,140	and Other	7,980

Adjustments on December 31 are required as follows:

    (a) The inventory on hand is $90,720.
    (b) The allowance for doubtful accounts is to be increased to a balance of $3,000.
    (c) Buildings are depreciated at the rate of 3⅓% per year.
    (d) Accrued selling expenses are $3,840.
    (e) There are supplies of $780 on hand.
    (f) Prepaid insurance relating to 1982 and 1983 totals $720.
    (g) Accrued interest on long-term investments is $240.
    (h) Accrued real estate, payroll and other taxes are $900.
    (i) Accrued interest on the mortgage is $480.
    (j) Income tax is estimated to be 45% of the income before income tax.

Instructions:

    (1) Prepare an eight-column work sheet.
    (2) Prepare adjusting, closing, and reversing entries.

3

The Conceptual Framework of Accounting

CHAPTER OBJECTIVES

Describe the need for a conceptual framework.

Identify the components of the FASB conceptual framework project.

Discuss the objectives of financial reporting.

Discuss the qualitative characteristics of accounting information.

Consider the nature of the traditional accounting model.

In Chapter 1 accounting was identified as a service activity designed to provide useful information, primarily financial in nature, for decision-making purposes. The accounting process was reviewed in Chapter 2, detailing the means by which entity transactions are measured and communicated. It is important to note that the accounting process generates information for a variety of potential users. Managers are the major "internal" users of the information produced by the accounting process. They use accounting information, as well as other data, in making a number of decisions concerning the operations of the business. "External" users of accounting information include owners, lenders, suppliers, potential investors and creditors, employees, financial analysts, representatives of labor unions and government agencies, and the general public. These external users are generally not directly involved in the daily management of the business and must rely to a significant extent on the periodic financial reports supplied by management to provide the information they need to make investment, lending, and other decisions. The objective of this text is primarily to consider external financial reporting requirements. This chapter explores the conceptual framework of accounting as a basis for understanding the theory and practice of financial reporting. The major accounting issues and current accounting practice are described in the remaining chapters of the text.

NEED FOR A CONCEPTUAL FRAMEWORK

As pointed out in Chapter 1, accounting has evolved to meet the needs of business in measuring and communicating the results of enterprise activity. As business has grown in size and complexity, so has accounting. A major factor in the growth and complexity of business was the introduction of the corporate form of organization, which encourages a broad base of ownership. The development of corporations has also increased the need for external financial reporting because the owners of the business entities — the stockholders — are seldom the managers of those entities and need periodic reports to evaluate the results of company operations and thus management's performance.

Accounting for large and complex organizations presents many challenges to accountants, such as establishing adequate accounting controls and ensuring the proper recording and classification of the thousands of transactions that occur yearly. From an external reporting viewpoint, another extremely important challenge is selecting the most appropriate methods for reporting enterprise activity. Often, there are several justifiable reporting alternatives for a particular transaction. Therefore, accountants are continually required to use their judgment in selecting from the reporting alternatives the one that most accurately reflects the financial position and results of operations for the entity given the specific circumstances involved. If businesses and their activities were identical, reporting alternatives could be eliminated. However, businesses are different. Even within a particular industry, companies are not organized in exactly the same way, they do not produce identical products or provide identical services, and their accounting systems and the reports generated therefrom are not uniform. Thus, accountants must exercise professional judgment in fulfilling their roles as suppliers of useful information for decision makers.

For some time, accountants and business executives have agreed that a broad framework of financial accounting and reporting concepts is needed to assist those charged with the responsibility of financial reporting. Such a framework should provide guidelines for proper reporting under particular circumstances. It should assist accountants and others in selecting among reporting alternatives that method which would best represent the economic reality of the situation and should, therefore, result in reporting the most useful information for decision making purposes.

A conceptual framework of generally accepted accounting principles will not solve all accounting or reporting problems, however. The conceptual framework should provide guidance and offer a standard or frame of reference. But it will not eliminate the need for judgment in terms of, for example, what information should be supplied, what specific method of reporting would be most appropriate under the circumstances, and in what form the information should be presented.

When the Financial Accounting Standards Board was established, it responded to this need for a general framework by undertaking a comprehensive project to develop a "conceptual framework for financial accounting and reporting." This project has been described as an attempt to provide a constitution for accounting. The result of the project hopefully will provide both support and guidance for individual financial accounting standards. Because of its potential impact on future accounting practice, all students interested in accounting should be aware of the elements of the FASB conceptual framework and should monitor the progress of this important project.

COMPONENTS OF THE FASB CONCEPTUAL FRAMEWORK: AN OVERVIEW

The conceptual framework project was one of the original FASB agenda items. It is viewed as a long-term, continuing project to be developed in stages. Because of its significant potential impact on many aspects of financial reporting, and therefore its controversial nature, progress must be deliberate. The project has high priority and receives a large share of FASB resources. Currently, there are eight specific components of the conceptual framework project, each in varying stages of completion. These components are listed below and are briefly discussed in the following paragraphs.

1. Objectives of financial reporting by business enterprises
2. Elements of financial statements of business enterprises
3. Qualitative characteristics: criteria for selecting and evaluating financial accounting and reporting policies
4. Measurement: changing prices
5. Accounting recognition criteria
6. Reporting earnings
7. Funds flow and liquidity
8. Information in financial statements and in financial reporting other than financial statements

Objectives of Financial Reporting by Business Enterprises

The starting point for the conceptual framework was determined to be the objectives of financial reporting. Study on this topic produced the first of a series of planned publications from the conceptual framework project. The results of this phase of the project were published in November 1978, as Statement of Financial Accounting Concepts No. 1 — "Objectives of Financial Reporting by Business Enterprises." The objectives are discussed in some detail later in the chapter.

Elements of Financial Statements of Business Enterprises

This phase of the conceptual framework is intended to develop definitions for the main elements of the general purpose financial statements: assets, liabilities, equity investments by owners, distributions to owners, comprehensive income, revenues, expenses, gains, and losses. These elements are defined by the FASB in Statement of Financial Accounting Concepts No. 3, "Elements of Financial Statements of Business Enterprises," and are incorporated throughout the text.

Qualitative Characteristics: Criteria for Selecting and Evaluating Financial Accounting and Reporting Policies

This part of the project is intended to identify and clarify qualitative characteristics that should be considered in adopting reporting standards for both business and nonbusiness enterprises. Results of this phase should be useful to standard-setting bodies, such as the FASB, and also to preparers, auditors, and users of financial statements in understanding and applying accounting standards. These results were published in May, 1980, as Statement of Financial Accounting Concepts No. 2, "Qualitative Characteristics of Accounting Information," and its main points are discussed later in the chapter.

Measurement: Changing Prices

This part of the framework is specifically concerned with the effects of changing prices on business enterprises. Historically, accountants have ignored the fact that the dollar, which is the common measuring unit in the United States, is unstable, i.e., its purchasing power fluctuates as general price levels change. Further, accountants have measured the results of transactions in terms of "historical cost," the exchange price at the date of a transaction; they have not reported current values, the exchange prices at dates subsequent to the transaction date. Thus, accountants have traditionally not measured and reported the impact of either general or specific price changes on business entities.

After considerable study, the FASB has issued Statement of Financial Accounting Standards No. 33 which requires most large companies to disclose supplementary information concerning the impact of both specific and general price changes on a business entity. The nature of these requirements and the issues involved in reporting price changes are discussed at length in Chapter 20.

Accounting Recognition Criteria

This component was added to the framework project in 1979. The intent is to develop criteria for accounting recognition of the elements of financial statements mentioned earlier. Statement of Financial Accounting Concepts No. 3 established *what* the elements are, and this phase of the project will establish criteria for determining *when* to recognize them.

Reporting Earnings

This phase of the study is designed to determine the kinds of earnings information that should be furnished based on the objectives of financial reporting. The results of this phase may dramatically change the format currently used for the income statement. A significant part of this phase of the study is to identify useful criteria for classifying revenues, gains, expenses, and losses. The issues involved in reporting earnings are discussed in several chapters, especially Chapters 4 and 18.

Funds Flow and Liquidity

This part of the framework project will reconsider APB Opinion No. 19 concerning the Statement of Changes in Financial Position. The objective is to determine the appropriate information to be reported about an enterprise's flow of funds and its liquidity position. Obviously, this phase is closely related to the reporting of earnings and will likely follow that project. The funds statement is discussed in Chapters 5 and 19.

Information in Financial Statements and in Financial Reporting Other Than Financial Statements

This is the last component of the conceptual framework as currently planned. Its objective is to determine where the information specified by the objectives of financial reporting should be disclosed — in the financial statements themselves or elsewhere. It is also concerned with who should disclose what information — should there be uniform disclosures for all business enterprises or selected disclosures for particular enterprises. A position paper is being developed to explain the criteria the FASB might use in making the above distinctions.

Definition, Recognition, Measurement, and Display

In considering the individual components of the conceptual framework, the interrelationships become apparent. Decisions concerning one part of the framework will, no doubt, influence other parts. However, the Board has made it clear that certain aspects must be considered independently. As shown in the illustration on page 65, definition, recognition, measurement, and display are four distinct aspects of the framework.[1]

To show the distinctness of each of these aspects of the framework, consider the problem of reporting a particular asset on the balance sheet. The item must first qualify as an asset, i.e., it must possess the characteristics of

---

[1]*Statement of Financial Accounting Concepts No. 3*, "Elements of Financial Statements of Business Enterprises" (Stamford: Financial Accounting Standards Board, December 1980), par. 16, 17 and 37–42.

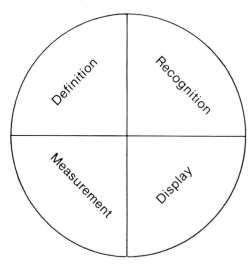

Aspects of the Conceptual Framework

an asset as defined by the FASB. However, it must also meet the criteria for recognition and have attributes that are capable of reliable measurement or estimation. If an item qualifies as an asset, meets the criteria for recognition, and is measurable, then it can be determined how best to display or report the asset on the balance sheet. Some items may qualify as elements of financial statements in terms of definition, but may not be reported on the statements because of recognition or measurement problems. The most appropriate means of reporting, the display aspect, is yet another independent consideration.

OBJECTIVES OF FINANCIAL REPORTING

In discussing the first component of the framework, the objectives of financial reporting, four points should be made initially. First, the objectives of financial reporting are important and have been given number one priority by the FASB because they determine the purposes and overall direction of accounting. Without identifying the goals for financial reporting, e.g., who needs what kind of information and for what reasons, accountants cannot determine the definitions or recognition criteria needed, which measurements are useful, or how best to report accounting information. The objectives presented in this section are those of the FASB as summarized and adapted from Statement of Financial Accounting Concepts No. 1.[2] Because the FASB is the primary standard-setting body for accounting in the private sector, the FASB objectives should be considered carefully. However, it should also be recognized that another group might identify somewhat different objectives for financial reporting. The objectives, as well as the other components of the conceptual framework, should therefore not be interpreted as "universal truths."

---

[2]*Statement of Financial Accounting Concepts No. 1,* "Objectives of Financial Reporting by Business Enterprises" (Stamford: Financial Accounting Standards Board, November 1978).

A second and related point is that the objectives of financial reporting are not immutable but are directly connected with the needs of those for whom the information is intended and must be considered in their environmental context. Financial reporting is not an end in itself but is directed toward satisfying the need for useful information in making business and economic decisions. Thus, the objectives of financial reporting may change in response to changes in the information needs of decision makers and in the economic, legal, political, and social aspects of the total business environment.

Third, the objectives of financial reporting are intended to be broad in nature. Financial reporting encompasses not only disclosures in financial statements, which are a primary means of communicating information to external parties, but also other information provided by the accounting system concerning an enterprise's resources, obligations, and earning ability. The objectives must be broadly based to satisfy a variety of user needs. Thus, they are objectives for general purpose financial reporting, attempting to satisfy the common interests of various potential users rather than to meet the specific needs of any selected group.

A fourth point is that the objectives of financial reporting are primarily directed toward the needs of those external users of accounting data who lack the authority to prescribe the information they desire. For example, the Internal Revenue Service or the Securities and Exchange Commission can require selected information from individuals and companies; investors and creditors must rely to a significant extent on the information contained in the periodic financial reports supplied by management, and, therefore, are the major users toward which financial reporting is directed.

Information for Decision Making

As already pointed out, the overall objective of financial reporting is to provide information for decision-making purposes. The FASB states:

> Financial reporting should provide information that is useful to present and potential investors and creditors and other users in making rational investment, credit, and similar decisions. The information should be comprehensible to those who have a reasonable understanding of business and economic activities and are willing to study the information with reasonable diligence.[3]

The emphasis in this overall objective is on investors and creditors as the primary external users because in satisfying their needs, most other general-purpose needs of external users will be met. This objective also recognizes a fairly sophisticated user of financial reports, one who has a reasonable understanding of accounting and business.

Assessing Cash Flow Prospects

The major concern of investors and creditors is in assessing future cash flows. Investment and lending decisions are made with the expectation of

---

[3]*Ibid.*, par. 34.

eventually increasing cash resources. An investor hopes to recover the initial investment, receive a return on that investment in the form of cash dividends, and ultimately sell the investment for more than it cost. Creditors seek to recover their cash outlays by repayments of the loans and to increase cash resources from interest payments. In making their decisions, investors and creditors must consider the amounts, timing, and uncertainty (risk) of these prospective cash flows.

A company is similar to an investor in desiring to recover its investment plus receive a return on that investment. A company invests cash in non-cash resources in order to produce a product or service for which it will receive cash inflows, with the amounts returned hopefully in excess of the amounts invested. To the extent a company is successful in generating favorable cash flows, it can pay dividends and interest, and the market prices of its securities will increase. Thus, the expected cash flows to investors and creditors are directly related to the expected cash flows of business enterprises. This relationship is captured in another key objective of financial reporting:

> . . . financial reporting should provide information to help investors, creditors, and others assess the amounts, timing, and uncertainty of prospective net cash inflows to the related enterprise.[4]

Information About Enterprise Resources and Claims Against Resources

Financial accounting does not purport to measure directly the value of a business. However, financial reporting should provide information that clearly identifies entity resources (assets) and the claims against those resources, both creditor claims (liabilities) and owner claims (owners' equity). By highlighting the relationships between assets, liabilities, and owners' equity items, investors, creditors, and others should be able to determine the financial strengths and weaknesses of an enterprise and assess its position of liquidity and solvency. Such information will help users determine the financial status of a company which, in turn, should provide insight into the prospects of future cash flows. It may also help individuals estimate the overall value of a business. To be complete, financial reports must disclose the significant changes in resources and claims against resources arising from transactions, events, and circumstances.

Information About Enterprise Performance and Earnings

The FASB states that "the primary focus of financial reporting is information about an enterprise's performance provided by measures of earnings and its components."[5] There are several aspects of this important objective. Clearly, investors and creditors are mostly concerned with expectations of future enterprise performance. However, to a large degree, they rely on evaluations of past performance as measures of future performance. The FASB

---

[4]*Ibid.*, par. 37.
[5]*Ibid.*, par. 43.

concludes that information about enterprise earnings, measured by accrual accounting, generally provides a better indicator of enterprise performance than does information about current cash receipts and disbursements. However, the FASB recognizes that investors and creditors primarily want information about earnings as an indicator of future cash-flow potential.

Investors and creditors use reported earnings and information concerning the components of earnings in a variety of ways. For example, earnings may be interpreted by users of financial statements as an overall measure of managerial effectiveness, as a predictor of future earnings and long-term "earning power," and as an indicator of the risk of investing or lending. The information may be used to establish new predictions, confirm previous expectations, or change past evaluations.

Additional Objectives

Notwithstanding the emphasis on earnings, another objective of financial reporting is to:

> . . . provide information about how an enterprise obtains and spends cash, about its borrowing and repayment of borrowing, about its capital transactions, including cash dividends and other distributions of enterprise resources to owners, and about other factors that may affect an enterprise's liquidity or solvency.[6]

Much of the information to satisfy this objective is provided in the Statement of Changes in Financial Position, although information about earnings and economic resources and claims against resources may also be useful in evaluating the liquidity and solvency of a firm.

Although the objectives of financial reporting are aimed primarily at the needs of external users, financial reporting should also provide information that allows managers and directors to make decisions which are in the best interest of the owners. A related objective is that sufficient information should be provided to allow the owners to assess how well management has discharged its stewardship responsibility over the entrusted resources.

In summary, if the objectives discussed in the preceding paragraphs are fully attained, the FASB believes those who make economic decisions will have better information upon which to evaluate alternative courses of action and the expected returns, costs, and risks of each. The result should be a more efficient allocation of scarce resources among competing uses by individuals, enterprises, markets, and the government.

QUALITATIVE CHARACTERISTICS OF ACCOUNTING INFORMATION

Individuals who are charged with a responsibility for financial reporting should continually seek to provide the best, i.e., most useful, information possible within reasonable cost constraints. The problem is very complex

---

[6]*Ibid.*, par. 49.

because of the many choices among acceptable reporting alternatives. The key aspects of definition, recognition, measurement, and display are again apparent. For example, what items should be capitalized as assets or reported as liabilities? Which revenues and costs should be assigned to a particular reporting period and on what basis? What are the attributes to be measured: historical costs, current values, or net realizable values? At what level of aggregation or disaggregation should information be presented? Where should specific information be disclosed — in the financial statements, in the notes to the financial statements, or perhaps not at all? These and similar choices must be made by policy makers, such as members of the FASB or SEC; by managements as they fulfill their stewardship roles; and by accountants as they assist management in reporting on a company's activities.

To assist in choosing among financial accounting and reporting alternatives, several criteria have been established by the FASB. These criteria relate to the qualitative characteristics of accounting information. The illustration below presents a hierarchy of these qualities and will be used as a frame of reference in discussing them.[7]

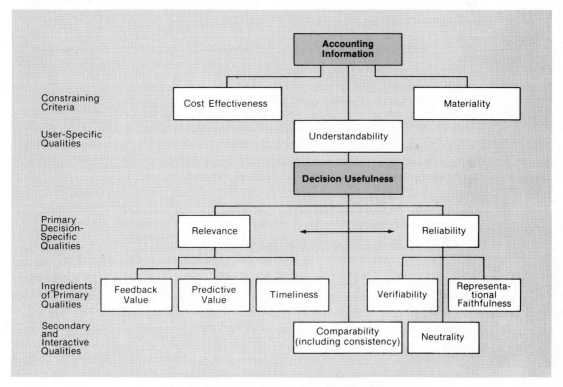

Hierarchy of Accounting Information Qualities

---

[7]The hierarchy presented in the illustration is adapted from Figure 1 of Statement of Financial Accounting Concepts No. 2, "Qualitative Characteristics of Accounting Information" (Stamford: Financial Accounting Standards Board, May 1980), page 15.

The quality of **decision usefulness** is central to the hierarchy. All other characteristics are viewed in terms of their contribution to the usefulness of information for decision making.

Constraining Criteria

In satisfying the informational qualities identified in the illustration on page 69, there are two overriding criteria that act as constraints. These two criteria are **cost effectiveness** and **materiality**. Both are pervasive criteria that impact on all of the other informational qualities.

Cost Effectiveness. Information is like other commodities in that it must be worth more than it costs to be desirable. Too often government regulators and others assume information is a "free" good. Obviously, it is not, and the cost-benefit relationship must always be kept in mind when selecting or requiring reporting alternatives. For example, when the Federal Trade Commission required large companies to disclose information about lines of business, a group of companies brought court action to nullify the requirement. A major argument of the companies was that the information requested would be very costly to prepare because it was not normally generated by the accounting system. It was also argued that the line-of-business disclosures in the form required by the FTC would not be beneficial to users because the segments to be reported on were artificial and not those the companies normally used to report on a less than company-wide basis. Unfortunately, in the authors' opinion, these reasons were not persuasive, but the point is that the cost of producing information (including, for example, additional modifications to the normal accounting system, or even additional printing and mailing costs) must be compared to the extra benefits (generally meaning an improvement in specific decisions to be made) to determine if the information should be reported.

The difficulty in assessing cost effectiveness is that the costs and especially the benefits are not always evident or easily measured. Notwithstanding this difficulty, the criterion of cost effectiveness is an important one and should be considered when selecting reporting alternatives.

Materiality. Financial reporting is concerned only with the information affecting the decisions to be made by users of the financial statements. Contrary to the belief of many readers of financial statements, the amounts reported in the statements are not comprehensive and are often not exact. For many decisions such completeness and exactness are not required. There is, of course, a point at which disclosures become relevant, when information that is incomplete or inexact does affect a decision. This point defines the boundary between information that is material and information that is immaterial.

Materiality is an overriding concept related to but distinguishable from the primary qualities of relevance and reliability. Materiality determines the threshold for recognition of accounting items and is primarily quantitative in nature. It is directed toward the specific question, Is the item large enough or the degree of accuracy precise enough to influence the decision of a user of the information? Of course, the degree of influence caused by the size of the item also depends on the nature of the item and the circumstances in which the judgment must be made. Certain information may be relevant to a decision, e.g., whether overtime is paid on a particular job. However, if the amount of overtime is negligible, that bit of information will have little or no influence on a decision to accept the job. Under those circumstances, information about overtime pay would be immaterial. Thus, relevance and materiality are both related to the concept of information usefulness. However, relevance is directed toward the *nature* of the information while materiality focuses on the *size* of a judgment item in a given set of circumstances.

At the present time, there are few guidelines to assist the preparers of financial reports in applying the concept of materiality. Where guidelines do exist, they are not uniform. For example, 10 percent is the materiality guideline for disclosing segment data for diversified companies, 3 percent is considered material in determining the significance of dilution for earnings per share computations, and there is a zero materiality threshold in the area of foreign corrupt practices. Managers and accountants must therefore exercise judgment in determining whether a failure to disclose certain data will affect the decisions of the users of financial statements.

Past court cases also help determine what is material by providing examples of where the lack of disclosure of certain information in the financial statements has been considered a material misstatement. The failure to disclose proper inventory values or pending sales of large amounts of assets, the failure to disclose the imminence of a highly profitable transaction or to disclose a significant downward readjustment of reported earnings are a few examples.[8]

In summary, the following point should be kept in mind in making judgments concerning materiality:

> The omission or misstatement of an item in a financial report is material if, in the light of surrounding circumstances, the magnitude of the item is such that it is probable that the judgment of a reasonable person relying upon the report would have been changed or influenced by the inclusion or correction of the item.[9]

User-Specific Qualities

The hierarchy illustrated on page 69 distinguishes user-specific qualities such as **understandability** from qualities inherent in accounting information or decision-specific qualities. The quality of understandability is essential to decision usefulness because information cannot be useful to decision makers if it is not understood, even though the information may be relevant and reliable. The understandability of information depends on both

---

[8]For additional examples of quantitative materiality considerations see Appendix C of FASB Statement of Concepts No. 2.

[9]*Statement of Financial Accounting Concepts No. 2,* "Qualitative Characteristics of Accounting Information" (Stamford: Financial Accounting Standards Board, May 1980), par. 132.

user characteristics and the inherent characteristics of the information presented. Hence, understandability can be evaluated only with respect to specific classes of decision makers. As indicated earlier, financial reporting is directed toward those users who have a reasonable understanding of business and economic activities and who are willing to study the information provided with reasonable diligence.

Primary Decision-Specific Qualities

In the following statement, the FASB identified **relevance** and **reliability** as the primary qualities inherent in useful accounting information:

> The qualities that distinguish "better" (more useful) information from "inferior" (less useful) information are primarily the qualities of relevance and reliability, with some other characteristics that those qualities imply.[10]

Relevance. The relevance of information may be judged only in relation to its intended use. If information is not relevant to the needs of decision makers, it is useless regardless of how well it meets other criteria. The objective of relevance, then, is to select methods of measuring and reporting that will aid those individuals who rely upon financial statements to make decisions. Many critics of financial statements have argued that traditionally prepared statements are irrelevant to many decisions that must be made. An increasing amount of research is being conducted to evaluate this criticism. What information is required by those who must make a decision? How can current practice be changed to improve the relevance, and thus the usefulness, of accounting information?

The FASB defines relevant information as that which will "make a difference." Information may confirm expectations or change them. In either case, a decision maker's assessment of the probability of occurrence of some event is affected by the information. If the decision maker's assessment is not affected by certain information, that information is not relevant and therefore not useful to the decision maker. Thus, the FASB relates relevance to the predictive or confirmation value of information. If a user can better predict future consequences based on information about past events and transactions, then such information is relevant.[11]

As shown in the illustration on page 69, two key ingredients of relevant information are its **feedback value** and **predictive value**. Information provides feedback on past actions that helps confirm or correct earlier expectations. Such information can then be used to help predict future outcomes. Normally relevant information provides both feedback and predictive value at the same time. Knowledge of previous activities and consequences generally improves a decision maker's ability to predict the results of similar future actions. As stated by the FASB, "Without a knowledge of the past, the basis for prediction will usually be lacking. Without an interest in the future, knowledge of the past is sterile."[12]

---

[10]*Ibid.*, par. 15.
[11]*Ibid.*, par. 46–50.
[12]*Ibid.*, par. 51.

Timeliness is another key ingredient of relevance, relating directly to decision usefulness. Information furnished after a decision has been made is of no value. All accounting systems should be established to provide information to users in a timely manner. In meeting this criterion, financial statements must be prepared prior to the time an accountant can be absolutely certain as to the results of an entity's operations. The entity is an ongoing enterprise with many interacting activities. Thus, any attempt to measure the success of an entity at some point in time before its dissolution must rely heavily on estimates. Decisions by investors, creditors, governmental authorities, managers, and others rely on these estimates. By convention, the year has been established as the normal period for reporting. Annual statements, as well as statements covering shorter intervals, such as quarters, have been provided by entities to satisfy the needs of those requiring financial information.

It is evident that the degree of relevance of information will vary for different users depending on their particular needs and circumstances. Therefore, trade-offs exist among the desirable qualities of useful information, including reliability and the other qualities yet to be discussed. As stated by the FASB:

> In the last analysis each decision maker judges what accounting information is useful, and that judgment is influenced by factors such as the decisions to be made, the methods of decision making used, the information already possessed or obtainable from other sources, and the decision maker's capacity (alone or with professional help) to process the information.[13]

Reliability. The second primary quality of accounting information is reliability. Accounting information is reliable if users can depend on it to represent the economic conditions or events that it purports to represent.[14] Reliability does not mean absolute accuracy. Obviously, there are degrees of reliability. Information that is based on judgments and includes estimates and approximations cannot be totally accurate, but it should be reliable. The objective, then, is to present the type of information in which users can have confidence. To accomplish this objective, information must contain the key ingredients of reliability: **verifiability** and **representational faithfulness**.

Verification implies consensus. Accountants seek to base their findings on facts that are determined objectively and that can be verified by other trained accountants. The FASB indicates that "verifiable financial accounting information provides results that would be substantially duplicated by independent measurers using the same measurement methods."[15]

All accounting measurements, however, cannot be completely free from subjective opinions and judgments. Cash receipts and disbursements can be adequately supported by vouchers, and cash on hand is determined by

---

[13]*Ibid.*, par. 36.
[14]*Ibid.*, par. 62.
[15]*Ibid.*, par. 82.

count; full support and verification for this element and its changes are available. Findings here can be readily verified. Purchases of goods and services, as well as sales, are also generally well supported by evidence and are subject to verification. There are a number of areas in accounting, however, where determinations must be based in part upon judgment, estimate, and other subjective factors. The recognition of depreciation is an example. But the degree of estimate can be minimized by the attempt to develop evidence lending objective support to conclusions. Verifiable determinations are encouraged as a means of reducing possible error, bias, or intentional distortion, and achieving an accounting that can be accepted with confidence.

Two kinds of bias are possible in accounting information: **measurer bias** and **measurement bias**. Verifiability protects against measurer bias. Representational faithfulness deals with measurement bias. That is, does the measurement show what it purports to show. The measurements reported on the balance sheet, for example, have been criticized because they do not reflect the value of a company. However, that has not been their purpose. If the purpose of balance sheet measurements is accepted in its traditional context of reporting on the financial status of a company as measured by historical costs based on past arms-length transactions, then such information can be said to exhibit the quality of representational faithfulness. The information may be rejected as not measuring the right thing, that is, as not being relevant, but the information would be reliable in the sense of not having measurement bias.

Secondary and Interactive Qualities

There are at least three additional qualities that directly influence accounting information. Listed in the order they are discussed, these concepts are: (1) neutrality, (2) comparability, and (3) consistency.

Neutrality. Financial statements should not be biased in favor of one group to the detriment of another. This may seem in conflict with the primary quality of relevance; however, the presumption of the FASB is that external financial reports are general purpose statements that should meet the common needs of a wide variety of users. Specialized needs must be met in other ways.

The concept of neutrality is similar to the all-encompassing principle of "fairness." It is also directly related to other informational criteria, especially reliability. As stated by the FASB,

> To be neutral, accounting information must report economic activity as faithfully as possible, without coloring the image it communicates for the purpose of influencing behavior in *some particular direction.*[16]

Comparability. The essence of comparability is that information becomes much more useful when it can be related to a benchmark or standard, that

---

[16]*Ibid.*, par. 100.

is, when it is compared to another firm or to similar information for the same firm but for other equivalent periods of time. Thus, comparability may be regarded as intra-comparability, or comparability within a single enterprise, and inter-comparability, or comparability between enterprises. The comparability within a single firm relates more to consistency which is discussed in the next section.

Financial reports should provide information permitting a comparison of one company with another. This requires that like things be accounted for in the same manner on the financial statements. Basic similarities and differences in the activities of companies should be clearly apparent from the financial statements. They should not be influenced by selection and use of different accounting methods.

One of the greatest unsolved problems in accounting is the present acceptance of alternative accounting methods under situations that do not appear to be sufficiently different to warrant different practices. Much current research in accounting is directed toward identifying circumstances justifying the use of a given method of accounting. If this research is successful, alternative methods can be eliminated where circumstances are found to be the same. In the meantime, current practice requires disclosure of the accounting methods used, as well as the impact of changes in methods when a change can be justified. There is also pressure on accountants to indicate the "preferability" of one accounting method over another. Although the disclosures currently made do not generally provide enough information for a user to convert the published financial information from one accounting method to another, they do provide information that can assist the user in determining the degree of inter-company comparability.

Consistency. Consistency is an important ingredient of intra-comparability and useful accounting information. In view of the number of reporting alternatives, such as the different procedures for cost allocation in measuring depreciation, the different approaches for pricing inventories in developing cost of goods sold, and the different forms and classifications for the presentation of operating and financial data, the methods adopted should be consistently employed if there is to be continuity and comparability in the accounting presentations. In analyzing statements one constantly seeks to identify and evaluate the changes and trends within the enterprise. Conclusions concerning financial position and operations may be materially in error if, for example, accelerated depreciation is applied against the revenue of one year and straight-line depreciation against the revenue of the next year, or if securities are reported under long-term investments in one year and under current assets in the following year. Consistency in the application of accounting procedures is also recognized as a means of ensuring integrity in financial reporting; the use of alternate procedures in succeeding periods opens the doors to manipulation of net income and asset and equity measurements.

This is not to suggest that methods once adopted should not be changed. A continuing analysis of the business activities, as well as changing conditions, may suggest changes in accounting methods and presentations leading to more informative statements. These changes should be incorporated in the accounting system and statements. But the financial statements should be accompanied by a clear explanation of the nature of the changes and their effects, where they are material, so current reporting can be properly interpreted and related to past reporting.

Both consistency and comparability are concepts relating to the relationships of two or more accounting numbers rather than to the informational quality of the number itself, as is true with the primary qualities of relevance and reliability.

NATURE OF THE ACCOUNTING MODEL: AN UNRESOLVED ISSUE

Perhaps one of the most important issues to be resolved by the conceptual framework is the nature of the accounting model to be used for financial reporting. The traditional accounting model is comprised of several basic features. First, the business enterprise is viewed as a specific **entity** separate and distinct from its owners and any other business unit. It is the entity and its activities that receive the focus of attention for accounting purposes.

Second, in the absence of evidence to the contrary, the entity is viewed as a **going concern**. This continuity assumption provides support for the preparation of a balance sheet reporting costs assignable to future activities rather than realizable values that would attach to properties in the event of voluntary liquidation or forced sale. This same assumption calls for the preparation of an income statement reporting only such portions of revenues and costs as are allocable to current activities.

Third, only the **arms-length transactions and events** are accounted for which impact upon an entity. Such transactions and events provide the basis for accounting entries, and any changes in resources and equity values are generally not recorded until a transaction has taken place.

A fourth and related point is that accounting, as it is practiced today, is founded upon the **cost valuation principle**. The amount of money actually exchanged in a transaction is the amount used as a basis for the recognition of goods or services acquired. Cost represents a value regarded as definite and immediately determinable, and thus also satisfies the criteria of verifiability and neutrality. The use of historical costs is supported as a means of closing the doors to possible error, bias, or even intentional misstatement, and achieving an accounting that can be accepted with confidence.

Fifth, transactions are measured in **monetary units**, and, in the United States at least, the dollar is used as the measuring unit. As mentioned earlier, value changes in the dollar have historically been ignored. Accounting systems are designed to account for the use of given units of money, that is, their inflow and their outflow. Thus, accounting systems tend to produce statements that summarize stewardship functions of management. Changes in the value of the monetary unit are not significant when a historical cost principle is adopted that regards only the accounting for original dollars as important. However, many accountants have felt uncomfortable about the relevance of accounting information that is insensitive to changes in the value of the measuring unit. Although all accounts shown on the balance sheet are labeled dollars, they are not dollars of equal purchasing power. These various dollars are added together as though the monetary units were stable. But when the value of the dollar fluctuates greatly over time, such an assumption obviously loses its validity.

Sixth, it is assumed that accounting information is needed on a timely basis and so the life of a business entity is divided in specific **accounting periods**. For each time period an income measure is determined on an **accrual basis**. This means that revenues are recognized as earned, not necessarily when cash is received; and expenses are recognized when incurred, not necessarily when cash is paid.

The revenues for a period are generally determined independently from expenses by application of the concept of **revenue recognition**. Essentially, the recognition of revenue is a timing problem. Revenue could be recognized at a number of points during the production and sales cycle of a product. The recognition principle, however, provides that before revenue is recorded (1) the earning process must be complete or virtually complete, and (2) an arms-length market exchange must have taken place. Based upon these criteria, revenue is generally recognized at **the point of sale**, that is, at the point when an arms-length transaction between two willing and competent parties has been completed. Other points in the cycle are sometimes used because of the special nature of the transactions.

Expenses for a period are determined by direct association with specific revenues or a particular time period. This process has frequently been referred to as **the matching process**. Many allocations of cost are arbitrary because of the artificiality of attaching a cost to each unit of revenue and because of the uncertainty that remaining unallocated costs will contribute to the realization of future revenue. It should be noted that since the point in time for the recognition of revenue and expense is identical with the point in time that changes in assets and liabilities are recognized, income determination is directly related to asset valuation.

Another concept often associated with the traditional accounting model is **conservatism**. This means that when there is genuine doubt concerning which of two or more reporting alternatives should be selected, business is best served by adopting a conservative approach, that is, by choosing the alternative with the least favorable effect upon owners' equity. However, conservatism does not mean deliberate and arbitrary understatement of net assets and earnings. Conservatism should be used to deal with uncertainties when a degree of skepticism is warranted. A common example in accounting practice is reporting inventories at the lower of cost or market values. Thus, the concept of conservatism is a useful one, but one that should be applied carefully and used only as a moderating and refining influence to the accounting process as a whole.

Many of the above assumptions and features of the accounting model are being questioned. If the conceptual framework relaxes these assumptions or otherwise changes the accounting model, financial reporting will be affected. Students should not only pay attention to the unresolved and controversial issues that will be discussed throughout the text, but they should also be prepared to monitor and keep pace with the changes that will occur in accounting in the future.

Establishing a conceptual framework for accounting is an on-going project. It is certainly not an easy task nor will its completion necessarily provide solutions to all accounting problems. The FASB has made commendable progress, but much remains to be done. Even some of the work already accomplished is being, and will continue to be, reconsidered and revised to correct weaknesses. Nevertheless, progress is being made. Meeting user needs for financial information in an increasingly complex environment will continue to be a major problem for accounting professionals. Increasing governmental regulation of business and accounting is another challenge to be faced. Furthermore, accountants are being asked to assume additional responsibilities, e.g., the detection of fraud and the reporting of the social impact of enterprise activity. And these responsibilities must be performed in a manner that will maintain high professional standards and thus avoid legal difficulties.

The challenges facing the accounting profession are significant. They provide an exciting opportunity for future accountants to make important contributions to their profession and to society. Resolution of problems may not be easy, but it will be rewarding and it will certainly make a career in accounting interesting.

QUESTIONS

1. Who are the primary "internal" and "external" users of accounting information?
2. What impact has the corporate form of business had on financial reporting?
3. Why is judgment required of accountants in fulfilling their role as suppliers of information?
4. The Conceptual Framework Project is receiving a large share of the FASB's resources. What is the project expected to accomplish? What is it not likely to do?
5. List the eight components that currently comprise the FASB conceptual framework.
6. Why are definition, recognition, measurement, and display considered separate and distinct aspects of the conceptual framework?
7. Identify the major objectives of financial reporting as specified by the FASB.
8. Identify and describe the two "constraining criteria" for accounting information.
9. Why is it so difficult to measure the cost effectiveness of accounting information?
10. What is the current materiality standard in accounting?
11. Distinguish between the primary informational qualities of relevance and reliability.

12. What characteristics directly affect the relevance of information? Explain.

13. Does reliability mean absolute accuracy? Explain.

14. Two types of bias may exist in accounting information. What are they and to which of the qualities of accounting information do they relate?

15. Define comparability. How does comparability differ from uniformity?

16. Of what value is consistency in financial reporting?

17. Identify and describe the basic features of the traditional accounting model.

18. What impact might the FASB conceptual framework have on the accounting model?

EXERCISES

exercise 3-1

As a student of accounting, you have noticed that a substantial portion of the literature deals with establishing a comprehensive set of concepts upon which accounting principles can be based. This is currently the case and has been for the past 50 years. Yet, in discussions with colleagues and friends, you have to admit that the accounting profession still cannot point to an authoritative set of accounting concepts and principles which are universally accepted within the business community. As you think about this problem, at least three questions come to mind: (1) Why have accountants not been able to develop a conceptual framework? (2) Is an overall conceptual framework of accounting even needed? and (3) What are the members of the FASB doing differently, if anything, so that they might expect to succeed in establishing a conceptual framework of accounting where others have failed? Discuss possible answers to these questions.

exercise 3-2

Teri Green has recently been promoted. She is now the chief financial officer of Teltrex, Inc., and has primary responsibility for the external reporting function. During the past three weeks, Green has met with Jeff Thalman, the senior vice president of Westmore First National Bank where Teltrex has a $1,000,000 line of credit; Susan David, a financial analyst for Stubbs, Jones, and McConkie, a brokerage firm; and Brian Ellis, who is something of a corporate gadfly and who owns 2 percent of Teltrex's outstanding common stock. Each of these individuals has commented on Teltrex's last year's annual report, pointing out deficiencies and suggesting additional information they would like to see presented in this year's annual report. From Green's point of view, explain the nature of general purpose financial statements and indicate the informational qualities of the accounting data that she must be concerned with in fulfilling Teltrex's external reporting responsibility.

4

The Statements of Income and Changes in Owners' Equity

CHAPTER OBJECTIVES

Explain the importance of measuring and reporting income and its components.

Describe the economic approach and the transaction approach to income determination.

Discuss the impact of changing prices on the measurement and reporting of earnings.

Describe and illustrate the content and form of the income statement.

Describe and illustrate the reporting of changes in owners' equity.

Accounting systems are designed to provide a variety of reports and analyses for internal and external use. Traditionally, the information made available for external use has been reported in a set of financial statements consisting of: (1) an **income statement** presenting the results of operations of an entity for a reporting period; (2) a **balance sheet** reporting the financial position of a business at a certain date; and (3) a **statement of changes in financial position** describing the changes in enterprise resources over the reporting period. When the change in owners' equity is not fully explained by the income statement, a supplemental **statement of changes in owners' equity** is usually presented to provide a complete reconciliation of the beginning and ending equity balances. This set of general-purpose financial statements is intended for the use of a wide variety of external users. Although there has been some discussion as to the need for special purpose statements directed to specific external users, there has been no significant movement toward this in practice.

The importance of measuring and reporting income, as well as the nature and the content of the income statement, is described in this chapter. Also discussed is the statement of changes in owners' equity. The balance sheet and statement of changes in financial position are discussed in Chapter 5.

IMPORTANCE OF MEASURING AND REPORTING INCOME

The **income statement**, alternately titled the *earnings statement*, the *statement of profit and loss*, or the *statement of operations*, summarizes business activities for a given period and reports the net income or loss resulting from operations and from certain other defined activities.

The measuring and reporting of business income and its components is generally regarded as one of the most important responsibilities of accountants. Reference is made to the income statement by many different groups who need to evaluate the results of business activities. As discussed in Chapter 3, information on past earnings may be used as a measure of overall managerial performance and as an indicator of future earnings potential. Information about earnings may also be useful in determining the worth of a business, for it is business earnings that ultimately validate asset values. Proper measurement of income promotes the flow of capital to the most profitable and presumably the most efficient enterprises, providing for optimal allocation of scarce economic resources.

The current emphasis on the income statement may be attributed primarily to (1) the information needs of investors and creditors, (2) an increase in the internal use of accounting information, and (3) the pervasive influence of the tax laws on business entities.

Needs of Investors and Creditors

As indicated by the FASB in *Statement of Financial Accounting Concepts No. 1*, the primary objective of financial reporting is to provide information useful for decision making.[1] The types of information to be supplied are therefore dependent on the needs of the users and their particular decisions.

Investors and creditors are considered to be among the most important external users of financial information. In today's business world most investors and creditors have very little direct contact with the companies in which they have holdings. Although they can attend annual stockholders' meetings, very few of them actually do. Instead, they rely on earnings infor-

---

[1] *Statement of Financial Accounting Concepts, No. 1*, "Objectives of Financial Reporting by Business Enterprises" (Stamford: Financial Accounting Standards Board, 1978).

mation published in financial statements, newspapers, and the financial press as a basis for evaluating management's performance and the company's ability to generate favorable cash flows in the future. Specifically, investors and creditors, and those who advise or represent them, must assess the amounts, timing, and uncertainty of prospective cash receipts. Such receipts take the form of dividends or interest and the proceeds from the sale of stock or the redemption or maturity of securities and loans.

While recognizing the importance of future cash flow prospects, the FASB has stated that accrual accounting provides a better indication of enterprise performance than information about current cash receipts and disbursements.[2] Thus, the income statement reports earnings and its components on an accrual basis. In the future, however, additional cash flow information, perhaps even on a projected basis, may be required.

Increased Internal Use of Accounting Information

Not only has there been increased interest in the income statement by outside users, but the same can also be said for the primary internal user — management. Years ago, proprietors often could acquire an intuitive feel as to how well things were going in an enterprise; but, today, in most situations, the complexity of modern business makes this impossible. Managements of large and growing corporate enterprises, dealing in many different product areas, need to have profitability information to answer questions relating to past, present, and projected programs. Questions arise such as: How effective was our past advertising policy? Should we make or buy certain component parts for our end-line products? Should we add to our product lines? Information systems within the enterprise must provide answers to these and related questions and often do so in the context of some version of an income report.

Income Tax Laws

Since 1913 when the 16th amendment to the Constitution was passed, taxes on income at both national and state levels have become increasingly significant. To comply with income tax laws, every business entity must have some system for the measurement of income. However, generally accepted accounting principles are not based on the tax law. Income measurement for tax purposes is related to governmental regulatory, social, and financial objectives and responsibilities. Income determination according to generally accepted accounting principles, however, is related primarily to the decision-making needs of investors, creditors, and managers. These differing objectives create many differences between taxable income and "book" income which must be accounted for and reconciled. The emphasis in this text is on proper reporting for financial accounting purposes and not on what may be appropriate or desirable for tax purposes. Significant dif-

---

[2] *Ibid.*, par. 44.

ferences between accounting for tax purposes and for financial accounting purposes are noted, however, where appropriate.

NATURE OF INCOME

With increasing attention being given to reporting earnings, it is only natural that certain questions have been raised: What purpose should the measurement of income serve in our economy? How can it best serve this purpose? Is the accountant's function limited to that of a historian reporting on the past? Or should accountants try to provide the best guide for estimating future earning power? All of these questions are appropriate; however, all of the answers may not be provided by the same income statement, and some purposes are being better satisfied than others by present accounting methods.

At least part of the reason why the measurement of income has presented problems to accountants is the lack of a precise definition of **income**. Another important factor is the need to exercise judgment on a great many matters in arriving at such a measurement. Thus, considerable research has been directed toward the subject of income determination. Two primary approaches to income measurement have been predominant: the **economic approach** and the **transaction approach**.

Economic Approach

A business entity commences activities in the attempt to increase its **net assets** (total assets − total liabilities) through profitable operations. This increase in net assets, referred to by many economists as a change in the *wealth* or *well-offness* of the entity, represents the *income* of the firm. Thus, the **economic approach** to the determination of income is to value the net assets of an entity at two different times and compute the change that has occurred. If the change is positive, after adjustment for any investment or withdrawal of assets by the owners, there has been income. If the change is negative, there has been a loss. Because income is determined by comparing the value of net assets at two different times, this method is sometimes referred to as the **valuation method**.

The valuation method is most commonly used by economists in their discussion of income. One of the most-quoted economists in accounting literature, J. R. Hicks, defined income as the maximum value which an entity can distribute during a period and still expect to be as well-off as it was at the beginning of the period.[3] The problem inherent in this concept of income is in defining the **value of net assets**. Is it the historical cost of the net assets reduced by some amount for their use? Is it the current value of the net assets determined by replacement or market values? Is it the historical cost of the net assets adjusted for the change in price levels since original acquisitions? All of these, as well as other concepts, may be regarded as satisfying the general term, value of net assets. Another question

---

[3]J. R. Hicks, *Value and Capital*, 2d ed. (Oxford University Press, 1946).

that must be resolved is what is to be included in net assets. Should intangible items, such as goodwill, patents, and leaseholds be included in assets? Should the value of employees be reported as an asset? Should estimated payments relating to warranties and pensions be included in liabilities?

For many years economists, and recently some accountants, have approached these difficult questions by attempting to define net assets in terms of the present value of the future cash benefits that net assets are expected to provide.

Advocates of this approach maintain that to measure the true economic income of a firm, we should determine the amounts of future cash flows at different points in time. Then, with the use of appropriate discount rates, the present worth of these streams of future benefits could be determined. Net assets thus computed could be compared at different time intervals in arriving at an income measure that would show increased (or decreased) well-offness.

Although this concept has some theoretical merit, it has had minor influence upon practice primarily because of the measurement problems involved. We live in an uncertain world with limited knowledge of future cash flows. Expectations as to these future flows vary among those individuals with interest in the company. Also, with limited knowledge of the future, what should be accepted as the appropriate discount rates to apply to cash flows in arriving at asset values? Because of these uncertainties, the accountant has turned to more direct ways of defining income.

Transaction Approach

The method of income determination that has proved most acceptable to the accountant has been the **transaction approach**, also sometimes referred to as the matching method. This approach measures the results of enterprise transactions and involves the determination of the amount of revenue earned by an entity during a given period and the amount of expired costs applicable to that revenue. The difference between these two items is recognized as **net income**. If users were willing to wait until the end of the life of a business unit for the full results of its operations, it would be an easy matter to compute the total revenues and total expenses of the business and the resulting net income or net loss. However, users of income statements, seeking to judge the progress of an entity, need periodic measurements of business profitability. In fact, users seem increasingly interested in receiving financial statements more frequently than at the traditional annual intervals. To satisfy this need, interim statements are also provided by most large companies. Thus, the element of timing, both for revenue and expense, becomes ever more significant. Rather than concentrating on asset valuations, the center of attention is thus transferred to a discussion of **revenue recognition** and **expense recognition**. It should be recognized, however, that because the financial statements are fundamentally interrelated, the point in time at which revenues and expenses are recognized is also the time when changes in amounts of net assets are recognized.

Revenue Recognition. Revenues may be defined as inflows of assets resulting from the normal operations of a business.[4] Generally, revenues are derived from normal recurring activities such as selling products, rendering services, or permitting others to use enterprise resources in exchange for interest, rent, royalties, or similar fees. Proceeds from the disposal of resources such as plant and equipment or long-term investments should not be included in regular revenues; however, if such assets are sold at a gain, the resulting increase in net assets should be reported as a separate component of operating earnings. Assets acquired by purchase, proceeds from borrowing, and capital contributions do not give rise to revenue.

Although the above description of revenues defines the activities that produce revenue, it does not specify the time period in which revenue should be recorded and recognized in the income statement. A general **revenue recognition rule** has evolved stating that revenue should be recorded when two conditions are met: (1) the earnings process is complete or virtually so; and (2) an exchange has taken place. These criteria have led to the conventional recognition of revenue at a specific point in the earnings process — when assets are sold or services are rendered. However, some accountants would argue that an exchange does not necessarily have to occur for recognition of revenue. What is critical is that objective measurement is possible, whether or not an exchange has taken place, in addition to the earning process being substantially complete. There are sufficient deviations from the general rule to justify a closer look into the nature of revenue recognition.

The revenue-producing cycle as it passes through an entity can be a long one. The beginning point is not well defined, but assume that it begins with the development of proposals for a certain product by an individual or by the research and development department of a business unit. From the idea stage, the future product is carefully described in plans and engineering specifications. Bills of material are prepared, a production schedule is agreed upon, and raw materials are ordered, delivered, and placed into production. Labor and factory overhead are added to the raw materials as the product proceeds through the manufacturing process. Once completed, the product is transferred to the finished goods warehouse. The product is listed in company catalogs, it is promoted in advertising campaigns, and it moves through the company's distribution system to the final sale. Frequently sales are on a credit basis, and, after a period of time, collections are made on the accounts. The product may be sold with a warranty for necessary repairs or replacements. The cycle thus extends from the original idea to the end of the warranty period. All these steps are involved in the recognition of the sales revenue. If there is a failure at any step, revenue may be seriously curtailed or possibly completely eliminated. And yet, there is only one aggregate revenue amount for the entire cycle, the sale price of the goods. The question then is: When should revenue be recognized?

---

[4]See *FASB Discussion Memorandum*, "An Analysis of the Issues Related to Reporting Earnings" (Stamford: Financial Accounting Standards Board, July 31, 1979).

Answers to the question of when revenue should be recognized can be divided into two broad categories: (1) at one specific point in the cycle, or (2) at two or more points in the cycle.[5] The prevailing practice provides for recognition of revenue at one specific point in the cycle. Of course, determining the specific point presents a problem. Applying the previously mentioned guidelines, revenue from sale of products is recognized at the **point of sale**, usually interpreted to mean the time of delivery to customers. It is felt that prior to the sale, there has not been an arm's-length determination of the market value of the goods. This makes any objective measure of revenue subject to dispute. In addition, most accountants feel that the **critical event** is the sale of an item, and that the earning process is not complete until the sales commitment has been substantially fulfilled. The same guidelines dictate that revenue from services is recognized *when services have been performed and are billable*, and that revenue from permitting others to use enterprise resources is recognized *as resources are used or as time passes*.

There are three notable exceptions to the general rule. One exception to the rule of recognition of revenue at the point of sale is found, for example, when market values are firmly established and the marketability of a given product is assured. Revenue in such instances is recognized at the **point of completed production**. Farm products with assured sales prices meet these criteria. In other instances, when uncertainty exists as to the collectibility of a receivable arising from the sale of goods or services, recognition of revenue may be deferred to the **point of actual cash collection**. The *installment sales method* of accounting is an example of the application of this practice. Although the installment sales method of deferring revenue beyond the point of sale is accepted as an alternate method for purposes of income taxation, it is not generally accepted for financial statement purposes "unless the circumstances are such that the collection of the sale price is not reasonably assured."[6]

The third exception is when revenue is recognized at two or more points in the cycle. Although conceptually one can maintain that revenue is being earned continuously throughout the cycle, the measurement of revenue on a continuous basis may be impractical. It also raises special questions, such as: Should revenue of an equal amount be assigned to each phase of the cycle? Or should revenue be recognized in proportion to the costs incurred in each phase of the cycle? In certain cases, however, the production phase of the cycle extends over more than one accounting period and some allocation of revenue over the periods involved is considered essential to meaningful statements. Construction contracts for buildings, roads, and dams requiring several periods to complete are often of this nature. The **percent-**

---

[5]This subject was considered by a special AAA Committee on Realization which was established in 1964 and published its conclusions in 1966. Some of their comments on the point of revenue recognition are included in this section. *Accounting Review* (Evanston, Illinois: American Accounting Association, April 1965), pp. 312–322.

[6]*Opinions of the Accounting Principles Board, No. 10*, "Omnibus Opinion — 1966" (New York: American Institute of Certified Public Accountants, 1967), par. 12.

age-of-completion method of accounting is used to meet these special conditions. This method requires a firm contract for sale prior to construction and an ability to estimate with reasonable accuracy the costs remaining to be incurred on the project. Portions of the total estimated revenue are recognized as the project progresses.

Thus, revenue recognition occurs at certain specifically defined points in the revenue-producing cycle. Generally, the recognition criteria are met and revenues are recorded at the point of sale. However, earlier or later recognition may be required due to the circumstances mentioned. Prior to revenue recognition, valuations are stated in terms of cost. After the recognition criteria are satisfied, use is made of *estimated or actual realizable values*. Discussion will certainly continue within the accounting profession as to the validity and acceptability of alternative points of revenue recognition. However, regardless of the point of revenue recognition selected, the relationship that has been defined between revenues and expenses will still hold.

Expense Recognition. Expenses may be defined as outflows or expirations of assets used or liabilities incurred to generate revenues in the normal course of business.[7] Some expenses may be directly associated with revenues as, for example, cost of goods sold. Other expenses are associated indirectly with revenue by assignment to particular periods of time during which the revenues have been recognized. Still other costs are not charged currently to the income statement because they relate to future revenues and, therefore, are shown as assets on the balance sheet. When the future service potential has expired, the costs are then associated with current revenues and reported as expenses. Expenses do not include repayment of borrowing, expenditures to acquire assets, distributions to owners (including the acquisition of treasury stock), or corrections of errors dealing with expenses of prior periods.

The FASB uses the terms **gains** and **losses** to reflect the net increases and decreases in net assets resulting from peripheral or incidental activities of a business.[8] As indicated earlier, gains from the sales of assets other than inventory are distinguished from revenues from normal operating activities. Similarly, losses from disposals of such assets are to be distinguished from expenses. While similar in some respects to revenues and expenses, gains and losses should be reported separately, but as a part of net income from continuing operations.

A primary difficulty in income determination is the decision as to how various expenses are, in fact, to be associated with revenues. It has not been possible to prescribe exact rules for *association* or *matching*.[9] Certain guidelines for the matching of expenses with revenues in arriving at net income or loss have evolved through time. When an accountant is faced with an

---

[7]*FASB Discussion Memorandum, loc. cit.*
[8]*Ibid.*
[9]Recent accounting pronouncements have been more specific in establishing guidelines for making these associations. Critics of this trend have stated their fear that accounting may become a set of rigid rules if such a trend continues.

absence of guidelines, judgment must be exercised. Three **expense matching principles** have been noted as being of special significance: (1) *associating cause and effect*; (2) *systematic and rational allocation*; and (3) *immediate recognition*.[10]

Associating Cause and Effect. Some costs can be associated directly with specific revenues. When this association is possible, the cost is recognized as an expense of the period in which the revenue is recognized. Thus, if an inventory item on hand at the end of a period represents a source of future revenue under the point of sale principle, the cost of producing the item is deferred to a future period and it is reported as an asset. Certain costs, such as labor and materials, usually can be directly related to the cost of producing the inventory item. Other costs, such as factory overhead, may be assumed to be associated with an inventory item on some logical basis such as the number of labor hours or the number of machine hours required to produce the item. Judgment plays an increasingly important part as the association becomes less direct.

Care must be taken to assure that proper recognition is made of all costs already incurred, as well as those yet to be incurred relative to any revenue currently recognized.

Systematic and Rational Allocation. In the absence of a direct cause and effect relationship, a different basis for expense recognition is commonly used. Here the attempt is made to associate costs in a systematic and rational manner with the products or the periods benefited. In arriving at period expense recognition, estimates must be made of the timing pattern of the benefits received from the individual costs and systematic allocation methods developed. The methods adopted should appear reasonable to an unbiased observer and should be followed consistently.

Some of the costs allocated to a period become expenses immediately and are associated with current revenue. Other costs *attach* to inventories and other assets on some logical basis and thus are associated with future revenue by being deferred as assets. Examples of costs that are associated with periods in a systematic way include costs of buildings and equipment, insurance, and taxes.

Immediate Recognition. Those costs that cannot be related to revenue either by associating cause and effect or by systematic and rational allocation, must be recognized as expenses of the current period. In some instances, prior period adjustments must be made, generally to correct past errors. These adjustments are discussed in Chapter 17. Most costs, however, are recognized as expenses in the period when no discernable future revenues can be associated with them.

Change in Estimates. In reporting periodic revenues and in attempting to properly match those expenses incurred to generate current period reve-

---

[10]*Statements of the Accounting Principles Board, No. 4*, "Basic Concepts and Accounting Principles Underlying Financial Statements of Business Enterprises" (New York: American Institute of Certified Public Accountants, 1970).

nues, accountants must continually make judgments. The numbers reported in the financial statements reflect these judgements and are based upon estimates of such factors as the number of years of useful life for depreciable assets, the amount of gas or oil to be produced, the amount of uncollectible accounts expected, or the amount of warranty liability to be recorded on the books. These and other estimates are made using the best available information at the statement date. However, conditions may change subsequently, and the estimates may need to be revised. Naturally, if either revenue or expense amounts are changed, the income statement is affected. The question is whether the previously reported income measures should be revised or whether the changes should impact only on the current and future periods.

The APB stated in Opinion No. 20 that adjustments in estimates should be made either in the current period or in the current and future periods. No retroactive adjustment or pro forma statements are to be prepared for a change in estimate.[11] These adjustments are felt to be part of the normal accounting process and not a change of past periods.

To illustrate, assume that for the past three years Mapleton Hardware, Inc., has estimated that 3 percent of its accounts receivable sales would be uncollectible. However, experience has shown that only about 2 percent of credit sales have actually gone bad. Company management should change its current and future provision for uncollectible accounts to the 2 percent guidelines but would not, according to APB Opinion No. 20, go back and retroactively adjust the reported income figures for the past three years. If the amount of the change is material, separate disclosure should be made concerning the change in estimate in the notes to the financial statements.

Effects of Changing Prices

As indicated in Chapter 3, accountants have traditionally ignored the impact of changing prices on financial statements. Thus, income has been measured by matching historical costs against recognized revenue, with none of the amounts being adjusted for the effects of inflation. Recognizing that the users of financial statements need to have an understanding of the impact of changing prices on a business enterprise, the FASB issued Statement No. 33, "Financial Reporting and Changing Prices."[12]

This statement, which applies primarily to certain large, publicly-held companies, requires disclosure of selected information on a supplemental basis. It does not affect the nature of the basic financial statements; income is still to be measured and reported on a historical cost basis, using the recognition and matching principles. The supplemental information to be disclosed reflects both general price changes (the impact of inflation) and specific price changes of selected items, primarily inventories and plant

---

[11]*Opinions of the Accounting Principles Board, No. 20*, "Accounting Changes" (New York: American Institute of Certified Public Accountants, 1971), par 31.

[12]*Statements of Financial Accounting Standards, No. 33*, "Financial Reporting and Changing Prices," (Stamford: Financial Accounting Standards Board, 1979).

assets. Price-level adjusted information must be disclosed for such items as income from continuing operations, gains and losses in purchasing power, and net assets at year-end. This and other selected information is to be reported for the current fiscal year and each of the preceding four years. The supplemental information must be included in any published annual report that contains the primary financial statements, although the information can be presented in several different formats.

Discussion of the details of these requirements and the mechanics of adjusting for price changes is deferred to Chapter 20. The main point to note here is that the accounting profession, in recognition of the needs of investors and creditors, now requires additional information concerning the components of earnings that reflect the impact of changing prices. Even though additional effort is required to prepare and interpret such information, the potential benefits for increased understanding of the results of enterprise activity seem to be well worth the effort.

REPORTING INCOME — THE INCOME STATEMENT

The importance of the revenue-expense relationships and the significance attached to the earnings of an entity by various users, especially investors and creditors, have been described in the first part of this chapter. In view of the importance attached to income measurement, the question continually arises: How can the components of net earnings be presented on the income statement in the most informative and useful manner?[13]

Reporting Results of Operations on an All-Inclusive Basis

Historically, there have been two generally accepted forms for income statement presentation, and the selection of the form reflected the manner in which the business unit preferred to recognize unusual or extraordinary items. One form, referred to as the **current operating performance income statement**, provided for reporting only normal and recurring operating items; other components, such as extraordinary items and prior period adjustments, were recorded directly in retained earnings and reported on an accompanying statement that summarized all of the changes in the retained earnings for the period. An alternative form, known as the **all-inclusive income statement**, provided for the presentation of unusual and extraordinary items on the face of the income statement after normal operating items. In employing the first form, the final amount was generally designated as net income; in the second form the final amount was designated by some as net income and by others as net income after extraordinary items. Because both of these income statement forms were being used in practice, there was a lack of consistency in the reporting by enterprises and thus a real danger of misinterpretation of the results of operations by statement users.

With the issuance of Accounting Principles Board Opinion No. 9, "Reporting the Results of Operations," a modified all-inclusive concept of income presentation was adopted. Both ordinary operations and extraordinary

---

[13]*FASB Discussion Memorandum, loc. cit.*

items were to be presented on the income statement, but as separate and distinct categories, with the nature and amounts of irregular or extraordinary items being disclosed net of tax. In effect, all items of income were to be recognized on the income statement with the exception of certain prior period adjustments.

Below-the-Line Items

With the adoption of the all-inclusive concept of reporting income came a recognition of the need to distinguish between certain income components. This led to the separate reporting of extraordinary items, discontinued operations, and the results from changing accounting principles. These special items are sometimes referred to as **below-the-line items**, i.e., the earnings components disclosed after income from continuing operations. These components of income are explained in Chapter 18.

The FASB is currently reviewing the entire area of income reporting. It is felt that the current "below-the-line" reporting practices are too narrow, and that there is not sufficient disclosure and emphasis on the effects of unusual events or transactions, and on the economic changes that affect the relationships between recurring revenues and expenses. While the suggested format for reporting the various earnings components has not yet been specified, there does seem to be a consensus that a distinction should be made between the regular earnings and the irregular earnings of a business. **Regular earnings** are those that can be expected to occur on a consistent basis over time. Most regular earnings are derived from the normal activities of a business, generally from the sale of goods and services. However, earnings may also be derived on a regular and consistent basis from activities that may be considered peripherally related to the main activities of a company, that is, from sources that are incidental to the normal business operations. An example would be interest revenue for a manufacturing enterprise. These peripheral earnings are reported as a part of income from continuing operations but generally as a separate category from normal operating income. The heading "Other revenues and other expenses" is often used to identify this component of regular earnings. Thus, the regular earnings of a business will generally result in the disclosures of sales, cost of sales, gross margins, contribution margins, other revenues and expenses, and an income from continuing operations figure.

Irregular earnings are those that occur infrequently, and also are the result of unusual activities or events. Examples of possible disclosures of irregular earnings include: items that are exceptionally large or small in comparison with corresponding amounts in previous years, results of activities that are undertaken infrequently, adjustments of past estimates, effects of accounting changes, and holding gains and losses.[14] The main objective of such disclosures is to provide users with additional information about the components of earnings so they will not confuse the effect of an irregular item with a change in earning ability of a more lasting nature.

---

[14]*Ibid.*

Content of the Income Statement

The income statement generally consists of a series of sections developing the net income for the period. As mentioned earlier, all elements of income, except for prior period adjustments, are to be included. However, a distinction should be made between the results of normal operations and other elements affecting net income. Major categories included within the normal operations section are: (1) revenues from the sale of goods and service; (2) cost of goods sold and expenses of providing services; (3) operating expenses; (4) other revenue and expense items; and (5) income tax relative to income from normal operations. Depending on individual circumstances, additional sections in the income statement would report other irregular earnings components all shown net of their tax effect. Illustrative statements are presented on pages 95 and 96.

Sales. Revenue from sales reports the total sales to customers for the period. This total should not include additions to billings for sales and excise taxes that the business is required to collect on behalf of the government. These billing increases are properly recognized as current liabilities. Sales returns and allowances and sales discounts should be subtracted from gross sales in arriving at net sales revenue. When the sales price is increased to cover the cost of freight to the customer and the customer is billed accordingly, freight charges paid by the company should also be subtracted from sales in arriving at net sales. Freight charges not absorbed by the buyer are recognized as selling expenses.

Cost of Goods Sold. When merchandise is acquired from outsiders, the cost of goods relating to sales of the period must be determined. **Cost of merchandise available for sale** is first determined. This is the sum of the beginning inventory, purchases, and all other buying, freight, and storage costs relating to the acquisition of goods. A net purchases balance is developed by subtracting purchase returns and allowances and purchase discounts from gross purchases. **Cost of goods sold** is calculated by subtracting the ending inventory from the cost of merchandise available for sale.

When the goods are manufactured by the seller, the **cost of goods manufactured** must first be calculated. Cost of goods manufactured replaces purchases in the summary just described. The determination of cost of goods manufactured begins with the cost of goods in process at the beginning of the period. To this is added the cost of materials put into production, the cost of labor applied to material conversions, and all of the other costs for services and facilities utilized in manufacturing, including factory supervision, indirect labor, depreciation and other costs relating to factory buildings and equipment, factory supplies used, patent amortization, and factory light, heat, and power. The total thus obtained represents the cost of goods completed and goods still in production. The goods in process inventory at the end of the period is subtracted from this total in arriving at the cost of the goods finished and made available for sale.

In practice, the distinction between those costs included in inventory as production costs and those classified as selling and administrative expenses is not always clear nor consistently applied among firms. This can result in differing income measures because some costs are included as part of the inventory while others are not.

Operating Expenses. *Operating expenses* are generally reported in two categories: (1) selling expenses and (2) general and administrative expenses. Selling expenses include such items as sales salaries and commissions and related payroll taxes, advertising and store displays, store supplies used, depreciation of store furniture and equipment, and delivery expenses. General and administrative expenses include officers' and office salaries and related payroll taxes, office supplies used, depreciation of office furniture and fixtures, telephone, postage, business licenses and fees, legal and accounting services, contributions, and similar items. Charges related to the use of buildings, such as rent, depreciation, taxes, insurance, light, heat, and power, should be allocated in some equitable manner to manufacturing activities and to selling and general and administrative activities. In the case of the merchandising concern, charges relating to buildings are generally reported in full in the general and administrative category.

Other Revenue and Expense Items. Other revenue and expense items include items identified with financial management and other miscellaneous recurring items. Other revenue includes earnings in the form of interest and dividends, gains from the sale of plant assets, and miscellaneous earnings from rentals, royalties, and service fees. Other expense includes interest expense, losses from the sale of plant assets, and other expenses related to the miscellaneous revenue items reported. These items are reported as a part of income from continuing operations, but as separate components of regular earnings.

Income Tax Relative to Income from Normal Operations. The income tax expense should report the tax on revenue and expense transactions included in pretax ordinary income from normal operations. This will require application of income tax allocation procedures described in Chapter 15. In reporting the tax, the components included in its determination should be disclosed. Parenthetical remarks or notes in the income statement may be considered appropriate in defining the nature and purpose of the allocations.

Earnings per Share. On the income statement for a corporation, the summary of net income is followed by a special presentation of earnings per share for the period in accordance with APB Opinion No. 15.[15] Earnings per share is computed by dividing income from normal operations, and any other major category of income subsequently disclosed, by the weighted average number of shares of common stock outstanding. For example, the

---

[15] *Opinions of the Accounting Principles Board, No. 15*, "Earnings per Share" (New York: American Institute of Certified Public Accountants, 1969).

Andersen Corporation income statement illustrated on page 95 shows earnings per share of 60¢ for net income. This figure is derived by dividing the amount of net income by 50,000 shares of common stock outstanding during the period.

APB Opinion No. 15 also requires the presentation of additional earnings-per-share information if there is a potential dilution of earnings due to the existence of convertible securities or stock options or warrants.

Form of the Income Statement

The income statement traditionally has been prepared in either multiple-step or single-step form. An example of an income statement in multiple-step form is presented on page 95 and in condensed single-step form on page 96.

In the **multiple-step form**, the ordinary operations are first summarized and designated as "Income from continuing operations before income tax." The income tax related to ordinary operations is computed and deducted. The title of the remaining figure varies depending upon whether there are other irregular components of income to be disclosed. The illustrations in this chapter assume no other income items and therefore identify the amount of after-tax income from continuing operations as net income. A more comprehensive illustration of reporting earnings is presented in Chapter 18.

Revenue and expense items are grouped to provide different income measurements as follows:

1. *Gross profit on sales* (or *gross margin*) — the difference between sales and the costs directly related to such sales.
2. *Operating income* — gross profit on sales less operating expenses.
3. *Income from continuing operations before income tax* — operating income increased by other revenue items and decreased by other expense items.
4. *Net income* — income less the income tax applicable to ordinary income.
5. *Earnings per common share* — the presentation of earnings per common share in terms of income by major category.

The **single-step form** may be in reality a modified single-step form if there are regular and irregular items to be disclosed separately. However, as illustrated, all ordinary revenue and expense items are listed and summarized without separate headings for cost of goods sold, gross profit, and other revenue and expense items.

Many accountants have raised objections to the multiple-step income statement form. They point out that the various income designations have no universal meaning and may prove a source of confusion to the reader. Quoting such designations in the absence of a complete income statement may prove ambiguous or actually misleading. They further maintain that multiple-step presentation implies certain cost priorities and an order for cost recoveries. But there is no such order and there can be no earnings unless all costs are recovered. These persons support the single-step form that minimizes sectional labeling. However, recent accounting pronouncements seem to be moving toward greater sectionalization of the income statement through separate identification of each significant irregular income component. Such disclosures should help investors and creditors in assessing the amounts and timing of future cash flows.

Andersen Corporation
Income Statement
For Year Ended December 31, 1981

Revenue from sales:			
Sales		$510,000	
Less: Sales returns and allowances	$ 7,500		
Sales discount	2,500	10,000	$500,000
Cost of goods sold:			
Merchandise inventory, January 1, 1981		$ 95,000	
Purchases	$320,000		
Freight in	15,000		
Delivered cost of purchases	$335,000		
Less: Purchases returns and allowances... $1,000			
Purchases discount	4,000	5,000	330,000
Merchandise available for sale		$425,000	
Less merchandise inventory, December 31, 1981		125,000	300,000
Gross profit on sales			$200,000
Operating expenses:			
Selling expenses:			
Sales salaries	$ 30,000		
Advertising expense	15,000		
Depreciation expense — selling and delivery equipment	5,000		
Miscellaneous selling expense	10,000	$ 60,000	
General and administrative expenses:			
Officers and office salaries	$ 48,000		
Taxes and insurance	20,000		
Miscellaneous supplies expense	5,000		
Depreciation expense — office furniture and fixtures	5,000		
Doubtful accounts expense	2,500		
Amortization expense	10,600		
Miscellaneous general expense	4,400	95,500	155,500
Operating income			$ 44,500
Other revenue and expense items:			
Interest revenue	$ 3,000		
Dividend revenue	5,000		
Gain on sale of investment	5,000	$ 13,000	
Interest expense		(7,500)	5,500
Income from continuing operations before income tax			$ 50,000
Income tax			20,000
Net income			$ 30,000
Earnings per common share[1]			$.60

[1]$30,000 ÷ 50,000 shares = $.60

Multiple-Step Income Statement

Andersen Corporation
Income Statement
For Year Ended December 31, 1981

Revenues:		
Net sales...	$500,000	
Other revenue — interest and dividends..	13,000	$513,000
Expenses:		
Cost of goods sold	$300,000	
Selling expense...	60,000	
General and administrative expense...	95,500	
Interest expense..	7,500	
Income tax..	20,000	483,000
Net income..		$ 30,000
Earnings per common share[1]		$.60

[1]$30,000 ÷ 50,000 shares = $.60

Condensed Single-Step Income Statement

The income statement is frequently prepared in condensed form and simply reports totals for certain classes of items, such as cost of goods sold, selling expenses, general expenses, and other revenue and expense. Additional detail may be provided by the use of supporting schedules and explanatory notes as illustrated in General Mills' income statement for 1979 in Appendix B. Notes to the financial statements are further discussed and illustrated in Chapter 5.

The use of condensed income statements by large units engaged in a number of diversified activities has been severely criticized. Income statements prepared in condensed form may tend to disguise the important trends operating within the individual segments of a diversified company. Because of this, the FASB, in Statement No. 14, and the Securities and Exchange Commission both require disclosure of sales and profit information by major segments of a company. This issue is further explored in Chapter 18.

When goods are manufactured by the seller, the cost of the goods manufactured must be determined before the cost of goods sold can be computed. If a summary of cost of goods manufactured is to accompany the financial statements, it should be presented as a schedule in support of the amount reported on the income statement. Assuming the merchandise available for sale in the example on page 95 was obtained by manufacture rather than by purchase, cost of goods sold on the income statement would be presented as shown below. The supporting schedule is shown at the top of page 97.

Cost of goods sold:		
Finished goods inventory, January 1, 1981	$ 40,000	
Add cost of goods manufactured per manufacturing schedule..	310,000	
Merchandise available for sale..	$350,000	
Less finished goods inventory, December 31, 1981.........	50,000	$300,000

Andersen Corporation
Manufacturing Schedule
For Year Ended December 31, 1981

Direct materials:			
Raw materials inventory, January 1, 1981		$ 30,000	
Purchases..	$105,000		
Freight in	10,000		
Delivered cost of raw materials	$115,000		
Less: Purchases returns and allowances $1,000			
Purchases discount 4,000	5,000	110,000	
Total cost of raw materials available for use................		$140,000	
Less raw materials inventory, December 31, 1981........		40,000	
Raw materials used in production.....................................			$100,000
Direct labor...			140,000
Factory overhead:			
Indirect labor..		$ 20,000	
Factory supervision...		14,500	
Depreciation expense — factory buildings and equipment		12,000	
Light, heat, and power		10,000	
Factory supplies expense		8,500	
Miscellaneous factory overhead		15,000	80,000
Total manufacturing costs			$320,000
Add goods in process inventory, January 1, 1981...........			25,000
			$345,000
Less goods in process inventory, December 31, 1981.....			35,000
Cost of goods manufactured			$310,000

Manufacturing Schedule

Frequently, only the cost of goods sold is reported on the income statement. If a schedule of the cost of goods sold is to be provided, it should summarize the cost of goods manufactured as well as the change in finished goods inventories. Instead of reporting beginning and ending inventories, it is possible simply to report inventory variations for the period in arriving at the cost of materials used, cost of goods manufactured, or cost of goods sold. For example, an increase in the finished goods inventory would be subtracted from the cost of goods manufactured in arriving at the cost of goods sold; a decrease in the finished goods inventory would be added to the cost of goods manufactured in arriving at the cost of goods sold.

REPORTING CHANGES IN OWNERS' EQUITY

When the only change in owners' equity arises from earnings for the period, the balance sheet prepared at the end of the period may report in the owners' equity section the balance of the equity at the beginning of the period, the change arising from earnings for the period, and the resulting balance at the end of the period. Usually, however, more than the earnings must be recognized in explaining the change in equity.

Changes in Retained Earnings

In the case of a corporation, if transactions affecting the stockholders' equity have been limited to changes in retained earnings, a **retained earnings statement** is prepared. This statement reports the beginning balance for retained earnings, any prior period adjustments shown net of tax to arrive at the adjusted retained earnings at the beginning of the period, earnings for the period, dividend declarations, and the ending retained earnings balance. Prior period adjustments are made primarily for corrections of errors in the financial statements of earlier periods. A retained earnings statement to accompany the income statement prepared on page 95 is shown below.

Andersen Corporation Retained Earnings Statement For Year Ended December 31, 1981	
Retained earnings, January 1, 1981	$149,000
Deduct prior period adjustment — correction of inventory overstatement, net of income tax refund of $9,000	9,000
Adjusted retained earnings, January 1, 1981..	$140,000
Add net income per income statement	30,000
	$170,000
Deduct dividends declared	20,000
Retained earnings, December 31, 1981	$150,000

Retained Earnings Statement

The income statement and retained earnings statement may be prepared in *combined* form. In preparing the combined statement, net income data are first listed and summarized. The amount of net earnings for the period is then combined with the retained earnings balance at the beginning of the period or the adjusted balance due to prior period adjustments. This total is adjusted for dividend declarations in arriving at the retained earnings balance at the end of the period. Data can be presented in either multiple-step or single-step form. The combined statement listing data in single-step form can be prepared in the form shown on page 99 (details for revenues and expenses have been omitted).

Other Significant Changes

Frequently, there are changes other than those affecting retained earnings that have an impact on the total owners' equity. The primary examples are increases and decreases in capital stock. When such is the case, companies should provide a statement of changes in owners' equity as a part of the financial statements. This statement would include the changes in retained earnings and other significant changes in the owners' equity of the business. Often the information is disclosed in the footnotes instead of a formal statement. An illustration of a statement of changes in owners' equity from the published financial statements of Levi Strauss & Co. appears on page 99.

Andersen Corporation Income and Retained Earnings Statement For Year Ended December 31, 1981		
Revenues		$513,000
Expenses...		483,000
Net income..		$ 30,000
Adjusted retained earnings, January 1, 1981:		
Retained earnings, January 1, 1981.............................	$149,000	
Deduct prior period adjustment — correction of inventory over- statement, net of income tax refund of $9,000...........................	9,000	140,000
		$170,000
Deduct dividends declared...		20,000
Retained earnings, December 31, 1981.............................		$150,000

Combined Income and Retained Earnings Statement

SUMMARY

The statement of earnings is certainly one of the most important statements prepared for the general use of creditors, investors, and others. The data reported provide a measure of a firm's past profitability and assist the user in assessing prospective future cash flows, either in the form of dividends, interest and repayment of loans, or appreciation in net asset values. There is currently considerable interest in the measurement and reporting of earnings which may lead the FASB to dramatically revise currently accepted accounting practice in this area.

Consolidated Statement of Stockholders' Equity
Levi Strauss & Co. and Subsidiaries
(Dollar amounts in thousands except per share data)

	Common Stock	Additional Paid-In Capital	Retained Earnings	Treasury Stock
Balance November 27, 1977	$21,999	$73,178	$374,950	$ (6,272)
Net income			144,969	
Purchases of treasury stock				(3,611)
Shares issued to employees		(1,283)		6,360
Cash dividends declared ($.80 per share)			(34,972)	
Balance November 26, 1978	$21,999	$71,895	$484,947	$ (3,523)
Net income			191,454	
Purchase of treasury stock				(87,451)
Shares issued to employees		(2,444)		7,443
Shares issued in connection with acquisition		12,973		24,288
Cash dividends declared ($1.00 per share)			(40,391)	
Balance November 25, 1979	$21,999	$82,424	$636,010	$(59,243)

QUESTIONS

1. Which accounting statements are considered general purpose financial statements?

2. Why is the measurement of business income considered to be one of the most important responsibilities of accountants?

3. What specific reasons can you offer for the increased importance of the income statement?

4. Why is the net income figure computed on the basis of generally accepted accounting principles often not the same as taxable income computed from IRS directives?

5. An article in a financial journal was titled "What are Earnings? The Growing Creditability Gap." What do you think was meant by this title?

6. What are the major differences between the economic and transaction approaches to income determination?

7. What concepts of the "value of net assets" might be applied in the economic approach to income determination?

8. What two conditions must normally be met for revenue to be recognized? At what point in the revenue cycle are these conditions usually met?

9. What are three specific exceptions to the general rule of revenue recognition?

10. Why is the process of matching costs with revenues in income determination so difficult?

11. Do you think matching expenses with revenues is more difficult to apply in a machine assembly plant than in a CPA firm? Why?

12. What guidelines are used to match costs with revenues in determining income?

13. Why are changes in estimates to be reported only in current and future periods and not retroactively adjusted?

14. How has the accounting profession responded to the need for recognizing the impact of changing prices?

15. What advantages are there to the distinction between regular and irregular earnings?

16. (a) What objections can be made to the multiple-step income statement? (b) What objections can be made to the single-step statement?

17. What information not found in the income statement or the balance sheet is disclosed in the retained earnings statement?

EXERCISES

exercise 4-1

Changes in account balances for the Flanigan Sales Co. during 1981 were as follows:

	Increase (Decrease)
Cash	$135,000
Accounts Receivable	15,000
Merchandise Inventory	120,000
Buildings and Equipment (net)	360,000

	Increase (Decrease)
Accounts Payable..	(105.000)
Bonds Payable...	300,000
Capital Stock	225,000
Additional Paid-In Capital..	45,000

Dividends paid during 1981 were $75,000. Calculate the net income for the year assuming there were no transactions affecting retained earnings other than the dividend payment.

exercise 4-2

Indicate which of the following items involves the recognition of revenue or gain. Give the reasons for your answer.

(a) Land acquired in 1952 at $15,000 is now conservatively appraised at $100,000.

(b) Timberlands show a growth in timber valued at $40,000 for the year.

(c) An addition to a building was self-constructed at a cost of $3,600 after two offers from private contractors for the work at $4,650 and $5,000.

(d) Certain valuable franchise rights were received from a city for payment of annual licensing fees.

(e) A customer owing $4,600, which was delinquent for one year, gave securities valued at $5,000 in settlement of the obligation.

(f) Merchandise, cost $1,000, is sold for $1,600 with a 50% down payment on a conditional sales contract, title to the merchandise being retained by the seller until the full contract price is collected.

(g) Cash is received on the sale of gift certificates redeemable in merchandise in the following period.

exercise 4-3

State the amount of revenue and/or expense for 1981 in each of the following transactions of the Kryton Tractor Co. The accounting period ends December 31, 1981. Treat each item individually.

(a) On December 15, 1981, Kryton received $12,000 as rental revenue for a 6-month period ending June 15, 1982.

(b) Kryton, on July 1, 1981, sold one of its tractors and received $10,000 in cash and a note for $50,000 at 12% interest, payable in one year. The fair market value of the tractor is $60,000.

(c) One of Kryton's steady customers is presently in a weak cash flow position. To maintain its goodwill with this customer, Kryton sells them 2 tractors with a normal combined selling price of $112,000, but allows them a special discount of $8,000.

(d) During 1981, tractors sold for $400,000 are accompanied by a Kryton guarantee for one year. Past experience indicates that repairs equal to 1% of sales revenue will be required in year of sale, and an additional 3% of sales revenue will be needed for repairs in the subsequent year.

(e) On December 28, 1981, Kryton sold 5 tractors for a total of $435,000. As of December 31, 1981, 3 of the tractors were still in Kryton's warehouse.

exercise 4-4

Where in a multiple-step income statement would each item be reported?

(a) Gain on sale of land.

(b) Purchases discount.

(c) Charge for doubtful accounts in anticipation of failure to collect receivables.

(d) Loss from long-term investments written off as worthless.

(e) Loss from a strike.

(f) Loss from inventory price decline.

(g) Depletion expense.

(h) Sales discount.

(i) Dividends received on long-term investments.

(j) Income tax for current period.

(k) Collection of life insurance policy upon death of officer.

(l) Vacation pay of office employee.

exercise 4-5

Using proper headings, prepare a manufacturing schedule in good form selecting the proper items from the following:

Purchases	$200,000	Indirect labor	$ 9,000
Purchases returns and allowances	20,000	Selling expenses	36,000
		Direct labor	52,000
Beginning inventory — finished goods	40,000	Other overhead	30,000
		Ending inventory — finished goods	32,000
Beginning inventory — goods in process	26,000	Ending inventory — goods in process	24,000
Beginning inventory — raw materials	30,000		
Accounts receivable	170,000	Ending inventory — raw materials	36,000
Equipment	52,000	Cash	22,000

exercise 4-6

The selling expenses of Robinson, Inc., for 1981 are 10% of sales. General expenses, excluding doubtful accounts, are 25% of cost of goods sold but only 15% of sales. Doubtful accounts are 2% of sales. The beginning merchandise inventory was $124,000 and it decreased 25% during the year. Income for the year before income tax of 45% is $104,000. Prepare an income statement, including earnings per share data, giving supporting computations. Robinson, Inc., has 104,000 shares of common stock outstanding.

exercise 4-7

From the chart of accounts presented below, prepare a multiple-step income statement in good form showing all appropriate items properly classified, including disclosure of earnings per share data. Assume a supporting manufacturing schedule has been prepared. (No monetary amounts are to be recognized.)

Accounts Payable
Accumulated Depreciation — Office Building
Accumulated Depreciation — Delivery Equipment
Accumulated Depreciation — Office Furniture and Fixtures
Accumulated Depreciation — Tools
Advertising Expense
Allowance for Doubtful Accounts
Amortization of Patents
Cash
Common Stock, $20 par (10,000 shares outstanding)
Delivery Salaries
Depreciation Expense — Office Building
Depreciation Expense — Delivery Equipment
Depreciation Expense — Office Furniture and Fixtures
Depreciation Expense — Tools
Direct Labor
Dividend Revenue
Dividends Payable
Dividends Receivable
Doubtful Accounts Expense
Factory Heat, Light, and Power
Factory Supervision
Factory Supplies
Factory Supplies Used
Finished Goods
Freight In
Federal Unemployment Tax Payable
Goods in Process
Goodwill
Income Tax
Income Tax Payable

Insurance Expense
Interest Expense — Bonds
Interest Expense — Other
Interest Payable
Interest Receivable
Interest Revenue
Miscellaneous Delivery Expense
Miscellaneous Factory Overhead
Miscellaneous General Expense
Miscellaneous Selling Expense
Office Salaries
Office Supplies
Office Supplies Used
Officers Salaries
Patents
Property Tax
Purchases Discount
Raw Materials
Raw Materials Purchases
Raw Materials Returns and Allowances
Retained Earnings
Royalties Received in Advance
Royalty Revenue
Salaries and Wages Payable
Sales
Sales Discount
Sales Returns and Allowances
Sales Salaries and Commissions
Sales Tax Payable
Tools

exercise 4-8

The Marville Steel Co. reports the following for 1981:

Retained earnings, January 1, 1981	$384,500
Selling expenses	212,200
Sales revenue	958,050
Interest expense	12,360
General and administrative expenses	237,800
Cost of goods sold	383,220
Dividends paid — 1981	23,000

Common stock outstanding: average for 1981, 30,000 shares

Prepare a single-step income statement (including earnings per share data) and a statement of retained earnings for Marville. Assume a 40% tax rate for all items.

exercise 4-9

The pre-audit income statement for the 10 months ended December 31, 1981, of Best Toy Company, a firm which started operations on March 1, 1981, revealed the following:

Best Toy Company
Income Statement
For Period Ended December 31, 1981

Sales			$497,000
Cost of goods sold:			
Completed units — 5,000		$401,000	
Ending inventory — 1,000		80,200	320,800
Gross profit on sales			$176,200
Selling expenses:			
Advertising	$13,200		
Miscellaneous selling expenses	60,000	$ 73,200	
General and administrative expenses:			
Officers salaries	$32,100		
Depreciation expense	16,900		
Miscellaneous general and administrative expenses	3,300	52,300	125,500
Income before income tax			$ 50,700

During the course of the year-end audit, the auditors observed the following:

(a) Factory depreciation of $11,200 was included in general and administrative expenses.
(b) Sales returns and allowances of $2,750 were not recorded.
(c) Accrued sales commissions of $5,230 were not recorded as of December 31, 1981.
(d) Advertising expense of $13,200, paid on March 1, 1981, was for newspaper ads appearing each month for the next 12 months.
(e) Income tax was charged at a 40 percent rate.

Prepare a corrected income statement for the period ended December 31, 1981. (Round amounts to the nearest dollar.)

exercise 4-10

From the following data for Jenneson Carpet Sales, prepare a statement of retained earnings for 1981.

Net loss — 1981	$ 97,775
Total assets at December 31, 1981	3,033,750
Common stock at December 31, 1981	750,000
Paid-in capital in excess of par at December 31, 1981	253,000
Dividends paid during 1981	35,600

The debt-to-equity ratio (liabilities ÷ owners' equity) is 50% at December 31, 1981.

PROBLEMS

problem 4-1

Rigby Investment Company purchased 100 shares of Stiles, Inc., and 100 shares of Mint Stores, Inc., on January 1, 1981. Data on these investments on a per share basis are as follows:

	Stiles	Mint
Cost	$61.25	$82.25
Net income reported — 1981	7.00	7.50
Dividend paid — 1981	6.00	5.50
Market value — December 31, 1981	54.25	79.75

Primary Investment Company and United Shares, Inc., each purchased 100 shares of Celector Manufacturing Co. and 100 shares of Omar Electronics, Inc., on January 1, 1981. Data on these investments, also on a per share basis, are as follows:

	Celector	Omar
Cost	$50.75	$90.25
Net income reported — 1981	4.00	6.00
Dividend paid — 1981	2.75	none
Market value — December 31, 1981	56.25	93.75

United Shares, Inc., sold its shares of Omar Electronics, Inc., on December 31, 1981, at the market value shown above. At the same time it purchased 200 shares of Melton, Inc., for $9,350. The other companies continued to hold their original investment.

Instructions:
(1) Compute the revenues for the three companies, using each of the following approaches to revenue recognition for each company (no expenses are to be recognized in computing your answers):
(a) Dividends received (plus gain on sales, if any).
(b) Share of net income reported by company whose stock is owned.
(c) Dividends received adjusted by any change in the market value of the stock.
(2) Evaluate each of the approaches to revenue recognition as to its informational value to investors.

problem 4-2

The Thompson Co. on July 1, 1980, reported a retained earnings balance of $1,525,000. The books of the company showed the following account balances on June 30, 1981:

Sales	$2,500,000
Inventory: July 1, 1980	160,000
June 30, 1981	165,000
Sales Returns and Allowances	30,000
Purchases	1,536,000
Purchases Discount	24,000
Dividends	260,000
Selling and General Expenses	250,000
Income Tax	285,200

Instructions: Prepare a single-step income statement accompanied by a retained earnings statement. The Thompson Co. has 400,000 shares of common stock outstanding.

problem 4-3

Selected account balances of the Edwards Company along with additional information as of December 31, 1981, are as follows:

Contribution to Employees Pension Fund	$ 290,000	Depreciation Expense — Store Equipment	$ 25,000
Delivery Expense	425,000	Dividends	150,000
Depreciation Expense — Delivery Trucks	29,000	Dividend Revenue	5,000
		Doubtful Accounts Expense	22,000
Depreciation Expense — Office Buildings and Equipment	35,000	Federal Income Tax, 1981	515,600
		Freight In	145,000

Gain on Sale of Office Equipment.. $	10,000	Officers and Office Salaries.......... $	950,000
		Purchases Discount	47,700
Interest Revenue...........................	1,500	Purchases	4,633,200
Loss on Sale of Marketable Securities..	50,000	Retained Earnings, Jan. 1, 1981...	550,000
		Sales	9,125,000
Loss from Write-Down of Obsolete Inventory.............................	125,000	Sales Discount..............................	55,000
		Sales Returns and Allowances.....	95,000
Merchandise Inventory, Jan. 1, 1981...	1,050,000	Sales Salaries	601,000
		State and Local Taxes..................	100,000
Miscellaneous General Expense..	45,000	Store Supplies Expense...............	50,000
Miscellaneous Selling Expense ...	50,000		

(a) Inventory at year-end was valued at $750,000 — $875,000 cost less the $125,000 write-down of obsolete inventory.

(b) Edwards Company has 100,000 shares of common stock outstanding.

Instructions: Prepare a combined statement of income and retained earnings for the year ended December 31, 1981. (Use a multiple-step form.)

problem 4-4

The London Supply Co. prepares a multiple-step income statement. The statement is supported by (1) a manufacturing schedule, (2) a selling expense schedule, and (3) a general and administrative expense schedule. You are supplied the data shown below.

Income tax for the current year:
Applicable to ordinary income... $30,404

Inventory balances at the end of the fiscal period as compared with balances at the beginning of the fiscal period were as follows:

Finished goods... $18,500 decrease
Goods in process .... 4,500 increase
Raw materials .... 10,000 decrease

Other account balances include the following:

Advertising Expense .... $	15,000	Interest Expense........................... $	10,200
Delivery Expense..........................	23,000	Miscellaneous Factory Costs	10,500
Depreciation Exp. — Machinery ..	5,600	Miscellaneous General Expense..	3,200
Direct Labor..................................	184,000	Miscellaneous Selling Expense ...	2,150
Dividend Revenue	300	Officers Salaries	116,200
Dividends	30,000	Office Salaries	70,000
Doubtful Accounts Expense.........	1,600	Office Supplies Expense...............	3,200
Factory Heat, Light, and Power....	26,990	Raw Materials Purchases	206,350
Factory Maintenance	15,000	Raw Materials Returns.................	2,000
Factory Supervision	60,000	Royalty Revenue...........................	2,700
Factory Supplies Expense............	14,000	Sales...	1,031,500
Factory Taxes	14,000	Sales Discount..............................	8,000
Freight In on Raw Materials	10,000	Sales Returns and Allowances.....	6,500
Gain on Sale of Land	8,000	Sales Salaries	65,000
Indirect Labor...............................	74,000		

London Supply Co. has 50,000 shares of common stock outstanding.

Instructions: Prepare an income statement with supporting schedules using the data for the year ended April 30, 1981, listed above.

problem 4-5

The Stinson Corporation was organized on March 21, 1981, 15,000 shares of no-par stock being issued in exchange for land, buildings and equipment valued at $60,000 and cash of $15,000. The following data summarize activities for the initial fiscal period ending December 31, 1981:

(a) Net income for the period ending December 31, 1981, was $20,000.

(b) Raw materials on hand on December 31 were equal to 25% of raw materials purchased in 1981.

(c) Manufacturing costs in 1981 were distributed as follows:

Materials used............50%
Direct labor 30%
Factory overhead.......20% (includes depreciation of building, $2,500)

(d) Goods in process remaining in the factory on December 31 were equal to 33⅓% of the goods finished and transferred to stock.

(e) Finished goods remaining in stock were equal to 25% of the cost of goods sold.

(f) Operating expenses were 30% of sales.

(g) Cost of goods sold was 150% of the operating expenses total.

(h) Ninety percent of sales were collected in 1981; the balance was considered collectible in 1982.

(i) Seventy-five percent of the raw materials purchased were paid for; there were no expense accruals or prepayments at the end of the year.

Instructions:

(1) Prepare an income statement and a supporting manufacturing schedule. (Disregard income tax.)

(2) Prepare a summary of cash receipts and disbursements to support the cash balance that would be reported on the balance sheet at December 31, 1981.

problem 4-6

On December 31, 1981, analysis of the Clancey Furniture Store's operations for 1981 revealed the following:

(a) Total cash collections from customers, $105,600.

(b) December 31, 1980 inventory balance, $10,020.

(c) Total cash payments, $87,364.

(d) Accounts receivable, December 31, 1980, $20,350.

(e) Accounts payable, December 31, 1980, $9,870.

(f) Accounts receivable, December 31, 1981, $10,780.

(g) Accounts payable, December 31, 1981, $4,130.

(h) General and administrative expenses total 20% of sales. This amount includes the depreciation on store and equipment.

(i) Selling expenses of $11,661 total 30% of gross profit on sales.

(j) No general and administrative or selling expense liabilities existed at December 31, 1981.

(k) Wages and salaries payable at December 31, 1980, $1,050.

(l) Depreciation expense on store and equipment total 13.5% of general and administrative expenses.

(m) Shares of stock issued and outstanding, 4,500.

(n) The income tax rate is 40%.

Instructions: Prepare a multiple-step income statement for the year ended December 31, 1981.

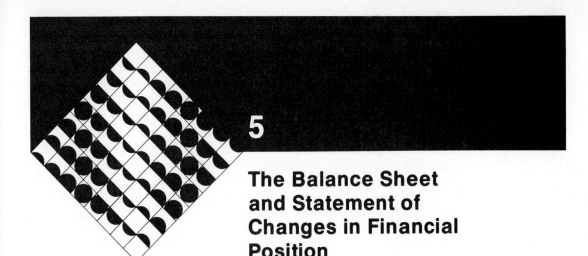

5

The Balance Sheet and Statement of Changes in Financial Position

CHAPTER OBJECTIVES

Describe the purposes and limitations of the balance sheet.

Identify and define the major elements on the balance sheet.

Discuss and illustrate the general reporting format for the balance sheet.

Present an overview of the nature and purposes of the statement of changes in financial position.

Chapter 4 discussed the statements of income and changes in owners' equity. The main subject of this chapter is the balance sheet. The statement of changes in financial position is also introduced but is explained in more detail in Chapter 19 when students are better able to understand its complexities.

PURPOSES AND LIMITATIONS OF THE BALANCE SHEET

The **balance sheet**, also known as the **statement of financial position**, reports as of a given point in time the resources of a business (**assets**), its obligations (**liabilities**), and the residual ownership claims against an entity's resources (**owners' equity**). By analyzing the relationships among these items, investors, creditors, and others can assess a firm's *liquidity*, i.e., its ability to meet short-term obligations, and *solvency*, i.e., its ability to pay all current and long-term debts as they come due. The balance sheet also shows the composition of assets and liabilities, the relative proportions of debt and equity financing, and how much of a firm's earnings have been retained in the business. Collectively, this information can be used by external parties to help assess the financial status of a firm at a particular date.

Following the traditional accounting model, the balance sheet is a historical report presenting the cumulative results of all past transactions of a business measured in terms of historical costs. It is an expression of the basic accounting equation — **Assets = Liabilities + Owners' Equity**. The balance sheet shows both the character and the amount of the assets, liabilities, and owners' equity.

For many years, the emphasis on earnings and profitability measures has resulted in the income statement receiving more attention than the balance sheet. While it does not appear that the prominence of reporting earnings is likely to decrease, the business community has shown a renewed interest in the balance sheet in recent years. Consider the following excerpts from an article entitled "Focus on Balance Sheet Reform."

> A quiet, but potentially explosive, revolution is sweeping the U.S. business world as lenders, investors, regulators, accountants, and corporate managers rediscover what should never have been lost: the balance sheet.
>
> ★ ★ ★
>
> Only by studying the balance sheet can a lender or an investor — or a regulator — measure a company's liquidity and its ability to generate profits and pay debts and dividends year after year. "The balance sheet is the anchor to windward," says John H. Kennedy, vice-president for finance at Alco Standard Corp. in Valley Forge, Pa. "It shows whether the company will survive, how profitable it can be, and whether it has a major obstacle to profits, like a pile of debt coming due."
>
> Because the balance sheet tells so much, it is astonishing that it could ever have gotten lost. Four decades ago, Benjamin Graham and David Dodd, the founding fathers of security analysis, stressed the balance sheet as they taught investors to look at a company's "intrinsic value" before they bought. Then came the go-go years of the late 1960s and early 1970s, when the only thing that seemed to matter was how fast a company could grow, a game that the biggest, most sophisticated institutional investors played as avidly as the rankest amateur in for a fast kill.
>
> But the go-go years ended in the inflation-recession agony of 1974–75, and people are focusing on the balance sheet as they have not in years . . .[1]

Balance sheets, especially when compared over time and with additional data, provide a great deal of useful information to those interested in analyzing the financial well-being of a company. Specific relationships, such as a company's current ratio, its debt to equity ratio, and its rate of return on investment can be highlighted.[2] Future commitments, favorable and unfavorable trends, problem areas in terms of collection patterns, and the rela-

---

[1] "Focus on Balance Sheet Reform," *Business Week*, June 7, 1976, p. 52.
[2] These ratios and relationships are discussed in detail in Chapter 21.

tive equity positions of creditors and owners can also be analyzed, all of which assist in evaluating the financial position of a company.

Notwithstanding its usefulness, the balance sheet has some serious limitations. External users often need to know a company's worth. The balance sheet, however, does not reflect the current values of a business. Instead, the entity's resources and obligations are shown at historical costs based on past transactions. The historical cost measurements represent market values existing at the dates the arms-length transactions occurred. However, when the prices of specific assets change significantly after the transaction date, as has certainly been the case recently in the United States, then the balance sheet numbers are not relevant for evaluating a company's current worth.

A related problem with the balance sheet is the instability of the dollar, the standard accounting measuring unit in the United States. Because of general price changes in the economy, the dollar does not maintain a constant purchasing power. Yet the historical costs of resources and equities shown on the balance sheet are not adjusted for changes in the purchasing power of the measuring unit. The result is a balance sheet which reflects assets, liabilities, and equities stated in terms of unequal purchasing power units, some elements being stated in terms of 1950 dollars, for example, and some in terms of 1980 dollars. This makes comparisons among firms and even within a single firm less meaningful.

An additional limitation of the balance sheet, also related to the need for comparability, is that all companies do not classify and report all like items similarly. For example, titles and account classifications vary; some companies provide considerably more detail than others; and some companies with apparently similar transactions report them differently. Such differences make comparisons difficult and diminish the potential value of balance sheet analysis.

The balance sheet may be considered deficient in another respect. Due primarily to measurement problems, some entity resources and obligations are not reported on the balance sheet. For example, the employees of a company may be one of its most valuable resources; yet, they are not shown on the balance sheet because their future service potentials are not measurable in monetary terms. Similarly, a company's potential liability for polluting the air would not normally be shown on its balance sheet. The assumptions of the traditional accounting model identified in Chapter 3, specifically the requirements of arms-length transactions measurable in monetary terms, add to the objectivity of balance sheet disclosures but at the same time cause some information to be omitted that is likely to be relevant to certain users' decisions.

The FASB has attempted to correct, at least partially, two of the above problems by requiring supplemental disclosures of both current values and general price-level adjusted amounts for selected items. These reporting requirements are discussed in detail in Chapter 20. As indicated in Chapter 3, the Board is also working on other reporting problems through their conceptual framework project.

CONTENT OF THE BALANCE SHEET

For accounting purposes, **assets** are defined as "probable future economic benefits obtained or controlled by a particular entity as a result of past transactions or events."[3] They include those costs that have not been applied to revenues in the past and are expected to afford economic utility in the production of revenues in the future. Assets include both *monetary assets*, such as cash, certain marketable securities, and receivables, and *nonmonetary assets* — those costs recognized as recoverable and hence properly assignable to revenues of future periods, such as inventories, prepaid insurance, equipment, and patents.

Liabilities are defined as "probable future sacrifices of economic benefits arising from present obligations of a particular entity to transfer assets or provide services to other entities in the future as a result of past transactions or events."[4] They measure the claims of creditors against entity resources. The method for settlement of liabilities varies. Liabilities may call for settlement by cash payment or settlement through goods to be delivered or services to be performed.

Owners' equity is defined as "the residual interest in the assets of an entity that remains after deducting its liabilities. In a business enterprise, the equity is the ownership interest."[5] It measures the interest of the ownership group in the total resources of the enterprise. This interest arises from investments by owners, and the equity increase or decrease from the change in net assets resulting from operations. An ownership equity does not call for settlement on a certain date; in the event of business dissolution, it represents a claim on assets only after creditors have been paid in full.

Balance sheet items are generally classified in a manner to facilitate analysis and interpretation of financial data. Information of primary concern to all parties is the business unit's liquidity and solvency — its ability to meet current and long-term obligations. Accordingly, assets and liabilities are classified as (1) **current** or **short-term** items and (2) **noncurrent, long-term**, or **fixed** items. When assets and liabilities are so classified, the difference between current assets and current liabilities may be determined. This is referred to as the company's **working capital** — the liquid buffer available in meeting financial demands and contingencies of the future.

Current Assets and Current Liabilities

Current assets include cash and resources which are reasonably expected to be converted into cash during the normal operating cycle of a business or within one year, whichever period is longer. As depicted on page 111, the **normal operating cycle** is the time required for cash to be

---

[3]*Statement of Financial Accounting Concepts No. 3*, "Elements of Financial Statements of Business Enterprises" (Stamford: Financial Accounting Standards Board, December 1980), par. 19.

[4]*Ibid.*, par. 28.

[5]*Ibid.*, par. 43.

converted to inventories, inventories into receivables, and receivables ultimately into cash. When the operating cycle exceeds twelve months, for example, in the tobacco, distillery, and lumber industries, the longer period is used.

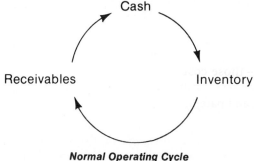

Normal Operating Cycle

Some exceptions to the general definition of current assets should be noted. Cash which is restricted as to use, e.g., designated for the acquisition of noncurrent assets or segregated for the liquidation of noncurrent debts, should not be included in current assets. Also, in classifying assets not related to the operating cycle, a one-year period is always used as the basis for current classification. For example, a note receivable due in 18 months which arose from the sale of land previously held for investment would be classified as noncurrent even if the normal operating cycle exceeds 18 months.

In addition to cash, receivables and inventories, current assets typically include such resources as prepaid expenses and marketable securities. Prepayments of such items as insurance and interest are not current assets in the sense they will be converted into cash but on the basis that, if they had not been prepaid, they would have required the use of cash or other current assets during the operating cycle period. Long-term prepayments should be reported as noncurrent assets and charged to the operations of several years. If securities of companies, whether marketable or not, are acquired for purposes of control rather than conversion back to cash during the normal operating cycle, they should not be designated as current assets. Other items which perhaps could be converted into cash, but are not expected to be converted and therefore should not be classified as current assets, include the cash surrender value of life insurance policies, land, and depreciable assets.

Current assets are normally listed on the balance sheet in the order of their liquidity. These assets, with the exception of marketable securities and inventories, are usually reported at their estimated realizable values. Thus, current receivable balances are reduced by allowances for estimated uncollectible accounts. Marketable equity securities should be reported at the lower of aggregate cost or market.[6] Inventories may be reported at cost or on the basis of "cost or market, whichever is lower."

---

[6]*Statement of Financial Accounting Standards, No. 12*, "Accounting for Certain Marketable Securities" (Stamford: Financial Accounting Standards Board, 1975), par. 8.

Current liabilities are those obligations which are reasonably expected to be paid using existing resources properly classified as current assets or by creating other current liabilities. Generally, if a liability will be paid within 12 months, it is properly classified as current. As with receivables, payables arising from the normal operating activities may be classified as current even if they are not to be paid within 12 months, but within the operating cycle if it exceeds 12 months. Items commonly included as current liabilities are accounts payable, collections received in advance of delivery of goods or services, and other debts which arise in the normal operations of a business and which are directly related to the operating cycle, for example, accruals for salaries and wages, rentals, interest, and taxes. The amount of a long-term liability coming due within the current period, such as the current portion of a long-term mortgage or the amount required to be paid within one year under sinking fund provisions, should also be classified as a current liability.

The current liability classification, however, generally does not include the following items, since these do not require the use of resources classified as current.

1. Short-term obligations expected to be refinanced.[7]
2. Debts to be liquidated from funds that have been accumulated and are reported as noncurrent assets.
3. Loans on life insurance policies made with the intent that these will not be paid but will be liquidated by deduction from the proceeds of the policies upon their maturity or cancellation.
4. Obligations for advance collections that involve long-term deferment of the delivery of goods or services.[8]

With respect to short-term obligations which normally would come due within the operating cycle but are expected to be refinanced, i.e., discharged by means of the issuance of new obligations in their place, the Financial Accounting Standards Board (FASB) has concluded such obligations should be excluded from current liabilities if the following conditions are met: (1) the intent of the company is to refinance the obligations on a long-term basis, and (2) the company's intent is supported by an ability to consummate the refinancing as evidenced by a post-balance-sheet-date issuance of long-term obligations or equity securities or an explicit financing agreement.[9]

In effect, the FASB is recognizing that certain short-term obligations will not require the use of working capital during a period even though they are scheduled to mature during that period. Thus, they should not be classified as current liabilities.

---

[7]*Statement of Financial Accounting Standards, No. 6*, "Classification of Short-Term Obligations Expected to be Refinanced" (Stamford: Financial Accounting Standards Board, 1975).

[8]*Accounting Research and Terminology Bulletins — Final Edition, No. 43*, "Restatement and Revision of Accounting Research Bulletins" (New York: American Institute of Certified Public Accountants, 1961), par. 8 and footnotes 2 and 3.

[9]*Statement of Financial Accounting Standards, No. 6, op. cit.*, par. 9–11.

Few problems are generally found in the valuation of current liabilities. Payables can usually be determined accurately, even though some items may require estimates as to the amounts ultimately to be paid. These claims, however determined, if payable currently, must be included under the current heading.

The importance of an adequate working capital position cannot be minimized. A business may not be able to survive in the absence of a satisfactory relationship between current assets and current liabilities. Furthermore, its ability to prosper is largely determined by the composition of the current asset pool. There must be a proper balance between liquid assets in the form of cash and temporary investments, and receivables and inventories. Activities of the business center around these assets. Cash and temporary investments, representing immediate purchasing power, are used to meet current claims and purchasing, payroll, and expense requirements; receivables are the outgrowth of sales effort and provide cash in the course of operations; merchandise is also a source of cash as well as the means of achieving a profit. Management, in setting policies with respect to selling, purchasing, financing, expansion, and dividends, must work within the limitations set by the company's working capital position.

Noncurrent Assets and Noncurrent Liabilities

Assets and liabilities not qualifying for presentation under the current headings are classified under a number of noncurrent headings. Noncurrent assets may be listed under separate headings, such as "Long-term investments," "Land, buildings, and equipment," "Intangible assets," and "Other long-term assets." Noncurrent liabilities are generally listed under separate headings, such as "Long-term liabilities," "Unearned revenues," and "Other long-term liabilities."

Long-Term Investments. Investments held for such long-term purposes as regular income, appreciation, or ownership control are reported under the heading "Long-term investments." Examples of items properly reported under this heading are long-term stocks, bonds, and mortgage holdings; securities of affiliated companies and advances to such companies; sinking fund assets consisting of cash and securities held for the redemption of bonds or stocks, the replacement of buildings, or the payment of pensions; land held for future use or sale; the cash surrender value of life insurance; and other miscellaneous investments not used directly in the operations of the business. Although many long-term investments are reported at cost, there are modifications to the valuation of some investments which will be discussed in later chapters.

Land, Buildings, and Equipment. Properties of a tangible and relatively permanent character that are used in the normal business operations are reported under "Land, buildings, and equipment" or other appropriate heading. Land, buildings, machinery, tools, furniture, fixtures, and vehicles are included under this heading. Buildings and equipment are normally reported at cost less accumulated depreciation.

Intangible Assets. The long-term rights and privileges of a nonphysical character acquired for use in business operations are reported under the heading "Intangible assets." Included in this class are such items as goodwill, patents, trademarks, franchises, copyrights, formulas, leaseholds, and organization costs. Intangible assets are normally reported at cost less amounts previously amortized.

Other Long-Term Assets. Those noncurrent assets not suitably reported under any of the previous classifications may be listed under the general heading "Other long-term assets" or may be listed separately under special descriptive headings. Such assets include long-term advances to officers, deposits made with vendors to secure contracts, and segregated cash funds representing long-term refundable deposits from customers.

Prepayments for services or benefits to be received over a number of periods are properly regarded as noncurrent. Among these are such items as plant rearrangement costs and developmental and improvement costs. These long-term prepayments are frequently reported under a "Deferred costs" or "Deferred charges" heading. However, objection can be raised to a deferred costs category since this designation could be applied to all costs assignable to future periods including inventories, buildings and equipment, and intangible assets. The deferred costs heading may be avoided by reporting long-term prepayments within the other long-term assets section or under separate descriptive headings.

A debit balance in the deferred income tax account may be shown under "Other long-term assets" or may be reported separately. Income tax is considered to be prepaid when paid on a computed taxable income that is more than the income reported on the financial statements. The difference between taxable income and "book" income may be a temporary one caused by a *timing* difference — a difference in the period in which revenue or expense is recognized on the tax return and on the books. Under these circumstances, matching of income tax expense with revenue requires that the tax paid on taxable income in excess of the book income be deferred and recognized as an addition to tax expense in the period when the income is ultimately recognized on the books. Most of the time, Deferred Income Taxes has a credit balance and, as indicated on page 116, is properly shown as a long-term liability. Accounting for income tax is considered in detail in Chapter 15.

Contingent Assets. Circumstances at the balance sheet date may indicate the existence of certain rights or claims that could materialize as valuable assets depending upon the favorable outcome of certain events. In the absence of a legal right to the properties at that time, these can be viewed only as **contingent assets.** Contingencies that might result in gains are not recorded in the accounts; they may be disclosed by a special note or by appropriate comment under a separate "Contingent assets" heading following the

"Other asset" classifications. Care should be exercised not to present misleading implications with respect to possible realization.[10] Tax claims, insurance claims, and claims against merchandise creditors may warrant such treatment. Reference to contingent assets in the balance sheet is rare in practice.

Long-Term Liabilities. Long-term notes, bonds, mortgages, and similar obligations not requiring the use of current funds for their retirement are generally reported on the balance sheet under the heading "Long-term liabilities."

When an amount borrowed is not the same as the amount ultimately required in settlement of the debt, and the debt is stated in the accounts at its maturity amount, a debt discount or premium is reported. The discount or premium should be related to the debt item: a discount, then, should be subtracted from the amount reported for the debt, and a premium should be added to the amount reported for the debt. The debt is thus reported at its present value as measured by the proceeds from its issuance. Amortization of the discount or premium brings the obligation to the maturity amount by the end of its normal term. When a note, a bond issue, or a mortgage formerly classified as a long-term obligation becomes payable within a year, it should be reclassified and presented as a current liability, except when the obligation is expected to be refinanced as discussed earlier or is to be paid out of a sinking fund.

Unearned Revenues. Cash may be received or other assets recognized for goods and services to be supplied in future periods. Such transactions are recognized in the accounts by debits to assets and credits to liability accounts reporting the advance payments. The latter balance is properly carried forward until the company meets its responsibilities through the delivery of goods or the performance of services. If, in subsequent periods, the expenses of providing the goods and services are less than the obligations that are discharged thereby, earnings will be recognized; on the other hand, if expenses are greater than the obligations that are discharged, losses will be incurred. Examples of transactions that call for revenue deferral and recognition as long-term obligations include fees received in advance on long-term service contracts, and long-term leasehold and rental prepayments. These prepayments are normally reported on the balance sheet under the heading of "Unearned revenues."

All revenues received in advance for goods and services are frequently reported under the "Unearned revenues" heading, including those calling for settlement in the near future. However, the noncurrent classification is appropriate only when an item represents no significant claim upon current assets. When significant costs are involved in satisfying a claim and these costs will be met from the company's current assets, the prepayment should

---

[10]*Statement of Financial Accounting Standards No. 5*, "Accounting for Contingencies" (Stamford: Financial Accounting Standards Board, 1975), par. 17.

be recognized as a current liability. The obligation arising from the receipt of cash in advance on magazine subscriptions, for example, is properly recognized as a current liability in view of the claim it makes upon current assets.

Other Long-Term Liabilities. Those noncurrent liabilities not suitably reported under the "Long-term liabilities" or "Unearned revenues" headings may be listed under the general heading "Other long-term liabilities" or may be listed separately under special descriptive headings. Such liabilities include obligations to customers in the form of long-term refundable deposits on returnable containers, long-term obligations to company officers or affiliated companies, matured but unclaimed bond principal and interest obligations, and long-term liabilities under pension plans.

A credit balance in the deferred income tax account may be shown under "Other long-term liabilities" or may be reported separately. Income tax is considered to have accrued when tax is paid on a computed income that is less than the income reported on the financial statements. The difference, as in the case of the deferred income tax expense previously mentioned, may be a temporary one caused by a timing difference. In this case, however, the timing difference has resulted in postponing income tax until a later period. Timing differences may occur, for example, in recognizing a different amount of depreciation on the tax return and on the books, and also in recognizing revenue on installment sales and on long-term construction contracts. A matching of income tax expense with revenue requires that postponed income tax be accrued and recognized as a subtraction from tax paid in the period when the revenue is ultimately recognized on the tax return.

Contingent Liabilities. Past activities or circumstances may have given rise to possible future liabilities, although legal obligations do not exist on the date of the balance sheet. These possible claims are known as **contingent liabilities**. They are potential obligations involving uncertainty as to possible losses. As future events occur or fail to occur, this uncertainty will be resolved. Thus, a contingent liability is distinguishable from an **estimated liability**. The latter is a definite obligation with only the amount of the obligation in question and subject to estimation at the balance sheet date. There may not be any doubt as to the amount of a contingent liability, for example, a pending lawsuit, but there is considerable uncertainty as to whether the obligation will actually materialize.

In the past, contingent liabilities were not recorded in the accounts nor presented on the balance sheet. When they were disclosed, it was in the notes to the financial statements. Since the issuance of FASB Statement No. 5, if a future payment is considered probable, the liability should be recorded by a debit to a loss account and a credit to a liability account.[11] Otherwise, the contingent nature of the loss would still be disclosed in a note to the financial statements or ignored depending on the degree of re-

---

[11]*Ibid.*, par. 8–13.

moteness of the expected occurrence. Examples of contingent liabilities and further discussion of their treatment are presented in Chapter 13.

Owners' Equity

The method of reporting the owners' equity varies with the form of the business unit. Business units are typically divided into three categories: (1) **proprietorships**, (2) **partnerships**, and (3) **corporations**. In the case of a proprietorship, the owner's equity in assets is reported by means of a single capital account. The balance in this account is the cumulative result of the owner's investments and withdrawals as well as past earnings and losses. In a partnership, capital accounts are established for each partner. Capital account balances summarize the investments and withdrawals and shares of past earnings and losses of each partner, and thus measure the partners' individual equities in the partnership assets.

In a corporation, the difference between assets and liabilities is referred to as **stockholders' equity, shareholders' equity**, or simply, **capital**. In presenting the stockholders' equity on the balance sheet, a distinction is made between the equity originating from the stockholders' investment, referred to as **paid-in capital** or **contributed capital**, and the equity originating from earnings, referred to as **retained earnings**.

The relationship and distinction between the amount of capital paid in or contributed by the owners of the corporation relative to the amount the company has earned and retained in the business is a significant one. Such disclosure helps creditors and investors assess the long-term ability of a company to internally finance its own operations. If the contributed capital of a corporation is large relative to the total owners' equity, it means the corporation has been financed primarily from external sources, usually from the sale of stock to investors. If the earned capital of a corporation is large relative to the total owners' equity, it means the company has been profitable in the past and has retained those earnings in the business to help finance its activities. This distinction between earned and contributed capital is not as important for a proprietorship or partnership because the owners of those types of businesses generally are also involved in their management and therefore are aware of how the company activities are being financed.

Contributed Capital. Contributed or paid-in capital is generally reported in two parts: (1) **capital stock** representing that portion of the contribution by stockholders assignable to the shares of stock issued; (2) **additional paid-in capital** representing investments by stockholders in excess of the amounts assignable to capital stock as well as invested capital from other sources.

Capital stock outstanding having a par value is shown on the balance sheet at par. Capital stock having no par value is stated at the amount received on its original sale or at some other value as stipulated by law or as assigned by action of the board of directors of the corporation. When more than a single class of stock has been issued and is outstanding, the stock of each class is reported separately. **Treasury stock,** which is stock issued but subsequently reacquired by the corporation, is subtracted from the total stock issued or from the sum of contributed capital and retained earnings balances. The capital stock balance is viewed as the **legal capital** or **permanent capital** of the corporation.

A premium received on the sale of par-value stock or the amount received in excess of the value assigned to no-par stock is recognized as additional paid-in capital. Additional paid-in capital may also arise from transactions other than the sale of stock, such as from the acquisition of property as a result of a donation or from the sale of treasury stock at more than cost. The additional paid-in capital balances are normally added to capital stock so the full amount of the contributed capital may be reported. Contributed capital is discussed in detail in Chapter 16.

Retained Earnings. The amount of undistributed earnings of past periods is reported as **retained earnings**. The total amount thus shown will probably not represent cash available for payment as dividends since past years' earnings will usually already have been reinvested in other assets. An excess of dividends and losses over earnings results in a negative retained earnings balance called a **deficit**. The balance of retained earnings is added to the contributed capital total in summarizing the stockholders' equity; a deficit is subtracted.

Portions of retained earnings are sometimes reported as restricted and unavailable as a basis for dividends. Restricted earnings may be designated as *appropriations*. Appropriations are sometimes made for such purposes as sinking funds, plant expansion, loss contingencies, and the reacquisition of capital stock. Often such appropriations are disclosed in a note rather than in the accounts. When appropriations have been made in the accounts, retained earnings on the balance sheet consists of an amount designated as *appropriated* and a balance designated as *unappropriated* or *free*. The term "reserve" should not generally be used to designate appropriations. Retained earnings is fully discussed in Chapter 17.

Offsets on the Balance Sheet

A number of balance sheet items are frequently reported at gross amounts calling for the recognition of offset balances in arriving at proper valuations. Such offset balances are found in asset, liability, and owners' equity categories. In the case of assets, for example, an allowance for doubtful accounts is subtracted from the sum of the customers' accounts in reporting the net amount estimated collectible; accumulated depreciation is subtracted from the related buildings and equipment balances in reporting the costs of the assets still assignable to future revenues. In the case of liabilities, reacquired bonds or *treasury bonds*, are subtracted from bonds issued in reporting the amount of bonds outstanding; a bond discount is subtracted from the face value of bonds outstanding in reporting the net amount of the debt. In the case of stockholders' equity in the corporation, a deficit is subtracted from contributed capital.

The types of offsets described above, utilizing contra accounts, are required for proper reporting of particular balance sheet items. Offsets are improper, however, if applied to different asset and liability balances or to asset and owners' equity balances even when there is some relationship between the items. For example, a company may accumulate cash in a special fund to discharge certain tax liabilities; but as long as control of the cash is retained and the liabilities are still outstanding, the company should continue to report both the asset and the liabilities separately. Or a company may accumulate cash in a special fund for the redemption of preferred stock outstanding; but until the cash is applied to the reacquisition of the stock, the company must continue to report the asset as well as the owners' equity item. A company may have made advances to certain salespersons while at the same time reporting accrued amounts payable to others; but a net figure cannot be justified here, just as a net figure cannot be justified for the offset of trade receivables against trade payables.

Form of the Balance Sheet

The form of the balance sheet presentation varies in practice. Its form may be influenced by the nature and size of the business, by the character of the business properties, and, in some instances, by requirements set by regulatory bodies. The balance sheet is generally prepared in **account form**, assets being reported on the left-hand side and liabilities and owners' equity on the right-hand side. It may also be prepared in **report form**, with assets, liabilities, and owners' equity sections appearing in vertical arrangement.

The order of asset and liability classifications may vary, but usually emphasis is placed upon a company's working capital position and liquidity, with asset and liability groups, as well as the items within such groups, presented in the order of liquidity. A balance sheet in account form with financial data reported in the order of liquidity is illustrated on pages 120 and 121.

When the report form is used, liability and owners' equity totals may be added together to constitute an amount equal to the asset total. In other instances, total liabilities are subtracted from total assets, and owners' equity is reported as the difference. A variation of the report form referred to as the **financial position form** has found some favor. This form emphasizes the current position and reports a working capital balance. The financial position form is illustrated at the top of page 122. (Individual assets and liabilities are omitted in the example.)

Related balance sheet items are frequently combined so the balance sheet may be prepared in condensed form. For example, land, buildings, and equipment may be reported as a single item; raw materials, goods in process, and finished goods inventories may be combined; and long-term investments may be reported in total. Consolidation of similar items within reasonable limits may actually serve to clarify the business position and data relationships. Supporting detail for individual items, when considered of particular significance or when required by law, may be supplied by

Assets

Current assets:			
Cash in bank and on hand..................................		$ 36,500	
Marketable securities (reported at cost; market value, $71,500)..		70,000	
Notes receivable, trade debtors (Note 2)..........	$ 15,000		
Accounts receivable.......................................	50,000		
	$ 65,000		
Less allowance for doubtful notes and accounts receivable..	5,000	60,000	
Claim for income tax refund.............................		9,000	
Creditors accounts with debit balances............		750	
Advances to employees		1,250	
Interest receivable..		250	
Inventories (Note 1a)...		125,000	
Prepaid expenses:			
Supply inventories..	$ 3,000		
Insurance..	4,250	7,250	$310,000
Long-term investments:			
Investment in land and unused facilities (Note 1d)...		$ 22,500	
Cash surrender value of officers' life insurance policies		9,000	31,500

Land, buildings, and equipment (Note 1b):

	Cost	Accumulated Depreciation	Book Value	
Land	$ 80,000		$ 80,000	
Buildings..	150,000	$ 35,000	115,000	
Equipment	100,000	45,000	55,000	
	$330,000	$ 80,000		250,000

Intangible assets (Note 1c):			
Patents...		$ 70,000	
Goodwill		18,500	88,500
Other long-term assets:			
Advances to officers....................................		$ 15,000	
Customer deposits on returnable containers........		5,000	20,000
Total assets...			$700,000

See accompanying notes to financial statements.

Account Form

means of special summaries referred to as **supplementary** or **supporting schedules**. For example, a listing of all long-term debt with appropriate interest rates and maturity dates might be shown as a useful supporting schedule to the notes payable account. Product segment data is another example of information often shown as a supplementary schedule. In Appendix B, Notes 5 and 16 and the product segment data schedule for General Mills demonstrate the effective use of supporting schedules.

Corporation
Sheet
31, 1981

Liabilities

Current liabilities:

Notes payable, trade creditors		$ 14,250	
Accounts payable		12,500	
Dividends payable		5,000	
Advances from customers		5,750	
Income tax payable		27,000	
Other liabilities:			
Salaries and wages payable	$ 1,000		
Taxes payable	1,500	2,500	$ 67,000

Long-term liabilities:

8% First-mortgage bonds due December 31, 1997 (Note 3)		$100,000	
Less unamortized bond discount		5,000	95,000

Unearned revenues:

Unearned lease revenue (Note 1d)	20,000

Other long-term liabilities:

Deferred income tax	$ 3,000	
Liability under pension plan (Note 4)	65,000	68,000
Total liabilities		$250,000

Stockholders' Equity

Contributed capital:

Common stock, $5 stated value, 100,000 shares authorized, 50,000 shares issued and outstanding	$250,000		
Paid-in capital from sale of common stock at more than stated value	45,000	$295,000	
Retained earnings		155,000	
Total stockholders' equity			450,000
Total liabilities and stockholders' equity			$700,000

Balance Sheet

Parenthetical notation is another technique commonly used in balance sheet presentations. For example, in the balance sheet shown on page 120 and above, the marketable securities are shown as follows:

Marketable securities (reported at cost; market value $71,500) 70,000

Such disclosure shows the current market value of the securities as well as their cost. Thus, parenthetical disclosures can add significantly to the total understanding of the reader.

Andersen Corporation
Balance Sheet
December 31, 1981

Current assets		$310,000
Less current liabilities..		67,000
Working capital		$243,000
Add:		
Long-term investments..	$ 31,500	
Land, buildings, and equipment...	250,000	
Intangible assets	88,500	
Other long-term assets	20,000	390,000
Total assets less current liabilities.......................................		$633,000
Deduct:		
Long-term liabilities less unamortized bond discount..................	$ 95,000	
Unearned revenues	20,000	
Deferred income tax..	3,000	
Liability under pension plan	65,000	183,000
Net assets...		$450,000
Stockholders' equity:		
Contributed capital..		$295,000
Retained earnings		155,000
Total stockholders' equity..		$450,000

Financial Position Form of Balance Sheet

Balance sheet data are generally presented in comparative form. With comparative reports for two or more dates, information is made available concerning the nature and trend of financial changes taking place within the periods between balance sheet dates. When a statement is presented in a special form, the heading should designate the nature of the form that is provided, as for example, "Condensed Balance Sheet," or "Comparative Balance Sheet."

Notes to the Financial Statements

Notes to the financial statements are an integral part of any formal financial statement presentation. They are essential in explaining the basic financial data and should be prepared and read with care. Notes are commonly used to provide additional information about balance sheet and income statement items that cannot conveniently be shown, parenthetically or otherwise, directly on the statements. Frequently, notes deal with methods of valuation, the existence and amounts of dividends in arrears, the existence of contingencies, special financing arrangements, significant accounting policies and changes in policies, or other unusual events or items which would be better understood with additional explanation.

The balance sheet for Andersen Corporation, on pages 120 and 121, refers to Note 2 in connection with the trade notes receivable. In that note, shown on page 123, the company discloses its contingent liability on $40,000 worth of guaranteed notes. Note 3, referenced under long-term liabilities, describes the nature of the bonds outstanding, especially with respect to the call option on the bonds.

Andersen Corporation
Notes to Financial Statements — Year Ended December 31, 1981

1. Summary of significant accounting policies:
   (a) Inventories are valued at cost or market, whichever is lower. Cost is calculated by the first-in, first-out method.
   (b) Depreciation is computed for both the books and tax return by the double-declining balance method.
   (c) Intangible assets are being amortized over the period of their estimated useful lives: patents, 10 years, and goodwill, 20 years.
   (d) The company leased Market Street properties for a 15-year period ending January 1, 1989. The lease does not meet criteria for capitalization and the leasehold payment received in advance is being recognized as revenue over the life of the lease.

2. The company is contingently liable on guaranteed notes and accounts totaling $40,000. Also, various suits are pending on which the ultimate payment cannot be determined. In the opinion of counsel and management, such liability, if any, will not be material.

3. Bonds may be called at the option of the board of directors at 105 plus accrued interest on or before December 31, 1983, and at gradually reduced amounts but at not less than 102½ plus accrued interest after January 1, 1989.

4. The pension plan covers all employees. The company funds all pension costs accrued. The liability under the company pension plan has been calculated on the basis of actuarial studies.

The overall objective of note disclosure is clarification of the information presented in the financial statements. It is a real challenge to present concisely and clearly the information needed by the various users of financial statements. The notes provided with General Mills' statements, presented as Appendix B, demonstrate how one company has attempted to meet that challenge. Disclosure requirements are so extensive that they cannot be completely discussed in a single chapter. Specific requirements will be noted as appropriate throughout the text. The notes to the financial statements illustrated in this chapter and in the end-of-chapter material do not necessarily provide complete disclosure, but are only illustrative of the general nature and content of notes included with financial statements.[12]

Summary of Significant Accounting Policies Followed

In addition to the other notes, a summary of the significant accounting policies followed should be presented with the financial statements. In this regard, the Accounting Principles Board concluded in APB Opinion No. 22:

> ... When financial statements are issued purporting to present fairly financial position, changes in financial position, and results of operations in accordance with generally accepted accounting principles, a description of all significant

---

[12]Notes to financial statements in end-of-chapter material need only be prepared when specifically required by the exercise or problem.

accounting policies of the reporting entity should be included as an integral part of the financial statements.[13]

The Board further stated:

> . . . In general, the disclosure should encompass important judgments as to appropriateness of principles relating to recognition of revenue and allocation of asset costs to current and future periods; in particular it should encompass those accounting principles and methods that involve any of the following: (a) A selection from existing acceptable alternatives; (b) Principles and methods peculiar to the industry in which the reporting entity operates, even if such principles and methods are predominantly followed in that industry; (c) Unusual or innovative applications of generally accepted accounting principles (and, as applicable, of principles and methods peculiar to the industry in which the reporting entity operates).[14]

Examples of disclosures of accounting policies required by this opinion would include, among others, those relating to depreciation methods, amortization of intangible assets, inventory pricing methods, the recognition of profit on long-term construction-type contracts, and the recognition of revenue from leasing operations.[15]

The exact format for reporting the summary of accounting policies was not specified by the APB. However, the Board recommended such disclosure be included as the initial note or as a separate summary preceding the notes to the financial statements. The summary of significant accounting policies for the Andersen Corporation is presented on page 123 as the first note to the financial statements.

Careful classification of items under descriptive headings, appropriate explanatory notes, and the presentation of data in comparative form provide more meaningful statements. Presentations in condensed forms and the rounding of numbers to the nearest dollar, hundred or thousands of dollars clarify relationships and facilitate analysis. A variety of different balance sheet disclosures are found in practice. As noted earlier, an illustrative set of financial statements, complete with applicable notes, is provided in Appendix B of this textbook. Included is a balance sheet illustrating one approach taken in the development of a statement summarizing financial status.

OVERVIEW OF THE STATEMENT OF CHANGES IN FINANCIAL POSITION

The **statement of changes in financial position**, also commonly referred to as the **funds statement**, is a condensed report of how the activities of a business have been financed and how the financial resources have been used. It is a flow statement, emphasizing the inflows and outflows of resources related to the significant financial events of an enterprise during a reporting period. The remainder of this chapter provides an overview of the statement of changes in financial position.

---

[13]*Opinions of the Accounting Principles Board, No. 22*, "Disclosure of Accounting Policies" (New York: American Institute of Certified Public Accountants, 1972), par. 8.

[14]*Ibid.*, par. 12.

[15]*Ibid.*, par 13.

Nature and Purpose of the Funds Statement

The funds statement provides a summary of the sources from which funds became available during a period and the purposes to which funds were applied. An important part of the summary is the presentation of data concerning the extent to which funds were generated by income-oriented operations of the business. In addition to reporting funds provided by operations, funds inflow is also related to such sources as the sale of property items, the issuance of long-term obligations, and the issuance of capital stock. Funds outflow is related to such uses as the acquisition of property items, the retirement of long-term obligations, the reacquisition of outstanding stock, and the payment of dividends.

These primary inflows and outflows are illustrated diagrammatically below:

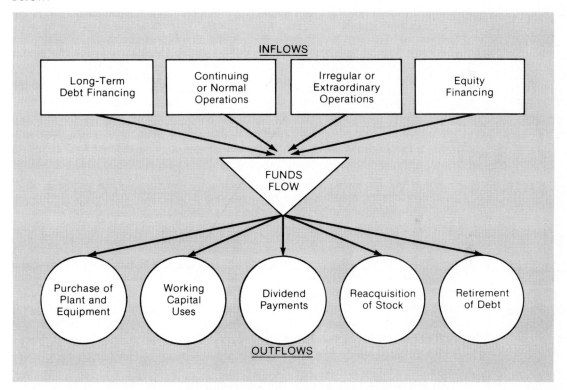

Although based on the same data as the balance sheet and the income statement, the statement of changes in financial position helps to answer questions not readily apparent from examination of either or both of the other two statements. For example, the funds statement helps the reader answer questions such as: Where did the profits go? Why were dividends not larger in view of rising earnings? How can dividends be distributed in excess of current earnings or when there was a reported net loss? Why are current assets decreasing when the results of operations are positive? How was the plant expansion financed? What use was made of the proceeds from the sale of stock? How was bonded indebtedness paid off even though there was a substantial operating loss? These questions require answers if the various users of financial statements are to be provided the means of fully evaluating the operations of the business unit and the management of its resources.

Thus, although related to the balance sheet and the income statement, the funds statement cannot be considered in any sense a duplication of or substitution for the other financial statements. The Accounting Principles Board, in Opinion No. 19, points out:

> The funds statement is related to both the income statement and the balance sheet and provides information that can be obtained only partially, or at most in piecemeal form, by interpreting them. An income statement together with a statement of retained earnings reports results of operations but does not show other changes in financial position. Comparative balance sheets can significantly augment that information, but the objectives of the funds statement require that all such information be selected, classified, and summarized in meaningful form. The funds statement cannot supplant either the income statement or the balance sheet but is intended to provide information that the other statements either do not provide or provide only indirectly about the flow of funds and changes in financial position during the period.[16]

To illustrate the special contribution made by the funds statement, consider the needs of a prospective creditor and the means for meeting these needs. An individual or group asked to make a long-term loan to a company is concerned with the company's proposed use of the loan, the ability of the company to meet the periodic interest payments on the loan, and the ability of the company ultimately to pay off the loan. Balance sheet analysis will provide answers to questions relative to the cash and near-cash items on hand, the working capital of the business — its amount and composition — present long-term indebtedness, and the implications on financial position if the loan is granted. Income statement analysis will provide answers to questions relative to the earnings of the company, the ability of earnings to cover current interest charges, and the implications as to earnings and interest charges if the loan is granted. Funds statement analysis will indicate the resources available to the company in the past and the uses made of those resources as well as the financing and investing implications if the loan is granted. Finally, funds data can be used in estimating the resources that will be generated in the future and the ability of the company to meet the added indebtedness.

It is obvious that in meeting the requirements of the users of financial statements, funds information will be most useful if offered in comparative form for two or more years. An additional statement reporting forecasted or budgeted funds-flow data may prove of equal or even greater value. Although suggestions have been made that the latter information be made available to the external users of financial information, this practice has not yet been adopted.

---

[16]*Opinions of the Accounting Principles Board, No. 19*, "Reporting Changes in Financial Position" (New York: American Institute of Certified Public Accountants, 1971), par. 5.

Concepts of Funds

The term **funds** has been defined in several different ways, and its definition will determine the character of the funds statement prepared. Funds are most frequently used to mean working capital, and when so defined, the funds statement reports financing and investing activities in terms of working capital. Defined in those terms, the funds statement provides a summary of the individual sources and uses of working capital for the period. Funds are sometimes used to denote cash, and a funds statement applying this concept simply provides a presentation of the individual sources and uses of cash for the period and the resulting change in the cash balance. A modification of the cash concept defines funds as net current monetary assets — current assets excluding inventory and prepaid items less current liabilities — all current monetary assets, or simply cash and temporary investments combined. In applying alternative definitions, the funds statement would report the sources and applications of such "funds" and reconcile their change in successive balance sheets. In practice, funds reporting generally employs the working capital or cash concepts, and subsequent discussions in this text will describe the preparation of funds statements using these concepts.

Illustration of a Funds Statement

By helping to answer questions such as those mentioned earlier, the funds statement serves an important function. The format of the statement, presented on a working capital basis, is illustrated below for the Andersen Corporation. Another example of a statement of changes in financial position is included in Appendix B.

Andersen Corporation			
Statement of Changes in Financial Position — Working Capital Basis			
For Year Ended December 31, 1981			
Working capital was provided by:			
Operations:			
Income before irregular or extraordinary items		$25,000	
Add items not requiring working capital:			
Depreciation	$10,000		
Amortization of patents and goodwill	10,600	20,600	
Working capital provided by operations		$45,600	
Issuance of bonds		95,000	
Issuance of common stock to acquire land		70,000	$210,600
Working capital was applied to:			
Dividends		$20,000	
Retirement of long-term debt		80,000	
Acquisition of land by issuance of common stock		70,000	170,000
Increase in working capital*			$ 40,600

*Details of increase in working capital are not given. The above figures are illustrative only. They cannot be derived from the financial statements presented because comparative statements are not provided.

Using the format illustrated, the funds statement has two main sections, showing the **sources** of funds and the **applications** or uses of funds. The difference between total sources and applications is the net increase or decrease in working capital or cash.

As highlighted in the funds statement for Andersen Corporation, working capital was provided by operations and from the issuance of bonds. Additional resources were obtained from the sale of stock and were used to acquire land. The working capital generated was applied to dividends and to retire long-term debt, with the balance increasing working capital. Thus, the funds statement has accomplished its main purpose — that of identifying the primary sources and applications of funds and, therefore, the major financing activities of the business during a period of time. In Chapter 19 the techniques of preparing and analyzing funds statements are discussed in detail.

QUESTIONS

1. What are the purposes and limitations of the balance sheet?

2. What is the composition of the balance sheet? How is it related to the income statement and the statement of changes in financial position?

3. What is the balance sheet equation? Define each of the elements of that equation.

4. Why is the distinction between current and noncurrent assets and liabilities so important?

5. What criteria are generally used (a) in classifying assets as current or noncurrent? (b) in classifying liabilities as current or noncurrent?

6. Barker's Inc., reports the cash surrender value of life insurance on company officials as a current asset in view of its immediate convertibility into cash. Do you support this treatment?

7. Indicate under what circumstances each of the following can be considered noncurrent: (a) cash, (b) receivables.

8. Under what circumstances may bonds payable due in six months be reported as a long-term liability, even though they will not be liquidated from accumulated noncurrent funds?

9. What objections can be made to the use of the heading "Deferred costs"?

10. What justification is there for treating intangible items as assets on the balance sheet?

11. Distinguish between the following: (a) contingent liabilities and estimated liabilities, (b) appropriated retained earnings and free retained earnings.

12. What are the major classifications of (a) assets, (b) liabilities, and (c) owners' equity items? Indicate the nature of the items reported within each major classification.

13. Under what circumstances may offset balances be properly recognized on the balance sheet?

14. What is the nature and purpose of notes to financial statements?

15. What is the basic purpose of the statement of changes in financial position? What kind of information does this statement provide that is not readily available from the other general purpose statements?

16. What are the major categories of funds flow for a business entity?

17. What are the most common concepts of funds applied in preparing the statement of changes in financial position? Describe the statement under each of the different fund concepts. Which approach do you support?

EXERCISES

exercise 5-1

A balance sheet contains the following classifications:

(a) Current assets
(b) Long-term investments
(c) Land, buildings, and equipment
(d) Intangible assets
(e) Other long-term assets
(f) Current liabilities

(g) Long-term liabilities
(h) Unearned revenues
(i) Capital stock
(j) Additional paid-in capital
(k) Retained earnings

Indicate by letter how each of the following accounts would be classified. Place a minus sign (−) after all accounts representing offset or contra balances.

___ (1) Discount on Bonds Payable
___ (2) Stock of Subsidiary Corporation
___ (3) 12% Bonds Payable (due in six months)
___ (4) U.S. Treasury Notes
___ (5) Income Tax Payable
___ (6) Sales Tax Payable
___ (7) Estimated Claims Under Guarantees for Service and Replacements
___ (8) Accounts Payable (debit balance)
___ (9) Unearned Rental Revenue (three years in advance)

___(10) Accumulated Depletion
___(11) Interest Receivable
___(12) Preferred Stock Retirement Fund
___(13) Trademarks
___(14) Allowance for Doubtful Accounts
___(15) Dividends Payable
___(16) Accumulated Depreciation
___(17) Petty Cash Fund
___(18) Prepaid Rent
___(19) Prepaid Interest
___(20) Organization Costs

exercise 5-2

State how each of the following accounts should be classified on the balance sheet.

(a) Accumulated Patent Amortization
(b) Retained Earnings
(c) Vacation Pay Payable
(d) Retained Earnings Appropriated for Loss Contingencies
(e) Allowance for Doubtful Accounts
(f) Liability for Pension Payments
(g) Marketable Securities
(h) Paid-In Capital from Sale of Stock at More Than Stated Value
(i) Unamortized Bond Issue Costs
(j) Goodwill
(k) Receivables — U.S. Government Contracts
(l) Advances to Salespersons

(m) Customers Accounts with Credit Balances
(n) Raw Materials
(o) Cash Representing Refundable Deposits on Returnable Containers
(p) Unclaimed Payroll Checks
(q) Employees Income Tax Payable
(r) Subscription Revenue Received in Advance
(s) Interest Payable
(t) Deferred Income Tax (debit balance)
(u) Tools
(v) Deferred Income Tax (credit balance)
(w) Loans to Officers
(x) Leasehold Improvements
(y) Patents

exercise 5-3

Indicate how each of the following items should be classified on the balance sheet:

(a) Cash surrender value of life insurance.
(b) Sinking fund cash for retirement of bonds.
(c) Bonds payable in six months out of sinking fund cash.
(d) Note receivable that will be collected in 10 annual installments.
(e) Cash deposited with broker on option to buy real estate.
(f) Land held as future plant site.
(g) Warehouse in process of construction.
(h) Cash fund representing customers' deposits on returnable containers.
(i) Cash fund representing sales tax collections.
(j) Goods in process that will require more than one year for completion.

exercise 5-4

For each of the following items, indicate the proper amount and account classification(s) for the

December 31, 1981 balance sheet.

(a) A serial note payable of $80,000 carries an interest rate of 12%, payable semiannually September 1, and March 1. On March 1 of each year $20,000 of the principal is paid.

(b) $30,000 cash has been restricted for the purchase of a factory addition.

(c) Excess cash on hand of $12,000 has been used to purchase securities. As soon as the need for cash arises, these securities will be sold.

(d) A short-term note payable of $15,000 coming due on August 1, 1982; probably will be refinanced during 1982 with a long-term note.

(e) Company's twenty-year bonds payable with a face value of $100,000 were sold on December 28, 1981, for $103,000.

exercise 5-5

Using the following data, prepare a balance sheet in financial position form for Facer Milling Company at December 31, 1981.

Accounts payable	$20,000
Accounts receivable	22,000
Accumulated depreciation	18,000
Bonds payable	23,000
Cash	10,000
Land, buildings, and equipment	50,000
Inventory	10,000
Contributed capital	15,000
Rent revenue received in advance	5,000
Retained earnings	11,000

exercise 5-6

The bookkeeper for Fuja, Inc., submitted the following balance sheet as of December 31, 1981.

Fuja, Inc.
Balance Sheet
December 31, 1981

Assets		Liabilities and Stockholders' Equity	
Cash	$ 60,000	Accounts payable — trade	$100,000
Accounts receivable — trade	100,000	Salaries payable	40,000
Inventories	160,000	Stockholders' equity	280,000
Machinery	40,000		
Goodwill	60,000		
	$420,000		$420,000

Reference to the records of the company indicated the following:

(a) Cash included:

Petty cash	$ 2,000
Payroll account	20,000
Savings account for cash to be used for building remodeling	20,000
General account	18,000
	$60,000

(b) State and local taxes of $4,800 were accrued on December 31. However, $4,800 had been deposited in a special cash account to be used to pay these and neither cash nor the accrued taxes were reported on the balance sheet.

(c) Twenty-five percent of Fuja, Inc.'s inventory is rapidly becoming obsolete. The obsolete portion of the inventory as of the balance sheet date was worth only one half of what Fuja, Inc., paid for it.

(d) Goods costing $6,000 were shipped to customers on December 30 and 31, at a sales price of $8,800. Goods shipped were not included in the inventory as of December 31. However, receivables were not recognized for the shipment since invoices were not sent out until January 3.

(e) One of Fuja, Inc.'s machines costing $16,000 is located on the Autonomous Island Republic, Tropicana. The dictator of Tropicana nationalized several foreign businesses during 1981 and is likely to expropriate Fuja, Inc.'s machinery for personal use. All machinery was acquired in July of 1981 and will not be depreciated this year.

(f) The corporation had been organized on January 1, 1981, by exchanging 22,000 shares of no-par stock with stated value of $10 per share for the net assets of the partnership Kazu and Komino.

Prepare a corrected balance sheet as of December 31, 1981.

exercise 5-7

From the following chart of accounts, prepare a balance sheet in account form showing all balance sheet items properly classified. (No monetary amounts are to be recognized.)

Accounts Payable	Interest Receivable
Accounts Receivable	Interest Revenue
Accumulated Depreciation — Building	Inventory
Accumulated Depreciation — Equipment	Investment in Bonds
Advertising Expense	Land
Allowance for Decline in Value of Marketable Securities	Loss on Purchase Commitments
Allowance for Doubtful Accounts	Marketable Securities
Bonds Payable	Miscellaneous General Expense
Buildings	Notes Payable
Cash	Paid-In Capital from Sale of Common Stock at More Than Stated Value
Common Stock	Paid-In Capital from Sale of Treasury Stock
Cost of Goods Sold	Patents
Deferred Income Tax (debit balance)	Pension Fund
Depreciation Expense — Buildings	Premium on Bonds Payable
Dividends	Prepaid Insurance
Doubtful Accounts Expense	Property Tax Expense
Equipment	Purchases
Estimated Warranty Expense Payable	Purchases Discount
Gain on Sale of Land	Retained Earnings
Gain on Sale of Marketable Securities	Salaries Payable
Goodwill	Sales
Income Summary	Sales Salaries
Income Tax Expense	Travel Expense
Income Tax Payable	

exercise 5-8

From the following information for the MJB Corporation, prepare a statement of changes in financial position on a working capital basis for the year ended December 31, 1981.

Amortization of patent	$ 2,200
Depreciation expense	7,000
Issuance of common stock	25,000
Issuance of new bonds payable	15,000
Net income	44,000
Payment of dividend	22,500
Purchase of equipment	33,200
Retirement of long-term debt	45,000
Sale of land (no gain or loss)	3,500
Net decrease in working capital for the period	4,000

PROBLEMS

problem 5-1

Booth Tractors, Inc., furnishes you with the following list of accounts.

Accounts Payable	$ 55,000	Advertising Expense	$ 72,000
Accounts Receivable	40,000	Allowance for Doubtful Accounts	8,000
Accumulated Depreciation	44,000	Bonds Payable	70,000
Advances to Salespersons	5,000	Cash	12,000

Certificates of Deposit	$ 20,000	Paid-In Capital in Excess of Par...	$ 45,000
Common Stock (par)	120,000	Premium on Bonds Payable	6,000
Customer Accounts with Credit Balances	4,000	Prepaid Interest Expense	3,000
		Rent Revenue	27,000
Deferred Income Tax (credit balance)	53,000	Rent Revenue Received in Advance	2,000
Equipment	184,000	Retained Earnings	40,000
Inventory	49,000	Retained Earnings Appropriated for Loss Contingencies	30,000
Investment in Kemp Oil Co. Stock (70% of outstanding stock)	85,000	Taxes Payable	10,000
		Tools	68,000
Investment in Tooke Co. Stock (current marketable securities)	21,000		

Instructions: From the above partial list of accounts determine working capital, total assets total liabilities, and stockholders' equity per share of stock (50,000 shares outstanding).

problem 5-2

Below is a list of account titles and balances for the Lott Company as of January 31, 1982.

Accounts Payable	$ 85,800	Interest Receivable	$ 400
Accounts Receivable	106,000	Investment in Undeveloped Properties	212,000
Accumulated Depreciation — Buildings	140,000	Land	130,000
Accumulated Depreciation — Machinery and Equipment	40,000	Machinery and Equipment	144,000
Allowance for Doubtful Notes and Accounts	4,200	Miscellaneous Supplies Inventories	6,200
Buildings	300,000	Notes Payable (current)	69,260
Cash in Banks	107,300	Notes Payable (due 1987)	50,000
Cash on Hand	8,880	Notes Receivable	22,400
Cash Surrender Value of Life Insurance	17,000	Preferred Stock, $6 par	300,000
		Premium on Common Stock	60,000
Claim for Income Tax Refund	5,000	Prepaid Insurance	4,500
Common Stock, $20 par	600,000	Raw Materials	33,800
Employees Income Tax Payable	3,640	Retained Earnings (debit balance)	11,740
Finished Goods	42,000	Salaries and Wages Payable	7,400
Goods in Process	78,800	Temporary Investments in Marketable Securities	156,880
Income Tax Payable	24,600		
Interest Payable	2,000		

Instructions: Prepare a properly classified balance sheet.

problem 5-3

Account balances and supplemental information for Sunshine Research Corp., as of December 31, 1981 are given below:

Accounts Payable	$ 32,160	Furniture, Fixtures, and Store Equipment	$769,000
Accounts Receivable — Trade	57,731	Inventory	201,620
Accumulated Depreciation — Leasehold Improvements and Equipment	579,472	Investment in Unconsolidated Subsidiary	80,000
Additional Paid-In Capital	100,000	Insurance Claims Receivable	120,000
Allowance for Doubtful Accounts	1,731	Land	6,000
Automotive Equipment	132,800	Leasehold Improvements	65,800
Cash	30,600	7½–12% Mortgage Notes	200,000
Cash Surrender Value of Life Insurance	3,600	Notes Payable — Banks	17,000
		Notes Payable — Trade	63,540
Common Stock	200,000	Patent Licenses	57,402
Deferred Income Tax (credit balance)	45,000	Prepaid Insurance	5,500
		Profit Sharing, Payroll, and Vacation Payable	40,000
Dividends Payable	37,500	Retained Earnings	225,800
Franchises	12,150	Tax Receivable — In Litigation	13,000

Supplemental information:

   (a) Depreciation is provided by the straight-line method over the estimated useful lives of the assets.
   (b) Common stock is $5 par, and 40,000 of the 100,000 authorized shares were issued and are outstanding.
   (c) The cost of an exclusive franchise to import a foreign company's ball bearings and a related patent license are being amortized on the straight-line method over their remaining lives: franchise, 10 years; patents, 15 years.
   (d) Inventories are stated at the lower of cost or market: cost was determined by the specific identification method.
   (e) Insurance claims based upon the opinion of an independent insurance adjustor are for property damages at the central warehouse. These claims are estimated to be one-half collectible in the following year and one-half collectible thereafter.
   (f) The company leases all of its buildings from various lessors. Estimated fixed lease obligations are $50,000 per year for the next ten years. The leases do not meet the criteria for capitalization.
   (g) The company is currently in litigation over a claimed overpayment of income tax of $13,000. In the opinion of counsel, the claim is valid. The company is contingently liable on guaranteed notes worth $17,000.

   Instructions: Prepare a properly classified balance sheet in account form. Include all notes and parenthetical notations necessary to properly disclose the essential financial data.

problem 5-4

The following balance sheet was prepared by the accountant for Pioneer Company.

Pioneer Company
Balance Sheet
June 30, 1982

Assets

Cash...	$ 25,500
Marketable securities (includes 25% ownership in stock of Pine Mountain Developers, at cost of $250,000)..	332,000
Inventories (net of amount still due suppliers of $75,980)...............................	624,600
Prepaid expenses (includes a deposit of $10,000 made on inventories to be delivered in 18 months)...	32,100
Plant assets (excluding $50,000 of equipment still in use, but fully depreciated)...	220,000
Goodwill (based upon estimate of President of Pioneer Company).................	50,000
Total assets..	$1,284,200

Liabilities and Stockholders' Equity

Notes payable ($75,000 due in 1984)	$ 135,000
Accounts payable (not including amount due to suppliers of inventory — see above)	142,000
Long-term liability under pension plan	80,000
Reserve for building expansion	75,000
Accumulated depreciation — fixed assets..	73,000
Taxes payable...	44,500
Bonds payable (net of discount of $30,000)...	270,000
Deferred income tax credit..	83,000
Common stock (20,000 shares @ $10 par)...	200,000
Premium on common stock	50,500
Reserve for loss contingencies...	15,000
Retained earnings — unappropriated	116,200
Total liabilities and stockholders' equity	$1,284,200

   Instructions: Prepare a corrected statement in good form using appropriate account titles.

problem 5-5

The Oakley Ranch summarizes its financial position in the following letter to their accountant.

January 20, 1982

Dear Collin:

The following information should be of value to you in preparing the balance sheet for Oakley Ranch as of December 31, 1981. The balance of cash as of December 31 as reported on the bank statement was $43,825. There were still outstanding checks of $9,320 that had not cleared the bank and cash on hand of $3,640 was not deposited until January 4, 1982.

Customers owed the company $40,500 at December 31. We estimated 5% of this amount will never be collected. We owe suppliers $32,000 for poultry feed purchased in November and December. About 80% of this feed was used before December 31.

Because we think the price of grain will rise in 1982, we are holding 10,000 bushels of wheat and 5,000 bushels of oats until spring. The market value at December 31 was $3.50 per bushel of wheat and $1.50 per bushel of oats. We estimate that both prices will increase 10% by selling time. We are not able to estimate the cost of raising this product.

Oakley Ranch owns 1,850 acres of land. Two separate purchases of land were made as follows: 1,250 acres at $200 per acre in 1963, and 600 acres at $400 per acre in 1969. Similar land is currently selling for $800 per acre. The balance of the mortgage on the two parcels of land is $270,000 at December 31; 10% of this mortgage must be paid in 1982.

Our farm buildings and equipment cost us $176,400 and on the average are 50% depreciated. If we were to replace these buildings and equipment at today's prices, we believe we would be conservative in estimating a cost of $300,000.

We have not paid property tax of $5,500 for 1982 billed us in late November. Our estimated income tax for 1981 is $18,500. A refund claim for $2,800 has been filed relative to the 1979 income tax return. The claim arose because of an error made on the 1979 return.

The operator of the ranch will receive a bonus of $7,000 for 1981 operations. It will be paid when the entire grain crop has been sold.

As you will recall, we issued 14,000 shares of $10 par stock upon incorporation. The ranch received $255,000 as net proceeds from the stock issue. Dividends of $45,000 were declared last month and will be paid on February 1, 1982.

The new year appears to hold great promise. Thanks for your help in preparing this statement.

Sincerely,
Alice Mahle
President — Oakley Ranch

Instructions: Based upon this information, prepare a properly classified balance sheet as of December 31, 1981.

problem 5-6

The balance sheet below is submitted to you for inspection and review.

Aaron Freight Company
Balance Sheet
December 31, 1981

Assets		Liabilities and Stockholders' Equity	
Cash	$ 50,000	Miscellaneous liabilities	$ 2,500
Accounts receivable	180,000	Loan payable	56,250
Inventories	220,000	Accounts payable	146,250
Prepaid insurance	12,500	Capital stock	250,000
Land, buildings, and		Paid-in capital	332,500
equipment	325,000		
	$787,500		$787,500

In the course of the review you find the data listed below:

(a) The possibility of uncollectible accounts on accounts receivable has not been considered. It is estimated that uncollectible accounts will total $5,000.

(b) $50,000 representing the cost of a large-scale newspaper advertising campaign completed in 1981 has been added to the inventories, since it is believed that this campaign will benefit sales of 1982. It is also found that inventories include merchandise of $16,250 received on December 31 that has not yet been recorded as a purchase.

(c) Prepaid insurance consists of $1,000, the cost of fire insurance for 1982, and $11,500, the cash surrender value on officers' life insurance policies.

(d) The books show that land, buildings, and equipment have a cost of $525,000 with depreciation of $200,000 recognized in prior years. However, these balances include fully depreciated equipment of $75,000 that has been scrapped and is no longer on hand.

(e) Miscellaneous liabilities of $2,500 represent salaries payable of $7,500, less noncurrent advances of $5,000 made to company officials.

(f) Loan payable represents a loan from the bank that is payable in regular quarterly installments of $6,250.

(g) Tax liabilities not shown are estimated at $11,250.

(h) Deferred income tax (credit) arising from timing differences in recognizing income totals $23,750. This tax was not included in the balance sheet.

(i) Capital stock consists of 6,250 shares of preferred 6% stock, par $20, and 12,500 shares of common stock, stated value $10.

(j) Capital stock had been issued for a total consideration of $312,500, the amount received in excess of the par and stated values of the stock being reported as paid-in capital.

Instructions: Prepare a corrected balance sheet in report form with accounts properly classified.

problem 5-7

The following data were taken from the records of Peabody Produce Company for the year ended June 30, 1981.

Borrowed on long-term notes	$20,000
Issued capital stock	50,000
Purchased equipment	27,000
Net income	37,000
Purchased treasury stock	2,000
Paid dividends	30,000
Depreciation expense	12,000
Retired bonds payable	70,000
Goodwill amortization	2,000
Sold long-term investment (at cost)	5,000
Decrease in net working capital	3,000

Instructions:

(1) From the information given, prepare in good form a statement of changes in financial position on a working capital basis.

(2) Briefly explain what an interested party would learn from studying Peabody Produce Company's Funds Statement.

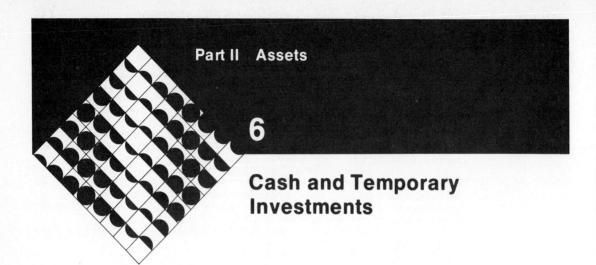

Part II Assets

6

Cash and Temporary Investments

CHAPTER OBJECTIVES

Identify criteria for classifying and disclosing the various components of cash.

Discuss potential problems in cash control and methods of reducing the probability of loss and misappropriation.

Describe and illustrate the imprest system of accounting for cash funds.

Describe and illustrate procedures for reconciling book cash balances and bank statement balances.

Discuss the nature of temporary investments.

Describe and illustrate accounting for purchases and sales of marketable securities.

Describe, illustrate, and evaluate alternative methods of accounting for changes in market values of marketable securities.

The first part of this book has established a perspective of accounting and its theoretical foundation. Part II explores items classified as **assets**, beginning with the most liquid assets, cash and temporary investments.

CASH

Cash is the most active item on accounting statements. It is involved in most business transactions. This is due to the nature of business transactions which include a price and conditions calling for settlement in terms of a medium of exchange. The standard medium of exchange is cash. Even if cash is not directly involved in a transaction, it provides the basis for measurement and accounting for all other items.

In striking contrast to the activity of cash is its unproductive nature. Since cash is the measure of value, it cannot expand or grow unless it is converted into other properties. Excessive balances of cash on hand are often referred to as **idle cash**. Efficient cash management requires available cash to be continuously working in one of several ways — e.g., as part of the operating cycle or as a short-term or long-term investment.

Composition of Cash

Cash is composed of commercial and savings deposits in banks and elsewhere and items on hand that can be used as a medium of exchange or that are acceptable for deposit at face value by a bank. **Cash on hand** would include petty cash funds, change funds, and other regularly used and unexpended funds, together with items such as personal checks, travelers' checks, cashiers' checks, bank drafts, and money orders.

"Acceptance at face value on deposit" is a satisfactory test in classifying as cash the items found in the cash drawer. It is assumed that deposits in a bank are made regularly and that deposits become the basis for disbursements by the depositor. Although postage stamps may in some instances pass for mail payments of small amounts, they are not accepted for deposit and should be classified as office supplies. Post-dated checks are in effect notes receivable and should not be recognized as cash until the time they can be deposited. Checks deposited but returned by the bank because of insufficient funds in the debtor's account are receivables. Cash-due memorandums for money advanced to officers and employees are receivable items, in some instances less satisfactory receivables than those of trade customers. A note or draft left at a bank for collection represents a receivable until collection is made and the amount is added to the depositor's account. Stocks, bonds, and United States securities, although immediately convertible into cash, generally are not used as a means for making payments, hence do not constitute cash but should be recognized as temporary or long-term investments.

Since the concept of cash embodies the standard of value, no valuation problems are encountered in reporting those items qualifying as cash. When cash is comprised solely of cash on hand and unrestricted demand deposits, the total generally appears on the balance sheet as a single item "Cash." Other components of cash, however, should be disclosed or reported as separate items.

Deposits that are not immediately available due to withdrawal restrictions require separate identification. Certificates of deposit (CDs), for example, generally may be withdrawn only at specified maturity dates. Thus, CDs are preferably reported parenthetically or separately as short-term or long-term investments.

Deposits in foreign banks subject to immediate and unrestricted withdrawal qualify as cash. Such balances should be converted into their U.S. dollar equivalents as of the date of the balance sheet. However, cash in foreign banks blocked or otherwise restricted as to use or withdrawal and cash in closed banks should be designated as claims or receivables of a current or noncurrent character and should be reported subject to allowances for losses on their realization.

Cash balances specifically designated by management for special purposes may be separately reported. Those cash balances to be applied to some current purpose or current obligation are properly reported in the current section on the balance sheet. For example, cash funds for employees' travel, payment of current interest and dividends, or payment of taxes or other obligations included in the current liabilities may be separately reported but are still classified as current.

Cash restricted as to use by agreement should be separately designated and reported. Restricted cash should be reported as a current item only if it is to be applied to some current purpose or obligation. Classification of the cash balance as current or noncurrent should parallel the classification applied to the liability.

Cash balances not available for current purposes require separate designation and classification under a noncurrent heading on the balance sheet. The noncurrent classification applies to items such as the following: time deposits not currently available as a result of withdrawal restrictions; cash deposits on bids or options that may be applied to the acquisition of noncurrent assets; and cash funds held by trustees for plant acquisitions, bond retirement, and pension payments.

A credit balance in the cash account resulting from the issuance of checks in excess of the amount on deposit is known as a **cash overdraft** and should be reported as a current liability. An overdraft does not necessarily embarrass a company if a number of checks are outstanding and deposits are made to cover the checks before clearance. When a company has two balances with a single bank, there can be no objection to the offsetting of the overdraft against an account with a positive balance; failure by the depositor to meet the overdraft will actually result in bank action to effect such an offset. However, when a company has accounts with two different banks and there is a positive balance in one account and an overdraft in the other, both an asset balance and a liability balance should be recognized in view of the claim against one bank and an obligation to the other; if recognition of an overdraft is to be avoided, cash should actually be transferred to cover the deficiency.

In summary, cash is a current asset comprised of coin, currency, and other items which (1) serve as a medium of exchange, and (2) provide the basis for measurement in accounting. Most negotiable instruments (e.g., checks, bank drafts, and money orders) qualify as cash because they can be converted to coin or currency on demand or are acceptable for deposit at face value by a bank. Components of cash restricted as to use or withdrawal should be disclosed or separately reported and classified as an investment, a receivable, or other asset. The objective of disclosure is to provide the user of financial statements with information to assist in evaluating the entity's ability to meet obligations and in assessing the effectiveness of cash management.

Compensating Balances. In connection with financing arrangements, it is common practice for a company to agree to maintain a minimum or average balance on deposit with a bank or other lending institution. These **compensating balances** are defined by the SEC as ". . . that portion of any demand deposit (or any time deposit or certificate of deposit) maintained by a corporation . . . which constitutes support for existing borrowing arrangements of the corporation . . . with a lending institution. Such arrangements would include both outstanding borrowings and the assurance of future credit availability."[1]

Compensating balances provide a source of funds to the lender as partial compensation for credit extended. In effect, such arrangements raise the interest rate because the borrower cannot use the entire amount on deposit with the lending institution. These balances present an accounting problem from the standpoint of disclosure. Readers of financial statements are likely to assume the entire cash balance is available to meet current obligations, when, in fact, part of the balance is restricted.

The solution to this problem is to disclose the extent of compensating balances. The SEC recommends any "legally restricted" deposits held as compensating balances be segregated and reported separately. If the balances are the result of short-term financing arrangements, they should be shown separately among the "cash items" in the current asset section; if the compensating balances are in connection with long-term agreements, they should be classified as noncurrent, either as investments or "other assets." Where deposits are not legally restricted, but where compensating balance agreements still exist, the amounts and nature of the arrangements should be disclosed in the footnotes to the financial statements.

Electronic Funds Transfer. During the past few years, some companies have experimented with a new method of transferring funds called **Electronic Funds Transfer (EFT)**. This is a method of transferring funds to and from a bank electronically with no paper (e.g., currency or checks) involved in the transaction. EFT also makes cash information available upon request at any time through the use of a computer hook-up between the bank and its client.

Current uses of EFT systems include:

1. *Balance reporting systems* which provide the user with the bank balance through terminal-based computers.
2. *Zero-balance receipt and disbursement accounts* where the bank has instructions from its customer to maintain the customer's demand account (non-interest-bearing) at zero and to transfer funds to these accounts from interest-

---

[1]Securities and Exchange Commission, *Accounting Series Release No. 148*, "Disclosure of Compensating Balances and Short-Term Borrowing Arrangements" (Washington: U.S. Government Printing Office, 1973).

bearing accounts only as needed. The purpose of these accounts is obviously to keep idle funds to a minimum.

3. *Direct payroll deposit*, which involves a corporation transferring electronically the amount due an employee to the employee's bank through an automated clearing house rather than issuing paychecks to its employees. Some corporations are not supportive of this use of EFT because the widely used "float period" is eliminated. The float period is the time required for the company's check to actually clear the bank. Usually it takes 2-5 days from the time the company issues a check to the time the check is deposited and eventually charged to the company's account.

4. *Individual-to-business bill payment*, an arrangement where the individual authorizes the business to electronically bill the individual's demand account for the amount due. The bank transfers the funds to the business and notifies the individual of the charge to the individual's account.

The future possibilities of EFT are limitless. While EFT will not alter the general nature of cash, if EFT is widely accepted, it will certainly impact on the manner of handling cash, especially where computer accounting systems are concerned. As one individual has stated, "With the development of electronic funds transfer systems (EFTS), electronic data processing in business is about to undergo a revolution as profound as that caused by the introduction of computers to accounting in the early 1960s."[2]

Control of Cash

The term **internal control** encompasses the systems, procedures, and policies employed by an enterprise to help assure that its transactions are properly authorized and are appropriately executed and recorded. It is a term that embraces both **administrative controls** and **accounting controls**. Administrative controls relate to the plan of organization and procedures required for management's authorization of transactions. This is the first step in establishing accounting controls which include the plans, procedures, and records necessary for safeguarding assets and producing reliable financial records. Accounting controls are specifically designed to provide reasonable assurance that:

a. Transactions are executed in accordance with management's general or specific authorization.
b. Transactions are recorded as necessary (1) to permit preparation of financial statements in conformity with generally accepted accounting principles or any other criteria applicable to such statements and (2) to maintain accountability for assets.
c. Access to assets is permitted only in accordance with management's authorization.
d. The recorded accountability for assets is compared with the existing assets at reasonable intervals and appropriate action is taken with respect to any differences.[3]

---

[2]Norman R. Lyons, "Segregation of Functions in EFTS," *Journal of Accountancy*, October 1978, p. 89. See also Sanford Rose, "Checkless Banking is Bound to Come," *Fortune*, June 1977.
[3]*Statement on Auditing Standards No. 1*, "Codification of Auditing Standards and Procedures" (New York: American Institute of Certified Public Accountants, 1973), par. 320.28.

Managers and auditors have long recognized the need for effective internal controls. However, with the passage of the Foreign Corrupt Practices Act of 1977, the emphasis on internal controls is significantly increased. This is due to a provision in the Act which requires all public companies, not just those with foreign operations, to keep good accounting records and to maintain a sufficient system of internal accounting controls. The Act amends the Securities and Exchange Act of 1934 and incorporates the definitions of internal control quoted above. Thus, by law, all companies falling under the jurisdiction of the SEC are now required to devise and maintain a "sufficient" system of internal control. The exact meaning of sufficient is not clear; to date specific guidelines have not been established. It is apparent, however, that managers, accountants, and others involved with public companies should consider carefully the increased responsibilities being imposed in the internal control area.

Obviously, the system of internal control must be developed with appropriate regard to the size and nature of the particular unit to be served. Its design should provide the maximum contributions practicable considering the special risks faced as well as the costs of providing controls. The increased use of data processing equipment for processing accounting transactions has not eliminated the need for carefully designed control systems; on the contrary, it may have increased the need. As new equipment is acquired and introduced into a system, the establishment or modification of controls should be considered.

In any system of internal accounting control, special emphasis must be placed on the procedures for handling and accounting for cash.

Problems in Cash Control. Because of the characteristics of cash — its small bulk, its lack of owner identification, and its immediate transferability — it is the asset most subject to misappropriation, intentional or otherwise. Losses can be avoided only by careful control of cash from the time it is received until the time it is spent.

Control over business cash normally requires as a minimum the separation of cash custodial functions and cash recording functions. When the same persons have access to cash and also to cash records, the business becomes vulnerable to the misappropriation of cash and to the manipulation or falsification of cash records. The following are representative of practices found under these circumstances: (1) cash receipts from sales, from recoveries of accounts previously written off, from refunds on invoice overpayments, and from other sources are understated, the unrecorded cash being pocketed; (2) receivables are not entered on the books and cash collected on these receivables is withheld; (3) customers' accounts are credited for remittances but Sales Returns or Doubtful Accounts Expense is debited and the cash is withheld; (4) checks for personal purposes are debited to business expense; (5) invoices, vouchers, receipts, payroll records, or vouchers once approved and paid are used in support of fictitious charges, and endorsements on checks issued in payment of these charges are subsequently forged; (6) the cash balance is misstated by erroneous footings in the cash receipts and disbursement records, cash equivalent to the misstatement being withheld.

Two additional practices, check kiting and lapping, may be found when those who handle cash also maintain the cash records of the business.

Check kiting occurs when at the end of a month a transfer of funds is made by check from one bank to another to cover a cash shortage, and the entry to record the issue of the check is held over until the beginning of the new period. A cash increase in the customer's balance is recognized by the second bank in the current month as a result of the receipt of the check, but a corresponding decrease in the customer's balance is not recognized by the first bank because the check has not yet been presented for payment. When the bank statements are received, the balance in the bank in which the check was deposited shows an increase. At the same time, the balance shown in the bank on which the check was drawn remains unchanged. A cash shortage is thus temporarily concealed.

Lapping occurs when a customer's remittance is misappropriated, the customer's account being credited when cash is collected from another customer at a later date. This process may be continued with further misappropriations and increasing delays in postings. To illustrate lapping, assume that on successive days cash is received from customers A, B, and C in amounts of $75, $125, and $120. A's payment is misappropriated. A is subsequently credited with $75 out of B's payment and the difference, $50, is misappropriated. B is credited for $125 upon C's $120 payment and $5 is returned on the amounts originally *borrowed*. The shortage at this point is $120, the unrecorded credit to C's account. This procedure can be continued with but slight delay in recording any customer's payment. The embezzler usually intends to return the money and avoid the strain of lapping after a profit has been made on the investments. Unable to make restitution, the embezzler may resort to a fictitious entry debiting Doubtful Accounts Expense or some other expense account and crediting the customers' balances to bring these up to date.

Cash Shortage and Overage. When cash records and summaries report a cash total differing from the amount available for deposit, and it is assumed that cash has been lost or errors have been made in making change, an adjustment is made to a **cash short and over** account. The offsetting part of the entry is to the regular cash account. Unless theft is involved, the cash short and over account will usually "net" to a nominal amount during the year. Any balance in this account may be reported as miscellaneous expense or revenue in summarizing net income. However, a cash shortage resulting from employee defalcation should be charged to an employee account or the bonding company liable for such losses. Failure to recover the shortage requires the recognition of a loss from this source.

Attributes of Cash Control Systems. The system for the control of cash must be adapted to a particular business. It is not feasible to attempt to describe all of the features and techniques employed in businesses of various kinds and sizes. In general, however, systems of cash control deny access to the records to those who handle cash. This reduces the possibility of improper entries to conceal the misuse of cash receipts and cash payments. The probability of misappropriation of cash is greatly reduced if two or more employees must conspire in the embezzlement. Further, systems normally provide for separation of the receiving and paying functions. The basic characteristics of a system of cash control are listed below:

1. Specifically assigned responsibility for handling cash receipts.
2. Separation of handling and recording cash receipts.
3. Daily deposit of all cash received.
4. Voucher system to control cash payments.
5. Internal audit at irregular intervals.

Specifically Assigned Responsibility for Handling Cash Receipts. A fundamental principle in controlling any asset is that the responsibility be specifically assigned to one person. This principle is especially vital in the area of cash. If more than one person must have access to the same cash fund at different times, a reconciliation of the cash on hand should be made each time the responsibility is shifted. Any shortage or questionable transaction can then be identified with a particular person.

Separation of Handling and Recording Cash Receipts. An adequate control system normally requires cash from sales and cash remittances from customers be made available directly to the treasurer or the cashier for deposit, while records related to these transactions, as well as records related to bank deposits, be made available directly to the accounting department. It is also desirable that comparisons of bank deposits with the book records of cash be made regularly by a third party who is engaged neither in the cash handling nor in the cash recording functions. Frequently, for example, a clerk opens the mail, prepares lists of remittances in duplicate, and then sends the cash and one copy of the list of remittances to the cashier and the second copy of the list to the accounting department. Readings of cash registers are made by some responsible individual other than the cashier at the end of the day. The cash, together with a summary of the receipts, is sent to the cashier; a summary of the receipts is also sent to the accounting department. Although deposits in the bank are made by the cashier or treasurer, entries on the books are made from lists of remittances and register readings prepared by individuals not otherwise involved in handling or recording cash. Members of the accounting or auditing staff compare periodic bank statements with related data on the books to determine whether the data are in agreement. If customers' remittances are not listed and the cash is misused, statements to customers will report excessive amounts and protests will lead to sources of the discrepancies; if cash receipts listed are not deposited properly, the bank record will not agree with cash records.

Daily Deposit of All Cash Received. The daily deposit of all cash received prevents sums of cash from lying around the office and being used for other than business purposes. Officers and employees have less opportunity to borrow on IOU's. Both the temptation for misappropriation of cash and the risk of theft of cash are avoided. The bank protects company funds and releases these only upon proper company authorization. When the full receipts are deposited daily, the bank's record of deposits must agree with the depositor's record of cash receipts. This double record provides an automatic check over cash receipts.

Voucher System to Control Cash Payments. The use of a voucher system to control cash payments is a desirable feature of cash control. Vouchers authorizing disbursements of cash by check are made at the time goods or services are received and found acceptable. Entries in the voucher register recording the expenditures and the authorizations for payment are made by the accounting department. Checks are also prepared and are sent, together with documents supporting the disbursements, to the person specifically authorized to make payment, normally the official designated as treasurer. This person signs and issues checks only after careful inspection of the vouchers supporting and authorizing payments. The accounting department, upon notification of the issuance of checks, makes appropriate records of this fact. Receiving and paying functions of the business are maintained as two separate systems. In each instance, custodial and recording activities are exercised by different parties.

Internal Audit at Irregular Intervals. Internal audits at irregular and unannounced intervals may be made a part of the system of cash control. A member of the internal auditing staff verifies the records and checks on the activities of those employees handling cash to make sure the provisions of the system are being carried out. Such control is particularly desirable over petty cash and other cash funds where cash handling and bookkeeping are generally combined.

Double Record of Cash. A preceding section listed the daily deposit of all cash received as an important factor in the control of cash. If all cash receipts are deposited daily, then the bank record of deposits will agree with the depositor's record of cash receipts. As a complementary device, all cash payments should be made by check; the bank's record for checks should agree with the depositor's record of cash payments. Two complete cash summaries are thus available, one in the cash account and the other on the monthly bank statement. In addition to the advantages resulting from organized and consistent routines applied to cash receipts and disbursements, a duplicate record of cash maintained by an outside agency is made available as a check upon the accuracy of the records kept by the company.

Petty Cash

Immediate cash payments and payments too small to be made by check may be made from a **petty cash fund** . Under an *imprest system*, the petty cash fund is created by drawing a check to Petty Cash for the amount of the fund. In recording the establishment of the fund, Petty Cash Fund is debited and Cash is credited. The cash is then turned over to a cashier or some person who is solely responsible for payments made out of the fund. The cashier should require a signed receipt for all payments made. These receipts may be printed in prenumbered form. Frequently, a bill or other memorandum is submitted when a payment is requested. A record of petty cash payments may be kept in a *petty cash journal*.

Whenever the amount of cash in the fund runs low and also at the end of each fiscal period, the fund is replenished by writing a check equal to the payments made. In recording replenishment, expenses and other appropriate accounts are debited for petty cash disbursements and Cash is credited. The cash short and over account, mentioned earlier, may be used when the fund fails to balance. Replenishment is necessary whenever statements are to be prepared since petty cash disbursements are recognized on the books only when the fund is replenished.

The request for cash to replenish the fund is supported by a summary and analysis of the signed receipts required at the time of the disbursement from the fund. This analysis is the basis for the debits recognized on the books when the replenishing check is issued. The signed receipts, together with appropriate documents, are filed as evidence supporting petty cash disbursements.

The cashier of the petty cash fund is held accountable for the total amount of the fund. The person responsible must have on hand at all times cash and signed receipts equal in amount to the original balance of the fund. The cashier should be discouraged from cashing employees' checks from petty cash or otherwise engaging in a banking function. If a banking function is to be undertaken, it should represent a separate activity with a fund established for this purpose.

The petty cash operation should be maintained apart from other cash funds employed for particular business purposes. For example, a retail store may require funds for making change. Certain sums of coins and currency are withheld from deposit at the end of each day to be carried forward as the change funds for the beginning of business on the next day. A separate account should be established to report a cash supply always on hand. Also, special funds or bank accounts may be established for payrolls, dividend distributions, and bond interest payments. Each fund requires a separate accounting.

Reconciliation of Bank Balances

When daily receipts are deposited and payments other than those from petty cash are made by check, the bank's statement of its transactions with the depositor can be compared with the record of cash as reported on the depositor's books. A comparison of the bank balance with the balance reported on the books is usually made monthly by means of a summary known as a **bank reconciliation statement**. The bank reconciliation statement is prepared to disclose any errors or irregularities in either the records of the bank or those of the business unit. It is developed in a form that points out the reasons for discrepancies in the two balances. It should be prepared by an individual who neither handles nor records cash. Any discrepancies should be brought to the immediate attention of appropriate company officials.

When the bank statement and the depositor's records are compared, certain items may appear on one and not the other, resulting in a difference in the two balances. Most of these differences result from timing lags, and are thus normal. Four common types of differences arise in the following situations:

1. A deposit made toward the end of the month and recorded on the depositor's books is not received by the bank in time to be reflected on the bank statement. This amount, referred to as a **deposit in transit**, has to be added to the bank statement balance to make it agree with the balance on the depositor's books.

2. Checks written toward the end of the month have reduced the depositor's cash balance, but have not cleared the bank as of the bank statement date. These **outstanding checks** must be subtracted from the bank statement balance to make it agree with the depositor's records.

3. The bank normally charges a monthly fee for servicing an account. The bank automatically reduces the depositor's account balance for this **bank service charge** and notes the amount on the bank statement. The depositor must deduct this amount from the recorded cash balance to make it agree with the bank statement balance. The return of a customer's check for which insufficient funds are available, known as a **not-sufficient-funds (NSF) check**, is handled in a similar manner.

4. An amount owed to the depositor is paid directly to the bank by a third party and added to the depositor's account. Upon receipt of the bank statement (assuming prior notification has not been received from the bank), this amount must be added to the cash balance on the depositor's book. Examples include, in the case of an individual, a direct payroll deposit by the individual's employer; or, in the case of a business, collection by the bank of a note receivable from a customer of the depositor. Banks often charge a fee for providing the latter type of collection service.

If, after considering the items mentioned, the bank statement and the book balances cannot be reconciled, a detailed analysis of both the bank's records and the depositor's books may be necessary to determine whether errors or other irregularities exist on the records of either party.

There are two common forms of the bank reconciliation statement: (1) reconciliation of bank and book balances to a corrected balance, and (2) reconciliation of the bank balance to the book balance. The first form is prepared in two sections, the bank statement balance being adjusted to the corrected cash balance in the first section, and the book balance being adjusted to the same corrected cash balance in the second section. The first section, then, contains items the bank has not recognized as well as any corrections for errors made by the bank; the second section contains items the depositor has not yet recognized and any corrections for errors made on the depositor's books.

The other form begins with the bank statement balance and reports the adjustments that must be applied to this balance to obtain the cash balance on the depositor's books. The second form, then, simply reports the items accounting for the discrepancy between the bank and book balances. Both forms are illustrated below.

Graham, Inc. Bank Reconciliation Statement November 30, 1981		
Balance per bank statement, November 30, 1981		$2,979.72
Add: Deposits in transit	$658.50	
Charge for interest made to depositor's account by bank in error	12.50	671.00
		$3,650.72
Deduct outstanding checks:		
No. 1125	$ 58.16	
No. 1138	100.00	
No. 1152	98.60	
No. 1154	255.00	
No. 1155	192.07	703.83
Corrected bank balance		$2,946.89
Balance per books, November 30, 1981		$2,552.49
Add: Proceeds of draft collected by bank November 30 ($500 face less $1.50 bank charges)	$498.50	
Check No. 1116 to Ace Advertising for $46 recorded by depositor as $64 in error	18.00	516.50
		$3,068.99
Deduct: Bank service charges	$ 3.16	
Customer's check deposited November 25 and returned marked NSF	118.94	122.10
Corrected book balance		$2,946.89

Reconciliation of Bank and Book Balances to Corrected Balance

Graham, Inc. Bank Reconciliation Statement November 30, 1981		
Balance per bank statement, November 30, 1981		$2,979.72
Add: Deposits in transit	$658.50	
Charge for interest made to depositor's account by bank in error	12.50	
Bank service charges	3.16	
Customer's check deposited November 25 and returned marked NSF	118.94	793.10
		$3,772.82
Deduct: Outstanding checks:		
No. 1125 .... $ 58.16		
No. 1138 .... 100.00		
No. 1152 .... 98.60		
No. 1154 .... 255.00		
No. 1155 .... 192.07	$703.83	
Check No. 1116 to Ace Advertising for $46 recorded by depositor as $64 in error	18.00	
Proceeds of draft collected by bank on November 30	498.50	1,220.33
Balance per books, November 30, 1981		$2,552.49

Reconciliation of Bank Balance to Book Balance

Although the reconciliation of bank and book balances to a corrected balance may be considered preferable because it develops a corrected cash figure and shows separately all of the items requiring adjustment on the depositor's books, some accountants prefer to use the second form, which is consistent with the nature of the reconciliation required for many other accounts.

After preparing the reconciliation, the depositor should record any items appearing on the bank statement and requiring recognition on the company's books as well as any corrections for errors discovered on its own books. The bank should be notified immediately of any bank errors. The following entries are required on the books of Graham, Inc., as a result of the reconciliation just made:

Cash	498.50	
Miscellaneous General Expense	1.50	
Notes Receivable		500.00
To record collection of a $500 time draft by the bank on which bank charges were $1.50.		
Cash	18.00	
Advertising Expense		18.00
To record correction for check in payment of advertising recorded as $64 instead of the actual amount, $46.		
Accounts Receivable	118.94	
Miscellaneous General Expense	3.16	
Cash		122.10
To record customer's uncollectible check and bank charges for November.		

After these entries are posted, the cash account will show a balance of $2,946.89. This is the amount to be reported on the balance sheet. As noted, these adjustments are clearly distinguishable when using the first form of bank reconciliation. They are shown separately as adjustments on the books. If the second form is used, adjustments can be determined only after careful analysis of all reconciling items.

Proper Disclosure of Cash and Current Condition

Although a system of internal control may provide for the effective safeguarding of cash, careful examination of the records is still necessary at the end of an accounting period to determine whether transactions have been satisfactorily recorded and cash and the current position of the business are properly presented. Certain practices designed to present a more favorable financial condition than is actually the case may be encountered. Such practices are sometimes referred to as *window dressing*. For example, cash records may be held open for a few days after the close of a fiscal period and cash received from customers during this period reported as receipts of the preceding period. An improved cash position is thus reported. If this balance is then used as a basis for drawing predated checks in payment of accounts payable, the ratio of current assets to current liabilities may be improved. For example, if current assets are $30,000 and current liabilities are $20,000 providing a current ratio of 1.5 to 1, recording payment to creditors of $10,000 will produce balances of $20,000 and $10,000, a current ratio of 2 to 1. The current ratio may also be improved by writing checks in payment of obligations and entering these on the books even though checks are not to be mailed until the following period. Or the current position, as well as earnings and owners' equity, may be overstated by predating sales made at the beginning of the new period. A careful review of the records will disclose whether improper practices have been employed. If such practices are discovered, the accounts should be corrected.

A companion function to cash control is cash planning. This is an important responsibility within a company and does not take place without management effort. Many companies which are basically sound in organization and product control frequently have financial problems because managements do not understand the basic importance of cash planning. A knowledge of the techniques of budgeting and forecasting is essential to sound financial control. These topics are important but are outside the scope of this book. They are considered in detail in managerial accounting texts.

TEMPORARY INVESTMENTS

Temporarily available excess cash may be invested in time deposits, certificates of deposit and similar instruments, or it may be used to purchase securities. As a result, revenue will be produced that would not be available if cash were left idle. Investments made during seasonal periods of low activity can be converted into cash in periods of expanding operations. Asset items arising from temporary conversions of cash are reported in the "Current assets" section of the balance sheet as "Temporary investments." Accounting and reporting considerations applicable to investments of a long-term nature are discussed in Chapters 12 and 14.

Criteria for Reporting Securities as Temporary Investments

Investments in securities qualify for reporting as **temporary investments** provided (1) there is a ready market for converting such securities into cash, and (2) it is management's intention to sell them if the need for cash arises.

Securities are considered marketable when a day-to-day market exists and when they can be sold on short notice. The volume of trading in the securities should be sufficient to absorb a company's holdings without materially affecting the market price. Generally, marketable securities include such items as listed stocks, high-grade bonds, and first-mortgage notes. United States government securities, despite their relatively low yield, are also a highly favored form of marketable security because of their stable prices and wide market. Securities having a limited market and which fluctuate widely in price are not suitable for temporary investments.

Marketable securities may be converted into cash shortly after being acquired or they may be held for some time. In either case, however, they are properly classified as temporary investments as long as management intends to sell them if the need for cash arises. The deciding factor is management's intent, not the length of time the securities are held. Therefore, the following types of investments do not qualify as temporary investments even though the securities may be marketable: (1) reacquired shares of a corporation's own stock; (2) securities acquired to gain control of a company; (3) securities held for maintenance of business relations; and (4) any other securities that cannot be used or are not intended to be used as a ready source of cash.

Recording Purchase and Sale of Marketable Securities

Stocks and bonds acquired as temporary investments are recorded at cost, which includes brokers' fees, taxes, and other charges incurred in their acquisition. Stocks are normally quoted at a price per single share; bonds are quoted at a price per $100 face value although they are normally issued in $1,000 denominations. The purchase of 100 shares of stock at 5⅛, then, would indicate a purchase price of $512.50; the purchase of a $1,000 bond at 104¼ would indicate a purchase price of $1,042.50.

When bonds are acquired between interest payment dates, the price is increased by a charge for accrued interest to the date of purchase. This charge should not be reported as part of investment cost. Two assets have been acquired — bonds and accrued interest — and should be reported in two separate asset accounts. Upon the receipt of interest, the accrued interest account is closed and Interest Revenue is credited for the excess. Instead of recording the interest as an asset (asset approach), Interest Revenue may be debited for the accrued interest paid. The subsequent collection of interest would then be credited in full to Interest Revenue. The latter procedure (revenue approach) is usually more convenient.

To illustrate the entries for the acquisition of securities, assume that $100,000 in U.S. Treasury notes are purchased at 104¼ on April 1. Interest is 9% payable semiannually on January 1 and July 1. Accrued interest of $2,250 would thus be added to the purchase price. The entries to record the purchase of the securities and the subsequent collection of interest under the alternate procedures would be as follows:

Asset Approach:

Apr. 1	Marketable Securities — 9% U.S. Treasury Notes	104,250	
	Interest Receivable	2,250	
	Cash		106,500
July 1	Cash	4,500	
	Interest Receivable		2,250
	Interest Revenue		2,250

Revenue Approach:

Apr. 1	Marketable Securities — 9% U.S. Treasury Notes	104,250	
	Interest Revenue	2,250	
	Cash		106,500
July 1	Cash	4,500	
	Interest Revenue		4,500

When such securities are acquired at a higher or lower price than their maturity value and it is expected that they will be held until maturity, periodic amortization of the premium or accumulation of the discount with corresponding adjustments to interest revenue is required. However, when securities are acquired as a temporary investment and it is not likely they will be held until maturity, such procedures are normally not necessary. When a temporary investment is sold, the difference between the sales proceeds and the cost is reported as a gain or loss on the sale. For example, if the U.S. Treasury notes in the preceding illustration were sold on July 1 for $105,000, the sale would be recorded as follows:

July 1 Cash..	105,000	
Marketable Securities — 9% U.S. Treasury Notes..............		104,250
Gain on Sale of Marketable Securities		750

The gain would be reported on the income statement as "Other revenue."

Valuation of Marketable Securities

Three different methods for the valuation of marketable securities have been advanced: (1) cost, (2) cost or market, whichever is lower, and (3) market.

Cost. Valuation of marketable securities at cost refers to the original acquisition price of a marketable security including all related fees, unless a new cost basis has been assigned to recognize a permanent decline in the value of the security. Cost is to be used unless circumstances require another method as is the case with marketable equity securities, to be explained in the next section. The recognition of gain or loss is deferred until the asset is sold, at which time investment cost is matched against investment proceeds. The cost basis is consistent with income tax procedures, recognizing neither gain nor loss until there is a sale or exchange.

Cost or Market, Whichever is Lower. When using the lower of cost or market method, if market is lower than cost, security values are written down to the lower value; if market is higher than cost, securities are maintained at cost, gains awaiting confirmation through sale.

Traditionally, the lower of cost or market method has been used only under special conditions when market was considered substantially lower than cost, and the decline was not considered temporary. Because of the difficulty in defining substantial and nontemporary declines, the lower of cost or market method was not widely used in practice prior to 1976.[4]

Significant fluctuations of the stock market in recent years have created many more situations where market values are lower than cost. After due consideration of the issues involved, the FASB issued Statement No. 12 which requires that **marketable equity securities** be carried at the lower of aggregate cost or market value.[5] An equity security is defined by the FASB in Statement No. 12 as

---

[4]In the AICPA trends and technique survey, only 25 out of 291 companies reported marketable securities at the lower of cost or market. *Accounting Trends & Techniques*, 30th ed. (New York: American Institute of Certified Public Accountants, 1976), p. 80.

[5]*Statement of Financial Accounting Standards, No. 12*, "Accounting for Certain Marketable Securities" (Stamford: Financial Accounting Standards Board, 1975), par. 8.

". . . any instrument representing ownership shares (e.g., common, preferred, and other capital stock), or the right to acquire (e.g., warrants, rights, and call options) or dispose of (e.g., put options) ownership shares in an enterprise at fixed or determinable prices. The term does not encompass preferred stock that by its terms either must be redeemed by the issuing enterprise or is redeemable at the option of the investor, nor does it include treasury stock or convertible bonds."[6]

FASB Statement No. 12 deals only with marketable equity securities. Other marketable securities, primarily marketable debt securities (corporate and government bonds), still may be carried at cost unless there is a substantial decline that is not due to temporary conditions. It seems logical, however, to treat all short-term marketable securities similarly. All temporary investments are acquired for the same reason — utilization of idle cash to generate a short-term return. Both equity securities and debt securities must meet the same criteria to qualify as temporary investments, and their valuation should reflect a similar concept, i.e., the amount of cash that could be realized upon liquidation at the balance sheet date. Therefore, in the illustrations and end-of-chapter material in this text, the lower of cost or market method is used for all short-term marketable securities. It should be recognized, however, that actual practice varies. Some companies interpret FASB No. 12 strictly and account for only marketable equity securities on the lower of cost or market basis.

The lower of cost or market method may be employed in two ways: (1) it may be applied to securities in the aggregate; or (2) it may be applied to individual items. To illustrate, assume marketable securities with cost and market values on December 31, 1981, as follows:

	Cost	Market	Lower of Cost or Market on Individual Basis
1,000 shares of Carter Co. common........	$20,000	$16,000	$16,000
$25,000 Emerson Co. 7% bonds..............	25,000	26,500	25,000
$10,000 Gardner Co. 8% bonds	10,000	7,500	7,500
	$55,000	$50,000	$48,500

The lower of cost or market value on an aggregate basis is $50,000; on an individual basis, $48,500.

In accounting for marketable equity securities, it should be noted that FASB Statement No. 12 requires the use of the **aggregate method**. An important factor in choosing the aggregate basis is that many companies consider their marketable securities portfolios as collective assets. Further, the Board felt that applying the lower of cost or market procedure on an individual security basis would be unduly conservative.

However, the FASB did recognize that many companies classify separately their current and noncurrent securities portfolios. Therefore, when a classified balance sheet is presented, the lower of aggregate cost or market is to be applied to the separate current and noncurrent portfolios. When an

---

[6]*Ibid*, par. 7a.

unclassified balance sheet is presented, the entire marketable equity securities portfolio is to be considered a noncurrent asset. The application of FASB Statement No. 12 to long-term marketable equity securities is discussed in detail in Chapter 12.

In adopting the lower of aggregate cost or market method for marketable equity securities, the FASB chose to recognize declines in the realizable value of short-term marketable equity securities portfolios as a charge against income of the current period. The possibility of a future recovery in the market value was not considered sufficient reason to maintain the carrying value at cost.

Recognition of a decline in value on the books calls for a reduction of the asset and a debit to a loss account. Various titles are used for the loss account: Unrealized Loss on Marketable Securities; Loss on Valuation of Marketable Equity Securities; Recognized Decline in Value of Current Marketable Securities. The authors prefer the last title to avoid confusion with the entry required upon the final sale of the securities or with the title used in accounting for long-term marketable equity securities. It should also be noted that the valuation loss is not recognized for income tax purposes, and the basis of the securities for measurement of the ultimate gain or loss upon final disposition continues to be cost. Cost can be preserved on the books by the use of a valuation account to reduce the securities to market. The following entry may be made to illustrate this procedure.

Recognized Decline in Value of Current Marketable Securities ..	5,000	
Allowance for Decline in Value of Current Marketable Securities		5,000

The balance sheet would show:

Current assets:		
Marketable securities (at cost)...	$55,000	
Less allowance for decline in value of current marketable securities	5,000	
Marketable securities (at market, December 31, 1981)...............		$50,000

In practice a shorter form is often used, such as the following:

Current assets:	
Marketable securities (reported at market; cost, $55,000)	$50,000

The $5,000 loss must be reported on the current income statement, probably as a charge related to financial management. If in the future there is an increase in the market value of the short-term marketable securities portfolio, the write-down should be reversed to the extent that the resulting carrying value does not exceed original cost. The original write-down is to be viewed as a valuation allowance, representing an estimated decrease in the realizable value of the portfolio. Any subsequent market increase reduces or eliminates this valuation allowance. The reversal of a write-down is considered a change in accounting estimate of an unrealized loss.[7]

---

[7] See *FASB Statement No. 5*, par. 2 and *APB Opinion No. 20*, par. 10.

Changes in estimates and other accounting changes are discussed in Chapter 18.

In subsequent periods, the portfolio of temporary investments will change through purchases and sales of individual securities. Because cost remains the accepted basis for recognition of gain or loss on final disposition and for income tax purposes, it is preferable to record the sale of marketable securities as though no valuation account existed; i.e., on a cost basis. At the end of each accounting period, an analysis can then be made of cost and aggregated market values for the securities held and the allowance account adjusted to reflect the new difference between cost and market. If market exceeds cost at a subsequent valuation date, the allowance account would be eliminated, and the securities would be valued at cost, the lower of the two values. The offsetting revenue account for the adjustment may be titled Recovery of Recognized Decline in Value of Current Marketable Securities.

To illustrate accounting for subsequent years' transactions, assume in the preceding example that in 1982 the Carter Co. stock is sold for $17,000 and $25,000 of 9% U.S. Treasury bonds are purchased for $24,500. The following entries are made:

Cash	17,000	
Loss on Sale of Marketable Securities	3,000	
Marketable Securities — Carter Co. Common		20,000
Marketable Securities — 9% U.S. Treasury Bonds	24,500	
Cash		24,500

Assuming the market value of the remaining securities in the portfolio is unchanged and the market value of the U.S. Treasury bonds remains at cost, the aggregate market value of the temporary investments is $58,500 ($26,500 + $7,500 + $24,500). When comparing the aggregate market value to the aggregate cost value of $59,500 ($25,000 + $10,000 + $24,500), the following adjusting entry would be made at the end of 1982:

Allowance for Decline in Value of Current Marketable Securities	4,000	
Recovery of Recognized Decline in Value of Current Marketable Securities		4,000

This entry leaves the valuation account with a balance of $1,000 which, when subtracted from cost of $59,500, will report the marketable securities at their aggregate market value of $58,500.

If the aggregate market value of the securities portfolio had fallen during 1982 to $53,000, the adjusting entry would be:

Recognized Decline in Value of Current Marketable Securities	1,500	
Allowance for Decline in Value of Current Marketable Securities		1,500

The entry increases the allowance account to $6,500 which, when subtracted from cost of $59,500, will report marketable securities at their aggregate market value of $53,000.

On the other hand, if the aggregate market value of the securities portfolio had risen to $60,000, the adjusting entry at year end would be:

Allowance for Decline in Value of Current Marketable Securities.......... 5,000
    Recovery of Recognized Decline in Value of Current Marketable Se-
    curities.. 5,000

This entry cancels the allowance account since the $59,500 original cost of securities is lower than their $60,000 aggregate market value.

If the classification of a marketable equity security changes from current to noncurrent or vice versa, the security must be transferred to the applicable portfolio at the lower of cost or market value at date of transfer. If the market value is lower than cost, the market value becomes the new cost basis and a realized loss is to be included in determining net income.[8] In essence, this procedure recognizes the loss upon transfer as though it had been realized. This should reduce the likelihood of income being manipulated through the transfer of securities between current and long-term portfolios.

To summarize the accounting for short-term marketable equity securities under FASB Statement No. 12, securities are originally recorded at cost. Subsequent valuation is at lower of cost or market on an aggregate basis. The adjustment is made at year-end through a valuation allowance account. Any reduction in value is recognized as a current period loss in the income statement; any recovery of the write-down, up to the original cost but no higher, is recognized as a current period recovery in the income statement. These gains or losses would be shown after operating income as "other revenues" or "other expenses." The amount of gain or loss on the ultimate sale of a marketable security is still the difference between the sales price and the original cost of the security without consideration for any previous year-end allowance adjustments. Then, at year-end, the allowance will be adjusted once again to reflect the proper lower of cost or market amount for the remaining securities portfolio. Any permanent declines in securities values are to be recognized as losses currently, just like any other asset, with the new value being considered cost from thence forward. No subsequent partial recovery would be allowed.

FASB Statement No. 12 requires extensive disclosure of information with respect to marketable equity securities, including aggregate cost and market values, gross unrealized gains and losses, and the amount of net realized gain or loss included in net income.[9]

Market. Market value refers to the current market price of the marketable security. Current market prices are recognized as affording an objective basis for the valuation of marketable securities. Securities on the balance sheet are reported at their current values whether higher or lower than cost. As with the lower of cost or market method, asset increases and decreases may be reported in a special valuation account.[10]

In applying market, it would be possible to recognize changes in secu-

---

[8]*Statement of Financial Accounting Standards No. 12, op. cit.,* par. 10.
   [9]*Ibid,* par. 12.
   [10]The valuation account is normally considered the same as an offset account. In adjusting for market, the amount in the valuation account is often added to instead of subtracted from the asset account, making the valuation account an adjunct account, rather than an offset account.

rity values by reporting the gain or the loss on the income statement. However, if it is felt that any increase in income, caused by market values in excess of cost, should await the sale of securities, a separate capital account, such as Unrealized Appreciation in Valuation of Marketable Securities, may be credited.

To illustrate the procedure that may be followed, assume at the end of 1981 securities costing $50,000 have quoted values of $60,000. The securities are sold in 1982 for $62,000. An unrealized gain is reported at the end of 1981. This is canceled when the securities are sold in 1982 and the effect of the sale is reported in the income statement. The entries are:

```
1981
Dec. 31 Marketable Securities — Increase to Current Market Value...  10,000
            Unrealized Appreciation in Valuation of Marketable Se-
               curities...............................................................................        10,000
1982
Mar.  5 Cash............................................................................................  62,000
            Unrealized Appreciation in Valuation of Marketable Securi-
               ties.......................................................................................  10,000
            Marketable Securities (at cost)..............................................        50,000
            Marketable  Securities — Increase  to  Current  Market
               Value....................................................................................        10,000
            Gain on Sale of Marketable Securities...................................        12,000
```

In the preceding illustration the valuation change is reflected only in the balance sheet. Alternatively, the change could be recognized in the income statement by crediting a revenue account such as Unrealized Gain on Marketable Securities instead of the capital account.

Market value has been and continues to be an acceptable method for valuing marketable securities within certain industries that follow specialized accounting practices with respect to marketable securities. Enterprises within these industries, such as securities brokers and dealers, that carry marketable equity securities at market value are not required by FASB Statement No. 12 to change to lower of cost or market.

Evaluation of Methods

Valuation at cost finds support on the grounds that it is an extension of the cost principle; the asset is carried at cost until a sale or exchange provides an alternative asset and confirms a gain or loss. The cost method offers valuation on a consistent basis from period to period. It is the simplest method to apply and adheres to income tax requirements. However, certain objections to cost can be raised. The use of cost means investments may be carried at amounts differing from values objectively determinable at the balance sheet date, and the integrity of both balance sheet and income statement measurements can be challenged. The use of cost also means identical securities may be reported at different values because of purchases at different prices. A further objection is that management, in controlling the sale of securities, can determine the periods in which gains or losses are to be recognized even though these changes may have accrued over a number of periods.

The use of market value is advocated on the basis that there is evidence of the net realizable value of the marketable securities held at the balance sheet date and any changes from previous carrying values should be recognized as gains or losses in the current period. Assuming marketable securities are defined as having a readily available sales price or bid and ask price from one of the national securities exchanges or over-the-counter markets, this method is objective and relatively simple to apply. The major drawback of this method is that gains or losses may be recognized prior to realization, i.e., prior to the actual sale of the securities. In addition, market values fluctuate, often significantly, which would require continual changing of the carrying value of marketable securities on the balance sheet. Market is also challenged as a departure from the cost principle and as lacking in conservatism. Furthermore, market is not acceptable for general income tax purposes.

The lower of cost or market procedure provides for recognizing market declines and serves to prevent potential mistakes arising in analyzing statements when these declines are not reported. The lower of cost or market is supported as a conservative procedure. This approach may be challenged on the basis that it may be the most complicated method to follow, and it fails to apply a single valuation concept consistently. Securities carried at cost at the end of one period may be reported at market value in the subsequent period. Critics argue that if net realizable value is a desirable measurement concept, its use should not depend on whether portfolio values are greater or less than original cost.

CASH AND TEMPORARY INVESTMENTS ON THE BALANCE SHEET

For statement purposes, cash may be reported as a single item or it may be summarized under several descriptive headings, such as cash on hand, commercial deposits, and savings deposits. Since current assets are normally reported in the order of their liquidity, cash is listed first, followed by temporary investments, receivables, and inventories. When temporary investments are pledged for some particular purpose, the nature and the purpose of the pledge should be disclosed parenthetically or by note.

Cash and temporary investments may be reported on the balance sheet in the following manner:

Current assets:			
Cash on hand and demand deposits in banks			$ 46,000
Special cash deposits (to pay interest and dividends)			24,000
Temporary investments:			
Certificates of deposit		$100,000	
Marketable securities:			
U.S. Government obligations (reported at cost; market, $158,500; $50,000 in bonds has been pledged as security on short-term bank loan)	$150,000		
Other stocks and bonds (reported at cost; market, $44,200)	35,000	185,000	285,000

QUESTIONS

1. Why is cash on hand both necessary and yet potentially unproductive?

2. State how each of the following items should be reported on the balance sheet: (a) demand deposits with bank, (b) restricted cash deposits in foreign banks, (c) payroll fund to pay accrued salaries, (d) change funds on hand, (e) cash in a special cash account to be used currently for the construction of a new building.

3. The following items were included as cash on the balance sheet for the Lawrence Co. How should each of the items have been reported?

(a) Customers' checks returned by the bank marked "Not Sufficient Funds."

(b) Customers' postdated checks.

(c) Cashier's note with no due date.

(d) Postage stamps received in the mail for merchandise.

(e) Postal money orders from customers awaiting deposit.

(f) Receipts for advances to buyers.

(g) Notes receivable in the hands of the bank for collection.

(h) Special bank account in which sales tax collections are deposited.

(i) Customers' checks not yet deposited.

4. Bartholomew Manufacturing is required to maintain a compensating balance of $15,000 with its bank to maintain a line of open credit. The compensating balance is legally restricted as to its use. How should the compensating balance be reported on the balance sheet and why?

5. What are some current and possible future uses of EFT?

6. (a) Explain check kiting and lapping. (b) Mention at least six other practices resulting in misappropriations of cash in the absence of an adequate system of internal control. (c) What is the basic principle of cash control making fraudulent practices extremely difficult?

7. As an auditor, what basic features would you hope to find in your client's system of cash control?

8. (a) What are the major advantages in using imprest petty cash funds? (b) What dangers must be guarded against when petty cash funds are used?

9. (a) Give at least four common sources of differences between depositor and bank balances. (b) Which of the differences in (a) require an adjusting entry on the books of the depositor?

10. (a) What two methods may be employed in reconciling the bank and the cash balances? (b) Which would you recommend? Why?

11. International Cosmetics Corporation engaged in the following practices at the end of a fiscal year:

(a) Sales on account from January 1–January 5 were predated as of the month of December.

(b) Checks in payment of accounts were prepared on December 31 and were entered on the books, but they were placed in the safe awaiting instructions for mailing.

(c) Customers' checks returned by the bank and marked "Not Sufficient Funds" were ignored for statement purposes.

(d) Amounts owed company officers were paid off on December 31 and reborrowed on January 2.

Explain what is wrong with each of the practices mentioned and give the entries that are required to correct the accounts.

12. Define *temporary investments*. What criteria must be met for a security to be considered a temporary investment?

13. What two methods may be used to record the payment for accrued interest on bond investments? Which method is preferable?

14. (a) What positions are held with respect to the valuation of marketable securities? (b) What arguments can be advanced in support of each and which position do you feel has greatest merit?

15. Resorts International reports marketable securities on the balance sheet at the lower of cost or market. What adjustments are required on the books at the end of the year in each situation below:

(a) Securities are purchased early in 1979 and at the end of 1979 their market value is more than cost.

(b) At the end of 1980 the market value of the securities is less than cost.

(c) At the end of 1981 the market value of the securities is greater than at the end of 1980 but is still less than cost.

(d) At the end of 1982 the market value of the securities is more than the amount originally paid.

16. One of the arguments advanced for using market as the valuation procedure for temporary investments is that it assists in a "proper evaluation of managerial decisions and activities relative to purchases, sales, and holdings of marketable securities." How might you support this statement using the following example? Marketable securities purchased for $500 rose in value to $900 as of the end of the fiscal year, and were sold in the subsequent year for $650.

17. On reconciling the cash account with the bank statement, it is found the general cash fund is overdrawn $436 but the bond redemption account has a balance of $5,400. The treasurer wishes to show cash as a current asset at $4,964. Discuss.

18. The Lehi Fence Company shows in its accounts a cash balance of $66,500 with Bank A, and an overdraft of $1,500 with Bank B on December 31. Bank B regards the overdraft as in effect a loan to the Lehi Fence Company and charges interest on the overdraft balance. How would you report the balances with Banks A and B? Would your answer be any different if the overdraft arose as a result of certain checks deposited and proved to be uncollectible and the overdraft was cleared promptly by the Lehi Fence Company at the beginning of January?

19. Under certain conditions it is proper to offset either assets against liabilities or liabilities against assets. Comment upon the following practices of the Pioneer Kitchens Company.

(a) An overdraft of $300 in the payroll fund kept with Farmers and Mechanics Bank is offset against a restricted savings account balance kept with the same bank.

(b) A mortgage of $130,000 is offset against the buildings account of $180,000 to reflect a net equity in the buildings of $50,000.

(c) Advances to employees of $500 are offset against Salaries Payable of $1,100.

EXERCISES

exercise 6-1

Mr. Walton, proprietor of the Bennett Fabricating Co., would like to know how much cash may be reported on Bennett's balance sheet. Bennett has the following bank accounts and balances:

Overdrawn checking account	$ (20)
United States savings bonds	400
Payroll account	100
Sales tax account	150

In addition to the bank accounts, Bennett has the following items in the office:

Postage stamps	$ 20
Employee's postdated check	30
IOU from Walton's brother	100
A wristwatch (reported at market value; surrendered as security by a customer who forgot his wallet)	30
Credit memo from a vendor for a purchase return	64
Traveler's check	40
Insufficient funds check	18
Ten cases of empty soft drink bottles (returnable value)	24
Petty cash fund ($16 in currency and expense receipts for $84)	100
Money order	36

How much may be reported as cash on Bennett's balance sheet?

exercise 6-2

In auditing the books of Star Corp. for 1981, you find a petty cash fund of $800 is maintained on the imprest basis, but the company has failed to replenish the fund on December 31. Replenishment was made and recorded on January 15, 1982, when a check for $740 was drawn to petty cash for expenses paid. Your analysis discloses $600 of petty cash was spent in 1981. What entry would be made in correcting the records, assuming the books for 1981 have been closed?

exercise 6-3

An examination on the morning of January 2 by the auditor for the Pearson Lumber Company discloses the following items in the petty cash drawer:

Currency and coin		$ 105.66
IOU's from members of the office staff		135.00
An envelope containing collections for a football pool, with office staff names attached		45.00
Petty cash vouchers for:		
Typewriter repairs	$24.00	
Stamps	45.00	
Telegram charges	28.50	97.50
Employee's check postdated January 15		150.00
Employee's check marked "NSF"		210.00
Check drawn by Pearson Lumber Company to Petty Cash		345.00
		$1,088.16

The ledger account discloses a $1,050 balance for Petty Cash. (1) What adjustments should be made on the auditor's working papers so petty cash may be correctly stated on the balance sheet? (2) What is the correct amount of petty cash for the balance sheet? (3) How could the practice of borrowing by employees from the fund be discouraged?

exercise 6-4

Kendall Home Repair borrowed $50,000 at 12%, but was required to maintain a compensating balance of $10,000.

(1) In this case, what is Kendall's actual rate of interest?
(2) How should this information be disclosed?

exercise 6-5

The following data are assembled in the course of reconciling the bank balance as of December 31, 1981, for Fuente, Inc. What cash balance will be found on the company books, assuming no errors on the part of the bank and the depositor?

Balance per bank statement	$607.80
Checks outstanding	880.00
December 31 receipts recorded but not deposited	175.00
Bank charges for December not recognized on books	3.75
Draft collected by bank but not recognized on books	275.00

exercise 6-6

The accounting department is furnished with the following data in reconciling the bank statement for Broberg Jewelers:

Cash balance per books	$14,692.71
Deposits in transit	2,615.23
Bank service charge	21.00
Outstanding checks	3,079.51
Note collected by bank including $45 interest (Broberg not yet notified)	1,045.00
Error by bank — check drawn by Brobert was charged to Broberg's account	617.08
Sale and deposit of $1,729.00 was entered in books as $1,792.00	

Give the journal entry required on the books to adjust the cash account.

exercise 6-7

The Blue Lake Manufacturing Co. receives its bank statement for the month ending June 30 on July 2. The bank statement indicates a balance of $2,550. The cash account as of the close of business on June 30 has a balance of $270. In reconciling the balances, the auditor discovers the following:

    (a) Receipts on June 30, $10,500, were not deposited until July 1.
    (b) Checks outstanding on June 30 were $13,290.
    (c) The bank has charged the depositor for overdrafts, $60.
    (d) A canceled check to H. M. Ship for $9,618 was entered in cash payments in error as $9,168.

    Prepare a bank reconciliation statement. (Use the form reconciling bank and depositor figures to corrected cash balance.)

exercise 6-8

The following information was included in the bank reconciliation for Ashman Plastics, Inc. for June. What was the total of the outstanding checks at the beginning of June? Assume all other reconciling items are listed below:

Checks and charges returned by bank in June, including a June service charge of $10	$16,435
Service charge made by bank in May and recorded on books in June	5
Total of credits to Cash in all journals during June	19,292
Customer's NSF check returned as a bank charge in June (no entry made on books)	100
Customer's NSF check returned in May and redeposited in June (no entry made on books in either May or June)	250
Outstanding checks at June 30	8,060
Deposit in transit at June 30	600

exercise 6-9

Give the entries necessary to record these transactions of Frampton, Inc., in 1981.

    (a) Purchased $100,000 U.S. Treasury 8% bonds, paying 102½ plus accrued interest of $3,000. Broker's fees were $740. Frampton, Inc., uses the revenue approach to record accrued interest on purchased bonds.
    (b) Purchased 1,000 shares of Byland Co. common stock at 256 plus brokerage fees of $1,200.
    (c) Received semiannual interest on the U.S. Treasury bonds.
    (d) Sold 300 shares of Byland Co. common at 261.
    (e) Sold $60,000 of U.S. Treasury 8% bonds at 103 plus accrued interest of $800.
    (f) Purchased a $20,000 six-month certificate of deposit.

exercise 6-10

During 1981, the John Curtis Novelty Shop purchased the following marketable securities:

	Cost	Year-End Market
Astpo Co. common	$12,000	$14,000
Bernard 8% bonds	18,000	11,000

Marketable securities are to be reported on the balance sheet at the lower of aggregate cost or market. (1) What entry would be made at year-end assuming the above values? (2) What entry would be made during 1982 assuming one half of the Astpo Co. common stock is sold for $7,000? (3) What entry would be made at the end of 1982 assuming: (a) the market value of remaining securities is $18,000? (b) The market value of remaining securities is $21,000? (c) The market value of remaining securities is $28,000?

exercise 6-11

Southern City Steel Corp. acquires marketable securities in 1980 at a cost of $225,000. Market values of the securities at the end of each year are as follows: 1980, $210,000; 1981, $219,000; 1982, $240,000. Give the entries at the end of 1980, 1981, and 1982 indicating how the securities would be reported on the balance sheet at the end of each year under each of the following assumptions:

    (a) Securities are reported at cost.
    (b) Securities are reported at the lower of cost or market on an aggregate basis.
    (c) Securities are reported at market.

exercise 6-12

State what effect the following practices would have on the ratio of current assets to current liabilities; increase, no effect, or decrease. (Assume the current ratio is in excess of 1:1.)

    (a) Hold books open to receive payment of outstanding accounts receivable thus increasing the cash balance.
    (b) Close books early so that payment of creditors would be in next period, thus maintaining a higher cash balance.
    (c) Hold books open to include a few days of sales of the following period in records of this period.
    (d) Hold books open so that payment of creditors would be in this period rather than the next period, thus decreasing the cash account.

PROBLEMS

problem 6-1

The balance of $147,000 in the cash account of Lisonbee, Inc., consists of these items:

Petty cash fund	$ 600
Receivable from an employee	300
Cash in bond sinking fund	13,500
Cash in a foreign bank unavailable for withdrawal	30,000
Cash in Central Bank	90,000
Currency on hand	12,600

The balance in the marketable securities account consists of:

U.S. Treasury bonds	31,260
Voting stock of a subsidiary company (70% interest)	366,000
Advances to a subsidiary company (no maturity date specified)	90,000
A note receivable from a customer	30,000
The company's own shares held as treasury stock	15,000
Stock of Western Telephone Co.	42,000

    Instructions: Calculate the correct Cash and Marketable Securities balances and state in what accounts and in what sections of the balance sheet the other items would be properly reported.

problem 6-2

The cash account of Stanford Glass Service, Inc., disclosed a balance of $17,056.48 on October 31, 1981. The bank statement as of October 31 showed a balance of $21,209.45. Upon comparing the statement with the cash records, the following facts were developed:

(a) Stanford's account had been charged for a customer's uncollectible check amounting to $1,143 on October 26.

(b) A two-month, 9%, $3,000 customer's note dated August 25, discounted on October 12, had been protested October 26, and the bank had charged Stanford for $3,050.83, which included a protest fee of $5.83.

(c) A customer's check for $725 had been entered as $625 both by the depositor and the bank but was later corrected by the bank.

(d) Check No. 661 for $1,242.50 had been entered in the cashbook as $1,224.50, and check No. 652 for $32.90 had been entered as $329. The company uses the voucher system.

(e) There were bank service charges for October of $39.43 not yet recorded on the books.

(f) A bank memo stated that M. Stum's note for $2,500 and interest of $62.50 had been collected on October 29, and the bank had made a charge of $12.50. (No entry had been made on the books when the note was sent to the bank for collection.)

(g) Receipts of October 29 for $6,850 were deposited November 1.

The following checks were outstanding on October 31:

No. 620	$1,250.00	No. 671	$ 732.50
621	3,448.23	673	187.90
632	2,405.25	675	275.72
670	1,775.38	676	2,233.15

Instructions:

(1) Construct a bank reconciliation statement, using the form where both bank and book balances are brought to a corrected cash balance.

(2) Give the journal entries required as a result of the information given above. (Assume the company makes use of the voucher system.)

problem 6-3

Analysis of the December bank statement for Sabertooth Cutlery Corp. discloses the following information:

(a) Statement balance at December 31, 1981, was $33,350.

(b) Check issued by Sabco, Inc., for $630 was charged to Sabertooth Cutlery Corp. in error.

(c) December bank charges were $60.

(d) Deposit of $1,400 was erroneously credited to Sabertooth Cutlery Corp., account by the bank.

(e) Outstanding checks at December 31, 1981, were $10,560. They included a $600 check outstanding for 8 months to Amco Products which was canceled in December and a new check issued. No entry was made for the cancellation.

(f) Receipts on December 31 were $9,000. Receipts were deposited on January 2.

(g) An error in addition was made on the December 23 deposit slip. This slip showed a total of $2,220. The correct balance as credited to the account by the bank was $2,020. A count of cash on hand showed an overage of $200 as of December 31.

(h) The Cash in Bank balance in the general ledger as of December 31, 1981, was $31,280.

Instructions:

(1) Prepare a bank reconciliation statement which reconciles the bank balance with the balance per books.

(2) Give all entries required on the books at December 31, 1981.

problem 6-4

A bank statement for Elkins Products shows a balance as of December 31, 1981, of $11,772.56. The cash account for the company as of this date shows an overdraft of $542.24. In reconciling the statement with the books, the following items are discovered:

(a) The cash balance includes $600 representing change cash on hand. When the cash on hand is counted, only $517 is found.

(b) The cash balance includes $800 representing a petty cash fund. Inspection of the petty cash fund reveals cash of $640 on hand and a replenishing check drawn on December 31 for $160.

(c) Proceeds from cash sales of $1,180 for December 27 were stolen. The company expects to recover this amount from the insurance company and has made no entry for the loss.

(d) The bank statement shows the depositor charged with a customer's NSF check for $94, bank service charges of $31.20, and a check for $260 drawn by Elkars Produce and incorrectly cleared through this account.

(e) The bank statement does not show receipts of December 31 of $3,330, which were deposited on January 3.

(f) Checks outstanding were found to be $18,610. This includes the check transferred to the petty cash fund and also two checks for $228 each payable to J. Miner. Miner had notified the company she had lost the original check and had been sent a second one, the company stopping payment on the first check.

Instructions:

(1) Prepare a bank reconciliation statement, using the form in which both bank and book balances are brought to a corrected cash balance.

(2) Give the correcting entries for Elkins Products required by the foregoing.

(3) List the cash items as they should appear on the balance sheet on December 31.

problem 6-5

The following data are furnished by the Laser Products, Inc. Laser uses the lower of cost or market method of reporting all current marketable securities, and has a fiscal year end of December 31.

1981

June 1 Purchased 30, $1,000 Landoth, Inc. 10% bonds at 103 plus brokerage fees of $200. Interest is paid January 1 and July 1. Laser uses the revenue approach to record accrued interest on purchased bonds.

July 1 Received semiannual interest from the Landoth, Inc. bonds.

Sept. 1 Purchased $50,000 of 9% U.S. Treasury bonds for $52,000 plus accrued interest. Brokerage fees were $350. Interest is paid semiannually on January 1 and July 1.

Oct. 31 Sold $20,000 of U.S. Treasury bonds for $22,000 plus accrued interest. Brokerage fees were $200.

Dec. 31 Accrual of interest on the marketable securities.

Dec. 31 Market prices of securities were: Landoth, Inc. bonds, 105; U.S. Treasury bonds, 101.

1982

Feb. 1 Sold all Landoth, Inc. bonds for $30,300 plus accrued interest. Brokerage fees were $200.

Instructions: Give the journal entries for the above data.

problem 6-6

Seletos, Inc., purchased marketable securities during 1981 with the following costs and year-end market values:

	Cost	Market
600 shares of Toko Machinery common	$ 33,600	$ 39,375
200 shares of Kit, Inc. common	51,960	46,770
$20,000 Goodplace Municipal 7% bonds	27,540	20,130
	$113,100	$106,275

Seletos, Inc., values marketable securities at the lower of cost or market on an aggregate basis. On August 10, 1982, Seletos, Inc., sold 150 shares of Kit, Inc., common for $35,325. Market prices of the remaining securities on December 31, 1982, were: Toko common, 63; Kit, Inc. common, 235½; and Goodplace Municipal 7% bonds, 106⅞.

Instructions: Give all required entries for the valuation and sale of securities in 1981 and 1982. Ignore entries for interest revenue on the bonds.

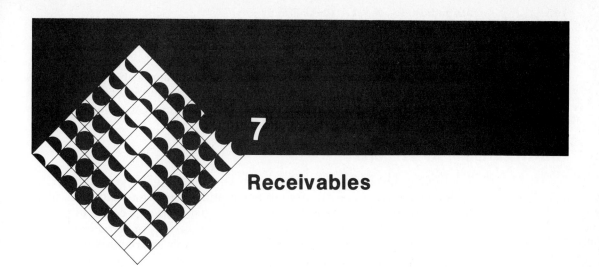

7

Receivables

CHAPTER OBJECTIVES

Identify the various types of receivables and the appropriate classifications for reporting purposes.

Explain the concept of net realizable value as it relates to accounts receivable.

Describe and illustrate methods of estimating collectibility of receivables.

Describe and illustrate the use of accounts receivable as a source of immediate cash.

Explain the concept of present value in accounting for notes receivable.

Describe and illustrate the discounting of notes receivable.

For many businesses, receivables are a significant item, often representing a major portion of the liquid assets of a company. Therefore, it is important to establish effective credit policies and collection procedures to ensure timely collection of receivables and to minimize losses from uncollectible accounts. Sound internal controls and proper accounting for receivables can be important influences on the profitability of company operations.

NATURE AND COMPOSITION OF RECEIVABLES

In its broadest sense, the term **receivables** is applicable to all claims against others for money, goods, or services. For accounting purposes, however, the term is generally employed in a narrower sense to designate claims expected to be settled by the receipt of cash.

Classification of Receivables

Usually, the chief source of receivables is the normal operating activities of the business, i.e., credit sales of goods and services to customers. These **trade receivables** may be evidenced by a formal written promise to pay and classified as **notes receivable**. In most cases, however, trade receivables are unsecured "open accounts," often referred to simply as **accounts receivable**.

Trade accounts receivable represent an extension of short-term credit to customers. Payments are generally due within thirty to ninety days. The credit arrangements are typically informal agreements between seller and buyer supported by such business documents as invoices, sales orders, and delivery contracts. Normally trade receivables do not involve interest, although an interest or service charge may be added if payments are not made within a specified period. Trade receivables are the most common type of receivable and are generally the most significant in total dollar amount.

Nontrade receivables include all other types of receivables. They arise from a variety of transactions such as: (1) sale of securities or property other than goods or services; (2) advances to stockholders, directors, officers, employees, and affiliated companies; (3) deposits with creditors, utilities, and other agencies; (4) purchase prepayments; (5) deposits to guarantee contract performance or expense payment; (6) claims for losses or damages; (7) claims for rebates and tax refunds; (8) subscriptions for capital stock; and (9) dividends and interest receivable. Nontrade receivables are generally supported by formal, often written, agreements. Nontrade receivables should be summarized in appropriately titled accounts and reported separately in the financial statements.

Another classification relates to the **current** or short-term vs **noncurrent** or long-term nature of receivables. As indicated in Chapter 5, the "Current assets" classification as broadly conceived includes all receivables identified with the normal operating cycle. Receivables arising outside of the inventory-to-cash cycle qualify as current only if they are expected to be collected within one year. Thus, for classification purposes, all trade receivables are considered current; each nontrade item requires separate analysis to determine whether it is reasonable to assume that it will be collected within one year. Noncurrent receivables are reported under the "Long-term investments" or "Other long-term assets" caption, whichever is appropriate.

Amounts due from officers, directors, and major stockholders arising out of sales and subject to the usual credit terms are normally considered current; however, when claims have arisen from transactions other than sales and current recovery is not assured, such items are properly classified as noncurrent. Sales to affiliated companies give rise to current claims, but advances are generally regarded as long-term in nature. Deposits on materials and merchandise ordered will soon represent inventories and are reported as current, but deposits on utility contracts are reported as long-term. Deposits for machinery and equipment ordered are noncurrent in view of the ultimate application of the deposit. Claims from the sale of assets other than merchandise and calling for periodic collections over a period exceeding one year require special analysis to determine the portion of the claim to be reported as current and the portion to be reported as noncurrent.

Subscriptions to capital stock are current only if they are currently collectible. When current collection is not probable, such balances are reported as noncurrent assets or as subtractions from capital balances so that only the amount actually paid by stockholders and subscribers is reported as contributed capital.

When income tax refund claims or other claims have been granted and collection is expected within one year, they qualify for current presentation. When claims are still being processed and recovery is assured although the period required for such processing is uncertain, they are shown under a noncurrent heading.

Receivables are established in the accounts only when supportable claims exist, and when it can be reasonably assumed that the claims will be realized. When a claim does not involve a material amount and there is little likelihood of recovery, no reference need be made to it on the balance sheet. On the other hand, if a material amount is involved and there is prospect of a favorable settlement, the claim is properly viewed as a contingent receivable and should be disclosed by a special note or by appropriate comment under a separate contingent asset heading.

In summary, receivables may be classified in various ways, e.g., as accounts or notes receivable, as trade or nontrade receivables, and as current or long-term receivables. These categories are not mutually exclusive. For example, accounts receivable are trade receivables and are current; notes receivable may also be trade receivables and may be current in some circumstances, but are nontrade, long-term receivables in other situations. The classifications used most often in practice and throughout this book will be simply accounts receivable, notes receivable, and other receivables.

Accounting Considerations

The basic problems in accounting for receivables include appropriate valuation, proper classification, and accurate reporting of receivables. The collection of receivables and their proper use in cash planning are also important considerations. These accounting issues are addressed in the remaining sections of this chapter.

ACCOUNTS RECEIVABLE

Accounts receivable broadly include all trade receivables not supported by some form of commercial paper. Although it would be appropriate to refer to open accounts with customers arising from the sale of goods and services as Trade Accounts Receivable to distinguish these from other receivables, it has become established practice to use Accounts Receivable to designate these claims. Accounts receivable for reporting purposes should be limited to trade accounts expected to be converted into cash in the regular course of business. The account balances, for example, should not include receivables arising from charges for reusable containers if such charges will be canceled when containers are returned.

Recognition and Reporting Considerations

A receivable arising from the sale of goods is generally recognized when the title to goods passes to the buyer. Because the point at which title passes may vary with the terms of the sale, it is general practice to recognize the receivable when goods are shipped to the customer. Receivables should not be recognized for goods shipped on approval where the shipper retains title to the goods until there is a formal acceptance, or for goods shipped on consignment where the shipper retains title to the goods until they are sold by the consignee.

Receivables for services to customers are properly recognized when the services are performed. When work under a contract has not been completed at the end of the period, the amount due as of the balance sheet date will have to be calculated. Receivables should be recognized for the portion of work completed under construction contracts and for reimbursable costs and accrued fees on cost-plus-fixed-fee contracts.

Ordinarily, detailed records of customer transactions and customers' balances are carried in subsidiary records. Entries to subsidiary records may be made from original business documents evidencing the transactions. With machine methods, subsidiary records are frequently maintained simultaneously with the preparation of invoices and remittance records.

Certain revenues accrue with the passage of time and are most conveniently recognized when collections are made. At the end of the period, it is necessary to calculate the amounts accrued since the last collections and to establish appropriate accrued receivables. Accrued interest is recognized on assets such as bank deposits, notes, bonds, and annuities. Rentals may accrue on real estate holdings. Royalties and patent fees may accrue on certain rights and properties. For some business units, accrued receivables may be small in total; for others, they may involve large amounts.

Creditor accounts with debit balances require special attention. These balances are found by an analysis of subsidiary ledger detail. For example, assume that the accounts payable control account reports a balance of $10,000. Inspection of subsidiary account detail reveals accounts with credit balances of $10,500 and accounts with debit balances of $500. The nature of the debit balances should be investigated. If the debit balances have arisen as a result of overpayments or returns and allowances after payment, they are reportable as current assets in view of the claims they represent for cash or merchandise from vendors. Such balances are properly reported under a title, such as Creditors' Accounts with Debit Balances or Sundry Claims. If debit balances represent advance payments on the purchase of raw materials or merchandise, these too are current assets reportable under some descriptive title, such as Advances on Purchase Contracts. In either case, Accounts Payable is reported at $10,500. Although both an asset and a liability are reported, no adjustment to the control account or the subsidiary ledger detail is required. Debit balances in the subsidiary ledger are carried forward and are ultimately canceled by purchases or cash settlement.

Customer ledger detail requires similar analysis. Customers' accounts with credit balances may result from overpayments, from customer returns after full payment, or from advance payments by customers. Such credits should be recognized as current liabilities, and accounts receivable should be reported at the sum of the debit balances in the subsidiary ledger.

When contra balances in customer and creditor accounts are not material in amount, they are frequently disregarded and only the net receivable or payable balance is reported on the balance sheet.

Credit Card Sales. An increasing amount of business is being transacted with credit cards. Credit cards issued by department stores, such as Sears or J. C. Penney, are essentially open accounts and are treated like other accounts receivable. Periodic bills are sent to cardholders for merchandise purchased, cash is collected, and any uncollectible amounts are recognized as bad debts. An interest or service charge is usually assessed for credit extended.

The major oil and gas companies follow similar procedures in accounting for their credit cards. The station owner periodically submits the credit card receipts to the company headquarters, using the receipts as though they were cash to pay for gas and other supplies received from the company. The company then bills the individual customers for their purchases, and follows procedures similar to those of a department store for accounts receivable.

Bank cards, such as VISA and MasterCard, are handled somewhat differently. When a retailer receives a bank credit card from a customer in payment for merchandise, the sale is treated like a cash sale. Periodically the credit card receipts are summarized, and the total is recorded on a regular, but separate, bank deposit slip. The receipts are then deposited as though they were cash.

When the bank receives the deposit slip and the credit card receipts, the retailer's bank account is credited for the amount of the deposit. Monthly, the bank debits the retailer's bank account for a credit card service fee which is usually a percentage (generally 3–5 percent) of net credit card sales. The customer pays the bank directly. In effect, it is the bank which holds the receivables.

As an example, assume that Hall & Nielsen, a small clothing retailer, had VISA credit card sales of $650 on June 9, 1981. The journal entry for these sales would be:

Cash	650	
Sales		650

Upon deposit, $650 would be added to Hall & Nielsen's bank account. Eventually, the customers purchasing the $650 worth of merchandise would pay their credit card balances to the bank. At the end of the month, assuming that Hall & Nielsen had monthly credit card sales of $14,300 and the bank charges a fee of 3 percent of net credit card sales, the journal entry to record the expenses charged by the bank would be:

Credit Card Service Fee	429	
Cash...		429
Credit card service fee, $14,300 × .03 = $429.		

Valuation of Accounts Receivable

Theoretically, receivables arising from the sale of goods or services should be reported at their **net realizable or expected cash value**. This would indicate that accounts receivable should be recorded net of any discounts expected to be taken and any anticipated sales returns or allowances. Further, it would suggest that the receivables should be reduced by any unearned finance or interest charges included in their face amounts, and any anticipated uncollectible items. The objective is to report the amount of claims from customers actually expected to be collected in cash.

Trade Discounts. Many companies bill their customers at a gross sales price less an amount designated as a **trade discount**. The discount may vary by customer depending on the volume of business or size of order from the customer. In effect, the trade discount reduces the gross or list sales price to the net price actually charged the customer. This net price is the amount at which the receivable and corresponding revenue should be recorded.

Cash Discounts. It is common business practice to offer **cash discounts** to customers to encourage prompt payment of bills. Cash discounts may be taken only if payment is received within a specified period of time, generally thirty days or less. It is almost always beneficial for customers to take all cash discounts, even if a short-term loan is required to raise sufficient cash to make the payment. Therefore, receivables may be recorded net of cash discounts on the assumption that all such discounts will be taken. If a discount is not taken and the gross amount is collected, the extra cash is considered additional revenue from discounts not taken. While this procedure is logical, the more common method followed in practice is to record the receivable at its gross amount. If payment is received within the discount period, Sales Discount is debited for the difference between the recorded amount of the receivable and the total cash collected. This method is simple and widely used. Cash discounts are explained more fully on page 204 of Chapter 8.

Sales Returns and Allowances. In the normal course of business, it is likely that some goods will be returned and some allowances will have to be made for such factors as goods damaged during shipment, spoiled or other-wise defective goods, or shipment of an incorrect quantity or type of goods. When goods are returned or an allowance is necessary, net sales and ac-counts receivable are reduced. To illustrate, assume merchandise costing $1,000 is sold and later returned. The return would be recorded in the fol-lowing manner:

Sales Returns and Allowances	1,000	
Accounts Receivable		1,000

While the charge could be made directly to Sales, the use of a separate account preserves information which may be useful to management.

In some instances an end-of-period adjustment should be made to recog-nize the estimated portion of outstanding receivables that will not be col-lected due to returns and allowances in the following period. Expected fu-ture returns and allowances should be recognized whenever failure to do so is likely to have a material impact on financial statements of the current period.

To illustrate, assume that the Byland Co. which began operating in Jan-uary, 1981, estimated that 3% of its $2 million accounts receivable out-standing at December 31, 1981, would not be collected due to returns and allowances adjustments. For illustrative purposes the amount is considered to have a material effect on the company's income. Therefore, the following year-end adjusting entry is made:

Sales Returns and Allowances	60,000	
Allowance for Sales Returns and Allowances		60,000

Computation:
3% × $2,000,000 = $60,000

During the following year, Byland would record various sales returns and allowances. Allowance for Sales Returns and Allowances, if not ad-justed during the year, would still have a $60,000 credit balance at the end of 1982. If the year-end Accounts Receivable balance is $1.5 million and 3% is still deemed an appropriate rate, the allowance account should be adjusted to a credit balance of $45,000 ($1,500,000 × 3% = $45,000) with the following entry:

Allowance for Sales Returns and Allowances	15,000	
Sales Returns and Allowances		15,000

The allowance account is a contra asset valuation account to be de-ducted from accounts receivable on the balance sheet. Therefore, accounts receivable are reported at their estimated net realizable value. The sales returns and allowances account is subtracted from sales on the income statement. This procedure is consistent with the fundamental matching principle. It is an attempt to recognize the proper amount of sales revenue for a particular period. The realized revenues can then be properly matched with appropriate expenses to produce a realistic income measurement for the period. Since a formal position was taken by the AICPA, the accrual of sales returns has been more widely used in practice, especially in those industries which experience significant amounts of returns.[1] Failure to anticipate sales returns and allowances or other charges affecting the realizable value of receivables will have little effect on periodic net income when sales volume and the rate of occurrence of such charges do not vary significantly from period to period. The anticipation of sales returns and allowances is not allowed for income tax purposes.

Unearned Finance Charges Included in Receivables. Amounts charged to customers on sales contracts often include finance, interest, and other charges related to the extension of credit. These charges are actually earned with the passage of time and should be recognized as unearned at the time of the sale. The Accounting Principles Board in Opinion No. 6 makes the following observation:

> Unearned discounts (other than cash or quantity discounts and the like), finance charges and interest included in the face amount of receivables should be shown as a deduction from the related receivables.[2]

The entry at the time of sale should establish the unearned customer charges, and periodic adjustments should be made to recognize the amounts earned. To illustrate, assume that installment sales contracts of $27,600 for a year include finance charges of 2% a month, or approximately $3,277. Payments are to be made in 12 equal monthly installments. Installment sales would be reported as follows:

Installment Accounts Receivable	27,600	
Sales		24,323
Unearned Customer Finance Charges		3,277
To record installment sales.		

Computation:
$PV_n = R(PVAF_{\overline{n}|i})$
$PV_n = (\$27,600 \div 12)(PVAF_{\overline{12}|2\%}); PV_n = \$2,300 (10.5753) = \$24,323.$
See Appendix A, Table IV.

As collections are made on installment accounts, the finance charges on the net receivable balance would be recognized as earned. Assuming that the monthly finance charge is 2%, the entry for the first month is shown below.

Cash	2,300.00	
Unearned Customer Finance Charges	486.46	
Installment Accounts Receivable		2,300.00
Revenue from Customer Finance Charges		486.46

Computation:
Finance charge:
2% × $24,323 ($27,600 − $3,277) = $486.46

As shown below, any unearned finance charge would be reported on the balance sheet as a deduction from the related receivable account. The reve-

---

[1]*Statement of Position 75-1*, "Revenue Recognition When Right of Return Exists" (New York: American Institute of Certified Public Accountants, 1975), p. 5.

[2]*Opinions of the Accounting Principles Board, No. 6*, "Status of Accounting Research Bulletins" (New York: American Institute of Certified Public Accountants, 1965), par. 14.

nue from customer finance charges will be included in "Other operating revenues" in the income statement.

Installment accounts receivable	$25,300.00	
Less unearned customer finance charges	2,790.54	$22,509.46

Estimating Collectibility of Accounts Receivable

Almost invariably some receivables will prove uncollectible. Uncollectible amounts must be anticipated if the charge for them is to be related to the period of the sale and if receivables are to be stated at their estimated realizable amounts.

The amount of receivables estimated to be uncollectible is recorded by a debit to expense and a credit to an allowance account. The terminology for these account titles has changed somewhat over time. The term Allowance for Doubtful Accounts has largely replaced the earlier term of Reserve for Bad Debts following the recommendation of the AICPA terminology bulletin regarding restrictive use of the term "reserve." Other possible terms besides Doubtful Accounts are Uncollectible Accounts or Bad Debts. The expense account title usually is consistent with that of the allowance account, and thus becomes Doubtful Accounts Expense, Uncollectible Accounts Expense, or Bad Debts Expense.

The charge for doubtful accounts may be reported as a deduction from sales on the theory that it is net sales — sales after uncollectibles — that must cover current charges and yield a profit. However, instead of being treated as a contra-sales balance, the bad debts item is usually regarded as a failure of management, and, hence, is reported as a selling, general and administrative, or financial charge, depending upon the division held responsible for approving sales on account. The allowance account is reported as a subtraction from accounts receivable. Use of the allowance account avoids premature adjustments to individual receivable accounts.

When positive evidence is available concerning the partial or complete worthlessness of an account, the account is written off by a debit to the allowance account and a credit to the receivable. Positive evidence of a reduction in value is found in the bankruptcy, death, or disappearance of a debtor, failure to enforce collection legally, or a barring of collection by the statute of limitations. Write-offs should be supported by evidence of the uncollectibility of the accounts from appropriate parties, such as courts, lawyers, or credit agencies, and should be authorized in writing by appropriate company officers.

Bases for Estimating Charge for Doubtful Accounts. The estimate for doubtful accounts may be based upon (1) the amount of sales for the period or (2) the amount of receivables outstanding at the end of the period. When sales are used as the basis for calculation, the problem of estimating the charge for doubtful accounts is viewed as one involving primarily the proper measurement of income. When receivables are used as the basis for calculation, the problem is viewed as one involving primarily the proper valuation of receivables.

If the sales basis is used in computing the periodic charge for doubtful accounts, any existing balance in the allowance account resulting from past period charges is disregarded. For example, if 2 percent of sales are considered doubtful in terms of collection and sales for the period are $100,000, the charge for doubtful accounts expense would be 2 percent of the current period's sales, or $2,000, regardless of the carryover balance in the allowance account. On the other hand, if the amount of receivables is used as a basis for estimating the charge for doubtful accounts, a corrected allowance figure is established each period by adjusting the existing balance. For example, if it is determined that the allowance for doubtful accounts should be $1,500 and the current credit balance in the allowance account is $600, the debit to Doubtful Accounts Expense and corresponding credit to the allowance account would be $900. These two methods, described in the paragraphs that follow, are applicable to notes receivable as well as accounts receivable.

Adjustment for Doubtful Accounts Based on Sales. The charges for doubtful accounts of recent periods are related to the sales of those periods in developing a percentage of the charge for doubtful accounts to sales. This percentage may be modified by expectations based on current experience. Since doubtful accounts occur only with credit sales, it would seem logical to develop a percentage of doubtful accounts to credit sales of past periods. This percentage would be applied to credit sales of the current period. However, since extra work may be required in maintaining separate records of cash and credit sales or in analyzing sales data, the percentage is frequently developed in terms of total sales. Unless there is considerable periodic fluctuation in the proportion of cash and credit sales, the total sales method will give satisfactory results.

The **sales percentage method** for anticipating doubtful accounts is widely used in practice because it is sound in theory and simple to apply. Although normally offering a satisfactory approach to income measurement by providing equitable charges to periodic revenue, the method may not offer a "cash realizable" valuation for receivables. This shortcoming can be overcome by analyzing receivables at different intervals and correcting the allowance for any significant excess or deficiency.

Adjustment for Doubtful Accounts Based on Receivables. There are two methods of establishing and maintaining an allowance for doubtful accounts when receivables are used as the basis for the adjustment:

1. The allowance is adjusted to a certain percentage of receivables.
2. The allowance is adjusted to an amount determined by aging the accounts.

In adjusting the allowance account to a certain **percentage of receivables**, the uncollectible accounts experiences of recent periods are related to accounts outstanding for those periods, and the data are considered in terms of special current conditions. An estimate of the probable uncollectibles is developed and Doubtful Accounts Expense is debited and Allowance for Doubtful Accounts credited for an amount bringing the allowance to the desired balance. To illustrate, assume that receivables are $60,000 and the allowance account has a credit balance of $200 at the end of the period. Doubtful accounts are estimated at 2% of accounts receivable, or $1,200. The following entry brings the allowance to the desired amount:

Doubtful Accounts Expense	1,000	
Allowance for Doubtful Accounts		1,000

Although this method provides a satisfactory approach to the valuation of receivables, it may fail to provide equitable period charges to revenue. This is particularly true in view of the irregular determinations of actual uncollectibles as well as the lag in their recognition. After the first year, periodic provisions are directly affected by the current reductions in the allowance resulting from a recognition of uncollectible accounts originating in prior periods.

The most commonly used method for establishing an allowance based on outstanding receivables involves **aging receivables**. Individual accounts are analyzed to determine those not yet due and those past due. Past-due accounts are classified in terms of the length of the period past due. An analysis sheet used in aging accounts receivable is shown below:

Cash and Carry, Inc.
Analysis of Receivables — December 31, 1981

Customer	Amount	Not Yet Due	Not More Than 30 Days Past Due	31–60 Days Past Due	61–90 Days Past Due	91–180 Days Past Due	181–365 Days Past Due	More Than One Year Past Due
A. B. Andrews	$ 450			$ 450				
B. T. Brooks	300				$ 100	$ 200		
B. Bryant	200		$ 200					
L. B. Devine	2,100	$ 2,100						
K. Martinez	200							$ 200
M. A. Young	1,400	1,000			100	300		
Total	$47,550	$40,000	$3,000	$1,200	$ 650	$ 500	$ 800	$1,400

It is desirable to review each overdue balance with an appropriate company official and to arrive at estimates concerning the degree of collectibility of each item listed. An alternative procedure is to develop a series of estimated loss percentages and apply these to the different receivable classifications. The calculation of the allowance on the latter basis is illustrated at the top of page 176.

Doubtful Accounts Expense is debited and Allowance for Doubtful Accounts is credited for an amount bringing the allowance account to the required balance. Assuming uncollectibles estimated at $2,870 as shown in

Cash and Carry, Inc.
Estimated Amount of Uncollectible Accounts — December 31, 1981

Classification	Balances	Uncollectible Accounts Experience Percentage	Estimated Amount of Uncollectible Accounts
Not yet due	$40,000	2%	$ 800
Not more than 30 days past due	3,000	5%	150
31–60 days past due	1,200	10%	120
61–90 days past due	650	20%	130
91–180 days past due	500	30%	150
181–365 days past due	800	50%	400
More than one year past due	1,400	80%	1,120
	$47,550		$2,870

the tabulation above and a credit balance of $620 in the allowance before adjustment, the following entry would be made:

Doubtful Accounts Expense	2,250	
Allowance for Doubtful Accounts		2,250

The aging method provides the most satisfactory approach to the valuation of receivables at their cash realizable amounts. Furthermore, data developed through aging receivables may be quite useful to management for purposes of credit analysis and control. On the other hand, application of this method may require considerable time and may prove expensive. The method still involves estimates, and the added refinement achieved by the aging process may not warrant the additional cost. As in the preceding method, charges based upon the recognizable impairment of asset values rather than upon sales may fail to provide equitable periodic charges against revenue.

Corrections in Allowance for Doubtful Accounts. As previously indicated, the allowance for doubtful accounts balance is established and maintained by means of adjusting entries at the close of each accounting period. If the allowance provisions are too large, the allowance account balance will be unnecessarily inflated and earnings will be understated; if the allowance provisions are too small, the allowance account balance will be inadequate and earnings will be overstated.

Care must be taken to see that the allowance balance follows the credit experience of the particular business. The process of aging receivables at different intervals may be employed as a means of checking the allowance balance to be certain that it is being maintained satisfactorily. Such periodic reviews may indicate the need for a correction in the allowance as well as a change in the rate or in the method employed.

When the uncollectible accounts experience approximates the anticipation of the losses, the allowance procedure may be considered satisfactory and no adjustment is required. When it appears there has been a failure to estimate uncollectible accounts satisfactorily, resulting in an allowance balance clearly inadequate or excessive, an adjustment is in order. Such an adjustment would be considered a change in accounting estimate under APB Opinion No. 20, and the effect would be reported in the current and future periods as an ordinary item on the income statement, usually as an addition to or subtraction from Doubtful Accounts Expense.

The recognition of current period receivables as uncollectible by debits to the allowance and credits to the receivable accounts may result in a debit balance in the allowance account. A debit balance arising in this manner does not indicate the allowance is inadequate; debits to the allowance simply predate the current provision for uncollectible accounts, and the adjustment at the end of the period should cover uncollectibles already determined as well as those yet to be recognized.

Occasionally, accounts that have been charged off as uncollectible are unexpectedly collected. Entries are required to reverse the original entry and record the collection. Assuming an account of $1,500 was determined to be uncollectible but was subsequently collected, the entries would be as follows:

Allowance for Doubtful Accounts	1,500	
Accounts receivable		1,500
To write off a customer's account as uncollectible.		
Accounts Receivable	1,500	
Allowance for Doubtful Accounts		1,500
To reverse the original entry made in writing off the account.		
Cash	1,500	
Accounts Receivable		1,500
To record collection of account.		

Direct Write-Off Method

Many businesses may feel that the accounting refinement to be gained by anticipating uncollectibles hardly warrants the additional work required. Instead of anticipating uncollectible accounts, these businesses may prefer simply to recognize them in the periods in which accounts are determined to be uncollectible. This is referred to as the **direct write-off method**. When the loss is not anticipated by the establishment of an allowance, uncollectible accounts are written off by a debit to Uncollectible Accounts Expense or Bad Debt Expense and a credit to the customer's account. Because the loss is now certain, and the write-off is made directly to the customer's account rather than to an allowance, the term Doubtful Accounts Expense is not appropriate.

The recognition of uncollectibles in the period of their discovery is simple and convenient. However, accounting theory supports the anticipation of uncollectibles so that current revenues may carry the full burden of related expenses. Failure to use the allowance method is a departure from generally accepted accounting principles.

Accounts Receivable as a Source of Cash

Accounts receivable are a part of the normal operating cycle of a business. Cash is used to purchase inventory which in turn is often sold on account. The receivables are then collected providing the cash to start the cycle over. Generally the operating cycle takes several months to complete. Sometimes companies find themselves in need of immediate cash and cannot wait for completion of the normal cycle. At other times companies are not in financial stress but want to accelerate the receivable collection process or shift the risk of credit and the effort of collection to someone else. In these circumstances, receivables from customers can be used as a source of financing.

Three types of financing arrangements are common using accounts receivable to obtain cash from a bank or finance company: (1) pledge of accounts receivable, (2) assignment of accounts receivable, and (3) sale of accounts receivable.

Pledge of Accounts Receivable. Advances are frequently obtained from banks or other lending institutions by **pledging accounts receivable** as security on a loan. Ordinarily, collections are made by the borrower who is required to use this cash in meeting the obligation to the lender. The lender may be given access to the borrower's records to determine whether remittances are being properly made on pledged accounts.

No special accounting problems are encountered in the pledge of receivables. When receivables are pledged, the books simply report the loan and the subsequent settlement. However, disclosure should be made on the balance sheet, by parenthetical comment or note, of the amount of receivables pledged to secure the obligation to the lender.

Assignment of Accounts Receivable. Finance companies may agree to advance cash over a period of time as accounts receivable are assigned to them. The assignments carry a guarantee on the part of the borrower (**assignor**) to make up any deficiency if the accounts fail to realize required amounts. **Assignments** are, in effect, sales of accounts on a **recourse basis**. The cash advanced by the finance company (**assignee**) is normally less than the assigned accounts by a percentage considered adequate to cover uncollectible items, returns and allowances, offsets, and amounts subject to dispute. When amounts actually recovered on assigned accounts exceed the sum of the advance and the finance company's charges, such excess accrues to the assignor. Charges made by the finance company frequently consist of a commission on the amount advanced, plus interest on the unrecovered balance of the advance computed on a daily basis. Assignments are usually made on a **non-notification basis**, customers remaining uninformed concerning the assignment; customers make their payments to the assignor who is then required to turn the collections over to the assignee. When assignments are made on a **notification basis**, customers are instructed to make their payments directly to the finance company.

The accounting treatment required for assignment of accounts receivable is illustrated by the following example. Assume that the Eckles Co. on March 1 assigns accounts receivable of $25,000 to the Far West Finance Co. and receives $19,500 representing an advance of 80% of receivables less a commission on the advance of 2½% or $500. Collections are to be made by the assignor who is to remit such receipts to the assignee with interest on the unpaid balance at an annual rate of 12%. The entries on the books of the assignor and assignee are given below.

Transaction	Entries on Assignor's Books (Eckles Company)	Entries on Assignee's Books (Far West Finance Co.)
March 1 Eckles Co. assigned accounts receivable of $25,000 to Far West Finance Co. receiving $19,500 representing an advance of 80% of receivables less a commission on the advance of 2½%.	Accounts Receivable Assigned ...... 25,000 — Accounts Receivable 25,000; Cash .... 19,500 — Commission Expense... 500 — Note Payable to Far West Finance Co. 20,000	Eckles Co. Accounts..... 25,000 — Equity of Eckles Co. in Assigned Accounts.............. 5,000 — Commission Revenue.............. 500 — Cash 19,500
March 31 Eckles Co. collected $15,000 on assigned accounts. This amount together with interest at 12% for one month on the amount advanced, or $200, was remitted to Far West Finance Co.	Cash .... 15,000 — Accounts Receivable Assigned .... 15,000; Note Payable to Far West Finance Co........... 15,000 — Interest Expense........... 200 — Cash 15,200	Cash .... 15,200 — Eckles Co. Accounts. 15,000 — Interest Revenue 200
March 31 Sales returns and allowances granted by Eckles Co. on assigned accounts during March totaled $1,000.	Sales Returns and Allowances.............. 1,000 — Accounts Receivable Assigned 1,000	Equity of Eckles Co. in Assigned Accounts....... 1,000 — Eckles Co. Accounts. 1,000
May 31 Eckles Co. collected $8,500 on assigned accounts. Balance due, $5,000, together with interest at 12% for two months on this amount, or $100, was remitted to Far West Finance Co. in final settlement; $3,500 was retained. Remaining account balances relative to assignment were closed.	Cash .... 8,500 — Accounts Receivable Assigned .... 8,500; Note Payable to Far West Finance Co........... 5,000 — Interest Expense........... 100 — Cash .... 5,100; Accounts Receivable.... 500 — Accounts Receivable Assigned 500	Cash .... 5,100 — Eckles Co. Accounts. 5,000 — Interest Revenue .... 100; Equity of Eckles Co. in Assigned Accounts....... 4,000 — Eckles Co. Accounts. 4,000

The assignor makes two entries at the time of assignment: one entry sets the assigned accounts receivable apart under separate control, a second entry establishes a credit representing a note payable to the finance company, accompanied by debits to Cash for the cash received, and to Commission Expense for the charges made by the assignee. Thereafter, as cash is collected on assigned accounts, the assigned receivables balance is reduced and cash is remitted to reduce the note payable. Entries are made to reduce the assigned receivables balance for such items as returns, allowances, and write-offs. Upon final settlement with the assignee, any balance in Accounts Receivable Assigned is returned to the unassigned accounts control. The equity of the assignor in the accounts is always the remaining balance in the assigned accounts less the note payable to the assignee.

On the books of the assignee, the advance of cash is recorded by a debit to an asset account for the total receivables assigned, a credit to an account with the assignor for the latter's equity in this total, a credit to Commission Revenue for the charges made, and a credit to Cash for the cash paid. As cash is received, Cash is debited and the assigned accounts and Interest Revenue are credited. Reductions in assigned accounts involving charges to be absorbed by the assignor are recognized by reductions in the assignor's equity. Upon final settlement, any balance remaining in the assignor's equity in assigned accounts is offset against the assigned receivables balance.

If a balance sheet is prepared before the finance company has received full payment, the assignor recognizes the difference between the total accounts assigned and the portion required to cover the claim of the finance company as an asset. Disclosure is also made of the responsibilities to the finance company if assigned accounts do not realize enough to liquidate the loan. The assignee in preparing a balance sheet would report the outstanding assigned accounts as an asset.

To illustrate, if in the preceding example balance sheets are prepared on March 31, information relating to assigned accounts may be reported as shown below.

Eckles Co. (Assignor)

Current assets:			
Accounts receivable — unassigned		$50,000	
Accounts receivable — assigned:			
Assigned accounts	$9,000		
Less note payable to Far West Finance Co. (company is contingently liable as guarantor of assigned accounts)	5,000	4,000	
Total accounts receivable			$54,000

Far West Finance Co. (Assignee)

Current assets:		
Eckles Co. accounts	$ 9,000	
Less equity of Eckles Co. in assigned accounts	4,000	$ 5,000

When customers are informed concerning the assignment of accounts and collections are made by the finance company, procedures similar to those illustrated can still be employed. However, entries would be made by the assignor when information is received from the finance company concerning collections, interest charges, and the return of accounts in excess of claims.

Sale of Accounts Receivable. Certain banks, dealers, and finance companies purchase accounts receivable outright on a **without recourse** basis. This is known as accounts receivable **factoring**, and the buyer is referred to as a **factor**. Customers are notified that their bills are payable to the factor, and this party assumes the burden of billing and collecting accounts. The flow of activities involved in factoring is presented below.

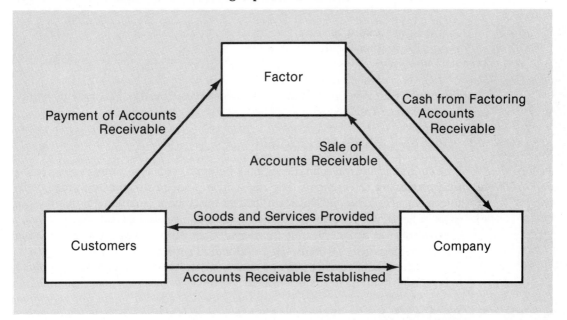

In many instances, factoring may involve more than the purchase and collection of accounts receivable. Factoring frequently involves a continuing agreement whereby a financing institution assumes the credit function as well as the collection function. Under such an arrangement, the factor grants or denies credit, handles the accounts receivable bookkeeping, bills customers, and makes collections. The business unit is relieved of all these activities. The sale of goods provides immediate cash for business use. Because the factor absorbs the losses from bad accounts and frequently assumes credit and collection responsibilities, the charge made exceeds the interest charge involved in borrowing cash or the commission and interest charges involved in the assignment of receivables. The factor may withhold a portion of the purchase price for possible future charges for customer returns and allowances or other special adjustments. Final settlement is made after receivables have been collected.

When receivables are sold outright, without recourse, Cash is debited, receivables and related allowance balances are closed, and an expense account is debited for factoring charges. When part of the purchase price is withheld by the factor, a receivable is established pending final settlement. Upon receipt of the total purchase price from the finance company, the receivable account is eliminated. To illustrate, assume that $10,000 of receivables are sold without recourse to a finance company for $8,500. An allowance for doubtful accounts equal to $300 was previously established. The finance company withheld 5% of the purchase price as protection against sales returns and allowances. The entry to record the sale of the accounts would be:

Cash..	8,075	
Receivable from Finance Company...	425	
Allowance for Doubtful Accounts...	300	
Factoring Expense..	1,200	
Accounts Receivable..		10,000

Computations:
Cash = $8,500 − $425 = $8,075; receivable = $8,500 × 5% = $425; factor expense = ($10,000 − $300) − $8,500 = $1,200.

Assuming there were no returns or allowances, the final settlement would be recorded as follows:

Cash..	425	
Receivable from Finance Company		425

Accounts receivable financing may be employed as a temporary or emergency measure after exhausting the limited line of unsecured credit available from a lending institution. On the other hand, management may engage in accounts receivable financing as a continuing policy. Recent years have witnessed an increasing number of factoring arrangements involving the full delegation of credit and collection responsibilities to specialists. Financial assistance to business through the factoring of open accounts today amounts to millions of dollars.

NOTES RECEIVABLE

A **note** is an unconditional written promise by one party to another to pay a certain sum of money at a specified time. The note may be negotiable or nonnegotiable. It is **negotiable**, i.e., legally transferable by endorsement and delivery, only if it provides for payment to the order of the second party or bearer. Such notes are commonly accepted by commercial banks for discount; hence, they are more liquid than other classes of receivables.

For reporting purposes notes receivable should include only negotiable short-term instruments acquired from trade debtors and not yet due. Trade notes generally arise from sales involving relatively high dollar amounts where the buyer wants to extend payment beyond the usual trade credit period of thirty to ninety days. Also, sellers sometimes request notes from customers whose open accounts are past due.

Nontrade notes receivable should be separately designated on the balance sheet under an appropriate title. For example, notes arising from loans to customers, officers, employees, and affiliated companies should be reported separately.

Valuation of Notes Receivable

Notes receivable are initially recorded at their **present value** which may be defined as the sum of future receipts discounted to the present date at an appropriate rate of interest.[3] In a lending transaction, the present value is the amount of cash received by the borrower. When a note is exchanged for property, goods, or services, the present value equals the current cash selling price of the items exchanged. The difference between the present value and the amount to be collected at the due date or **maturity date** is a charge for interest.

All notes arising in arm's length transactions between unrelated parties involve an element of interest. However, a distinction as to form is made between interest-bearing and non-interest-bearing notes. **Interest-bearing notes** are written as a promise to pay a **face amount** plus interest at a specified rate. In the absence of special valuation problems, the face amount of an interest-bearing note is the present value upon issuance of the note.

Non-interest-bearing notes do not specify an interest rate, but the face amount includes the interest charge. Thus, present value is the difference between the face amount and the interest included in that amount.

In recording receipt of a note, Notes Receivable is debited for the face amount of the note. When the face amount differs from the present value, as is the case with non-interest-bearing notes, the difference is recorded as a premium or discount and amortized over the life of the note.

To illustrate, assume the Alpha Corporation sells goods on January 1, 1981, with a price of $1,000. The buyer gives Alpha a promissory note due December 31, 1982. The maturity value of the note includes interest at 10%. Thus, Alpha will receive $1,210 ($1,000 × 1.21)[4] when the note is paid. The following entries show the accounting procedures for an interest-bearing note and one written in a non-interest-bearing form.

	Interest-Bearing Note Face Amount = Present Value = $1,000 Stated Interest Rate = 10%			Non-Interest-Bearing Note Face Amount = Maturity = $1,210 No Stated Interest Rate		
1981 Jan. 1	Notes Receivable	1,000		Notes Receivable	1,210	
	Sales		1,000	Sales		1,000
				Discount on Notes Receivable ...		210
	To record note received in exchange for goods selling for $1,000.					
Dec. 31	Interest Receivable	100		Discount on Notes		
	Interest Revenue		100	Receivable	100	
				Interest Revenue		100
	To recognize interest earned for one year; $1,000 × .10.					
1982 Dec. 31	Cash	1,210		Cash	1,210	
	Notes Receivable		1,000	Discount on Notes		
	Interest Receivable		100	Receivable	110	
	Interest Revenue		110	Notes Receivable		1,210
				Interest Revenue		110
	To record settlement of note at maturity and recognize interest earned for one year: ($1,000 + $100) × .10.					

[3]See Appendix A for a discussion of present value concepts and applications.

[4]The future value of $1 due in two years at an annual rate of 10% is $1.21. See Table I of Appendix A.

If the non-interest-bearing note were recorded at face value with no recognition of the interest included therein, the sales price and profit to the seller would be overstated. In subsequent periods interest income would be understated. Failure to record the discount would also result in an overstatement of assets. At December 31, 1981, the unamortized discount of $110 would be deducted from notes receivable on the balance sheet.

Although the proper valuation of receivables calls for the amortization procedure just described, exceptions may be appropriate in some situations due to special limitations or practical considerations. The Accounting Principles Board in Opinion No. 21 provided guidelines for the recognition of interest on receivables and payables and the accounting subsequently to be employed. However, the Board indicated that this process is not to be regarded as applicable under all circumstances. Among the exceptions are the following:

> . . . receivables and payables arising from transactions with customers or suppliers in the normal course of business which are due in customary trade terms not exceeding approximately one year.[5]

Accordingly, short-term notes and accounts receivable arising from trade sales may be properly recorded at the amounts collectible in the customary sales terms.

Notes, like accounts receivable, are not always collectible. If notes receivable comprise a significant portion of regular trade receivables, a provision should be made for uncollectible amounts and an allowance account established using procedures similar to those for accounts receivable already discussed.

Discounting Notes Receivable

As indicated earlier in the chapter, accounts receivable can be a source of immediate cash. Notes receivable can also provide a source of cash for a company through the process of **bank discounting**. Bank discounting is the sale of notes receivable for cash to a bank or to some other agency willing to accept such instruments. If a note is non-interest-bearing, cash is received for the face value of the note less a charge for interest, known as **discount**, for the period from the date the note is discounted to the date of its maturity. If the note is interest-bearing, the maturity value of the note is first determined. The amount received from the bank (**proceeds**) is the maturity value of the note less a discount calculated on this maturity value from the date the note is discounted to its maturity.

To illustrate entries for a non-interest-bearing note, assume a 90-day, $1,000 note dated December 1 is received; the note is discounted on December 16 at 18%. The following entries are made:

---

[5]*Opinions of the Accounting Principles Board, No. 21*, "Interest on Receivables and Payables" (New York: American Institute of Certified Public Accountants, 1971), par. 3(a). It may be noted that the primary objective of the Opinion was not to suggest new principles but simply to clarify and refine the manner of applying existing principles.

Dec.	1	Notes Receivable	1,000.00	
		Accounts Receivable...		1,000.00
	16	Cash	962.50	
		Interest Expense	37.50	
		Notes Receivable..		1,000.00

Computation:
Discount: $1,000 × .18 × 75/360 = $37.50

To illustrate the accounting for an interest-bearing note, assume that the note received in the previous example provides for the payment of interest at 10% at its maturity and it is discounted at the bank at 18%. Under these circumstances, the following entries would be appropriate:

Dec.	1	Notes Receivable	1,000.00	
		Accounts Receivable...		1,000.00
	16	Cash	986.56	
		Interest Expense	13.44	
		Notes Receivable..		1,000.00

Computation:

Maturity value of note:
$1,000 + interest ($1,000 × .10 × 90/360) = $1,025
Discount:
$1,025 × .18 × 75/360 = $38.44

Proceeds:
$1,025 − $38.44 = $986.56
Net interest expense:
$1,000 − $986.56 = $13.44

A note endorsed "without recourse" relieves the endorser of any liability for the inability of the maker of the note or any prior endorser to pay the note upon its maturity. When a note is endorsed without making any qualification, the endorser becomes liable to subsequent holders of the note if it is not paid at maturity. However, if the endorser is held liable on the note, that person has the right to recover amounts paid from the maker of the note or prior endorsers who failed to comply with its terms.

Normally, endorsement without qualification is required in discounting a note, and the endorser becomes contingently liable on the note. Under these circumstances Notes Receivable Discounted instead of Notes Receivable may be credited when the note is discounted. Pending final settlement on the note, the discounted portion of notes receivable would be regarded as a contingent asset. Notes Receivable Discounted, in turn, would be an accompanying contingent liability. When the person who holds the note at maturity receives payment from the maker, both payment and recovery contingencies are ended, and Notes Receivable Discounted can be applied against Notes Receivable.

The use of the notes receivable discounted account gives the same final result as that obtained when Notes Receivable is credited for notes discounted. Since data concerning the contingent liability are of concern only on the balance sheet date and these can be determined readily at the end of the period from an examination of the detailed record of notes discounted, the extra work involved in maintaining a notes receivable discounted account may not be warranted. When a notes receivable discounted balance is carried in the accounts, this balance is subtracted from Notes Receivable in reporting the notes receivable balance. When a notes receivable discounted account is not used, information concerning the contingent liability is provided on the balance sheet by means of a parenthetical remark or note or by special reference under a separate contingent liabilities heading.

If a note is not paid when it is due, the holder of the note must give the endorser prompt notice of such dishonor. The endorser is then required to make payment to the holder. Payment consists of the face value of the note plus interest and any fees and costs relating to collection. The full amount paid is recoverable from the maker of the note, and Accounts Receivable, Notes Receivable Dishonored, or Notes Receivable Past Due may be debited. If Notes Receivable Discounted were credited at the time the note was discounted, this balance, together with the original notes receivable balance, should be canceled. Subsequent recovery on the note is recorded by a debit to Cash and a credit to the account with the debtor. It should be noted that this subsequent payment by the debtor would generally include additional interest from date of dishonor to date of payment as well as the protest fee which the endorser has had to pay. Failure to recover any portion of the balance due would call for writing off the unpaid balance.

To illustrate, assume that in the preceding example Notes Receivable Discounted instead of Notes Receivable was credited when the note was discounted. The following entry would be made when the note is paid at maturity.

Notes Receivable Discounted	1,000	
Notes Receivable		1,000

If the note was not paid at maturity and the bank charged the endorser with a $10 protest fee, an entry would be made as follows:

Accounts Receivable	1,035	
Notes Receivable Discounted	1,000	
Cash		1,035
Notes Receivable		1,000

Computation:
  Maturity value of note, $1,025 + $10 protest fee = $1,035

Subsequent payment from the customer, assuming 30 days of additional interest, is recorded as follows:

Cash	1,043.63	
Accounts Receivable		1,035.00
Interest Revenue		8.63

Computation:
  Value of receivable at dishonor date: $1,035 \times .10 \times 30/360 = $8.63 interest + $1,035 = $1,043.63

PRESENTATION OF RECEIVABLES ON THE BALANCE SHEET

Normally, the receivables qualifying as current items are grouped for presentation in the following classes: (1) accounts — trade debtors, (2) notes — trade debtors, (3) other receivables, and (4) accrued receivables. Reporting should disclose nonnegotiable notes. The detail reported for other and accrued receivables depends upon the relative significance of the various items included. When trade accounts or installment contracts are properly reported as current but involve collections beyond one year, particulars of such deferred collections should be provided. Valuation accounts are deducted from the individual receivable balances or combined balances to which they relate. Notes receivable may be reported gross with notes receivable discounted shown as a deduction from this balance, or notes may be reported net with appropriate reference to the contingent liability arising from notes discounted. Accounts receivable assigned may be reported gross with the interest of the assignee in such balance shown as a subtraction item, or the company's interest in receivables may be reported net. When receivables are supported by pledges of collateral to assure their collectibility, the nature of the pledge and the fact that the receivables are wholly or partly secured should be disclosed.

Current receivable items as they might appear on the balance sheet are shown below. An alternative to parenthetical disclosure would be to present the supplemental information in a note to the financial statements.

Receivables:

Trade notes receivable (notes of $20,000 have been pledged to secure bank borrowing)..............................	$ 39,500	
Less notes receivable discounted......................................	1,500	$ 38,000
Accounts receivable — unassigned (including installment contracts of approximately $30,000 not due for 12–18 months)..	$112,000	
Less allowance for doubtful accounts and repossession charges..	2,500	109,500
Accounts receivable — assigned......................................	$ 42,000	
Less note payable to finance company..........................	8,500	33,500
Miscellaneous notes and accounts, including short-term loans to employees of $6,500		12,000
Accrued receivables..		4,500
Total receivables		$197,500

QUESTIONS

1. Explain how each of the following factors affects the classification of a receivable: (a) the form of the receivable, (b) the source of the receivable, and (c) the expected length of time to maturity or collection.

2. The Summer Corporation shows on its balance sheet one receivable balance including the following items: (a) advances to officers, (b) deposits on machinery and equipment being produced by various companies for the Summer Corporation, (c) advances for traveling expenses, (d) damage claims against transportation companies approved by such companies, (e) estimated federal income tax refunds, (f) accrued interest on notes receivable, (g) overdue notes, (h) receivables from a foreign subsidiary company, (i) subscriptions receivable on a new bond issue, and (j) creditor overpayments. Suggest the proper treatment of each item.

3. The Collin Co. includes in its current receivable total an investment in a joint venture with the Lars Corporation. Officials of the Collin Co. justify this practice on the grounds the assets of the joint venture are all in current form. Comment on this practice.

4. The Clarke Manufacturing Co. has filed a lawsuit against a competitor for alleged patent infringement. Clarke is seeking a very large sum in damages. The president of Clarke feels that the potential proceeds should "show up somewhere on the balance sheet." How would you respond to this comment?

5. (a) Give three methods for the establishment and the maintenance of an allowance for doubtful accounts. (b) What are the advantages and disadvantages of each method?

6. How would the percentages used in estimating uncollectible accounts be determined under any of the methods of maintaining an allowance for doubtful accounts?

7. What entries are necessary when an account previously written off is collected?

8. An analysis of the accounts receivable balance of $8,702 on the records of Bookkeepers, Inc., on December 31 reveals the following:

Accounts from sales of last three months (appear to be fully collectible)	$7,460
Accounts from sales prior to October 1 (of doubtful value)	1,312
Accounts known to be worthless	320
Dishonored notes charged back to customers' accounts	800
Credit balances in customers' accounts	1,190

    (a) What adjustments are required?
    (b) How should the various balances be shown on the balance sheet?

9. How do the accounting procedures for recognizing uncollectible accounts in the period of discovery (direct write-off) differ from those of anticipating uncollectible accounts?

10. List and explain three items that may be deducted under certain circumstances in reducing accounts receivable to a net realizable value.

11. If unearned customer finance charges for installment receivables are carried as a separate valuation account balance, what difficulties do you foresee in calculating a proper allowance for doubtful accounts?

12. In what section of the income statement would you report (a) doubtful accounts expense, (b) sales discounts?

13. (a) Distinguish between the practices of (1) pledging, (2) assigning, and (3) selling accounts receivable. (b) Describe the accounting procedures to be followed in each case.

14. The Dunn Co. enters into a continuing agreement with H & S Finance, Inc., whereby the latter company buys without recourse all of the trade receivables as they arise and assumes all credit and collection functions. (a) Describe the advantages that may accrue to the Dunn Co. as a result of the factoring agreement. (b) Are there any disadvantages? Explain.

15. Comment on the statement, "There is no such thing as a non-interest-bearing note."

16. The Lambert Optical Co. discounts at 20% the following three notes at the Security First Bank on July 1 of the current year. Compute the proceeds on each note using 360 days to a year.
    (a) A 90-day, 11% note receivable for $10,000 dated June 1.
    (b) A 6-month, 12% note receivable for $14,000 dated May 13.
    (c) Its own 4-month note payable dated July 1 with face value of $5,000 and no stated interest rate.

17. Indicate several methods for presenting information on the balance sheet relating to (a) notes receivable discounted, and (b) accounts receivable assigned.

EXERCISES

exercise 7-1

The accounts receivable control account for the Brix Corporation shows a debit balance of $123,800; the Allowance for Doubtful Accounts shows a credit balance of $7,600. Subsidiary ledger detail reveals the following:

Trade accounts receivable — assigned (note payable to finance company is $16,000)	$21,000
Subscriptions receivable for common stock due in 60 days	45,000
Interest receivable on bonds	3,750
Installment receivables due 1–18 months hence (including unearned finance charge of $1,000)	6,000
Trade receivables from officers, due currently	700
Customers' accounts reporting credit balances arising from sales returns	250
Advance payments to creditors on purchase orders	7,500
Advance payments to creditors on orders for machinery	12,000
Customers' accounts reporting credit balances arising from advance payments	1,500
Accounts known to be worthless	900
Trade accounts on which post-dated checks are held (no entries were made on receipt of checks)	700
Advances to affiliated companies	15,000
Other trade accounts receivable — unassigned	13,000

Show how this information would be reported on the balance sheet.

exercise 7-2

The information below, pertaining to the Selker Company's first year of operations, is to be used in testing the accuracy of Accounts Receivable, which has a balance of $33,000 at December 31, 1980.

    (a) Collections from customers, $50,000
    (b) Merchandise purchased, $80,000
    (c) Ending merchandise inventory, $20,000
    (d) Goods sell at 50% above cost
    (e) All sales are on account

Compute the balance that Accounts Receivable should show and determine the amount of any shortage or overage.

exercise 7-3

José Rubio's Mexican Restaurant accepts only cash or VISA and MasterCard credit cards. During June, total sales amounted to $16,800, including $10,000 worth of net bank card sales. The bank charges a 3.5% fee on net credit card sales. Record the monthly summary entry to reflect the above transactions.

exercise 7-4

Accounts Receivable of the Fakler Manufacturing Co. on December 31, 1981, had a balance of $150,000. The Allowance for Doubtful Accounts had a $4,500 debit balance. Sales in 1981 were $1,125,000 less sales discounts taken of $9,000.
    Give the adjusting entry for estimated doubtful accounts expense, assuming:

    (1) One half of 1% of 1981 net sales will probably never be collected.
    (2) Two percent of outstanding accounts receivable are doubtful.
    (3) An aging schedule shows that $7,500 of the outstanding accounts receivable are doubtful.

exercise 7-5

Willie's Gas Station had sales of $605,000 during 1981, 30% of which were on credit. Accounts receivable outstanding at December 31, 1981 totaled $30,000, and the allowance for doubtful accounts had a $500 credit balance. Willie had cash discounts (for credit customers who paid within the discount period) of $10,000. He also had $5,000 of merchandise returned by dissatisfied customers, 30% of which were by credit customers.

Give the adjusting entry for estimated doubtful accounts expense, assuming:

(1) One percent of net credit sales will be uncollectible.
(2) Two and one-half percent of current accounts receivable are doubtful.

exercise 7-6

Prior to 1982, Jeske Inc., followed the percentage-of-sales method of estimating doubtful accounts. The following data are gathered by the accounting department:

	1978	1979	1980	1981
Total sales	$1,050,000	$2,100,000	$3,600,000	$6,300,000
Credit sales	600,000	960,000	1,950,000	3,600,000
Accounts receivable (end-of-year balance)	186,000	234,000	360,000	750,000
Allowance for doubtful accounts (end-of-year credit balance)	3,000	18,000	12,000	66,000
Accounts written off	27,000	6,000	42,000	9,000

(1) What amount was debited to expense for 1979, 1980, and 1981?
(2) Compute the balance in the valuation account at the beginning of 1978 assuming there has been no change in the percentage of sales used over the four-year period.
(3) What explanation can be given for the fluctuating amount of write-off?
(4) Why do the actual write-offs fail to give the correct charge to expense?

exercise 7-7

As you check the adequacy of the allowance for doubtful accounts for Hite Corporation, you find the following information:

	1978	1979	1980
Total sales	$600,000	$675,000	$720,000
Credit sales	330,000	410,000	500,000
Accounts receivable (end-of-year balance)	80,000	105,000	130,000
Allowance for doubtful accounts (end-of-year credit balance)	1,000	6,000	8,500

Hite has not made the entry to update Allowance for Doubtful Accounts for 1980. Make the adjusting entry under the following assumptions:

(1) The doubtful accounts expense is to be 1% of total sales.
(2) The allowance for doubtful accounts is to be 5% of end-of-year accounts receivable.
(3) The allowance for doubtful accounts is to be 7% of end-of-year accounts receivable.

exercise 7-8

The Technical Publishing Company follows the procedure of debiting Doubtful Accounts Expense for 2% of all new sales. Sales for four consecutive years and year-end allowance account balances were as follows:

Year	Sales	Allowance for Doubtful Accounts (end-of-year credit balance)
1978	$2,100,000	$21,500
1979	1,975,000	35,500
1980	2,500,000	50,000
1981	2,350,000	66,000

(1) Compute the amount of accounts written off for the years 1979, 1980, and 1981.
(2) The external auditors are concerned with the growing amount in the allowance account. What action do you recommend the auditors take?
(3) What arguments might Technical use to justify the balance in the valuation account? Allowance for Doubtful Accounts is the only accounts receivable valuation account used by Technical Publishing.

exercise 7-9

Johnson Corporation sells equipment with a book value of $6,000, receiving a non-interest-bearing note due in three years with a face amount of $8,000. There is no established market value for the equipment. The interest rate on similar obligations is estimated at 12%. Compute the gain or loss on the sale and the discount on notes receivable, and make the necessary entry to record the sale.

exercise 7-10

Brady, Inc., sold a piece of machinery with an original cost of $40,000 and accumulated depreciation of $15,000. The buyer, lacking sufficient cash to pay for the machine, issued a 6-month, 10% note for $28,000. Make the entries for Brady to record (1) the sale and (2) settlement of the note at maturity.

exercise 7-11

Hillcrest Co. assigned accounts of $130,000 to L. M. Finance, Inc., and received an 85% advance, less a 3% commission on the amount of the advance. The following occurred with respect to the assigned accounts.

    (a) $60,000 was collected and forwarded to L. M. Finance along with interest of $300.
    (b) Merchandise which had been sold for $1,500 was returned for full credit.
    (c) $55,000 was collected; the balance due the finance company, plus interest of $650, was paid by Hillcrest.

Of the remaining accounts assigned, 90% are considered collectible; the others are to be written off against the allowance for doubtful accounts. Make all entries for Hillcrest Co. pertaining to the assigned accounts.

exercise 7-12

Smokey Beef Processing Co. assigns accounts of $90,000 to the Liston Finance Co., guaranteeing these accounts and receiving an 80% advance less a flat commission of 2% on the amount of the advance. Accounts of $67,500 are collected and remittance is made to the finance company. Uncollectible accounts of $3,000 are written off against an allowance for doubtful accounts; remaining accounts are collected and settlement is made with the finance company together with payment of $1,800 for interest. What entries are required on the books of Smokey Beef Processing Co. and on the books of Liston Finance Co. to record the assignment and the subsequent transactions?

exercise 7-13

The Beta Corporation decides to use accounts receivable as a basis for financing. Its current position is as follows:

Accounts receivable .	$80,000	Cash overdraft............	$ 400
Inventories.................	81,000	Accounts payable......	57,500

Prepare a statement of its current position, assuming cash is obtained as indicated in each case below:

    (1) Cash of $60,000 is borrowed on short-term notes and $35,000 is applied to the payment of creditors; accounts of $70,000 are pledged to secure the loan.
    (2) Cash of $60,000 is advanced to the company by Eakins Finance Co., the advance representing 80% of accounts assigned to it; assignment is made on a with recourse basis, and amounts collected in excess of loan balance and charges accrue to Beta Corporation.
    (3) Cash of $60,000 is received on the sale of accounts receivable of $70,800 on a nonrecourse basis.

exercise 7-14

On December 21, the following notes are discounted by the bank at 16%. Determine the cash proceeds from each note.

    (1) 30-day, $3,500, non-interest-bearing note dated December 15.
    (2) 60-day, $2,379, 9% note dated December 1.
    (3) 60-day, $10,000, 13% note dated November 6.
    (4) 90-day, $6,775, 19% note dated November 24.

exercise 7-15

Glen Larsen sold Andersen Farm Machinery a used tractor and received a 90-day, 10% note for $5,000 on May 13, 1980. On May 29, Larsen discounted the note at 11%. On August 11 the bank notified Larsen that the note was not paid and charged Larsen a $10 protest fee. On September 1 Larsen collected the note plus 12% interest from the maturity date on the account receivable balance. Record the entries for the above events on Larsen's books.

exercise 7-16

Bill Richmond received from Jane Harman, a customer, a 90-day, 12% note for $4,000, dated June 6, 1981. On July 6, Richmond had Harman's note discounted at 10% and recorded the contingent liability. The bank protested nonpayment of the note and charged the endorser with protest fees of $10 in addition to the amount of the note. On September 28, 1981, the note was collected with interest at 14% from the maturity date on the account receivable balance. What entries would appear on Richmond's books as a result of the foregoing?

exercise 7-17

On June 1, 1981, J. Sparks received a $4,107 note from a customer on an overdue account. The note matures on August 30 and bears interest at 10%. On July 1, Sparks discounted the note at 11% and applied the proceeds to the payment of creditors. On August 30, the customer is unable to make payment to the bank and the bank charges Sparks' account for the maturity value of the note plus a $6 protest fee. On September 29, Sparks accepted the customer's offer to cancel the liability in exchange for marketable securities valued at $4,290. Give all entries on Sparks' books to record the foregoing.

PROBLEMS

problem 7-1

The balance sheet for the Ashley Cosmetic Corporation on December 31, 1980, includes the following receivable balances:

Interest receivable...		$ 325
Notes receivable...	$47,500	
Less notes receivable discounted...............	15,500	32,000
Accounts receivable..	$90,000	
Less allowance for doubtful accounts........	3,950	86,050

Transactions during 1981 included the following:

    (a) Sales on account were $767,800.
    (b) Cash collected on accounts totaled $571,000, which included accounts of $97,000 on which cash discounts of 2% were allowed.
    (c) Notes received in payment of accounts totaled $84,000.
    (d) Notes receivable discounted as of December 31, 1980, were paid at maturity with the exception of one $8,000 note on which the company had to pay $8,090, which included interest and protest fees. It is expected that recovery will be made on this note in 1982.
    (e) Customers' notes of $50,000 were discounted during the year, proceeds from their sale being $48,500. Of this total, $34,500 matured during the year without notice of protest.
    (f) Customers' accounts of $8,420 were written off during the year as worthless.
    (g) Recoveries of doubtful accounts written off in prior years were $1,020.
    (h) Notes receivable collected during the year totaled $26,000 and interest collected was $2,150.
    (i) On December 31, accrued interest on notes receivable was $635.

(j) Uncollectible accounts are estimated to be 5% of the December 31, 1981, Accounts Receivable balance.

(k) Cash of $35,000 was borrowed from the bank, accounts receivable of $42,000 being pledged on the loan. Collections of $19,500 had been made on these receivables (included in the total given in transaction [b]) and this amount was applied on December 31, 1981, to payment of accrued interest on the loan of $500, and the balance to partial payment of the loan.

Instructions:

(1) Prepare journal entries summarizing the transactions and information given above.

(2) Prepare a summary of current receivables for balance sheet presentation.

problem 7-2

The Tammarack Co., which began business on January 1, 1981, decided to establish an allowance for doubtful accounts. It was estimated that uncollectibles would amount to 1% of credit sales. At the end of each month, an entry was made to record doubtful accounts expense equal to 1% of credit sales for the month. On December 31, 1981, outstanding receivables are $23,000; Allowance for Doubtful Accounts has a credit balance of $500 after recording estimated doubtful accounts expense for December and after $250 of uncollectible accounts had been written off. Following is additional data for 1981.

(a) Collections from customers (excluding cash purchases), $60,000.
(b) Merchandise purchased, $90,000.
(c) Ending merchandise inventory, $15,000.
(d) Goods were sold at 40% above cost.
(e) 80% of sales were on account.

Instructions: Determine if accounts receivable and the allowance for doubtful accounts are correctly stated at December 31, 1981.

problem 7-3

The following transactions affecting the accounts receivable of Southern States Manufacturing Corporation took place during the year ended January 31, 1981.

Sales (cash and credit) .... $	591,050
Cash received from credit customers (customers who paid $298,900 took advantage of the discount feature of the corporation's credit terms, 2/10, n/30)...	302,755
Cash received from cash customers	205,175
Accounts receivable written off as worthless	4,955
Credit memoranda issued to credit customers for sales returns and allowances..	56,275
Cash refunds given to cash customers for sales returns and allowances	16,972
Recoveries on accounts receivable written off as uncollectible in prior periods (not included in cash amount stated above)	10,615

The following two balances were taken from the January 31, 1980 balance sheet:

Accounts receivable..	$95,842
Allowance for doubtful accounts....................	9,740

The corporation provides for its net uncollectible account losses by crediting Allowance for Doubtful Accounts for 1½% of net credit sales for the fiscal period.

Instructions:

(1) Prepare the journal entries to record the transactions for the year ended January 31, 1981.

(2) Prepare the adjusting journal entry for estimated uncollectible accounts on January 31, 1981.

problem 7-4

Kohler Pipe Company completed the following transactions during 1981 related to accounts receivable.

April 1 Assigned accounts of $100,000 to Irwin Finance Co. for a cash advance of 70% of receivables less a commission on the advance of 2%.

April 30 Collections during April on assigned accounts were $32,440. This amount plus 12% interest for one month on the amount advanced was remitted to Irwin Finance Co.

April 30 Wrote off against the allowance account, $4,750 of uncollectible accounts of which $2,000 were assigned accounts.

May 31 Collections during May on assigned accounts were $35,000. This amount plus 12% interest for one month on the unpaid balance was remitted to Irwin Finance Co.

May 31 Granted sales returns of $8,500 on assigned accounts during May.

June 30 Collections during June on assigned accounts were $9,500. Balance due Irwin Finance Co. plus 12% interest for one month on the unpaid balance was remitted. Remaining account balances relative to assignment were closed.

Instructions:

(1) Give the entries required to record the above transactions on the Kohler Pipe Company's books.

(2) Give the entries required to record the same transactions on the books of the Irwin Finance Company.

problem 7-5

Live-Wire Electric Supply Company has run into financial difficulties. It decides to improve its cash position by factoring one third of its accounts receivable and assigning one half of the remaining receivables to the local bank. Details of these arrangements were as follows:

Accounts receivable, December 31, 1980...............$420,000   (before financing)
Allowance for doubtful accounts, December 31, 1980.. 3,000   (credit)
Estimated uncollectibles, December 31, 1980 ....   3% of accounts receivable balance
Factor discount rate ....   20% of gross receivables financed
Assignment withholding rate...................................   16% of gross receivables financed
Assignment service charge rate ....   3% of amount advanced, payable in advance

Instructions:

(1) Prepare the journal entries to record the receipt of cash from (a) factoring, and (b) assigning the accounts receivable.

(2) Prepare the journal entry to record the necessary adjustment to Allowance for Doubtful Accounts.

(3) Prepare the accounts receivable section of the balance sheet as it would appear after these transactions.

(4) What entry would be made on the company books of the Live-Wire Electric Supply Company when factored accounts have been collected?

problem 7-6

Parco Marketing Corporation completed the following transactions, among others:

May   5 Received a $5,000, 60-day, 10% note dated May 5 from C. I. Parker, a customer.

     24 Received a $1,800, 90-day, non-interest-bearing note dated May 23 from E. Silva as settlement for unpaid balance of $1,752.

     25 Had Parker's note discounted at the bank at 13%.

June 7 Had Silva's note discounted at the bank at 15%.

     25 Received from B. Avery, a customer, a $7,000, 90-day, 12% note dated June 5, payable to B. Avery and signed by the Barlow Corp. Upon endorsement, gave the customer credit for the maturity value of the note less discount at 13%.

     29 Received a $3,500, 60-day, 9% note dated June 29 from P. L. Edwards, a customer.

July 5 Received notice from the bank that Parker's note was not paid at maturity. Protest fees of $7.50 were charged by the bank.

     21 Received payment from Parker on the dishonored note, including interest at 16% on the account receivable balance from maturity date.

Instructions:

(1) Give the journal entries to record the above transactions, showing contingent liabilities in the accounts. (Show data used in calculations with each entry.)

(2) Give the adjusting entries required on July 31.

problem 7-7

On December 31, 1981, the notes receivable account of the Imbler Company consisted of the following notes:

Trade notes receivable, considered good:
Due in 12 months or less .... $ 27,000
Due in more than 12 months 46,000
Trade notes receivable, considered 80% collectible:
Due in 12 months or less 22,000
Trade notes receivable, considered worthless... 4,500
Trade notes receivable, considered good, and discounted with the First National Bank (with offsetting credits to Notes Receivable Discounted). Of these notes, $44,000 have been paid 98,000
Notes receivable accepted on sale of diesel equipment (plant asset), $72,000. This amount was payable $2,000 plus interest monthly, and the purchaser was considered a good credit risk.. 72,000
Note receivable of Ivan Imbler, president, payable on demand. This note was received in payment of his subscription to 1,000 shares of common stock of Imbler Company at par. Upon receipt of this note, the corporation issued a certificate of capital stock for 1,000 shares 120,000
$389,500

Instructions: Indicate how each of the company's notes receivable would be classified on the balance sheet of December 31, 1981.

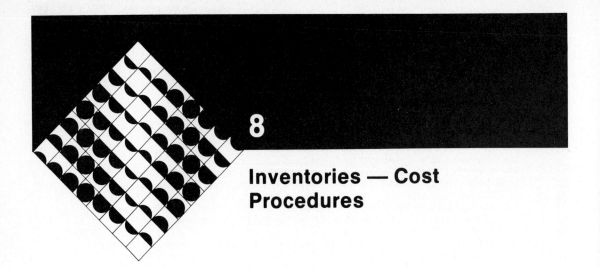

8

Inventories — Cost Procedures

CHAPTER OBJECTIVES

Describe the nature, classification, and cost of items included in inventory.

Explain the basic accounting problem of allocating inventory costs between the balance sheet and income statement.

Describe the impact of changing price levels on inventory cost allocation.

Describe and illustrate the traditional methods for allocating inventory costs.

Compare and evaluate inventory cost allocation methods.

Describe and illustrate the effects of inventory errors on financial statements.

The primary source of revenue for a business entity is the sale of goods or services. The selling price of the goods or services must exceed all directly and indirectly related expenses in order for a company to realize a profit on its operations. For a nonservice enterprise, the cost of goods sold and the cost of those held for future sale are significant items in the measurement of income and the determination of financial position.

NATURE OF INVENTORIES

The term **inventories** designates goods held for sale in the normal course of business and, in the case of a manufacturer, goods in production or to be placed in production. The nature of goods classified as inventory varies widely with the nature of business activities, and in some cases includes assets not normally thought of as inventories. For example, land and buildings held for resale by a real estate firm, partially completed buildings to be sold in the future by a construction firm, and marketable securities held for resale by a stockbroker are all properly classified as inventories by the respective firms.

Inventories represent one of the most active elements in business operations, being continuously acquired or produced and resold. A large part of a company's resources is frequently invested in goods purchased or manufactured. The cost of these goods must be recorded, grouped, and summarized during the accounting period. At the end of the period, costs must be allocated between current and future activities, i.e., between goods sold during the current period and those on hand to be sold in future periods. This allocation is a major element in financial reporting. Failure to allocate costs properly can result in serious distortions of financial progress and position.

IMPACT OF INFLATION ON INVENTORIES

Of the many accounting problems that complicate the allocation procedure, one of the most perplexing is the effect of changing prices. In recent decades, economies throughout most of the world have experienced moderate to extensive inflation. When prices increase while inventory is being held or produced, a higher than normal profit is recognized when the inventory is sold. Increases in the value of inventories due to rising prices have been labeled **holding gains** in the accounting literature. These are distinguished from **operating gross profit**, which reflects the normal markup between cost and selling price. The holding gain share of profits must be used to replace the sold inventory. Thus, a portion of the reported profit is really illusory and is not available for return to stockholders as dividends.

For example, assume that a company purchased 100 units of inventory for $10 each or a total of $1,000. At the time of purchase, it was anticipated that the inventory would be sold for $12.50 per unit, a markup on cost of 25%. Assume further that, prior to resale, the cost to acquire identical goods increased to $12 per unit, and the resale price was increased to $15 to maintain the 25% markup. If the 100 units were sold, historical cost accounting would recognize sales revenue of $1,500 and cost of $1,000, or a gross profit of $500. However, replacement of the 100 units now requires $1,200 of the proceeds. Thus, $200 of the reported profit is really a holding gain, and $300 is the true gross profit from operations.

As discussed in Chapter 4, historical cost reporting fails to reflect the fact that a company's real position is improved only to the extent of the true operating profit. In addition to the impact on cost of sales, the increased cost of inventory replacement is not reflected in the balance sheet under the historical cost system. Failure to recognize the holding gains as a separate revenue item occurring at the time of the price increase produces a balance sheet with asset values lower than their current replacement cost. To continue the above example, assume that the inventory was not sold in the current period. Historical cost accounting would require the asset to be reported at its cost of $1,000. However, if the unrealized holding gain were recognized, the inventory would be reported at $1,200. The $200 unrealized holding gain could be reported either as a revenue item on the income statement or as a direct increase to owners' equity. The choice between these alternatives would depend upon the income recognition rule being applied.

As discussed in Chapter 3, the accounting standards currently accepted in the United States are still based upon historical costs. However, because of the increasingly significant influence of inflation on our economy, the Securities and Exchange Commission ruled in 1976 that certain large companies must report the replacement cost of inventories as supplemental information.[1] The SEC stopped short of requiring adjustment of the actual income statement and balance sheet accounts. The FASB extended this supplementary information requirement in 1979 to include computation of a supplemental net income figure that includes a cost of sales computation based upon current replacement costs.[2] In response to the FASB's action, the SEC agreed to phase out its own replacement cost disclosure requirements.

Pending a more complete acceptance of accounting for inflation, accountants in the United States have developed some unique methods of inventory valuation in their attempt to cope with the deteriorating value of the dollar. These methods, only partially successful, are explored in both this and the subsequent chapter. If prices remained constant, inventory valuation would prove to be rather simple. But when prices continually change, which is the current situation, the allocation of a constant cost to present and future periods' revenue challenges the most experienced accountant.[3]

CLASSES OF INVENTORIES

The term **merchandise inventory** is generally applied to goods held by a merchandising firm, either wholesale or retail, when such goods have been acquired in a condition for resale. The terms **raw materials**, **goods in process**, and **finished goods** refer to the inventories of a manufacturing enterprise. The latter items require description.

Raw materials

Raw materials are goods acquired for use in the productive process. Some raw materials are obtained directly from natural sources. More often,

---

[1]Securities and Exchange Commission, *Accounting Series Release No. 190*, "Disclosure of Certain Replacement Cost Data" (Washington: U.S. Government Printing Office, 1976).
[2]*Statement of Financial Accounting Standards, No. 33*, "Financial Reporting and Changing Prices" (Stamford: Financial Accounting Standards Board, 1979), par. 29–30.
[3]See Chapter 20 for in-depth discussion of accounting for inflation.

however, raw materials are acquired from other companies and represent the finished products of the suppliers. For example, newsprint is the finished product of the paper mill but represents raw material to the printer who acquires it.

Although the term raw materials can be used broadly to cover all materials used in manufacturing, this designation is frequently restricted to materials that will be physically incorporated in the products being manufactured. The term **factory supplies**, or **manufacturing supplies**, is then used to refer to auxiliary materials, i.e., materials that are necessary in the productive process but are not directly incorporated in the products. Oils and fuels for factory equipment, cleaning supplies, and similar items fall into this grouping since these items are not incorporated in a product but simply facilitate production as a whole. Raw materials directly used in the production of certain goods are frequently referred to as **direct materials**; factory supplies are referred to as **indirect materials**.

Although factory supplies may be summarized separately, they should be reported as a part of a company's inventories since they will ultimately be consumed in the productive process. Supplies used in the delivery, sales, and general administrative functions of the enterprise should not be reported as part of the inventories, but as prepaid expenses.

Goods in Process

Goods in process, alternately referred to as **work in process**, consists of materials partly processed and requiring further work before they can be sold. This inventory includes three cost elements: (1) **direct materials**, (2) **direct labor**, and (3) **factory overhead** or **manufacturing overhead**. The cost of materials directly identified with the goods in production is included under (1). The cost of labor directly identified with goods in production is included under (2). The portion of factory overhead assignable to goods still in production forms the third element of cost.

Factory overhead consists of all manufacturing costs other than direct materials and direct labor. It includes factory supplies used and labor not directly identified with the production of specific products. It also includes general manufacturing costs such as depreciation, maintenance, repairs, property taxes, insurance, and light, heat, and power, as well as a reasonable share of the managerial costs other than those relating solely to the selling and administrative functions of the business. Overhead may be designated as **fixed**, **variable**, or **semivariable**. Overhead charges that remain constant in amount regardless of the volume of production are referred to as **fixed**. Depreciation, insurance, rent, and property taxes normally fall into this category. Overhead charges that fluctuate in proportion to the volume of production are called **variable**. Some indirect materials and labor vary directly with production. Some charges vary, but the variations are not in direct proportion to the volume. These charges have both fixed and variable components and are designated as **semivariable** or **mixed** costs. Factory supervision is an example of a semivariable item when it is fixed within a certain range of production but changes when production is not within this range.

Finished Goods

Finished goods are the manufactured products awaiting sale. As products are completed, the costs accumulated in the production process are transferred from Work in Process to the finished goods inventory account. The diagram below illustrates the basic flow of product costs through the inventory accounts of a manufacturer.

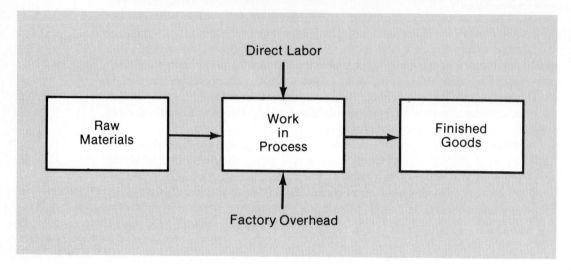

INVENTORY SYSTEMS

Inventory records may be maintained on either a **periodic** or **perpetual** basis. A **periodic inventory system** requires a **physical inventory**, i.e., a counting, measuring, or weighing of goods, at the end of the accounting period to determine the quantities on hand. Values are then assigned to the quantities to determine the portion of the recorded costs to be carried forward.

The **perpetual inventory system** requires the maintenance of records that offer a continuous summary of inventory items on hand. Individual accounts are kept for each class of goods. Inventory increases and decreases are recorded in the individual accounts, the resulting balances representing the amounts on hand. Perpetual records may be kept in terms of quantities only or in terms of both quantities and costs. In a manufacturing organization, a perpetual system applied to inventories requires recording the full movement of goods through individual accounts for raw materials, goods in process, and finished goods. Illustrative entries to account for these movements of goods appear on pages 38–39.

When the perpetual system is employed, physical counts of the units on hand should be made at least once a year to confirm the balances on the books. The frequency of physical inventories will vary depending upon the nature of the goods, their rate of turnover, and the degree of internal control. A plan for continuous counting of inventory items on a rotation basis is frequently employed. Variations may be found between the book record and the amounts actually on hand as a result of recording errors, shrinkage, breakage, theft, and other causes. The book inventories should be adjusted to agree with the physical count when a discrepancy exists. To illustrate, assume that a physical inventory of raw materials resulted in a value which is $2,500 less than the recorded book inventory. The entry to adjust the book inventory would be as follows:

Inventory Adjustment	2,500	
Raw Materials Inventory		2,500

Normal adjustments for shrinkage and breakage are reported as adjustments to cost of goods sold. Abnormal shortages or thefts may be reported separately as operating expenses.

Practically all large trading and manufacturing enterprises and many relatively small organizations have adopted the perpetual inventory system as an integral part of their record keeping and internal control. This system offers a continuous check and control over inventories. Purchasing and production planning are facilitated, adequate inventories on hand are assured, and losses incurred through damage and theft are fully disclosed. The additional costs of maintaining such a system are usually well repaid by the benefits provided to management.

ITEMS TO BE INCLUDED IN INVENTORY

As a general rule, goods should be included in the inventory of the party holding title. The passing of title is a legal term designating the point at which ownership changes. In some situations, the legal rule may be waived for practical reasons or because of certain limitations in its application. When the rule of passing of title is not observed, there should be appropriate disclosure on the statements of the special practice followed and the factors supporting such practice. Application of the legal test under a number of special circumstances is described in the following paragraphs.

Goods in Transit

When terms of sale are **FOB (free on board) shipping point**, title passes to the buyer with the loading of goods at the point of shipment. Under these terms, application of the legal rule to a year-end shipment calls for recognition of a sale and an accompanying decrease in goods on hand on the books of the seller. Since title passes at the shipping point, **goods in transit** at year-end should be included in the inventory of the buyer despite the lack of physical possession. A determination of the goods in transit at year-end is made by a review of the incoming orders during the early part of the new period. The purchase records may be kept open beyond the fiscal period to permit the recognition of goods in transit as of the end of the period, or goods in transit may be recorded by means of an adjusting entry.

When terms of a sale are **FOB destination**, application of the legal test calls for no recognition of the transaction until goods are received by the buyer. In this case, because of the difficulties involved in ascertaining whether goods have reached their destination at year-end, the seller may prefer to ignore the legal rule and employ shipment as a basis for recognizing a sale and the accompanying inventory decrease. In some cases, title to goods may pass before shipment takes place. For example, if the parties agree that the buyer will pick up the goods at the seller's place of business, and if the goods are **segregated** awaiting pick-up, title has passed and the goods should be recognized as in transit to the buyer. If the sale is recognized upon segregation by the seller, care must be taken to exclude such goods from the seller's inventory. The buyer, on the other hand, could recognize the in-transit goods as a purchase and thus part of its inventory.

Goods on Consignment

Goods are frequently transferred to a dealer (**consignee**) on a consignment basis. The shipper (**consignor**) retains title and includes the goods in inventory until their sale by the consignee. **Consigned goods** are properly reported at the sum of their cost and the handling and shipping costs incurred in their transfer to the consignee. The goods may be separately designated on the balance sheet as merchandise on consignment. The consignee does not own the consigned goods; hence neither consigned goods nor obligations for such goods are reported on the consignee's financial statements. Other merchandise owned by a business but in the possession of others, such as goods in the hands of salespersons and agents, goods held by customers on approval, and goods held by others for storage, processing, or shipment, should also be shown as a part of the owner's ending inventory.

Conditional and Installment Sales

Conditional sales and installment sales contracts may provide for a retention of title by the seller until the sales price is fully recovered. Under these circumstances, the seller, who retains title, may continue to show the goods, reduced by the buyer's equity in such goods as established by collections; the buyer, in turn, can report an equity in the goods accruing through payments made. However, in the usual case when the possibilities of returns and defaults are very low, the test of passing of title should be relinquished and the transaction recorded in terms of the expected outcome: the seller, anticipating completion of the contract and the ultimate passing of title, recognizes the transaction as a regular sale involving deferred collections; the buyer, intending to comply with the contract and acquire title, recognizes the transaction as a regular purchase.

DETERMINATION OF INVENTORY COST

After the goods to be included as inventory have been identified, the accountant must assign a dollar value to the physical units. As indicated earlier, the profession has historically favored retention of some measure of

incurred cost for this purpose. Attention is directed in this chapter to identifying the elements that comprise cost, and to a consideration of how to determine the portion of historical costs to be retained as the inventory amount reported on the balance sheet and the amount to be charged against current revenues.

Items Included in Cost

Inventory cost consists of all expenditures, both direct and indirect, relating to inventory acquisition, preparation, and placement for sale. In the case of raw materials or goods acquired for resale, cost includes the purchase price, freight, receiving, storage, and all other costs incurred to the time goods are ready for sale. Certain expenditures can be traced to specific acquisitions or can be allocated to inventory items in some equitable manner. Other expenditures may be relatively small and difficult to allocate. Such items are normally excluded in the calculation of inventory cost and are thus charged in full against current revenue as **period costs**.

The charges to be included in the cost of manufactured products have already been mentioned. Proper accounting for materials, labor, and factory overhead items and their identification with goods in process and finished goods inventories is best achieved through adoption of a cost accounting system designed to meet the needs of a particular business unit. Certain costs relating to the acquisition or the manufacture of goods may be considered abnormal and may be excluded in arriving at inventory cost. For example, costs arising from idle capacity, excessive spoilage, and reprocessing are normally considered abnormal items chargeable to current revenue. Only those portions of general and administrative costs that are clearly related to procurement or production should be included in inventory cost.

In practice, companies take different positions in classifying certain costs. For example, costs of the purchasing department, costs of accounting for manufacturing activities, and costs of pensions for production personnel may be treated as inventoriable costs by some companies and period costs by others.

Discounts as Reductions in Cost

Discounts treated as a reduction of cost in recording the acquisition of goods should similarly be treated as a reduction in the cost assigned to the inventory. **Trade discounts** are discounts converting a catalog price list to the prices actually charged to a buyer. The discount available may vary with such factors as the quantity purchased. Thus, trade discounts are frequently stated in a series. For example, given trade discount terms based on the quantity ordered of 30/20/10, a customer would be entitled to a discount of either 30%, 30% and 20%, or 30% and 20% and 10%, depending on the size of the order. Each successive discount is applied to the net invoice cost after deducting any earlier discounts. To illustrate, assume that an inventory item is listed in a catalog for $5,000 and a buyer is given terms of 20/10/5. The net invoice price is calculated as follows:

	Discount	*Net Invoice Amount*
$5,000 × 20%	$1,000	$5,000 − $1,000 = $4,000
$4,000 × 10%	$ 400	$4,000 − $ 400 = $3,600
$3,600 × 5%	$ 180	$3,600 − $ 180 = $3,420

An alternative approach to the above computation is to compute a composite discount rate which can be applied to the initial gross amount. The following computation could be made for the above invoice:

Discount Rate ×	*Percentage of Original Invoice Cost* =	*Composite Discount Rate*
20%	100%	20.00%
10%	80% (100% − 20%)	8.00
5%	72% (80% − 8%)	3.60
Composite Rate		31.60%

Computation of discount: $5,000 × 31.6% = $1,580 discount
Net price = $5,000 − $1,580 = $3,420

The advantage of the composite approach is that once a composite rate is computed, it can be used directly for all purchases that have the same trade discount terms.

Cost is defined as the list price less the trade discount. No record needs to be made of the discount, and the purchases should be recorded at the net price.

Cash discounts are discounts granted for payment of invoices within a limited time period. Business use of such discounts has declined in popularity over the past years, although they are still found in some industries. Cash discounts are usually stated as a certain percentage rate to be allowed if the invoice is paid within a certain number of days, with the full amount due within another time period. For example, 2/10, n/30 (two ten, net thirty) means that 2% is allowed as a cash discount if the invoice is paid within 10 days after the invoice date, but that the full or "net" amount is due within 30 days. Terms of 3/10 eom mean a 3% discount is allowed if the invoice is paid within 10 days after the end of the month in which the invoice is written.

Theoretically, inventory should be recorded at the discounted amount, i.e., the gross invoice price less the allowable discount. This **net method** reflects the fact that discounts not taken are in effect credit-related expenditures incurred for failure to pay within the discount period. They are recorded in the discounts lost account and reported as a separate item on the income statement. Discounts lost represent a relatively high rate of interest and indicate a failure on the part of financial management due to either carelessness in considering payment alternatives or financial inability to avoid the extra charge.

This inefficiency is not reflected when inventory records are maintained at the gross unit price for convenience, as is often the case. Under the **gross method** cash discounts taken are reflected through a contra purchases account, Purchases Discount. There is no recognition of the amount of available discounts not taken.

Because of its control features, the net method of accounting for purchases is strongly preferred; however, many companies still follow the historical practice of recognizing cash discounts only as payments are made. If the payment is made in the same period the inventory is sold, use of either method will result in the same net income. However, if inventory is sold in one period and payment is made in a subsequent period, net income is affected and a proper matching of costs against revenue will not take place. If the net method is used, an adjusting entry should be made at the end of each period to record the discounts lost for invoices which have not yet been paid.

The entries required for both the gross and net methods are illustrated below. A perpetual inventory method is assumed.

Transaction	Purchases Reported Net		Purchases Reported Gross	

Purchase of merchandise priced at $2,500 less trade discount of 30/20 and a cash discount of 2%:
$2,500 less 30% = $1,750
$1,750 less 20% = $1,400
$1,400 less 2% = $1,372
	Inventory............................ 1,372
	   Accounts Payable.........
		1,372	Inventory........................... 1,400
			   Accounts Payable.........
				1,400

(a) Assuming payment of the invoice within discount period.	Accounts Payable 1,372
	   Cash ....
		1,372	Accounts Payable 1,400
			   Purchases Discount .....
			   Cash.............................
				28
				1,372

(b) Assuming payment of the invoice after discount period.	Accounts Payable 1,372
	Discounts Lost 28
	   Cash..............................
		1,400	Accounts Payable 1,400
			   Cash..............................
				1,400

(c) Required adjustment at the end of the period assuming that the invoice was not paid and the discount period has lapsed.	Discounts Lost .... 28 Accounts Payable.........	28	No entry required	

Purchases Returns and Allowances

Adjustments to invoice cost are also made when merchandise is either damaged or is of a lesser quality than ordered. Sometimes the merchandise is physically returned to the supplier. In other instances, a credit is allowed to the buyer by the supplier to compensate for the damage or the inferior quality of the merchandise. In either case, the liability is reduced and a credit is made either directly to the inventory account under a perpetual inventory system, or to a contra purchases account, Purchases Returns and Allowances, under a physical inventory system.

TRADITIONAL COST ALLOCATION METHODS

Four commonly applied allocation methods are discussed in this section: (1) **specific identification**, (2) **first-in, first-out (fifo)**, (3) **weighted average**, and (4) **last-in, first-out (lifo)**. Each has certain characteristics that make it preferable under certain conditions. One of them, the last-in, first-out method was specifically developed as an attempt to reduce the impact of inventory inflation on net income. All four methods have in common the fact that inventory cost, as defined in this chapter, is allocated between the income statement and the balance sheet. No adjustment for price changes is made to the total amount to be allocated.

Specific Identification

Costs may be allocated between goods sold during the period and goods on hand at the end of the period according to the actual cost of specific units. This **specific identification** procedure requires a means of identifying the historical cost of each unit of inventory up to the time of sale. When perpetual inventory records are maintained, Cost of Goods Sold is debited and Inventory is credited for the actual cost of each item sold. In a periodic system, cost allocation is based on the identified cost of items on hand at the end of the period. Thus, under either system the flow of recorded costs matches the physical flow of goods.

The specific identification procedure is a highly objective approach to matching historical costs with revenues. As stated in Accounting Research Study No. 13, "There appears to be little theoretical argument against the use of specific identification of cost with units of product if that method of determining inventory costs is practicable."[4] Application of this method, however, is often difficult or impossible. When inventory is composed of a great many items or identical items acquired at different times and at different prices, cost identification procedures are likely to be slow, burdensome, and costly. Furthermore, when units are identical and interchangeable, this method opens the doors to possible profit manipulation through the selection of particular units for delivery. Finally, significant changes in costs during a period may warrant charges to revenue on a basis other than past identifiable costs.

First-In, First-Out Method

The **first-in, first-out (fifo) method** is based on the assumption that costs should be charged to revenue in the order in which incurred. Inventories are thus stated in terms of most recent costs. To illustrate the application of this method, assume the following data:

Jan.	1	Inventory	200 units at $10	$ 2,000
	12	Purchase	400 units at 12	4,800
	26	Purchase	300 units at 11	3,300
	30	Purchase	100 units at 12	1,200
		Total	1,000	$11,300

A physical inventory on January 31 shows 300 units on hand. The most recent costs would be assigned to the units as follows:

Most recent purchase, Jan. 30	100 units at $12	$1,200
Next most recent purchase, Jan. 26	200 units at 11	2,200
Total	300	$3,400

[4]Horace G. Barden, *Accounting Research Study No. 13*, "The Accounting Basis of Inventories" (New York: American Institute of Certified Public Accountants, 1973) p. 83.

If the ending inventory is recorded at $3,400, cost of goods sold is $7,900 ($11,300 − $3,400). Thus, revenue is charged with the earliest costs incurred.

When perpetual inventory accounts are maintained, a form similar to that illustrated below is used to record the cost assigned to units issued and the cost relating to the goods on hand. The columns show the quantities and values of goods acquired, goods issued, and balances on hand. It should be observed that identical values for physical and perpetual inventories are obtained when fifo is applied.

COMMODITY: X **(fifo)**

DATE	RECEIVED QUANTITY	UNIT COST	TOTAL COST	ISSUED QUANTITY	UNIT COST	TOTAL COST	BALANCE QUANTITY	UNIT COST	TOTAL COST
Jan. 1							200	$10	$2,000
12	400	$12	$4,800				200	10	2,000
							400	12	4,800
16				200	$10	$2,000			
				300	12	3,600	100	12	1,200
26	300	11	3,300				100	12	1,200
							300	11	3,300
29				100	12	1,200			
				100	11	1,100	200	11	2,200
30	100	12	1,200				200	11	2,200
							100	12	1,200

Fifo can be supported as a logical and realistic approach to the flow of costs when it is impractical or impossible to achieve specific cost identification. Fifo assumes a cost flow closely paralleling the usual physical flow of goods sold. Revenue is charged with costs considered applicable to the goods actually sold; ending inventories are reported in terms of most recent costs — costs closely approximating the current value of inventories at the balance sheet date. Fifo affords little opportunity for profit manipulation because the assignment of costs is determined by the order in which costs are incurred.

Average Cost Methods

The **weighted average method** is based on the assumption that goods sold should be charged at an average cost, such average being influenced or *weighted* by the number of units acquired at each price. Inventories are stated at the same weighted average cost per unit. Using the cost data in the preceding section, the weighted average cost of a physical inventory of 300 units on January 31 would be as follows:

Jan. 1	Inventory	200 units at $10		$ 2,000
12	Purchase	400 units at 12		4,800
26	Purchase	300 units at 11		3,300
30	Purchase	100 units at 12		1,200
	Total	1,000		$11,300

Weighted average cost ....$11,300 ÷ 1,000 = $11.30.
Ending inventory...300 units at $11.30 = $3,390.

The ending inventory is recorded at a cost of $3,390, cost of goods sold is $7,910 ($11,300 − $3,390), and revenue is charged with a weighted average cost. The calculations above were made for costs of one month. Similar calculations could be developed in terms of data for a quarter or for a year.

When perpetual records of quantities issued are maintained but the costs of units issued are not recorded until the end of a period, a weighted average cost for the period, such as that discussed above, is calculated at that time and the accounts are credited for the cost of total units issued. Frequently, however, costs relating to issues are recorded currently, and it is necessary to calculate costs on the basis of the weighted average on the date of issue. This requires calculating a new weighted average cost immediately after the receipt of each additional purchase. This method of successive average recalculations is referred to as the **moving average method**. The use of this method is illustrated below.

COMMODITY: X **(moving average)**

DATE	RECEIVED QUANTITY	UNIT COST	TOTAL COST	ISSUED QUANTITY	UNIT COST	TOTAL COST	BALANCE QUANTITY	UNIT COST	TOTAL COST
Jan. 1							200	$10.00	$2,000
12	400	$12	$4,800				600	11.33	6,800
16				500	$11.33	$5,665	100	*11.35	1,135
26	300	11	3,300				400	11.09	4,435
29				200	11.09	2,218	200	11.09	2,217
30	100	12	1,200				300	11.39	3,417

*Increase in unit cost due to rounding.

On January 12 the new unit cost of $11.33 was found by dividing $6,800, the total cost, by 600, the number of units on hand. Then on January 16, the balance of $1,135 represented the previous balance of $6,800, less $5,665, the cost assigned to the 500 units issued on this date. New unit costs were calculated on January 26 and 30 when additional units were acquired.

With successive recalculations of cost and the use of such different costs during the period, the cost identified with the ending inventory will differ from that determined when cost is assigned to the ending inventory in terms of average cost for all goods available during the period. A physical inventory and use of the weighted average method resulted in a value for the ending inventory of $3,390; a perpetual inventory and use of the moving average method resulted in a value for the ending inventory of $3,417.

The average cost approach can be supported as realistic and as paralleling the physical flow of goods, particularly where there is an intermingling of identical inventory units. Unlike the other inventory methods, the average approach provides the same cost for similar items of equal utility. The method does not permit profit manipulation. Limitations of the average method are inventory values that perpetually contain some degree of influence of earliest costs and inventory values that may lag significantly behind current prices in periods of rapidly rising or falling prices.

Last-In, First-Out Method

The **last-in, first-out (lifo) method** is based on the assumption that the latest costs of a specific item should be charged to cost of goods sold. Inventories are thus stated at earliest costs. Using the cost data in the preceding section, a physical inventory of 300 units on January 31 would have a cost as follows:

Earliest costs relating to goods, Jan. 1	200 units at $10	$2,000
Next earliest cost, Jan. 12	100 units at 12	1,200
Total	300	$3,200

The ending inventory is recorded at a cost of $3,200 and cost of goods sold is $8,100 ($11,300 − $3,200). Thus, revenue is charged with the most recently incurred costs.

When perpetual inventories are maintained, it is necessary to calculate costs on a last-in, first-out basis using the cost data on the date of each issue as illustrated at the top of the next page.

It should be noted that lifo values obtained under a periodic system will usually differ from those determined on a perpetual basis. In the example, a cost of $3,200 was obtained for the periodic inventory, whereas $3,300 was obtained when costs were calculated as goods were issued. This difference results because it was necessary to "dip into" the beginning inventory layer and charge 100 units of the beginning inventory at $10 to the issue of January 16. The ending inventory thus reflects only 100 units at the beginning unit cost.

These temporary liquidations of inventory frequently occur during the year, especially for companies with seasonal business. These liquidations

COMMODITY: X **(lifo)**

DATE	RECEIVED			ISSUED			BALANCE		
	QUANTITY	UNIT COST	TOTAL COST	QUANTITY	UNIT COST	TOTAL COST	QUANTITY	UNIT COST	TOTAL COST
Jan. 1							200	$10	$2,000
12	400	$12	$4,800				200	10	2,000
							400	12	4,800
16				400	$12	$4,800			
				100	10	1,000	100	10	1,000
26	300	11	3,300				100	10	1,000
							300	11	3,300
29				200	11	2,200	100	10	1,000
							100	11	1,100
30	100	12	1,200				100	10	1,000
							100	11	1,100
							100	12	1,200

cause monthly reports prepared on the lifo basis to be unrealistic and meaningless. Because of this, most companies using lifo maintain their internal records using other inventory methods, such as fifo or weighted average, and adjust the statements to lifo at the end of the year with a lifo allowance account. Companies frequently refer to this account as the **lifo reserve** account. Because the profession has recommended that the word **reserve** not be used for asset valuation accounts, the term allowance is used in this text.

The lifo inventory method was developed in the United States during the late 1930's as a method to permit deferral of illusory inventory profits during periods of rising prices. Petition was made to Congress by companies desiring to use this method, and in 1939 Congress agreed to allow the use of lifo for income tax purposes *if* companies also used the method for financial reporting. This represents one of the few accounting areas in which tax and book accounting must agree.

Because lifo developed primarily as a tax shelter, the Internal Revenue Service controls the method of computing and applying this inventory method. As the IRS changes its rules, book accounting for inventories must also change. This has proven to be a serious disadvantage to the use of lifo.

Specific-Goods Lifo Pools. With large and diversified inventories, application of the lifo procedures to specific goods proved to be extremely burdensome. Because of the complexity and cost involved, companies frequently selected only a few very important inventory items, usually raw materials, for application of the lifo method. As a means of simplifying the valuation process and extending its applicability to more items, an adaptation of lifo applied to specific goods was developed, and approved by the

IRS. This adaptation permitted the establishment of **inventory pools** of substantially identical goods. At the end of a period, the quantity of items in the pool is determined, and costs are assigned to those items. Units equal to the beginning quantity in the pool are assigned the beginning unit costs. If the number of units in ending inventory exceeds the number of beginning units, the additional units are regarded as an incremental **layer** within the pool. The unit cost assigned to the items in the new layer may be based on (1) actual costs of earliest acquisitions within the period (lifo), (2) the weighted average cost of acquisitions within the period, or (3) actual costs of the latest acquisitions within the period (fifo). Increments in subsequent periods form successive inventory layers. A decrease in the number of units in an inventory pool during a period is regarded as a reduction in the most recently added layer, then in successively lower layers, and finally in the original or base quantity. Once a specific layer is reduced or eliminated, it is not restored.

To illustrate the above lifo valuation process, assume there are three inventory pools, and the changes in the pools are as listed below. The inventory calculations that follow the listing are based on the assumption that weighted average costs are used in valuing annual incremental layers.

Inventory pool increments and liquidations:

	Class A Goods	Class B Goods	Class C Goods
Inv., Dec. 31, 1980	3,000 @ $6	3,000 @ $5	2,000 @ $10
Purchases — 1981	3,000 @ $7	2,000 @ $6	3,000 @ $11
	1,000 @ $9		
Total available for sale	7,000	5,000	5,000
Sales — 1981	3,000	1,000	3,500
Inv., Dec. 31, 1981	4,000	4,000	1,500
Purchases — 1982	1,000 @ $8	2,000 @ $6	3,000 @ $11
	3,000 @ $10		
Total available for sale	8,000	6,000	4,500
Sales — 1982	3,500	2,500	2,000
Inv., Dec. 31, 1982	4,500	3,500	2,500

Inventory valuations using specific-goods lifo pools:

	Class A Goods		Class B Goods		Class C Goods	
Inv., Dec. 31, 1980	3,000 @ $6	$18,000	3,000 @ $5	$15,000	2,000 @ $10	$20,000
Inv., Dec. 31, 1981	3,000 @ $6	$18,000	3,000 @ $5	$15,000	1,500 @ $10	$15,000
	1,000 @ $7.50[1]	7,500	1,000 @ $6	6,000		
	4,000	$25,500	4,000	$21,000	1,500	$15,000
Inv., Dec. 31, 1982	3,000 @ $6	$18,000	3,000 @ $5	$15,000	1,500 @ $10	$15,000
	1,000 @ $7.50	7,500	500 @ $6	3,000	1,000 @ $11	11,000
	500 @ $9.50[2]	4,750				
	4,500	$30,250	3,500	$18,000	2,500	$26,000

[1]Cost of units acquired in 1981, $30,000, divided by number of units acquired, 4,000, or $7.50.
[2]Cost of units acquired in 1982, $38,000, divided by number of units acquired, 4,000, or $9.50.

The layer process for lifo inventories may be further illustrated in the following manner:

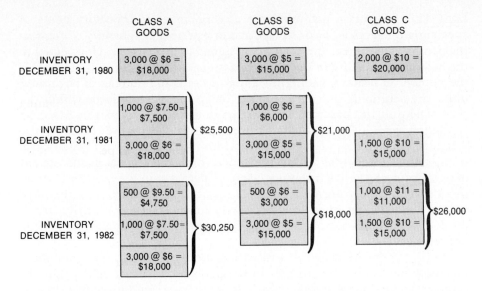

A new layer was added to the inventory of Class A goods each year. Previously established layers were reduced in 1982 for Class B goods and in 1981 for Class C goods.

Dollar-Value Lifo Pools. Even the grouping of substantially identical items into quantity pools does not produce all the benefits desired from the use of the lifo method. Technological changes sometimes introduce new products thus requiring the elimination of inventory in old pools, and requiring the establishment of new pools for the new product that no longer qualifies as being substantially identical. For example, the introduction of synthetic fabrics to replace cotton meant that "cotton" pools were eliminated and new "synthetic fabric" pools established. This change resulted in the loss of lower lifo bases by companies changing the type of fabrics they used. To overcome this type of problem and to further simplify the clerical work involved, the **dollar-value lifo inventory method** was developed. Under this method, the unit of measurement is the dollar rather than the quantity of goods. All similar items, such as all raw materials for a given line of business, are grouped into a pool and layers are determined based upon total dollar changes. The dollar-value method is currently the most widely used adaptation of the lifo concept and is now acceptable for tax purposes.[5] The procedures to apply this adaptation of lifo are discussed in Chapter 9.

COMPARISON OF COST ALLOCATION PROCEDURES

In using the first-in, first-out procedure, inventories are reported on the balance sheet at or near current costs. With last-in, first-out, inventories not

---

[5]Maurice E. Stark, "A Survey of LIFO Inventory Application Techniques," *The Accounting Review* (January, 1978), pp. 182–185.

changing significantly in quantity are reported at more or less fixed amounts relating back to the earliest purchases. Use of the average method generally provides inventory values closely paralleling first-in, first-out values, since purchases during a period are normally several times the opening inventory balance and average costs are thus heavily influenced by current costs. Specific identification can produce any variety of results depending upon the desires of management. When the prices paid for merchandise do not fluctuate significantly, alternative inventory methods may provide only minor differences on the financial statements. However, in periods of steadily rising or falling prices, the alternative methods may produce material differences. Differences in inventory valuations on the balance sheet are accompanied by differences in earnings on the income statement for the period.

Use of first-in, first-out in a period of rising prices matches oldest low-cost inventory with rising sales prices, thus expanding the gross profit margin. In a period of declining prices, oldest high-cost inventory is matched with declining sales prices, thus narrowing the gross profit margin. On the other hand, use of last-in, first-out in a period of rising prices relates current high costs of acquiring goods with rising sales prices, and in a period of falling prices, low costs of acquiring goods with declining sales prices. Average methods that provide inventory costs closely comparable with first-in, first-out costs offer operating results approximating first-in, first-out results.

The application of the different methods, excluding specific identification, in periods of rising and falling prices is illustrated in the following example. Assume that the Welch Sales Co. sells its goods at 50% over prevailing costs from 1979 to 1982. The company sells its inventories and terminates activities at the end of 1982. Sales, costs, and gross profits using each of the three methods are shown in the following tabulation.

	Fifo		Weighted Average[1]			Lifo		
1979:								
Sales, 500 units @ $9		$4,500			$4,500			$4,500
Inventory, 200 units	@ $5 $1,000		200 @ $5	$1,000		200 @ $5	$1,000	
Purchases, 500 units	@ $6 3,000		500 @ $6	3,000		500 @ $6	3,000	
Goods available for sale	$4,000			$4,000			$4,000	
Ending Inv., 200 units	@ $6 1,200		200 @ $5.71 ($4,000 ÷ 700)	1,142		200 @ $5	1,000	
Cost of goods sold		2,800		2,858				3,000
Gross profit on sales		$1,700		$1,642				$1,500
1980:								
Sales, 450 units @ $12		$5,400			$5,400			$5,400
Inventory, 200 units	@ $6 $1,200		200 @ $5.71	$1,142		200 @ $5	$1,000	
Purchases, 500 units	@ $8 4,000		500 @ $8	4,000		500 @ $8	4,000	
Goods available for sale	$5,200			$5,142			$5,000	
Ending Inv., 250 units	@ $8 2,000		250 @ $7.35 ($5,142 ÷ 700)	1,838		200 @ $5} 50 @ $8}	1,400	
Cost of goods sold		3,200		3,304				3,600
Gross Profit on Sales		$2,200		$2,096				$1,800

[1]Totals in the illustration are calculated to the nearest dollar.

	Fifo		Weighted Average		Lifo	

1981:

	Fifo		Weighted Average		Lifo	
Sales, 475 units @ $10.50		$4,988		$4,988		$4,988
Inventory, 250 units	@ $8 $2,000		250 @ $7.35 $1,838		200 @ $5 ⎱ 50 @ $8 ⎰ $1,400	
Purchases, 450 units	@ $7 3,150		450 @ $7 3,150		450 @ $7 3,150	
Goods available for sale	$5,150		$4,988		$4,550	
Ending Inv., 225 units	@ $7 1,575		225 @ $7.13 ($4,988 ÷ 700) 1,604		200 @ $5 ⎱ 25 @ $8 ⎰ 1,200	
Cost of goods sold		3,575		3,384		3,350
Gross profit on sales		$1,413		$1,604		$1,638

1982:

	Fifo		Weighted Average		Lifo	
Sales, 625 units @ $7.50		$4,688		$4,688		$4,688
Inventory, 225 units	@ $7 $1,575		225 @ $7.13 $1,604		200 @ $5 ⎱ 25 @ $8 ⎰ $1,200	
Purchases, 400 units	@ $5 2,000		400 @ $5 2,000		400 @ $5 2,000	
Cost of goods sold		3,575		3,604		3,200
Gross profit on sales		$1,113		$1,084		$1,488

The foregoing transactions are summarized below:

Year	Sales	FIFO Cost of Goods Sold	FIFO Gross Profit on Sales	FIFO Gross Profit % to Sales	WEIGHTED AVERAGE Cost of Goods Sold	WEIGHTED AVERAGE Gross Profit on Sales	WEIGHTED AVERAGE Gross Profit % to Sales	LIFO Cost of Goods Sold	LIFO Gross Profit on Sales	LIFO Gross Profit % to Sales
1979	$ 4,500	$ 2,800	$1,700	37.8%	$ 2,858	$1,642	36.5%	$ 3,000	$1,500	33.3%
1980	5,400	3,200	2,200	40.7	3,304	2,096	38.8	3,600	1,800	33.3
1981	4,988	3,575	1,413	28.3	3,384	1,604	32.2	3,350	1,638	32.8
1982	4,688	3,575	1,113	23.7	3,604	1,084	23.1	3,200	1,488	31.7
	$19,576	$13,150	$6,426	32.8%	$13,150	$6,426	32.8%	$13,150	$6,426	32.8%

Although the different methods give the same total gross profit on sales for the four-year period, use of first-in, first-out resulted in increased gross profit percentages in periods of rising prices and a contraction of gross profit percentages in a period of falling prices, while last-in, first-out resulted in relatively steady gross profit percentages in spite of fluctuating prices. The weighted average method offered results closely comparable to those obtained by first-in, first-out. Assuming operating expenses at 30% of sales, use of last-in, first-out would result in a net income for each of the four years; first-in, first-out would result in larger net incomes in 1979 and 1980, but net losses in 1981 and 1982. Inventory valuation on the last-in, first-out basis tends to smooth the peaks and fill the troughs of business fluctuations.

Income Tax Consequences of Lifo

The above comparison was made without considering the income tax impact of the method used. As indicated earlier, if a company elects to use lifo for tax purposes, it must also use lifo in its financial reporting. In a period of inflation, the lower reported profit using lifo results in lower income taxes. Thus, the tax liability on gross profit, assuming a 45% tax rate, for the three illustrated methods over the four-year period would be as follows:

	Fifo	Weighted Average	Lifo
1979	$ 765	$ 739	$ 675
1980	990	943	810
1981	636	722	737
1982	501	488	670
Total	$2,892	$2,892	$2,892

In this example, a complete cycle of price increases and decreases occurred over the four-year period; thus the total income tax liability for the four years was the same under each method. However, by using lifo to defer part of the tax during 1979 and 1980, more cash was available to the company for operating purposes. In periods of constantly increasing inflation, the deferral tends to become permanent and is a condition sought by many companies. When inflation started to accelerate in the United States in the mid 1970's, many companies began to report larger net incomes primarily caused by the illusory influence of holding gains. To protect their cash flows, a significant number of companies changed to lifo inventory to reduce their present and future tax liabilities. These changes had to be approved by the Internal Revenue Service, and were subject to specific rules governing adoption of the lifo method. The complexity of some of these rules deterred other companies from making the change even though the tax consequences promised to be favorable.

Evaluation of Lifo as a Cost Allocation Method

Because so many companies have resorted to lifo as a means of reducing income and, consequently, their income tax liability, it is important to identify the advantages and disadvantages of this unique inventory method. Because it allocates only the incurred cost between the balance sheet and the income statement, it can only partially account for the effects of inflation.

Major Advantages of Lifo. The advantages of lifo may be summarized as follows:

Tax Benefits. As mentioned earlier, temporary or permanent deferrals of income taxes can be achieved with lifo, resulting in current cash savings. These deferrals continue as long as the price level is increasing and inventory quantities do not decline. The improved cash flow enables a company to either decrease its borrowing and reduce interest cost, or invest the savings to produce revenue.

Better Measurement of Income. Because lifo allocates the most recently incurred costs to cost of sales, this method produces an income figure that tends to report only the operating income and defers recognition of the holding gain until prices or quantities decline. The illusory inflation profits discussed earlier tend not to appear as part of net income when lifo inventory is used.

Major Disadvantages of Lifo. The disadvantages of lifo are more subtle than the advantages. Companies adopting lifo sometimes realize too late that lifo can produce some severe side effects.

Reduced Income. The application of the most recent prices against current revenue produces a decrease in net income in an inflationary period. If management's goal is to maximize reported income, the adoption of lifo will produce results that are in opposition to that goal.

Investors and other users of financial statements frequently base their evaluations of a company's performance on the "bottom line" or net income. Failure on the part of users to recognize that a lower net income is due to the use of lifo rather than a decline in operating proficiency may have a depressing effect on the market price of a company's stock. The reduced income may be perceived as a failure on the part of management. Further, the use of lifo will reduce bonus payments to employees that are based on net income and could reduce the amount of dividends distributed to shareholders.

Unrealistic Inventory Balances on the Balance Sheet. The allocation of older inventory costs to the balance sheet can cause a serious understatement of inventory values. Depending upon the length of time the lifo layers have been developing, and the severity of the price increase, the reported inventory values can be substantially lower than current replacement values. For example, Note 3 to the General Mills statements reproduced in Appendix B states that if the fifo method had been used, inventories would be $46.5 million higher in 1979 than the reported lifo inventory. This is approximately 22% of the lifo valued inventory. Because inventory costs enter into the determination of working capital, the current ratio can be seriously distorted under a lifo inventory system. Although this discussion of lifo assumes an inflationary economy, if prices were to decrease, lifo would produce inventory values higher than current replacement costs. It is fair to assume that should this occur, there would be strong pressure for special action to permit the write-down of inventory balances to replacement cost.

Unanticipated Profits Created by Failing to Maintain Inventory Quantities. The income advantages summarized above will be realized only if inventory quantity levels are maintained. If the ending inventory quantities decline, the layers of cost eliminated are charged against current revenue. If the inventory costs of these layers are significantly less than the current replacement costs, the reported profit will be artificially increased by the failure to maintain inventory levels.

Two specific examples may clarify this weakness.

1. Many companies who rely upon steel as a basic raw material for their production processes use the lifo inventory method. Assume that during an extended

steel strike many manufacturing companies find their steel stock dwindling as their fiscal year-end approaches. Unless they can restock their inventories, they will be forced to match lower inventory costs against current revenue, thus reporting a substantial holding gain in current profit. Assume, for instance, that company sales for the year are $6,000,000 and that the cost of goods sold using current year prices is $5,000,000, but using a mixture of current year and earlier years lower priced lifo layers, the cost of goods sold is $4,000,000. The resulting increase in profit of $1,000,000 is caused solely by the inability of the company to replace its normal stocks.

2. The failure to protect lifo layers may be caused by a timing error in requesting shipments of purchases. Assume that a lumber company normally received its lumber by ship, but that at year-end orders were mishandled and a boat load was not received as planned. The company, in failing to record the boat load of lumber as a current year purchase, would have to apply older lifo costs against sales. The resulting profit could lead to conclusions that would not be justified by the facts.

To avoid the distortion caused by a temporary reduction of lifo layers at the end of a year, some accountants advocate establishing a replacement allowance that charges the current period for the extra replacement cost expected to be incurred in the subsequent period when the inventory is replenished. However, the use of an allowance for temporary liquidation of lifo layers, sometimes referred to as the **base-stock method**, is not currently acceptable for financial reporting or tax purposes. The use of this type of allowance on the books could disqualify a company from filing its tax returns on the lifo basis, and therefore, it is seldom used in practice.

Unrealistic Flow Assumptions. The cost assignment resulting from the application of lifo does not normally approximate the physical movement of goods through the business. One would seldom encounter in practice the actual use or transfer of goods on a last-in, first-out basis.

Artificial Adjustments for Inflation. Although lifo comes the closest of the four cost allocation methods discussed to recognizing the impact of inflation on inventories, it fails to recognize the full impact. As discussed earlier, a full recognition of the effects of inflation on inventory would require a balance sheet valuation at current cost, as well as the use of current replacement cost as the cost of each sale. If the last purchase of inventory was made before a significant price rise, lifo would still fail to properly match current cost and current income. Only a replacement cost or a next-in, first-u t system would fully reflect the effects of inflation on the income statement.

OTHER COST PROCEDURES

The methods previously described for arriving at inventory cost are the ones most widely used. Several other procedures are sometimes encountered and deserve mention.

Cost of Latest Purchases

Sometimes goods are valued at cost of the latest purchase regardless of quantities on hand. When the inventory consists largely of recent purchases, this method may give results closely approximating those obtained through specific cost identification or first-in, first-out procedures with considerably less work. However, when the quantities of goods on hand are significantly in excess of the latest quantities purchased and major price changes have taken place, use of latest costs may result in significant cost misstatement.

Standard Costs

Manufacturing inventories are frequently reported at **standard costs** — predetermined costs based upon representative or normal conditions of efficiency and volume of operations. Differences between actual costs and standard costs for materials, labor, and factory overhead result in **standard cost variances** indicating favorable and unfavorable operational or cost experiences. Excessive materials usage, inefficient labor application, excessive spoilage, and idle time, for example, produce unfavorable variances, and these would be separately summarized in variance accounts.

Standard costs are developed from a variety of sources. Past manufacturing experiences may be carefully analyzed; time and motion studies, as well as job and process studies, may be undertaken; data from industry and economy-wide sources may be consulted. Standards should be reviewed at frequent intervals to determine whether they continue to offer reliable cost criteria. Changing conditions require adjustment in the standards, so that at the balance sheet date, standard costs will reasonably approximate costs computed under one of the recognized costing methods.

Direct Costing

A practice widely debated for many years is referred to as **direct costing, marginal costing**, or **variable costing**. Inventories under direct costing are assigned only the variable costs incurred in production — direct materials, direct labor, and the variable components of factory overhead. Fixed costs are treated as periodic charges and assigned to current revenue. Only costs directly related to output are assigned to goods and charged to the period in which the goods are sold; costs that are a function of time and that are continuing regardless of the volume of output — for example, supervisory salaries, depreciation, and property tax — are charged against revenue of the period in which they are incurred.

These differences are illustrated by the information given at the top of the next page.

With conventional **full costing** applied to inventories, a high gross profit may emerge in a period of high production even though sales are declining. With direct costing, cost of goods sold varies directly with sales and a high gross profit emerges in a period of high sales; changes in the volume of

	Full Costing		Direct Costing	
Sales..		$200,000		$200,000
Variable cost of goods sold	$110,000		$110,000	
Fixed cost of goods sold	55,000		62,500	
Total cost of goods sold		165,000		172,500
Gross profit..		$ 35,000		$ 27,500
Inventory value:				
Variable costs..		$ 15,000		$ 15,000
Fixed costs...		7,500		——
Total cost of inventory..........................		$ 22,500		$ 15,000

production have no effect upon gross profit. For example, assume in the illustration above that, although sales remained the same, production had been greater and as a result the ending inventory was double the amount shown. Variable costs identified with the inventory would amount to $30,000. Under full costing, a different allocation of fixed costs would be appropriate. Assuming that $12,500 in fixed costs is allocated to the inventory reducing the fixed costs assigned to operations by $5,000, the gross profit would increase to $40,000. Under direct costing, the gross profit would remain unchanged at $27,500.

Support for direct costing is made on the grounds that it provides more meaningful and useful data to management than full costing. Direct costing enables management to appraise the effects of sales fluctuations on net income. Sales, current and potential, can be evaluated in terms of out-of-pocket costs to achieve such sales. The direct costing approach becomes a valuable tool for planning and control and is used by management to analyze cost, price, and volume relationships.

Although no objection can be raised to the use of direct costing when it is used for internal reporting and as a means for assisting management in decision-making, objection can be raised to the extension of direct costing procedures to the annual financial statements. In measuring financial position and the results of operations, inventories must carry their full costs including a satisfactory allocation of the fixed overhead costs. Fixed costs, no less than variable costs, are incurred in contemplation of future benefits and should be matched against the revenues ultimately produced through such efforts. When inventories are valued by direct costing procedures for internal reporting, they should be restated in terms of full costing whenever financial statements are to be prepared.

SELECTION OF AN INVENTORY METHOD

As indicated in this chapter, companies have many alternative ways to value inventories. Guidelines for the selection of a proper method are very broad, and a company may justify almost any accepted method. After a lengthy study of inventory practices, Horace Barden, retired partner of Ernst and Whinney, concluded his Research Study by stating:

> . . . one must recognize that no neat package of principles or other criteria exists to substitute for the professional judgment of the responsible accoun-

tant. The need for the exercise of judgment in accounting for inventories is so great that I recommend to authoritative bodies that they refrain from establishing rules that, in isolation from the conditions and circumstances that may exist in practice, attempt to determine the accounting treatment to be applied under any and all circumstances.[6]

Many companies use more than one method. For example, General Mills values its grain and flour inventories at market, some domestic inventories at lifo, and other inventories at the lower of fifo cost and market.[7] The decision as to which method to use depends not only upon the tax consequences, but also the nature of the inventories themselves. Except for lifo, a company may use a different inventory method for tax purposes than it uses for reporting purposes.

As indicated earlier in this chapter, companies sometimes change their inventory methods, especially as economic conditions change. When inventories are a material item, a change in the inventory method by a company may impair comparability of that company's financial statements with prior years' statements and with the financial statements of other entities. Such changes require careful consideration and should be made only when management can clearly demonstrate the preferability of the alternative method. This position was emphasized by the Accounting Principles Board in Opinion No. 20 with the statement, "The burden of justifying other changes rests with the entity proposing the change."[8] If a change is made, complete disclosure of the impact of the change is encouraged by the FASB.

If the lifo method is used, practice includes disclosure of the inventory value as if fifo had been used. General Mills' statements referred to earlier illustrate this disclosure. The impact of the inventory difference on net income cannot be specifically reported because of Internal Revenue Service restrictions designed to prevent the implication in the statements that the lifo income is not the preferred one. This restriction makes it somewhat difficult for financial statement readers to make the conversion necessary to compare the statements of different reporting entities.

EFFECTS OF ERRORS IN RECORDING INVENTORY POSITION

Failures to report the inventory position accurately result in misstatements on both the balance sheet and the income statement. The effect on the income statement is sometimes difficult to evaluate because of the different amounts which can be affected by an error. Analysis of the impact is aided by recalling the structure of the cost of goods sold section of the income statement:

---

[6]Barden, *op. cit.*, p. 141.

[7]See Appendix B, Note 1C and Note 3.

[8]*Opinions of the Accounting Principles Board, No. 20*, "Accounting Changes" (New York: American Institute of Certified Public Accountants, 1971), par. 16.

Beginning Inventory

+

Purchases

=

Goods Available for Sale

−

Ending Inventory

=

Cost of Goods Sold

An overstatement of the beginning inventory will thus result in an overstatement of goods available for sale and cost of goods sold. Because the cost of goods sold is deducted from sales to determine the gross profit, the overstated cost of goods sold results in an understated gross profit and finally an understated net income. Sometimes an error may affect two of the above amounts in such a way that they offset each other. For example, if a purchase in transit under the fifo method is not recorded as a purchase *or* included in the ending inventory, the understatement of purchases results in an understatement of goods available for sale; however, the understatement of ending inventory subtracted from goods available for sale offsets the error and creates a correct cost of goods sold, gross profit, and net income. Inventory and accounts payable, however, will be understated on the balance sheet.

Because the ending inventory of one period becomes the beginning inventory of the next period, undetected accounting errors affect two accounting periods. If left undetected, the errors will offset each other under a fifo or average method. Errors in lifo layers may, however, perpetuate themselves until the layer is eliminated.

This type of analysis is required for all inventory errors. It is unwise to try to memorize the impact an error has on the income statement. It is preferable to analyze each situation as illustrated. The following analyses of four typical inventory errors, with their impact on both the current and succeeding years, provides additional opportunity for students to practice the above type of analysis.

1. Overstatement of the ending inventory through errors in the count of goods on hand, pricing, or the inclusion in inventory of goods not owned or goods already sold:

    Current year:
    Income statement — overstatement of the ending inventory will cause the cost of goods sold to be understated and the net income to be overstated.
    Balance sheet — the inventory will be overstated and the owners' equity will be overstated.
    Succeeding year:
    Income statement — overstatement of the beginning inventory will cause

the cost of goods sold to be overstated and the net income to be understated.

Balance sheet — the error of the previous year will have been counter-balanced on the succeeding income statement and the balance sheet will be correctly stated.

2. Understatement of ending inventory through errors in the count of goods on hand, pricing, or the failure to include in inventory goods purchased or goods transferred but not yet sold:

    Misstatements indicated in (1) above are reversed.

3. Overstatement of ending inventory accompanied by failure to recognize sales and corresponding receivables at end of period:

    Current year:

    Income statement — sales are understated by the sales price of the goods and cost of goods sold is understated by the cost of the goods relating to the sales; gross profit and net income are thus understated by the gross profit on the sales.

    Balance sheet — receivables are understated by the sales price of the goods and the inventory is overstated by the cost of the goods that were sold; current assets and owners' equity are thus understated by the gross profit on the sales.

    Succeeding year:

    Income statement — sales of the preceding year are recognized in this year in sales and cost of sales; gross profit and net income, therefore, are overstated by the gross profit on such sales.

    Balance sheet — the error of the previous year is counterbalanced on the succeeding income statement and the balance sheet will be correctly stated.

4. Understatement of ending inventory accompanied by failure to recognize purchases and corresponding payables at end of period:

    Current year:

    Income statement — purchases are understated, but this is counterbalanced by the understatement of the ending inventory; gross profit and net income are correctly stated as a result of the counterbalancing effect of the error.

    Balance sheet — although owners' equity is reported correctly, both current assets and current liabilities are understated.

    Succeeding year:

    Income statement — the beginning inventory is understated, but this is counterbalanced by an overstatement of purchases, as purchases at the end of the prior year are recognized currently; gross profit and net income are correctly stated as a result of the counterbalancing effect of the error.

    Balance sheet — the error of the previous year no longer affects balance sheet data.

This analysis can be summarized in tabular form as follows. (+) indicates overstatement, (−) indicates understatement, and (0) indicates no effect.

The correcting entry for each of these errors depends upon when the error is discovered. If it is discovered in the current year, adjustments can be made to current accounts, and the reported net income and balance sheet amounts will be correct. If the error is not discovered until the subsequent period, the correcting entry qualifies as a prior period adjustment if the net

	Current year						Subsequent year					
	Assets	Liabil-ities	Equity	Sales	Cost of goods sold	Net income	Assets	Liabil-ities	Equity	Sales	Cost of goods sold	Net income
Overstatement of ending inventory	+	0	+	0	−	+	0	0	0	0	+	−
Understatement of ending inventory	−	0	−	0	+	−	0	0	0	0	−	+
Overstatement of ending inventory and understatement of sales	−	0	−	−	−	−	0	0	0	+	+	+
Understatement of ending inventory and understatement of purchases	−	−	0	0	0	0	0	0	0	0	0	0

Summary of Impact of Inventory Errors on Financial Statements

income of the prior period was misstated. The error to the prior years' income is corrected through retained earnings. To illustrate these entries, assume that error number three above has occurred. The correcting entries required, depending upon when the error is discovered, would be as follows. Assume the use of a perpetual inventory system.

Error discovered in current year (Cost of inventory $1,000; sales price of inventory, $1,500).

Accounts Receivable	1,500	
Cost of Goods Sold	1,000	
Inventory		1,000
Sales		1,500

Error discovered in subsequent year (sale has been recorded in subsequent year).

Sales	1,500	
Cost of Goods Sold		1,000
Retained Earnings		500

If trend statistics are included in the annual reports, prior years' balances should be adjusted to reflect the correction of the error. Present-day audit techniques can substantially reduce the probability of material inventory errors.

QUESTIONS

1. (a) Distinguish between holding gains and operating profit. (b) Are holding gains really "gains"? Explain.

2. (a) What are the three cost elements entering into goods in process and finished goods?

(b) What items enter into factory overhead?

(c) Define fixed overhead, variable overhead, and semivariable or mixed overhead and give an example of each.

3. Distinguish between raw materials and factory supplies. Why are the terms direct materials and indirect materials often used to refer to raw materials and factory supplies, respectively?

4. What are the advantages of using the perpetual inventory system as compared with the periodic system?

5. Does the adoption of a perpetual inventory system eliminate the need for a physical count or measurement of inventories? Explain.

6. Under what normal conditions is merchandise in transit reported as inventory by the (a) seller? (b) buyer?

7. Under what conditions would an accounting failure to recognize incoming merchandise in transit that was shipped FOB shipping point have no effect on the income statement?

8. The Miller Company has followed the practice of recording all goods shipped on consignment as current period sales and has not carried consigned goods as inventory. Under what conditions would this practice have no effect on income?

9. How should the following items be treated in computing year-end inventory costs: (a) segregated goods? (b) conditional sales?

10. State how you would report each of the following items on the financial statements:

(a) Manufacturing supplies.

(b) Goods on hand received on a consignment basis.

(c) Materials of a customer held for processing.

(d) Goods received without an accompanying invoice.

(e) Goods in stock to be delivered to customers in subsequent periods.

(f) Goods in hands of agents and consignees.

(g) Deposits with vendors for merchandise to be delivered next period.

(h) Goods in hands of customers on approval.

(i) Defective goods requiring reprocessing.

11. (a) What types of expenditures are included in inventory costs? (b) What distinguishes a cost that is treated as a period cost from one included in inventory?

12. (a) What are the two methods of accounting for cash discounts? (b) Which method is generally preferred? Why?

13. Describe and explain the year-end adjustments necessary under the net method of accounting for cash discounts assuming: (a) The discount period has not elapsed and it is assumed that the invoice will be paid before the period expires. (b) The discount period has elapsed.

14. Theoretically, there is little wrong with inventory costing by the specific cost identification method. What objections can be raised to the use of this method?

15. What is meant by inventory layers? Why are they significant with respect to the fifo and lifo methods?

16. In recent years, some companies have changed from fifo to lifo for computing their inventory values. What effect does a change from fifo to lifo during an inflationary period have on net earnings and working capital? Explain.

17. Discuss the advantages and disadvantages of lifo as a cost allocation method.

18. As stated in the text, lifo can only partially account for the effects of inventory inflation. Explain this statement. (Include in your explanation the concept of incurred costs.)

19. (a) What type of company is likely to use standard costs? (b) What precautions are necessary in the use of standard costs?

20. What effect would each of the following situations have upon the current year's net income for a company manufacturing a single product if it used direct costing to value its ending inventory rather than full costing? Assume fixed costs are the same for each year.

(a) Quantity of items produced and sold are the same for the year.

(b) Quantity of items produced exceeds the quantity sold.

(c) Quantity of items sold exceeds the quantity produced.

21. State the effect of each of the following errors made by Cole, Inc., upon the balance sheet and the income statement (1) of the current period and (2) of the succeeding period:

(a) The company fails to record a sale of merchandise on account; goods sold are excluded in recording the ending inventory.

(b) The company fails to record a sale of merchandise on account; the goods sold are included, however, in recording the ending inventory.

(c) The company fails to record a purchase of merchandise on account; goods purchased are included in recording the ending inventory.

(d) The company fails to record a purchase of merchandise on account; goods purchased are not recognized in recording the ending inventory.

(e) The ending inventory is understated as the result of a miscount of goods on hand.

EXERCISES

exercise 8-1

J & D Lawn Products purchased a large piece of machinery for $15,000. The machine was placed in inventory awaiting sale. Prior to resale, the cost of similar equipment had increased by 10%. J & D sells all inventory at 50% over the cost necessary to replace the inventory.

(1) Determine the gross profit on the sale of the machine.

(2) Break the gross profit from part (1) into (a) the holding gain and (b) the operating profit.

(3) What argument might be made for presenting the two components of gross profit separately in the financial statements?

exercise 8-2

The management of Ledbetter Company has engaged you to assist in the preparation of year-end (December 31) financial statements. You are told that on November 30, the correct inventory level was 120,000 units. During the month of December sales totaled 50,000 units including 25,000 units shipped on consignment to Farnsworth Company. A letter received from Farnsworth indicates that as of December 31, they had sold 10,000 units and were still trying to sell the remainder. A review of the December purchase orders, to various suppliers, shows the following:

Date of Purchase Order	Invoice Date	Quantity in Units	Date Shipped	Date Received	Terms
12-2-81	1-3-82	10,000	1-2-82	1-3-82	FOB shipping point
12-11-81	1-3-82	8,000	12-22-81	12-24-81	FOB destination
12-13-81	1-2-82	13,000	12-28-81	1-2-82	FOB shipping point
12-23-81	12-26-81	12,000	1-2-82	1-3-82	FOB shipping point
12-28-81	1-10-82	10,000	12-31-81	1-5-82	FOB shipping point
12-31-81	1-10-82	15,000	1-3-82	1-6-82	FOB destination

Ledbetter Company uses the "passing of legal title" for inventory recognition. Compute the number of units which should be included in the year-end inventory.

exercise 8-3

The Carol Manufacturing Company reviewed its in-transit inventory and found the following items. Indicate which items should be included in the inventory balance at December 31, 1981. Give your reasons for the treatment you suggest.

(a) Merchandise costing $2,350 was received on January 3, 1982, and the related purchase invoice was recorded January 5. The invoice showed the shipment was made on December 29, 1981, FOB destination.

(b) Merchandise costing $625 was received on December 28, 1981, and the invoice was not recorded. The invoice was in the hands of the purchasing agent; it was marked "on consignment."

(c) A packing case containing a product costing $816 was standing in the shipping room when the physical inventory was taken. It was not included in the inventory because it was marked "Hold for shipping instructions." The customer's order was dated December 18, but the case was shipped and the customer billed on January 10, 1982.

(d) Merchandise received on January 6, 1982, costing $720 was entered in the purchase register on January 7. The invoice showed shipment was made FOB shipping point on December 31, 1981. Since it was not on hand during the inventory count, it was not included.

(e) A special machine, fabricated to order for a particular customer, was finished and in the shipping room on December 30. The customer was billed on that date and the machine was excluded from inventory although it was shipped January 4, 1982. (AICPA adapted)

exercise 8-4

Taylor Carpet Service regularly buys merchandise from Mountain Suppliers and is allowed a trade discount of 10/20/5 from the list price. Taylor uses the net method to record purchases and discounts. On August 15, Taylor Carpet purchased material from Mountain Suppliers. The invoice, received by Taylor, showed a list price of $2,500, and terms of 2/10, n/30. Payment was sent to Mountain Suppliers on August 28. Prepare the journal entries to record the purchase and subsequent payment.

exercise 8-5

On December 3, Thomas Photo purchased inventory listed at $8,550 from Ewing Photo. Terms of the purchase were 2/10, n/20. Thomas Photo also purchased inventory from Terry Wholesale on December 10, for a list price of $7,450. Terms of this purchase were 2/10 eom. On December 16, Thomas paid both suppliers for these purchases.

(1) Give the entries to record the purchases and invoice payments assuming that (a) the net method is used, (b) the gross method is used.

(2) Assume that Thomas had not paid either of the invoices at December 31. Give the year-end adjusting entries, if the net method is being used. Also assume that Thomas plans to pay Terry Wholesale within the discount period.

exercise 8-6

The Hansen Store shows the following information relating to Product A:

Inventory, January 1	300 units @ $17.50
Purchases, January 10	900 units @ $18.00
Purchases, January 20	1200 units @ $18.25
Sales, January 8	150 units
Sales, January 18	600 units
Sales, January 25	1000 units

What are the values of ending inventory under (1) perpetual and (2) periodic methods assuming the cost flows below? (Carry your unit costs to four places and round to three.)

(a) Fifo
(b) Lifo
(c) Average

exercise 8-7

Rushforth Farm Supply's records for the first three months of its existence show purchases of Commodity A as follows:

	Number of units	Cost
August	5,500	$29,975
September	8,000	41,600
October	4,370	24,035

The inventory at the end of October of Commodity A using fifo is valued at $33,811. Assuming that none of Commodity A was sold during August and September, what value would be shown at the end of October if a lifo cost flow was assumed?

exercise 8-8

The following data are for Product 102, stocked by the Merrill Company.

Date		Units	Unit Cost	Unit Sales Price
July 1	Balance..........	150	$6.50	
July 3	Purchase........	250	6.20	
July 11	Sale	120		$10.00
July 12	Sale	100		10.20
July 15	Purchase........	110	6.70	
July 21	Purchase........	70	6.80	
July 22	Sale	95		10.15
July 28	Sale	105		10.25
July 30	Purchase........	100	6.67	

Using the appropriate average costing method compute (1) cost of goods sold and (2) ending inventory value for the month of July under the following assumptions. (Carry unit costs to four places and round to three. Round totals to nearest dollar.)

(a) Periodic inventory method is used by the Merrill Company.
(b) Perpetual inventory method is used by the Merrill Company.

exercise 8-9

Flex Corporation had the following transactions relating to Product 500 during September.

Date		Units	Unit Cost
September 1	Balance on hand	500 units	$5.00
September 6	Purchase	100 units	4.50
September 12	Sale.............................	300 units	
September 13	Sale.............................	200 units	
September 18	Purchase	200 units	6.00
September 20	Purchase	300 units	4.00
September 25	Sale.............................	200 units	

Determine the ending inventory value under each of the following costing methods:

(1) Fifo (perpetual)
(2) Fifo (periodic)
(3) Lifo (perpetual)
(4) Lifo (periodic)

exercise 8-10

A flood recently destroyed many of the financial records of Hymas Manufacturing Company. Management has hired you to re-create as much financial information as possible for the month of October. You are able to find out that the company uses a weighted average inventory costing system. You also learn that Hymas makes a physical count at the end of each month in order to determine monthly ending inventory values. By examining various documents you are able to gather the following information:

Ending inventory at October 31	50,000 units
Total cost of units available for sale in October..........................	$118,800
Cost of goods sold during October	$ 99,000
Cost of beginning inventory, October 1	35¢ per unit
Gross margin on sales for October...	$101,000

October Purchases

Date	Units	Unit Cost
October 4	60,000	$0.40
October 11	50,000	0.41
October 15	40,000	0.42
October 16	50,000	0.45

You are asked to provide the following information:

(1) Number of units on hand, October 1.
(2) Units sold during October.
(3) Unit cost of inventory at October 31.
(4) Value of inventory at October 31.

exercise 8-11

The Lopez Company sells Product A. During a move to a new location, the inventory records for Product A were misplaced. The bookkeeper has been able to gather some information from the sales records, and gives you the data shown below:

July sales: 53,500 units at $10.00
July purchases:

Date	Quantity	Unit Price
July 5	10,000	$6.50
July 9	12,500	6.25
July 12	15,000	6.00
July 25	14,000	6.20

On July 31, 18,000 units were on hand with a total value of $110,800. Lopez has always used a periodic fifo inventory costing system. Gross profit on sales for July was $205,875. Reconstruct the beginning inventory (quantity and dollar value) for the month of July.

exercise 8-12

Calder Lumber Company uses a periodic lifo method for inventory costing. The following information relates to the plywood inventory carried by Calder Lumber.

Plywood Inventory

	Quantity	Lifo Costing Layers
May 1	500 Sheets	300 Sheets at $ 8.00
		125 Sheets at 11.00
		75 Sheets at 13.00

Plywood Purchases

May 8	115 Sheets at $14.00
May 17	95 Sheets at $15.00
May 29	200 Sheets at $13.00

All sales of plywood during May were at $20 per sheet. On May 31, there were 310 sheets of plywood in the storeroom.

(1) Compute the gross profit on sales for May, as a dollar value and as a percent of sales.
(2) Assume that because of a lumber strike, Calder Lumber is not able to purchase the May 29 order of lumber until June 10. If sales remained the same, recompute the gross profit on sales for May, as a dollar value and as a percent of sales.
(3) Compare the results of part (1) and part (2) and explain the difference.

exercise 8-13

First-in, first-out has been used for inventory valuation by the Harper Co. since it was organized in 1978. Using the data that follow, redetermine the net incomes for each year on the assumption of inventory valuation on the last-in, first-out basis:

	1978	1979	1980	1981
Reported net income	$ 15,500	$ 30,000	$ 34,250	$ 44,000
Reported ending inventories — fifo basis	61,500	102,000	126,000	130,000
Inventories — lifo basis	59,000	75,100	95,000	105,000

exercise 8-14

Parson Battery Company began operations on January 1, 1981. Sales for 1981 amounted to $500,000 (50,000 batteries). Because of an expected increase in demand during the coming year, production was increased and 80,000 units were manufactured during 1981. Variable costs for 1981 were $6.00 per battery. Depreciation, salaries, and other fixed factory overhead costs totaled $87,488 for the year.

Determine (1) the gross profit on sales, and (2) the value of remaining inventory (as of December 31) under:

      (a) the full costing method,
      (b) the direct costing method.

exercise 8-15

The following data relate to the Pratt Company's first three years of operations.

	1979	1980	1981
Net income under fifo	$20,000	$30,000	$12,000
Net income under lifo	15,000	17,000	13,000
Ending inventory under fifo	70,000	76,000	70,000

Compute the ending inventory under lifo for each year.

exercise 8-16

Annual income for the Robinson Co. for the period 1977–1981 appears below. However, a review of the records for the company reveals inventory misstatements as listed. Calculate corrected net income for each year.

	1977	1978	1979	1980	1981
Reported net income (loss)	$18,000	$20,000	$2,000	$(7,500)	$16,000
Inventory overstatement, end of year	2,500		2,800		1,600
Inventory understatement, end of year				4,000	

exercise 8-17

The Penner Corporation has been experiencing fluctuating profits over the past several years. Management is concerned and is wondering if the reason for the wide variation could be the company's use of fifo for inventory costing. The gross profit in 1979, 1980, and 1981, was $48,000, $16,000, and $39,000 respectively. An analysis of the past few years shows the following values for the ending inventory under two different costing assumptions.

	Ending inventory under:	
	Fifo	Lifo
December 31, 1978	$16,000	$16,000
December 31, 1979	24,000	14,000
December 31, 1980	62,400	72,500
December 31, 1981	41,000	46,400

Management is wondering if changing to a lifo inventory costing method would stabilize profits. Compute the gross profit for (1) 1979, (2) 1980, and (3) 1981, assuming that lifo had been used for inventory control.

exercise 8-18

The Evans Company reported income before taxes of $105,000 for 1979, and $120,000 for 1980. A later audit produced the following information:

      (a) The ending inventory for 1979 included 200 units erroneously priced at $5.90 per unit. The correct cost was $9.50 per unit.

(b) Merchandise costing $1,800 was shipped to the Evans Company, FOB shipping point, on December 26, 1979. The purchase was recorded in 1979, but the merchandise was excluded from the ending inventory since it was not received until January 4, 1980.

(c) On December 28, 1979, merchandise costing $1,200 was sold to Cole Paint Shop. Cole had asked Evans to keep the merchandise for him until January 2, when he would come and pick it up. Because the merchandise was still in the store at year-end, the merchandise was included in the inventory count. The sale was correctly recorded in December 1979.

(d) Holt Company sold merchandise costing $1,500 to Evans Company. The purchase was made on December 29, 1979, and the merchandise was shipped on December 30. Terms were FOB shipping point. Because the Evans Co. bookkeeper was on vacation, neither the purchase nor the receipt of goods was recorded on the books until January 1980.

Assuming all amounts are material and a physical count is taken every December 31,

(1) Compute the corrected income before taxes for each year.
(2) By what amount did the total net income change for the two years combined?
(3) Assume all errors were found in January 1981, before the books were closed for 1980; what journal entry would be made?

PROBLEMS

problem 8-1

The Ashbury Corporation uses Material 100 in a manufacturing process. Information as to balances on hand, purchases, and requisitions of Material 100 are given in the following table:

	Quantities			
Date	Received	Issued	Balance	Unit Price of Purchase
January 8	—	—	200	$1.55
January 29	200	—	400	1.70
February 8	—	80	320	—
March 20	—	160	160	—
July 10	150	—	310	1.75
August 18	—	110	200	—
September 6	—	110	90	—
November 14	200	—	290	2.00
December 29	—	110	180	—

Instructions: What is the closing inventory under each of the following pricing methods? (Carry unit costs to four places and round.)

(1) Perpetual fifo
(2) Periodic fifo
(3) Perpetual lifo

(4) Periodic lifo
(5) Moving average
(6) Weighted average

problem 8-2

Records of the Murray Sales Co. show the following data relative to Product A:

March 2 Inventory...........325 units at $25.50	March 3 Sales ....300 units at $37.50
6 Purchase...........300 units at 26.00	20 Sales ....200 units at 35.70
13 Purchase...........350 units at 27.00	28 Sales ....125 units at 36.00
25 Purchase........... 50 units at 27.50	

Instructions: Calculate the inventory balance and the gross profit on sales for the month on each of the following bases:
  (1) First-in, first-out. Perpetual inventories are maintained and costs are charged out currently.
  (2) First-in, first-out. No book inventory is maintained.
  (3) Last-in, first-out. Perpetual inventories are maintained and costs are charged out currently.
  (4) Last-in, first-out. No book inventory is maintained.
  (5) Moving average. Perpetual inventories are maintained and costs are charged out currently. (Carry calculations to four places and round to three.)
  (6) Weighted average. No book inventory is maintained.

problem 8-3

The Lay Manufacturing Co. was organized in 1979 to produce a single product. The company's production and sales records for the period 1979–1981 are summarized below:

	Units Produced		Sales	
	No. of Units	Production Costs	No. of Units	Sales Revenue
1979...........................	320,000	$144,000	200,000	$160,500
1980...........................	310,000	161,200	290,000	230,000
1981...........................	270,000	156,600	260,000	210,300

Instructions: Calculate the gross profit for each of the three years assuming that inventory values are calculated in terms of:
  (1) Last-in, first-out. (Average cost used for incremental layers.)
  (2) First-in, first-out.

problem 8-4

The Fellner Company sells three different products. Five years ago management adopted the lifo inventory method and established three specific pools of goods. Fellner values all incremental layers of inventory at the average cost of purchases within the period. Information relating to the three products for the first quarter of 1981 is given below.

	Product 102	Product 103	Product 104
Purchases:			
January...	1,000 @ $12.00	500 @ $25	5,000 @ $5.30
February...	1,500 @ $12.50	250 @ $26	4,850 @ $5.38
March	1,200 @ $12.25	——	3,500 @ $5.42
First quarter sales (units)	2,850	825	10,750
January 1, 1981 inventory	950 @ $11.50	155 @ $24	3,760 @ $5.00

Instructions: Compute the ending inventory value for the first quarter of 1981. (Round unit inventory values to the nearest cent and final inventory values to the nearest dollar.)

problem 8-5

The Bramble Products Company's inventory record appears below:

	Purchases		Sales
	Quantity	Unit Cost	Quantity
1979..	9,000	$5.60	6,500
1980..	9,500	5.75	10,000
1981..	7,200	5.78	5,000

The company uses a lifo cost flow assumption. It reported ending inventories as follows:

1979..	$14,000
1980..	11,600
1981..	24,410

Instructions: Determine if the Bramble Products Company has reported their inventory correctly. Assuming that 1981 accounts are not yet closed, make any necessary correcting entries.

problem 8-6

A portion of the Mower's Company balance sheet appears below:

	December 31, 1981	December 31, 1980
Assets:		
Cash	$353,300	$ 50,000
Notes receivable	–0–	25,000
Inventory	To be determined	199,875
Liabilities:		
Accounts payable	To be determined	$ 50,000

Mower Company pays for all operating expenses with cash, and purchases all inventory on credit. During 1981, cash totaling $471,700 was paid on accounts payable. Operating expenses for 1981 totaled $200,000. All sales are cash sales. The inventory was restocked by purchasing 1,500 units per month, and valued by using periodic fifo. The unit cost of inventory was $32.60 during January 1981 and increased $.10 per month during the year. All sales are made for $50 per unit. The ending inventory for 1980 was valued at $32.50 per unit.

Instructions:

(1) Compute the number of units sold during 1981.
(2) Compute the December 31, 1981 accounts payable balance.
(3) Compute the beginning inventory quantity.
(4) Compute the ending inventory quantity and value.
(5) Prepare an income statement for 1981 (including a detailed cost of goods sold section). Ignore income tax.

problem 8-7

The Weimer Corporation sells household appliances and uses lifo for inventory costing. The inventory contains ten different products, and historical lifo layers are maintained for each of them. The lifo layers for one of their products, Wonder Blender, were as follows at December 31, 1981:

1980 layer	4,000 @ $100
1975 layer	3,500 @ $ 85
1971 layer	1,000 @ $ 75
1969 layer	3,000 @ $ 52

Instructions:

(1) What was the value of the ending inventory of Wonder Blenders at December 31, 1981?
(2) How did the December 31, 1981 quantity of blenders compare with the December 31, 1980 quantity of blenders?
(3) What was the value of the ending inventory of Wonder Blenders at December 31, 1982, assuming that there were 10,500 blenders on hand?
(4) How would income in part (3) be affected if, in addition to the quantity on hand, 1,250 blenders were in transit to Weimer Corporation at December 31, 1982? The shipment was made on December 26, 1982, terms FOB shipping point. Total invoice cost was $131,250.

problem 8-8

The Wallace Corporation has adjusted and closed its books at the end of 1981. The company arrives at its inventory position by a physical count taken on December 31 of each year. In March of 1982, the following errors were discovered during an audit of the company's books.

(a) Merchandise which cost $2,500 was sold for $3,200 on December 29, 1981. The order was shipped December 31, 1981, with terms of FOB shipping point. The merchandise was not included in the ending inventory. The sale was recorded on January 12, 1982, when the customer made payment on the sale.

(b) On January 3, 1982, Wallace Corporation received merchandise which had been shipped to them on December 30, 1981. The terms of the purchase were FOB shipping point. Cost of the merchandise was $1,750. The purchase was recorded and the goods included in the inventory when payment was made in January of 1982.

(c) On January 8, 1982, merchandise which had been included in the ending inventory was returned to Wallace because the consignee had not been able to sell it. The cost of this merchandise was $1,200 with a selling price of $1,800.

(d) Merchandise costing $950, located in a separate warehouse, was overlooked and excluded from the 1981 inventory count.

(e) On December 26, 1981, Wallace Corporation purchased merchandise from a supplier costing $1,175. The order was shipped December 28 (terms FOB destination) and was still "in-transit" on December 31. Since the invoice was received on December 31, the purchase was recorded in 1981. The merchandise was not included in the inventory count.

(f) The corporation failed to make an entry for a purchase on account of $835 at the end of 1981, although it included this merchandise in the inventory count. The purchase was recorded when payment was made to the supplier in 1982.

(g) The corporation included in its 1981 ending inventory, merchandise with a cost of $1,290. This merchandise had been custom-built and was being held until the customer could come and pick up the merchandise. The sale, for $1,425, was recorded in 1982.

Instructions: Give the entry required in 1982 to correct each error. Assume that the errors were made during 1981 and all amounts are material.

problem 8-9

The Jennings Corporation adjusted and closed its books on December 31, 1981. Net income of $52,000 was reported for the year. Several months later, the independent auditors discovered the following material errors. Jennings used a periodic inventory method.

(a) 3,000 units of Product A, costing $8.95, were recorded at a unit cost of $8.59 in summarizing the ending inventory.

(b) A sale of merchandise shipped on January 3, 1982, was included in the ending inventory count. The cost of this merchandise was $4,750, and the sale was properly recorded at $5,950 on December 31, 1981.

(c) Merchandise costing $5,550 was included in the inventory although it was shipped to a customer on December 31, 1981, with terms of FOB shipping point. The corporation recorded the sale ($7,400) on January 3, 1982.

(d) Merchandise in the storeroom on December 31 (costing $1,500) was included in the 1981 ending inventory although the purchase invoice was not received or recorded until January 5, 1982.

(e) Merchandise in the hands of a consignee, costing $4,000, was included in the inventory; however, $2,400 of the merchandise had been sold as of December 31. The sale was not recorded until January 31, 1982, when the consignee made a full remittance of $3,200 on the merchandise sold.

(f) On December 31, 1981, a purchase of merchandise costing $2,500 was still in a delivery truck parked in the corporation's receiving dock. Because of the rush at year-end, the truck had not been unloaded. The terms of the purchase were FOB destination. The merchandise was not included in the ending inventory, but the purchase was recorded in the books in 1981.

Instructions:

(1) Compute the corrected net income for 1981.

(2) Give the entries that are required in 1982 to correct the accounts.

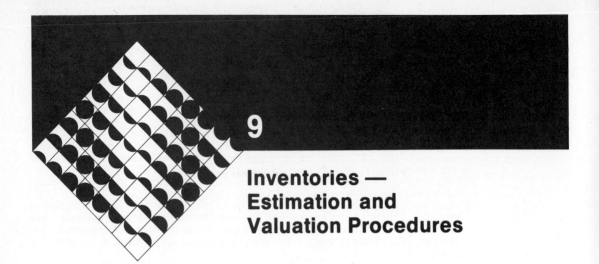

9

Inventories — Estimation and Valuation Procedures

CHAPTER OBJECTIVES

Explain and illustrate the use of estimating techniques in determining inventory quantities and costs.

Identify and describe alternatives to cost as a basis for valuing inventories.

Describe and illustrate currently accepted accounting procedures for recognizing declines in the value of goods on hand.

Describe and illustrate the presentation of inventories on the balance sheet and the required disclosure of supplemental information.

The basic concepts and methods of inventory cost allocation were presented in Chapter 8. Some specialized cost methods and departures from valuation at cost are discussed in Chapter 9.

GROSS PROFIT METHOD

Estimates are frequently employed in developing inventory quantities and costs. The **gross profit method** of estimation is based on an assumed relationship between gross profit and sales. A gross profit percentage is applied to sales to determine cost of goods sold; cost of goods sold is subtracted from the cost of goods available for sale to arrive at an estimated inventory balance.

234

The gross profit method is useful when:

1. A periodic system is in use and inventories are required for interim statements, or for the determination of the week-to-week or month-to-month inventory position, and the cost of taking physical inventories would be excessive for such purposes.
2. An inventory has been destroyed or lost by fire, theft, or other casualty, and the specific data required for its valuation are not available.
3. It is desired to test or check the validity of inventory figures determined by other means. Such application is referred to as the **gross profit test**.

The gross profit percentage used must be a reliable measure of current experience. In developing a reliable rate, reference is made to past rates and these are adjusted for variations considered to exist currently. Past gross profit rates, for example, may require adjustment when inventories are valued at last-in, first-out, and significant fluctuations in inventory position and/or prices have occurred. Current changes in cost-price relationships or in the sales mix of specific products also create a need for modifying past rates.

The calculation of cost of goods sold depends upon whether the gross profit percentage is developed and stated in terms of sales or in terms of cost. The procedures to be followed in each case are illustrated below.

Example 1 — Gross profit as a percentage of sales. Assume sales are $100,000 and goods are sold at a gross profit of 40% of sales.

If gross profit is 40% of sales, then cost of goods sold must be 60% of sales:

Sales	100%		Sales	100%
Cost of goods sold	?	=	Cost of goods sold	60%
Gross profit	40%		Gross profit	40%

Cost of goods sold, then, is 60% of $100,000, or $60,000. Goods available for sale less the estimated cost of goods sold gives the estimated cost of the remaining inventory. Assuming the cost of goods available for sale is $85,000, this balance less the estimated cost of goods sold, $60,000, gives an estimated inventory of $25,000.

Example 2 — Gross profit as a percentage of cost. Assume sales are $100,000 and goods are sold at a gross profit that is 60% of their cost.

If sales are made at a gross profit of 60% of cost, then sales must be equal to the sum of cost, considered 100%, and the gross profit on cost, 60%. Sales, then, are 160% of cost:

Sales	?		Sales	160%
Cost of goods sold	100%	=	Cost of goods sold	100%
Gross profit	60%		Gross profit	60%

To find cost, or 100%, sales may be divided by 160 and multiplied by 100, or sales may simply be divided by 1.60. Cost of goods sold, then, is $100,000 ÷ 1.60 = $62,500. This amount is subtracted from the cost of goods available for sale to determine the estimated inventory.

When various lines of merchandise are sold at different gross profit rates, it may be possible to develop a reliable inventory value only by making separate calculations for each line. Under such circumstances, it is necessary to develop summaries of sales, goods available for sale, and gross profit data for the different merchandise lines.

Use of Gross Profit Method for Interim Inventory Calculations

The gross profit method can be employed to provide management with information not otherwise available when a periodic inventory system is used. For example, assume that inventory values are needed to compute the merchandise turnover for a business whose gross profit calculation for the year is as follows:

Sales..		$500,000
Cost of goods sold:		
Merchandise inventory, January 1	$ 20,000	
Purchases..	310,000	
Merchandise available for sale..	$330,000	
Merchandise inventory, December 31	30,000	
Cost of goods sold		300,000
Gross profit on sales..		$200,000

If only these data are available, the average inventory is $25,000, the sum of the beginning and ending balances divided by 2. Using this inventory, the merchandise turnover, the number of times the average inventory has been replenished during the year, is 12 times, calculated as follows:

$$\frac{\text{Cost of goods sold}}{\text{Average inventory (using year-end balances)}} = \frac{\$300,000}{\$25,000} = 12$$

A more representative average inventory to use for computing turnover can be obtained by analyzing sales and purchases and computing estimated monthly inventories by the gross profit method. These computations are given below.

	A Purchases	B Sales	Cost of Goods Sold			
			C Cost as a Percentage of Sales	D Cost of Goods Sold (B × C)	E Inventory Increase or (Decrease) (A − D)	F Inventory (F + E)
January 1						$ 20,000
January	$ 20,000	$ 30,000	60%	$ 18,000	$ 2,000	22,000
February	20,000	30,000	60	18,000	2,000	24,000
March	20,000	30,000	60	18,000	2,000	26,000
April	20,000	30,000	60	18,000	2,000	28,000
May	30,000	40,000	60	24,000	6,000	34,000
June	30,000	40,000	60	24,000	6,000	40,000
July	30,000	60,000	60	36,000	(6,000)	34,000
August	30,000	40,000	60	24,000	6,000	40,000
September	40,000	40,000	60	24,000	16,000	56,000
October	40,000	50,000	60	30,000	10,000	66,000
November	20,000	50,000	60	30,000	(10,000)	56,000
December	10,000	60,000	60	36,000	(26,000)	30,000
	$310,000	$500,000	60%	$300,000	$ 10,000	$476,000

The average inventory can now be calculated from the monthly inventory balances and the merchandise turnover determined as follows:

$$\frac{\text{Total of inventories}}{\text{Number of inventories}} = \frac{\$476,000}{13} = \$36,615$$

$$\frac{\text{Cost of goods sold}}{\text{Average inventory (using monthly balances)}} = \frac{\$300,000}{\$36,615} = 8.2$$

This figure is more accurate than the one developed on the basis of the year-end inventories which were unrepresentative of the inventory activity during the year.

Use of the gross profit method to estimate inventories on a monthly, weekly, or other basis can also (1) serve as a control measure to avoid overstocking or shortages of goods and (2) provide information for the preparation of interim financial statements.

Use of Gross Profit Method for Computation of Casualty Loss

A common application of the gross profit method is the estimation of inventory when a physical count is impossible due to the loss or destruction of goods. For example, assume that on October 31, 1981, a fire in the warehouse of a wholesale distributing company totally destroyed the contents, including many accounting records. Remaining records indicated that the last physical inventory was taken on December 31, 1980, and that the inventory at that date was $329,500. Microfilm bank records of canceled checks disclosed that during 1981 payments to suppliers for inventory items were $1,015,000. Unpaid invoices at the beginning of 1981 amounted to $260,000, and communication with suppliers indicated a balance due at the time of the fire of $315,000. Bank deposits for the ten months amounted to $1,605,000. All deposits came from customers for merchandise purchased except for a loan of $100,000 obtained from the bank during the year. Accounts receivable at the beginning of the year were $328,000, and an analysis of the available records indicated that accounts receivable on October 31 totaled $275,000. Gross profit percentages on sales for the preceding four years were:

1977	28%	1979	23%
1978	25%	1980	24%

From these facts, the inventory in the warehouse at the time of the fire could be estimated as follows:

Estimate of sales January 1 to October 31, 1981	
Collection of accounts receivable ($1,605,000 − $100,000)....	$1,505,000
Add accounts receivable at October 31, 1981	275,000
	$1,780,000
Deduct accounts receivable at January 1, 1981	328,000
Estimate of sales January 1 to October 31, 1981......................	$1,452,000
Average gross profit percentage on sales for past 4 years......	25%
Average cost percentage on sales for past 4 years.................	75%
Estimate of cost of goods sold to October 31, 1981 ($1,452,000 × 75%)...	$1,089,000

Estimate of inventory on October 31, 1981

Merchandise inventory January 1, 1981...................................		$ 329,500
Add: Payments to suppliers — 1981	$1,015,000	
Amounts payable to suppliers, October 31, 1981	315,000	
	$1,330,000	
Deduct accounts payable to suppliers, January 1, 1981	260,000	
Estimate of purchases January 1 to October 31, 1981		1,070,000
Merchandise available for sale...		$1,399,500
Estimate of cost of goods sold for 1981 (from page 237)		1,089,000
Estimated merchandise inventory, October 31, 1981..............		$ 310,500

RETAIL INVENTORY METHOD

The **retail inventory method** is widely employed by retail concerns, particularly department stores, to arrive at reliable estimates of inventory position whenever desired. This method, like the gross profit method, permits the calculation of an inventory amount without the time and expense of taking a physical inventory or maintaining a detailed perpetual inventory record for each of the thousands of items normally included in a retail inventory. When this method is used, records of goods purchased are maintained at two amounts — cost and retail. A **cost percentage** is computed by dividing the goods available for sale at cost by the goods available for sale at retail. This cost percentage can then be applied to the ending inventory at retail, an amount that can be readily calculated by subtracting sales for the period from the total goods available for sale at retail.

The computation of a retail inventory at the end of a month is illustrated by the following example:

	Cost	Retail
Merchandise inventory, January 1	$30,000	$45,000
Purchases in January	20,000	35,000
Merchandise available for sale..	$50,000	$80,000
Cost percentage ($50,000 ÷ $80,000) = 62.5%		
Deduct sales for January..		25,000
Merchandise inventory, January 31, at retail...................................		$55,000
Merchandise inventory, January 31, at estimated cost ($55,000 × 62.5%)...	$34,375	

The effect of the above procedure is to provide an inventory valuation in terms of average cost. No cost sequence, such as lifo or fifo, is recognized; the percentage of cost to retail for the ending inventory is the same as the percentage of cost to retail for goods sold.

Use of the retail inventory method offers the following advantages:

1. Estimated interim inventories can be obtained without a physical count.
2. When a physical inventory is actually taken for periodic statement purposes, it can be taken at retail and then converted to cost without reference to individual costs and invoices, thus saving time and expense.
3. Shoplifting losses can be determined and monitored. Since physical counts of inventory should agree with the calculated retail inventory, any difference

not accounted for by clerical errors in the company records must be attributable to actual physical loss by shoplifting or employee theft.

Although this method permits the estimation of a value for inventory,
errors can occur in accounting for the dual prices and in applying the retail
method. Thus, a physical count of the inventory to be reported on the annual financial statements is generally required at least once a year. Retail
inventory records should be adjusted for variations shown by the physical
count so that records reflect the actual status of the inventory for purposes
of future estimates and control.

The accounting entries for the retail inventory method are similar to
those made using a periodic inventory system. The retail figures are part of
the analysis necessary to compute the cost of the inventory; however, they
do not actually appear in the accounts. Thus, the following entries would
be made to record the inventory data included in the example on page 238.

Purchases	20,000	
Accounts Payable		20,000
Accounts Receivable	25,000	
Sales		25,000
Income Summary	30,000	
Inventory		30,000
To close the beginning inventory.		
Inventory	34,375	
Income Summary		34,375
To record the ending inventory.		

After closing out the above nominal accounts, the income summary account has a balance of $9,375. This is the gross profit on sales that would
be reported on the income statement.

Markups and Markdowns

In the earlier inventory calculations, it was assumed that there were no
changes in retail prices after the goods were originally recorded. Frequently, however, retail prices do change because of changes in the price
level, shifts in consumer demand, or other factors. The terms listed below
are used in discussing the retail method:

1. **Original retail** — the initial sales price, including the original increase over
   cost referred to as the **markon** or **initial markup**.
2. **Additional markups** — increases that raise sales prices above original retail.
3. **Markup cancellations** — decreases in additional markups that do not reduce
   sales prices below original retail.
4. **Net markups** — Additional markups less markup cancellations
5. **Markdowns** — decreases that reduce sales prices below original retail.
6. **Markdown cancellations** — decreases in the markdowns that do not raise the
   sales prices above original retail.
7. **Net markdowns** — markdowns less markdown cancellations

The difference between cost and actual selling price as adjusted for the
described changes is referred to as the **maintained markup**.

To illustrate the use of these terms, assume that goods originally placed
for sale are marked at 50% above cost. Merchandise costing $4 a unit, then,

is marked at $6, which is the **original retail**. The **initial markup** of $2 is referred to as a "50% markup on cost" or a "33⅓% markup on sales price." In anticipation of a heavy demand for the article, the retail price is subsequently increased to $7.50. This represents an **additional markup** of $1.50. At a later date the price is reduced to $7. This is a **markup cancellation** of 50 cents and not a markdown since the retail price has not been reduced below the original sales price. But assume that goods originally marked to sell at $6 are subsequently marked down to $5. This represents a **markdown** of $1. At a later date the goods are marked to sell at $5.25. This is a **markdown cancellation** of 25 cents and not a markup, since sales price does not exceed the original retail.

Retail inventory results will vary depending upon whether net markdowns are used in computing the cost percentage. When applying the most commonly used retail method, net markups are added to goods available for sale at retail before calculating the cost percentage; net markdowns, however, are not deducted in arriving at the percentage. This method is sometimes referred to as the **conventional retail inventory method**. It results in a lower cost percentage and correspondingly a lower inventory amount and a higher cost of goods sold than would be obtained if net markdowns were deducted before calculating the cost percentage. This can be illustrated as follows:

Net markdowns not deducted to calculate cost percentage (Conventional retail):

	Cost	Retail
Beginning inventory	$ 8,600	$ 14,000
Purchases	72,100	110,000
Additional markups		13,000
Markup cancellations		(2,500)
Goods available for sale	$80,700	$134,500
Cost percentage ($80,700 ÷ $134,500) = 60%		
Deduct: Sales		$108,000
Markdowns		4,800
Markdown cancellations		(800)
		$112,000
Ending inventory at retail		$ 22,500
Ending inventory at estimated cost ($22,500 × 60%)	$13,500	

Net markdowns deducted to calculate cost percentage:

	Cost	Retail
Beginning inventory	$ 8,600	$ 14,000
Purchases	72,100	110,000
Net markups		10,500
Net markdowns		(4,000)
Goods available for sale	$80,700	$130,500
Cost percentage ($80,700 ÷ $130,500) = 61.84%		
Deduct sales		108,000
Ending inventory at retail		$ 22,500
Ending inventory at estimated cost ($22,500 × 61.84%)	$13,914	

The lower inventory obtained with the conventional method approximates a **lower of average cost or market** valuation. The lower of cost or market concept, discussed in detail later in this chapter, requires recognition of declines in the value of inventory in the period such declines occur. Under the conventional retail method, markdowns are viewed as indicating a decline in the value of inventory and are deducted as a current cost of sales. When markdowns are included in the cost percentage computation, the result is an average cost allocated proportionately between cost of sales and ending inventory. Thus, only a portion of the decline in value is charged in the current period. The remainder is carried forward in ending inventory to be charged against future sales.

Markdowns may be made for special sales or clearance purposes, or they may be made as a result of market fluctuations and a decline in the replacement cost of goods. In either case their omission in calculating the cost percentage is necessary in order to value the inventory at the lower of cost or market. This is illustrated in the two examples below:

Example 1 — Markdowns for special sales purposes. Assume that merchandise costing $50,000 is marked to sell for $100,000. To dispose of part of the goods immediately, one fourth of the stock is marked down $5,000 and is sold. The cost of the ending inventory is calculated as follows:

	Cost	Retail
Purchases	$50,000	$100,000
Cost percentage (50,000 ÷ $100,000) = 50%		
Deduct: Sales..		$ 20,000
Markdowns..		5,000
		$ 25,000
Ending inventory at retail		$ 75,000
Ending inventory at estimated cost ($75,000 × 50%)...............	$37,500	

If cost, $50,000, had been related to sales price after markdowns, $95,000, a cost percentage of 52.6% would have been obtained, and the inventory, which is three fourths of the merchandise originally acquired, would have been reported at 52.6% of $75,000, or $39,450. The inventory would thus be stated above the $37,500 cost of the remaining inventory and cost of goods sold would be understated by $1,950. A markdown relating to goods no longer on hand would have been recognized in the development of a cost percentage to be applied to the inventory. Reductions in the goods available at sales prices resulting from shortages or damaged goods should likewise be disregarded in calculating the cost percentage.

Example 2 — Markdowns as a result of market declines. Assume that merchandise costing $50,000 is marked to sell for $100,000. With a drop in replacement cost of merchandise to $40,000, sales prices are marked down to $80,000. Three fourths of the merchandise is sold. The cost of the ending inventory is calculated as follows:

	Cost	Retail
Purchases	$50,000	$100,000
Cost percentage ($50,000 ÷ $100,000) = 50%		
Deduct: Sales...		$ 60,000
Markdowns		20,000
		$ 80,000
Ending inventory at retail		$ 20,000
Ending inventory at estimated cost ($20,000 × 50%)...............	$10,000	

If cost, $50,000, had been related to sales price after markdowns, $80,000, a cost percentage of 62.5% would have been obtained and the inventory would have been reported at 62.5% of $20,000, or $12,500. The use of the 50% cost percentage in the example reduces the inventory to $10,000, a balance providing the usual gross profit in subsequent periods if current prices and relationships between cost and retail prices prevail.

Freight, Discounts, Returns, and Allowances

In calculating the cost percentage, freight in should be added to the cost of the purchase; purchase discounts and returns and allowances should be deducted. A purchase return affects both the cost and the retail computations, while a purchase allowance affects only the cost total unless a change in retail price is made as a result of the allowance. Sales returns are proper adjustments to gross sales since the inventory is returned; however, sales discounts and sales allowances are not deducted to determine the estimated ending retail inventory. The deduction is not made because the sales price of an item is added into the computation of the retail inventory when it is purchased and deducted when it is sold, all at the gross sales price. Subsequent price adjustments included in the computation would leave a balance in the inventory account with no inventory on hand to represent it. For example, assume the sales price for 100 units of Product A is $5,000. When these units are sold for $5,000, the retail inventory balance would be zero. Subsequently, if an allowance of $100 is granted to the customer, the allowance would not be included in the computation of the month-end retail inventory balance. It would be recorded on the books, however, in the usual manner: debit Sales Allowances and credit Accounts Receivable.

Limitations of Retail Method

The calculation of a cost percentage for all goods carried is valid only when goods on hand can be regarded as representative of the total goods handled. Varying markon percentages and sales of high- and low-margin items in proportions that differ from purchases will require separate records and the development of separate cost percentages for different classes of goods. For example, assume that a store operates three departments and that for July the following information pertains to these departments:

	Department A		Department B		Department C		Total	
	Cost	*Retail*	*Cost*	*Retail*	*Cost*	*Retail*	*Cost*	*Retail*
Beginning inventory	$20,000	$ 28,000	$10,000	$15,000	$16,000	$ 40,000	$ 46,000	$ 83,000
Net purchases	57,000	82,000	20,000	35,000	20,000	60,000	97,000	177,000
Goods available for sale..	$77,000	$110,000	$30,000	$50,000	$36,000	$100,000	$143,000	$260,000
Cost percentage..............		70%		60%		36%		55%
Sales...............................		80,000		30,000		40,000		150,000
Inventory at retail		$ 30,000		$20,000		$ 60,000		$110,000
Inventory at cost..............		$ 21,000		$12,000		$ 21,600		$ 60,500

$54,600

Because of the range in cost percentages from 36% to 70% and the difference in mix of the purchases and ending inventory, the ending inventory balance, using an overall cost percentage, is $5,900 higher ($60,500 − $54,600), than when the departmental rates are used. When material variations exist in the cost percentages by departments, separate departmental rates should be computed and applied.

The retail method is acceptable for income tax purposes, provided the taxpayer maintains adequate and satisfactory records supporting inventory calculations and applies the method consistently on successive tax returns.

DOLLAR-VALUE LIFO METHOD

The concept of dollar-value lifo pools was introduced in Chapter 8 on page 212. The **dollar-value method** of applying lifo has become the most popular of the lifo methods.[1] The greatest flexibility in using lifo is available under this method, and it can apply to almost any kind of inventory.

The income tax regulations specify that a taxpayer may ordinarily use only the **double extension method** for computing the base-year and the current-year cost of a dollar-value inventory pool. This method requires extending all items in the ending inventory at *both* the base-year prices *and* the end-of-year prices. The beginning inventory at base-year prices is then compared with the ending inventory at base-year prices to determine whether an increase or decrease in base-year prices has occurred. If a decrease has occurred, a reduction is required in the most recent layers equal to the base-year decrease. If an increase has occurred, a new layer is created.

In many cases it is impractical to double-extend all items because of the large number of items involved or because of changing products due to technological or other changes. In these situations, the taxpayer may use an **index method** for computing all or a part of the base-year values of the inventories. One method of arriving at an index is to double-extend a representative sample of the ending inventory and compute from this an index between the base-year and current-year prices. A modification of the **double-extension index**, known as the **link-chain index method**, is also ac-

---

[1] In a study made in 1975 of companies using lifo inventory, 76% reported use of the dollar-value method. See Maurice E. Stark, "A Survey of LIFO Inventory Application Techniques," *The Accounting Review* (January 1978), pp. 182–185.

cepted. In some limited situations, the regulations permit the use of published price indexes that show price movements for a specific type of business. In this chapter, the index method is used to illustrate dollar-value lifo procedures.

General Procedures — Dollar-Value Lifo

All goods in the inventory or in the separate pools to which dollar-value lifo is to be applied are viewed as though they were identical items. Physical inventories are valued in terms of current replacement prices. Beginning and ending inventory values are then converted by means of appropriate price indexes to base-year prices, i.e., price levels existing at the time the lifo method was adopted. The difference between the converted beginning and ending dollar balances is a measure of the inventory **quantity change** for the year. An inventory increase is recognized as an inventory layer to be added to the beginning inventory, and such increase is converted to current prices and added to the dollars identified with the beginning balance.

As discussed in Chapter 8, the Internal Revenue Service allows the incremental lifo layer to be valued using fifo, average, or lifo costing. Thus, the index used to convert the new layer may be (1) the year-end index as representative of the most recent purchases, (2) an average index, or (3) an index representing purchases at the beginning of the year. The examples in this chapter will assume conversion of the incremental layers on a fifo basis, i.e., at year-end prices. A strict lifo system in an inflationary economy, however, would convert the added layer at beginning-of-year prices to obtain maximum benefits from using the lifo method to account for inventory inflation.

An inventory decrease is recognized as a shrinkage to be applied to the most recent or top layer and to successively lower layers of the beginning inventory. This decrease is converted at the price indexes applying to such layers and subtracted from the dollars identified with the beginning inventory. The example on page 245 illustrates dollar-value lifo calculations. The index numbers and inventories at end-of-year prices are as follows:

Date	Price Index[1]	Inventory at End-of-Year Prices
December 31, 1977	1.00	$38,000
December 31, 1978	1.20	54,000
December 31, 1979	1.32	66,000
December 31, 1980	1.40	56,000
December 31, 1981	1.25	55,000

[1]Many published indexes appear as percentages without decimals, e.g., 100, 120, 132, 140, 125.

This example can also be illustrated by highlighting the layers as shown. The amount of each layer is determined by multiplying the amounts in the corner boxes. The amount in the upper left-hand box is the cost of the layer expressed in base-year dollars; the amount in the upper right hand box is the price index for the layer year.

Date	Inventory at End-of-Year Prices		Year-end Index		Inventory at Base-Year Prices	Layers in Base-Year Prices		Incremental Layer Conversion Index		Dollar-Value Lifo Cost
December 31, 1977	$38,000	÷	1.00	=	$38,000	$38,000	×	1.00	=	$38,000
December 31, 1978	$54,000	÷	1.20	=	$45,000	$38,000	×	1.00	=	$38,000
						7,000	×	1.20	=	8,400
						$45,000				$46,400
December 31, 1979	$66,000	÷	1.32	=	$50,000	$38,000	×	1.00	=	$38,000
						7,000	×	1.20	=	8,400
						5,000	×	1.32	=	6,600
						$50,000				$53,000
December 31, 1980	$56,000	÷	1.40	=	$40,000	$38,000	×	1.00	=	$38,000
						2,000	×	1.20	=	2,400
						$40,000				$40,400
December 31, 1981	$55,000	÷	1.25	=	$44,000	$38,000	×	1.00	=	$38,000
						2,000	×	1.20	=	2,400
						4,000	×	1.25	=	5,000
						$44,000				$45,400

1977	1978	1979	1980	1981
$38,000	$46,400	$53,000	$40,400	$45,400

The following items should be observed in the example:

December 31, 1978 — With an ending inventory of $45,000 in terms of base prices, the inventory has increased in 1978 by $7,000; however, the $7,000 increase is stated in terms of the pricing when lifo was adopted and needs to be restated in terms of 1978 year-end prices which are 120% of the base level.

December 31, 1979 — With an ending inventory of $50,000 in terms of base prices, the inventory has increased in 1979 by another $5,000; however, the $5,000 increase is stated in terms of the pricing when lifo was adopted and needs to be restated in terms of 1979 year-end costs which are 132% of the base level.

December 31, 1980 — When the ending inventory of $40,000 (expressed in base-year dollars) is compared to the beginning inventory of $50,000 (also expressed in base-year dollars), it is apparent that the inventory has been decreased by $10,000, in base-year terms. Under lifo procedures, the decrease is assumed to take place in the most recently added layers, reducing or eliminating them. As a result, the 1979 layer, priced at $5,000 in base-year terms, is completely eliminated, and $5,000 of the $7,000 layer from 1978 is eliminated. This leaves only $2,000 of the 1978 layer, plus the base-year amount. The remaining $2,000 of the 1978 layer is multiplied by 1.20 to restate it to 1978 dollars, and is added to the base-year amount to arrive at the ending inventory amount of $40,400.

December 31, 1981 — The ending inventory of $44,000 in terms of the base prices indicates an inventory increase for 1981 of $4,000; this increase requires restatement in terms of 1981 year-end prices which are 125% of the base level.

In some cases, the index for the first year of the lifo layers is not 1.00. This is especially true when an externally generated index is used. When this occurs, it is simpler to convert all inventories to a base of 1.00 rather than to use the index for the initial year of the lifo layers. The computations are done in the same manner as in the previous example except the inventory is stated in terms of the base year of the index, not the first year of the inventory layers. To illustrate, assume the same facts as stated for the example on page 244 except that the base year of the external index is 1974; in 1977, the index is 1.20; and, in 1978, it is 1.44. The schedule showing the lifo inventory computations would be modified as follows for the first two years. Note that the inventory cost is the same under either situation.

Date	Inventory at End-of-Year Prices		Year-End Index		Inventory at Base = 1.00 (1974 Prices)	Layers in Base = 1.00 (1974 Prices)		Incremental Layer Conversion Index		Dollar-Value Lifo Cost
December 31, 1977	$38,000	÷	1.20	=	$31,667	$31,667	×	1.20	=	$38,000
December 31, 1978	$54,000	÷	1.44	=	$37,500	$31,667	×	1.20	=	$38,000
						5,833	×	1.44	=	8,400
						$37,500				$46,400

INVENTORY VALUATIONS AT OTHER THAN COST

The basic cost procedures for determining inventory values have been discussed in this and the previous chapter. In some cases, generally accepted accounting principles permit deviations from cost, especially if a write-down of inventory values is warranted. The remainder of this chapter discusses some of these departures from historical cost and the circumstances under which they are appropriate.

Inventory Valuation at Lower of Cost or Market

As discussed in the preceding chapter, the accounting profession has not permitted the recognition of unrealized holding gains on inventories, i.e., goods on hand cannot be "written up" to reflect price-level increases prior to sale. Conversely, however, the recognition of unrealized losses is required under generally accepted accounting principles. This is a reflection of the long-standing and often debated tradition of conservatism in asset valuation and income recognition.

Recognition of a decline in the value of inventory as a loss in the period in which the decline occurs is referred to as **valuation at cost or market, whichever is lower,** or simply **valuation at the lower of cost or market.** The AICPA sanctioned this departure from cost in the following statement:

A departure from the cost basis of pricing the inventory is required when the utility of the goods is no longer as great as its cost. Where there is evidence that the utility of goods, in their disposal in the ordinary course of business, will be less than cost, whether due to physical deterioration, obsolescence, changes in price levels, or other causes, the difference should be recognized as a loss of the current period. This is generally accomplished by stating such goods at a lower level commonly designated as market.[2]

In applying the lower of cost or market method, the cost of the ending inventory, as determined under an appropriate cost allocation method, is compared with market value at the end of the period. If market is less than cost, an adjusting entry is made to record the loss and restate ending inventory at the lower value. It should be noted that no adjustment to lifo cost is permitted for tax purposes; thus, lower of cost or market is not acceptable when cost is computed on a lifo basis.

Definition of Market. Market in "lower of cost or market" is interpreted as replacement cost with upper and lower limits which reflect estimated realizable values. This concept of market was stated by the American Institute of Certified Public Accountants as follows:

> As used in the phrase *lower of cost or market*, the term *market* means current replacement cost (by purchase or by reproduction, as the case may be) except that:
> (1) Market should not exceed the net realizable value (i.e., estimated selling price in the ordinary course of business less reasonably predictable costs of completion and disposal); and
> (2) Market should not be less than net realizable value reduced by an allowance for an approximately normal profit margin.[3]

Replacement cost, sometimes referred to as **entry cost**, includes the purchase price of the product or raw materials plus all other costs incurred in the acquisition or manufacture of goods. Because wholesale and retail prices are generally related, declines in entry costs usually indicate declines in selling prices or **exit values**. However, exit values do not always respond immediately and in proportion to changes in entry costs. If selling price does not decline, there is no loss in utility and a write-down of inventory values would not be warranted. On the other hand, selling prices may decline in response to factors unrelated to replacement costs. Perhaps an inventory item has been used as a demonstrator which reduces its marketability as a new product. Or perhaps an item is damaged in storage or becomes shopworn from excessive handling.

The AICPA definition considers exit values as well as entry costs by establishing a ceiling for the market value at sales price less costs of completion and disposal and a floor for market at sales price less both the costs of completion and disposal and the normal profit margin. The ceiling limitation is applied so the inventory is not valued at more than its net realiz-

---

[2]*Accounting Research and Terminology Bulletins — Final Edition*, "No. 43, Restatement and Revision of Accounting Research Bulletins" (New York: American Institute of Certified Public Accountants, 1961), Ch. 4, statement 5.

[3]*Ibid.*, statement 6.

able value. Failure to observe this limitation would result in charges to future revenue that exceed the utility carried forward and an ultimate loss on the sale of the inventory. The floor limitation is applied so the inventory is not valued at less than its net realizable value minus a normal profit. The concept of normal profit is a difficult one to measure objectively. Profits vary by item and over time. Records are seldom accurate enough to determine a normal profit by individual inventory item. Despite these difficulties, however, the use of a floor prevents a definition of market that would result in a write-down of inventory values in one period to create an abnormally high profit in future periods.

To illustrate, assume that a certain commodity sells for one dollar; selling expenses are twenty cents; the normal profit is 25% or twenty-five cents. The lower of cost or market as modified by the AICPA is developed in each case as shown in the illustration below.

Case	Cost	Market				Lower of Cost or Market
		Replacement Cost	Floor (Estimated sales price less selling expenses and normal profit)	Ceiling (Estimated sales price less selling expenses)	Market (Limited by floor and ceiling values)	
A	$.65	$ .70	$.55	$.80	$.70	$.65
B	.65	.60	.55	.80	.60	.60
C	.65	.50	.55	.80	.55	.55
D	.50	.45	.55	.80	.55	.50
E	.75	.85	.55	.80	.80	.75
F	.90	1.00	.55	.80	.80	.80

A: Market is not limited by floor or ceiling; cost is less than market.
B: Market is not limited by floor or ceiling; market is less than cost.
C: Market is limited to floor; market is less than cost.
D: Market is limited to floor; cost is less than market.
E: Market is limited to ceiling; cost is less than market.
F: Market is limited to ceiling; market is less than cost.

The dollar line below graphically illustrates the floor and ceiling range. B and A replacement costs clearly are within bounds and therefore are defined as market. D and C are below the floor and thus the market is the floor; E and F are above the ceiling and market therefore is the ceiling.

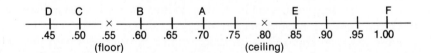

The market value is always the middle value of three amounts; replacement cost, floor, and ceiling.

Applying Lower of Cost or Market Method. The lower of cost or market method may be applied to each inventory item, to the major classes or categories of inventory items, or to the inventory as a whole. Application of this procedure to the individual inventory items will result in the lowest inventory value. However, application to inventory groups or to the inventory as a whole may provide a more representative valuation with considerably less effort. For example, assume that balanced stocks of raw materials are on hand, some have declined in value and others have gone up. When raw materials are used as components of a single finished product, a loss in the value of certain materials may be considered to be counterbalanced by the gains that are found in other materials, and the lower of cost or market applied to this category as a whole may provide an adequate measure of the utility of the goods.

The illustration below shows the valuation procedure applied to (1) individual inventory items, (2) independent classes of the inventory, and (3) inventory as a whole.

	Quantities	Unit Cost	Market	Total Cost	Total Market	Cost or Market, Whichever is Lower (1) If Applied to Individual Inventory Items	Cost or Market, Whichever is Lower (2) If Applied to Inventory Classes	Cost or Market, Whichever is Lower (3) If Applied to Inventory as a Whole
Material A............................	4,000	$1.20	$1.10	$ 4,800	$ 4,400	$ 4,400		
Material B............................	5,000	.50	.40	2,500	2,000	2,000		
Material C............................	2,000	1.00	1.10	2,000	2,200	2,000		
Total raw materials...........				$ 9,300	$ 8,600		$ 8,600	
Goods in Process D..........	10,000	1.60	1.40	$16,000	$14,000	14,000		
Goods in Process E..........	12,000	1.00	1.20	12,000	14,400	12,000		
Total goods in process......				$28,000	$28,400		28,000	
Finished Goods F	3,000	2.00	1.70	$ 6,000	$ 5,100	5,100		
Finished Goods G.............	2,000	1.50	1.60	3,000	3,200	3,000		
Total finished goods..........				$ 9,000	$ 8,300		8,300	
				$46,300	$45,300			$45,300
Inventory valuation...........						$42,500	$44,900	$45,300

In valuing manufacturing inventories, raw materials declines are applicable to the raw materials inventory and also to raw materials costs in goods in process and finished goods inventories. Declines in direct labor and factory overhead costs also affect the values of goods in process and finished goods, but these are usually ignored when they are relatively minor.

The method that is chosen for reducing an inventory to a lower value should be applied consistently in successive valuations. When valuing inventories by individual items, a lower market value assigned to goods at the end of a period is considered to be its cost for purposes of inventory valuation in subsequent periods; cost reductions once made, then, are not restored in subsequent inventory determinations. This restriction cannot be applied to inventories valued by major classes or as a whole when a record of the individual price changes is not maintained.

Conflict Between Tax Laws and Lower of Cost or Market Rule. A decline in inventory value may be deducted for federal income tax purposes as a loss in the taxable year in which such decline occurs. However, the deductible loss must be computed on an individual item basis. Thus, a company which applies lower of cost or market to classes of inventory or to inventory as a whole for financial reporting purposes must make a separate item-by-item computation to obtain a tax deduction.

Disputes between taxpayers and IRS as to what constitutes a recognizable decline in inventory value have led to a number of court decisions. An important tax case in this area was settled by the U.S. Supreme Court in 1979.[4] The taxpayer, Thor Power Tool Co., had followed the practice of writing down the value of spare parts inventories that were being held to cover future warranty requirements. Although the sales price did not decline, the probability of the parts being sold, and thus the net realizable value, decreased as time passed. The write-down to reflect the current decline in value is consistent with the accounting principle of matching current costs and revenues. The Supreme Court, however, upheld the IRS position that recognition of declines in inventory values for tax purposes must await actual decline in the sales price for the parts in question.

This case is another illustration of a situation in which tax and financial accounting practices differ. Because the objective of levying taxes is not always compatible with an attempt to measure results of operations, differences will probably always exist. As explained in Chapter 15, this creates a constant need for interperiod tax allocation under the assumption that taxes are accruable as an expense. The U.S. Supreme Court recognized this difference in objectives in their conclusion to the Thor case as follows:

> Given this diversity, even contrariety, of objectives, any presumptive equivalency between tax and financial accounting would be unacceptable.[5]

Evaluation of Lower of Cost or Market Method. As mentioned earlier, the lower of cost or market method is evidence of the concept of accounting conservatism. Its strict application has been applied to avoid valuing inventory on the balance sheet at more than replacement cost. As discussed earlier, the AICPA replaced this strict entry valuation with a utility measure that relies partially upon the exit prices. If selling prices for the inventory have declined and the decline is expected to hold until the inventory is sold, the adjustment of income in the period of the decline seems justified. The

---

[4]Thor Power Tool Company vs. Commissioner of Internal Revenue, *United States Supreme Court Reports*, Vol. 439, p. 532 (1979).

[5]*Ibid.*, pp. 542–3.

value of the inventory has been impaired which requires current adjustment. However, care must be taken in using this method not to manipulate income by allowing excessive charges against income in one period to be offset by excessive income in the next period.

Some accountants have argued against the use of lower of cost or market because it violates the cost concept. Market valuations are often subjective and based upon expectations. To the extent these expectations are not realized, misleading financial statements will be produced. To illustrate, assume that activities summarized in terms of cost provide the following results over a three year period:

	1980		1981		1982	
Sales...........................		$200,000		$225,000		$250,000
Cost of goods sold:						
Beginning inventory.....	$ 60,000		$ 80,000		$127,500	
Purchases	120,000		160,000		90,000	
Goods available for sale............................	$180,000		$240,000		$217,500	
Less ending inventory..	80,000	100,000	127,500	112,500	92,500	125,000
Gross profit on sales........		$100,000		$112,500		$125,000
Operating expenses.........		80,000		90,000		100,000
Net income		$ 20,000		$ 22,500		$ 25,000
Rate of income to sales...		10%		10%		10%

Assume estimates as to the future utility of ending inventories indicated market values as follows:

1980	1981	1982
$75,000	$110,000	$92,500

If the expected decline in selling prices did not occur, inventory valuation at the lower of cost or market would provide the following results.

	1980		1981		1982	
Sales...............................		$200,000		$225,000		$250,000
Cost of goods sold:						
Beginning inventory.....	$ 60,000		$ 75,000		$110,000	
Purchases	120,000		160,000		90,000	
Goods available for sale............................	$180,000		$235,000		$200,000	
Less ending inventory..	75,000	105,000	110,000	125,000	92,500	107,500
Gross profit on sales........		$ 95,000		$100,000		$142,500
Operating expenses.........		80,000		90,000		100,000
Net income		$ 15,000		$ 10,000		$ 42,500
Rate of income to sales...		7.5%		4.4%		17.0%

Reduction of an inventory below cost reduces the net income of the period in which the reduction is made and increases the net income of a subsequent period over what it would have been. In the example just given, total net income for the three-year period is the same under either set of calculations. But the reduction of inventories to lower market values reduced the net income for 1980 and for 1981 and increased the net income for 1982. The fact that inventory reductions were not followed by decreases in the sales prices resulted in net income determinations that varied considerably from those that might reasonably have been expected from increasing sales and costs that normally vary with sales volume.

Objection to valuation at the lower of cost or market is also raised on the grounds it produces inconsistencies in the measurements of both the financial position and the operations of the enterprise. Market decreases are recognized but increases are not. Although this system does produce some inconsistent application to the upward and downward movement of market, the authors feel that the lower of cost or market concept is preferable to a strict cost measurement. A loss in the utility of any asset should be reflected in the period the impairment is first recognized and a reasonable estimate of its significance can be determined. However, the lower of cost or market method fails to meet the needs of an inflationary economy as emphasized in Chapter 8. Most prices are increasing in our present economy; therefore, there is a reduced probability that, in any situation, the inventory market values will be lower than incurred cost.

Valuation at Market

As discussed in Chapter 8, due to inflationary conditions, there has been increasing pressure on accountants to move from the cost method of valuing inventories toward replacement cost or some other form of market valuation. Advocates of a market approach to inventory valuation argue that if market is a relevant measure of value when it is less than cost, it is equally valid when greater than cost.

Although the market method has not become *generally* accepted for statement presentation, it has been adopted for valuing certain types of inventories. Market valuation has become an accepted practice within the mining industry for products such as gold and silver for which market is readily defined and tends to fluctuate dramatically, often in response to speculative trading activity. Similar conditions have led to the wide-spread use of market in valuing inventories of agricultural commodities. For example, General Mills, whose statements appear in Appendix B, values its grain and flour inventories at current market prices. As discussed in Chapter 6, market is an acceptable method for valuing inventories of securities held by financial institutions and brokers and dealers in securities. These have been recognized by the accounting profession as special cases, acceptable within the framework of GAAP.

In applying the market method, the market price replaces cost regardless of whether market is greater or less than cost. Increases and decreases are normally reflected in the income statement. Some companies, however, credit a special equity account for unrealized holding gains and charge only losses against income. Thus, net income would be the same as that reported using a lower of cost or market valuation.

Although the current recommendations of the FASB require supplemental disclosure of market values, the authors believe that financial information would be more realistic and relevant if a market-based accounting system were adopted for use on the books and in the general statements. Only when market valuation is uniformly adopted for all purposes can users of financial statements clearly evaluate the impact of inflation on a specific company. Such a procedure would eliminate the various alternative cost allocation methods currently acceptable. Because market can be defined in different ways, the use of market valuation will not totally eliminate differences among companies, nor will it eliminate completely opportunities for manipulation of net income. However, issuance of specific guidelines by the FASB for applying market valuation should reduce the severity of these problems.

INVENTORIES ON THE BALANCE SHEET

It is customary to report both trading and manufacturing inventories as current assets even though in some situations, considerable time will elapse before portions of such inventories are realized in cash. Among the items that are generally reported separately under the inventories heading are merchandise inventory or finished goods, goods in process, raw materials, factory supplies, goods and materials in transit, goods on consignment, and goods in the hands of agents and salespersons. Inventories are normally listed in the order of their liquidity. Any advance payments on purchase commitments should be reported separately and should not be included with inventories. Such advances are preferably listed after inventories in the current asset section since they have not entered the inventory phase of the operating cycle.

The valuation procedures employed must be disclosed in a note to the financial statements outlining all significant accounting policies followed.[6] The basis of valuation (such as cost or lower of cost or market), together with the method of arriving at cost (lifo, fifo, average, or other method), should be indicated. The reader of a statement may assume that the valuation procedures indicated have been consistently applied and financial statements are comparable with those of past periods. If this is not the case, a special note should be provided stating the change in the method and the effects of the change upon the financial statements. Further discussion of reporting changes in accounting methods is found in Chapter 18.

If significant inventory price declines take place between the balance sheet date and the date the statement is prepared, such declines should be disclosed by parenthetical remark or note. When relatively large orders for merchandise have been placed by the reporting company in a period of widely fluctuating prices, but the title to such goods has not yet passed, such commitments should be described by special note. Information should also be provided concerning possible losses on purchase commitments.

---

[6]*Opinions of the Accounting Principles Board, No. 22,* "Disclosure of Accounting Policies" (New York: American Institute of Certified Public Accountants, 1972), par. 12.

Similar information may be appropriate for possible losses on sales commitments.

Replacement cost of inventories is now required to be included as a footnote to balance sheets of the larger corporations.[7] Until such time as market valuation of inventories becomes generally acceptable for reporting purposes, only supplemental disclosure of such values is required.

When inventories or sections of an inventory have been pledged as security on loans from banks, finance companies, or factors, the amounts pledged should be disclosed parenthetically in the inventory section of the balance sheet.

Inventory items may be reported as follows:

Inventories:		
Raw materials:		
On hand	$210,000	
In transit from supplier	30,000	$240,000
Goods in process		300,000
Finished goods:		
On hand (goods of $100,000 have been pledged as security on loans of $75,000 from First State Bank)	$300,000	
On consignment	15,000	315,000
Factory supplies		12,000
Total inventories		$867,000

QUESTIONS

1. What is your understanding of the meaning of the "gross profit test"?

2. Distinguish between: (a) gross profit as a percentage of cost and gross profit as a percentage of sales; (b) the gross profit method of calculating estimated inventory cost and the retail inventory method of calculating estimated inventory cost.

3. What effect would the use of the lifo inventory method have upon the applicability of the gross profit method of valuing inventory?

4. Define (a) initial markup, (b) additional markup, (c) markup cancellation, (d) markdown, (e) markdown cancellation, and (f) maintained markup.

5. How are purchase discounts and sales discounts treated in using the retail inventory method?

---

[7]*Statement of Financial Accounting Standards, No. 33*, "Financial Reporting and Changing Prices" (Stamford: Financial Accounting Standards Board, 1979).

6. A merchant taking inventory by the retail method maintains no separate record of markup cancellations and markdown cancellations. Instead the former is included in markdowns and the latter in markups, as "these represent price decreases and increases respectively." How will this procedure affect the inventory at (a) retail? (b) cost?

7. What are the major advantages of dollar-value lifo?

8. Under what circumstances would a decline in replacement cost of an item not justify a departure from the cost basis of valuing inventory?

9. The use of cost or market, whichever is lower, is an archaic continuation of conservative accounting. Comment on this view.

10. Why is a ceiling and floor limitation on replacement cost considered necessary by the AICPA?

11. The inventory of the Prince Co. on December 31, 1981, had a cost of $85,000. However, prices had been declining and the replacement cost of the inventory on this date was $70,000. Prices continued to decline and in early March, 1982, when the statements were being drawn up, the replacement cost for the inventory was only $55,000. How would you recommend that the inventory be reported on the statements for 1981?

12. The Berg Corporation began business on January 1, 1980. Information about inventories, as of December 31 for three consecutive years, under different valuation methods is shown below. Using this information and assuming that the same method is used each year, you are to choose the phrase which best answers each of the following questions:

	Lifo Cost	Fifo Cost	Market	Lower of Cost or Market*
1980	$10,200	$10,000	$ 9,600	$ 8,900
1981	9,100	9,000	8,800	8,500
1982	10,300	11,000	12,000	10,900

*Fifo cost, item by item valuation.

(a) The inventory basis that would result in the highest net income for 1980 is: (1) Lifo cost, (2) Fifo cost, (3) Market, (4) Lower of cost or market.

(b) The inventory basis that would result in the highest net income for 1981 is: (1) Lifo cost, (2) Fifo cost, (3) Market, (4) Lower of cost or market.

(c) The inventory basis that would result in the lowest net income for the three years combined is: (1) Lifo cost, (2) Fifo cost, (3) Market, (4) Lower of cost or market.

(d) For the year 1981, how much higher or lower would net income be on the fifo cost basis than on the lower of cost or market basis? (1) $400 higher, (2) $400 lower, (3) $600 higher, (4) $600 lower, (5) $1,000 higher, (6) $1,000 lower, (7) $1,400 higher, (8) $1,400 lower.

13. There has been increasing support for the use of market values in reporting inventories on the financial statements. What are the major arguments that are raised in supporting such use?

14. How would you recommend that the following items be reported on the balance sheet?

(a) Unsold goods in the hands of consignees.

(b) Purchase orders outstanding.

(c) Raw materials pledged by means of warehouse receipts on notes payable to bank.

(d) Raw materials in transit from suppliers.

(e) Merchandise produced by special order and set aside to be picked up by customer.

(f) Finished parts to be used in the assembly of final products.

(g) Office supplies.

EXERCISES

exercise 9-1

On August 15, 1981, a hurricane damaged a warehouse of RP & JS Merchandise Company. The entire merchandise inventory and many accounting records stored in the warehouse were completely destroyed. Although the inventory was not insured, a portion could be sold for scrap. Through the use of microfilmed records, the following data are assembled:

Inventory, January 1	$ 250,000
Purchases, January 1–August 15	1,150,000
Cash sales, January 1–August 15	225,000
Collection of accounts receivable, January 1– August 15	1,562,500
Accounts receivable, January 1	187,500
Accounts receivable, August 15	250,000
Salvage value of inventory	5,000
Gross profit percentage on sales	30%

Compute the inventory loss as a result of the hurricane.

exercise 9-2

On June 30, 1981, a flash flood damaged the warehouse and factory of Padway Corporation, completely destroying the work-in-process inventory. There was no damage to either the raw materials or finished goods inventories. A physical inventory taken after the flood revealed the following valuations:

Finished goods	$119,000
Work in process	–0–
Raw materials	62,000

The inventory on January 1, 1981, consisted of the following:

Finished goods	$140,000
Work in process	100,000
Raw materials	30,000
	$270,000

A review of the books and records disclosed that the gross profit margin historically approximated 25% of sales. The sales for the first six months of 1981 were $340,000. Raw material purchases were $115,000. Direct labor costs for this period were $80,000, and factory overhead has historically been applied at 50% of direct labor.

Compute the value of the work-in-process inventory lost at June 30, 1981. Show supporting computations in good form.

(AICPA adapted)

exercise 9-3

"Big D" Department Store uses the retail inventory method. On December 31, 1981, the following information relating to the inventory was gathered:

	Cost	Retail
Inventory, January 1, 1981	$ 21,625	$ 40,500
Sales		350,000
Purchases	280,000	400,000
Freight in	4,200	
Net markups		30,000
Net markdowns		10,000
Sales discounts		5,000

Compute the ending inventory value at December 31, 1981, using the retail inventory method.

exercise 9-4

The Supreme Clothing Store values its inventory under the retail inventory method at the lower of cost or market. The following data are available for the month of November 1981:

	Cost	Selling Price
Inventory, November 1.....................	$ 53,800	$ 80,000
Markdowns		21,000
Markups		29,000
Markdown cancellations		13,000
Markup cancellations		9,000
Purchases	173,200	223,600
Sales...		244,000
Purchase returns............................	3,000	3,600
Sales returns..................................		12,000

Based upon the data presented above, prepare a schedule in good form to compute the estimated inventory at November 30, 1981, at the lower of cost or market under the retail inventory method.

(AICPA adapted)

exercise 9-5

The Rumsey Manufacturing Company manufactures a single product. The management of Rumsey decided on December 31, 1978, to adopt the dollar-value lifo inventory method. The inventory value on that date using the newly adopted dollar-value lifo method was determined to be $500,000. Additional information follows:

	Inventory at Respective Year-End prices	Relevant Price Index
December 31, 1979.................................	$583,000	1.10
December 31, 1980.................................	598,000	1.15
December 31, 1981.................................	664,900	1.22

Compute the inventory value at December 31 of each year using the dollar-value lifo method.

exercise 9-6

Rawlins Inc., adopted dollar-value lifo in 1978. Information for each year since 1978 follows:

	Inventory at End-of-Year Prices	Year-End Index
December 31, 1978	$250,000	1.00
December 31, 1979	299,750	1.10
December 31, 1980	330,960	1.20
December 31, 1981	346,240	1.28

(1) Compute the inventory value for each year under the dollar-value lifo method.
(2) Compute the inventory value for 1981 assuming dollar-value lifo procedures were adopted in 1980 rather than in 1978.

exercise 9-7

Determine the proper carrying value of the following inventory items if priced in accordance with the recommendations of the AICPA.

Item	Cost	Replacement Cost	Sales Price	Cost of Completion	Normal Profit
Product 501	$1.65	$1.82	$2.30	$.35	$.20
Product 502	.69	.65	1.00	.30	.04
Product 503	.31	.24	.59	.15	.07
Product 504	.92	.84	1.05	.27	.05
Product 505	.79	.82	1.00	.19	.09
Product 506	1.19	1.15	1.25	.13	.11

exercise 9-8

Ron's Candy Company carries five products. Units on hand, costs, and market prices of these items on January 31, 1981, are as follows:

	Units	Unit Cost	Unit Market
Product 100	4,200	$2.50	$2.30
Product 101	1,800	1.75	1.65
Product 102	5,750	2.90	3.10
Product 103	3,100	5.60	5.05
Product 104	1,600	1.65	1.85

Prepare a statement to show the calculation of the inventory on the basis of cost or market, whichever is lower, as applied to individual products.

PROBLEMS

problem 9-1

Norris Manufacturing began operations five years ago. On August 13, 1981, a fire broke out in the warehouse destroying all inventory and many accounting records relating to the inventory. The information available is presented below. All sales and all purchases are on account.

	January 1, 1981	August 13, 1981
Inventory	$128,590	
Accounts receivable	130,590	$107,320
Accounts payable	88,140	122,850
Collection on accounts receivable, January 1–August 13		$697,250
Payments to suppliers, January 1–August 13		487,500
Goods on consignment at August 13, at cost		45,000

Summary of previous years sales:

	1978	1979	1980
Sales.............................	$626,000	$675,000	$680,000
Gross profit on sales.......	200,320	175,500	217,600

Instructions: Determine the inventory loss suffered as a result of the fire.

problem 9-2

The following information was taken from the records of the Card Company.

	1/1/80–12/31/80	1/1/81–9/30/81
Sales (net of returns)	$2,500,000	$1,500,000
Beginning inventory...	420,000	730,000
Purchases...	2,152,000	1,061,000
Freight in..	116,000	72,000
Purchases discounts...	30,000	15,000
Purchases returns	40,000	13,000
Purchases allowances	8,000	5,000
Ending inventory...	730,000	
Selling and general expenses.....................................	450,000	320,000

Instructions: Compute by the gross-profit method the value to be assigned to the inventory as of September 30, 1981, and prepare an interim statement summarizing operations for the nine-month period ending on this date.

problem 9-3

In December, 1981, Bullseye Merchandise, Inc., had a significant portion of its inventory stolen. The company determined the cost of inventory not stolen to be $38,046. The following information was taken from the records of the company.

	January 1, 1981 to Date of Theft	1980
Purchases...	$154,854	$161,320
Purchases returns and allowances	7,225	8,420
Sales..	236,012	243,980
Sales returns and allowances..	2,882	2,600
Salaries	9,600	10,800
Rent..	6,480	6,480
Insurance...	1,160	1,178
Light, heat, and water...	1,361	1,525
Advertising...	5,100	3,216
Depreciation expense...	1,506	1,536
Beginning inventory	57,456	59,040

Instructions: Estimate the cost of the stolen inventory.

problem 9-4

The following information was taken from the records of Locust, Inc., for the years 1980 and 1981.

	1981	1980
Sales	$138,600	$135,600
Sales discounts...	1,840	1,200
Sales returns	2,040	1,600
Freight in	4,000	3,640
Purchases (at cost)..	78,000	68,560
Purchases (at retail)...	100,560	92,480
Purchases discounts	1,178	1,000
Beginning inventory (at cost)		65,600
Beginning inventory (at retail).......................................		87,520

Instructions: Compute the value of the inventory at the end of 1980 and 1981 using the conventional retail inventory method.

problem 9-5

The Reed Clothing Store values its inventory under the retail inventory method. The following data are available for 1981:

	Cost	Selling Price
Inventory, January 1	$ 50,673	$ 79,100
Additional markdowns..		21,000
Additional markups..		40,600
Markdown cancellations..		13,000
Markup cancellations..		9,000
Purchases	170,000	221,600
Sales..		246,500
Purchases Returns...	3,600	6,000
Sales Allowances..		12,000
Freight in...	14,600	

Instructions:

(1) Prepare a schedule to compute the estimated inventory at December 31, 1981, at the lower of average cost or market under the retail method.

(continued)

   (2) Prepare the summary accounting journal entries to record the above inventory data (include entries to record the purchases, sales, and closing of inventory to income summary).
   (3) What gross profit on sales would be reported on the income statement for 1981?

problem 9-6

Do-It-Yourself Repair Shop began operations on January 1, 1976. Management concluded that dollar-value lifo should be used for inventory costing. Information concerning the inventory of Do-It-Yourself is shown below:

	Index	Inventory at Year-End Prices
December 31, 1976	1.00	$15,000
December 31, 1977	1.20	31,200
December 31, 1978	1.35	54,000
December 31, 1979	1.15	34,500
December 31, 1980	1.70	72,250
December 31, 1981	2.00	39,400

   Instructions: Compute the December 31 inventory value for each year (1976–1981) under the dollar-value lifo method.

problem 9-7

The Acute Company manufactures a single product. On December 31, 1976, Acute adopted the dollar-value inventory method. The inventory on that date using the dollar-value lifo inventory method was determined to be $300,000; the price index at the end of 1976 (the base year) was 1.20. Inventory data for succeeding years are as follows:

	Inventory at End-of-Year Prices	Price Index
December 31, 1977	$363,000	1.320
December 31, 1978	420,000	1.440
December 31, 1979	430,000	1.500
December 31, 1980	416,640	1.536
December 31, 1981	452,232	1.584

   Instructions: Compute the inventory amounts at December 31 of each year using the dollar-value lifo inventory method.

   (AICPA Adapted)

problem 9-8

Red Robin Lawn Supplies Co. uses the first-in, first-out method in calculating cost of goods sold for three of the products that Red Robin handles. Inventories and purchase information concerning these three products are given for the month of August.

		SHOVELS	FERTILIZER	LAWN SEED
Aug. 1	Inventory	5,000 units at $6.00	3,000 units at $10.00	6,500 units at $ .90
Aug. 1–15	Purchases	7,000 units at $6.50	4,500 units at $10.50	3,000 units at $1.25
Aug. 16–31	Purchases	3,000 units at $7.50		
Aug.	Sales	10,000 units	5,000 units	4,500 units
Aug. 31	Sale Price	$8.00 per unit	$11.00 per unit	$2.00 per unit

On August 31, Red Robin's suppliers reduced their price from the last purchase price by the following percentages: Shovels, 20%; Fertilizer, 10%; Lawn Seed 8%. Accordingly Red Robin decided to reduce their sales prices on all items by 10% effective September 1. Red Robin's selling cost is 10% of sales price. Shovels and fertilizer have a normal profit (after selling costs) of 30% on sales prices, while the normal profit on lawn seed (after selling costs) is 15% of sales price.

   Instructions:
   (1) Calculate the value of the inventory at August 31, using the lower of cost or market method (applied to individual items).
   (2) Calculate the cost of goods sold for August.

problem 9-9

Austin, Inc., carries four items in inventory. The following data are relative to such goods at the end of 1981:

			Per Unit			
	Units	Cost	Replacement Cost	Estimated Sales Price	Selling Cost	Normal Profit
Commodity A	2,000	$5.50	$5.00	$ 8.00	$ .90	$2.00
Commodity B	1,650	6.00	6.00	10.00	.80	1.25
Commodity C	5,000	2.50	2.00	4.75	.95	.50
Commodity D	3,250	7.00	7.50	7.50	1.20	1.75

Instructions: Calculate the value of the inventory under each of the following methods:

(1) Cost.
(2) The lower of cost or market without regard to market floor and ceiling limitations, applied to the individual inventory items.
(3) The lower of cost or market without regard to market floor and ceiling limitations applied to the inventory as a whole.
(4) The lower of cost or net realizable value applied to the individual inventory items.
(5) The lower of cost or market recognizing floor and ceiling limitations applied to the individual inventory items.

10

Plant and Intangible Assets — Acquisition

CHAPTER OBJECTIVES

Distinguish between capital and revenue expenditures.

Describe the nature and classification of plant assets and intangible assets.

Describe and illustrate the recording of asset acquisitions under various acquisition methods — purchase, exchange, issuance of securities, and donation or discovery.

Discuss by asset category special accounting problems in determining the cost of plant assets and intangible assets.

Describe the treatment of expenditures made subsequent to asset acquisition.

Many expenditures made by an entity are for the acquisition of resources which will contribute to the production of revenue for more than one fiscal period. The basic accounting concept of **matching costs with revenues** requires that this type of expenditure be charged against all of the periods benefited rather than allocated entirely to the period in which the expenditure is made. Such an expenditure is properly "capitalized," i.e., recognized as an asset on the balance sheet, and is commonly referred to as a **capital expenditure** or a **deferred cost**. The expenditure is then allocated against future revenue in some pattern which attempts to reflect the value received from the use of the asset acquired.

The first critical accounting question is what degree of assurance is there that a future direct benefit will actually be realized from the expenditure. If the future benefit is highly uncertain, the expenditure is not capitalized, but written off as an expense of the period. The expenditure is then commonly referred to as a **revenue expenditure**. Once an expenditure is identified as a capital expenditure, the next accounting question is what portion of the total expenditure should be considered part of the asset cost and thus capitalized. This chapter considers these questions for both tangible and intangible assets. The allocation of acquisition cost over time and the accounting for the eventual retirement or abandonment of assets are considered in the next chapter.

CLASSIFICATION OF PLANT AND INTANGIBLE ASSETS

Assets may be tangible or intangible. **Tangible assets** can be observed by one or more of the physical senses. They may be seen and touched and, in some environments, heard and smelled. **Plant assets**, sometimes referred to as fixed assets, are tangible assets of a durable nature employed in the operating activities of an enterprise. The term **plant** includes land, buildings, fixtures, machinery, and other equipment used to produce or facilitate the sale of goods and services. Plant assets may be reported on the balance sheet under the heading "Land, buildings, and equipment." Other common classifications include "Property, plant, and equipment" and "Plant and equipment," with the term *plant* used in a restricted sense to designate buildings only or land and buildings.

Intangible assets cannot be directly observed. Evidence of the asset in the form of agreements, contracts, or patents sometimes exists, but the asset itself has no physical existence. Intangible assets include such items as copyrights, patents, goodwill, and franchise agreements. The "most intangible" asset is goodwill. Unlike other intangible assets, goodwill does not represent any specific contractual future rights or privileges. Goodwill is recorded on the accounting records only when one business entity acquires another business entity, and then only if the purchase price exceeds the total fair market value of the net assets of the company acquired. Because of the relatively greater uncertainty concerning the ultimate benefit of most intangible assets, they are generally classified near the end of the asset section of the balance sheet.

CAPITAL AND REVENUE EXPENDITURES

The decision as to whether a given expenditure is a capital or revenue expenditure is one of many areas in which an accountant must exercise judgment. Generally, expenditures must be individually analyzed. In some companies, however, a lower limit to the definition of capital expenditure is established to avoid excessive costs of accounting for relatively small deferred costs. Thus, any expenditure under the established limit is always expensed currently even though future benefits are expected from that expenditure. This practice is justified on the grounds of expediency. The amount of the limit varies with the size of the company. Limits of $100, $500, and $1,000 are not unusual. This treatment is acceptable as long as it is consistently applied and no material misstatements arise due to unusual expenditure patterns or other causes.

Income cannot be fairly measured unless expenditures are properly identified and recorded as revenue or capital expenditures. For example, an incorrect debit to an equipment account instead of an expense account results in the overstatement of current earnings on the income statement and the overstatement of assets and owners' equity on the balance sheet. As the charge is assigned to operations in subsequent periods, earnings of such periods will be understated; assets and equity on the successive balance sheets will continue to be overstated, although by lesser amounts each year, until the asset is written off and the original error is fully counterbalanced. On the other hand, an incorrect debit to an expense instead of an equipment account results in the understatement of current earnings and the understatement of assets and equity. Earnings of subsequent periods will be overstated in the absence of debits for depreciation or amortization; assets and equity will continue to be understated, although by lesser amounts each year, until the original error is completely offset.

Because of the need to exercise judgment in some situations in determining the revenue or capital nature of expenditures, there is considerable diversity in practice as to which expenditures are capitalized. Two areas in which the FASB has attempted to reduce or eliminate such diversity are accounting for development stage expenditures and accounting for research and development expenditures.

Accounting for Development Stage Expenditures

In the past, some development stage companies deferred many costs without regard to recoverability or matching on the basis that they were not yet fully operating enterprises. Advocates of this approach maintain that all charges for interest, taxes, and general and administrative services during the development stage of a new company should be capitalized. Support for this procedure is based on the theory that future periods are benefited by necessary initial costs and it is unreasonable to assume losses have been incurred before sales activities begin. The Financial Accounting Standards Board reviewed this practice and concluded that accounting principles for companies in the organizational or developmental stage should be the same as for more mature companies. No special rules or principles should apply. Therefore, capitalization policies would not be different for these companies, and the above expenditures should be expensed in the period incurred, unless their deferral can be justified by identifiable future benefits.[1]

---

[1] *Statement of Financial Accounting Standards, No. 7*, "Accounting and Reporting by Development Stage Enterprises" (Stamford: Financial Accounting Standards Board, 1975), par. 10.

Accounting for Research and Development Expenditures

Historically, expenditures for research and development purposes were reported sometimes as capital expenditures and sometimes as revenue expenditures. The FASB inherited this problem from the Accounting Principles Board, and made this area the subject of their first definitive standard.[2] The Board defined **research** activities as those undertaken to discover new knowledge that will be useful in developing new products, services, or processes or that will result in significant improvements of existing products or processes. **Development** activities involve the application of research findings to develop a plan or design for new or improved products and processes. Development activities include the formulation, design, and testing of products, construction of prototypes, and operation of pilot plants.

In general, the FASB concluded that research and development expenditures should be treated as revenue expenditures and expensed in the period incurred.[3] This decision was reached after much analysis and after many attempts to establish criteria for selectively capitalizing some research and development expenditures and expensing others. Among the arguments for expensing these costs was the frequent inability to find a definite causal relationship between the expenditures and future revenues. Sometimes very large expenditures do not generate any future revenue, while relatively small expenditures lead to significant discoveries that generate large revenues. The Board found it difficult to establish criteria that would distinguish between those research and development expenditures that would most likely benefit future periods and those that would not.

As defined by the FASB in Statement No. 2, research and development costs include those costs of materials, equipment, facilities, personnel, purchased intangibles, contract services, and a reasonable allocation of indirect costs which are specifically related to research and development activities and which have no alternative future uses.[4] Such activities include:

1. Laboratory research aimed at discovery of new knowledge.
2. Searching for applications of new research findings or other knowledge.
3. Conceptual formulation and design of possible product or process alternatives.
4. Testing in search for or evaluation of product or process alternatives.
5. Modification of the formulation or design of a product or process.
6. Design, construction, and testing of pre-production prototypes and models.
7. Design of tools, jigs, molds, and dies involving new technology.
8. Design, construction, and operation of a pilot plant that is not of a scale economically feasible to the enterprise for commercial production.
9. Engineering activity required to advance the design of a product to the point that it meets specific functional and economic requirements and is ready for manufacture.[5]

---

[2]*Statement of Financial Accounting Standards, No. 2*, "Accounting for Research and Development Costs" (Stamford: Financial Accounting Standards Board, 1974).

[3]*Ibid.*, par. 12.

[4]*Ibid.*, par. 11.

[5]*Ibid.*, par. 9.

The Board stipulated, however, that expenditures for certain items having alternative future uses, either in additional research projects or for productive purposes, can be capitalized and allocated against future projects or periods. This exception permits the deferral of costs incurred for materials, equipment, facilities, and purchased intangibles, but only if an alternative use can be identified.

Research and development costs vary widely among companies. Many expenditures do have future worth, while others are so highly uncertain as to future worth that capitalization is clearly improper. For the FASB to ignore these differences and issue a blanket rule that all research and development expenditures should be handled the same seems arbitrary and without theoretical support. The International Accounting Group studying this area disagreed with the FASB and identified general situations in which they felt capitalization and deferral of development costs would be justified:

> Development costs of a project may be deferred to future periods if all the following criteria are satisfied:
> (a) the product or process is clearly defined and the costs attributable to the product or process can be separately identified;
> (b) the technical feasibility of the product or process has been demonstrated;
> (c) the management of the enterprise has indicated its intention to produce and market, or use, the product or process;
> (d) there is a clear indication of a future market for the product or process or, if it is to be used internally rather than sold, its usefulness to the enterprise can be demonstrated; and
> (e) adequate resources exist, or are reasonably expected to be available, to complete the project and market the product or process.[6]

While guidelines to help distinguish between capital and revenue expenditures are desirable, specific rules, such as those issued for research and development expenditures, that mandate by definition the treatment of all expenditures ignore the reality of the great diversity of conditions existing in practice.

RECORDING ACQUISITION OF PLANT AND INTANGIBLE ASSETS

Plant assets and intangible assets are recorded initially at cost — the initial bargained or cash sales price. The **cost** of property includes not only the original purchase price or equivalent value, but also any other expenditures required in obtaining and preparing it for its intended use. Any taxes and duties, freight, installation, and other expenditures related to the acquisition should be included in the asset cost.

In a competitive economy, the cost should be representative of the market value of the asset as of the acquisition date. While "bargain purchases" can occur in our less-than-perfect competitive economy, they are generally ignored and the cash or equivalent price is used to record the acquisition.

---

[6]*International Accounting Standard, No. 9*, "Accounting for Research and Development Activities" (London, England: International Accounting Standards Committee, 1978), par. 17.

There are a number of different arrangements that can be used to acquire assets, some of which present special problems relating to asset cost. The acquisition of assets is discussed under the following headings: (1) purchase for cash, (2) purchase on long-term contract, (3) exchange, (4) issuance of securities, and (5) donation or discovery.

Purchase for Cash

An asset acquired for cash is recorded at the amount of cash paid, including all incidental outlays relating to its purchase or preparation for use.

As suggested in Chapter 8, sound accounting theory requires discounts on purchases to be regarded as reductions in costs: earnings arise from sales, not from purchases. In applying this theory, any available discounts on property acquisitions should be treated as reductions to asset cost. Failure to take such discounts should be reported as Discounts Lost or Interest Expense.

A number of assets may be acquired for one lump sum. Some of the assets may be depreciable, others nondepreciable. Depreciable assets may have different useful lives. If there is to be accountability for the assets on an individual basis, the total purchase price must be allocated among the individual assets. When part of a purchase price can be clearly identified with specific assets, such a cost assignment should be made and the balance of the purchase price allocated among the remaining assets. When no part of the purchase price can be related to specific assets, the entire amount must be allocated among the different assets acquired. Appraisal values or similar evidence provided by a competent independent authority should be sought to support such allocation.

To illustrate the allocation of a joint asset cost, assume that land, buildings, and equipment are acquired for $80,000. Assume further that assessed values for the individual assets as reported on the property tax bill are considered to provide an equitable basis for cost allocation. The allocation is made as shown below.

	Assessed Values	Cost Allocation According to Relative Assessed Values	Cost Assigned to Individual Assets
Real properties:			
Land..	$14,000	14,000/50,000 × $80,000	$22,400
Improvements (building)......	30,000	30,000/50,000 × $80,000	48,000
Personal property (equipment)	6,000	6,000/50,000 × $80,000	9,600
	$50,000		$80,000

An asset acquired in secondhand or used condition should be recorded at its cost without reference to the balance on the seller's books. Expenditures to repair, recondition, or improve the asset before it is placed in use should be capitalized as part of the cost. It must be assumed that the buyer knew additional expenditures would be required when the purchase was made.

Purchase on Long-Term Contract

The acquisition of real estate or other property frequently involves deferred payment of all or part of the purchase price. The indebtedness of the buyer is usually evidenced by a note, debenture, mortgage, or other contract which specifies the terms for settlement of the obligation. The debt instrument may call for one payment at a given future date or a series of payments at specified intervals. Interest charged on the unpaid balance of the contract should be recognized as an expense. To illustrate the accounting for a long-term purchase contract, assume that land is acquired for $100,000; $35,000 is paid at the time of purchase and the balance is to be paid in semiannual installments of $5,000, plus interest on the unpaid principal at an annual rate of 10%. Entries for the purchase and for the first payment on the contract are shown below.

Transaction	Entry		
January 2, 1981 Purchased land for $100,000 paying $35,000 down, the balance to be paid in semiannual payments of $5,000 plus interest at 10%.	Land .... 100,000 Cash.. Contract Payable		35,000 65,000
June 30, 1981 Made first payment. Amount of payment: $5,000 + $3,250 (5% of $65,000) = $8,250	Interest Expense............................... 3,250 Contract Payable............................. 5,000 Cash..		8,250

In the preceding example, the contract specified both a purchase price and interest at a stated rate on the unpaid balance. Sometimes, however, a contract may simply provide for a payment or series of payments without reference to interest or may provide for a stated interest rate that is unreasonable in relation to the market. APB No. 21, "Interest on Receivables and Payables," requires that in these circumstances, the note, sales price, and cost of the property, goods, or services exchanged for the note should be recorded at the fair market value of the property, goods, or services or at the current market value of the note, whichever value is more clearly determinable.[7] The following example illustrates the accounting by the purchaser.

Assume that certain equipment, which has a cash price of $50,000, is acquired under a long-term contract. The contract specifies a down payment of $15,000 plus seven annual payments of $7,189.22 each, or a total price, including interest, of $65,324.54. Although not stated, the effective interest rate implicit in this contract is 10%, the rate that discounts the annual payments of $7,189.22 to a present value of $35,000, the cash price

---

[7]The term *notes* is used by the Board in Opinion No. 21 as a general term for contractual rights to receive money or contractual obligations to pay money at specified or determinable dates.

less the down payment.[8] As specified in APB Opinion No. 21, if the cash equivalent price, that is, the fair market value of the asset varies from the contract price because of delayed payments, the difference should be recorded as a discount and amortized over the life of the contract using the implicit or effective interest rate. The entries to record the purchase, the amortization of the discount for the first two years, and the first two payments would be as follows:

Transaction	Entry		

January 2, 1981
Purchased equipment with a cash price of $50,000 for $15,000 down plus seven annual payments of $7,189.22 each, or a total contract price of $65,324.54.
	Equipment.................................
	Discount on Equipment
	  Contract Payable....................
	    Equipment Contract Payable.................................
	    Cash.....................................
		50,000.00
		
		15,324.54
			
			50,324.54
			15,000.00

December 31, 1981
  Made first payment of $7,189.22.
  Amortization of debt discount:
    10% × $35,000 = $3,500
    ($50,324.54 − $15,324.54 = $35,000)
	Equipment Contract Payable.....
	  Cash.....................................
	Interest Expense........................
	  Discount on Equipment
	  Contract Payable..............
		7,189.22
		
		3,500.00
			
			7,189.22
			
			3,500.00

December 31, 1982
  Made second payment of $7,189.22.
  Amortization of debt discount:
    10% × $31,310.78* = $3,131.08
	Equipment Contract Payable.....
	  Cash.....................................
	Interest Expense........................
	  Discount on Equipment
	  Contract Payable..............
		7,189.22
		
		3,131.08
			
			7,189.22
			
			3,131.08

*$50,324.54 − $7,189.22 = $43,135.32 Equipment contract payable
$15,324.54 − $3,500.00 = <u>11,824.54</u> Discount on equipment contract payable
                $31,310.78 Present value of equipment contract payable end of first year

Property may be acquired under a conditional sales contract whereby legal title to the asset is retained by the seller until payments are completed. The failure to acquire legal title may be disregarded by the buyer and the transaction recognized in terms of its substance — the acquisition of an asset and assumption of a liability. The buyer has the possession and use of the asset and must absorb any decline in its value; title to the asset is retained by the seller simply as a means of assuring payment on the purchase contract.

---

[8]The effective or implicit interest rate is computed as follows:

$PV_n = R(PVAF_{\overline{n}|i})$
$\$50,000 - \$15,000 = \$7,189.22 (PVAF_{\overline{7}|i})$
$PVAF_{\overline{7}|i} = \dfrac{\$35,000.00}{\$\ 7,189.22}$
$PVAF_{\overline{7}|i} = 4.8684$

From Table IV, Appendix A, the interest rate for the present value of 4.8684 when n = 7 is 10%. For further examples of computing an implicit rate of interest, see page 653.

Acquisition by Exchange — General Case

When one **nonmonetary asset**[9] is traded for another, the new asset should generally be recorded at the fair market value of the asset given up, or the fair market value of the asset received if its fair market value is more clearly evident.[10] If a used asset is surrendered for a new asset, the fair market value of the new asset is often more clearly evident than the market value of the old asset, and thus would be used to value the exchange. Care must be taken to determine the true market value of the new asset. Frequently, the quoted price is not a good indicator of market and is higher than the actual cash price for the new asset. A higher list price permits the seller to increase the trade-in allowance for the used asset. The price for which the asset could be acquired in a strictly cash transaction is the fair market value that should be used.

Any difference between the fair market value assigned to the asset received and the book value (carrying value) of the old asset should be recognized as a gain or loss on the exchange. If the exchange involves a monetary consideration, or **boot**, the new asset should be recorded at the fair market value of the surrendered asset plus boot paid or minus boot received. Any trade-in allowance should be carefully examined to determine whether it measures fairly the value of the asset exchanged. The use of an inflated trade-in allowance as representative of the market value of the surrendered asset will result in the overstatement of the newly acquired asset and also in the subsequent overstatement of depreciation charges.

To illustrate an exchange involving nonmonetary assets under the general case, assume that a new truck with a fair market value of $8,200 is acquired in exchange for $600 cash and used equipment which originally cost $10,000 and has a book value of $8,000. The following entry would be made to record the exchange:

Trucks	8,200	
Accumulated Depreciation — Equipment	2,000	
Loss on Exchange of Equipment	400	
Equipment		10,000
Cash		600

Computation:
Trade-in allowance: $8,200 − $600 = $7,600
Accumulated depreciation: $10,000 cost − $8,000 book value = $2,000 accumulated depreciation
Loss:
$8,000 book value − $7,600 trade-in allowance = $400 loss

In the example, the asset was assumed to have been exchanged at the beginning of a fiscal period. When a depreciable asset is exchanged within a fiscal period, depreciation should be recognized to the time of the exchange,

---

[9]*Monetary assets* are those whose amounts are fixed in terms of units of currency by contract or otherwise. Examples include cash and short or long-term accounts receivable. *Nonmonetary assets* include all other assets, such as inventories, land, buildings, and equipment.

[10]*Opinions of the Accounting Principles Board, No. 29*, "Accounting for Nonmonetary Transactions" (New York: American Institute of Certified Public Accountants, 1973), par. 18.

and the entry to record the exchange should recognize the book value of the asset at that date.

Acquisition by Exchange — Special Cases

The Accounting Principles Board recognized three exceptions to the general rule of using market values to determine the gain or loss on exchange of nonmonetary assets.[11] They are:

1. If market values are not determinable within reasonable limits.
2. If the exchange indicates a gain, but does not culminate the earnings process:
   a. Exchange of inventory between dealers to facilitate sales to customers other than the parties involved in the exchange.
   b. Exchange of *similar productive assets* not held for sale.
3. If nonmonetary assets are transferred to owners in a spin-off, or other form of reorganization.[12]

In the first case, since there are no market values available, the new asset is recorded at the book value of the old asset and no gain or loss is recognized. In the second case, market values are available and indicated gains or losses can be computed. However, the Board concluded that both the exchanges identified above are interim transactions, and do not culminate the earnings process. Inventories are often swapped between dealers or other firms to obtain a different model, style, or color for a specific sale. The Board felt that no income should be recognized until a sale actually was made to an external customer. Likewise, they felt that income from an exchange of **similar productive assets**[13] occurs from the sale of items produced by the productive assets, not from their exchange. Thus, any **gain** indicated by comparing market values with book values is deferred unless boot is received. The asset acquired is valued at the book value of the asset relinquished. However, if a **loss** is indicated because the fair market value of the asset given up is less than its book value, the general case would apply and the entire loss should be recognized. If boot is *received* in the exchange, the Board felt that a partial culmination of the earnings process has occurred and part of the gain represented by the boot should be recognized immediately. Because of the complexities of accounting for exchanges not culminating the earning process, the following examples will illustrate journal entries for exchange with and without monetary asset transfers.

Exchanges Not Culminating the Earnings Process — No Boot Involved. To illustrate the exchange of similar assets when no boot is involved, assume that Company A exchanged equipment costing $9,000, with accumulated depreciation of $6,000 and a fair market value of $5,000, for similar equipment from Company B costing $12,000, with accumulated de-

---

[11]*Ibid.*, par. 20–23.
[12]Further discussion of Exception 3 is beyond the scope of this textbook.
[13]*Similar productive assets* are assets of the same general type, that perform the same function, or that are employed in the same line of business.

preciation on Company B's books of $7,500, and a fair market value of $5,000. The entries on the books of Company A and Company B would be:

Company A

Equipment	3,000	
Accumulated Depreciation — Equipment...	6,000	
Equipment..		9,000

Computation:

$9,000 cost of old equipment − $6,000 accumulated depreciation = $3,000 carrying value of the old equipment.

Company B

Equipment	4,500	
Accumulated Depreciation — Equipment...	7,500	
Equipment..		12,000

Computation:

$12,000 cost of old equipment − $7,500 accumulated depreciation = $4,500 carrying value of the old equipment.

Since the fair market value ($5,000) exceeded the book value of each asset involved in the exchange, each company had an indicated gain ($2,000 for Company A and $500 for Company B), but it is deferred and not recognized.

If the fair market values of the assets exchanged had been $4,000 at the time of the exchange, Company A would still have an indicated gain ($1,000) and would record the exchange as above with the gain deferred. However, Company B would have an indicated loss of $500 on the exchange, $4,500 − $4,000, and would value the new equipment at $4,000 after recognizing the loss of $500. This latter treatment differs from the income tax treatment for exchanges with an indicated loss. Under income tax regulations, no gain *or* loss is recognized on exchange of productive, like-kind assets.[14]

Exchange Not Culminating the Earnings Process — Boot Involved.

When a small amount of monetary consideration (boot) is *given* in an exchange, the same procedures apply as when no boot is involved.[15] No indicated gain is recognized and the new asset is recorded at the carrying value of the old asset plus the cash given. However, if boot is *received* in the exchange, and there is an indicated gain on the transaction, a portion of the gain is recognized. The formula for the amount of gain recognized is as follows:[16]

$$\text{Recognized Gain} = \frac{\text{Boot}}{\text{Boot} + \text{Fair Market Value of Acquired Asset}} \times \text{Total Indicated Gain}$$

The total indicated gain is the difference between the fair market value of the asset given up and its book value. The recognized gain is determined by

[14]Internal Revenue Code, Sec. 1031.

[15]Opinion No. 29 does not define a "small amount of monetary consideration." Presumably, if the monetary amount exceeds the concept of being small, the transaction no longer qualifies as a nonmonetary exchange and the exchange would be accounted for as a monetary exchange with any gain or loss recognized.

[16]*Opinions of the Accounting Principles Board, No. 29, op. cit.*, par. 22.

computing the percentage the boot received is of the total consideration received and applying this percentage to the indicated gain. This is a somewhat arbitrary rule, and difficult to justify in theory. It also differs from the income tax rule which requires recognition of the gain to the extent boot is received.

To illustrate this situation, assume that Company A exchanged equipment costing $15,000 with accumulated depreciation of $9,000 and a fair market value of $8,000 plus cash of $500 for similar equipment from Company B costing $12,000 with accumulated depreciation on Company B's books of $5,000 and a fair market value of $8,500. Company A would have an indicated gain of $2,000 ($8,000 fair market value of the asset given up less its carrying value of $6,000). The gain can also be determined by reference to the fair market value of the asset received ($8,500 fair market value of the asset received less $6,500, the book value of the asset exchanged plus boot paid). Because the exchange is not viewed as culminating the earnings process, the gain is deferred. The entries on the books of Company A would be as follows:

Company A (boot given in exchange)

Equipment	6,500	
Accumulated Depreciation — Equipment..	9,000	
Cash...		500
Equipment..		15,000

Computation:
$15,000 cost of old equipment − $9,000 accumulated depreciation + $500 cash = $6,500 carrying value of the old equipment plus cash paid.

Company B would have an indicated gain of $1,500 ($8,500 − $7,000, the carrying value of the asset exchanged). However, since Company B received the boot, a portion of the gain will be recognized and the balance deferred. The recognized gain is computed from the formula as follows:

$$\text{Recognized Gain} = \frac{\$500}{\$500 + \$8,000} \times \$1,500$$
$$= 1/17 \times \$1,500 = \underline{\underline{\$88}}$$

The entries on the books of Company B would be as follows:

Company B (boot received in exchange)

Equipment	6,588	
Accumulated Depreciation — Equipment..	5,000	
Cash	500	
Equipment..		12,000
Gain on Exchange of Equipment......................................		88

Computation:
$12,000 cost of old equipment − $5,000 accumulated depreciation − $500 cash = $6,500 carrying value of the old equipment minus cash paid. $6,500 + $88 gain = $6,588.

The accounting for nonmonetary exchanges is summarized in the flowchart on page 274.

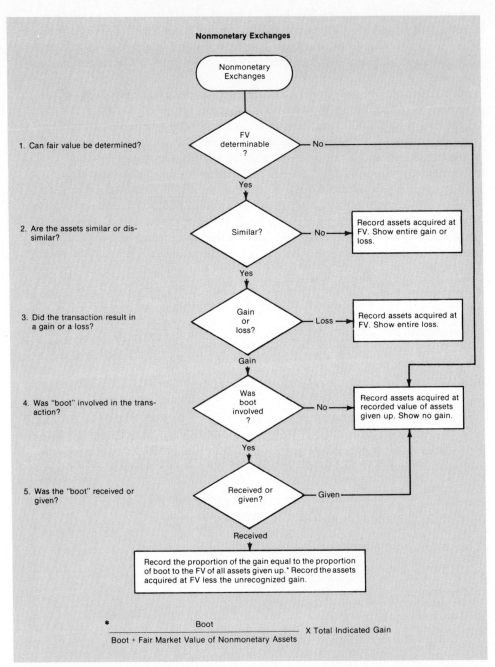

Nonmonetary Exchanges

1. Can fair value be determined?

2. Are the assets similar or dissimilar?

3. Did the transaction result in a gain or a loss?

4. Was "boot" involved in the transaction?

5. Was the "boot" received or given?

Nonmonetary Exchanges

FV determinable?

No → Record assets acquired at recorded value of assets given up. Show no gain.

Yes

Similar?

No → Record assets acquired at FV. Show entire gain or loss.

Yes

Gain or loss?

Loss → Record assets acquired at FV. Show entire loss.

Gain

Was boot involved?

No → Record assets acquired at recorded value of assets given up. Show no gain.

Yes

Received or given?

Given →

Received

Record the proportion of the gain equal to the proportion of boot to the FV of all assets given up.* Record the assets acquired at FV less the unrecognized gain.

$$* \frac{\text{Boot}}{\text{Boot} + \text{Fair Market Value of Nonmonetary Assets}} \times \text{Total Indicated Gain}$$

Reprinted with permission of *The CPA Journal,* © 1979, New York State Society of Certified Public Accountants.

Accounting for Nonmonetary Exchanges[17]

[17]Bruce E. Collier and Paul Munter, "A Flowchart of APB Opinion No. 29 — Accounting for Nonmonetary Transactions," *CPA Journal* (September 1979), p. 84.

Acquisition by Issuance of Securities

A company may acquire certain property by issuing its own bonds or stock. When a market value for the securities can be determined, such value is assigned to the asset; in the absence of a market value for the securities, the fair market value of the asset would be sought. If bonds or stock are selling at more or less than par value, Bonds Payable or Capital Stock should be credited at par and the difference recorded as a premium or discount. To illustrate, assume that a company issues 1,000 shares of $25 par stock in acquiring land; the stock is currently selling on the market at $45. An entry should be made as follows:

Land	45,000	
Common Stock		25,000
Premium on Common Stock		20,000

When securities do not have an established market value, appraisal of the assets by an independent authority may be required to arrive at an objective determination of their fair market value. If satisfactory market values cannot be obtained for either securities issued or the assets acquired, values as established by the board of directors may have to be accepted for accounting purposes. Disclosure should be provided on the balance sheet of the source of the valuation. The assignment of values by the board of directors is normally not subject to challenge unless it can be shown that the board has acted fraudulently. Nevertheless, evidence should be sought to validate the fairness of original valuations, and if within a short time after an acquisition, the sale of stock or other information indicates that original valuations were erroneous, appropriate action should be taken to restate asset and owners' equity accounts.

Property is frequently acquired in exchange for securities pursuant to a corporate merger or consolidation. When such combination represents the transfer of properties to a new owner, the combination is designated a *purchase* and acquired assets are reported at their cost to the new owner. But when such combination represents essentially no more than a continuation of the original ownership in the enlarged entity, the combination is designated a *pooling of interests* and accounting authorities have approved the practice of recording properties at the original book values as shown on the books of the acquired company. Specific guidelines for distinguishing between a purchase and a pooling of interests are included in APB Opinion No. 16 and are discussed in detail in advanced accounting texts.[18]

Acquisition by Donation or Discovery

When property is received through donation by a governmental unit or other source, there is no cost that can be used as a basis for its valuation. It is classified as a **nonreciprocal transfer of a nonmonetary asset**.[19] Even

---

[18]See Paul M. Fischer, William James Taylor, and J. Arthur Leer, *Advanced Accounting* (Cincinnati: South-Western Publishing Co., 1978).

[19]*Opinions of the Accounting Principles Board, No. 29, op. cit.*, par. 3(d).

though certain expenditures may have to be made incident to the gift, these expenditures are generally considerably less than the value of the property. Here cost obviously fails to provide a satisfactory basis for asset accountability as well as for future income measurement.

Property acquired through donation should be appraised and recorded at its fair market value.[20] A donation increases owners' equity, therefore Donated Capital is credited. To illustrate, if the Beverly Hills Chamber of Commerce donates land and buildings appraised at $50,000 and $150,000 respectively, the entry on the books of the donee would be:

Land	50,000	
Buildings	150,000	
Donated Capital		200,000

Depreciation of an asset acquired by gift should be recorded in the usual manner; the value assigned to the asset providing the basis for the depreciation charge.

If a gift is contingent upon some act to be performed by the donee, the contingent nature of the asset and the capital item should be indicated in the account titles. Account balances should be reported "short" or a special note should be made on the balance sheet. When conditions of the gift have been met, both the increase in assets and in owners' equity should be recognized in the accounts and on the financial statements.

Occasionally, valuable resources are discovered on already owned land. The discovery greatly increases the value of the property. However, because the cost of the land is not affected by the discovery, it is common practice to ignore this increase in value. Similarly, the increase in value for assets that change over time, such as growing timber or aging wine, is ignored in common practice. Failure to recognize these discovery or accretion values ignores the economic reality of the situation and tends to materially understate the assets of the entity. More meaningful decisions could probably be made if the user of the statements was aware of these changes in value.

Recently, special attention has been focused on the discovery value of oil and gas reserves. Most of the increased attention has been caused by the energy shortages experienced in the United States, and the rapid increase in oil and gas prices charged by oil-producing companies in the Near East and Mexico. Exploration and drilling costs in the oil industry have historically been recorded in one of two ways; either as an asset to be written off against revenue from producing wells (**full cost**), or as an immediate write-off unless successful discoveries of oil are made (**successful efforts**). In an attempt to increase comparability among oil and gas producing companies, the FASB established guidelines in FASB Statement No. 19 that would have allowed deferral of these drilling costs only for a reasonable period or, until the productivity of an oil well could be determined. This was a form of successful efforts accounting. These guidelines were suspended by the FASB before they could be put into effect. The suspension resulted from extreme pressure from the Securities and Exchange Commission, the Fed-

---

[20]*Ibid.*, par. 18.

eral Trade Commission, and small oil producers who did not want to show large losses on their income statement for the write-offs of these developmental costs. In the place of establishing a common method for handling these costs, the SEC proposed experimenting with the use of a new method of accounting referred to as **Revenue Recognition Accounting (RRA)**. In effect, this proposal would permit a company to place a current value on proven recoverable oil reserves which can then be used to offset developmental costs. This is in reality a form of discovery value accounting that would recognize revenue when the reserves are found, not when they are actually withdrawn from the ground. For the present, RRA figures may be reported as supplemental information to a company's financial statements.

RECORDING ACQUISITION OF SPECIFIC ASSETS

Special accounting problems arise in recording the acquisition of certain property items. Attention is directed in the following sections to specific properties and their special problems.

Real Property

All property is divided into two basic categories — real property and personal property. **Real property**, alternatively referred to as realty or real estate, includes land and most things affixed to it. The latter element includes buildings, building fixtures such as plumbing that cannot be removed without damage to the structure, and most land improvements such as trees, shrubs, and sidewalks. All other property is **personal property**.

Land. Rights to land arising from purchase should be distinguished from rights under leaseholds and under easements. With a **purchase**, the buyer acquires title and ownership **in fee simple**, and the property is properly recognized as an asset. A **leasehold** provides rights to the possession and profits of land for a certain period. An **easement** provides rights for the use of land as in the case of rights-of-way or other special privileges. Recognition of asset balances for leaseholds and easements is limited to prepayments of rents and fees to the owners of land for the acquired rights unless the leasehold or easement is in substance a purchase. In this case, the present value of future rental payments is capitalized.

When land is purchased, its cost includes not only the negotiated purchase price but also all other costs related to the acquisition including brokers' commissions, legal fees, title, recording, and escrow fees, and surveying fees. Any existing unpaid tax, interest, or other liens on the property assumed by the buyer are added to cost.

Costs of clearing, grading, subdividing, or otherwise permanently improving the land after its acquisition should also be treated as increases in the cost of land. When a site secured for a new plant is already occupied by a building that must be torn down, the cost of removing the old structure less any recovery from salvage is added to land cost. If salvage exceeds the cost of razing buildings, the excess may be considered a reduction of land cost. Special assessments by local governments for certain local benefits, such as streets and sidewalks, lighting, and sewers and drainage systems that will be maintained by the government, may be regarded as permanently improving land and thus chargeable to this asset. When expenditures are incurred for land improvements having a limited life and requiring ultimate replacement as, for example, paving, fencing, water and sewage systems, and landscaping, such costs should be summarized separately in an account entitled Land Improvements and depreciated over the estimated useful life of the improvements. The useful life of some improvements may be limited to the life of the buildings on the land; other improvements may have an independent service life.

Land qualifies for presentation in the land, buildings, and equipment category only when it is being used in the normal activities of the business. Land held for future use or for speculation should be reported under the long-term investments heading; land held for current sale should be reported as a current asset. A descriptive account title should be used to distinguish land not used in normal operations from the land in use.

Buildings. A purchase involving the acquisition of both land and buildings requires the cost to be allocated between the two assets. Allocable cost consists of the purchase price plus all charges incident to the purchase. The cost allocated to buildings is increased by expenditures for reconditioning and repairs in preparing the asset for use as well as by expenditures for improvements and additions.

When buildings are constructed, their costs consists of materials, labor, and overhead related to construction. Costs of excavation or grading and filling required for purposes of the specific project, rather than for making land usable, are charged to buildings. Charges for architects' fees, building permits and fees, workers' compensation and accident insurance, fire insurance for the period of construction, and temporary buildings used for construction activities, form part of the total building cost. Tax on property improvements, as well as financing costs during a period of construction, are generally capitalized as a cost of buildings.

It was suggested earlier that when land and buildings are acquired and buildings are immediately demolished, the cost of demolishing buildings is added to land as a cost of preparing land for its intended use. However, the cost of demolishing buildings that have been previously occupied by the company requires different treatment. This is a cost that should be identified with the original buildings. The recovery of salvage upon asset retirement serves to reduce the cost arising from the use of an asset and is frequently anticipated in calculating periodic charges for depreciation; a cost arising from asset retirement serves to increase the cost of asset use but is seldom anticipated in developing periodic charges.

In many instances, careful analysis is required in determining whether an expenditure should be recognized as buildings or whether it should be identified with the land or equipment categories. For example, expenditures for sidewalks and roads that are part of a building program are normally reported as buildings, but these would be properly reported as land improvements when they improve land regardless of its use; expenditures for items such as shelving, cabinets, or partitions in the course of building construction are normally reported as buildings, but these would be properly reported as equipment items when they are movable, can be used in different centers, and are considered to have independent lives. Particular care should be directed to charges against revenues under different classification and recording alternatives. Frequently alternative classifications can be supported and the ultimate choice will be a matter of judgment.

If depreciation on buildings is to be recognized satisfactorily, separate accounts should be maintained for each building with a different life as well as for those structural elements of a building requiring modification or replacement before the building is fully depreciated, such as loading and shipping quarters, storage facilities, and garages. Separate recording should also be extended to building equipment and appurtenances requiring replacement before the building is fully depreciated, such as boilers, heating and ventilating systems, plumbing and lighting systems, elevators, and wiring and piping installations. The latter items are frequently summarized in an account titled Building Equipment or Building Improvements, but detailed records will be required in support of this balance of the different service lives of the individual items.

Equipment

Equipment covers a wide range of items that vary with the particular enterprise and its activities. The discussion in the following paragraphs is limited to machinery, tools, patterns and dies, furniture and fixtures, motor vehicles, and returnable containers.

Machinery of the manufacturing concern includes such items as lathes, stamping machines, ovens, and conveyor systems. The machinery account is debited for all expenditures identified with the acquisition and the preparation for use of factory machines. Machinery cost includes the purchase price, tax and duties on purchase, freight charges, insurance charges while in transit, installation charges, expenditures for testing and final preparation for use, and costs for reconditioning used equipment when purchased.

Two classes of **tools** are employed in productive activities: (1) **machine tools**, representing detachable parts of a machine, such as dies, drills, and punches; and (2) **hand tools**, such as hammers, wrenches, and saws. Both classes of tools are normally of small individual cost and are relatively short-lived as a result of wear, breakage, and loss. These factors frequently suggest that these items be accounted for as a single asset. Replacement of these small tools may then either be charged directly to expense or added to the single asset account and written off by reasonable annual depreciation charges.

Patterns and dies are acquired for designing, stamping, cutting, or forging out a particular object. The cost of patterns and dies is either a purchase cost or a developmental cost composed of labor, materials, and overhead.

When patterns and dies are used in normal productive activities, their cost is reported as an asset and the asset values are written off over the period of their usefulness. When the use of such items is limited to the manufacture of a single job, their cost is recognized as a part of the cost of that job.

Furniture and fixtures include such items as desks, chairs, carpets, showcases, and display fixtures. Acquisitions should be identified with production, selling, or general and administrative functions. Such classification makes it possible to assign depreciation accurately to the different business activities. Furniture and fixtures are recorded at cost, which includes purchase price, tax, freight, and installation charges.

Automobile and truck acquisitions should also be identified with production, selling or general and administrative functions. Depreciation can then be accurately related to the different activities. Automotive equipment is recorded at its purchase price increased by any sales and excise tax and delivery charges paid. When payment for equipment includes charges for items, such as current license fees, personal property tax, and insurance, these should be recognized separately as expenses relating to both the current and the future use of the equipment.

Goods are frequently delivered in **containers** to be returned and reused. Returnable containers consist of such items as tanks, drums, and barrels. Containers are depreciable assets used in the business and are included in the equipment group. Adjustments must be made periodically to reduce the asset account and its related accumulated depreciation for containers not expected to be returned. The reduction is reported as a current loss.

Leaseholds

A **leasehold** is a contractual agreement whereby a **lessee** is granted a right to use property owned by the **lessor** for a specified period of time for a specified periodic cost. Many leases are in effect purchases of property. In such cases, the property should be recorded on the lessee's books as an asset at the present value of the future lease payments. Even when a lease is not considered to be the same as a purchase and the periodic payments are written off as rental expense, certain lease prepayments or improvements to the property by the lessee may be treated as capital expenditures. Since leasehold improvements, such as partitions in a building, additions, and attached equipment, revert to the owner at the expiration of the lease, they are properly capitalized on the books of the lessee and amortized over the remaining life of the lease. Some lease costs are really expenses of the period and should not be capitalized. This includes improvements that are made in lieu of rent; e.g., a lessee builds partitions in a leased warehouse for storage of its product. The lessor allows the lessee to offset the cost against rental expense for the period. These costs should be expensed by the lessee.

Patents

A **patent** is an exclusive right granted by the government to an inventor enabling the inventor to control the manufacture, sale, or other use of the invention for a specified period of time. The United States Patent Office issues patents which are valid for **seventeen years** from the date of issuance. Patents are not renewable although effective control of an invention is frequently maintained beyond the expiration of the original patent through new patents covering improvements or changes. The owner of a patent may grant its use to others under royalty agreements or the patent may be sold.

The issuance of a patent does not necessarily indicate the existence of a valuable right. The value of a patent stems from whatever advantage it might afford its owner in excluding competitors from utilizing a process resulting in lower costs or superior products. Many patents cover inventions that cannot be exploited commercially and may actually be worthless.

Patents are recorded at their **acquisition costs.** When a patent is purchased, it is recorded at the new owner's purchase price. When a patent is developed through company-sponsored research, the accounting treatment falls under FASB Statement No. 2, "Accounting for Research and Development Costs," described previously. Only patent licensing and related legal fees are included as its costs. All related experimental and developmental expenditures, along with the cost of models and drawings not required by the patent application, are considered research and development costs and are to be debited to expense when incurred.[21]

The validity of a patent may be challenged in the courts. The cost of successfully prosecuting or defending infringement suits is regarded as a cost of establishing the legal rights of the holder and may be added to the other costs of the patent. In the event of unsuccessful litigation, the litigation cost, as well as other patent costs, should be written off as a loss.

Copyrights

A **copyright** is an exclusive right granted by the federal government permitting an author, composer, or artist to publish, sell, license, or otherwise control a literary, musical, or artistic work. In 1978, a new copyright law became effective in the United States. Under the new law, a copyright expires fifty years after the death of the creator of the work. Formerly, copyrights expired after a maximum of 56 years from the time they were granted. The new law permits the United States to be part of the Bern Union, the most widely recognized international copyright agreement.

The cost assigned to a copyright consists of those charges required to establish the right. When a copyright is purchased, it is recorded at its purchase price. The cost of any subsequent litigation to protect the copyright, if successful, should be capitalized as an additional cost of the copyright.

Trademarks and Trade Names

Trademarks and **trade names,** together with distinctive symbols, labels, and designs, are important to all companies that depend upon a public de-

---

[21]*Statement of Financial Accounting Standards, No. 2,* "Accounting for Research and Development Costs" (Stamford, Conn.: Financial Accounting Standards Board, 1974), par. 10(i).

mand for their products. It is by means of these distinctive markings that particular products are differentiated from competing brands. In building up the reputation of a product, relatively large costs may be incurred. The federal government offers legal protection for trademarks through their registry with the United States Patent Office. Prior and continuous use is the important factor in determining the ownership of a particular trademark. The right to a trademark is retained as long as continuous use is made of it. Protection of trade names and brands that cannot be registered must be sought in the common law. Distinctive trademarks, trade names, and brands can be assigned or sold.

The cost of a trademark consists of those expenditures required to establish it, including filing and registry fees, and expenditures for successful litigation in defense of the trademark. When a trademark is purchased, it is recorded at its purchase price.

Organization Costs

In forming a corporation, certain expenditures are incurred including legal fees, promotional costs, stock certificate costs, underwriting costs, and state incorporation fees. The benefits to be derived from these expenditures normally extend beyond the first fiscal period. Further, the recognition of these expenditures as expenses at the time of organization would commit the corporation to a deficit before it actually begins operations. These factors support the practice of recognizing the initial costs of organization as an intangible asset.

Expenditures relating to organization may be considered to benefit the corporation during its entire life. Thus, there is theoretical support for carrying organization costs as an intangible asset until the corporation is dissolved or becomes inactive. On the other hand, it may be argued that the organizational and start-up costs of a business are of primary benefit during the first few years of operation. Beyond that point, these costs generally become insignificant in terms of impact on the success or failure of the enterprise.

It is sometimes suggested that operating losses of the first few years should be capitalized as organization costs or as goodwill. It is argued that the losses cannot be avoided in the early years when the business is being developed, and hence it is reasonable that these losses should be absorbed in later years. Although losses may be inevitable, they do not necessarily carry any future service potential. To report these losses as intangible assets would result in the overstatement of assets, net income, and owners' equity. This practice cannot be condoned.

Franchises

A **franchise** is an exclusive right or privilege received by a business or individual (**franchisee**) to perform certain business functions or use certain products or services, usually in a specified geographical area. The **grantor** of the franchise (**franchisor**) usually specifies a period of time over which the right may be exercised and the conditions under which the franchise can be revoked. Some grantors are governmental units such as municipalities, that frequently grant business concerns the right to use public property to provide services such as utilities, refuse collection, and public transportation. Other grantors are private companies who grant exclusive rights to market their products or to use their name.

The cost of a franchise includes any sum paid specifically for a franchise as well as legal fees and other costs incurred in obtaining it. Although the value of a franchise at the time of its acquisition may be substantially in excess of its cost, the amount recorded should be limited to actual outlays. When a franchise is purchased from another company, the amount paid is recorded as the franchise cost.

A franchise agreement may require that periodic payments be made to the grantor. Payments may be fixed amounts or they may be variable amounts depending upon revenue, utilization, or other factors. These payments should be recognized by the franchisee as charges to periodic revenue. When certain property improvements are required under terms of the franchise, the costs of the improvements should be capitalized and charged to revenue over the life of the franchise.

Goodwill

Goodwill is generally regarded as the summation of all the special advantages, not otherwise identifiable, related to a going concern. It includes such items as a good name, capable staff and personnel, high credit standing, reputation for superior products and services, and favorable location. Unlike most other assets, tangible or intangible, goodwill cannot be transferred without transferring the entire business.

From an accounting point of view, goodwill is recognized as the ability of a business to earn above-normal earnings with the identifiable assets employed in the business. Above-normal earnings mean a rate of return greater than that normally required to attract investors into a particular type of business.

The recording of goodwill has been the subject of many discussions and publications. Under currently accepted accounting principles, goodwill is recorded on the books only when it is **acquired by purchase** or otherwise established through a business transaction. The latter condition includes its recognition in connection with a merger or a reorganization of a corporation or a change of partners in a partnership.

Although goodwill is recognized on the company books only when it is acquired in an arm's-length transaction, this procedure makes it more difficult to compare a company that has recorded goodwill and one that doesn't. Just because a company has not purchased another company does not mean it does not have goodwill as defined above. Thus, current accounting principles may result in misleading users as far as goodwill is concerned. On the other hand, to allow companies to place a value on their own goodwill would undoubtedly lead to abuse. These difficulties have led some accountants to suggest that all purchased goodwill should be written off to expense as soon as it is acquired. Advocates of this position include the authors of Accounting Research Study No. 10, "Accounting for Goodwill," whose justification for immediate write-off was given as follows:

1. Goodwill is not a resource or property right that is consumed or utilized in the production of earnings. It is the result of expectations of future earnings by investors and thus is not subject to normal amortization procedures.
2. Goodwill is subject to sudden and wide fluctuations. That value has no reliable or continuing relation to costs incurred in its creation.
3. Under existing practices of accounting, neither the cost nor the value of non-purchased goodwill is reported in the balance sheet. Purchased goodwill has no continuing, separately measurable existence after the combination and is merged with the total goodwill value of the continuing business entity. As such, its write-off cannot be measured with any validity.
4. Goodwill as an asset account is not relevant to an investor. Most analysts ignore any reported goodwill when analyzing a company's status and operations.[22]

This position has been consistently rejected by the accounting principles-setting bodies, and the immediate write-off of purchased goodwill is strongly discouraged. They maintain that a price has been paid for the excess earnings power, and it should be recognized as an asset. Because of the poor connotative image the term goodwill has acquired, some companies have avoided the use of it. For example, General Mills refers to its goodwill as "Excess of Cost over Net Assets of Acquired Companies."[23]

In the purchase of a going business, the actual price paid for goodwill usually results from bargaining and compromises between the parties concerned. A basis for negotiation in arriving at a price for goodwill could involve many variables:

1. The level of projected future earnings.
2. An appropriate rate of return.
3. Current valuation of the net business assets other than goodwill.

These are not really accounting methods, but financial models that utilize accounting data.

When a lump-sum amount is paid for an established business and no explicit evaluation is made of goodwill, goodwill may still be recognized. In this case the identifiable net assets require appraisal, and the difference between the full purchase price and the value of identifiable net assets can be attributed to the purchase of goodwill. In appraising properties for this purpose, current market values should be sought rather than the values reported in the accounts. Receivables should be stated at amounts estimated to be realized. Inventories and securities should be restated in terms of current market values. Land, buildings, and equipment may require special

---

[22]George R. Catlett and Norman O. Olson, "Accounting for Goodwill," *Accounting Research Study No. 10* (New York: American Institute of Certified Public Accountants, 1968).

[23]See Appendix B.

appraisals in arriving at their present replacement or reproduction values. Intangible assets, such as patents and franchises, should be included at their current values even though, originally, expenditures were reported as expenses or were reported as assets and amortized against revenue. Care should be taken to determine that liabilities are fully recognized. Assets at their current fair market values less the liabilities to be assumed provide the net assets total that, together with estimated future earnings, is used in arriving at a purchase price.

To the extent possible, the amount paid for an existing company should be related to identifiable assets. If an excess does exist, the use of a term other than goodwill can avoid the implication that only companies that purchase other companies have goodwill. The term used by General Mills seems to overcome this difficulty.

EXPENDITURES SUBSEQUENT TO ACQUISITION

During the lives of property items, regular as well as special expenditures are incurred. Certain expenditures are required to maintain and repair assets; others are incurred to increase their capacity or efficiency or to extend their useful lives. Each expenditure requires careful analysis to determine whether it should be assigned to revenue of the current period, hence charged to an expense account, or whether it should be assigned to revenue of more than one period, which calls for a debit to an asset account or to an accumulated depreciation account. In many cases the answer may not be clear, and the procedure chosen may be a matter of judgment.

The terms maintenance, repairs, betterments, improvements, additions, and rearrangements are used in describing expenditures made in the course of asset use. These are described in the following sections.

Maintenance

Expenditures to maintain plant assets in fit condition are referred to as **maintenance**. Among these are expenditures for painting, lubricating, and adjusting equipment. Maintenance items are ordinary and recurring and do not improve the asset or add to its life; therefore, they are recorded as expenses.

Repairs

Expenditures to restore assets to a fit condition upon their breakdown or to restore and replace broken parts are referred to as **repairs**. When these expenditures are ordinary and benefit only current operations, they are debited to expense. When they are extraordinary and **extend the life of the asset,** they may be debited to the accumulated depreciation account. The depreciation rate is then redetermined in view of changes in the asset book value and estimated life. Debits for repairs extending the useful life of the asset are made against the accumulated depreciation account to avoid a build-up of gross asset values. The book value of the asset will be the same whether the debit is made to the asset account directly or to the accumulated depreciation account.

Repairs involving the overhauling of certain assets are frequently referred to as **renewals**. Substitutions of parts or entire units are referred to as **replacements**. The cost of the replacement may be expensed or capitalized depending upon how the property unit is defined. For example, components of a major piece of equipment, such as the motor, the frame, and the attachments, may be considered separate property units, or the entire machine may be considered the property unit. If the component parts are the property units, replacement of a component requires entries cancelling the book value related to the old component and capitalizing the cost of new equipment. If the property unit is the entire machine, the replacement of the component would be debited to an expense if it is considered to be a normal replacement, or debited to accumulated depreciation if it is considered to be an extraordinary replacement. General criteria as to what constitutes a property unit have not been developed by the profession. Companies have had to establish their own guidelines and consistently apply them. Research indicates that companies do not feel that this lack of guidelines has led to serious abuses in practice.[24]

Repairs arising from flood, fire, or other casualty require special analysis. An expenditure to restore an asset to its previous condition should be reported as a loss from casualties.

Betterments or Improvements

Changes in assets designed to provide increased or improved services are referred to as **betterments** or **improvements**. Installation of improved lighting systems, heating systems, or sanitary systems represent betterments. Minor expenditures for betterments may be recorded as ordinary repairs. Major expenditures call for entries to cancel the book value related to the old asset and to establish the new, or entries to reduce the accumulated depreciation related to the original asset. The latter method is sometimes required when the cost of the item replaced is not readily separable from the whole unit.

Additions

Enlargements and extensions of existing facilities are referred to as **additions**. A new plant wing, additional loading docks, or the expansion of a paved parking lot represent additions. These expenditures are capitalized, and the cost is written off over the service life of the addition.

Another type of addition occurs with intangible assets such as patents, copyrights, trademarks, and franchises. Sometimes legal costs are incurred to protect a patent or a copyright. If the legal action is successful, the legal cost could be deferred over the remaining life of the asset. This would be proper because the successful conclusion of the suit means the asset will

---

[24]Charles Lamden, Dale L. Gerboth, and Thomas McRae, "Accounting for Depreciable Assets," *Accounting Research Monograph No. 1* (New York: American Institute of Certified Public Accountants, 1975), pp. 48–49.

still be a valuable piece of property to the company. On the other hand, if the suit is lost, the costs should be expensed and the remaining value of the asset should be written off against revenue.

Rearrangements

Movement of machinery and equipment items and reinstallations to secure economies or greater efficiencies are referred to as **rearrangements**. Costs related to rearrangements should be assigned to those periods benefiting from such changes. When more than one period is benefited, an asset account — appropriately designated to indicate the nature of the cost deferral — should be established and this balance allocated systematically to revenue. When rearrangements involve reinstallation costs, the portion of asset book value related to an original installation should be written off; the cost of the new installation should be added to the asset and written off over its remaining life.

SUMMARY

The most challenging issue facing accountants in the area of asset acquisitions is which costs should be deferred and matched against future revenue, and which should be expensed immediately. Costs to acquire new property items with lives in excess of one fiscal period should clearly be capitalized and charged against future periods. Accounting for repairs, additions, and similar costs incurred subsequent to the initial acquisition is less clear, and such expenditures must be individually evaluated in light of existing conditions. The historical acquisition cost of the asset is widely accepted as the basis for the gross investment, whether for tangible or intangible assets. Methods for matching these costs against future revenues will be discussed in the next chapter, as well as accounting for the retirement of assets.

QUESTIONS

1. What are the characteristics that distinguish intangible assets from tangible assets?

2. (a) Distinguish between capital expenditures and revenue expenditures. (b) Give five examples of each.

3. Which of the following items would be recorded as a revenue expenditure and which would be recorded as a capital expenditure?
  (a) Cost of installing machinery.
  (b) Cost of moving and reinstalling machinery.
  (c) Extensive repairs as a result of fire.
  (d) Cost of grading land.
  (e) Insurance on machinery in transit.
  (f) Bond discount amortization during construction period.
  (g) Cost of major overhaul on machinery.
  (h) New safety guards on machinery.
  (i) Commission on purchase of real estate.
  (j) Special tax assessment for street improvements.
  (k) Cost of repainting offices.

4. Indicate the effects of the following errors on the balance sheet and the income statement in the current year and in succeeding years:
  (a) The cost of a depreciable asset is incorrectly recorded as a revenue expenditure.
  (b) A revenue expenditure is incorrectly recorded as an addition to the cost of a depreciable asset.

5. What types of activities are considered research and development activities?

6. How are identifiable intangible assets more similar to tangible assets than to the intangible asset, goodwill?

7. What additional accounting problems are introduced when a company purchases equipment on a long-term contract rather than with cash?

8. Under what circumstances is a gain or loss recognized when a productive asset is exchanged for a similar productive asset?

9. How should development stage enterprises report (a) their organization costs and (b) any net operating losses?

10. The Parkhurst Corporation acquires land and buildings valued at $250,000 as a gift from Industrial City. The president of the company maintains that since there was no cost for the acquisition, neither cost of the facilities nor depreciation needs to be recognized for financial statement purposes. Evaluate the president's position assuming (a) the donation is unconditional; (b) the donation is contingent upon the employment by the company of a certain number of employees for a ten-year period.

11. In the balance sheets of many companies, the largest classification of assets in amount is plant assets. Name the items, in addition to the amount paid to the former owner or contractor, that may be properly included as part of the acquisition cost of the following property items: (a) land, (b) buildings, and (c) equipment.

12. How would a trademark worth $5,000,000 be reported on the balance sheet if (a) the trademark were purchased for $5,000,000 or (b) the trademark gradually became identified over the years as a company symbol?

13. (a) What items are normally considered to comprise the organization costs of a company? (b) Would you approve the inclusion of the following items: (1) first-year advertising costs; (2) first-year loss from operations?

14. What costs are capitalized as (a) copyrights, (b) franchises, (c) trademarks?

15. (a) Under what conditions may goodwill be reported as an asset? (b) The Radcliff Company engages in a widespread advertising campaign on behalf of new products, charging above-normal expenditures to goodwill. Do you approve of this practice? Why or why not?

16. Distinguish between (a) maintenance and repairs, (b) ordinary repairs and extraordinary repairs, (c) betterments and additions.

EXERCISES

exercise 10-1

In 1981 the MSA Corporation incurred research and development costs as follows:

Materials and equipment	$100,000
Personnel	100,000
Indirect costs	50,000
	$250,000

These costs relate to a product that will be marketed in 1982. It is estimated that these costs will be recouped by December 31, 1985.

(1) What is the amount of research and development costs which should be charged to income in 1981?
(2) Assume that of the above costs, equipment of $60,000 can be used on other research projects. Estimated useful life of the equipment is five years, and it was acquired at the beginning of 1981. What is the amount of research and development costs which should be charged to income in 1981 under these conditions. Assume depreciation on all equipment is computed on a straight-line basis. (AICPA adapted)

exercise 10-2

Spencer, Inc., acquires a machine priced at $82,000. Payment of this amount may be made within 60 days; a 5% discount is allowed if cash is paid at time of purchase. Give the entry to record the acquisition, assuming:

(a) Cash is paid at time of purchase.
(b) Payment is to be made at the end of 60 days.
(c) A long-term contract is signed whereby a down payment of $25,000 is made with 12 payments of $6,000 to be made at monthly intervals thereafter.

exercise 10-3

The Red Sky Shipping Co. acquired land, buildings, and equipment at a lump-sum price of $380,000. An appraisal of the assets at the time of acquisition disclosed the following values:

Land... $150,000
Buildings 225,000
Equipment... 125,000

What cost should be assigned to each asset?

exercise 10-4

The Dixon Corporation purchased land, a building, a patent, and a franchise for the lump sum of $950,000. A real estate appraiser estimated the building to have a resale value of $400,000 (⅔ of the total worth of land and building). The franchise had no established resale value. The patent was valued by management at $300,000. Give the journal entry to record the acquisition of the assets.

exercise 10-5

Braithwaite Hot Dog Co. purchases equipment costing $120,000 with a down payment of $30,000 and sufficient semiannual installments of $7,000 (including interest on the unpaid principal at 10% per year) to pay the balance.

(1) Give the entries to record the purchase and the first two semiannual payments.
(2) Assume that there was no known cash price and twenty semiannual installments were to be made. Give the entries to record the purchase and the first two semiannual payments.

exercise 10-6

Moore Math Analysis, Inc., purchased a new computer. The following data relate to the purchase:

(a) List price of new computer with trade-in — $60,000.
(b) Cash price of new computer with no trade-in — $53,700.
(c) Moore Math Analysis, Inc., received a trade-in allowance (based on list price) of $15,000 on a dissimilar machine costing $25,000 new and having a present book value of $12,000.
(d) The Express Delivery Service charged Moore $1,200 to deliver the computer.

Give the entry to record the acquisition of the new computer.

exercise 10-7

Assume that Alpine Corporation has a machine that cost $22,000, has a book value of $16,000, and has a market value of $20,000. For each of the following situations, indicate the value at which Alpine should record the new asset and why it should be recorded at that value.

(a) Alpine exchanged the machine for a truck with a list price of $25,000.

(b) Alpine exchanged the machine for another machine qualifying as a similar productive asset with a list price of $20,500.

(c) Alpine exchanged the machine for a newer model machine with a list price of $24,000. Alpine paid $1,000 in the transaction.

(d) Alpine exchanged the machine plus $750 cash for a similar machine from Payson Co. The newly acquired machine is carried on Payson's books at $25,000 with accumulated depreciation of $15,000; its fair market value is $20,750. In addition to determining the value, give the journal entries for both companies to record the exchange.

exercise 10-8

On January 31, 1981, Cherrytown Corp. exchanged 10,000 shares of its $25 par common stock for the following assets:

(a) A trademark valued at $150,000

(b) A building, including land, valued at $650,000 (20% of the value is for the land).

(c) A franchise right. No estimate of value at time of exchange.

Cherrytown Corp. stock is selling at $95 per share on the date of the exchange. Give the entries to record the exchange on Cherrytown's books.

exercise 10-9

The Rabbit Co. enters into a contract with the Taulbee Construction Co. for construction of an office building at a cost of $720,000. Upon completion of construction the Taulbee Construction Co. agrees to accept in full payment of the contract price Rabbit Co. 10% bonds with a face value of $400,000 and common stock with a par value of $300,000 and no established fair market value. Rabbit Co. bonds are selling on the market at this time at 98. How would you recommend the building acquisition be recorded?

exercise 10-10

The following expenditures were incurred by the Merrill Food Co. in 1982: purchase of land, $300,000; land survey, $1,500; fees for search of title for land, $350; building permit, $500; temporary quarters for construction crews, $10,750; payment to tenants of old building for vacating premises, $2,000; razing of old building, $25,000; excavation of basement, $10,000; special assessment tax for street project, $2,000; dividends, $5,000; damages awarded for injuries sustained in construction, $4,200 (no insurance was carried; the cost of insurance would have been $200); costs of construction, $750,000; cost of paving parking lot adjoining building, $25,000; cost of shrubs, trees, and other landscaping, $5,000. What is the cost of the land, land improvements, and building?

exercise 10-11

Wong and Fong Enterprises, Inc., developed a new machine which reduces the time required to insert the fortunes into their fortune cookies. Because the process is considered very valuable to the fortune cookie industry, Fong had the machine patented. The following expenses were incurred in developing and patenting the machine.

Research and development laboratory expenses	$15,000
Metal used in the construction of machine	5,000
Blueprints used to design the machine	500
Legal expenses to obtain patent	10,000
Wages paid for Fong's work on the research, development, and building of the machine (60% of the time was spent in actually building the machine)	30,000
Expense of drawings required by the patent office to be submitted with the patent application	150
Fees paid to government patent office to process patent application	500

One year later, Wong and Fong Enterprises, Inc., paid $12,000 in legal fees to successfully defend the patent against an infringement suit by the Golden Dragon Cookie Co.

Give the entries on Wong and Fong's books indicated by the above events. Ignore any amortization of the patent or depreciation of the machine.

exercise 10-12

Brookstone Corporation acquired the following assets at the beginning of 1981. Give the entries to record the acquisition of the assets.

(a) Paperback copyright to a best seller novel in exchange for 120 shares of Brookstone Corporation stock; $50 par, common stock selling for $224 per share.
(b) A fast food franchise in exchange for one acre of prime real estate. Franchises of this type are selling for $50,000 cash. The land was purchased 10 years ago for $2,500. The franchise has an unlimited life as long as Brookstone Corporation maintains the quality standards of the grantor.
(c) Enoc Enterprises for $212,500 cash. Net identifiable assets of Enoc Enterprises are fairly valued at $187,500. The purchased goodwill is expected to grow every year as Brookstone Corporation plans to expend substantial resources for advertising and other promotional activities.

exercise 10-13

The Mustang Manufacturing Co. was incorporated on January 1, 1981. In reviewing the accounts in 1982, you find the organization costs account appears as follows:

ACCOUNT   Organization Costs

Item	Debit	Credit	Balance Debit	Balance Credit
Incorporation fees	3,750		3,750	
Legal fees relative to organization	21,150		24,900	
Stock certificate cost...	6,000		30,900	
Cost of rehabilitating building acquired at end of 1981...	165,600		196,500	
Advertising expenditures to promote company products...	18,000		214,500	
Amortization of organization costs for 1981, 20% of balance of organization cost (per board of directors' resolution).........................		42,900	171,600	
Net loss for 1981	54,000		225,600	

Give the entry or entries required to correct the account.

exercise 10-14

One of the most difficult problems facing an accountant is the determination of which expenditures should be deferred as assets and which should be immediately charged off as expenses. What position would you take in each of the following instances?

(a) Painting of partitions in a large room recently divided into four sections.
(b) Labor cost of tearing down a wall to permit extension of assembly line.
(c) Replacement of motor on a machine. Life used to depreciate the machine is 8 years. The machine is 4 years old. Replacement of the motor was anticipated when the machine was purchased.
(d) Cost of grading land prior to construction.
(e) Assessment for street paving.
(f) Cost of moving and reinstalling equipment.
(g) Cost of tearing down a previously occupied old building in preparation for new construction; old building is fully depreciated.

PROBLEMS

problem 10-1

The Parowan Wholesale Company incurred the following expenses in 1981 for their office building acquired on July 1, 1981, the beginning of its fiscal year:

Cost of land	$ 75,000
Cost of building	425,000
Remodeling and repairs prior to occupancy	67,500
Escrow fee	15,000
Landscaping	25,000
Unpaid property tax for period prior to acquisition	20,000
Real estate commission	30,000

The company signed a non-interest-bearing note for $500,000 on the acquisition. The implicit interest rate is 12%. Payments of $25,000 are to be made semiannually beginning January 1, 1982, for 10 years.

Instructions: Give the required journal entries to record (1) the acquisition of the land and building (assume that cash is paid to equalize the cost of the assets and the present value of the note), and (2) the first two semiannual payments, including amortization of note discount.

problem 10-2

The following transactions were completed by the Terry Toy Co. during 1981:

Mar. 1	Purchased real property for $536,775 which included a charge of $11,775 representing property tax for March 1–June 30 that had been prepaid by the vendor; 20% of the purchase price is deemed applicable to land and the balance to buildings. A mortgage of $375,000 was assumed by the Terry Toy Co. on the purchase.
2–30	Previous owners had failed to take care of normal maintenance and repair requirements on the building, necessitating current reconditioning at a cost of $24,900.
June 1	The company exchanged its own stock with a fair market value of $35,000 (par $30,000) for a patent and a new plastic doll-making machine. The machine has a market value of $25,000.
July 1	The new machinery for the new building arrived. In addition to the machinery a new franchise was acquired from the manufacturer of the machinery to produce Double Duck dolls. Payment was made by issuing bonds with a face value of $50,000 and by paying cash of $15,000. The value of the franchise is set at $20,000 while the fair market value of the machine is $40,000.
Nov. 5–20	The company contracted for parking lots and landscaping at a cost of $45,000 and $9,600 respectively. The work was completed and billed on November 20.
Dec. 29–31	The business was closed to permit taking the year-end inventory. During this period, required redecorating and repairs were completed at a cost of $4,500.

Instructions: Give the journal entries to record each of the preceding transactions. (Disregard depreciation.)

problem 10-3

The Carter Co. planned to open a new store. The company narrowed the possible sites to two lots and decided to take purchase options on both lots while they studied traffic densities in both areas. They paid $7,200 for the option on Lot A and $14,400 for the option on Lot B. After studying traffic densities, they decided to purchase Lot B. The company opened a single real estate account that shows the following:

Debits:	Option on Lot A	$ 7,200
	Option on Lot B	14,400
	Payment of balance on Lot B	120,000
	Title insurance	2,100
	Assessment for street improvements	5,100
	Recording fee for deed	300
	Cost of razing old building on Lot B	9,000
	Payment for erection of new building	300,000
Credit:	Sale of salvaged materials from old building	9,000

The salvage value of material obtained from the old building and used in the erection of the new building was $7,500. The depreciated value of the old building, as shown by the books of the company from which the purchase was made, was $54,000. The old building was razed immediately after the purchase.

Instructions:

(1) Determine the cost of the land, listing the items included in the total.
(2) Determine the cost of the new building, listing the items included in the total.

problem 10-4

The Union Development Co. acquired the following assets in exchange for various nonmonetary assets.

1981

Mar. 15 Acquired a new computerized lathe in exchange for 3 old lathes. The old lathes had a total cost of $35,000 and had a remaining book value of $13,000. The new lathe had a market value of $20,000, approximately the same value as the three old lathes.

June 1 Acquired 200 acres of land by issuing 2,000 shares of common stock with par value of $10 and market value of $90. Market analysis reveals that the market value of the stock was a reasonable value for the land.

July 15 Acquired a used piece of heavy earth-moving equipment, market value $25,000, by exchanging a used molding machine with a market value of $5,000 (book value $2,000; cost $10,000) and land with a market value of $25,000 (cost $10,000). Cash of $5,000 was received by Union Development Co. as part of the transaction.

Aug. 15 Acquired a patent, franchise, and copyright for 2 used milling machines. The book value of each milling machine was $1,500 and each had originally cost $10,000. The market value of each machine is $12,500. It is estimated that the patent and franchise have about the same market values, and the market value of the copyright is 50% of the market value of the patent.

Nov. 1 Acquired a new packaging machine for 4 old packaging machines. The old machines had a total cost of $50,000 and a total remaining book value of $30,000. The new packaging machine has an indicated market value of $25,000, approximately the same value of the four old machines.

Instructions: Prepare the journal entries required on Union Development Co. books to record the exchanges.

problem 10-5

A review of the books of Busbee Electric Co. disclosed that there were five transactions involving gains and losses on the exchange of fixed assets. The transactions were recorded as indicated in the following ledger accounts.

Cash				Plant Assets				Accumulated Depreciation			
(2)	5,000	(5)	1,000	(1)	10,000	(3)	118,000	(3)	110,000		
(3)	6,000			(2)	25,000	(4)	300,000	(4)	390,000		

Intangible Assets		Gain on Exchange — Plant Assets			Loss on Exchange — Plant Assets		
(5)	1,000		(1)	10,000	(3)	2,000	
			(2)	30,000			
			(4)	90,000			

Investigation disclosed the following facts concerning these transactions:

(1) Exchanged a piece of equipment with a $50,000 original cost, $20,000 book value, and $30,000 current market value for a piece of similar equipment owned by Creer Electric that had a $60,000 original cost, $10,000 book value, and a $30,000 current market value.

(2) Exchanged 20 acres of land, cost $10,000, current market value $40,000, for 10 acres of land, market value $35,000, and $5,000 in cash.

(3) Exchanged a building, cost $150,000, book value $40,000, current market value $30,000, for a used building with market value of $24,000 plus cash of $6,000.

(4) Exchanged a factory building, cost $850,000, book value $460,000, current market value $550,000, for equipment owned by Crestwood, Inc. that had an original cost of $900,000, accumulated depreciation of $325,000, and current market value of $550,000.

(5) Exchanged a patent, cost $12,000, book value $6,000, current market value $3,000 and cash of $1,000 for another patent with market value of $4,000.

Instructions: Analyze each recorded transaction as to its compliance with generally accepted accounting principles. Prepare adjusting journal entries where required.

problem 10-6

In your audit of the books of Quist Corporation for the year ending September 30, 1981, you found the following items in connection with the company's patents account:

(a) The company had spent $102,000 during its fiscal year ended September 30, 1980, for research and development costs and debited this amount to its patent account. Your review of the company's cost records indicated the company had spent a total of $123,500 for the research and development of its patents, of which only $21,500 spent in its fiscal year ended September 30, 1979, had been debited to Research and Development Expense.

(b) The patents were issued on April 1, 1980. Legal expenses in connection with the issuance of the patents of $14,280 were debited to Legal and Professional Fees.

(c) The company paid a retainer of $7,500 on October 5, 1980, for legal services in connection with an infringement suit brought against it. This amount was debited to Deferred Costs.

(d) A letter dated October 15, 1981, from the company's attorneys in reply to your inquiry as to liabilities of the company existing at September 30, 1981, indicated that a settlement of the infringement suit had been arranged. The other party had agreed to drop the suit and to release the company from all future liabilities for $16,000. Additional fees due to the attorneys amounted to $590.

Instructions: From the information given, prepare correcting journal entries as of September 30, 1981.

problem 10-7

Transactions during 1981 of the newly organized Barstow Corporation included the following:

Jan. 2 Paid legal fees of $10,000 and stock certificate costs of $3,200 to complete organization of the corporation.

15 Hired a clown to stand in front of the corporate office for two weeks and hand out pamphlets and candy to create goodwill for the new enterprise. Clown cost $800; candy and pamphlets, $500.

Apr. 1 Patented a newly developed process with the following costs:

Legal fees to obtain patent	$22,400
Patent application and licensing fees	3,200
Total	$25,600

It is estimated that in five years other companies will have developed improved processes making the Barstow Corporation process obsolete.

May 1 Acquired both a license to use a special type of container and a distinctive trademark to be printed on the container in exchange for 600 shares of Barstow Corporation common stock selling for $80 per share. The license is worth twice as much as the trademark, both of which may be used for 6 years.

July 1 Acquired a shed for $50,000 to house prototypes of experimental models to be developed in future research projects.

Dec. 31 Salaries for an engineer and a chemist involved in product development totaled $100,000 in 1981.

Instructions:

(1) Give journal entries to record the foregoing transactions. (Give explanations in support of your entries.)

(2) Present in good form the "Intangible assets" section of the Barstow Corporation balance sheet at December 31, 1981.

11

Plant and Intangible Assets — Utilization and Retirement

CHAPTER OBJECTIVES

Explain the concept of periodic charges to represent the utilization of assets in producing revenue.

Discuss the allocation of historical asset cost versus periodic charges based on current cost.

Identify and describe the factors determining the periodic depreciation charge.

Describe, illustrate, and evaluate alternative methods of depreciation.

Discuss the amortization of intangible assets and the depletion of wasting assets.

Describe and illustrate the accounting for asset retirements.

A fundamental characteristic of most plant and intangible assets is that as they are used to produce revenue, their utility for future services declines. A notable exception to this generalization is land — even farm land can be kept productive indefinitely with proper fertilization and care. Other plant assets, however, have limited lives and are literally "used up" in producing revenue. Intangible assets, although not physically used up or exhausted, tend to decline in utility with the passage of time.

As an asset is used to produce revenue, a charge against revenue to represent the usage is required if proper matching is to occur and a meaningful income figure is to be reported. In practice, three different terms have evolved to describe this charge depending upon the type of asset involved. For plant assets, generally the charge is referred to as **depreciation**. For mineral and other natural resources, sometimes referred to as *wasting assets*, the charge that describes the depleting of the source of the revenue is appropriately called **depletion**. For intangible assets, such as patents, copyrights and goodwill, the charge is referred to as **amortization**. Sometimes the latter term is used generically to encompass all of the other terms. Because the principles underlying each of these terms are similar, they are discussed together in this chapter.

HISTORICAL COST VERSUS CURRENT COST ALLOCATION

A difficult problem in accounting for plant and intangible asset utilization arises in determining the periodic charges to revenues, especially in periods of changing prices. In accounting practice, depreciation, depletion, and amortization have traditionally been viewed as an allocation of the acquisition cost over the life of the asset. This meaning can be observed in the definition of depreciation accounting adopted by the Committee on Terminology in the 1940's and still accepted today:

> *Depreciation accounting* is a system of accounting which aims to distribute the cost or other basic value of tangible capital assets, less salvage (if any), over the estimated useful life of the unit (which may be a group of assets) in a systematic and rational manner. It is a process of allocation, not of valuation. *Depreciation for the year* is the portion of the total charge under such a system that is allocated to the year. Although the allocation may properly take into account occurrences during the year, it is not intended to be a measurement of the effect of all such occurrences.[1]

Under this view, the total amount charged against revenue is fixed by the acquisition cost less any estimated recoverable salvage or residual value. While the pattern of charges may vary with the allocation method used, the total amount charged against revenue cannot exceed the historical cost of the asset. For any group of assets at any given time, the cumulative amount charged against past revenue plus the remaining asset carrying or book value will equal the original acquisition cost adjusted by any additions or betterments.

There are many who advocate a charge against revenue based on a current asset value referred to as **replacement cost** or **current cost**. This allocation approach matches current rather than past costs against current revenues, resulting in a net income figure that better reflects income available for dividends and is more useful for estimating future cash flows of the business entity. The concept of replacement cost was discussed in conjunction with inventories in Chapter 8. Plant assets, like inventories, must be

---

[1]*Accounting Research and Terminology Bulletins — Final Edition*, "Accounting Terminology Bulletins, No. 1, Review and Résumé" (New York: American Institute of Certified Public Accountants, 1961), par. 56.

replaced, and that portion of current and future earnings needed for replacement will not be available for distribution to owners or for payments to creditors.

Replacement costs reflect changes in the prices of specific assets. Another approach to accounting for the impact of price changes is **constant-dollar adjustment** of historical costs. This approach restates historical costs to reflect general price-level changes, i.e., changes in the value of the monetary unit measured by a general index.

As discussed in previous chapters, increasing inflationary pressures prompted the SEC, and later the FASB, to require supplemental disclosure of the effects of changing prices. Currently, under FASB Statement No. 33, companies with inventories and tangible fixed assets totaling more than $125 million or total assets exceeding $1 billion are required to report, as supplemental information, both constant-dollar and current-cost information. For plant assets, disclosure requirements apply to both the remaining asset cost and the charge against current revenue.

Historical cost is still the basis for financial statement reporting. However, various attempts have been made to modify the application of historical cost allocation to partially soften the impact of changing price levels. Emphasis in this chapter is on the methods used to allocate the historical acquisition cost against revenue and the modifications made to consider price changes. Supplemental disclosures for price changes are discussed and illustrated in Chapter 20.

DEPRECIATION OF PLANT ASSETS

Depreciation is the allocation of asset cost over the periods benefited by the use of the asset. There has been a tendency, however, on the part of many readers of financial statements to interpret depreciation accounting as somehow related to the accumulation of a fund for asset replacement. The use of such terms as "provision for depreciation" and "reserve for depreciation" has contributed toward this misinterpretation.

The charge for depreciation is the recognition of the declining service value of an asset. The nature of this charge is no different from those made to recognize the expiration of insurance premiums or patent rights. It is true that revenues equal to or in excess of expenses for a period result in a recovery of these expenses; salary expense is thus recovered by revenues, as is insurance expense, patent amortization, and charges for depreciation. But this does not mean that cash equal to the recorded depreciation will be segregated for property replacement. Revenues may be applied to many uses: to the increase in receivables, inventories or other working capital items; to the acquisition of new property or other noncurrent items; to the retirement of debt or the redemption of stock; or to the payment of dividends. If a special fund is to be available for the replacement of property, special authorization by management would be required. Such a fund is seldom found, however, because fund earnings would usually be less than the return from alternative uses of the resources.

Factors Determining the Periodic Depreciation Charge

Four factors must be recognized in arriving at the periodic charge for the use of a depreciable asset: (1) **asset cost**, (2) **residual or salvage value**, (3) **useful life**, and (4) **pattern of use**.

Asset Cost. The **cost** of an asset includes all of the expenditures relating to its acquisition and preparation for use as described in Chapter 10. The cost of an asset less the expected residual value, if any, is the depreciable cost or depreciation base, i.e., the portion of asset cost to be charged against future revenue.

Residual or Salvage Value. The **residual** or **salvage value** of a plant asset is the amount which can reasonably be expected to be realized upon retirement of the asset. This may depend upon the retirement policy of the company as well as market conditions and other factors. If, for example, the company normally uses equipment until it is physically exhausted and no longer serviceable, the residual value, represented by the scrap or junk that may be salvaged, may be nominal. But if the company normally trades its equipment after a relatively short period of use, the residual value, represented by the value in trade, may be relatively high. In some cases there may be a cost to dismantle and remove an asset. The residual value should be adjusted to a lower amount to reflect these anticipated costs. From a theoretical point of view, any net estimated residual value should be subtracted from cost in arriving at the cost of the asset to be allocated. Therefore, if dismantling and removal costs are expected to exceed the ultimate salvage value, the excess or "negative salvage value" should be added to the cost in arriving at the total cost to be allocated.

In practice, both salvage values and dismantling and removal costs are frequently ignored in determining periodic depreciation charges. Disregard of these items is not objectionable when they are relatively small or not subject to reasonable estimation and when it is doubtful whether greater accuracy will be gained through such refinement.

A theoretical question related to residual or salvage values is whether the effects of changing prices should be anticipated in its estimation. The general approach to this question by the accounting principles-setting bodies has been that if price changes are ignored in the allocation process, they should be ignored in the estimation of residual or salvage values. Thus, the salvage value used to determine the depreciable cost is based upon the conditions existing at the date of asset acquisition.

Useful Life. Plant assets other than land have a limited **useful life** as a result of certain physical and functional factors. The **physical factors** that limit the service life of an asset are (1) *wear and tear*, (2) *deterioration and decay*, and (3) *damage or destruction*. Everyone is familiar with the processes of wear and tear that render an automobile, a typewriter, or furniture no longer usable. A tangible asset, whether used or not, is also subject to deterioration and decay through aging. Finally, fire, flood, earthquake, or accident may reduce or terminate the useful life of an asset.

The **functional factors** limiting the lives of these assets are (1) *inadequacy* and (2) *obsolescence*. An asset may lose its usefulness when, as a result of altered business requirements or technical progress, it no longer can produce sufficient revenue to justify its continued use. Although the asset is still usable, its inability to produce revenue has cut short its service life. An example of rapid obsolescence can be observed in the computer industry. The rapid technological changes in this field have rendered perfectly good electronic equipment obsolete for efficient continued use long before the physical asset itself wore out.

Both physical and functional factors must be recognized in estimating the useful life of a depreciable plant asset. This recognition requires estimating what events will take place in the future and requires careful judgment on the part of the accountant.[2] Physical factors are more readily apparent than functional factors in predicting asset life. But when functional factors are expected to hasten the retirement of an asset, these must also be recognized.

Both physical and functional factors may operate gradually or may emerge suddenly. Recognition of depreciation is usually limited to the conditions that operate gradually and are reasonably foreseeable. For example, a sudden change in demand for a certain product may make an asset worthless, or an accident may destroy an asset, but these are unforeseeable events requiring recognition when they occur.

Since the service life of a depreciable plant asset is affected by maintenance and repairs, the policy with respect to these matters must be considered in estimating useful life. Low standards of maintenance and repair keep these charges at a minimum but may hasten the physical deterioration of the asset, thus requiring higher-than-normal allocations for depreciation. On the other hand, high standards of maintenance and repairs will mean higher charges for these items; but with a policy prolonging the usefulness of assets, periodic allocations for depreciation may be reduced.

The useful life of a depreciable plant asset may be expressed in terms of either an estimated time factor or an estimated use factor. The time factor may be a period of months or years; the use factor may be a number of hours of service or a number of units of output. The cost of the asset is allocated in accordance with the lapse of time or degrees of use. The rate of cost allocation may be modified by other factors, but basically depreciation must be recognized on a time or use basis.

The useful life of assets has sometimes been used by Congress and the Treasury Department to offset the effects of inflation on the tax return and to stimulate investment and economic growth. For example, during World War II, a tax provision was passed by Congress permitting companies that had provided facilities and equipment to produce emergency war products to depreciate these assets over a very short period of time. This enabled a

---

[2]Although the concept of useful life is generally recognized to be difficult to apply, there has been relatively little written on it in accounting literature. For a thorough discussion of the topic, see Charles Lamden, Dale L. Gerboth, and Thomas McRae, "Accounting for Depreciable Assets," *Accounting Research Monograph No. 1* (New York: American Institute of Certified Public Accountants, 1975), Ch. 5.

company to write off its cost against revenue rapidly, thus reducing taxable income and deferring payment of income tax on current revenues until after the short life had expired. In 1971 the Treasury Department introduced the Asset Depreciation Range (ADR) system which allowed companies to vary the lives of their depreciable assets over a range 20% above or below the guideline lives provided in the regulations for different types of depreciable assets. This permitted greater flexibility on the part of users to adjust their depreciation charge by altering useful lives.

In 1979 Congress considered a proposal similar to the emergency facility write-off provisions of World War II that would drastically reduce the useful life for tax purposes. This bill, referred to as the Jones-Conable bill, would reduce all depreciable plant assets into three classes: (1) buildings, (2) equipment, and (3) light trucks and automobiles. The bill would allow depreciation over ten years for buildings, five years for equipment, and three years for light trucks and automobiles. The objectives of this bill were to stimulate economic growth through increased capital investment and to allow United States businesses the same advantages many foreign competitors have who can write off their capital investment against revenue for tax purposes very rapidly. Although this law was not passed in 1979, its introduction illustrates how useful life is used by the public sector to partially adjust for the impact of inflation on a company's cost of replacing existing facilities and to promote economic growth. Modifications of asset lives for tax purposes are generally not acceptable for financial reporting purposes. Their justification is not based upon sound accounting theory, but upon national economic policy goals. Thus periodic depreciation charges on the tax return often differ from those on financial statements.

Pattern of Use. In order to match service cost against revenue, it is necessary to consider how an asset's services are actually expected to be used over the life of the asset. Periodic depreciation charges should reflect as closely as possible the **pattern of use**. If the asset produces a varying revenue pattern, then the depreciation charges should vary in a corresponding manner. When depreciation is measured in terms of a time factor, the pattern of use must be estimated. Several somewhat arbitrary methods have come into common use. Each method represents a different pattern and is designed to make the time basis approximate the use basis. The time factor is employed in two general classes of methods, *straight-line depreciation* and *decreasing-charge depreciation*. When depreciation is measured in terms of a use factor, the units of use must be estimated. The depreciation charge varies periodically in accordance with the services provided by the asset. The use factor is employed in *service-hours depreciation* and in *productive-output depreciation*.

Recording Periodic Depreciation

The periodic allocation of plant asset costs is made by debiting either a production overhead cost account or a selling or administrative expense account, and crediting an allowance or contra asset account. If the charge is made to a production overhead account, it becomes part of the cost of the finished and unfinished goods inventories and is deferred to the extent inventory has not been sold or completed. If the charge is made to selling or administrative expenses, it is considered to be a period cost and is written off against revenue as an operating expense of the current period.

The valuation or allowance account that is credited in recording periodic depreciation is commonly titled Accumulated Depreciation. The accumulation of expired cost in a separate account rather than crediting the asset account directly permits identification of the original cost of the asset and the accumulated depreciation. The FASB requires disclosure of both cost and accumulated depreciation for plant assets on the balance sheet or notes to the financial statements. This enables the user to estimate the relative age of all assets and provides some basis for evaluating the effects of price-level changes on the company's plant assets.

A separate valuation account is maintained for each asset or class of assets requiring the use of a separate depreciation rate. When a subsidiary property ledger is maintained for land, buildings, and equipment, it normally provides for the accumulation of depreciation allocations on the individual assets. Such records are variously termed Unit Property Records, Property Ledger, or Plant Asset Control Records. They usually involve the control account principle; assets being summarized in the general ledger, and detail being recorded in subsidiary ledgers.

The use of a property record consisting of cards or separate sheets provides a flexible record since assets can be arranged in any desired order. One card or one sheet is provided for each asset on which all information with respect to the item is listed. For buildings and equipment, this information usually includes a description of the asset, location, name of the vendor, guarantee period, insurance carried, date acquired, original cost, transportation charges, installation cost, estimated life, estimated residual value, depreciation rate, depreciation to date, major expenditures for repairs and improvements, and proceeds from final disposal. Property files are frequently maintained on tabulating cards, magnetic tapes, or in the memory of an electronic computer. When the information is maintained and stored in this form, it may be easily sorted and used to make depreciation computations and accounting entries.

Separate debits relating to individual property items in the subsidiary ledger support the land, buildings, and equipment balance in the general ledger; separate credits representing individual property item cost allocations in the subsidiary ledger support the accumulated depreciation balance in the general ledger. When a property item consists of a number of units or structural elements with varying lives and these units are recorded separately, depreciation is recognized in terms of the respective lives of the different units.

Methods of Depreciation

As mentioned earlier, there are a number of different methods for allocating the costs of depreciable assets. The method used in any specific instance is a matter of judgment and should be selected to most closely approximate the actual pattern of use expected from the asset. The following methods are described in this chapter:

Time-Factor Methods
1. Straight-line depreciation
2. Decreasing-charge depreciation
   (a) Sum-of-the-years-digits method
   (b) Declining-balance method
   (c) Double-declining-balance method

Use-Factor Methods
1. Service-hours method
2. Productive-output method

Group-Rate and Composite-Rate Methods
1. Group depreciation
2. Composite depreciation

Two other time-factor methods each providing for increasing charges, the *annuity method* and the *sinking fund method*, require the use of compound interest calculations. These methods are rarely encountered in practice.

The examples that follow assume the acquisition of a machine at a cost of $10,000 with a salvage value at the end of its useful life of $500. The following symbols are employed in the formulas for the development of depreciation rates and charges:

C = Asset cost
S = Estimated salvage value
n = Estimated life in years, hours of service, or units of output
r = Depreciation rate per period, per hour of service, or per unit of output
D = Periodic depreciation charge

Time-Factor Methods. The most common methods of cost allocation are related to the passage of time. In general, a productive asset is used up over time. Possible obsolescence due to technological changes is also a function of time. Of the time-factor methods, straight-line depreciation is the most popular. Decreasing-charge methods are widely used for tax purposes, however, because they provide for the highest charge in the first year of asset use and declining charges in later years. The result is a deferral of income tax due to the higher deductions for depreciation in the earlier years. These "accelerated depreciation" methods are based largely on the assumption that there will be rapid reductions in asset efficiency, output, or other benefits in the early years of an asset's life. Such reductions may be accompanied by increased charges for maintenance and repairs. Charges for depreciation decline, then, as the economic advantages afforded through ownership of the asset decline. The most commonly used decreasing-charge methods are sum-of-the-years-digits and some variation of a declining-balance method.

Decreasing-charge methods, like asset lives, have been used by Congress and the Treasury Department to provide some relief for companies when price levels change and replacement costs of existing facilities greatly increase. The most popular method used to achieve this goal is double-declining balance. Although an attempt was made by Congress to justify its use on the basis of the pattern of asset use, this relationship is very difficult to show. Many companies use double-declining balance or other accelerated depreciation methods for tax purposes, but compute depreciation on a straight-line basis for financial reporting purposes. This is the policy followed by General Mills as disclosed in Note 1B, page 669. The difference between taxable income and income reported in the financial statements requires interperiod tax allocation as discussed in Chapter 15.

Straight-Line Depreciation. **Straight-line depreciation** relates cost allocation to the passage of time and recognizes equal periodic charges over the life of the asset. The allocation assumes equal usefulness per time period, and in applying this assumption, the charge is not affected by asset productivity or efficiency variations. In developing the periodic charge, an estimate is made of the useful life of the asset in terms of months or years. The difference between the asset cost and residual value is divided by the useful life of the asset in arriving at the cost assigned to each time unit.

Using data for the machine referred to earlier and assuming a 10-year life, annual depreciation is determined as follows:

$$D = \frac{C - S}{n}, \text{ or } \frac{\$10,000 - \$500}{10} = \$950$$

The depreciation rate is commonly expressed as a percentage to be applied periodically to asset cost. The depreciation rate in the example is calculated as follows: $(100\% - 5\%) \div 10 = 9.5\%$. This percentage applied to cost provides a periodic charge of $950. The rate may also be expressed as a percentage to be applied to depreciable cost — cost less residual value. Expressed in this way the rate is simply the reciprocal value of the useful life expressed in periods, or r (per period) $= 1 \div n$. In the example, then, the annual rate would be $1 \div 10 = 10\%$, and this rate applied to depreciable cost, $9,500, gives an annual charge of $950. A table to summarize the process of cost allocation follows:

End of Year	Asset Cost Allocation — Straight-Line Method		
	Debit to Depreciation Expense and Credit to Accumulated Depreciation	*Balance of Accumulated Depreciation*	*Asset Book Value*
			$10,000
1	$ 950	$ 950	9,050
2	950	1,900	8,100
3	950	2,850	7,150
4	950	3,800	6,200
5	950	4,750	5,250
6	950	5,700	4,300
7	950	6,650	3,350
8	950	7,600	2,400
9	950	8,550	1,450
10	950	9,500	500
	$9,500		

It was indicated earlier that residual value is frequently ignored when this is a relatively minor amount. If this were done in the example, depreciation would be recognized at $1,000 per year instead of $950.

Sum-of-the-Years-Digits Method. The **sum-of-the-years-digits method** provides decreasing charges by applying a series of fractions, each of a smaller value, to depreciable asset cost. Fractions are developed in terms of the sum of the asset life periods. Weights for purposes of developing reducing fractions are the years-digits listed in reverse order. The denominator for the fraction is obtained by adding these weights; the numerator is the weight assigned to the specific year. The denominator for the fraction can be obtained by an alternate calculation: the sum of the digits for the first and last years can be divided by 2 and multiplied by the number of years of asset life. In the example, the denominator can be determined as follows: $([10 + 1] \div 2) \times 10 = 55$. Periodic charges for depreciation using the sum-of-the-years-digits method for the asset previously described are developed as follows:

	Reducing Weights	Reducing Fractions
First year	10	10/55
Second year	9	9/55
Third year	8	8/55
Fourth year	7	7/55
Fifth year	6	6/55
Sixth year	5	5/55
Seventh year	4	4/55
Eighth year	3	3/55
Ninth year	2	2/55
Tenth year	1	1/55
	55	55/55

Depreciation computed by the application of reducing fractions to depreciable cost is summarized in the table below:

Asset Cost Allocation — Sum-of-the-Years-Digits Method

End of Year	Debit to Depreciation Expense and Credit to Accumulated Depreciation		Balance of Accumulated Depreciation	Asset Book Value
				$10,000.00
1	(10/55 × $9,500)	$1,727.27	$1,727.27	8,272.73
2	(9/55 × 9,500)	1,554.55	3,281.82	6,718.18
3	(8/55 × 9,500)	1,381.82	4,663.64	5,336.36
4	(7/55 × 9,500)	1,209.09	5,872.73	4,127.27
5	(6/55 × 9,500)	1,036.36	6,909.09	3,090.91
6	(5/55 × 9,500)	863.64	7,772.73	2,227.27
7	(4/55 × 9,500)	690.91	8,463.64	1,536.36
8	(3/55 × 9,500)	518.18	8,981.82	1,018.18
9	(2/55 × 9,500)	345.45	9,327.27	672.73
10	(1/55 × 9,500)	172.73	9,500.00	500.00
		$9,500.00		

Declining-Balance Method. The **declining-balance method** provides decreasing charges by applying a constant percentage rate to a declining asset book value. The rate to be applied to the declining book value in producing the estimated salvage value at the end of the useful life of the asset is calculated by the following formula:

$$r \text{ (rate per period applicable to declining book value)} = 1 - \sqrt[n]{S \div C}$$

Using the previous asset data and assuming a 10-year asset life, the depreciation rate is determined as follows:

$$1 - \sqrt[10]{\$500 \div \$10,000} = 1 - \sqrt[10]{.05} = 1 - .74113 = .25887, \text{ or } 25.887\%$$

Dividing the estimated salvage value by cost in the formula above gives .05, the value that the salvage value at the end of 10 years should bear to cost. The tenth root of this value is .74113. Multiplying cost and the successive declining book values by .74113 ten times will reduce the asset to .05 of its cost. The difference between 1 and .74113, or .25887, then, is the rate of decrease to be applied successively in bringing the asset down to .05 of its original balance. Since it is impossible to bring a value down to zero by a constant multiplier, a residual value must be assigned to the asset in using the formula. In the absence of an expected residual value, a nominal value of $1 can be assumed for this purpose.

Depreciation calculated by application of the 25.887% rate to the declining book value is summarized in the following table:

Asset Cost Allocation — Declining-Balance Method

End of Year	Debit to Depreciation Expense and Credit to Accumulated Depreciation		Balance of Accumulated Depreciation	Asset Book Value
				$10,000.00
1	(25.887% × $10,000.00)	$2,588.70	$2,588.70	7,411.30
2	(25.887% × 7,411.30)	1,918.56	4,507.26	5,492.74
3	(25.887% × 5,492.74)	1,421.91	5,929.17	4,070.83
4	(25.887% × 4,070.83)	1,053.82	6,982.99	3,017.01
5	(25.887% × 3,017.01)	781.01	7,764.00	2,236.00
6	(25.887% × 2,236.00)	578.83	8,342.83	1,657.17
7	(25.887% × 1,657.17)	428.99	8,771.82	1,228.18
8	(25.887% × 1,228.18)	317.94	9,089.76	910.24
9	(25.887% × 910.24)	235.63	9,325.39	674.61
10	(25.887% × 674.61)	174.61*	9,500.00	500.00
		$9,500.00		

*Discrepancy due to rounding.

Instead of developing an exact rate that will produce a salvage value of $500, it is usually more convenient to approximate a rate that will provide satisfactory cost allocation; since depreciation involves an estimate, there is little assurance that rate refinement will produce more accurate results. In the previous illustration, the use of a rate of 25% is more convenient than 25.887%; differences are not material.

Double-Declining-Balance Method. Federal income tax regulations provide that for certain assets, depreciation is allowed at a fixed percentage equal to double the straight-line rate. This is referred to as the **double-declining-balance method**. Although a residual value is not taken into account in employing this method as in other methods, depreciation charges should not be made after reaching the residual balance. The double-declining-balance method was initially introduced into the income tax laws in 1954. The percentage is readily calculated as follows:

Estimated Life in Years	Straight-Line Rate	Double-Declining-Balance Rate
3	33⅓%	66⅔%
5	20	40
6	16⅔	33⅓
8	12½	25
10	10	20
20	5	10

Depreciation using the double-declining-balance method for the asset described earlier is summarized in the table that follows:

Asset Cost Allocation — Double-Declining-Balance Method

End of Year	Debit to Depreciation Expense and Credit to Accumulated Depreciation		Balance of Accumulated Depreciation	Asset Book Value
				$10,000.00
1	(20% × $10,000.00)	$2,000.00	$2,000.00	8,000.00
2	(20% × 8,000.00)	1,600.00	3,600.00	6,400.00
3	(20% × 6,400.00)	1,280.00	4,880.00	5,120.00
4	(20% × 5,120.00)	1,024.00	5,904.00	4,096.00
5	(20% × 4,096.00)	819.20	6,723.20	3,276.80
6	(20% × 3,276.80)	655.36	7,378.56	2,621.44
7	(20% × 2,621.44)	524.29	7,902.85	2,097.15
8	(20% × 2,097.15)	419.43	8,322.28	1,677.72
9	(20% × 1,677.72)	335.54	8,657.82	1,342.18
10	(20% × 1,342.18)	268.44	8,926.26	1,073.74
		$8,926.26		

It should be noted that the rate of 20% is applied to the book value of the asset each year. In applying this rate, the book value after ten years exceeds the residual value by $573.74 ($1,073.74 − $500.00). This condition arises wherever residual values are relatively low in amount. One way to make the book value equal the residual value is to change from the double-declining-balance method to another acceptable method prior to the end of the asset's useful life. This change is permitted for tax purposes.

The optimal time to make the change is at the point when depreciation for the year using another acceptable method exceeds that computed using the double-declining-balance method. This comes earliest by changing to the sum-of-the-years-digits method. The exact time to change depends upon the estimated residual value of the asset. In the above example, the change should be made in the third year when the depreciation using the sum-of-the-years-digits method for the remaining life of the asset would be $1,311.11 rather than $1,280 under the double-declining-balance method. The determination of which year is the best time to change can be made each year by comparing the depreciation using the sum-of-the-years-digits method for the remaining life of the asset to the depreciation using the double-declining-balance method. This is illustrated at the top of page 307.

Year	Reducing Fraction Based Upon Remaining Life		Asset Book Value Less Salvage at Beginning of Year Using Double-Declining-Balance Depreciation	Depreciation Expense Using Sum-of-the-Years-Digits Method for Remaining Life of the Asset	Depreciation Expense Using Double-Declining-Balance Method (See Preceding Schedule)
1	10/55	×	$9,500	$1,727.27	$2,000
2	9/45	×	7,500	1,500.00	1,600
3	8/36	×	5,900	1,311.11	1,280

A new schedule combining both methods can be prepared. The reducing fraction for the sum-of-the-years-digits method will be 8/36, 7/36, 6/36, etc., since the asset has eight years of remaining life when the change takes place.

End of Year	Debit to Depreciation Expense and Credit to Accumulated Depreciation		Balance of Accumulated Depreciation	Asset Book Value
				$10,000.00
1	(20% × $10,000)	$2,000.00	$2,000.00	8,000.00
2	(20% × 8,000)	1,600.00	3,600.00	6,400.00
3	8/36($9,500 − 3,600)	1,311.11	4,911.11	5,088.89
4	7/36(9,500 − 3,600)	1,147.22	6,058.33	3,941.67
5	6/36(9,500 − 3,600)	983.33	7,041.66	2,958.34
6	5/36(9,500 − 3,600)	819.44	7,861.10	2,138.90
7	4/36(9,500 − 3,600)	655.56	8,516.66	1,483.34
8	3/36(9,500 − 3,600)	491.67	9,008.33	991.67
9	2/36(9,500 − 3,600)	327.78	9,336.11	663.89
10	1/36(9,500 − 3,600)	163.89	9,500.00	500.00

Federal income tax laws permit the use of double-declining balance only for certain types of assets — primarily new tangible personal property and new residential rental property. Some other types of assets, however, may be depreciated at a rate not exceeding 1.5 times the straight-line rate. In general, this **150% declining balance method** is applicable to used personal property and new nonresidential buildings. The 150% rate is applied in the same manner as the 200% declining balance rate.

Evaluation of Time-Factor Methods. Using the straight-line method, depreciation is a constant or fixed charge each period. When the life of an asset is affected primarily by the lapse of time rather than by the degree of use, recognition of depreciation as a constant charge is generally appropriate. However, net income measurements become particularly sensitive to changes in the volume of business activity. With above-normal activity, there is no increase in the depreciation charge; with below-normal activity, revenue is still charged with the costs of assets standing ready to serve.

Straight-line depreciation is a widely used procedure. It is readily understood and frequently parallels observable asset deterioration. It has the advantage of simplicity and under normal conditions offers a satisfactory means of cost allocation. Normal asset conditions exist when (1) assets have been accumulated over a period of years so that the total of depreciation plus maintenance is comparatively even from period to period, and (2) service potentials of assets are being steadily reduced by functional as well as physical factors. The absence of either of these conditions may suggest the use of some depreciation method other than straight line.

Decreasing-charge methods can be supported as reasonable approaches to asset cost allocation when the annual benefits provided by a property item decline as it grows older. These methods, too, are suggested when an asset requires increasing maintenance and repairs over its useful life.[3] When straight-line depreciation is employed, the combined charges for depreciation, maintenance, and repairs will increase over the life of the asset; when the decreasing-charge methods are used, the combined charges will tend to be equalized.

Other factors suggesting the use of a decreasing-charge method include: (1) the anticipation of a significant contribution in early periods with the extent of the contribution to be realized in later periods less definite; (2) the possibility that inadequacy or obsolescence may result in premature retirement of the asset. In the event of premature retirement, depreciation charges will have absorbed what would otherwise require recognition as a loss.

Depreciation for Partial Periods. The discussion thus far has assumed that assets were purchased on the first day of a company's fiscal period. In reality, of course, asset transactions occur throughout the year. When a time-factor method is used, depreciation on assets acquired or disposed of during the year may be based on the number of days the asset was held during the period. When the level of acquisitions and retirements is significant, however, companies often adopt a less burdensome policy for recognizing depreciation for partial periods. Some alternatives found in practice include the following:

1. Depreciation is recognized to the nearest whole month. Assets acquired on or before the 15th of the month are considered owned for the entire month; assets acquired after the 15th are not considered owned for any part of the month. Conversely, assets sold on or before the 15th of the month are not considered owned for any part of the month; assets sold after the 15th are considered owned for the entire month.
2. Depreciation is recognized to the nearest whole year. Assets acquired during the first six months are considered held for the entire year; assets acquired during the last six months are not considered in the depreciation computation. Conversely, no depreciation is recorded on assets sold during the first six months and a full year's depreciation is recorded on assets sold during the last six months.
3. One-half year's depreciation is recognized on all assets purchased or sold during the year. A full year's depreciation is taken on all other assets.

---

[3]The AICPA Committee on Accounting Procedure has stated, "The declining-balance method is one of those which meets the requirements of being 'systematic and rational.' In those cases where the expected productivity or revenue-earning power of the asset is relatively greater during the earlier years of its life, or where maintenance charges tend to increase during the later years, the declining-balance method may well provide the most satisfactory allocation of cost." The Committee would apply these conclusions to other decreasing-charge methods, including the sum-of-the-years-digits method, that produce substantially similar results. See *Accounting Research and Terminology Bulletins — Final Edition*, "No. 44 (Revised), Declining-Balance Depreciation" (New York: American Institute of Certified Public Accountants, 1961), par. 2.

4. No depreciation is recognized on acquisitions during the year but depreciation for a full year is recognized on retirements.
5. Depreciation is recognized for a full year on acquisitions during the year but no depreciation is recognized on retirements.

Methods 2 through 5 are attractive because of their simplicity. However, Method 1 provides greater accuracy and its use is assumed in the examples and problems in the text unless otherwise specified.

If a company uses the sum-of-the-years-digits method of depreciation and recognizes partial year's depreciation on assets purchased or sold, each year's computation after the first year must be divided into two parts. The depreciation expense for each full year must be computed and then prorated over the partial periods. For example, assume the asset discussed on page 302 was acquired midway through a fiscal period. The computation of depreciation for the first two years recognizing partial period depreciation would be as follows:

First Year:		
Depreciation for first full year (see page 304)	$1,727.27	
One-half year's depreciation		$ 863.64
Second Year:		
Depreciation for balance of first year		$ 863.63
Depreciation for second full year (see page 304)	$1,554.55	
One-half year's depreciation		777.28
Total depreciation — second year		$1,640.91

Use-Factor Methods. Use-factor methods view asset exhaustion as related primarily to asset use or output and provide periodic charges varying with the degree of such service. Service life for certain assets can best be expressed in terms of hours of service; for others in terms of units of production.

Service-Hours Method. **Service-hours depreciation** is based on the theory that purchase of an asset represents the purchase of a number of hours of direct service. This method requires an estimate of the life of the asset in terms of service hours. Depreciable cost is divided by total service hours in arriving at the depreciation rate to be assigned for each hour of asset use. The use of the asset during the period is measured, and the number of service hours is multiplied by the depreciation rate in arriving at the periodic depreciation charge. Depreciation charges against revenue fluctuate periodically according to the contribution the asset makes in service hours.

Using asset data previously given and an estimated service life of 20,000 hours, the rate to be applied for each service hour is determined as follows:

$$r \text{ (per hour)} = \frac{C - S}{n}, \text{ or } \frac{\$10,000 - \$500}{20,000} = \$.475$$

Allocation of asset cost in terms of service hours is summarized in the following table:

Asset Cost Allocation — Service-Hours Method

End of Year	Service Hours	Debit to Depreciation Expense and Credit to Accumulated Depreciation		Balance of Accumulated Depreciation	Asset Book Value
					$10,000.00
1	1,500	(1,500 × $.475)	$ 712.50	$ 712.50	9,287.50
2	2,500	(2,500 × .475)	1,187.50	1,900.00	8,100.00
3	2,500	(2,500 × .475)	1,187.50	3,087.50	6,912.50
4	2,000	(2,000 × .475)	950.00	4,037.50	5,962.50
5	1,500	(1,500 × .475)	712.50	4,750.00	5,250.00
6	1,500	(1,500 × .475)	712.50	5,462.50	4,537.50
7	3,000	(3,000 × .475)	1,425.00	6,887.50	3,112.50
8	2,500	(2,500 × .475)	1,187.50	8,075.00	1,925.00
9	2,000	(2,000 × .475)	950.00	9,025.00	975.00
10	1,000	(1,000 × .475)	475.00	9,500.00	500.00
	20,000		$9,500.00		

It is assumed that the original estimate of service hours is confirmed and the asset is retired after 20,000 hours are reached in the tenth year. Such precise confirmation would seldom be found in practice.

It should be observed that straight-line depreciation resulted in an annual charge of $950 regardless of fluctuations in productive activity. When asset life is affected directly by the degree of use, and when there are significant fluctuations in such use in successive periods, the service-hours method, which recognizes hours used instead of hours available for use, normally provides the more equitable charges to operations.

Productive-Output Method. **Productive-output depreciation** is based on the theory that an asset is acquired for the service it can provide in the form of production output. This method requires an estimate of the total unit output of the asset. Depreciable cost divided by the total estimated output gives the equal charge to be assigned for each unit of output. The measured production for a period multiplied by the charge per unit gives the charge to be made against revenue. Depreciation charges fluctuate periodically according to the contribution the asset makes in unit output.

Using the previous asset data and an estimated productive life of 2,500,000 units, the rate to be applied for each thousand units produced is determined as follows:

$$r \text{ (per thousand units)} = \frac{C - S}{n}, \text{ or } \frac{\$10,000 - \$500}{2,500} = \$3.80$$

Asset cost allocation in terms of productive output is summarized in the tabulation at the top of page 311.

Evaluation of Use-Factor Methods. When quantitative uses of plant assets can be reasonably estimated and readily measured, the use-factor methods provide highly satisfactory approaches to asset cost allocation. Depreciation as a fluctuating charge tends to follow the revenue curve: high depreciation charges are assigned to periods of high activity; low charges are assigned to periods of low activity. When the useful life of an asset is affected primarily by the degree of its use, recognition of depreciation as a variable charge is particularly appropriate.

Asset Cost Allocation — Productive-Output Method

End of Year	Unit Output	Debit to Depreciation Expense and Credit to Accumulated Depreciation		Balance of Accumulated Depreciation	Asset Book Value
					$10,000
1	80,000	(80 × $3.80)	$ 304	$ 304	9,696
2	250,000	(250 × 3.80)	950	1,254	8,746
3	400,000	(400 × 3.80)	1,520	2,774	7,226
4	320,000	(320 × 3.80)	1,216	3,990	6,010
5	440,000	(440 × 3.80)	1,672	5,662	4,338
6	360,000	(360 × 3.80)	1,368	7,030	2,970
7	280,000	(280 × 3.80)	1,064	8,094	1,906
8	210,000	(210 × 3.80)	798	8,892	1,108
9	120,000	(120 × 3.80)	456	9,348	652
10	40,000	(40 × 3.80)	152	9,500	500
	2,500,000		$9,500		

However, certain limitations in using the use-factor methods need to be pointed out. Asset performance in terms of service hours or productive output is often difficult to estimate. Measurement solely in terms of these factors could fail to recognize special conditions, such as increasing maintenance and repair costs as well as possible inadequacy and obsolescence. Furthermore, when service life expires even in the absence of use, a use-factor method may conceal actual fluctuations in earnings; by relating periodic depreciation charges to the volume of operations, periodic operating results may be smoothed out, thus creating a false appearance of stability.

Group-Rate and Composite-Rate Methods. It was assumed in preceding discussions that depreciation expense is associated with individual assets and is applied to each separate unit. This practice is commonly referred to as **unit depreciation**. However, there may be certain advantages in associating depreciation with a group of assets and applying a single rate to the collective cost of the group at any given time. Group cost allocation procedures are referred to as **group depreciation** and **composite depreciation**.

Group Depreciation. When useful life is affected primarily by physical factors, a group of similar items purchased at one time should have the same expected life, but in fact some will probably remain useful longer than others. In recording depreciation on a unit basis, the sale or retirement of an asset before or after its anticipated lifetime requires recognition of a gain or loss. Such gains and losses, however, can usually be attributed to normal variations in useful life rather than to unforeseen disasters and windfalls.

The **group-depreciation** procedure treats a collection of similar assets as a single group. Depreciation is accumulated in a single valuation account, and the depreciation rate is based on the average life of assets in the group. Because the accumulated depreciation account under the group procedure applies to the entire group of assets, it is not related to any specific asset. Thus, no book value can be calculated for any specific asset and there are no fully depreciated assets. The depreciation rate is applied to the recorded cost of all assets remaining in service, regardless of age, in arriving at the periodic depreciation charge.

When an item in the group is retired, no gain or loss is recognized; the asset account is credited with the cost of the item and the valuation account is debited for the difference between cost and any salvage. With normal variations in asset lives, the losses not recognized on early retirements are offset by the continued depreciation charges on those assets still in service after the average life has elapsed. Group depreciation is generally computed as an adaptation of the straight-line method, and the illustrations in this chapter assume this approach.

To illustrate, assume that 100 similar machines having an average expected useful life of 5 years are purchased at a total cost of $2,000,000. Of this group, 30 machines are retired at the end of four years, 40 at the end of five years, and the remaining 30 at the end of the sixth year. Based on the average expected useful life of 5 years, a depreciation charge of 20% is reported on those assets in service each year. The charges for depreciation and the changes in the group asset and accumulated depreciation accounts are summarized below.

Asset Cost Allocation — Group Depreciation

End of Year	Debit to Depreciation Expense (20% of Cost)	Asset Debit	Asset Credit	Asset Balance	Accumulated Depreciation Debit	Accumulated Depreciation Credit	Accumulated Depreciation Balance	Asset Book Value
		$2,000,000		$2,000,000				$2,000,000
1	$ 400,000			2,000,000		$ 400,000	$ 400,000	1,600,000
2	400,000			2,000,000		400,000	800,000	1,200,000
3	400,000			2,000,000		400,000	1,200,000	800,000
4	400,000		$ 600,000	1,400,000	$ 600,000	400,000	1,000,000	400,000
5	280,000		800,000	600,000	800,000	280,000	480,000	120,000
6	120,000		600,000	—	600,000	120,000	—	—
	$2,000,000	$2,000,000	$2,000,000		$2,000,000	$2,000,000		

It should be noted that the depreciation charge is exactly $4,000 per machine-year. In each of the first four years, 100 machine-years of service[4] are utilized, and the annual depreciation charge is $400,000. In the fifth year, when only 70 machines are in operation, the charge is $280,000 (20% of $1,400,000). In the sixth year, when 30 units are still in service, a proportionate charge for such use of $120,000 (20% of $600,000) is made.

If the 30 machines retired after four years had been sold for $50,000, the entry to record the sale using the group depreciation method would have been as follows:

Cash	50,000	
Accumulated Depreciation — Equipment	550,000	
Equipment		600,000

---

[4]It should be observed that in the example the original estimates of an average useful life of 5 years is confirmed in the use of the assets. Such precise confirmation would seldom be the case. In instances where assets in a group are continued in use after their cost has been assigned to operations, no further depreciation charges would be recognized. On the other hand, where all of the assets in a group are retired before their cost has been assigned to operations, a special charge related to such retirement would have to be recognized.

If unit depreciation had been used for these 100 machines, the retirement entry would have reflected four years depreciation expense charged for the machines sold, and a loss of $70,000 would be charged against revenue as follows:

Cash	50,000	
Accumulated Depreciation — Equipment	480,000	
Loss on Sale of Equipment	70,000	
Equipment		600,000

If additional assets are purchased and added to the group, the depreciation rate is applied to the larger gross cost of all assets in the group. Application of the group depreciation procedure under circumstances such as the foregoing provides an annual charge that is more closely related to the quantity of productive facilities being used. Gains and losses due solely to normal variations in asset lives are not recognized, and operating results are more meaningfully stated. The convenience of applying a uniform depreciation rate to a number of similar items may also represent a substantial advantage.

Composite Depreciation. The basic procedures employed under the group method for allocating the cost of substantially identical assets may be extended to include dissimilar assets. This special application of the group procedure is known as **composite depreciation**. The composite method retains the convenience of the group method, but because assets with varying service-lives are aggregated to determine an average life, it is unlikely to provide all the reporting advantages of the group method.

A composite rate is established by analyzing the various assets or classes of assets in use and computing the depreciation as an average of the straight-line annual depreciation as follows:

Asset	Cost	Residual Value	Depreciable Cost	Estimated Life in Years	Annual Depreciation Expense (Straight-line)
A	$ 2,000	$ 120	$ 1,880	4	$ 470
B	6,000	300	5,700	6	950
C	12,000	1,200	10,800	10	1,080
	$20,000	$1,620	$18,380		$2,500

Composite depreciation rate to be applied to cost: $2,500 ÷ $20,000 = 12.5%.
Composite or average life of assets: $18,380 ÷ $2,500 = 7.35 years.

It will be observed that a rate of 12.5% applied to the cost of the assets, $20,000, results in annual depreciation of $2,500. Annual depreciation of $2,500 will accumulate to a total of $18,380 in 7.35 years; hence 7.35 years may be considered the composite or average life of the assets. Composite depreciation would be reported in a single accumulated depreciation account. Upon the retirement of an individual asset, the asset account is credited and Accumulated Depreciation is debited with the difference between cost and residual value. As with the group procedure, no gains or losses are recognized at the time individual assets are retired.

After a composite rate has been set, it is ordinarily continued in the absence of significant changes in the lives of assets or asset additions and retirements having a material effect upon the rate. It is assumed in the preceding example that the assets are replaced with similar assets when retired. If they are not replaced, continuation of the 12.5% rate will misstate depreciation charges.

AMORTIZATION OF INTANGIBLE ASSETS

The life of an intangible asset is usually limited by the effects of obsolescence, shifts in demand, competition, and other economic factors. Because of the difficulty in estimating such highly uncertain future events, companies sometimes did not amortize the cost of intangible assets, but assumed their value was never used up. This practice was frequently followed for trademarks, goodwill and some franchises. The Accounting Principles Board, however, felt that eventually all intangible assets became of insignificant worth to the company. The Board, therefore, issued Opinion No. 17, requiring that the recorded costs of all intangible assets acquired after October 31, 1970 — the effective date of the Opinion — be amortized over the estimated useful life.[5] Many companies do not amortize certain intangibles, notably goodwill, acquired prior to November 1, 1970, although amortization of these assets was encouraged by the Board.[6]

The useful life of an intangible asset may be affected by a variety of factors, all of which should be considered in determining the amortization period. Useful life may be limited by legal, regulatory, or contractual provisions. These factors, including options for renewal or extension, should be evaluated in conjunction with the economic factors noted above and other pertinent information. A patent, for example, has a legal life of 17 years; but if the competitive advantages afforded by the patent are expected to terminate after 5 years, then the patent cost should be amortized over the shorter period.

Although the life of an intangible asset is to be estimated by careful analysis of the surrounding circumstances, a maximum life of 40 years was established for amortization purposes. APB Opinion No. 17 included this limitation as follows:

> The cost of each type of intangible asset should be amortized on the basis of the estimated life of that specific asset and should not be written off in the period of acquisition. . . .
> The period of amortization should not, however, exceed forty years. Analysis at the time of acquisition may indicate that the indeterminate lives of some intangible assets are likely to exceed forty years and the cost of those assets should be amortized over the maximum period of forty years, not an arbitrary shorter period.[7]

---

[5]*Opinions of the Accounting Principles Board, No. 17*, "Intangible Assets" (New York: American Institute of Certified Public Accountants, 1970).

[6]See, for example, the notes to financial statements for The Bendix Corporation and General Mills, Inc., reproduced on page 322 and in Appendix B, respectively.

[7]*Opinions of the Accounting Principles Board, No. 17, op. cit.,* par 28–29.

The requirement that the recorded cost of all intangible assets be amortized and the arbitrary selection of a 40-year life are of questionable theoretical merit. An analysis of the expected future benefits to be derived from a particular asset should be the basis for capitalizing and amortizing the cost of any asset, whether tangible or intangible.

Recording Periodic Amortization

Amortization, like depreciation, may be charged as an operating expense of the period or allocated to production overhead if the asset is directly related to the manufacture of goods. In practice the credit entry is often made directly to the asset account rather than to a separate allowance account. This practice is arbitrary, and there is no reason why charges for amortization cannot be accumulated in a separate account in the same manner as depreciation. The FASB requires disclosure of both cost and accumulated depreciation for plant assets, but does not require similar disclosure for intangible assets. When amortization is recorded in a separate account, such account is typically called Accumulated Amortization.

Method of Amortization

Amortization of intangible assets is made evenly in most instances, or on a straight-line allocation basis. APB Opinion No. 17 states:

> The Board concludes that the straight-line method of amortization — equal annual amounts — should be applied unless a company demonstrates that another systematic method is more appropriate.[8]

Although practice favors straight-line amortization, analysis of many intangibles such as patents, franchises, and even goodwill suggests that greater benefit is often realized in the early years of the asset's life than in the later years. In those instances, a decreasing-charge amortization seems justified.

DEPLETION OF NATURAL RESOURCES

Natural resources, also called **wasting assets,** move toward exhaustion as the physical units representing these resources are removed and sold. The withdrawal of oil or gas, the cutting of timber, and the mining of coal, sulphur, iron, copper, or silver ore are examples of processes leading to the exhaustion of natural resources. Depletion expense is a charge for the using up of the resources.

Recording Periodic Depletion

Because depletion expense is recognized as the cost of the material that becomes directly embodied in the product of the company, it is always charged to inventory. If the inventory is sold, depletion expense becomes part of the cost of goods sold. If it is unsold at the end of an accounting

---

[8]*Ibid.*, par. 30.

period, it is deferred in the cost of inventory. The credit is made to either Accumulated Depletion or directly to the natural resource asset account.

Computing Periodic Depletion

The computation of depletion expense is an adaptation of the productive-output method of depreciation. Perhaps the most difficult problem in computing depletion expense is estimating the amount of resources available for economical removal from the land. Generally, a geologist, mining engineer, or other expert is called upon to make the estimate, and it is subject to continual revision as the resource is extracted or removed.

Developmental costs, such as costs of drilling, sinking mine shafts, and constructing roads should be capitalized and added to the original cost of the property in arriving at the total cost subject to depletion. These costs are often incurred before normal activities begin.

To illustrate the computation of depletion expense, assume the following facts: Land containing natural resources is purchased at a cost of $5,500,000. The land has an estimated value after removal of the resources of $250,000; the natural resource supply is estimated at 1,000,000 tons. The unit depletion charge and the total depletion charge for the first year, assuming the withdrawal of 80,000 tons are calculated as follows:

Depletion charge per ton: ($5,500,000 − $250,000) ÷ 1,000,000 = $5.25
Depletion charge for the first year: 80,000 tons × $5.25 = $420,000

If the 80,000 tons are sold, the entire $420,000 becomes a part of the cost of goods sold. If only 60,000 tons are sold in the current period, $105,000 becomes part of the inventory shown on the ending balance sheet.

When buildings and improvements are constructed in connection with the removal of natural resources and their usefulness is limited to the duration of the project, it is reasonable to recognize depreciation on such properties on an output basis consistent with the charges to be recognized for the natural resources themselves. For example, assume buildings are constructed at a cost of $250,000; the useful lives of the buildings are expected to terminate upon exhaustion of the natural resource consisting of 1,000,000 units. Under these circumstances, a depreciation charge of $.25 ($250,000 ÷ 1,000,000) should accompany the depletion charge recognized for each unit. When improvements provide benefits expected to terminate prior to the exhaustion of the natural resource, the cost of such improvements may be allocated on the basis of the units to be removed during the life of the improvements or on a time basis, whichever is considered more appropriate.

CHANGES IN ESTIMATES OF VARIABLES

The allocation of asset costs benefiting more than one period cannot be precisely determined at acquisition because so many of the variables cannot be known with certainty until a future time. Only one factor in determining the periodic charge for depreciation, amortization or depletion is based upon historical information — asset cost. Other factors — residual value, useful life or output, and the pattern of use or benefit — must be estimated. The question frequently facing accountants is how adjustments to these estimates, which arise as time passes should be reflected in the accounts. As indicated in Chapter 4, a change in estimate is normally reported in the current and future periods rather than as an adjustment of prior periods. This type of adjustment would be made for residual value and useful life changes. However, a change in the cost allocation method based on a revised expected pattern of use, is a change in accounting principle and is accounted for in a different manner. Changes in accounting principles are discussed in Chapter 18.

To illustrate the procedure for a change in estimate affecting allocation of asset cost, assume that a company purchased $50,000 of equipment and estimated a ten-year life for depreciation purposes. Using the straight-line method with no residual value, the annual depreciation would be $5,000. After four years, accumulated depreciation would amount to $20,000, and the remaining undepreciated book value would be $30,000. Assume in the fifth year, a re-evaluation of the life indicates only four more years of service can be expected from the asset. An adjustment must therefore be made for the fifth and subsequent years to reflect the change. A new annual depreciation charge is calculated by dividing the remaining book value by the remaining life of four years. In the illustration above, this would result in an annual charge of $7,500 for the fifth through eighth years ($30,000 ÷ 4 = $7,500).

A change in the estimated life of an intangible asset is accounted for in the same manner, i.e., the unamortized cost is allocated over the remaining life based upon the revised estimate. Because of the uncertainties surrounding the estimation of the life of an intangible asset, frequent evaluation of the amortization period should be made to determine if a change in estimated life is warranted.

Another change in estimate occurs in accounting for wasting assets when the estimate of the recoverable units changes as a result of further discoveries, improved extraction processes, or changes in sales prices that indicate changes in the number of units that can be extracted profitably. A revised depletion rate is established by dividing the remaining resource cost balance by the estimated remaining recoverable units.

To illustrate, assume the same facts as enumerated on page 316. Land is purchased at a cost of $5,500,000 with estimated residual value of $250,000. The original estimated supply of natural resources in the land is 1,000,000 tons. As indicated previously, the depletion rate under these conditions would be $5.25 per ton, and the depletion charge for the first year when 80,000 tons were mined would be $420,000. Assume that in the second year of operation, 100,000 tons of ore are withdrawn, but before the books are closed at the end of the second year, appraisal of the expected recoverable tons indicates a remaining tonnage of 950,000. The new depletion rate and the depletion charge for the second year would be computed as follows:

Cost assignable to recoverable tons at the beginning of the second year:
Original costs applicable to depletable resources $5,250,000
Deduct depletion charge for the first year.. 420,000

Balance of cost subject to depletion $4,830,000

Estimated recoverable tons as of the beginning of the second year:
Number of tons withdrawn in the second year 100,000
Estimated recoverable tons as of the end of the second year....................... 950,000

Total recoverable tons at the beginning of the second year 1,050,000

Depletion charge per ton for the second year: $4,830,000 ÷ 1,050,000 = $4.60
Depletion charge for the second year: 100,000 × $4.60 = $460,000.

Sometimes an increase in estimated recoverable units arises from additional expenditures for capital developments. When this occurs, the additional costs should be added to the remaining recoverable cost and divided by the number of tons remaining to be extracted. To illustrate this situation, assume in the above example that $525,000 additional costs had been incurred at the beginning of the second year. The above computation of depletion rate and depletion expense would be changed as follows:

Cost assignable to recoverable tons as of the beginning of the second year:
Original costs applicable to depletable resources..................................... $5,250,000
Add additional costs incurred in the second year...................................... 525,000

$5,775,000
Deduct depletion charge for the first year 420,000

Balance of cost subject to depletion... $5,355,000

Estimated recoverable tons as of the beginning of the second year; as
above:.. 1,050,000

Depletion charge per ton for the second year: $5,355,000 ÷ 1,050,000 = $5.10
Depletion charge for the second year: 100,000 × $5.10 = $510,000

Accounting is made up of many estimates. The procedures outlined in this section are designed to prevent the continual restating of reported income from prior years. Adjustments to prior period income figures are made only if actual errors have occurred, not when reasonable estimates have been made that later prove inaccurate.

PERIODIC COST ALLOCATION ON THE INCOME STATEMENT

Because depreciation, depletion, and amortization expenses are different from other expenses since they do not require current cash disbursements, and because of their significance monetarily for most companies, practice has favored reporting all of these charges as a separate item on a single-step income statement. This approach can be observed in the General Mills financial statements in Appendix B. Note that depreciation expense and amortization expense are itemized separately, and include any such charges that for inventory purposes were included in production operating costs.

ASSET RETIREMENTS

Assets may be retired by sale, trade, or abandonment. Generally, when an asset is disposed of, the asset account and allowance account balance if applicable are canceled, and a gain or loss is recognized for the difference between the amount recovered on the asset and its book value. The gain or loss would be reported as "other income" in the year of asset disposition. As noted earlier, however, no gain or loss is recognized on the retirement of plant assets depreciated using the group or composite method.

Recording Asset Retirements

In recording a disposal, depreciation, amortization, or depletion should be recognized to the date of disposition. To illustrate the accounting for an asset retirement, assume that certain machinery is sold on April 10, 1981, for $1,250. The machinery was originally acquired on November 20, 1972, for $10,000 and had been depreciated at 10% per year. The company's policy is to recognize depreciation to the nearest month in the period of acquisition and disposal. The entries to record depreciation for 1981 and sale of the machinery are as follows:

Depreciation Expense — Machinery	250.00	
Accumulated Depreciation — Machinery		250.00
To record depreciation for three months in 1981.		

Computation:
$10,000 × 10% × 3/12 = $250.

Cash	1,250.00	
Accumulated Depreciation — Machinery	8,333.33	
Loss on Sale of Machinery	416.67	
Machinery		10,000.00
To record sale of machinery.		

Computation:

Cost		$10,000.00
Depreciation to date of sale:		
November 20, 1972 — April 10, 1981 (10% per year for 8 4/12 years)		8,333.33
Asset book value		$ 1,666.67
Proceeds from sale		1,250.00
Loss on sale		$ 416.67

The preceding entries can be combined in the form of a single compound entry as follows:

Cash	1,250.00	
Depreciation Expense — Machinery	250.00	
Accumulated Depreciation — Machinery	8,083.33	
Loss on Sale of Machinery	416.67	
Machinery		10,000.00

If an asset is scrapped or abandoned without cash recovery, a loss would be recognized equal to the asset book value; if the full cost of the asset has been written off, the asset and its offset balance would simply be canceled. When an asset is retired from active or standby service but is not immediately disposed of, the asset and accumulated depreciation balances should be closed and the lesser of book value or salvage value of the asset established as a separate asset account. If the estimated salvage value is less than book value, the difference should be recognized as a loss on the retirement. Prior to ultimate disposition of the asset, the salvage value should be reported as an asset but separately from the land, buildings, and equipment section of the balance sheet.

Property Damage or Destruction

Special accounting problems arise when property is damaged or destroyed as a result of fire, flood, storm, or other casualty. When a company owns many properties and these are widely distributed, the company itself may assume the risk of loss. However, companies ordinarily carry insurance for casualties that may involve large sums.

When uninsured properties are partly or wholly destroyed, asset book values should be reduced or canceled and a loss recorded for such reductions. When property items are insured and these are damaged or destroyed, entries on the books must be made to report asset losses and also the insurance claims arising from such losses.

The most common casualty loss incurred by a business is that from fire. Of all of the various types of protection offered by insurance, fire is the risk most widely covered. Because of the importance of fire insurance in business and because of special accounting problems that arise in the event of fire, a discussion of this matter is included in this chapter.

Fire Insurance. Fire insurance policies are usually written in $100 or $1,000 units for a period of three years. Insurance premiums are normally paid annually in advance. The amount of the premium is determined by the conditions prevailing in each case.

The insurance contract may be canceled by either the insurer or the insured. When the insurance company cancels the policy, a refund is made on a pro rata basis. When the policyholder cancels the policy, a refund may be made on what is known as a short-rate basis that provides for a higher insurance rate for the shorter period of coverage.

Accounting for Fire Losses. When a fire occurs and books of account are destroyed, account balances to the date of the fire will have to be reconstructed from the best available evidence. As the first step in summarizing the fire loss, books as maintained or as reconstructed are adjusted as of the date of the fire. With accounts brought up to date, the loss may be summarized in a fire loss account. The fire loss account is debited for the book value of properties destroyed, and it is credited for amounts recoverable from insurance companies and amounts recoverable from salvage. The balance of the account is normally recognized as an ordinary loss and is closed into the income summary account.

A number of special problems are encountered in arriving at the charges to be made to the fire loss account. When depreciable assets are destroyed, the book values of the properties must be brought up to date and these balances in total or in part transferred to the fire loss account. When merchandise is destroyed, the estimated cost of the merchandise on hand at the time of the fire must be determined. If perpetual inventory records are available, the goods on hand may be obtained from this source. In the absence of such records, the inventory is generally calculated by the gross profit method. The inventory may be set up by a debit to the inventory account and a credit to the income summary account. The inventory total or portion destroyed may now be transferred to the fire loss account.

Insurance expired to the date of the fire is recorded as an expense. The balance in the unexpired insurance account is carried forward when policies continue in force and offer original protection on rehabilitated properties or newly acquired replacements. If a business does not plan to repair or replace the assets, it may cancel a part or all of a policy and recover cash on a short-rate basis. The difference between the unexpired insurance balance and the amount received on the short-rate basis is a loss from insurance cancellation brought about by the fire and is recorded as an addition to the fire loss balance.

Because the insurance proceeds are based upon appraised values, insurance proceeds may exceed the book value of assets destroyed, resulting in a credit balance in the fire loss account. If the assets destroyed must be replaced at current market prices, the credit balance can hardly be viewed as indicating an economic gain. The credit balance may be designated for reporting purposes as "Excess of Insurance and Salvage over Book Value of Assets Lost by Fire."

BALANCE SHEET PRESENTATION AND DISCLOSURE

Plant assets, natural resources, and intangible assets are usually shown separately on the balance sheet. As indicated earlier in this chapter, both the gross cost and accumulated depreciation must be disclosed for plant assets. Such disclosure is not required for intangible and wasting assets, and many companies report only net values for these assets. Because of the alternative methods available to compute the asset cost allocation charge, the method used must be disclosed in the financial statements. Without this information, a user of the statements might be misled in trying to compare the financial results of one company with another. Cost allocation methods are normally reported in the first note to the financial statements, "Summary of Significant Accounting Policies."

Selected portions of the financial statements published in the 1979 Annual Report of The Bendix Corporation are reproduced on page 322. In the condensed Consolidated Balance Sheet, plant assets, natural resources, and intangible assets are reported at their net values. Plant asset cost and accumulated depreciation are disclosed in Details to Consolidated Balance Sheet. Though not required, similar information is provided for intangible

The Bendix Corporation and Consolidated Subsidiaries
Consolidated Balance Sheet

September 30	1979	1978
	(in millions)	
Total Current Assets	**1,401.0**	1,237.2
Investments	**171.8**	137.4
Land, Buildings, and Equipment—Net	**600.3**	532.7
Timber and Timberlands (Less Depletion)	**38.0**	32.5
Goodwill and Other Intangibles (Less Amortization)	**65.7**	70.7
Miscellaneous Assets	**34.2**	26.9
Total	**$2,311.0**	$2,037.4

Details to Consolidated Balance Sheet

	September 30	
	1979	1978
	(in millions)	
Land, Buildings, and Equipment		
Land and improvements	**$ 45.0**	$ 38.8
Buildings	**242.4**	230.1
Machinery and equipment	**563.1**	506.5
Construction in progress	**75.9**	64.3
Total	**926.4**	839.7
Less—Accumulated depreciation	**326.1**	307.0
Land, Buildings, and Equipment—Net	**$600.3**	$532.7

	September 30	
	1979	1978
	(in millions)	
Goodwill and Other Intangibles		
Goodwill and other intangibles	**$ 73.2**	$ 77.4
Patents	**3.6**	3.2
Total	**76.8**	80.6
Less—Accumulated amortization	**11.1**	9.9
Remainder	**$ 65.7**	$ 70.7

The Bendix Corporation and Consolidated Subsidiaries

Notes to Consolidated Financial Statements

Summary of Significant Accounting Policies

Land, Buildings, and Equipment Land, buildings, and equipment are stated at cost. Depreciation is provided generally on a straight-line basis over the estimated service lives of the respective classes of property. Because of the numerous classifications of property and equipment, it is impracticable to enumerate depreciation rates. Fully depreciated assets still in service are not included in the property accounts. Amortization of leasehold improvements is credited to the asset accounts and is based upon the terms of the respective leases.

Maintenance, repairs, and renewals, including replacement of minor items of physical properties, are charged to income; major additions to physical properties are capitalized.

For physical properties not fully depreciated, the cost of the assets retired or sold is credited to the asset accounts and the related accumulated depreciation is charged to the accumulated depreciation accounts. The gain or loss from sale or retirement of property is taken into income.

Timber and Timberlands Timber and timberlands are stated at cost, less depletion which is credited directly to the asset accounts. Depletion of timber is provided on footages removed at rates based on estimated recoverable timber in each tract.

Goodwill and Other Intangibles Goodwill arising prior to November 1970 represents the excess of cost over the amount ascribed to the net assets of going businesses purchased and is not amortized; goodwill and other intangibles arising from acquisitions entered into after October 1970 are amortized on a straight-line basis over periods up to forty years.

Purchased patents are stated at cost, less amortization, and are amortized over their estimated economic lives. The cost of internally developed patents is charged to income as incurred.

assets. As stated in the Summary of Significant Accounting Policies, depletion is credited directly to the asset accounts. Appendix B provides another illustration of reporting and disclosure practices for plant and intangible assets.[9]

QUESTIONS

1. Distinguish between depreciation, depletion, and amortization.

2. What has been the historical definition of depreciation, depletion, and amortization commonly used by accountants?

3. (a) What arguments can be made for charging more than an asset's cost against revenue? (b) What methods have been suggested to adjust cost allocation for inflation?

4. The president of the Vega Co. recommends that no depreciation be recorded for 1981 since the depreciation rate is 5% per year and price indexes show that prices during the year have risen by more than this figure. Evaluate this argument.

5. The policy of the Lyons Co. is to recondition its building and equipment each year so they may be maintained in perfect repair. In view of the extensive periodic costs involved in keeping the property in such condition, officials of the company feel the need for recognizing depreciation is eliminated. Evaluate this argument.

6. Distinguish between functional depreciation and physical depreciation of assets.

7. What factors must be considered to determine the periodic depreciation charges that should be made for a company's depreciable plant assets?

8. The computer has greatly simplified accounting for buildings and equipment. In what ways has this simplification taken place?

9. In what ways, if any, do accelerated methods of depreciation increase the flow of cash into a company?

10. There are several different methods that may be used to allocate the cost of assets against revenue. Wouldn't it be better to require all companies to use the same method? Discuss briefly.

11. The Egnew Manufacturing Company purchased a new machine especially built to perform one particular function on their assembly line. A difference of opinion has arisen as to the method of depreciation to be used in connection with this machine. Three methods are now being considered:
   (a) The straight-line method.
   (b) The productive-output method.
   (c) The sum-of-the-years-digits method.
List separately the arguments for and against each of the proposed methods from both the theoretical and the practical viewpoints. In your answer, you need not express your preference and you are to disregard income tax consequences.

12. The certified public accountant is frequently called upon by management for advice regarding methods of computing depreciation. Although the question arises less frequently, of comparable importance is whether the depreciation method should be based on the consideration of the property items as units, as groups, or as having a composite life.
   (a) Briefly describe the depreciation methods based on recognizing property items as (1) units, (2) groups, or (3) as having a composite life.
   (b) Present the arguments for and against the use of each of these methods.
   (c) Describe how retirements are recorded under each of these methods.

13. Wells, Inc., has valuable patent rights that are being amortized over their legal lives. The president of the company believes these patents are contributing sub-

---

[9]See the Consolidated Balance Sheet and Notes 1B and 1D.

stantially to company goodwill and recommends patent amortization be capitalized as company goodwill. What is your opinion of this proposal?

14. What factors should be considered in estimating the useful lives of intangible
assets?

15. (a) What method is commonly used to amortize the cost of intangible assets?
(b) Under what circumstances might an alternative method be appropriate?

16. What procedures must be followed when the estimate of recoverable wasting
assets is changed due to subsequent development work?

17. Machinery in the finishing department of the Gerhardt Co., although less than
50% depreciated, has been replaced by new machinery. The company expects to
find a buyer for the old machinery, and on December 31 the machinery is in the
yards and available for inspection. How should it be reported on the balance
sheet?

18. How should plant assets, wasting assets, and intangibles be reported on the
balance sheet? What footnote disclosure should be made for these assets?

EXERCISES

exercise 11-1

A machine is purchased at the beginning of 1981 for $31,000. Its estimated life is 6 years. Freight in
on the machine is $1,400. Installation costs are $800. The machine is estimated to have a residual
value of $2,000, and a useful life of 40,000 hours. It was used 6,000 hours in 1981.

(1) What is the cost of the machine for accounting purposes?
(2) Compare the depreciation charge for 1981 using (a) the straight-line method, and (b) the
service-hours method.

exercise 11-2

The Table Company purchased a machine for $90,000 on June 15, 1981. It is estimated that the
machine will have a 10-year life and will have a salvage value of $9,000. Its working hours and
production in units are estimated at 36,000 and 600,000 respectively. It is the company's policy to
take a half-year's depreciation on all assets for which they use the straight-line or double-declining-balance depreciation method in the year of purchase. During 1981, the machine was operated
4,000 hours and produced 67,000 units. Which of the following methods will give the greatest
depreciation expense for 1981: (1) double-declining balance; (2) productive-output; or (3) service-
hours. (Show computations for all three methods.)

exercise 11-3

Plastics Manufacturing Co. acquired machinery at a cost of $200,000. The asset had a 10-year life
and a scrap value of $14,000. Depreciation was to be recorded at a rate double the straight-line
rate. However, realizing that a continuation of depreciation at the same rate would require the
recognition of a significant loss in the last year of asset life, the company decided to change to the
sum-of-the-years-digits method and write off the remaining asset book value over the remaining
asset life beginning with the year in which the declining-balance method produced a smaller
charge than the sum-of-the-years-digits depreciation. Prepare a table indicating the optimum year
to change methods and listing annual depreciation charges and the accumulated depreciation for
the 10-year period. Round depreciation to the nearest dollar amount.

exercise 11-4

On July 1, 1980, Benjamin Corporation purchased factory equipment for $25,000. Salvage value
was estimated to be $3,000. The equipment will be depreciated over ten years, counting the year of
acquisition as one-half year. What should Benjamin Corporation record for depreciation expense
for 1981 using the (a) double-declining-balance method? (b) sum-of-the-years-digits method?

exercise 11-5

Equipment was purchased at the beginning of 1979 for $50,000 with an estimated product life of 300,000 units. The equipment has a salvage value of $5,000. During 1979, 1980, and 1981, the unit production of the equipment was 80,000 units, 120,000 units, and 40,000 units respectively. The machine was damaged at the beginning of 1982, and the equipment was scrapped with no salvage value.

    (1) Determine depreciation using the productive-output method for 1979, 1980, and 1981.
    (2) Give the entry to write off the equipment.

exercise 11-6

The Medallion Co. records show the following assets:

	Acquired	Cost	Salvage	Estimated Useful Life
Machinery	7/1/80	$105,000	$7,500	10 years
Equipment	1/1/81	33,000	1,500	7 years
Fixtures	1/1/81	45,000	4,500	4 years

What is (a) the composite depreciation rate to be applied to cost and (b) the composite life of the asset?

exercise 11-7

A schedule of machinery owned by Lester Manufacturing Company is presented below:

	Total Cost	Estimated Salvage Value	Estimated Life in Years
Machine A	$550,000	$50,000	20
Machine B	200,000	20,000	15
Machine C	40,000	——	5

Lester computes depreciation on the straight-line method. Based upon the information presented, calculate the composite depreciation rate and the composite life of these assets.   (AICPA adapted)

exercise 11-8

The Box Manufacturing Co. acquired a machine at a cost of $19,080 on March 1, 1975. The machine is estimated to have a life of 10 years except for a special unit that will require replacement at the end of 6 years. The asset is recorded in two accounts, $14,400 being assigned to the main unit, and $4,680 to the special unit. Depreciation is recorded by the straight-line method to the nearest month, salvage values being disregarded. On March 1, 1981, the special unit is scrapped and is replaced with a similar unit; the cost of the replacement at this time is $11,200 and it is estimated that the unit will have a residual value of approximately 25% of cost at the end of the useful life of the main unit. What are the depreciation charges to be recognized for the years 1975, 1981, and 1982.

exercise 11-9

The Qualis Co. applied for and received numerous patents at a total cost of $30,345 at the beginning of 1976. It is assumed the patents will be useful evenly during their full legal life. At the beginning of 1978, the company paid $7,875 in successfully prosecuting an attempted infringement of these patent rights. At the beginning of 1981, $25,200 was paid to acquire patents that could make its own patents worthless: the patents acquired have a remaining life of 15 years but will not be used.

    (1) Give the entries to record the expenditures relative to patents.
    (2) Give the entries to record patent amortization for the years, 1976, 1978, and 1981.

exercise 11-10

On July 1, 1981, Stubs Mining, a calendar-year corporation, purchased the rights to a copper mine. Of the total purchase price, $1,400,000 was appropriately allocable to the copper. Estimated reserves were 400,000 tons of copper. Stubs expects to extract and sell 5,000 tons of copper per month. Production began immediately. The selling price is $25 per ton.

To aid production, Stubs also purchased some new equipment on July 1, 1981. The equipment cost $152,000 and had an estimated useful life of 8 years. However, after all the copper is removed from this mine, the equipment will be of no use to Stubs and will be sold for an estimated $8,000.

If sales and production conform to expectations, what is Stubs' depletion expense on this mine and depreciation expense on the new equipment for financial accounting purposes for the calendar year 1981?

exercise 11-11

Indec Corporation purchased a machine on January 1, 1975, for $150,000. At the date of acquisition, the machine had an estimated useful life of 15 years with no salvage value. The machine is being depreciated on a straight-line basis. On January 1, 1980, as a result of Indec's experience with the machine, it was decided that the machine had an estimated useful life of 10 years from the date of acquisition. What is the amount of depreciation expense on this machine in 1980 using a new annual depreciation charge for the remaining 5 years?

exercise 11-12

The Manning Mining Company in 1978 paid $3,200,000 for property with a supply of natural resources estimated at 2,000,000 tons. The property was estimated to be worth $400,000 after removal of the natural resource. Developmental costs of $600,000 were incurred in 1979 before withdrawals of the resources could be made. In 1980 resources removed totaled 400,000 tons. In 1981 resources removed totaled 600,000 tons. During 1981 discoveries were made indicating that available resources subsequent to 1981 will total 3,000,000 tons. Additional developmental costs of $880,000 were incurred in 1981. What entries should be made to recognize depletion for 1980 and 1981?

exercise 11-13

Star, Inc., purchased equipment costing $100,000 on June 30, 1981, having an estimated life of 5 years and a residual value of $10,000. The company uses the sum-of-the-years-digits method of depreciation, and takes one-half year's depreciation on assets in the year of purchase. The asset was sold on December 31, 1983, for $31,000. Give the entry to record the sale of the equipment.

PROBLEMS

problem 11-1

A delivery truck was acquired by Sports, Inc., for $10,000 on January 1, 1980. The truck was estimated to have a 3-year life and a trade-in value at the end of that time of $1,000. The following depreciation methods are being considered.

(a) Depreciation is to be calculated by the straight-line method.
(b) Depreciation is to be calculated by the sum-of-the-years-digits method.
(c) Depreciation is to be calculated by applying a fixed percentage to the declining book value of the asset that will reduce the asset book value to its residual value at the end of the third year. (The third root of .10 = .464.)
(d) Repair charges are estimated at $70 for the first year and are estimated to increase by $50 in each succeeding year; depreciation charges are to be made on a diminishing scale so that the sum of depreciation and estimated repairs is the same for each year over the life of the asset.

Instructions: Prepare tables reporting periodic depreciation and asset book value over the 3-year period for each assumption listed above.

problem 11-2

A company buys a machine for $9,600. The maintenance costs for the years 1979–1982 are as follows:

1979 .. $ 100
1980 .. 110
1981 .. 2,548 (Includes $2,496 for cost of a new motor installed in December, 1981.)
1982 .. 140

Instructions:

(1) Assume the machine is recorded in a single account at a cost of $9,600. No record is kept of the cost of the component parts. Straight-line depreciation is used and the asset is estimated to have a useful life of 8 years. It is assumed there will be no residual value at the end of the useful life. What is the sum of the depreciation and maintenance charges for each of the first four years?

(2) Assume the cost of the frame of the machine was recorded in one account at a cost of $7,200 and the motor was recorded in a second account at a cost of $2,400. Straight-line depreciation is used with a useful life of 10 years for the frame and 4 years for the motor. Neither item is assumed to have any residual value at the end of its useful life. What is the sum of depreciation and maintenance charges for each of the first four years?

(3) Evaluate the two methods.

problem 11-3

The Beckham Company purchased a machine costing $110,000 in 1980. The machine had an estimated salvage value of $20,000 and a useful life of 20 years. It is the company policy to take a full year's depreciation in the year of purchase. At the beginning of 1983, the company changed the method of depreciation on the machine from double-declining balance to sum-of-the-years-digits in order to fully depreciate it. On December 31, 1984, the machine was sold for $74,500.

Instructions:

(1) Determine the gain or loss on the sale of the machine.
(2) Prepare the journal entry to record the sale.

problem 11-4

The Omrat Manufacturing Co. acquired 25 similar machines at the beginning of 1976 for $50,000. Machines have an average life of 5 years and no residual value. The group-depreciation method is employed in writing off the cost of the machines. Machines were retired as follows:

2 machines at the end of 1978   11 machines at the end of 1980
6 machines at the end of 1979   6 machines at the end of 1981

Instructions: Give the entries to record the retirement of machines and the periodic depreciation for the years 1976–1981 inclusive.

problem 11-5

Machines are acquired by McArthur, Inc., on March 1, 1981, as follows:

	Cost	Estimated Salvage Value	Estimated Life in Years
Machine 101	$54,000	$12,000	6
102	20,000	2,000	8
103	2,000	800	8
104	18,000	1,700	10
105	7,500	None	10

Instructions:

(1) Calculate the composite depreciation rate for this group.
(2) Calculate the composite or average life in years for the group.
(3) Give the entry to record the depreciation for the year ending December 31, 1981.

problem 11-6

On January 10, 1973, the Briggs Company spent $24,000 to apply for and obtain a patent on a newly developed product. The patent had an estimated useful life of 10 years. At the beginning of 1977, the company spent $18,000 in successfully prosecuting an attempted infringement of the patent. At the beginning of 1978, the company purchased for $50,000 a patent that was expected to prolong the life of its original patent by 5 years. On July 1, 1981, a competitor obtained rights to a patent which made the company's patent obsolete.

Instructions: Give all the entries that would be made relative to the patent for the period 1973–1981, including entries to record the purchase of the patent, annual patent amortization, and ultimate patent obsolescence. (Assume the company's accounting period is the calendar year.)

problem 11-7

The Dutch Corp. was organized on January 2, 1981. It was authorized to issue 80,000 shares of common stock, par $50. On the date of organization it sold 20,000 shares at par and gave the remaining shares in exchange for certain land bearing recoverable ore deposits estimated by geologists at 800,000 tons. The property is deemed to have a value of $3,000,000 with no residual value.

During 1981 mine improvements totaled $45,000. Miscellaneous buildings and sheds were constructed at a cost of $99,000. During the year 50,000 tons were mined; 4,000 tons of this amount were on hand unsold on December 31, the balance of the tonnage being sold for cash at $17 per ton. Expenses incurred and paid for during the year, exclusive of depletion and depreciation, were as follows:

Mining	$151,750
Delivery	15,000
General and administrative	12,800

Cash dividends of $2 per share were declared on December 31, payable January 15, 1982.

It is believed that buildings and sheds will be useful only over the life of the mine; hence depreciation is to be recognized in terms of mine output.

Instructions: Prepare an income statement and a balance sheet for 1981. Submit working papers showing the development of statement data.

problem 11-8

The Silver Mining Company paid $2,700,000 in 1980 for property with a supply of natural resources estimated at 2,000,000 tons. The estimated cost of restoring the land for use after the resources are exhausted is $225,000. After the land is restored, it will have an estimated value of $562,500. Development costs, such as drilling and road construction, were $825,000. Buildings, such as bunk houses and mess hall, were constructed on the site for $112,500. The useful lives of the buildings are expected to terminate upon exhaustion of the natural resources. Operations were not begun until January 1, 1981. In 1981, resources removed totaled 600,000 tons. During 1982, an additional discovery was made indicating that available resources subsequent to 1982 will total 1,800,000 tons. Because of a strike, only 400,000 tons of resources were removed during 1982.

Instructions: Compute the debits to Depletion Expense for 1980, 1981, and 1982. (Include depreciation expense as a part of depletion expense.)

problem 11-9

The Lakeview Company entered into the following transactions involving its plant and intangible assets in 1981. Lakeview uses the calendar year as its fiscal year.

Jan. 1 The Lakeview Company sold land to the Falls Company which originally cost Lakeview $600,000. There was *no* established exchange price for this property. Falls gave Lakeview a $1,000,000 noninterest-bearing note payable in five equal annual installments of $200,000 with the first payment due December 31, 1981. The note has *no* ready market. The prevailing interest rate for a note of this type is 10%.

Mar. 1 Lakeview sold a machine for $800. The machine had been purchased on May 1, 1972, for $25,000. At the time of acquisition, the machine was estimated to have a useful life of ten years and a salvage value of $1,000. The company has recorded monthly depreciation using the straight-line method.

July 1 Lakeview sold a machine for $27,000. It was acquired for $74,000 on November 1, 1975. At the time of acquisition, the machine was estimated to have a useful life of 8 years and a salvage value of $2,000.

Dec. 31 Lakeview had purchased patents on January 1, 1978, at a cost of $56,000. The patents had been estimated to have a 10-year life. It is now estimated that the remaining benefit from the patents will be negligible after 1984.

Instructions: Prepare journal entries to record each of the given transactions or adjustments required by the information provided.

problem 11-10

The following account balances pertain to the North Ice Company.

Account Title	Dr.	Cr.
Equipment	675,000	
Goodwill	435,000	
Inventory	90,000	
Land	200,000	
Franchises	575,000	
Cash	65,000	
Accounts Receivable	137,000	
Buildings	1,400,000	
Patents	15,000	
Notes Receivable	456,000	
Accumulated Depreciation — Equipment		235,000
Accounts Payable		147,000
Notes Payable		1,500,000
Accumulated Depreciation — Buildings		385,000

Additional information:

(a) $600,000 of the notes payable are secured by a direct lien on the building.

(b) The company uses the sum-of-the-years-digits method of cost allocation for buildings and equipment and uses straight-line for patents, franchises, and goodwill.

(c) Inventory valuation was made using the retail method.

Instructions: Prepare the land, buildings, and equipment section and the intangible asset section of the balance sheet.

12

Long-Term Investments in Equity Securities

CHAPTER OBJECTIVES

Explain the nature and classification of long-term investments.

Describe and illustrate the accounting for acquisitions of equity securities under various acquisition methods.

Explain the concepts underlying the recognition of revenue from long-term investments in common stock, and illustrate the application of the cost and equity methods of revenue recognition.

Discuss the accounting treatment of corporate distributions in the form of stock dividends, stock splits, and stock rights.

Describe and illustrate the valuation of equity securities subsequent to acquisition.

Describe and illustrate the accounting for dispositions of stock by sale, redemption, and exchange.

A company invests funds in inventories, receivables, land, buildings, equipment, and other assets in order to engage in the sale of goods and services. Some available funds, however, may be applied to the acquisition of assets not directly identified with a company's primary activities. These assets, referred to as **investments**, are expected to contribute to the success of the business either by exercising a favorable influence on sales and operations generally, or by making an independent contribution to business earnings over the long term.

CLASSIFICATION OF INVESTMENTS

From the standpoint of the owner, investments are either temporary or long-term. As discussed in Chapter 6, investments are classified as current only where they are (1) readily marketable and (2) it is management's intent to use them in meeting current cash requirements. Investments not meeting both of these tests are considered **long-term** or **permanent investments** and are usually reported on the balance sheet under a separate noncurrent heading.

The accounting problems relating to long-term investments in equity securities are considered in this chapter; those relating to bonds in Chapter 14. Long-term investments also include such diverse items as: special purpose funds; real estate investments; interests in life insurance contracts; advances to subsidiaries that are of a permanent nature; deposits made to guarantee contract performance; and equity interests in partnerships, trusts, and estates. Most of these assets either produce current revenue or have a favorable business effect in some other way. Although cost is the underlying basis for these miscellaneous investments, the accounting procedure varies according to the type of investment involved.

LONG-TERM INVESTMENTS IN EQUITY SECURITIES

One of the characteristics of our free enterprise financial community is the considerable level of intercorporate investment. A corporation may acquire securities of another established corporation to obtain instant growth in assets and earning power and/or a diversification in the products or services sold. In other cases, the investment insures the acquiring company a source for its raw materials or a distribution outlet for its finished product. Whatever the objective, an investment in equity securities of another corporate entity is expected to enhance the economic well-being of the acquiring company.

Acquisition of Equity Securities

Shares of stock are usually acquired through brokers on the New York Stock Exchange, the American Stock Exchange, regional exchanges, or over the counter. Stock may also be acquired directly from an issuing company or from a private investor.

Cash Purchase. Stock purchased for cash is recorded at the amount paid, including brokers' commissions, taxes, and other fees incidental to the purchase. When payment of all or part of the purchase price is deferred, the full cost of the stock should be recorded as an asset. An agreement or **subscrip-**

tion entered into with a corporation for the purchase of its stock is recognized by a debit to an asset account for the securities to be received and a credit to a liability account for the amount to be paid. A purchase of stock that is partially financed by a broker is referred to as a purchase **on margin**. Stock acquired on margin should be recorded at its purchase price and a liability recognized for the unpaid balance.

To illustrate, assume a company purchases 2,000 shares of common stock in another company at a price of $30 per share. Existing margin requirements call for an initial payment of two thirds of the purchase price or $20 per share. The purchase would be recorded as follows:

Investment in Common Stock	60,000	
Cash		40,000
Payable to Broker		20,000

To report only the initial cash invested would be, in effect, to offset the obligation to the broker against the investment account. A charge for interest on any obligation arising from a stock purchase should be reported as an expense.

Noncash Acquisition. When stock is acquired in exchange for properties or services, the fair market value of such considerations or the value at which the stock is currently selling, whichever is more clearly determinable, should be used as a basis for recording the investment. In the absence of clearly defined values for assets or services exchanged or a market price for the security acquired, appraisals and estimates are required in arriving at cost. Any gain or loss is recognized as an ordinary item in the period of the exchange. To illustrate, assume that a company purchases common stock with inventory; cost is $20,000, normal selling price, $30,000. The market value of the securities is not well established. If the company uses the perpetual inventory system the exchange would be recorded as follows:

Cost of Sales	20,000	
Investment in Common Stock	30,000	
Inventory		20,000
Sales		30,000

The $10,000 gross profit on the exchange would be included in total gross profit reported for the period of the exchange.

Lump-Sum Purchase. When two or more securities are acquired for a lump-sum price, this cost should be allocated in some equitable manner to the different acquisitions. When market prices are available for each security, cost can be apportioned on the basis of the relative market prices. When there is a market price for one security but not for the other, it may be reasonable to assign the market price to one and the cost excess to the other. When market prices are not available for either security, cost apportionment may have to be postponed until support for an equitable division becomes available. In some cases, it will be necessary to carry the two securities in a single account until disposition, and to treat the proceeds from the sale of one as a subtraction from total cost. The residual cost can then be identified with the other security. To illustrate these procedures, assume the purchase of 100 units of preferred and common stock at $75 per unit; each unit consists of one share of preferred and two shares of common. Market prices at the time the stock is acquired are $60 per share for preferred and $10 per share for common. The investment cost is recorded in terms of the relative market values of the securities, as follows:

Investment in Preferred Stock..	5,625	
Investment in Common Stock..	1,875	
Cash		7,500

Computation:
Value of preferred: 100 × $60 = $6,000
Value of common: 200 × $10 = 2,000
$8,000

Cost assigned to preferred: 6,000/8,000 × $7,500 = $5,625.
Cost assigned to common: 2,000/8,000 × $7,500 = $1,875.

If there is no market value for common stock, the investment may be recorded as follows:

Investment in Preferred Stock..	6,000	
Investment in Common Stock..	1,500	
Cash		7,500

Computation:
Cost of preferred and common stock...........................	$7,500
Cost identified with preferred stock (market)	6,000
Remaining cost identified with common stock	$1,500

If the division of cost must be deferred, the following entry is made:

Investment in Preferred and Common Stock..	7,500	
Cash		7,500

The joint investment balance may be eliminated when a basis for apportionment is established and costs can be assigned to individual classes.

In some limited situations, stock is subject to special calls or assessments requiring additional capital contributions from stockholders. Such payments to the corporation are recorded as additions to the costs of the holdings. Pro rata contributions by the stockholders to the corporation to eliminate a deficit, to retire bonds, or to effect a reorganization, are also treated as additions to investment cost.

Revenue from Long-Term Investments in Common Stocks

The accounting profession has developed a variety of methods to account for investments in common stock. The key concept in accounting for and reporting equity investments subsequent to purchase is the **degree of influence** exercised by the acquiring company (**investor**) over the acquired company (**investee**).

When a company acquires a majority voting interest in another company through acquisition of **more than 50%** of its voting common stock, the investor and investee are referred to respectively as the **parent** company and

subsidiary company. Financial statement balances of the parent and subsidiary are added together or **consolidated** after necessary adjustments are made. This treatment reflects the fact that majority ownership of common stock assures control by the parent over the decision-making processes of the subsidiary. In certain limited situations, the financial statements of a subsidiary are not consolidated with those of the parent. Generally, however, the reporting entity is the economic unit consisting of the parent and all its subsidiaries. Accounting for consolidated entities is covered in advanced accounting texts.[1]

The Cost and Equity Methods of Revenue Recognition. Consolidated financial statements are appropriate only when the investor holds a majority voting interest in the investee. A considerable degree of control, however, may be exercised by an investor owning **50% or less** of the common stock of the investee. If conditions indicate that the acquiring company exercises **significant influence** over the financial and operational decisions of the other company, the basic accounting principle of substance over form suggests that accounting procedures should be designed to parallel as closely as possible those followed when voting control exists and consolidated statements are prepared. The **equity method** of accounting is used to produce these results. Because adjustments are made directly to a single investment account, this method is often referred to as a "one-line consolidation."

When the acquiring company does not exercise significant influence over the acquired company, accounting for the investment should recognize the separate identities of the companies. At present, this is accomplished by the **cost method** of accounting; subsequent to acquisition, adjustments are made to the carrying value of the investment only to recognize a decline in market value below cost. Since preferred stock does not provide for significant influence, the cost method is used for these investments.

The ability to exercise significant influence over such decisions as dividend distribution and operational and financial administration may be indicated in several ways: e.g., representation on the investee's board of directors, participation in policy-making processes, material intercompany transactions, interchange of managerial personnel, or technological dependency. Another important consideration is the extent of ownership by an investor in relation to the concentration of other shareholdings. While it is clear that ownership of over 50% of common stock assures control by the acquiring company, ownership of a lesser percentage may give effective control if the balance of the stock is widely held and no significant blocks of stockholders are consistently united in their ownership.

The Accounting Principles Board in Opinion No. 18 recognized that the degree of influence and control will not always be clear and that judgment will be required in assessing the status of each investment. To

---

[1]See Paul M. Fischer, William James Taylor, and J. Arthur Leer, *Advanced Accounting* (Cincinnati: South-Western Publishing Co., 1978).

achieve a reasonable degree of uniformity in the application of its position, the Board set 20% as an ownership standard; the ownership of 20% or more of the voting stock of the company carries the presumption, in the absence of evidence to the contrary, that an investor has the ability to exercise significant influence over that company. Conversely, ownership of less than 20% leads to the presumption that the investor does not have the ability to exercise significant influence unless such ability can be demonstrated.[2]

Because other control factors are usually very subjective, the percentage-of-ownership rule set forth in APB Opinion No. 18 has been widely accepted as the criterion for determining the appropriate method of revenue recognition for investments in equity securities when the investor does not possess absolute voting control. Thus, in the absence of persuasive evidence to the contrary, the **cost method** is used when ownership is **less than 20%**; the **equity method**, when ownership is **20% to 50%**. The financial statements of General Mills, Inc., reproduced in Appendix B provide an example of the application of this rule. As indicated in Note 1A, companies more than 50% owned by General Mills, Inc., have been consolidated and companies which are between 20% and 50% owned are reported as separate investments on the balance sheet.

Applying the Equity Method. The equity method of recognizing revenue reflects the economic substance of the relationship between the investor and investee rather than the legal distinction of the separate entities. Although the earnings of the investee are not legally available to stockholders until their distribution as dividends has been authorized by the board of directors, the timing of the distribution can be affected by a stockholder with significant influence over the dividend decision. Failure to recognize income as earned by the investee would permit such a stockholder to affect its own income by the distribution policy followed.

Under the equity method of accounting for controlled investments, a proportionate share of the earnings or losses of the investee is recognized by the investor in the year earned or incurred. The earnings are generally reflected in a single account unless the investee has special items such as extraordinary gains or losses or cumulative adjustments from changing accounting methods. Separate revenue accounts should be used for ordinary income and for these special items. The investment account is increased by the proportionate share of the earnings and decreased by the proportionate share of the losses and the proportionate distribution of dividends.

For example, assume that Probert Manufacturing Co. held a 40% interest in the common stock of Stewart, Inc. In 1981, Stewart, Inc., reported net income of $150,000, which included an extraordinary gain of $30,000. Dividends of $70,000 were distributed to stockholders. The following entries would be made on the books of Probert Manufacturing Co. to record its share of the 1981 earnings of Stewart, Inc.

---

[2]*Opinions of the Accounting Principles Board, No. 18*, "The Equity Method of Accounting for Investments in Common Stock" (New York: American Institute of Certified Public Accountants, 1971).

Investment in Stewart, Inc., Common Stock......................................	60,000	
Share of Ordinary Income — Stewart, Inc., Common Stock		48,000
Share of Extraordinary Income — Stewart, Inc., Common Stock..		12,000
To recognize 40% of the income earned by Stewart, Inc., common stock.		
Cash	28,000	
Investment in Stewart, Inc., Common Stock....................................		28,000
To record receipt of cash dividend.		

If the investee company has preferred stock outstanding, dividends on this stock must be deducted from income before the investor computes the proportionate share of income earned.

One of the objectives of the equity method is that the recorded investment reflect as closely as possible a proportionate share of the underlying value of the investee company as if 100% of the company had been purchased. When a company is purchased, the purchase price often differs from the recorded book values of the company. If the purchase price exceeds the recorded value, the acquiring company must allocate this purchase price among the assets acquired using their current market values as opposed to the amounts carried on the books of the acquired company. If part of the purchase price is still unallocated after this division, the difference is identified as goodwill. If the recorded value exceeds the purchase price, asset values must be reduced to equal the purchase price. Future income determination for the acquired company will use the new recorded values to determine the depreciation and amortization charges.

When only a portion of a company is purchased and the equity method is used to reflect the income of the partially owned company, a similar adjustment may be required to the reported income. In order to determine whether such an adjustment is necessary, the acquiring company must compare the implied value of the company based upon the purchase price of the common stock with the recorded book value of the company at the date of purchase. If the implied value exceeds the reported value, the computed excess must be analyzed in the same way as described above for a 100% purchase, although no entries are made to the books for the new values. To the extent assets have limited lives, the proportionate share of additional depreciation or amortization implied in the purchase price must be deducted from the income reported by the acquired company. This adjustment serves to meet the objective of computing the income reported using the equity method in the same manner as would be done if the company were 100% purchased.

For example, assume that the total common stockholders' equity of Stewart, Inc., was $500,000 at the time Probert Manufacturing Co. purchased 40% of its common shares of $250,000. The implied value of the total common stockholders' equity of Stewart, Inc., would be $625,000 ($250,000 ÷ .40), or $125,000 in excess of common stockholders' equity. Assume that review of the asset values discloses that the market value of depreciable properties with an average remaining life of ten years exceeds the carrying value of these assets by $50,000. The remaining $75,000 difference ($125,000 − $50,000) is attributed to goodwill. The adjustment to

Stewart, Inc.'s revenue to be recognized by Probert Manufacturing Co. would be a deduction of $2,000 for the proportionate depreciation of the excess market value on depreciable property, ($50,000 × .40) ÷ 10, and a deduction of $750 for the proportionate amortization of goodwill over a 40-year period, ($75,000 × .40) ÷ 40. The entry for this adjustment would be as follows:

```
Share of Ordinary Income — Stewart, Inc., Common Stock..............   2,750
    Investment in Stewart, Inc., Common Stock...................................          2,750
    To adjust share of ordinary income on Stewart, Inc., common
    stock for proportionate depreciation on excess market value
    of depreciable property, $2,000, and for amortization of im-
    plied goodwill from acquisition, $750.
```

This illustration assumes that the fiscal years of the two companies coincide and that the purchase of the stock is made at the first of that year. If a purchase is made at other times, the income earned up to the date of the purchase is assumed to be included in the cost of purchase. Only income earned subsequent to acquisition should be recognized as revenue on the books of the investor.

If the purchase cost is less than the underlying book value at the time of acquisition, it is assumed that specific assets of the investee are overvalued and an adjustment is necessary to reduce the depreciation or amortization taken by the investee. The journal entry to reflect this adjustment is the reverse of the one just illustrated.

If the investor and the investee are engaged in intercompany revenue producing activities, adjustments must also be made to eliminate intercompany profits. These adjustments are similar to those made when consolidated statements are prepared for parents and 50% or more owned subsidiaries. A more complete description of these intercompany problems is found in advanced accounting texts.

Applying the Cost Method. When investment in another company's stock does not involve either a controlling interest or significant influence, the revenue recognized is limited to the distribution of the dividends declared by the investee. The receipt of cash dividends by a stockholder is recorded by a debit to Cash and a credit to Dividend Revenue. Three dates are generally included in the formal dividend announcement: (1) date of declaration, (2) record date, and (3) date of payment. The formal dividend announcement may read somewhat as follows: "The Board of Directors at their meeting on November 5, 1981, declared a regular quarterly dividend on outstanding common stock of 50 cents per share payable on January 15, 1982, to stockholders of record at the close of business, December 29, 1981." The stockholder becomes aware of the dividend action upon its announcement. If stock is sold and a new owner is recognized by the corporation prior to the record date, the dividend is paid to the new owner. If a stock transfer is not recognized by the corporation until after the record date, the dividend will be paid to the former owner, i.e., the shareholder of record. After the record date, stock no longer carries a right to dividends and sells **ex-dividend**.[3] Accordingly, a stockholder is justified in recognizing the corporate dividend action on the record date. At this time a receivable account may be debited and Dividend Revenue credited. Upon receipt of the dividend, Cash is debited and the receivable credited. Practice frequently omits accrual and recognizes revenue as the cash is received.

If dividends paid by the investee exceed the income earned by the investee since the stock was acquired, the excess represents a return of the investment price. This portion should be credited to the investment account rather than to Dividend Revenue. For example, assume that a 15% interest in Security Manufacturing Co. is acquired by Midwest Manufacturing Co. for $100,000. At the end of the first full year of ownership, Security Manufacturing reports an income of $50,000 and pays a dividend to its shareholders of $80,000. The $12,000 dividend received by Midwest Manufacturing Co. should be recorded as follows:

Cash ($80,000 × 15%)	12,000	
Dividend Revenue ($50,000 × 15%)		7,500
Investment in Security Manufacturing Co. Common Stock		4,500

A similar allocation of dividends between revenue and investment is required when an investee makes distributions in excess of current and prior years' accumulated earnings. Although these **liquidating dividends** can occur in any company, they are most common in a company consuming natural resources in its operations. When natural resources are limited and irreplaceable, the company may choose to distribute full proceeds becoming available from operations. Dividends paid, then, represent in part a distribution of earnings and in part a distribution of invested capital. Distributions involving both earnings and invested capital may also be found when a company makes full distribution of the proceeds from the sale of certain properties, such as land or securities, or when a distribution represents the proceeds from business liquidation.

Information regarding the portion of dividends representing earnings and the portion representing invested capital should be reported to the stockholder by the corporation making the distribution. This is necessary because return *of* capital is not taxable income; however, return *on* capital is recognized as taxable income. This report may not accompany each dividend check but instead may be provided annually and may cover the total dividends paid during the year. If dividends have been recorded as revenue during the year, the revenue account is debited and the investment account is credited when notification is received of the amount to be recognized as a distribution of invested capital.

When liquidating dividends exceed investment cost, excess distributions are reported as a gain from the investment. If liquidation is completed and the investment cost is not fully recovered, the balance of the investment account should be written off as a loss.

---

[3] Stock on the New York Stock Exchange is normally quoted ex-dividend or ex-rights four full trading days prior to the record date because of the time required to deliver the stock and to record the stock transfer.

Property Dividends. Dividend distribution under either the cost or equity method may involve assets other than cash. Such dividends are referred to as **property dividends**. In distributing earnings by means of a property dividend, the corporation credits the asset account for the cost of the asset distributed, debits Retained Earnings for the market value of the asset distributed, if determinable, and accounts for the difference as a gain or a loss. APB Opinion No. 29 defines this type of transaction as a nonreciprocal transfer to an owner and recommends that it be treated as a dividend.[4] The stockholder debits an asset account and credits Dividend Revenue or the investment account depending on whether the cost or equity method is being used. The stockholder also recognizes the dividend in terms of the market value of the property item at the date of its distribution. To illustrate these situations, assume that the Wells Corporation with 1,000,000 shares of common stock outstanding distributes as a dividend its holdings of 50,000 shares of Barnes Co. stock acquired at a cost of $11 per share. The distribution of one share of Barnes Co. stock for every 20 shares of Wells Corporation held is made when Barnes Co. shares are selling at $16. Wells Corporation would record the dividend as follows:

```
Retained Earnings................................................................. 800,000
   Investment in Barnes Co. Common Stock .......................................       550,000
   Gain from Distribution of Barnes Co. Common Stock....................       250,000
      To record distribution of 50,000 shares of Barnes Co. stock as
      a property dividend.
```

A stockholder owning 100 shares of Wells Corporation stock would make the following entry in recording the receipt of the dividend:

```
Investment in Barnes Co. Common Stock.......................................   80
   Dividend Revenue..............................................................           80
      Received 5 shares of Barnes Co. common stock, market price
      $16 per share, as a dividend on 100 shares of Wells Corpora-
      tion.
```

Nonrevenue Distributions from Investee

Certain types of distributions or stock adjustments do not produce immediate revenue for investors, but may enhance the value of their investment over time. The most common of these are stock dividends, stock splits, and stock rights. Although differing in nature, each requires a recomputation of cost per share of the investment. In some cases, an allocation of the investment cost is necessary to reflect the additional investment securities held.

Stock Dividends. A company may distribute a dividend in the form of additional shares that are the same as those held by its stockholders. Such a dividend does not affect company assets but simply results in the transfer of retained earnings to invested capital. The increase in total shares outstand-

---

[4]*Opinions of the Accounting Principles Board, No. 29,* "Accounting for Nonmonetary Transactions" (New York: American Institute of Certified Public Accountants, 1973), par. 3.

ing is distributed pro rata to individual stockholders. The receipt of additional shares by stockholders leaves their respective equities exactly as they were. Although the number of shares held by individual stockholders has gone up, there are now a greater number of shares outstanding and proportionate interests remain unchanged. The division of equities into a greater number of parts cannot be regarded as giving rise to revenue. To illustrate, assume that Eagle Corporation has 10,000 shares of common stock outstanding. Total stockholders' equity is $330,000; the book value per share is $33. If a 10% stock dividend is declared, an additional 1,000 shares of stock will be issued and the book value per share will decline to $30. A stockholder who held 10 shares with a book value of $330 (10 × $33) will hold 11 shares after the stock dividend, with the book value remaining at $330 (11 × $30).

The market value of the stock may or may not react in a similar manner. Theoretically, the same relative decrease should occur in the market value as occurred in the book value; however, there are many variables influencing the market price of securities. If the percentage of the stock dividend issued is comparatively low, under 20–25%, there is generally less than a pro rata immediate effect on the stock market price. This means that while a stockholder after receiving a stock dividend will have no greater interest in the company, the investment may have a greater market value.

Because no assets are distributed, there is no effect on the underlying book value of the investment; only a memorandum entry needs to be made by the stockholder in recognizing the receipt of additional shares. Original investment cost applies to a greater number of shares, and this cost is divided by the total shares now held in arriving at the cost per share to be used upon subsequent disposition of holdings. The new per-share cost basis is indicated in the memorandum entry.

When stock has been acquired at different dates and at different costs, the stock dividend will have to be related to each different acquisition. Adjusted costs for shares comprising each lot held can then be developed. To illustrate, assume that H. C. De Soto owns stock of the Banner Corporation acquired as follows:

	Shares	Cost per Share	Total Cost
Lot 1	50	$120	$6,000
Lot 2	30	90	2,700

A stock dividend of 1 share for every 2 held is distributed by the Banner Corporation. A memorandum entry on De Soto's books to report the number of shares now held and the cost per share within each lot would be made as follows:

Received 40 shares of Banner Corporation stock, representing a 50% stock dividend on 80 shares held. Number of shares held and costs assigned to shares are now as follows:

	Shares	Total Cost	Revised Cost per Share
Lot 1	75 (50 + 25)	$6,000	$80 ($6,000 ÷ 75)
Lot 2	45 (30 + 15)	2,700	60 ($2,700 ÷ 45)

The number of shares to be issued as a stock dividend may include fractional shares. Usually a cash payment is made to the stockholder by the issuing company in lieu of issuing fractional shares.

Receipt of a dividend in the form of stock of a class different from that held should not be regarded as revenue. As in the case of a like dividend, a portion of the retained earnings relating to the original holdings is formally labeled invested capital. All owners of the stock on which the dividend is declared participate pro rata in the distribution and now own two classes of stock instead of a single class. A book value can now be identified with the new stock, but this is accompanied by a corresponding decrease in the book value identified with the original holdings. A similar position can be taken when an investor receives dividends in the form of bonds or other contractual obligations of the corporation.

One difference between the receipt of stock of the same class and securities of a different class should be noted. When common stock is received on common, all shares are alike and original cost may be equitably assigned in terms of the total number of units held after the dividend. When different securities are received whose value is not the same as that of the shares originally held, it would not be proper to assign an equal amount of original cost to both old and new units. Instead, equitable apportionment of cost would require use of the relative market values of the two classes of securities. To illustrate, assume the ownership of 100 shares of Bell Co. common stock acquired at $100 per share. A stock dividend of 50 shares of $25 par preferred stock is received on the common stock held. On the date of distribution the common stock is selling for $65 and the preferred stock for $20. The receipt of the dividend and the apportionment of the $10,000 investment cost is recorded as follows:

Investment in Bell Co. Preferred Stock..	1,333.33	
Investment in Bell Co. Common Stock		1,333.33
To record receipt of 50 shares of preferred stock as a dividend on 100 shares of common.		

Computation:
Cost of common apportioned to common and preferred shares on the basis of relative market values of the two securities on the date of distribution:
Value of preferred: 50 × $20 = $1,000
Value of common: 100 × $65 = 6,500
                                              $7,500
Cost assigned to preferred: 1,000/7,500 × $10,000 = $1,333.33.
(Cost per share: $1,333.33 ÷ 50 = $26.67.)
Cost assigned to common: 6,500/7,500 × $10,000 = $8,666.67.
(Cost per share: $8,666.67 ÷ 100 = $86.67.)

Stock dividends may be reported as revenue if they are regarded as having been made in lieu of cash. The distribution is regarded as having been made in lieu of cash if (1) it is made in discharge of preference dividends for the current year or for the preceding taxable year, or (2) the stockholder is given the option of receiving cash or other property instead of stock.

Stock Splits. A corporation may effect a **stock split** by reducing the par or stated value of capital stock and increasing the number of shares outstanding accordingly. For example, a corporation with 1,000,000 shares outstanding may decide to split its stock on a 3-for-1 basis. After the split the corporation will have 3,000,000 shares outstanding: each stockholder will have three shares for every share originally held. However, each share will now represent only one third of the interest previously represented; furthermore, each share of stock can be expected to sell for approximately one third of its previous value.

The stockholders ledger is revised to show the increased number of shares identified with each stockholder and the reduced par value, if any. Accounting for a stock split on the books of the investor is the same as that for a stock dividend. With an increase in the number of shares, each share now carries only a portion of the original cost. When shares have been acquired at different dates and at different prices, the shares received in a split will have to be associated with the original acquisitions and per-share costs for each lot revised. A memorandum entry is made to report the increase in the number of shares and the allocation of cost to the shares held after the split.

Stock Rights. A corporation that wishes to raise cash by the sale of additional stock may be required to offer existing stockholders the right to subscribe to the new stock. This privilege attaching to stock is called the **preemptive right** and is designed to enable stockholders to retain their respective interest in the corporation. For example, assume that a stockholder owns 50% of a company's outstanding stock. If the stock is doubled and the additional shares are offered and sold to other parties, that stockholder's interest in the company would drop to 25%. With the right to subscribe to the pro rata share of any new offering, the stockholder can maintain the same proportionate interest in the corporation. Although the preemptive right is a general requirement in most state corporation laws, the right may be nullified in the articles of incorporation of a company. There is an increasing movement by corporations to eliminate the preemptive right.

In order to make subscription privileges attractive and to insure sale of the stock, it is customary for corporations to offer the additional issues to its stockholders at less than the market price of the stock. Certificates known as **rights** or **warrants** are issued to stockholders enabling them to subscribe for stock in proportion to the holdings on which they are issued. One right is offered for each share held. But more than one right is generally required in subscribing for each new share. Rights may be sold by stockholders who do not care to exercise them.

As in the case of cash and other dividends, the directors of the corporation in declaring rights to subscribe for additional shares designate a record date that follows the declaration date. All stockholders on the record date are entitled to the rights. Up to the record date, stock sells **rights-on**, since parties acquiring the stock will receive the rights when they are issued; after the record date, the stock sells **ex-rights**, and the rights may be sold separately by those owning the rights as of the record date. A date on which the rights expire is also designated when the rights are declared. Rights not exercised are worthless beyond the expiration date. Generally, rights have a limited life of only a few weeks.

The receipt of stock rights is comparable to the receipt of a stock dividend in that the corporation has made no asset distribution and stockholders' equities remain unchanged. However, the stockholders' investment is now evidenced by shares originally acquired and by rights that have a value of their own since they permit the purchase of shares at less than market price. These circumstances call for an **allocation of cost** between the original shares and the rights. Since the shares and the rights have different values, an apportionment should be made in terms of the relative market values as of the date the stock sells ex-rights. A separate accounting for each class of security is subsequently followed. The accounting for stock rights is illustrated in the following example.

Assume that in 1978 Interior Design Co. acquired 100 shares of Superior Products no-par common at $180 per share. In 1982 the corporation issues rights to purchase 1 share of common at $100 for every 5 shares owned. Interior Design Co. thus receives 100 rights — one right for each share owned. However, since 5 rights are required for the acquisition of a single share, the 100 rights enable Interior to subscribe for only 20 new shares. Interior's original investment of $18,000 now applies to two assets, the shares and the rights. This cost is apportioned on the basis of the relative market values of each security as of the date that the rights are distributed to the stockholders. The cost allocation may be expressed as follows:

$$\text{Cost assigned to rights:} \frac{\text{Market Value of Rights}}{\text{Market Value of Stock Ex-rights} + \text{Market Value of Rights}} \times \begin{array}{l}\text{Original}\\\text{Cost of}\\\text{Stock}\end{array}$$

$$\text{Cost assigned to stock:} \frac{\text{Market Value of Stock Ex-rights}}{\text{Market Value of Stock Ex-rights} + \text{Market Value of Rights}} \times \begin{array}{l}\text{Original}\\\text{Cost of}\\\text{Stock}\end{array}$$

Assume that Superior Products common is selling ex-rights at $121 per share and rights are selling at $4 each. The cost allocation would be made as follows:

To rights: $\dfrac{4}{121 + 4} \times \$18,000 = \$576$ ($576 ÷ 100 = $5.76, cost per right)

To stock (balance): $18,000 − $576 = $17,424 ($17,424 ÷ 100 = $174.24, cost per share)

The following entry may be made at this time:

Investment in Superior Products Stock Rights.. 576
    Investment in Superior Products Common Stock..................................... 576
    Received 100 rights permitting the purchase of 20 shares at $100.
    Cost of stock was apportioned on the basis of the relative market
    values of stock and rights on the date rights were distributed.

The cost apportioned to the rights is used in determining the gain or the loss arising from the sale of rights. Assume that the rights in the preceding example are sold at 4½. The following entry would be made:

Cash	450	
Loss on Sale of Superior Products Stock Rights	126	
Investment in Superior Products Stock Rights		576
Sold 100 rights at 4½.		

If the rights are exercised, the cost of the new shares acquired consists of the cost assigned to the rights plus the cash that is paid in the exercise of rights. Assume that, instead of selling the rights, Interior Design Co. exercises its privilege to purchase 20 additional shares at $100. The following entry is made.

Investment in Superior Products Common Stock	2,576	
Investment in Superior Products Stock Rights		576
Cash		2,000
Exercised rights acquiring 20 shares at $100.		

Upon exercising the rights, Interior Design's records show an investment balance of $20,000 consisting of two lots of stock as follows:

Lot 1 (1978 acquisition) 100 shares:	
($17,424 ÷ 100 = $174.24, cost per share as adjusted)	$17,424
Lot 2 (1982 acquisition) 20 shares:	
($2,576 ÷ 20 = $128.80, cost per share acquired through rights)	2,576
Total	$20,000

These costs provide the basis for calculating gains or losses upon subsequent sales of the stock.

Frequently the receipt of rights includes one or more rights that cannot be used in the purchase of a whole share. For example, assume that the owner of 100 shares receives 100 rights; 6 rights are required for the purchase of 1 share. Here the holder uses 96 rights in purchasing 16 shares. Several options are available to the holder: allow the remaining 4 rights to lapse; sell the rights and report a gain or a loss on such sale; or supplement the rights held by the purchase of 2 or more rights making possible the purchase of an additional share of stock.

If the owner of valuable rights allows them to lapse, it would appear that the cost assigned to such rights should be written off as a loss. This can be supported on the theory that the issuance of stock by the corporation at less than current market price results in some dilution in the equities identified with original holdings. However, when changes in the market price of the stock make the exercise of rights unattractive to all investors and none of the rights can be sold, no dilution has occurred and any cost of rights reported separately should be returned to the investment account.

Valuation of Marketable Equity Securities

The valuation of marketable equity securities held as a temporary investment and included with current assets was discussed in Chapter 6. In general, current marketable equity securities are valued at the lower of aggregate cost or market, and an allowance is used to reduce the cost to market.

Any change in the allowance account is recognized in the income statement in the period of change.

When marketable equity securities are classified as long-term investments because management's intent is not to use the securities as a current source of cash, the advantages of market valuations are less certain. Stock market prices can fluctuate greatly while the stock is being held, and if the investment is to be retained for long-range purposes, the impact of gains or losses on the net income could be misleading. The Financial Accounting Standards Board in its Statement No. 12 considered this classification difference to be significant, and recommended a slightly different treatment for valuation of noncurrent equity investments than for current equity investments.[5]

Temporary Changes in Market Value. If the investor can exercise significant influence over the decisions of the investee, the equity method described earlier in this chapter is used and no recognition is given for temporary fluctuations in the market price. If the cost method is appropriate because significant influence does not exist, the lower of aggregate cost or market is to be used for valuation thus following the recommended procedures for marketable equity securities classified as current assets. Temporary declines in value are reflected in an allowance account which is deducted from the investment account on the balance sheet.

Adjustments for temporary changes in value of noncurrent marketable equity securities do not affect current income as do adjustments for current marketable equity securities. Instead, a **contra stockholders' equity** account is created. This account, which in FASB Statement No. 12 is entitled Net Unrealized Loss on Noncurrent Marketable Equity Securities, is to be deducted from the total stockholders' equity balance in the balance sheet. Both the allowance account that reduces the cost to market and the contra stockholders' equity account should have the same balance at all times. As the market price of the noncurrent equity security portfolio varies, these accounts will be adjusted to bring the valuation to the lower of aggregate cost or market. When equity securities are sold, the transaction is recorded on the historical cost basis and a gain or loss recognized. These procedures are illustrated in the following example.

A company carries a long-term investment marketable equity portfolio that has a cost of $125,000. At December 31, 1981, the market value of the securities held has fallen to $110,000. The decline is judged to be temporary. The following entries would be required to reduce the securities valuation from cost to market.

Net Unrealized Loss in Noncurrent Marketable Equity Securities.....	15,000	
Allowance for Decline in Value of Noncurrent Marketable Equity		
Securities...		15,000

Assume that at the end of 1982, the portfolio has increased through additional purchases to an original cost of $155,000. The market value of the

---

[5]*Statement of Financial Accounting Standards, No. 12,* "Accounting for Certain Marketable Securities" (Stamford: Financial Accounting Standards Board, 1975), par. 9.

portfolio is $148,000. The amount in the allowance account and in the contra equity account can now be reduced to $7,000 as follows:

Allowance for Decline in Value of Noncurrent Marketable Equity Securities	8,000	
Net Unrealized Loss in Noncurrent Marketable Equity Securities		8,000

Permanent Declines in Market Value. If a decline in the market value of an individual security in the portfolio is judged to be other than temporary, the cost basis of that security should be reduced by crediting the investment rather than the allowance account. The write-down should be recognized as a loss and charged against income.[6] The new cost basis for the security may not be adjusted upward to its original cost for any subsequent increases in market value.

To illustrate the accounting for a permanent decline, assume the long-term marketable equity securities portfolio of a company at the end of its first year of operations contains the following securities:

	Cost	Market
Company A	$ 50,000	$ 40,000
Company B	30,000	35,000
Company C	100,000	60,000
Total	$180,000	$135,000

On an aggregate basis, the allowance adjustment would be for the difference between cost and market, or $45,000. However, if evaluation of market conditions for the securities of Company C indicates the decline in value is other than temporary, the security should be written down to market, and a reevaluation made of the portfolio to determine the need for an allowance. The write-down entry would be as follows:

Recognized Loss from Permanent Decline in Market Value of Noncurrent Marketable Equity Securities	40,000	
Long-Term Investment in Marketable Securities		40,000

The recognized loss account would be closed to Income Summary at the end of the year. The portfolio of long-term securities would now appear as follows:

	Cost	Market
Company A	$ 50,000	$ 40,000
Company B	30,000	35,000
Company C	60,000	60,000
Total	$140,000	$135,000

The $5,000 difference would be recognized as a charge against the unrealized loss account and as a credit to the allowance for decline.

The valuation of marketable equity securities as discussed on the preceding pages is summarized in the flowchart on page 347. By studying the flowchart carefully in conjunction with the discussion and examples, the decision points and accounting treatment can be more clearly understood.

---

[6]*Ibid.*, par. 21.

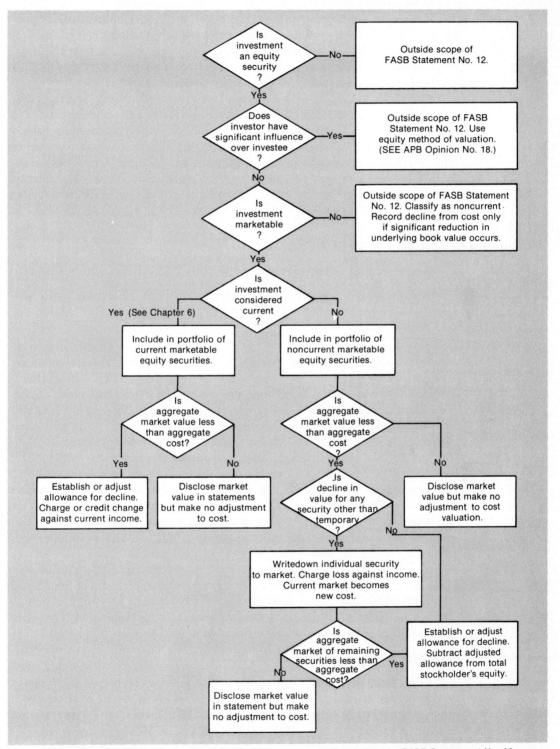

Flowchart of Valuation for Marketable Equity Securities as Prescribed by FASB Statement No. 12

If there is a change in the classification of a marketable equity security between current and noncurrent assets, the transfer should be made at the lower of cost or market at the date of the transfer, and the lower figure is defined as the new cost basis with a realized loss being recorded in the current period as was done for permanent declines in value.

The above action of the Financial Accounting Standards Board places a high premium on the classification of marketable equity securities. Because the classification is determined on the basis of subjective criteria, such as the intent of management to hold or sell, there is much concern that the classification can be used to manipulate the net income. The adoption of a consistent valuation for all investments, regardless of their classification, seems preferable to the differentiated treatment outlined in Statement No. 12.

Valuation of Nonmarketable Equity Securities

A marketable equity security is defined by FASB Statement No. 12 as

> . . . an equity security as to which sales prices or bid and ask prices are currently available on a national securities exchange (i.e., those registered with the Securities and Exchange Commission) or in the over-the-counter market.[7]

Equity securities traded in foreign markets that have breadth and scope comparable to that indicated for trading in the United States would also be classified as marketable. A nonmarketable equity security must be classified as a long-term investment. Either the cost or equity method is applied to the investment depending upon the degree of influence over the investee. Accounting for nonmarketable equity securities is outside the scope of FASB Statement No. 12. However, the accounting principle of conservatism would indicate that if a significant decline in the underlying book value of the investment occurs, a write-down of the investment would be required. Any write-down would be accounted for in the same manner as described for a market decline in the value of marketable equity securities where the decline is judged to be other than temporary. Thus a loss would be recognized in the current year.

If a nonmarketable security becomes marketable *and* the classification changes to current, the current market becomes the new cost of the security if the market is lower than cost. If the security remains classified as noncurrent, it is included in the portfolio of noncurrent marketable equity securities for purposes of lower of cost or market valuation.

Disposition of Equity Securities

Long-term investments in equity securities may be disposed of by sale, redemption, or exchange for another type of security. It is necessary to maintain sufficient records so the cost basis of the stock can be determined.

---

[7]*Ibid.*, par. 7.

Sale of Stock. If there is a difference between the sales proceeds and the cost basis of the investment, the sale of stock results in a recognition of a gain or loss. The gain or loss is considered to be realized when the sale occurs. Any prior adjustments for unrealized valuation losses for the investment portfolio are disregarded when recording the sale unless a new cost basis had been assigned to reflect a permanent decline in value. Valuation adjustments are made at each statement date and are reflections of existing portfolio values at that date. Since only realized gains and losses are recognized for tax purposes, this method of accounting produces amounts needed on the tax return.

To illustrate the accounting for realized and unrealized gains and losses, assume that a company had the following portfolio of noncurrent marketable equity securities as of December 31, 1981:

	Cost	Market
A Company	$ 50,000	$ 40,000
B Company	30,000	35,000
C Company	100,000	60,000
Total	$180,000	$135,000

If none of the decline were considered permanent, an adjusting entry would be made as follows:

Unrealized Loss in Value of Noncurrent Marketable Equity Securities	45,000	
Allowance for Decline in Value of Noncurrent Marketable Equity Securities		45,000

Assume that Company A stock is sold in 1982 for $35,000. The entry to record the sale would be:

Cash	35,000	
Loss on Sale of Noncurrent Marketable Equity Securities	15,000	
Long-Term Investments in Marketable Securities		50,000

At the end of 1982, the long-term portfolio would again be evaluated and adjustments made to the contra asset and contra equity accounts to reflect the new cost and market value amounts. Assume that the cost of the portfolio at December 31, 1982, was $110,000 and the market value was $90,000. The new balance in the valuation account should be $20,000, and the valuation entry at that date would be as follows:

Allowance for Decline in Value of Noncurrent Marketable Equity Securities	25,000	
Unrealized Loss in Value of Noncurrent Marketable Equity Securities		25,000

As indicated earlier, if a decline in market value of the noncurrent marketable equity securities is considered permanent, market becomes the new cost or carrying value. Gains and losses upon sale of the security are measured from the new carrying value. If, for example, the decline in value of A Company securities at the end of 1981 had been considered permanent, the loss on the sale in 1982 would have been $5,000 instead of $15,000. For income tax purposes, the 1982 loss would still be $15,000.

Redemption of Stock. Stock, particularly preferred issues, may be called in for redemption and cancellation by the corporation under conditions set by the issue. The call price is ordinarily set at a figure higher than the price at which the stock was originally issued, but this call price may be more or less than the cost to the holder who acquired the stock after its original issue. When stock is surrendered to the corporation, an entry is made debiting Cash and crediting the investment account. Any difference between the cash proceeds and the investment cost is recorded as a gain or a loss. For example, assume that an investor acquires 100 shares of Y Co. 6%, $100 par preferred stock at 97. These shares are subsequently called in at 105. The redemption is recorded on the stockholder's books by the following entry.

Cash	10,500	
Investment in Y Co. 6% Preferred Stock		9,700
Gain on Redemption of Y Co. Preferred Stock..............................		800
Received $10,500 on call of Y Co. preferred stock, cost $9,700.		

Exchange of Stock. When shares of stock are exchanged for other securities, the investor opens an account for the newly acquired security and closes the account of the security originally held. The new securities should be recorded at their fair market value or at the fair market value of the shares given up, whichever may be more clearly determinable, and a gain or loss is recognized on the exchange for the difference between the value assigned to the securities acquired and the carrying value of the shares given up. In the absence of a market value for either old or new securities, the carrying value of the shares given up will have to be recognized as the cost of the new securities. To illustrate, assume that the Z Co. offers its preferred stockholders two shares of no-par common stock in exchange for each share of $100 par preferred. An investor exchanges 100 shares of preferred stock carried at a cost of $10,000 for 200 shares of common stock. Common shares are quoted on the market at the time of exchange at $65. The exchange is recorded on the books of the stockholder by the following entry:

Investment in Z Co. Common Stock..	13,000	
Investment in Z Co. Preferred Stock..		10,000
Gain on Conversion of Z Co. Preferred Stock		3,000
Acquired 200 shares of common stock valued at $65 in exchange for 100 shares of preferred stock costing $100.		

LONG-TERM INVESTMENTS ON THE BALANCE SHEET

Long-term investments are generally reported on the balance sheet following the current assets classification. The long-term investment section should not include temporary investments held as a ready source of cash. Headings should be provided for the different long-term investment categories and individual long-term investments reported within such groupings. Detailed information relative to individual long-term investments may be provided in separate supporting schedules. Long-term investment costs should be supplemented by market quotations in parenthetical or note form if market exceeds cost. Information concerning the pledge of long-term investments as collateral on loans should be provided. When long-term investments are carried at amounts other than cost, the valuation that is employed should be described.

The "Long-term investments" section of a balance sheet might appear as follows:

Long-term investments:
Affiliated companies:
Investment in Wilson Co. common stock, reported by the equity method (Investment consists of 90,000 shares representing a 40% interest acquired on July 1, 1977, for $1,500,000. Retained earnings of the subsidiary since date of acquisition have increased by $120,000; 40% of this amount, or $48,000, is identified with the parent company equity and has been recognized in the accounts.) ... $1,548,000
Advances to Wilson Co. 115,000 $1,663,000

Miscellaneous stock investments, at cost (stock has an aggregate quoted market value of $112,000; stock has been deposited as security on bank loan — refer to notes payable, contra).   100,000

Total long-term investments $1,763,000

QUESTIONS

1. Why would a manufacturing company invest funds in stocks, bonds, and other securities?

2. How should each of the following be classified on the balance sheet?
  (a) Stock held for purposes of controlling the activities of a subsidiary.
  (b) Listed stock rights to be sold.
  (c) Stock intended to be transferred to a supplier in cancellation of an amount owed.

3. David Giles purchases 1,000 shares of Bart Motors at $90 a share in November, paying his broker $65,000. The market value of the stock on December 31 is $125 a share; Giles has made no further payment to his broker. On this date he shows on his balance sheet Bart Motors stock, $100,000, the difference between market value and the unpaid balance to the broker. Do you approve of this report? Explain.

4. How would you record the purchase of stock and bond units acquired for a lump sum when (a) only one of the securities is quoted on the market? (b) both securities are quoted? (c) neither security is quoted?

5. Define: (a) parent company, (b) subsidiary company.

6. (a) What factors may indicate the ability of an investor owning less than a majority voting interest to exercise significant influence over the investee's operating and financial policies? (b) What percentage of stock ownership is required to exercise significant influence?

7. A corporation is a legal entity, separate and distinct from its owners and any other business unit. In view of this legal entity concept, how can use of the equity method by an investor be justified?

8. What is the difference between consolidated financial statements and a one-line consolidation achieved by using the equity method?

9. Distinguish between the following types of dividends: (a) cash, (b) stock, (c) property.

10. What reasons may be offered for the infrequent use of property dividends by a corporation?

11. Some accounting writers have suggested that certain stock dividends should constitute revenue to the recipients. What is the basis for this view?

12. Distinguish between the valuation method recommended for current marketable equity securities and that recommended for noncurrent marketable equity securities.

13. How are nonmarketable equity securities classified and valued on the balance sheet?

EXERCISES

exercise 12-1

Metal Magic, Inc., acquired on margin 2,500 shares of Ferrus Co. preferred stock and 25,000 shares of Ferrus Co. common stock for $500,000 plus broker's commission of 1%. Market prices at the time the stock was acquired were $40 per share for preferred and $16 per share for common. Terms of the margin agreement provided for payment at acquisition date of the broker's commission plus 25% of the stock purchase price. The balance due the broker, plus 10% interest, must be paid within six months.

      (1) What entry should have been made to record the purchase?
      (2) What entry would be made to pay the balance due the broker three months after purchase?

exercise 12-2

National Environment Technologies purchased 12,000 shares of common stock of Landreth, Inc., on May 13, 1980, for $15 per share. At the time of the purchase, Landreth Inc., had outstanding 40,000 shares, and the total stockholders' equity was $600,000. Thereafter, the following took place:

(a) On July 5, 1981, National Environment Technologies received from Landreth, Inc., a dividend of $2 per share.

(b) On December 31, 1981, Landreth, Inc., reported net income of $250,000 for the calendar year 1981.

Give the entries that would be required to reflect the purchase and subsequent events on National Environment Technologies' books.

exercise 12-3

In 1980, Frost Corporation acquired 22,500 shares of Al-Artica, Inc., for a cost of $360,000. Although this purchase represented only 15% of the 150,000 shares of Al-Artica, Inc., common voting stock outstanding, it allowed Frost Corporation to elect its president, Harold Baca, chairman of Al-Artica, Inc.'s board of directors. What entries would Frost make to record the following events?

1981

Dec. 31 Al-Artica announces net income of $275,000 for the year ended December 31, 1981 and pays a dividend of 80¢ per share.

1982

Jan. 2 Frost Corporation acquires an additional 37,500 shares of Al-Artica for $600,000.

Dec. 31 Al-Artica announces ordinary income of $325,000 for the year ended December 31, 1981, an extraordinary gain of $75,000, and pays a dividend of $1.00 per share.

exercise 12-4

Darl Co. purchased 100,000 shares of Washburn Manufacturing Co. stock on July 1, 1981, at book value as of that date. Washburn Manufacturing Co. had 400,000 shares outstanding at the time of the purchase. Prior to this purchase, Darl Co. had no interest in Washburn Manufacturing Co. In its second quarterly statement, Washburn Manufacturing Co. reported net income of $56,000 for the six months ended June 30, 1981. Darl Co. received a dividend of $7,000 from Washburn Manufacturing Co. on August 1, 1981. Washburn Manufacturing Co. reported net income of $120,000 for the year ended December 31, 1981. Give the entries Darl Co. would make to reflect its share of Washburn Manufacturing Co.'s earnings for the year and the receipt of the dividends.

exercise 12-5

On January 1, 1981, Western Co. purchased 8,000 shares of Colvin Corporation common stock for $40,000. At that date there were 40,000 shares of Colvin common stock authorized and outstanding. The net assets of Colvin at January 1 were valued at $150,000. You determine that fixed assets with a remaining life of 10 years have a fair market value of $20,000 above their net book value, and that the remainder of the excess is attributed to goodwill and amortized over 40 years.

Give the entries required in 1981 and 1995 on Western's books if the investment in Colvin permits Western to exercise significant influence and if (a) net income in 1981 of Colvin is $60,000; and (b) net loss in 1995 is $10,000.

exercise 12-6

Prado, Inc., purchases 10,000 shares of Darron, Inc., which represents 25% of its outstanding common voting stock. The purchase price was $35,000. The carrying value of the net assets of Darron Co. at the time of purchase was $120,000. Assets with an average remaining life of 5 years have a current market value which is $35,000 in excess of their carrying values. The remaining difference between the purchase price and the value of the underlying stockholder's equity cannot be attributable to any tangible asset; however, the company is carrying Goodwill on its books valued at $40,000, which is being amortized at the rate of $1,250 per year for 32 more years. At the end of the year of purchase, Darron reports net income of $30,000. Give the entries necessary to reflect Prado, Inc.'s share of the income, and any necessary adjusting entries. (Carry computations to nearest dollar.)

exercise 12-7

Harold Gividen owns stock of Hjorth Bros., Inc. acquired in two lots as follows:

	Shares	Cost per Share	Total Cost
January 29, 1979	75	$24	$1,800
June 22, 1980	100	30	3,000

In 1981, a stock dividend of 35 shares was received. Because Gividen needed cash, he sold the 35 shares at $15 per share and credited the proceeds to a revenue account, Gain on Sale of Hjorth Bros., Inc. Stock. If the first-in, first-out method is used to record stock sales, what correction in the accounts is necessary assuming (a) the books are still open for 1981; (b) the error is not detected until 1982 after the 1981 financial reports were prepared?

exercise 12-8

Carma Fellows owns 240 shares of Poulson Co. common acquired at $20 per share. Give the cost basis per share for Fellows' investment holdings if:

(a) A common stock dividend of 1 for 3 is received.
(b) Common stock is exchanged in a 4-for-1 split.
(c) A preferred stock dividend of 1 share for every 5 shares of common held is received; common is selling ex-dividend at $25; preferred is selling at $125.
(d) A property dividend of 1 share of Jasper Co. common, market price $10, for every 6 shares held is received.

exercise 12-9

The long-term marketable equity securities portfolio for Valley Industries, Inc., contained the following securities at December 31, 1981. No previous market declines had been recorded.

	Cost	Market Value
Salt Valley common	$32,000	$39,000
Pinkerton Co. common	20,000	14,000
Layton Oil Co. common	40,000	33,000

(1) Give the December 31, 1981 valuation entry required under FASB Statement No. 12 if none of the declines in market value are considered permanent.
(2) Assume the Pinkerton Co. common was sold for $17,000 in 1982 and that the market value of the remaining securities in the portfolio was the same at December 31, 1982, as it was at December 31, 1981. Give the journal entries to record the sale of the stock and the valuation entries necessary at December 31, 1982.
(3) Give the December 31, 1981 valuation entries required under FASB Statement No. 12 if the decline in value of the Layton Oil Co. stock is considered permanent.

exercise 12-10

Bridgeman Paper Co. reported the following selected balances on its financial statements for each of the four years 1979–1982.

	1979	1980	1981	1982
Allowance for Decline in Value of Noncurrent Marketable Equity Securities	0	$25,000	$18,000	$30,000
Recognized Loss from Permanent Decline in Market Value of Noncurrent Marketable Equity Securities	0	0	$ 4,000	0
Allowance for Decline in Value of Current Marketable Equity Securities	0	$ 5,000	$ 8,000	$ 3,000

Based upon the above balances, reconstruct the valuation journal entries that must have been made each year.

exercise 12-11

The Clapson Co. holds stock of Waico, Inc. acquired as follows:

	Shares	Total Cost
1980...	200	$6,200
1981...	100	2,800
1982...	100	2,900

Give the entries that would be made upon the sale of 100 shares in 1983 at $29 per share assuming that cost is determined by (a) the first-in, first-out method, (b) the weighted average cost method, (c) identification of lot sold as the 1981 purchase.

exercise 12-12

In 1971, the Lockland Manufacturing Co. purchased for $108,000 ten acres adjoining its manufacturing plant to provide for possible future expansion. From 1971–1981 the company paid a total of $25,000 in taxes and $20,000 in special assessments. In 1981 it sold one half of the land for $120,000 and erected a building at a cost of $450,000 on the other half. All of these transactions were recorded in a "plant" account. The company books on December 31, 1981, show a "plant" account balance of $483,000. Give the journal entries to correct the accounts.

PROBLEMS

problem 12-1

Galland Inc., and the Noble Corp. each have 200,000 shares of no-par stock outstanding. Rollins Inc., acquired 20,000 shares of Galland stock and 50,000 shares of Noble stock in 1976. Changes in retained earnings for Galland and Noble for 1979 and 1980 are as follows:

		Galland, Inc.		Noble Corp.
Retained earnings (deficit), January 1, 1979..		$200,000		$(35,000)
Cash dividends, 1979		(25,000)		——
		$175,000		$(35,000)
Income before extraordinary items.................	$40,000		$20,000	
Extraordinary gain..	——		45,000	
Net income, 1979...		40,000		65,000
Retained earnings, December 31, 1979..........		$215,000		$30,000
Cash dividends, 1980		(30,000)		(10,000)
Market value of stock dividends issued — 10,000 shares (transferred to paid-in capital section)..		(30,000)		
Net income, 1980 (no extraordinary items)....		60,000		25,000
Retained earnings, December 31, 1980..........		$215,000		$45,000

> **Instructions:** Give the entries required on the books of Rollins Inc., for 1979 and 1980 to account for its investments.

problem 12-2

On March 31, 1978, Desert Products purchased 45,000 shares of Hastings, Inc., for $15 per share. Hastings had 150,000 shares outstanding at the time. Its net assets on that date had a book value of $2,125,000. The excess of cost over the underlying equity is attributable to equipment, which has a fair market value of $50,000 in excess of book value and a remaining useful life of 10 years; the remainder of the excess is attributable to goodwill, which is amortized over 30 years. Net income from operations for the first quarter for Hastings was $125,000. Thereafter, the following took place:

1978
Dec. 31 Hastings, Inc., reported net income of $400,000 for the year.
1979
Jan. 2 Hastings, Inc., sold 30,000 shares in a public offering for $17 per share. Desert Products did not purchase any of these shares.
Jan. 31 Desert Products received a dividend of $48,000 from Hastings, Inc.
Dec. 31 Hastings, Inc., reported net income of $560,000 for the year.
1980
Jan. 2 Hastings, Inc., sold 70,000 shares in a public offering for $20 per share. Desert Products did not purchase any of the shares. Significant influence is considered lost due to dilution of ownership.
Jan. 31 Desert Products received a dividend of $56,000 from Hastings, Inc. The dividend was declared in 1979. No entry was made by Desert Products at declaration date.
Dec. 31 Hastings, Inc. reported net income for the year of $750,000.
1981
Jan. 31 Desert Products received a dividend of $54,000.

Instructions: Give the entries to record the foregoing transactions assuming Desert Products and Hastings, Inc., maintain their books on a calendar year basis.

problem 12-3

On January 2, 1980, Jenkins Co. purchased 15% of Walt Enterprises common voting stock for $75,000 when the net carrying value of Walt Enterprises assets was $400,000. The excess of the implied fair market value over the net carrying value is attributable to goodwill. On December 31, 1980, Walt Enterprises reported net income of $50,000 for the year then ended; Jenkins Co. received $1,500 in dividends in 1980. On January 2, 1981, Jenkins Co. purchased an additional 5% of Walt Enterprises stock for $27,000 when the net carrying value of Walt Enterprises assets was $440,000. The excess of implied fair market value over carrying value is attributable to goodwill. Dividends received from Walt Enterprises for 1981 totaled $5,000; net income reported by Walt Enterprises for the year ended December 31, 1981, was $85,000. Jenkins Co. amortizes goodwill on a straight-line basis over 40 years.

Instructions: Give the entries necessary to record the above transactions on the books of Jenkins Co.

problem 12-4

Transactions in the Manning Corp. investment account during 1980 included the following (assume the specific identification method is used in accounting for stock transactions):

Jan. 7 Purchased 750 units of Gomez Co. preferred and common stock at $90 per unit. Each unit consisted of one share of preferred and three shares of common. No market costs were available.
Feb. 1 Common stock market value became established at $14 per share. No market price is yet available for preferred stock.
Mar. 15 Received stock rights permitting the purchase of one share of common at $10 for every 4 shares held. On this day, rights were being traded at $1 each and stock was being traded ex-rights at $14 per share.
Mar. 26 Exercised 1,800 rights and sold the remainder at $1 each less $25 brokerage costs.
May 10 Sold the Gomez Co. preferred stocks at $50 per share.
July 22 Received a 10% stock dividend on Gomez Co. common and one share of Gomez Co. 8% preferred stock for every 50 shares of Gomez Co. common held before the 10% stock dividend. On this date, preferred stock was selling for $60 per share, and common stock was selling for $15 per share. Costs were allocated first to preferred stock dividend, then to the common stock dividend.
Oct. 13 Sold 500 shares of Gomez Co. common; 495 shares of Lot 2 and 5 shares from Lot 1. The sales price was $14 per share.
Dec. 10 Gomez Co. redeemed 25 shares of the preferred stock at a call price of $65 per share. These came from the preferred identified with Lot 1.

Instructions:

(1) Give the journal entries to record the foregoing transactions. (Give computations in support of your entries.)

(2) Give the investment account balance on December 31, 1980, and the shares and costs making up this balance.

problem 12-5

The Clawson Co. has the following securities on hand on January 1, 1980.

Hicken, Inc., 8% preferred stock, par $100, 50 shares	$5,500
Mangum, Inc., common stock, 200 shares	$6,600

During 1980, the following transactions were completed relative to investments.

Jan. 29 Purchased 75 shares of Randall, Inc., common for $2,700.

Feb. 14 Received a cash dividend of 60¢ and stock dividend of 20% on Mangum, Inc., common.

Apr. 25 Purchased 125 shares of Randall, Inc., common for $5,000.

June 30 Received the semiannual dividend on Hicken, Inc., 8% preferred.

July 1 Randall, Inc., common was split on a 4-for-1 basis.

Aug. 14 Received a dividend of 50¢ on Randall, Inc., common.

Aug. 21 Received a cash dividend of 60¢ and a stock dividend of 10% on Mangum, Inc., common.

Sept. 13 Sold 100 shares of Randall, Inc., common for $2,000 and also sold 25 shares of Hicken, Inc., 8% preferred for $3,000.

Oct. 26 Received rights on Randall, Inc., common to subscribe for additional shares as follows: 1 share could be acquired at $15 for every 4 shares held. On this date stock was selling for 23 and rights were selling at 2; stock cost was apportioned on this basis.

Nov. 16 Exercised the Randall, Inc., rights.

Dec. 1 Received a special year-end dividend on Mangum, Inc., common of $2.

Instructions:

(1) Assuming the use of first-in, first-out in assigning costs to sales, give journal entries to record the foregoing transactions. (Give calculations in support of your entries.)

(2) Give the investment account balance as of December 31, 1980, including the number of shares and costs comprising such balances.

problem 12-6

Transactions of Valley Corp. in securities during 1980 were as follows:

Jan. 29 Purchased 1,500 shares of Colton, Inc., common stock for $45,000.

June 22 Purchased 10,000 shares of Riggs Co. preferred stock for $140,000.

Aug. 5 Sold 750 shares of Colton, Inc., common stock for $18,750.

The fair market value of Riggs Co. preferred and Colton, Inc., common stock on December 31, 1980, the date of the annual audit, was $12 and $20 per share respectively. The president of the company recommends that the cost balance in the investments account be retained because the investments are in reality long-term and the declines in market values seem to be temporary. The auditor counters that since one half of the Colton, Inc., common stock has been sold during the year and since the investment in Riggs Co. is in preferred stock, the investments appear to be current assets rather than long-term investments.

Instructions:

(1) Give journal entries to record any valuation adjustments that would be made if the auditor's recommendations are followed.

(2) Give journal entries to record any valuation adjustments that would be made if the president's recommendations are followed.

(3) Give journal entries to record any valuation adjustments that would be made if the Colton, Inc., common is identified as long-term, but the decline is felt to be permanent. The Riggs Co. stock is still classified as a current asset.

problem 12-7

The long-term investment portfolio of Roylance, Inc., at December 31, 1981, contains the following securities:

Arnold Company common, 1% ownership, 2,000 shares; cost, $45,000; market value $35,000.
Graves Inc., preferred, 1,000 shares; cost $80,000; market value $85,000.
Wilson, Inc., 10% bonds, $10,000 face value; cost $12,000; market value $12,400.
Affiliated, Inc., common, 30% ownership; carrying value $120,000; market value $115,000.
Parry Company common, 10% ownership, 10,000 shares; cost $67,500; market value $50,000.
Jones Company common, 5% ownership, 6,000 shares; cost $35,000; no market value.

Instructions:

(1) Give the valuation adjustment required at December 31, 1981, assuming market values in the past for the long-term investment portfolio have always exceeded cost and none of the indicated declines in market value are considered permanent.

(2) Assume the Parry Company common stock market decline is considered permanent. Give the valuation entries required at December 31, 1981, under this change in assumption.

(3) Assume the market values for the long-term investment portfolio at December 31, 1982, were as follows:

Arnold Co. common	$ 48,000
Graves, Inc., preferred	82,000
Wilson, Inc., bonds	12,500
Affiliated, Inc., common	125,000
Parry Company common	45,000
Jones Company common	no market

Give the valuation entries at December 31, 1982, assuming the conditions at December 31, 1981, were as described in (2) above.

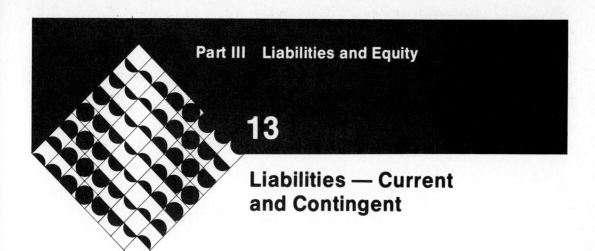

Liabilities — Current and Contingent

CHAPTER OBJECTIVES

Define liabilities and describe how the definition is applied in practice.

Describe how liabilities are reported in the financial statements.

Identify liabilities that are definite in amount and describe how they are recorded and reported.

Identify liabilities that are estimated in amount, and describe how they are estimated, recorded, and reported.

Identify contingent liabilities and describe how they are reported.

Part II focused on the accounts comprising the assets of a company, or the debit side of the balance sheet. Liabilities and owners' equity, the credit side of the balance sheet, are considered in Part III. In this chapter, liabilities in general and some specific current and contingent liabilities are discussed. Subsequent chapters focus on noncurrent liabilities that are relatively complex in nature and, in some cases, directly related to asset accounts. These include bonds, long-term notes, and income taxes.

DEFINITION OF LIABILITIES

Liabilities have been defined by the FASB as "probable future sacrifices of economic benefits arising from present obligations of a particular entity to transfer assets or provide services to other entities in the future as a result of past transactions or events."[1] This definition contains significant elements that need to be explored before individual liability accounts are discussed.

A liability is a result of **past transactions or events**. Thus, a liability is not recognized until incurred. This part of the definition excludes contractual obligations from an exchange of promises if performance by both parties is still in the future. Such contracts are referred to as *executory contracts*. This aspect of the liability definition has been subject to much discussion in accounting. The signing of a labor contract that obligates both the employer and the employee does not give rise to a liability in current accounting practice, nor does the placing of an order for the purchase of merchandise. However, under some conditions, the signing of a lease is recognized as an event that requires the current recognition of a liability even though a lease is essentially an executory contract. Clarification of this area is needed.

A liability represents an **obligation**. Generally, the obligation rests on a foundation of legal rights and duties. However, obligations created, inferred, or construed from the facts of a particular situation are also recognized as liabilities. For example, if a company regularly pays vacation pay or year-end bonuses, accrual of these items as a liability is warranted even though no legal agreement exists to make these payments.

A liability must involve a **probable future transfer of assets or services**. Although liabilities result from past transactions or events, an obligation may be contingent upon the occurrence of another event sometime in the future. When occurrence of the future event seems probable, the obligation is defined as a liability. Although the majority of liabilities are satisfied by payment of cash, some obligations are satisfied by transferring other types of assets or by providing services. For example, revenue received in advance requires recognition of an obligation to provide goods or services in the future. Usually, the time of payment is specified by a debt instrument, e.g., a note requiring payment of interest and principal on a given date or series of dates. Some obligations, however, require the transfer of assets or services over a period of time, but the exact dates cannot be determined when the liability is incurred, e.g., obligations to provide parts or service under a warranty agreement.

A liability is the **obligation of a particular entity**, i.e., the entity that has the responsibility to transfer assets or provide services. As long as the payment or transfer is probable, it is not necessary that the entity to whom the

---

[1] *Statement of Financial Accounting Concepts No. 3*, "Elements of Financial Statements of Business Enterprises" (Stamford: Financial Accounting Standards Board, December 1980), par. 28.

obligation is owed be identified. Thus, a warranty to make any repairs necessary to an item sold by an entity is an obligation of that entity even though it is not certain which customers will receive benefits. It is usually not difficult to identify the entity having the obligation.

CLASSIFICATION OF LIABILITIES

Liabilities may be classified as **current** or **noncurrent**. Generally, the distinction between current and noncurrent liabilities is an important one. Such distinction is necessary for the computation of working capital, a measure of the liquidity of an enterprise. However, for some types of entities, such as banks and other financial institutions, the distinction between current and noncurrent assets and liabilities has little or no significance. All assets and liabilities must be considered together to evaluate the liquidity and solvency of these entities.

Generally, the same rules apply for the classification of liabilities as for assets. If a liability arises in the course of an entity's normal operating cycle, it is considered current if it must be satisfied with current assets before the operating cycle is completed or within one year, whichever period is longer. On the other hand, bank borrowings, notes, mortgages and similar obligations are related to the general financial condition of the entity rather than directly to the operating cycle, and are classified as current only if they are to be paid with current assets within one year.

When debt that has been classified as noncurrent will mature within the next year, the liability should be reported as a current liability in order to reflect the expected drain on current assets. However, if the liability is to be paid by transfer of noncurrent assets that have been accumulated for the purpose of liquidating the liability, the obligation continues to be classified as noncurrent.

Short-term obligations expected to be refinanced on a long-term basis should not be included in current liabilities. This applies to the currently maturing portion of long-term debt and to all other short-term obligations except those arising in the normal course of operations that are due in customary terms. The refinancing must be more than a mere possibility. The FASB has ruled that noncurrent classification is appropriate only if one of the following conditions is met: (1) the refinancing must actually take place in the period between the balance sheet date and the date the balance sheet is issued or (2) a definite agreement for the refinancing must have been reached prior to issuance of the balance sheet.[2]

Timing is an important factor. If the obligation is paid prior to the actual refinancing, the obligation should be included in current liabilities on the balance sheet.[3] To illustrate, assume that the liabilities of Donnelly,

[2]*Statement of Financial Accounting Standards No. 6,* "Classification of Short-Term Obligations Expected to be Refinanced" (Stamford: Financial Accounting Standards Board, 1975), par. 11.

[3]*FASB Interpretation No. 8,* "Classification of a Short-Term Obligation Repaid Prior to Being Replaced by a Long-Term Security" (Stamford: Financial Accounting Standards Board, 1976).

Inc., at December 31, 1981, include a note payable for $200,000 due January 15, 1982. The management of Donnelly intends to refinance the note by issuing 10-year bonds. The bonds are actually issued before the issuance of the December 31, 1981, balance sheet on February 15, 1982. If the bonds were issued prior to payment of the note, the note should be classified as noncurrent on the December 31, 1981, balance sheet. If payment of the note preceded the sale of the bonds, however, the note should be included in current liabilities.

MEASUREMENT OF LIABILITIES

The definition of liabilities adopted by the FASB does not include measurement considerations. As outlined in Chapter 3, the measurement of the defined elements is a separate part of the conceptual framework project yet to be completed. Before liabilities can be included in the traditional balance sheet, they must be measured in financial terms. They should normally be reported at the amount necessary to liquidate the claim if it were being paid today. Thus, if the claim isn't to be paid until sometime in the future, the claim should either provide for interest to be paid on the debt, or the obligation should be reported at the discounted value of its maturity amount. Only in recent years have discounted values been used in accounting practice. Obligations arising in the course of normal business operations involving the buying and selling of merchandise or raw materials, and due within a one-year period, normally are not discounted.[4] Thus, regular accounts payable are not discounted even though they carry no interest provision. However, nonoperating business transactions such as the borrowing of money, selling of assets over time, and long-term leases, do involve the discounting process. The obligation in these instances is the present value of the future resource outflows.

Some liabilities, such as the principal payments on notes, are definite in amount. Other liabilities, such as warranty obligations, are estimated. Liabilities in both categories are normally reported on a balance sheet as claims against recorded assets. Some items that resemble liabilities are contingent upon the occurrence of some future event, and are not recorded until it is probable that the event will occur. If no reasonable basis exists for estimating the amount of a liability or a probable contingent liability, no recording of the obligation can take place. However, disclosure of the obligation should be made in a note to the financial statements.

The remaining sections of this chapter are divided into liabilities that are definite in amount, liabilities that are estimated in amount, and contingent liabilities. Several examples of liabilities in each area are presented to clarify the accounting issues involved.

---

[4]*Opinions of the Accounting Principles Board No. 21,* "Interest on Receivables and Payables" (New York: American Institute of Certified Public Accountants, 1971), par. 3.

LIABILITIES THAT ARE DEFINITE IN AMOUNT

Representative of liabilities that are definite in amount and are frequently found on the balance sheet are notes payable, accounts payable, and miscellaneous operating payables including salaries, payroll taxes, property and sales taxes, and income taxes. Some liabilities accrue as time passes. Most notable in this category are interest and rent, although the latter is frequently paid in advance. Some of the problems arising in determining the balances to be reported for liabilities that are definite in amount are described in the following sections.

Short-Term Notes Payable

Notes payable may include notes issued to trade creditors for the purchase of goods and services, to banks for loans, to officers and stockholders for advances, and to others for the purchase of plant assets. It is normally desirable to classify current notes payable on the balance sheet in terms of their origin. Such presentation provides information concerning the sources of business indebtedness and the extent to which the business has relied upon each source in financing its activities.

The problems encountered in the valuation of notes payable are similar to those discussed in Chapter 7 with respect to notes receivable. In reporting notes receivable, it was recognized that theoretical accuracy would require reporting at present values. It was further observed that valuation accounts should be established for amounts estimated to be uncollectible to arrive at the net realizable value of the asset. In reporting notes payable, similar considerations apply.

Individual notes are frequently secured by the pledge of certain assets. Assets pledged may consist of marketable securities, notes receivable, accounts receivable, inventories, or plant assets. The pledge of an asset limits the use or the disposition of the asset or its proceeds until the related obligation is liquidated. In the event of bankruptcy, the cash realized on a pledged asset must first be applied to the satisfaction of the related obligation. A liability is **partly secured** or **fully secured** depending upon whether the value of the pledged property is less than the amount of the obligation or whether such value is equal to or in excess of the obligation. As stated earlier, reference is made to a lien on an asset by a parenthetical remark in the "Assets" section of the balance sheet. It is also desirable to provide a parenthetical remark in connection with the secured liability identifying the asset pledged and its present market value.

There are many kinds of notes. However, two types frequently create difficulty in recording: (1) a note payable with no stated interest rate or an unreasonable rate, and (2) a note payable that is discounted at a financial institution. An example of each type is included in the following paragraphs:

1. Assume that equipment is purchased in exchange for a $10,000 non-interest-bearing note for one year. If the equipment and the related obligation are

recorded at $10,000, this would fail to recognize the charge for interest implicit in the deferred payment arrangement and both asset and liability balances would be overstated. If the prevailing interest rate on similar obligations is 10%, the asset, as well as the liability, must be recognized at a cash-equivalent value of $9,090.91 ($10,000 ÷ 1.10). The following entry should be made:

Equipment	9,090.91	
Discount on Notes Payable	909.09	
Notes Payable		10,000.00

In reporting the note on the balance sheet prior to its payment, an adjustment should be made to recognize the accrual of interest at 10% on the amount of the debt of $9,090.91 to the date of the balance sheet. The accrual of interest is recorded by a debit to Interest Expense and a credit to Discount on Notes Payable. The balance of the discount on the notes payable is subtracted from notes payable in reporting the liability on the balance sheet. A similar procedure would be required if a note provided for a nominal interest rate that was substantially lower than the current market rate.

2. Assume that a company borrows $10,000 by discounting its own $10,000 one-year note at the bank, receiving $10,000 less a discount of 10% or $9,000. If the amount of the discount is recognized as prepaid interest and the note is recorded at $10,000, both asset and liability balances would be overstated: interest has not been paid in advance but is still to be paid; the obligation at the time of borrowing is no greater than the amount borrowed. The following entry should be made:

Cash	9,000	
Discount on Notes Payable	1,000	
Notes Payable		10,000

In reporting the note on the balance sheet prior to its payment, an adjustment should be made to recognize the accrual of interest just as in the first example. However, a discount of 10% is, in effect, a charge for interest at the rate of 11.1% ($1,000 ÷ $9,000). The accrual of interest, then, is computed at 11.1% on the amount of the debt of $9,000 to the date of the balance sheet.

Accounts Payable

Most goods and services in today's economic environment are purchased on credit. The term **accounts payable** usually refers to the amount due for the purchase of materials by a manufacturing company or merchandise by a wholesaler or retailer. Other obligations, such as salaries and wages, rent, interest, and utilities are reported as separate liabilities in accounts descriptive of the nature of the obligation. Accounts payable are not recorded when purchase orders are placed, but only when legal title to the goods passes to the buyer. The rules for the customary recognition of legal passage of title were presented in Chapter 8. If goods are in transit at year-end, the purchase must be recorded if the shipment terms indicate that title has passed. This means that care must be exercised to review the purchase of goods and services near the end of an accounting period to assure a proper cut-off and reporting of liabilities and inventory.

It is customary to report accounts payable at the expected amount of the payment. Because the payment period is normally short, no recognition of interest by reporting the present value of the liability is required. As indicated in Chapter 8, if cash discounts are available, the liability should be reported net of the expected cash discount. Failure to use the net method in recording purchases reports liabilities in excess of the payment finally made.

Miscellaneous Operating Payables

Many miscellaneous payables arise in the course of a company's operating activities. Three of these are specifically discussed in this section. They are indicative of other specific liabilities that could be reported by a given entity. In general, the points made in discussing the definition of liabilities in the opening section of this chapter apply to these miscellaneous operating liabilities.

Salaries and Bonuses Payable. In an ongoing entity, salaries and wages of officers and other employees accrue daily. Normally, no entry is made for these expenses until payment is made. A liability for unpaid salaries and wages is recorded, however, at the end of an accounting period when a more precise matching of revenues and expenses is desired. An estimate of the amount of unpaid wages and salaries is made, and an adjusting entry is prepared to recognize the amount due. Usually the entire accrued amount is identified as salaries payable with no attempt to identify the withholdings associated with the accrual. When payment is made in the subsequent period, the amount is allocated between the employee and other entities such as government taxing units, unions, and insurance companies.

For example, assume that a company has 15 employees who are paid every two weeks. At December 31, four days of unpaid wages have accrued. Analysis reveals that the 15 employees earn a total of $1,000 a day. Thus the adjusting entry at December 31 would be:

Salaries and Wages Expense	4,000	
Salaries and Wages Payable		4,000

This entry may be reversed at the beginning of the next period, or, when payment is made, Salaries and Wages Payable may be debited for $4,000.

Additional compensation in the form of accrued bonuses or commissions should also be recognized. Bonuses are often based upon some measure of the employer's income. Employee bonuses, even those viewed as a sharing of profits with employees, are deductible expenses for the purposes of income tax.

An agreement may provide for a bonus computed on the basis of gross revenue or sales or on the basis of income. When income is used, the computation will depend upon whether the bonus is based on: (1) income before deductions for bonus or income tax, (2) income after deduction for bonus but before deduction for income tax, (3) income after deduction for income tax but before deduction for bonus, or (4) net income after deductions for both bonus and income tax. The degree of difficulty in computing a bonus based on income varies with the measure of income used. To illustrate the computations required in each case, assume the following: Barker Sales, Inc., gives the sales managers of its individual stores a bonus of 10% of store earnings. Income for 1981 for store No. 1 before any charges for bonus or income tax was $100,000. The income tax rate is 40%.

$$\text{Let B = Bonus}$$
$$\text{T = Income Tax}$$

1. *Assuming the bonus is based on income before deductions for bonus or income tax:*

$$B = .10 \times \$100,000$$
$$B = \$10,000$$

2. *Assuming the bonus is based on income after deduction for bonus but before deduction for income tax:*

$$B = .10 (\$100,000 - B)$$
$$B = \$10,000 - .10B$$
$$B + .10B = \$10,000$$
$$1.10B = \$10,000$$
$$B = \$9,090.91$$

Calculation of the bonus may be proved as follows:

Income before bonus and income tax	$100,000.00
Deduct bonus	9,090.91
Income after bonus but before income tax	$ 90,909.09
Bonus rate	10%
Bonus	$ 9,090.91

3. *Assuming the bonus is based on income after deduction for income tax but before deduction for bonus:*

$$B = .10 (\$100,000 - T)$$
$$T = .40 (\$100,000 - B)$$

Substituting for T in the first equation and solving for B:

$$B = .10 [\$100,000 - .40 (\$100,000 - B)]$$
$$B = .10 (\$100,000 - \$40,000 + .40B)$$
$$B = \$10,000 - \$4,000 + .04B$$
$$B - .04B = \$6,000$$
$$.96B = \$6,000$$
$$B = \$6,250$$

Substituting for B in the second equation and solving for T:

$$T = .40\ (\$100,000 - \$6,250)$$
$$T = .40 \times \$93,750$$
$$T = \$37,500$$

Calculation of the bonus may be proved as follows:

Income before bonus and income tax	$100,000
Deduct income tax	37,500
Income after income tax but before bonus	$ 62,500
Bonus rate	10%
Bonus	$ 6,250

4. *Assuming the bonus is based on net income after deductions for bonus and income tax:*

$$B = .10\ (\$100,000 - B - T)$$
$$T = .40\ (\$100,000 - B)$$

Substituting for T in the first equation and solving for B:

$$B = .10\ [\$100,000 - B - .40\ (\$100,000 - B)]$$
$$B = .10\ (\$100,000 - B - \$40,000 + .40B)$$
$$B = \$10,000 - .1B - \$4,000 + .04B$$
$$B + .1B - .04B = \$10,000 - \$4,000$$
$$1.06B = \$6,000$$
$$B = \$5,660.38$$

Substituting for B in the second equation and solving for T:

$$T = .40\ (\$100,000 - \$5,660.38)$$
$$T = .40 \times \$94,339.62$$
$$T = \$37,735.85$$

Calculation of the bonus is proved in the following summary:

Income before bonus and income tax		$100,000.00
Deduct: Bonus	$ 5,660.38	
Income tax	37,735.85	43,396.23
Net income after bonus and income tax		$ 56,603.77
Bonus rate		10%
Bonus		$ 5,660.38

The bonus should be reported on the income statement as an expense before arriving at net income regardless of the method employed in its computation.

Payroll Taxes and Income Tax Withheld. Social security and income tax legislation impose four taxes based upon payrolls:

1. Federal old-age, survivors, disability and hospital insurance
2. Federal unemployment insurance
3. State unemployment insurance
4. Income tax withheld

Federal Old-Age, Survivors, Disability, and Hospital Insurance. The Federal Insurance Contributions Act (FICA), generally referred to as social security legislation, provides for taxes on employers and employees to provide funds for federal old-age, survivors, disability, and hospital insurance benefits for certain individuals and members of their families. At one time only employees were covered by this legislation; however, coverage now includes most individuals who are self-employed.

Provisions of the legislation require equal contributions by the employee and the employer. The contribution is based upon a tax rate applied to annual gross wages up to a designated maximum. Both the tax rate and the wage base have greatly increased since the inception of the social security legislation to provide for increasing benefits. In the mid-thirties, an employer and employee each contributed one per cent of the employee's annual earnings up to $3,000. In 1980, the rate was 6.13% on earnings up to $25,900, with additional increases projected for subsequent years.

Employers of one or more persons, with certain exceptions, come under the law. The amount of the employee's tax is withheld from the wage payment by the employer. The employer remits this amount together with a matched amount. The employer is required to maintain complete records and submit detailed support for the tax remittance. The employer also is responsible for the full amount of the tax even when the employee contributions are not withheld. Self-employed persons who carry on a trade or business are assessed a tax rate somewhat higher than the employee's rate but less than the sum of the employee and employer contributions.

Federal Unemployment Insurance. The Federal Social Security Act and the Federal Unemployment Tax Act provide for the establishment of unemployment insurance plans. Employers with covered workers employed in each of 20 weeks during a calendar year or who pay $1,500 or more in wages during any calendar quarter are affected.

Under present provisions of the law, the federal government taxes eligible employers on the first $6,000 paid to every employee during the calendar year at 3.4% but allows the employer a tax credit limited to 2.7% for taxes paid under state unemployment compensation laws. No tax is levied on the employee. When an employer is subject to a tax of 2.7% or more as a result of state unemployment legislation, the federal unemployment tax, then, is 0.7% of the wages. Payment to the federal government is required quarterly. Unemployment benefits are paid by the individual states. Revenues collected by the federal government under the acts are used to meet the cost of administering state and federal unemployment plans as well as to provide supplemental unemployment benefits.

State Unemployment Insurance. State unemployment compensation laws are not the same in all states. In most states, laws provide for tax only on employers; but in a few states, taxes are applicable to both employers and employees. Each state law specifies the classes of exempt employees, the number of employees required, or the amount of wages paid before the tax is applicable, and the contributions that are to be made by employers and employees. Exemptions are frequently similar to those under the federal act. Tax payment is generally required on or before the last day of the month following each calendar quarter.

Although the normal tax on employers may be 2.7%, states have merit rating or experience plans providing for lower rates based upon employers' individual employment experiences. Employers with stable employment records are taxed at a rate in keeping with the limited amount of benefits required for their former employees; employers with less satisfactory employment records contribute at a rate more nearly approaching 2.7% in view of the greater amount of benefits paid to their former employees. Savings under state merit systems are allowed as credits in the calculation of the federal contribution, so the federal tax does not exceed 0.7% even though payment of less than 2.7% is made by an employer entitled to a lower rate under the merit rating system.

Income Tax Withheld. Federal income tax on the wages of an individual are collected in the period in which the wages are paid. The "pay-as-you-go" plan requires employers to withhold income tax from wages paid to their employees. Most states and many local governments also impose income taxes on the earnings of employees which must be withheld and remitted by the employer. Withholding is required not only of employers engaged in a trade or business, but also of religious and charitable organizations, educational institutions, social organizations, and governments of the United States, the states, the territories, and their agencies, instrumentalities, and political subdivisions. Certain classes of wage payments are exempt from withholding although these are still subject to income tax.

An employer must meet withholding requirements under the law even if wages of only one employee are subject to such withholdings. The amounts to be withheld by the employer are developed from formulas provided by the law or from tax withholding tables made available by the government. Withholding is based upon the length of the payroll period, the amount earned, and the number of withholding exemptions claimed by the employee. Taxes required under the Federal Insurance Contributions Act (both employees' and employer's portions) and income tax that has been withheld by the employer are paid to the federal government at the same time. These combined taxes are deposited in an authorized bank quarterly, monthly, or quarter-monthly (four deposits a month) depending upon the amount of the liability. Quarterly and annual statements must also be filed providing a summary of all wages paid by the employer.

Accounting for Payroll Taxes and Income Tax Withheld. To illustrate the accounting procedures for payroll taxes and income tax withheld, assume that in January, 1981, salaries for a retail store with 15 employees are $15,000. The state unemployment compensation law provides for a tax on employers of 2.7%. Income tax withholdings for the month are $1,600. Assume FICA rates are 6% for employer and employee. Entries for the payroll and the employer's payroll taxes follow:

Salaries Expense	15,000	
FICA Tax Payable		900
Employees Income Tax Payable		1,600
Cash		12,500
To record payment of payroll.		
Payroll Taxes Expense	1,410	
FICA Tax Payable		900
State Unemployment Tax Payable		405
Federal Unemployment Tax Payable.......................................		105
To record the payroll tax liability of the employer.		

Computation:

Tax under Federal Insurance Contributions Act: 6% × $15,000	$ 900
Tax under state unemployment insurance legislation: 2.7% × $15,000...........	405
Tax under Federal Unemployment Tax Act: 0.7% (3.4% − credit of 2.7%) × $15,000	105
Total payroll taxes expense...	$1,410

When tax payments are made to the proper agencies, the tax liability accounts are debited and Cash is credited.

The employer's payroll taxes, as well as the taxes withheld from employees, are based upon amounts paid to employees during the period regardless of the basis employed for reporting income. When financial reports are prepared on the accrual basis, the employer will have to recognize both accrued payroll and the employer's payroll taxes relating thereto by adjustments at the end of the accounting period.

For example, assume that the salaries and wages accrued at December 31 were $4,000. Of this amount, $1,000 was subject to unemployment tax and $2,500 to FICA tax. The accrual entry for the employer's payroll taxes would be as follows:

Payroll Taxes Expense..	184	
FICA Tax Payable..		150
State Unemployment Tax Payable		27
Federal Unemployment Tax Payable		7
To accrue the payroll tax liability of the employer.		

Computation:

Tax under Federal Insurance Contributions Act: 6% × $2,500...........................	$150
Tax under state unemployment insurance legislation: 2.7% × $1,000	27
Tax under Federal Unemployment Tax Act: 0.7% × $1,000................................	7
	$184

As was true with the accrual entry for the salaries and wages discussed on page 365, the above entry may be reversed at the beginning of the new period, or the accrued liabilities may be debited when the payments are made to the taxing authorities.

Agreements with employees may provide for payroll deductions and employer contributions for other items, such as group insurance plans, pension plans, savings bonds purchases, or union dues. Such agreements call for accounting procedures similar to those described for payroll taxes and income tax withholdings.

Other Tax Liabilities. There are many different types of taxes imposed on business entities. In addition to the several payroll taxes discussed in the previous section, a company usually must pay property taxes, federal and state income taxes on their earnings, and serve as an agent for the collection of sales taxes. Each of these liabilities has some unusual features that can complicate accounting for them.

Property Taxes. Real and personal property taxes are based upon the assessed valuation of properties as of a given date. This has given rise to the view held by courts and others that taxes accrue as of a given date. Generally the date of accrual has been held to be the date of property assessment. However, accounting treatment, in general, has been to charge taxes ratably over a tax year rather than to recognize these at the time the legal obligation arises.

Real and personal property taxes have been charged against revenue of various periods, including (1) the year in which paid (cash basis), (2) the year ending (or beginning) on the assessment (or lien) date, and (3) the fiscal year of the governing body levying the tax. Generally, the most acceptable basis of providing for property taxes is monthly accrual on the taxpayer's books during the fiscal period of the taxing authority for which the taxes are levied. This would relate the tax charge to the period in which taxes provide benefits through governmental services. Special circumstances may suggest the use of alternative accrual periods, but consistent application from year to year is the important consideration.

The cash payment of the property taxes may not coincide with the accrual period. For example, assume the taxing authority is on a July 1 to June 30 fiscal year, but the entity paying the tax is on a calendar year basis. If the full-year tax of $60,000 is paid on November 15, there is no tax liability at December 31, and the prepaid property tax account balance should be $30,000. If the tax payment is not made until after December 31, the property tax payable account should have a $30,000 balance. Each company's property tax status must be carefully reviewed to reflect the proper liability or prepayment according to the system used by the entity involved.

Income Taxes. Both federal and state governments raise a large portion of their revenue from income taxes assessed against both individuals and businesses. The taxable income of a business entity is determined by applying the tax rules and regulations to the operations of the business. As indicated in Chapter 3, the income tax rules do not always follow generally accepted accounting principles. Thus, the income reported for tax purposes may differ from that reported on the income statement. This difference can give rise to deferred income taxes, a special liability item discussed more fully in Chapter 15. The actual amount payable for the current year must be determined after all adjusting entries are made at the close of a fiscal period. Federal and some state income tax regulations require companies to estimate their tax liability, and make periodic payments during the year in advance of the final computation and submission of the tax returns. Thus, the amount of income tax liability at year-end is usually much lower than the total tax computed for the year. Because income tax returns are always subject to government audit, a contingent liability exists for any year within the statute of limitations and not yet reviewed by the Internal Revenue Service. If an additional liability arises as a result of an audit, the additional assessment should be reported as a liability until the payment is made.

Sales and Use Taxes. With the passage of sales and use tax laws by state and local governments, additional duties are required of a business unit. Laws generally provide that the business unit must act as an agent for the governmental authority in the collection from customers of sales tax on the transfers of tangible personal properties. Laws may also provide that the business unit is additionally liable for sales tax or use tax on goods it buys for its own use. The buyer is responsible for the payment of sales tax to the seller when both buyer and seller are in the same tax jurisdiction; however, the buyer is responsible for the payment of use tax directly to the tax authority when the seller is outside the jurisdiction of such authority. Provision must be made in the accounts for the liability to the government for the tax collected from customers and the additional tax that the business must absorb.

The sales tax payable is generally a stated percentage of sales. The actual sales total and the sales tax collections are usually recorded separately at the time of sale. The sales tax payable account then is used to accumulate the sales tax liability. The amount of sales tax to be paid to the taxing authority is computed on the recorded sales. If sales tax collections are not exactly equal to the sales tax liability because either more or less sales tax was collected than was required by law, the payable account will require adjustment to bring it to the balance due. In making this adjustment, a gain or a loss on sales tax collection is recognized. In some cases, sales tax collections as well as sales are recorded in total in the sales account. Under these conditions it becomes necessary to divide this amount into its component parts, sales and sales tax payable. For example, if the sales tax is 5% of sales, then the amount recorded in the sales account is equal to sales + .05 of sales, or 1.05 times the sales total. The amount of sales is obtained by dividing the sales account balance by 1.05, and 5% of the sales amount as thus derived is the tax liability. To illustrate, assume that the sales account balance is $100,000, which includes sales tax of 5%. Sales, then, are $100,000 ÷ 1.05 = $95,238.10. The sales tax liability is then 5% of $95,238.10 = $4,761.90. The liability can also be determined by subtracting the sales figure, $95,238.10 from $100,000.00. To record the liability, Sales would be debited and Sales Tax Payable would be credited for $4,761.90.

The recognition in the accounts of obligations for sales tax, use tax, or for tax on goods purchased by a business unit for its own use should be accompanied by debits to the asset or expense accounts in which the original purchases are recorded. For example, sales or use tax on the purchase of furniture and fixtures is recorded as a part of the cost of the asset; sales or use tax on the purchase of supplies representing a selling expense would be recorded as such.

Unearned Revenues

A significant class of liabilities is represented by **unearned revenues**. Frequently, these liabilities represent an obligation to provide services rather than tangible resources. Common types of unearned revenue include advances from customers, unearned rent, unearned subscription revenue for publishing companies, unearned interest, and unearned commissions. Unearned revenue accounts are classified as current or noncurrent liabilities depending upon when the revenue will be earned. When the revenue is earned, e.g., when services are performed, the unearned revenue account is debited and an appropriate revenue account is credited. If advances are refunded without providing goods or services, the liability is reduced by the payment, and no revenue is recognized.

LIABILITIES ESTIMATED IN AMOUNT

The amount of an obligation is generally established by contract or accrues at a specified rate. There are instances, however, when an obligation clearly exists on a balance sheet date but the amount ultimately to be paid cannot be definitely determined. Because the amount to be paid is not definite does not mean the liability can be ignored or given a contingent status. The claim must be estimated from whatever data are available. Obligations arising from current operations, for example, the cost of meeting warranties for service and repairs on goods sold, must be estimated when prior experience indicates there is a definite liability. Here, uncertainty as to the amount and timing of expenditures is accompanied by an inability to identify the payees; but the fact that there are charges yet to be absorbed is certain.

Representative of liabilities that are estimated in amount and frequently found on financial statements are the following:

1. Refundable deposits, reporting the estimated amount to be refunded to depositors.
2. Warranties for service and replacements, reporting the estimated future claims by customers as a result of past guarantees of services or product or product part replacement.
3. Customer premium offers, reporting the estimated value of premiums or prizes to be distributed as a result of past sales or sales promotion activities.
4. Tickets, tokens, and gift certificates, reporting the estimated obligations in the form of services or merchandise arising from the receipt of cash in past periods.
5. Compensated absences, reporting the estimated future payments attributable to past services of employees.

Refundable Deposits

Liabilities of a company may include an obligation to refund amounts previously collected from customers as deposits. **Refundable deposits** may be classified as current or noncurrent liabilities depending on the purpose of the deposit. If deposits are made to protect the company against non-payment for future services to be rendered, and the services are expected to be provided over a long period, the deposit should be reported as a noncurrent liability. Utility companies characteristically charge certain customers, such as those renting their homes, a deposit that is held until a customer discontinues the service, usually because of a move.

Another type of customer deposit is one made for reusable containers, such as bottles or drums, that hold the product being purchased. When a sale is recorded, a liability is recognized for the deposit. When a container is returned, a refund or credit is given for the deposit made. Periodically, an adjustment is recorded for containers not expected to be returned. The asset "containers" and the related accumulated depreciation account should be reduced to eliminate the book value of containers not expected to be returned, and any gain or loss is recognized on the "sale" of the containers. Because accounting for returnable containers is more complex than ordinary deposits, a detailed example is included.

Assume that the Molin Corporation sells its products in drums that cost $10 each. The estimated life of a drum is four years. The selling price for each drum filled with product is $100 which includes $9 as a deposit on the drum. It is estimated that 60% of the drums will be returned for a refund, and the remaining 40% will be kept by customers. Depreciation is computed on a straight-line basis on containers on hand and those expected to be returned. Assume that 1,000 drums are purchased by Molin in the first year of operations, and 800 units are sold for cash. Prior to the end of the year, 360 of the drums are returned for cash refunds. The entries to record the above information would be as follows:

Returnable Drums	10,000	
Cash		10,000
Purchase of 1,000 drums at $10 each.		
Cash	80,000	
Sales		72,800
Deposit on Returnable Drums		7,200
Sale of 800 units at $100 each, of which $9 is a deposit on the drum.		
Deposit on Returnable Drums	3,240	
Cash		3,240
Return of 360 drums and a refund made of $9 per drum.		
Deposit on Returnable Drums	2,880	
Loss on Nonreturn of Returnable Drums	320	
Returnable Drums		3,200
Recognize estimated loss from nonreturn of drums. No accumulated depreciation since this is first year of operation and depreciation is computed only on containers expected to be returned. (40% × 800 = 320 drums. $10 cost − $9 deposit = $1 loss per drum.)		
Depreciation Expense	1,700	
Accumulated Depreciation — Returnable Drums		1,700
Depreciation (4-year life or 25%) for one year on drums still on hand (200 + 360) plus estimated drums to be returned [(60% × 800) − 360 = 120], or 680 × $10 × .25 = $1,700.		

Drums not returned in subsequent years would result in a gain because the deposit would exceed the book value of the drums.

Warranties for Service and Replacements

Many companies agree to provide free service on units failing to perform satisfactorily or to replace defective goods. When agreements involve only minor costs, such costs may be recognized in the periods incurred. When agreements involve significant future costs and when experience indicates a definite future obligation exists, estimates of such costs should be made and matched against current revenues. Such estimates are usually recorded by a debit to an expense account and a credit to a liability account. Subsequent costs of fulfilling warranties are debited to the liability account and credited to an appropriate account, e.g., Cash or Inventory. To illustrate accounting for warranties, consider the following example. Supersonic Sound, Inc., sells compact stereo systems with a two-year warranty. Past experience indicates that 10% of all sets sold will need repairs in the first year, and 20% will need repairs in the second year. The average repair cost is $50 per system. The number of systems sold in 1981 and 1982 was 5,000 and 6,000, respectively. Actual repair costs were $12,500 in 1981 and $55,000 in 1982; it is assumed that all repair costs involved cash expenditures.

1981	Warranty Expense..	75,000	
	Estimated Liability Under Warranties..............................		75,000
	Estimated warranty expense based on systems sold: 5,000 × .30 × $50 = $75,000.		
	Estimated Liability Under Warranties..................................	12,500	
	Cash..		12,500
	Repairs actually made in 1981.		
1982	Warranty Expense..	90,000	
	Estimated Liability Under Warranties..............................		90,000
	Estimated warranty expense based on systems sold: 6,000 × .30 × $50 = $90,000.		
	Estimated Liability Under Warranties..................................	55,000	
	Cash..		55,000
	Repairs actually made in 1982.		

Periodically, the warranty liability account should be analyzed to see if the actual repairs approximate the estimate. Adjustment to the liability account will be required if experience differs appreciably from the estimates. These adjustments are changes in estimates and are reported in the period of change. If sales and repairs in the preceding example are assumed to occur evenly through the year, analysis of the liability account at the end of 1982 shows the ending balance of $97,500 ($75,000 + $90,000 − $12,500 − $55,000) is reasonably close to the predicted amount of $100,000 based upon the 10% and 20% estimates.

Computation:

1981 sales still under warranty for 6 months: $50 × [5,000 ($\frac{1}{2}$ × .20)].....	$ 25,000
1982 sales still under warranty for 18 months: $50 × [6,000 ($\frac{1}{2}$ × .10) + 6,000 (.20)]...	75,000
Total..	$100,000

Assume, however, that warranty costs incurred in 1982 were only $35,000. Then the ending balance of $117,500 would be much higher than the $100,000 estimate. If the $17,500 difference were considered to be material, an adjustment to warranty expense would be made in 1982 as follows:

Estimated Liability Under Warranties	17,500	
Warranty Expense		17,500
Adjustment of estimate for warranty repairs.		

In certain cases, customers are charged special fees for a service or replacement warranty covering a specific period. When fees are collected, an unearned revenue account is credited. The unearned revenue is then recognized as revenue over the warranty period. Costs incurred in meeting the contract requirements are debited to expense, and Cash, Inventory, or other appropriate account is credited. The service contract is in reality an insurance contract, and the amount charged for the contract is based upon the past repair experience of the company for the item sold. The fee usually is set at a rate that will produce a profit margin on the contract if expectations are realized.

To illustrate accounting for service contracts, assume a company sells three-year service contracts covering its product. During the first year, $50,000 was received on contracts, and expenses incurred in connection with these contracts totaled $5,000 all of which was for replacement parts. It is estimated from past experience that the pattern of repairs, based upon the total dollars spent for repairs, is 25% in the first year of the contract, 30% in the second year, and 45% in the third year. In addition, it is assumed that sales of the contracts are made evenly during the year. The following entries would be made in the first year of the warranty.

Cash	50,000	
Unearned Revenue from Service Contracts		50,000
Sale of service contracts.		
Unearned Revenue from Service Contracts......................................	6,250	
Revenue from Service Contracts...		6,250
Estimated revenue earned from contracts. 12½% (½ of 25%) of $50,000, or $6,250.		
Service Contract Expense	5,000	
Inventory		5,000
Repairs actually made during the year.		

Based upon the above entries, a profit of $1,250 on service contracts would be recognized in the first year. If future expectations change, adjustments will be necessary to the unearned revenue account to reflect the change in estimate.

The accounts Estimated Liability Under Warranties and Unearned Revenue from Service Contracts are classified as current or noncurrent liabilities depending upon the period remaining on the warranty. Those warranty costs expected to be incurred within one year or unearned revenues expected to be earned within one year are classified as current; the balance as long-term. In the above illustration, the expected revenue percentage for the second year would be 27½% of the contract price, i.e., 12½% for balance of first year expectations and 15% (½ of 30%) for one-half of the second year expectations, or $13,750. This amount would be classified as current. The remaining 60%, or $30,000, of unearned revenue would be classified as noncurrent.

The method of accounting illustrated above does not recognize any income on the initial sale of the contract, but only as the period of the service contract passes and the actual costs are matched against an estimate of the earned revenue. Alternatively, a company could estimate in advance the cost of the repairs and recognize the difference between the amount of the service contract and the expected repair cost in the period of the contract sale. The choice of which method to use depends upon the degree of confidence in the estimated repair cost. Revenue recognition varies with the facts involved. When collection is reasonably assured and future costs are known with a high degree of certainty, immediate income recognition is recommended. In the case of service contracts, the uncertainty of future expenses usually dictates use of the illustrated method.

Customer Premium Offers

Many companies offer special premiums to customers to stimulate the regular purchase of certain products. These offers may be open for a limited time or may be of a continuing nature. The premium is normally made available when the customer submits the required number of product labels or other evidence of purchase. In certain instances the premium offer may provide for an optional cash payment.

If a premium offer expires on or before the end of the company's fiscal period, adjustments in the accounts are not required. Premium obligations are fully met and the premium expense account summarizes the full charge for the period. However, when a premium offer is continuing, an adjustment must be made at the end of the period to recognize the liability for future redemptions — Premium Expense is debited and an appropriate liability account is credited. The expense is thus charged to the period benefiting from the premium plan and current liabilities reflect the claim for premiums outstanding. If premium distributions are debited to an expense account, the liability balance may be reversed at the beginning of the new period.

To illustrate the accounting for a premium offer, assume the following: Smart Foods offers a set of breakfast bowls upon the receipt of 20 certificates, one certificate being included in each package of the cereal distributed by this company. The cost of each set of bowls to the company is $2. It is estimated that only 40% of the certificates will be redeemed. In 1981, the company purchased 10,000 sets of bowls at $2 per set; 400,000 packages of cereal containing certificates were sold at a price of $1.20 per package. By the end of 1981, 30% of the certificates had been redeemed. Entries for 1981 are as follows:

Transaction	Entry
1981: Premium purchases: 10,000 sets × \$2 = \$20,000	Premiums — Bowl Sets .... 20,000 Cash.. 20,000
Sales: 400,000 packages × \$1.20 = \$480,000	Cash .... 480,000 Sales 480,000
Premium claim redemptions: 120,000 certificates, or 6,000 sets × \$2 = \$12,000.	Premium Expense .... 12,000 Premiums — Bowl Sets............... 12,000

December 31, 1981:
Coupons estimated redeemable in future periods:
Total estimated redemptions —
 40% of 400,000 160,000
 Redemptions in 1981 120,000
Estimated future redemptions..................... 40,000
 	
Estimated claims outstanding:
 40,000 certificates, or 2,000 sets @ \$2..... \$ 4,000
	Premium Expense 4,000
	  Estimated Premium Claims Out-
	  standing....................................... 4,000

January 1, 1982 (optional):
Reversal of accrued liability balance.
	Estimated Premium Claims Out-
	  standing.. 4,000
	  Premium Expense..................... 4,000

The balance sheet at the end of 1981 will show premiums of \$8,000 as a current asset and estimated premium claims outstanding of \$4,000 as a current liability; the income statement for 1981 will show premium expense of \$16,000 as a selling expense.

Experience indicating a redemption percentage that differs from the assumed rate will call for an appropriate adjustment in the subsequent period and the revision of future redemption estimates.

The estimated cost of the premiums may be shown as a direct reduction of sales by recording the premium claim at the time of the sale. This requires an estimate of the premium cost at the time of the sale. For example, in the previous illustration, the summary entry for sales recorded during the year, employing the sales reduction approach, would be as follows:

```
Cash ........................................................................................ 480,000
   Sales ................................................................................          464,000
   Estimated Premium Claims Outstanding ................................           16,000
```

The redemption of premium claims would call for debits to the liability account. Either the expense method or the sales reduction method is acceptable and both are found in practice.

Some organizations have adopted plans for the issuance to customers of trading stamps, cash register tapes, or other media redeemable in merchandise, premiums, or cash. The accounting procedure followed will depend upon the nature of the plan. A business may establish its own plan, prepare its own stamps or other trading media, and assume redemption responsibilities. Under these circumstances, the accounting procedure would parallel that just illustrated for specific premium offers. On the other hand, a business unit may enter into an agreement for a stamp plan with a trading-stamp company. The latter normally assumes full responsibility for the redemption of stamps and sells the trading stamps for a set unit price whether they are redeemed or not. The business would report stamps purchased as an asset and stamps issued as a selling expense; the trading-stamp company would recognize on its books the sale of stamps, purchase of premiums, distributions of premiums, and the estimated liability for the costs of merchandise and related services identified with stamps expected to be redeemed.

To illustrate accounting for trading stamps, assume that on January 3, 1981, Quik Mart Grocery Store purchased trading stamps from Silver Streak Stamp Company for $10,000. During the month of January, $2,000 worth of the stamps were issued to customers. The purchase and distribution of stamps would be recorded on Quik Mart's books as follows:

Trading Stamp Inventory	10,000	
Cash		10,000
Trading Stamp Expense	2,000	
Trading Stamp Inventory		2,000

Continuing the example, assume that Silver Streak's total stamp sales during January, 1981, amounted to $100,000. Past experience indicates that approximately 95% of the stamps are eventually redeemed for merchandise. The cost of the merchandise is on the average 90% of the price charged to merchants for the stamps. Assume also that during January, 1981, $30,000 worth of the stamps sold in January are redeemed for merchandise. The summary entries for Silver Streak Stamp Company relating to stamp activity in January would be:

Cash	100,000	
Revenue from Sale of Stamps		100,000
Cost of Sales — Trading Stamps	85,500	
Estimated Liability for Stamp Sales		85,500
Recognition of estimated cost to redeem trading stamps; 95% redemption rate, 90% cost: ($100,000 × .95 × .90 = $85,500).		
Estimated Liability for Stamp Sales	27,000	
Inventory		27,000
Issuance of merchandise: ($30,000 × .90 = $27,000).		

In the above example, it is assumed that the cost of the merchandise to be issued is known with sufficient certainty to enable the company to recognize the income of $14,500 ($100,000 − $85,500) immediately. As discussed on page 377 dealing with service contracts, when this certainty does not exist, income should be deferred and recognized as the merchandise is redeemed. Again, the particular practice followed depends upon the specific circumstances.

One of the more difficult questions in accounting for the liability for unredeemed trading stamps is the expected redemption rate. Past experience provides the best basis for making this determination.[5]

---

[5]For an illustration of models used to estimate the liability, see Davidson, Neter, and Petran, "Estimating the Liability for Unredeemed Stamps," *Journal of Accounting Research*, Autumn 1967, pages 186–207.

Tickets, Tokens, and Gift Certificates Outstanding

Many companies sell tickets, tokens, and gift certificates that entitle the owner to services or merchandise: for example, airlines issue tickets used for travel; local transit companies issue tokens good for fares; department stores sell gift certificates redeemable in merchandise.

When instruments redeemable in services or merchandise are outstanding at the end of the period, accounts should be adjusted to reflect the obligations under such arrangements. The nature of the adjustment will depend upon the entries originally made in recording the sale of the instruments.

Ordinarily, the sale of instruments redeemable in services or merchandise is recorded by a debit to Cash and a credit to a liability account. As instruments are redeemed, the liability balance is debited and Sales or an appropriate revenue account is credited. Certain claims may be rendered void by lapse of time or for some other reason as defined by the sales agreement. In addition, experience may indicate a certain percentage of outstanding claims will never be presented for redemption. These factors must be considered at the end of the period, when the liability balance is reduced to the balance of the claim estimated to be outstanding and a revenue account is credited for the gain indicated from forfeitures. If Sales or a special revenue account is originally credited on the sale of the redemption instrument, the adjustment at the end of the period calls for a debit to the revenue account and a credit to a liability account for the claim still outstanding.

Compensated Absences

Compensated absences include payments by employers for vacation, holiday, illness, or other personal activities. Employees often earn paid absences based upon the time employed. Generally, the longer an employee works for a company, the longer the vacation allowed, or the more liberal the time allowed for illnesses. At the end of any given accounting period, a company has a liability for earned but untaken compensated absences. The matching principle requires that this payment be charged against current revenue, and a liability established for the amount calculated.[6] The difficult part of this accounting is estimating how much should be accrued. In Statement No. 43, the FASB requires a liability to be recognized for compensated absences that (1) had been earned through services already rendered, (2) can be carried forward to subsequent years and (3) are estimable and probable. Minimum liability would be vested amounts when estimates cannot be made.

For example, assume a company has a vacation pay policy for all employees. If all employees had the same anniversary date for computing time in service, the computations would not be too difficult. However, most plans provide for a flexible employee starting date. In order to compute the

---

[6]*Statement of Financial Accounting Standards No. 43*, "Accounting for Compensated Absences" (Stamford: Financial Accounting Standards Board, 1980), par. 6.

liability, a careful inventory of all employees must be made that includes the number of years of service, rate of pay, carryover of unused vacation from prior periods, turnover, and the probability of taking the vacation.

Although compensated absences are not deductible for income tax purposes until the vacation, holiday, or illness is taken and the payment is made, they are required to be recognized as liabilities on the financial statements if the FASB requirements are met.

CONTINGENT LIABILITIES

Contingencies are defined in FASB Statement No. 5 as:

> . . . an existing condition, situation, or set of circumstances involving uncertainty as to possible gain . . . or loss . . . to an enterprise that will ultimately be resolved when one or more future events occur or fail to occur.[7]

As defined, contingencies may apply broadly to either assets or liabilities, and to either a gain or a loss. In this chapter, attention is focused on contingent losses that might give rise to a liability. Historically, liabilities classified as contingent were not recorded on the books, but were disclosed in notes to financial statements. The distinction between a recorded liability and a contingent liability was not always clear. If a legal liability existed and the amount of the obligation was either definite *or* could be estimated with reasonable certainty, the liability was recorded on the books. If the existence of the obligation depended upon the happening of a future event, recording of the liability was deferred until the event occurred. In an attempt to make the distinction more precise, the FASB used three terms in FASB Statement No. 5 to identify the range of likelihood possibilities of the event occurring. Different accounting action was recommended for each term. The terms, their definition, and the accounting action recommended are as follows:[8]

Term	Definition	Accounting Action
Probable	The future event or events are likely to occur	Record the probable event in the accounts if the amount can be reasonably estimated. If not estimable, disclose facts in note.
Reasonably possible	The chance of the future event or events occurring is more than remote but less than likely	Report the contingency in a note.
Remote	The chance of the future event or events occurring is slight	No recording or reporting unless contingency represents a guarantee. Then note disclosure is required.

If the happening of the event that would create a liability is probable, and if the amount of the obligation can be reasonably estimated, the contingency should be recognized as a liability. Some of the liabilities already presented

[7]*Statement of Financial Accounting Standards No. 5*, "Accounting for Contingencies" (Stamford: Financial Accounting Standards Board, 1975), par. 1.

[8]*Ibid.*, par. 3.

as estimated liabilities may be considered probable contingent liabilities because the existence of the obligation is dependent on some event occurring, e.g., warranties are dependent on the need for repair or service to be given, gift certificates are dependent upon the certificate being turned in for redemption, and vacation pay is dependent upon a person taking a vacation. These liabilities are not included in this section, however, because historically they have been recognized as recorded liabilities. Other liabilities, such as unsettled litigation claims, self insurance, and loan guarantees have more traditionally been considered as unrecorded contingent liabilities, and thus will be explored separately in the following pages. Inasmuch as all liabilities have some element of contingency associated with them, the authors feel that the classification "contingent liability," should be reserved for those items that fit into the latter two terms, i.e., reasonably possible and remote. If the happening of the event is probable, the liability is no longer a contingent liability, but a recorded estimated liability. Such liabilities meet the definition for liabilities presented at the beginning of this chapter. This approach avoids having to say that some contingent liabilities are recorded and others are not. By this definition, a contingent liability is never recorded but is either disclosed in a footnote or ignored depending upon the degree of remoteness of its expected occurrence.

The FASB statement provided no specific guidelines as to how these three terms should be interpreted in probability percentages. Surveys made of statement preparers and users disclosed a great diversity in the probability interpretation of the terms. It is unlikely, therefore, that FASB Statement No. 5 has greatly reduced the diversity in practice in recording some of these contingent items.

Litigation

An increasing number of lawsuits are being filed against companies and individuals. Lawsuits may result in substantial liabilities to successful plaintiffs. Typically, litigation takes a long time to conclude. For example, a U.S. Government anti-trust suit against IBM has been in court for several years. Even after a decision has been rendered by a lower court, there are many appeal opportunities available. Thus, both the amount and timing of a loss arising from litigation are generally highly uncertain. Some companies carry insurance to protect them against these losses, so the impact of the losses on the financial statements is minimized. For uninsured risks, however, a decision must be made as to when the liability for litigation becomes probable, and thus a recorded loss.

FASB Statement No. 5 identifies several key factors to consider in making the decision. These include:[9]

1. The nature of the litigation.
2. The period when the cause of action occurred. (Liability is not recognized in any period before the cause of action occurred.)
3. Progress of the case in court, including progress between date of the financial

---

[9]*Ibid.*, par. 36.

statements and their issuance date.

4. Views of legal counsel as to the probability of loss.
5. Prior experience with similar cases.
6. Management's intended response to the litigation.

If analysis of these and similar factors results in the judgment that a loss is probable, and the amount of the loss can be reasonably estimated, the liability should be recorded. A settlement after the balance sheet date but before the statements are issued would be evidence that the loss was probable at the year-end, and would result in a reporting of loss in the current financial statements.

Another area of potential liability involves unasserted claims, i.e., a cause of action has occurred but no claim has yet been asserted. For example, a person may be injured on the property of the company, but as of the date the financial statements are issued, no legal action has been taken; or a violation of a government regulation may occur, but no federal action has yet been taken. If it is probable that a claim will be filed, and the amount of the claim can be reasonably estimated, accrual of the liability should be made. If the amount cannot be reasonably estimated, note disclosure is required. If assertion of the claim is not judged to be probable, no accrual or disclosure is necessary.

The following example illustrates accounting for litigation that is judged to be probable of adverse settlement. Assume a claim for $10 million is filed in 1981 against Sky-Ways Limited for injuries suffered in an airplane crash. The case is in court, and an out-of-court settlement is in the process of being negotiated. Even though the nature of the accident made the loss uninsured, Sky-Ways has agreed to a payment of $2 million. Attorneys for Sky-Ways believe an eventual settlement will be reached for about that amount. Based upon these facts, management decides the $2 million loss is probable, and the estimated loss is recorded as follows:

1981	Loss from Damage Suit	2,000,000	
	Estimated Liability Arising from Damage Suit		2,000,000

Assume further that in 1982 a settlement is finally made for $2,500,000. Since the entry in the preceding year was based upon an estimate, the additional $500,000 is recorded as a loss in 1982.

1982	Loss from Damage Suit	500,000	
	Estimated Liability Arising from Damage Suit	2,000,000	
	Cash		2,500,000

If the actual loss is less than the amount recorded, the adjustment is made to the current year's income statement as would be true for revision of any estimates. Reference to General Mills' financial statements in Appendix B reveals no identified recorded liability for litigation. Reference to Note 14, however, implies there has been a provision for some liability in the accounts. The note also describes a contingent loss from litigation with the FTC. This disclosure indicates that adverse settlement is considered to be reasonably possible.

Self Insurance

Some large companies with widely distributed risks may decide not to purchase insurance for protection against the normal business risks of fire, explosion, flood, or damage to other persons or their property. These companies in effect insure themselves against these risks. The accounting question that arises is whether a liability should be accrued and a loss recognized for the possible occurrence of the uninsured risk. Sometimes companies have recorded as an expense an amount equal to the insurance premium that would have been paid had commercial insurance been carried. The FASB considered this specific subject in Statement No. 5, and concluded that no loss or liability should be recorded until the loss has occurred. Fires, explosions, or other casualties are random in occurrence, and as such, are not accruable. Further, they stated that

> . . . unlike an insurance company, which has a contractual obligation under policies in force to reimburse insureds for losses, an enterprise can have no such obligation to itself and, hence, no liability.[10]

Thus, although an exposed condition does exist, it is a future period that must bear any loss that occurs, not a current period.

Loan Guarantees

Enterprises sometimes enter into a contract guaranteeing a loan for another enterprise, frequently a subsidiary company, a supplier, or even a favored customer. These guarantees obligate the entity to make the loan payment if the principal borrower fails to make the payment. A similar contingent obligation exists when the payee of a note receivable discounts it at a bank, but is held contingently liable in the event the maker of the note defaults. Discussion of discounted notes receivable was included in Chapter 7. If the default on the loan or the note is judged to be probable based upon the events that have occurred prior to the issuance date of the financial statements, the loss and liability should be accrued in accordance with the general guidelines discussed in this section. Otherwise, note disclosure is required even if the likelihood of making the payment is remote. This exception to not disclosing remote contingencies arose because companies have traditionally disclosed guarantees in notes to the financial statements, and the FASB did not want to reduce this disclosure practice.

Future Commitments

Various types of contracts or agreements may be entered into that could result in losses to the entity making them. For example, a contract for a future sale of a product may be made with the selling price fixed. If a rapid rise in prices occurs before the date of the sale, a loss rather than a profit may be incurred by the seller on the contract. When a loss arising from such a commitment is probable, it should be accrued in the current period

---

[10]*Ibid.*, par. 28.

rather than waiting for it to be recognized when the commitment is ful-filled. For example, assume a $10,000 sale of a product is made with the item to be purchased and delivered in six months. The present cost of the product is $9,000. The financial statements are prepared after four months, and the cost of the product has risen rapidly and is now $11,000. Since the inventory must still be purchased, the $1,000 loss is probable and should be recognized as follows:

Loss from Future Sales Commitment	1,000	
Estimated Loss Arising from Sales Commitment		1,000

Assume further that the sale is made in the next year, and the purchase cost of the inventory was $11,000. The entry to record the sale and its cost under a perpetual inventory system would be as follows:

Inventory	11,000	
Cash		11,000
Accounts Receivable	10,000	
Sales		10,000
Cost of Sales	10,000	
Estimated Loss Arising from Sales Commitment	1,000	
Inventory		11,000

Other commitments, such as purchase commitments discussed in Chapter 8, would be recorded similarly.

Companies sometimes **hedge** their future commitments to avoid a loss. This means that at the same time a sales contract is entered into for six months in the future, a purchase contract for the item or its major compo-nent parts is entered into for delivery also in the future. A hedge enables a company to avoid the risk of loss. Of course, future commitments can result in profits, and a hedge prevents this from occurring as well. Probable gains arising from future commitments are not recognized in current practice until the event occurs. Thus, in the above example, if the cost fell to $8,000, the extra $1,000 profit would be recognized in 1982 when the sale was made.

BALANCE SHEET PRESENTATION

The liability section of the balance sheet is usually divided between cur-rent and noncurrent liabilities as previously discussed. The nature of the detail to be presented for current liabilities depends upon the use to be made of the financial statement. A balance sheet prepared for stockholders might report little detail; on the other hand, creditors may insist on full detail concerning current debts.

Assets are normally recorded in the order of their liquidity, and consis-tency would suggest liabilities be reported in the order of their maturity. The latter practice may be followed only to the extent it is practical: obser-vance of this procedure would require an analysis of the different classes of obligations and separate reporting for classes with varying maturity dates. A bank overdraft should be listed first in view of the immediate demand it makes on cash. In some cases a distinction is made between liabilities that have matured and are presently payable and others that have not matured though they are current.

Liabilities should not be offset by assets to be applied to their liquidation. Disclosure as to future debt liquidation, however, may be provided by an appropriate parenthetical remark or note. Disclosure of liabilities secured by specific assets should also be made by a parenthetical remark or note.

The current liabilities section of a balance sheet prepared on December 31, 1981, might appear as shown below:

Current liabilities:
Notes payable:
Trade creditors.. $12,000
Banks (secured by assignment of monies to become due under certain contracts totaling $36,000 included in asset section)........ 20,000
Officers... 10,000
Miscellaneous... 2,500 $44,500

Accounts payable:
Trade creditors.. $30,500
Credit balances in customers' accounts.......... 1,250
Miscellaneous... 3,500 35,250
Long-term liability installments due in 1982.... 10,000
Cash dividends payable....................................... 4,500
Income tax payable... 6,000

Other liabilities:
Salaries and wages payable .... $ 1,250
Real and personal property taxes 1,550
Miscellaneous liabilities 1,400
Customer advances.. 7,500
Estimated repair costs on goods sold with service warranties... 2,500 14,200 $114,450

Because most of the noncurrent liabilities are discussed in separate chapters that follow, illustration of the details of the noncurrent liabilities section is deferred until Chapter 17 and illustrated with owner's equity. For a further illustration of a liabilities section of a balance sheet with related notes, see the General Mills statements reproduced in Appendix B.

QUESTIONS

1. Identify the major elements included in the definition of liabilities recommended by the FASB.
2. (a) What is meant by an executory contract? (b) Do these contracts fit the definition of liabilities included in this chapter?
3. (a) Distinguish between the definition of liabilities and their measurement. (b) Why is present value used so extensively in liability accounting?
4. Distinguish between current and noncurrent liabilities.
5. Under what conditions would debt that will mature within the next year be reported as a noncurrent liability?

6. The Cable Co. issues a non-interest-bearing note due in one year in payment for equipment. Describe the accounting procedures that should be employed for the purchase.

7. Why is the use of the net method of recording purchases preferred over the gross method?

8. The sales manager for Bonneville Sales Co. is entitled to a bonus of 12% of profits. What difficulties may arise in the interpretation of this profit-sharing agreement?

9. How is depreciation computed on returnable containers when it is not known how many containers will be returned?

10. Under what circumstances can a company earn a profit on returnable containers?

11. How should a company account for revenue received in advance for a service contract?

12. What uncertainties are present when accounting for trading stamps?

13. What information must a firm accumulate in order to adequately account for estimated liabilities on tickets, tokens and gift certificates?

14. How should contingent liabilities that are reasonably possible of becoming liabilities be reported on the financial statements?

15. What factors are important in deciding whether a lawsuit in process should be reported as a liability on the balance sheet?

16. Why does accounting for self-insurance differ from accounting for insurance premiums with outside carriers?

17. Under what circumstances can a future sales commitment give rise to a loss? How can the possibility of loss be eliminated?

EXERCISES

exercise 13-1

The following notes were issued by the Yale Marble Company:

(a) Note issued to purchase office equipment. Face amount $25,000; no stated interest rate; market rate of interest, 12%; term of note, one year; date of note, November 1, 1981.

(b) Note issued to bank for a cash loan. Maturity value of note, $25,000; bank discount rate, 12%; term of note, one year; date of note, October 1, 1981.

(1) Give the entries required at the time the notes were issued. Round to nearest dollar.

(2) Give the adjusting entries required on December 31, 1981, to recognize the accrual of the interest on each note.

exercise 13-2

Bart Manufacturing Co. purchased two new company automobiles from Easy-Terms Auto Sales. The purchase was made on September 1, 1981. The terms of the sale called for Bart to pay $19,992 to Easy-Terms on September 1, 1982. At the date of purchase, the interest rate for short-term loans was 12%. Prepare the journal entries necessary on September 1, 1981, December 31, 1981 (year-end adjusting), and September 1, 1982.

exercise 13-3

Riggs Wholesale Company, has an agreement with its sales manager whereby the latter is entitled to 6% of company earnings as a bonus. Company income for a calendar year before bonus and income tax is $150,000. Income tax is 45% of income after bonus. Compute the amount of the bonus under each of the conditions below.

(a) The bonus is calculated on income before deductions for bonus and income tax.

(b) The bonus is calculated on income after deduction for bonus but before deduction for income tax.

(c) The bonus is calculated on income after deduction for income tax but before deduction for bonus.

(d) The bonus is calculated on net income after deductions for both bonus and income tax.

exercise 13-4

The Rodriguez Furniture Company provides a special bonus for its executive officers based upon income before bonus or income tax. Income before bonus and income tax for 1982 was $1,250,000. The combined state and federal income tax rate is 55% and the total income tax liability for 1982 is $632,500. What was the bonus rate?

exercise 13-5

Quickie Cleaners paid one week's wages of $10,600 in cash (net pay after all employment taxes and deductions) to its 40 employees. Income tax withholdings were equal to 17% of the gross payroll and the only other deductions were 6.1% for FICA tax and $160 for union dues. Give the entries that should be made on the books of the store to record the payroll and the tax accruals to be recognized by the employer, assuming that the company is subject to unemployment taxes of 2.7% (state) and .7% (federal).

exercise 13-6

On November 20, 1981, Red Rose Floral Shop received a property tax assessment of $144,000 for the fiscal year ending June 30, 1982. No entry was made to record the assessment. Several months later, Red Rose's accountant was preparing the yearly financial statements (based on a February 1 to January 31 fiscal year) and came across the property tax assessment. Give the journal entries to record the tax payment (if any) and any adjusting entries necessary on January 31, assuming:

(a) The full tax of $144,000 had been paid on January 5, 1982.
(b) The full tax of $144,000 had not been paid.
(c) A portion of the tax ($90,500) had been paid on January 20, 1982.

exercise 13-7

Total sales plus sales tax for the Universal Power Company in 1981 was $122,850; 70% of the sales are normally made on account. Prepare an entry summarizing these data for 1981 if the sales tax rate is 5%.

exercise 13-8

Woodsman Wholesale Camping Supplies, Inc., began selling large containers of white gas to various sporting goods stores on January 2, 1981. Each container of gas is sold for $42.50. In addition, a deposit of $7.50 is charged on the container. Based on conversations with other wholesalers, Woodsman expects approximately 80% of the containers that are sold to eventually be returned to Woodsman for a refund of the deposit. During 1981, Woodsman purchased 1,500 containers at a unit cost of $6.25. Each container has an estimated useful life of five years and is depreciated on a straight-line basis. By December 31, 1981, Woodsman had sold 1,200 containers of gas (all on a cash basis), and 734 had been returned and a refund made. Give the journal entries to record the above information.

exercise 13-9

In 1981 Daynes Office Supply began selling a new calculator which carried a two-year warranty against defects. Based on the manufacturer's recommendations, Daynes projects the estimated warranty costs (as a percent of dollar sales) as follows:

First year of warranty...	4%
Second year of warranty	10%

Sales and actual warranty repairs for 1981 and 1982 are presented below:

	1981	1982
Sales..	$250,000	$475,000
Actual warranty repairs	4,750	26,175

(1) Give the necessary journal entries to record the liability at the end of 1981 and 1982.
(2) Analyze the warranty liability account as of the year ending December 31, 1982, to see if the actual repairs approximate the estimate. Should Daynes revise the manufacturer's warranty estimate? (Assume sales and repairs occur evenly throughout the year).

exercise 13-10

Quick Service Appliance Company's accountant has been reviewing the firm's past television sales. For the past two years, Quick Service has been offering a special service warranty on all televisions sold. With the purchase of a television, the customer has the right to purchase a three-year service contract for an extra $50. Information concerning past television and warranty contract sales is given below:

Color-All Model II Television

	1981	1982
Television sales in units...	450	525
Sales price per unit	$ 400	$ 500
Number of service contracts sold	300	350
Expenses relating to television warranties......................	$2,950	$7,360

Quick Service's accountant has estimated from past records that the pattern of repairs has been 40% in the first year after sale, 36% in the second year, and 24% in the third year. Give the necessary journal entries related to the service contracts for 1981 and 1982. In addition, indicate how much profit on service contracts would be recognized in 1982. Assume sales of the contracts are made evenly during the year.

exercise 13-11

On January 2, 1981, the Russell Beverage Company began marketing a new soft drink called "TINGLE." To help promote TINGLE, the management of Russell is offering a special TINGLE T-shirt to each customer who returns 24 bottle caps. Russell estimates that out of the 450,000 bottles of TINGLE sold during 1981, only 60% of the bottle caps will be redeemed. On December 31, 1981, the following information was collected.

	Units	Amount
T-Shirts purchased by Russell	14,250	$18,525
T-Shirts distributed to customers	5,000	

(1) What is the amount of the liability which Russell should record on their 1981 financial statements?
(2) Give the journal entries to record the purchase, distribution, and year-end liability relating to the T-shirts.

exercise 13-12

Reliance Food Stores purchases trading stamps from Checkerboard Stamp Company. Checkerboard has agreed to handle full responsibility for the redemption of the stamps. During 1981, Reliance issued $7,025 worth of stamps to their customers. Reliance's records show the following information relating to their trading stamp inventory:

Trading Stamp Inventory — Reliance

| January 1, 1981.. | $12,750 |
| December 31, 1981... | 9,225 |

Besides selling to Reliance, Checkerboard also sells to other grocery outlets. During 1981, Checkerboard sold $175,000 worth of stamps to other grocery stores. Checkerboard estimates that 94% of the stamps will be eventually redeemed for merchandise. Checkerboard uses various household items as gifts to customers returning a predetermined number of stamps. The cost of the gifts averages 80% of the price paid by the merchants for the redeemed stamps. During 1981, $65,000 worth of stamps were redeemed by Checkerboard. Give the journal entries to record the sale and redemption of trading stamps during 1981 for Checkerboard and the purchase and distribution of stamps in 1981 for Reliance Foods.

exercise 13-13

Rosenbaum Builders, Inc., employs five people. Each employee is entitled to two weeks' paid vacation every year the employee works for the company. The conditions of the paid vacation are: (a) for each full year of work, an employee will receive two weeks of paid vacation (no vacation accrues for a portion of a year), (b) each employee will receive the same pay for vacation time as the regular pay in the year taken, and (c) unused vacation pay can be carried forward. The following data were taken from the firm's personnel records:

Employee	Starting Date	Cumulative Vacation Taken as of December 31, 1982	Weekly Salary
John Palermo	December 21, 1975	11 weeks	$375
Robert Gorman	March 6, 1980	2 weeks	500
Mary Ann Tyler	August 13, 1981	none	350
Frank Huang	December 17, 1980	3 weeks	300
Rebecca Lewis	March 29, 1982	none	400

Compute the liability for vacation pay as of December 31, 1982.

exercise 13-14

Conrad Corporation sells motorcycle helmets. In 1981, Conrad sold 4 million helmets before discovering a significant defect in the helmet's construction. By December 31, 1981, two lawsuits had been filed against Conrad. The first lawsuit, which Conrad has little chance of winning, is expected to be settled out of court for $900,000 in January of 1982. In the second lawsuit, which is for $400,000, Conrad's attorneys think the company has a fifty-fifty chance of winning. What accounting treatment should Conrad give the pending lawsuits in the year-end financial statements? (Include any necessary journal entries.)

exercise 13-15

Whipple Corporation is a wholesale distributor of lumber products. On September 4, an agreement was reached to deliver a large shipment of plywood to Gaffin, Inc., on February 4 of the following year. The sales price was firmly established at $16,500. The cost to Whipple at September 4 would have been $13,750, but they decided not to purchase at this price because they hoped prices would fall. A severe shortage of plywood during December drastically increased prices. By December 31, the date of Whipple's financial statements, the purchase price of the plywood had risen to $17,000. On February 3, the plywood was purchased for $18,000. Give the journal entries required to record the above transactions. (Assume a perpetual inventory system.)

exercise 13-16

Prepare the current liabilities section of the balance sheet for the McQueen Mattress Company on December 31, 1981, from the information appearing below:

(a) Notes payable: arising from purchases of goods, $58,680; arising from loans from banks, $18,000, on which marketable securities valued at $26,100 have been pledged as security; arising from short-term advances by officers, $21,600.
(b) Accounts payable arising from purchase of goods, $55,800.
(c) Cash balance with Farmers Bank, $9,900; cash overdraft with Merchants Bank, $5,976.
(d) Dividends in arrears on preferred stock, $32,400.
(e) Employees income tax payable, $1,584.
(f) First-mortgage serial bonds, $125,000, payable in semiannual installments of $5,000 due on March 1 and September 1 of each year.
(g) Advances received from customers on purchase orders, $4,140.
(h) Customers' accounts with credit balances arising from purchase returns, $1,500.
(i) Estimated expense of meeting warranty for service requirements on merchandise sold, $4,860.

PROBLEMS

problem 13-1

The following information comes from the books of D. E. Calder Supply Co. at December 31, 1981.

Sales on account (including sales tax of 5%)	$262,500
Net income	30,500
Cash dividends (declared December 30, 1981)	20,000
Machinery purchased, October 1, 1981 (a one-year non-interest-bearing note was issued in payment)	60,000

Notes payable (a one-year note for $10,000 was discounted at the bank at 13% on September 1, 1981)..	$10,000
Marketable securities	8,000
Common stock, $100 par	50,000

Instructions: Prepare necessary journal entries to record the following transactions: Round to nearest dollar.

(1) Discounting the note payable.
(2) Purchase of machinery (money is worth 12% per year).
(3) Declaration of cash dividend.
(4) Sales and sales tax.
(5) Record the interest to be charged to this year at year end as a result of the issuance of the notes.

problem 13-2

Miller Manufacturing Corporation pays bonuses to its sales manager and two sales agents. The company had income for 1981 of $1,500,000 before bonuses and income tax. Income taxes average 45%.

Instructions: Compute the bonuses assuming:

(1) Sales manager gets 6% and sales agents get 5% of income before tax and bonuses.
(2) Each bonus is 9% of income after income tax but before bonuses.
(3) Each bonus is 12% of net income after income tax and bonuses.
(4) Sales manager gets 12% and sales agents get 10% of income after bonuses but before income tax.

problem 13-3

Kingston Clothiers' employees are paid on the 10th and 25th of each month for the period ending the previous 5th and 20th respectively. An analysis of the payroll on Thursday, November 5, 1981, revealed the following data:

	Gross Pay	FICA	Federal Income Tax	State Income Tax	Insurance	Net Pay
Office salaries	$10,500	$ 504	$1,200	$ 200	$ 270	$ 8,326
Officers' salaries	27,000	324	5,100	1,500	510	19,566
Sales salaries	18,000	648	3,000	750	390	13,212
Total	$55,500	$1,476	$9,300	$2,450	$1,170	$41,104

It is determined that for the November 5 pay period, no additional employees exceeded the wage base for FICA purposes than had done so in prior periods. All of the officers' salaries, 70% of the office salaries, and 60% of the sales salaries for the payroll period ending November 5 were paid to employees that had exceeded the wage base for unemployment taxes. Assume the rates in force are as follows: FICA, 6%; federal unemployment tax, .7% and state unemployment tax, 2.3%.

Instructions: Prepare the adjusting entries that would be required at October 31, the end of Kingston's fiscal year, to reflect the accrual of the payroll and any related payroll taxes. Separate salary and payroll taxes expense accounts are used for each of the three employee categories; office, officers', and sales salaries.

problem 13-4

The Marston Corporation closes its books and prepares financial statements on an annual basis. The following information is gathered by the chief accountant to assist in preparing the liability section of the balance sheet:

(a) Property taxes of $45,000 were assessed on the property in May 1981, for the subsequent period of July 1 to June 30. The payment of the taxes is divided into three equal installments, November 1, February 1, and May 1. The November 1 payment was made and charged to Property Tax Expense. No other entries have been made for property taxes relative to the 1981–82 assessment. Assume prior year's property taxes were accrued properly at December 31, 1980, and the accrual entry was reversed on January 1, 1981.

(b) The estimated 1981 pretax income for Marston is $629,000. The effective tax rates for

Marston have been 42% federal and 10% state. Income tax payments of $280,000 were made by Marston during 1981, including $50,000 as the final payment on 1980 federal income taxes, $20,000 for 1981 state estimated taxes, the balance for 1981 federal estimated taxes.

(c) Taxable sales for 1981 were $7,500,000. The state sales tax rate is 4.5%. Quarterly statements have been filed, and the following tax payments were made with the return.

1st Quarter	$76,000
2d Quarter	80,000
3d Quarter	70,000

The balance in the account Sales Tax Payable is $110,800 at December 31, 1981.

Instructions:

(1) Based upon the given data, what amounts should be reported on the balance sheet as liabilities at December 31, 1981?

(2) Prepare the necessary adjusting entries to record the liabilities.

problem 13-5

Wondercoat, Inc., sells a special sealer in thirty-gallon reusable drums. To encourage the return of the drums, Wondercoat charges its customers a deposit of $20 for each drum. The cost of purchasing new drums in large quantities from its suppliers is $10 per drum. It is estimated that the drums have, on the average, a four-year life. The sealer sells for $4 per gallon. The following transactions occurred in 1981 and 1982. The business began at the beginning of Jan. 1981.

	1981	1982
Drums purchased	5,000	2,000
Drums filled with sealer sold	20,000	25,000
Empty drums returned	18,000	24,000
Drums not expected to be returned	500	400
Drums scrapped after return because of damage	100	600

Instructions: Prepare the journal entries for 1981 and 1982 to record the sales, returns, depreciation, and write-offs for unreturned and damaged drums. Assume purchases, sales, and returns are made evenly throughout the year. Compute depreciation on a straight-line basis. One-half year's depreciation is to be taken on all containers purchased, sold, or retired in a given year. A fifo flow is assumed. All sales and purchases are made on account.

problem 13-6

The Cascade Corp. manufactures a special type of low-suds laundry soap. A dish towel is offered as a premium to customers who send in two proof-of-purchase seals from these soap boxes and a remittance of $2. Data for the premium offer are summarized below:

	1981	1982
Soap sales ($2.50 per package)	$2,500,000	$3,125,000
Dish towel purchases ($2.50 per towel)	$ 130,000	$ 156,250
Number of dish towels distributed as premiums	40,000	60,000
Number of dish towels expected to be distributed in subsequent periods	7,500	2,000

Mailing costs are 26¢ per package.

Instructions:

(1) Give the entries for 1981 and 1982 to record product sales, premium purchases and redemptions, and year-end adjustments.

(2) Present "T" accounts with appropriate amounts as of the end of 1981 and 1982.

problem 13-7

Card Electronics, Inc., has a plan to compensate its employees for certain absences. Each employee can receive five days' sick leave each year plus 10 days' vacation. The benefits carry over for two additional years, after which the provision lapses on a fifo flow basis. Thus the maximum accumulation is 45 days. In some cases, the company permits vacations to be taken before they are earned. Payments are made based upon current compensation levels, not on the level in effect when the absence time was earned.

Employee	Days Accrued Jan. 1, 1981	Daily Rate Jan. 1, 1981	Days Earned 1981	Days Taken 1981	Days Accrued Dec. 31, 1981	Daily Rate Dec. 31
A	10	$36	15	10	15	$40
B	—	$46	15	10	5	$50
C	30	$40	7	37	—	Terminated June 15 — Rate = $45
D	−5	$34	15	20	−10	$40
E	40	$60	15	5	50	$70
F	Hired July 1 — Rate = $40	—	8	0	8	$40

Instructions:

(1) How much is the liability for compensated absences at December 31, 1981?

(2) Prepare a summary journal entry to record compensation absence payments during the year and the accrual at the end of the year. Assume the payroll liability account is charged for all payments made during the year for both sickness and vacation leaves. The average rate of compensation for the year may be used to value the hours taken except for Employee C who took his leaves at the date of termination. The end-of-year rate should be used to establish the ending liability.

problem 13-8

The Western Supply Co. has several contingent liabilities at December 31, 1981. The following brief description of each liability is obtained by the auditor.

(a) In May 1980, Western Supply became involved in litigation. In December 1981, a judgment for $800,000 was assessed against Western by the court. Western is appealing the amount of the judgment. Attorneys for Western feel it is probable that they can reduce the assessment on appeal by 50%. No entries have been made by Western pending completion of the appeal process, which is expected to take at least a year.

(b) In July 1981, Morgan County brought action against Western for polluting the Jordan River with its waste products. It is reasonably possible that Morgan County will be successful, but the amount of damages Western might have to pay should not exceed $200,000. No entry has been made by Western to reflect the possible loss.

(c) Western Supply has elected to self-insure its fire and casualty risks. At the beginning of the year, the account Reserve for Insurance, had a balance of $2,500,000. During 1981, $750,000 was debited to insurance expense and credited to the reserve account. After payment for losses actually sustained in 1981, the reserve account had a balance of $2,800,000 at December 31, 1981. The opening balance was a result of several years activity similar to 1981.

(d) Western Supply has signed as guarantor for a $50,000 loan by Guaranty Bank to Midwest Parts, Inc., a principal supplier to Western. Because of financial problems at Midwest, it is probable that Western Supply will have to pay the $50,000 with only a 40% recovery anticipated from Midwest. No entries have been made to reflect the contingent liability.

Instructions:

(1) What amount should be reported as a liability on the December 31, 1981 balance sheet?

(2) What note disclosure should be included as part of the balance sheet for each of the above items?

(3) Prepare the journal entries necessary to adjust Western's books to reflect your answers in (1) and (2).

14

Accounting for Bonds and Long-Term Notes

CHAPTER OBJECTIVES

Describe the various types of long-term debt used to finance an entity's operations.

Explain and illustrate currently accepted accounting procedures followed by both investors and issuers for the issuance and servicing of long-term debt, including bonds and notes.

Describe and illustrate currently accepted accounting procedures for the conversion and termination of long-term debt.

Illustrate the presentation of long-term debt on the balance sheets of both investors and issuers.

Long-term financing of a corporation is accomplished either through the issuance of long-term debt instruments, usually bonds or notes, or through the sale of additional stock. The issuance of bonds or notes instead of stock may be preferred by stockholders for the following reasons: (1) the charge against earnings for interest is normally less than the share of earnings that would be payable as dividends on a new issue of preferred stock or on the sale of additional common stock; (2) present owners continue in control of the corporation; and, (3) interest is a deductible expense in arriving at taxable income while dividends are not.

But there are certain limitations and disadvantages of financing through bonds and long-term notes. Debt financing is possible only when a company is in a satisfactory financial condition and can offer adequate security to a new creditor group. Furthermore, interest must be paid regardless of the company's earnings and financial position. With operating losses and the inability of a company to raise sufficient cash to meet periodic interest payments, bondholders may take legal action to assume control of company properties.

Most bonds and long-term notes differ only in terms of the time to maturity. Generally speaking, bonds carry a maturity date five years or more after issue. Some bonds may not mature for twenty-five years or more. Long-term notes, however, generally mature in a period of one to seven years from issuance date. Other characteristics of bonds and long-term notes are usually identical. Therefore, in the discussion that follows, references to bonds can also be applied to long-term notes.

Bonds and notes are purchased for both short-term and long-term purposes by corporations, principally insurance companies, banks, trust companies, and educational and charitable institutions. Because of the similarity in accounting for bonds and notes by issuers and investors, both sides of bond and long-term note transactions will be presented in this chapter.

NATURE OF BONDS

The power of a corporation to create bonded indebtedness is found in the corporation laws of a state and may be specifically granted by charter. In some cases formal authorization by a majority of stockholders is required before a board of directors can approve a bond issue.

Borrowing by means of bonds involves the issuance of certificates of indebtedness. Bond certificates may represent equal parts of the bond issue or they may be of varying denominations. Bonds of a business unit are commonly issued in $1,000 denominations, referred to as the **bond face, par,** or **maturity value**.

The group contract between the corporation and the bondholders is known as the **bond** or **trust indenture**. The indenture details the rights and obligations of the contracting parties, indicates the property pledged as well as the protection offered on the loan, and names the bank or trust company that is to represent the bondholders.

Bonds may be sold by the company directly to investors, or they may be underwritten by investment bankers or a syndicate. The underwriters may agree to purchase the entire bond issue or that part of the issue which is not sold by the company, or they may agree simply to manage the sale of the security on a commission basis.

Most companies attempt to sell their bonds to underwriters to avoid a loss occurring after the bonds are placed on the market. An interesting example of this occurred in 1979 when IBM Corporation went to the bond market for the first time and issued a record one billion dollars worth of bonds and long-term notes. After the issue was released by IBM to the underwriters, interest rates soared as the Federal Reserve Bank sharply increased its rediscount rate. The market price of the IBM securities fell, and the brokerage houses and investment bankers participating in the underwriting incurred a loss in excess of 50 million dollars on the sale of the securities to investors.

Issuers of Bonds

Bonds and similar debt instruments are issued by private corporations, the United States Government, state, county and local governments, school districts, and government sponsored organizations such as the Federal Home Loan Bank and the Federal National Mortgage Association. The total amount of debt issued by these organizations is now well in excess of one trillion dollars.

The U.S. debt includes not only Treasury bonds, but also Treasury bills, which are notes with less than one year to maturity date, and Treasury notes, which mature in one to seven years. Both Treasury bills and Treasury notes are more in demand in the marketplace than Treasury bonds.

Debt securities issued by state, county, and local governments and their agencies are collectively referred to as **municipal debt**. A unique feature of municipal debt is that the interest received by investors in such securities is exempt from federal income tax. Because of this tax advantage, "municipals" generally carry lower interest rates than debt securities of other issuers, enabling these governmental units to borrow at favorable interest rates. The tax exemption is in reality a subsidy granted by the federal government to encourage capital investment in state and local governments.

Types of Bonds

Bonds may be classified in many different ways. When all of the bonds mature on a single date, they are called **term bonds**; when bonds mature in installments, they are known as **serial bonds**. Bonds issued by private corporations may be **secured** or **unsecured**. Secured bonds provide protection to the investor in the form of a mortgage covering the company's real estate and perhaps other property, or a pledge in the form of certain collateral. A **first-mortgage bond** represents a first claim against the property of a corporation in the event of the company's inability to meet bond interest and principal payments. A **second-mortgage bond** is a secondary claim ranking only after the claim of the first-mortgage bonds or senior issue has been completely satisfied. A **collateral trust bond** is usually secured by stocks and bonds of other corporations owned by the issuing company. Such securities are generally transferred to a trustee who holds them as collateral on behalf of the bondholders and, if necessary, will sell them to satisfy the bondholders' claim.

Unsecured bonds are not protected by the pledge of certain property and are frequently termed **debenture bonds**. Holders of debenture bonds simply rank as general creditors with other unsecured parties. The risk involved in these securities varies with the financial strength of the debtor. Debentures issued by a strong company may involve little risk; debentures issued by a weak company whose properties are already heavily mortgaged may involve considerable risk. Quality ratings for bonds are made by both Moody's and

Standard and Poor's investment publication companies. For example, Moody's bond ratings range from Aaa, or highest quality, to C for a high-risk bond.

When another party promises to make payment on bonds if the issuing company fails to do so, the bonds are referred to as **guaranteed bonds**. A parent company, for example, may guarantee payment of the bonds issued by its subsidiaries.

Obligations known as **income bonds** have been issued when business failure has resulted in corporate reorganization. These bonds require the payment of interest only to the extent of a company's current earnings. Income bonds may be cumulative or noncumulative. If cumulative, interest that cannot be paid in one year is carried over as a lien against future earnings; if noncumulative, no future lien arises from inability to meet interest payments.

The investor acquiring government obligations looks to the taxing authority of the issuing unit for the measure of its ability to raise money to meet debt service requirements. Certain government obligations are identified with government-owned enterprises, and principal and interest payments are made from the revenues accruing from such operations. These are known as **revenue bonds**. Bonds secured by the general credit of the governmental unit are referred to as **general obligation (go) bonds**.

Bonds may provide for their conversion into some other security at the option of the bondholder. Such bonds are known as **convertible bonds**. The conversion feature generally permits the owner of bonds to exchange them for common stock. The bondholder is thus able to convert the claim into an ownership interest if corporate operations prove successful and conversion becomes attractive; in the meantime the special rights of a creditor are maintained.

Other bond features may serve the issuer's interests. For example, bond indentures frequently give the issuing company the right to call and retire the bonds prior to their maturity. Such bonds are termed **callable bonds**. When a corporation wishes to reduce its outstanding indebtedness, bondholders are notified of the portion of the issue to be surrendered, and they are paid in accordance with call provisions. Interest does not accrue after the call date.

Bonds may be classified as (1) **registered bonds** and (2) **bearer** or **coupon bonds**. Registered bonds call for the registry of the owner's name on the corporation books. Transfer of bond ownership is similar to that for stock. When a bond is sold, the corporate transfer agent cancels the bond certificate surrendered by the seller and issues a new certificate to the buyer. Interest checks are mailed periodically to the bondholders of record. Bearer or coupon bonds are not recorded in the name of the owner, title to such bonds passing with delivery. Each bond is accompanied by coupons for individual interest payments covering the life of the issue. Coupons are clipped by the owner of the bond and presented to a bank for deposit or collection. The issue of bearer bonds eliminates the need for recording bond ownership changes and preparing and mailing periodic interest checks. But coupon bonds fail to offer the bondholder the protection found in registered bonds in the event bonds are lost or stolen. In some cases, bonds provide interest coupons but require registry as to principal. Here, ownership safeguards are afforded while the time-consuming routines involved in making interest payments are avoided. Most bonds of recent issue are registered.

Recently, some bonds and long-term notes have been issued with **floating interest rates**. Because of the wide fluctuations in interest rates that have occurred in the past few years, the floating interest rate security reduces the risk to the investor when interest rates are rising and to the issuer when interest rates are falling. For example, in 1979, Mellon National Corporation issued 200 million dollars of floating rate notes due in 1989. Interest on these notes was 11.5% per year until December 14, 1979. For each semiannual period thereafter, the rate was set at .50% above the current interest yield equivalent of the market discount rate for six month U.S. treasury bills, subject to a minimum per annum interest rate of 6%.

Bond Market Price

The market price of bonds varies with the safety of the investment. When the financial condition and earnings of a corporation are such that payment of interest and principal on bonded indebtedness is virtually assured, the interest rate a company must offer to dispose of a bond issue is relatively low. As the risk factor increases, a higher interest return is necessary to attract investors. The amount of interest paid on bonds is a specified percentage of the face value. This percentage is termed the **stated** or **contract rate**. This rate, however, may not be the same as the prevailing or **market rate** for bonds of similar quality and length of time to maturity at the time the issue is sold. Furthermore, the market rate constantly fluctuates. These factors often result in a difference between bond face values and the prices at which the bonds sell on the market.

The purchase of bonds at face value implies agreement between the bond rate of interest and the prevailing market rate of interest. If the bond rate exceeds the market rate, the bonds will sell at a **premium**; if the bond rate is less than the market rate, the bonds will sell at a **discount**. The premium or the discount is the discounted value of the difference between the stated rate and the market rate of the series of interest payments. A declining market rate of interest subsequent to issuance of the bonds results in an increase in the market value of the bonds; a rising market rate of interest results in a decrease in their market value. The stated rate adjusted for the premium or the discount on the purchase gives the actual rate of return on the bonds, known as the **effective interest rate**. Bonds are quoted on the market as a percentage of face value. Thus, a bond quotation of 96.5 means the market price is 96.5% of face value, or at a discount; a bond quotation of 104 means the market price is 104% of face value, or at a premium. U.S. Government note and bond quotations are made in 32's rather than 100's. Thus a Government bond selling at 98.16 is selling at 98 16/32, or in terms of decimal equivalents, 98.5%.

The market price of a bond at any date can be determined by discounting the maturity value of the bond and each remaining interest payment at the effective rate of interest for similar debt on that date. Present value tables that can be used for discounting are included in Appendix A.

To illustrate the computation of a bond market price from the tables, assume 10-year, 8% bonds of $100,000 are to be sold on the bond issue date. The effective interest rate for these bonds is 10%, compounded semiannually. The computation may be divided into two parts:

1. *Present Value of Maturity Value:*
Maturity value of bonds after ten years or twenty semiannual periods = $100,000
Effective interest rate — 10% per year, or 5% per semiannual period:
$PV_n = A(PVF_{\overline{n}|\,i}) = \$100,000(\text{Table II}_{\overline{20}|\,5\%}) = \$100,000(.3769) = \$37,690.$
2. *Present Value of Twenty Interest Payments:*
Semiannual payment, 4% of $100,000 = $4,000
Effective interest rate — 10% per year, or 5% per semiannual period:
$PV_n = R(PVAF_{\overline{n}|\,i}) = \$4,000(\text{Table IV}_{\overline{20}|\,5\%}) = \$4,000(12.4622) = \$49,849.$

The market price for the bonds would thus be $87,539, the sum of the two parts. Because the effective interest rate is higher than the stated interest rate, the bonds would sell at a $12,461 discount at the issuance date.

Special adaptation of present value tables are available to determine the price to be paid for the bonds if they are to provide a certain return. A portion of such a bond table is illustrated below.

Note that the present value from the table of 8% bonds to return 10% in 10 years is $87,539, the same amount computed above. If the effective rate were 7.5%, the present value would be $103,476.

Values to the Nearest Dollar of 8% Bond for $100,000
Interest Payable Semiannually

Yield	8 years	8½ years	9 years	9½ years	10 years
7.00	$106,046	$106,325	$106,595	$106,855	$107,107
7.25	104,495	104,699	104,896	105,090	105,272
7.50	102,971	103,100	103,232	103,360	103,476
7.75	101,472	101,537	101,595	101,658	101,718
8.00	100,000	100,000	100,000	100,000	100,000
8.25	98,552	98,494	98,437	98,372	98,325
8.50	97,141	97,012	96,893	96,787	96,678
8.75	95,746	95,568	95,398	95,232	95,070
9.00	94,383	94,147	93,920	93,703	93,496
9.25	93,042	92,757	92,480	92,214	91,953
9.50	91,723	91,380	91,055	90,751	90,452
9.75	90,350	89,960	89,588	89,238	88,902
10.00	89,162	88,726	88,310	87,914	87,539

The table can also be used to determine the effective rate on a bond acquired at a certain price. To illustrate, assume that a $1,000, 8% bond due in 10 years is selling at $951. Reference to the column "10 years" for $95,070 shows a return of 8.75% is provided on an investment of $950.70.

BOND ISSUANCE

Bonds may be sold directly to investors by the issuer or they may be sold on the open market through securities exchanges or through investment bankers. Over 50% of bond issues are privately placed with large investors.

An issuer normally records bonds at their face value — the amount that the company must pay at maturity. Hence, when bonds are issued at an amount other than face value, a bond discount or premium balance is established for the difference between the cash received and the bond face value. The premium is added to or the discount is subtracted from the bond face value in the liability section of the balance sheet. This results in bonds being reported at their present value.

The issuance of bonds normally involves costs to the issuer for legal services, printing and engraving, taxes and underwriting. Traditionally, these costs have been either (1) summarized separately as bond issuance costs, classified as deferred charges and charged to revenue over the life of the bond issue, or (2) offset against any premium or added to any discount arising on the issuance and thus netted against the face value of the bonds. The Accounting Principles Board in Opinion No. 21 recommended that these costs be reported on the balance sheet as deferred charges.[1] However, in the FASB statement defining elements of financial statements issued in 1980, the Board stated that such costs fail to meet their definition of assets, and therefore changes in this APB Opinion could be forthcoming.[2] The authors agree with the position of the FASB, and favor netting the issuance costs against the bonds payable as part of the premium or discount on the bonds. Until such time as the FASB specifically addresses the issue, however, the APB Opinion governs generally accepted practice.

Although an investor could record the investment in bonds at their face value with a premium or discount account as described for the issuer, traditionally investors record their investment at cost, or net of any premium or discount. Cost includes brokerage fees and any other costs incident to the purchase. Bonds acquired in exchange for noncash assets or services are recorded at the fair market value of the bonds, unless the value of the exchanged assets or services is more clearly determinable. When bonds and other securities are acquired for a lump sum, an apportionment of such cost among the securities is required. Purchase of bonds on a deferred payment basis calls for recognition of both the asset and the liability balances.

When bonds are issued or sold between interest dates, an adjustment is made for the interest accrued between the last interest payment date and the date of the transaction. A buyer of the bonds adds the amount of accrued interest to the purchase price and then receives this payment back plus interest earned subsequent to the purchase date when the next interest payment is made. This practice avoids the problem an issuer of bonds would have in trying to split interest payments for a given period between two or more owners of the securities. For example, if the interest dates of 10% bonds are March 1 and September 1, and $600,000 of bonds are sold at par on May 1, the two months' interest from March 1 to May 1 of $10,000

---

[1]*Opinions of the Accounting Principles Board, No. 21,* "Interest on Receivables and Payables" (New York: American Institute of Certified Public Accountants, 1971), par. 16.

[2]*Statement of Financial Accounting Concepts No. 3,* "Elements of Financial Statements of Business Enterprises" (Stamford: Financial Accounting Standards Board, December 1980), par. 161.

would be added to the amount paid by the investor to the issuer. When the September 1 payment of $30,000 is made to the investor, the $10,000 is offset against the $30,000 received, and the net difference of $20,000 is reported as interest earned for the period from May 1 to September 1. Similarly, $20,000 is reported as interest expense by the issuer. The $10,000 interest payment may be debited to Interest Receivable on the investor's books and credited to Interest Payable on the issuer's books as shown below:

Issuer's Books

May 1	Cash	510,000	
	Bonds Payable		500,000
	Interest Payable		10,000
Sept. 1	Interest Payable	10,000	
	Interest Expense	20,000	
	Cash		30,000

Investor's Books

May 1	Interest Receivable	10,000	
	Investment in Bonds	500,000	
	Cash		510,000
Sept. 1	Cash	30,000	
	Interest Receivable		10,000
	Interest Revenue		20,000

Alternatively, as illustrated in the example below, the accrued interest could be initially credited to Interest Expense by the issuer and debited to Interest Revenue by the investor.

To further illustrate the accounting for bond issuance, assume a 10-year, $200,000, 8% bond issue is sold at 103, on May 1. Interest payment dates are February 1 and August 1. The entries on the books of the issuer and the investor would be as follows:

Issuer's Books

May 1	Cash	210,000	
	Bonds Payable		200,000
	Premium on Bonds		6,000
	Interest Expense		4,000
	To record issuance of bonds.		

Computation:
$200,000 × 1.03 = $206,000 purchase price.
Interest: $200,000 × .08 × 3/12 = $4,000

Investor's Books

May 1	Investment in Bonds	206,000	
	Interest Revenue	4,000	
	Cash		210,000
	To record investment in bonds.		

A 360-day year (12 months, 30 days per month) was assumed in the illustration for convenience. With the aid of computers, a 365-day year is increasingly being used for bond accounting.

When bonds are issued in exchange for property, the transaction should be recorded at the cash price at which the bonds could be issued. When difficulties are encountered in arriving at a cash price, the market or appraised value of the property acquired would be used. A difference between the face value of the bonds and the cash value of the bonds or the value of the property acquired is recognized as bond discount or bond premium.

BOND INTEREST

When coupon bonds are issued, cash is paid by the company in exchange for interest coupons on the interest dates. Payments on coupons may be made by the company directly to bondholders, or payments may be cleared through a bank or other disbursing agent. Subsidiary records with bondholders are not maintained since coupons are redeemable by bearers. In the case of registered bonds, interest checks are mailed either by the company or its agent. When bonds are registered, the bonds account requires subsidiary ledger support. The subsidiary ledger shows holdings by individuals and changes in such holdings. Checks are sent to bondholders of record as of the interest payment dates.

When an agent is to make interest payments, the company normally transfers cash to the agent in advance of the interest payment date. Since the company is not freed from its obligation to bondholders until payment has been made by its agent, it records the cash transfer by a debit to Cash Deposited with Agent for Bond Interest and a credit to Cash. On the date the interest is due, the company debits Interest Expense and credits Interest Payable. Upon receipt from the agent of paid interest coupons, a certificate of coupon receipt and appropriate disposal, or other evidence that the interest was paid, the company debits Interest Payable and credits Cash Deposited with Agent for Bond Interest.

Amortization of Premium or Discount

When bonds are issued at a premium or discount, the market acts to adjust the stated interest rate to a market or effective interest rate. Because of the initial premium or discount, the periodic interest payments made over the bond life by the issuer to the investors do not represent the complete revenue and expense for the periods involved. An adjustment to the cash transfer for the periodic write-off of the premium or discount is necessary to reflect the effective interest rate being incurred or earned on the bonds, and is referred to as **bond premium** or **discount amortization**. The periodic adjustment of bonds results in a gradual adjustment of the carrying value toward the bond's face value.

A premium on issued bonds recognizes that the stated interest rate is higher than the market interest rate. Amortization of the premium reduces the interest revenue or expense below the amount of cash transferred. A discount on issued bonds recognizes that the stated interest rate is lower than the market interest rate. Amortization of the discount increases the amount of interest revenue or expense above the amount of cash transferred.

Two principal methods are used to amortize the premium or discount: (1) the straight-line method and (2) the interest method.

Straight-Line Method. The straight-line method provides for the recognition of an equal amount of premium or discount amortization each period. The amount of monthly amortization is determined by dividing the premium or discount at purchase or issuance by the number of months remaining to the bond maturity date. For example, if a 10-year, 10% bond issue with a maturity value of $200,000 were sold on the issuance date at 103, the $6,000 premium would be amortized evenly over the 120 months until maturity, or at a rate of $50 per month, ($6,000 ÷ 120). If the bonds were sold three months after the issuance date, the $6,000 premium would be amortized evenly over 117 months, or a rate of $51.28 per month, ($6,000 ÷ 117). The amortization period is always the time from original sale to maturity. The premium amortization would reduce both interest expense on the issuer's books and interest revenue on the investor's books. A discount amortization would have the opposite results: both accounts would be increased.

It is necessary to set some arbitrary minimum time unit in the straight-line amortization of bond premium or bond discount. The month is used in this text as the minimum unit. Transactions occurring during the first half of the month are treated as though they were made at the beginning of the month; transactions occurring during the second half are treated as though made at the start of the following month. Use of a longer term, such as the quarter or half year, is possible, although this offers less accuracy than the use of a shorter time unit.

Interest Method. The interest method of amortization uses a uniform interest rate based upon a changing investment balance and provides for an increasing premium or discount amortization each period. In order to use this method, the effective interest rate for the bonds must first be determined. This is the rate of interest at bond issuance that discounts the maturity value of the bonds and the periodic interest payments to the market price of the bonds. This rate is used to determine the effective revenue or expense to be recorded on the books.

For example, as shown on page 399, $100,000, 10-year, 8% bonds sold to return 10% would sell for $87,539, or at a discount of $12,461. If the bonds were sold on the issuance date, the straight-line discount amortization for each six month period would be $623.05 [($100,000 − $87,539) ÷ 20]. The discount amortization for the first six months using the interest method would be computed as follows:

Investment balance at beginning of first period...	$87,539
Effective rate per semiannual period..	5%
Stated rate per semiannual period	4%
Interest amount based on effective rate ($87,539 × .05)	$ 4,377
Interest payment based on stated rate ($100,000 × .04)....................................	4,000
Difference between interest amount based on effective rate and stated rate ..	$ 377

This difference is the discount amortization for the first period using the interest method. For the second semiannual period, the bond carrying value increases by the discount amortization. The amortization for the second semiannual period would be computed as follows:

Investment balance at beginning of second period ($87,539 + $377)...............	**$87,916**
Interest amount based on effective rate ($87,916 × .05)	$ 4,396
Interest payment based on stated rate ($100,000 × .04)...................................	4,000
Difference between interest amount based on effective rate and stated rate ..	$ 396

The amount of interest for each period is computed at a uniform rate on an increasing balance. This results in an increasing discount amortization over the life of the bonds that is graphically demonstrated and compared with straight line amortization below.

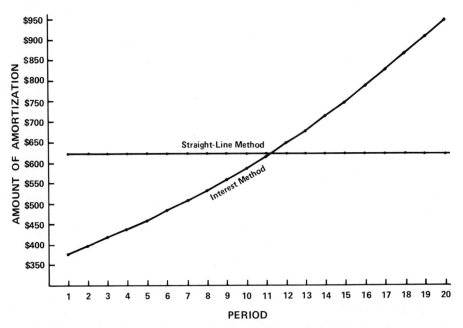

Premium amortization would be computed in a similar way except that the interest amount based on the stated interest rate would be higher than the amount based on the effective rate. For example, $100,000, 10-year, 8% bonds sold to return 6% would sell for $114,880, or at a premium of $14,880. If the bonds were sold on the issuance date, the premium amortization for the first and second six-month periods would be computed as follows:

Investment balance at beginning of first period...	**$114,880**
Effective rate per semiannual period..	3%
Stated rate per semiannual period..	4%
Interest payment based on stated rate ($100,000 × .04).................................	$ 4,000
Interest amount based on effective rate ($114,880 × .03)................................	3,446
Difference between interest amount based on stated rate and effective rate, or premium amortization	$ 554

Investment balance at beginning of second period ($114,880 − $554).......... $114,326

Interest payment based on stated rate ($100,000 × .04)................................ $ 4,000
Interest amount based on effective rate ($114,326 × .03)............................... 3,430

Difference between interest amount based on stated rate and effective rate $ 570

As illustrated, as the investment or liability balance is reduced by the premium amortization, the interest based upon the effective rate also decreases. The difference between the interest payment and the interest based upon the effective rate increases in a manner similar to discount amortization. Special bond amortization tables, such as the partial one illustrated below, may be prepared to determine the periodic adjustments to the bond carrying value.

Amortization of Premium — Interest Method
$100,000, 10-Year Bonds, Interest at 8% Payable Semiannually,
Sold at $114,880 to Yield 6%

Interest Payment	A Interest Paid (4% of Face Value)	B Interest Expense (3% of Bond Carrying Value)	C Premium Amortization (A − B)	D Unamortized Premium (D − C)	E Bond Carrying Value ($100,000 + D)
				$14,880	$114,880
1	$4,000	$3,446 (3% of $114,880)	$554	14,326	114,326
2	4,000	3,430 (3% of 114,326)	570	13,756	113,756
3	4,000	3,413 (3% of 113,756)	587	13,169	113,169
4	4,000	3,395 (3% of 113,169)	605	12,564	112,564
5	4,000	3,377 (3% of 112,564)	623	11,941	111,941
6	4,000	3,358 (3% of 111,941)	642	11,299	111,299
7	4,000	3,339 (3% of 111,299)	661	10,638	110,638
8	4,000	3,319 (3% of 110,638)	681	9,957	109,957
9	4,000	3,299 (3% of 109,957)	701	9,256	109,256
10	4,000	3,278 (3% of 109,256)	722	8,534	108,534
.	.	.	.	.	.
.	.	.	.	.	.
.	.	.	.	.	.

Because the interest method adjusts the stated interest rate to an effective interest rate, it is theoretically more accurate as an amortization method than is the straight-line method. Since the issuance of APB Opinion No. 21, the effective interest method is the recommended amortization method. The more popular straight-line method may be used by a company if the results of using it do not differ materially from the amortization using the interest method.[3]

Accounting for Bond Interest

Entries for premium or discount amortization may be made as adjusting entries at the end of a company's fiscal year or interim period, or as each interest payment is made. The accounting entries for bond interest and first

---

[3]*Opinions of the Accounting Principles Board, No. 21,* "Interest on Receivables and Payables" (New York: American Institute of Certified Public Accountants, 1972), par. 15.

year discount amortization on both the issuer's and investor's books would be as follows. Assume the bonds are issued at a discount as described on page 403, and the discount is amortized by the interest method when each payment is made or received.

Issuer's Books

First payment:	Interest Expense..	4,377	
	Cash..		4,000
	Discount on Bonds Payable....................................		377
Second payment:	Interest Expense..	4,396	
	Cash..		4,000
	Discount on Bonds Payable....................................		396

Investor's Books

First payment:	Cash..	4,000	
	Investment in Bonds......................................	377	
	Interest Revenue		4,377
Second payment:	Cash..	4,000	
	Investment in Bonds......................................	396	
	Interest Revenue...		4,396

If the bonds were sold at a premium, the investment or liability balance would be reduced over the life of the bonds to maturity value. Assume a 10-year, $200,000, 8% bond issue is sold at 103 on May 1 and is recorded as shown on page 401. Interest payment dates are February 1 and August 1, and the straight-line method of amortization is used. The following entries on both the issuer's and investor's books for the first year would be required. (Adjusting entries at the end of fiscal year are not included.)

Issuer's Books

Aug. 1	Interest Expense...	7,846
	Premium on Bonds Payable	154
	Cash	8,000

Computation:
Premium amortization for 3 months:
$6,000/117 = $51.28 per month
$51.28 × 3 = $153.84, or $154

Feb. 1	Interest Expense...	7,692
	Premium on Bonds Payable	308
	Cash	8,000

Computation:
Premium amortization for 6 months:
$51.28 × 6 = $307.68, or $308

Investor's Books

Aug. 1 Cash...	8,000	
Investment in Bonds...		154
Interest Revenue		7,846
Feb. 1 Cash...	8,000	
Investment in Bonds...		308
Interest Revenue		7,692

When bonds are acquired as a temporary investment, investment cost is maintained in the accounts without adjustment for premium or discount amortization. Any difference between the purchase and sales price is recognized as a gain or loss at the time of the sale.

BOND TRANSFERS BETWEEN INVESTORS

Bonds are negotiable, and thus may be sold on the market after purchase. As explained earlier, any accrued interest is paid for by the purchaser, thus giving the seller interest revenue for the period the investment was held. For example, assume Alco, Inc. owns Jessup Co. bonds with a maturity value of $100,000 and a carrying value of $98,000. Accrued interest of $2,500 is due on the bonds at the date of sale to Majestic, Inc. The bonds are sold at 99 plus accrued interest. The following entries on the seller's and buyer's books would be made.

Alco, Inc. (Seller)

Cash	101,500	
Investment in Jessup Co. Bonds		98,000
Interest Revenue		2,500
Gain on Sale of Bond Investment		1,000

Majestic, Inc. (Buyer)

Investment in Jessup Co. Bonds	99,000	
Interest Revenue	2,500	
Cash		101,500

CONVERSION OF BONDS

Convertible bonds grant to an investor the right to convert debt to equity under certain conditions. The conversion privilege is granted when the bonds are sold, but the value of the conversion privilege is normally combined with the cost of the debt instrument. When conversion takes place, a special valuation question must be answered. Should the market value of the securities be used to compute a gain or loss on the transaction? If the security is viewed as debt, then the conversion to equity would seem to be a significant economic transaction and a gain or loss would be recognized. If, however, the security is viewed as equity, the conversion is really an exchange of one type of equity capital for another, and the historical cost principle would seem to indicate that no gain or loss would be recognized. In practice, the latter approach seems to be most commonly followed by both the issuer and investor of the bonds. No gain or loss is recognized either for book or tax purposes. The book value of the bonds is transferred to become the book value of the stock issued.

If an investor viewed the security as debt, conversion of the debt could be viewed as an exchange of one asset for another. The general rule for the exchange of nonmonetary assets is that the market value of the asset exchanged should be used to measure any gain or loss on the transaction.[4] If there is no market value of the asset surrendered or if its value is undeter-

---

[4]*Opinions of Accounting Principles Board, No. 29,* "Accounting for Nonmonetary Transactions" (New York: American Institute of Certified Public Accountants, 1973), par. 18.

minable, the market value of the asset received should be used. The market value of convertible bonds should reflect the market value of the stock to be issued on the conversion, and thus the market value of the two securities should be similar. Before an exchange is recorded, the investment account should be brought up to date for premium or discount amortization.

To illustrate bond conversion for the investor recognizing a gain or loss on conversion, assume Carl Co. offers bondholders 40 shares of Carl Co. common stock, $25 par, in exchange for each $1,000, 8% bond held. An investor exchanges bonds of $10,000 (book value as brought up to date, $9,850) for 400 shares of common stock having a market price at the time of the exchange of $26 per share. The exchange is completed three months after an interest payment date. The exchange is recorded as follows:

Cash	200	
Investment in Carl Co. Common Stock	10,400	
Investment in Carl Co. Bonds		9,850
Gain on Conversion of Carl Co. Bonds		550
Interest Revenue		200

If the investor chose not to recognize a gain or loss, the journal entry would be as follows:

Cash	200	
Investment in Carl Co. Common Stock	9,850	
Investment in Carl Co. Bonds		9,850
Interest Revenue		200

Similar differences would occur on the issuer's books depending upon the viewpoint assumed. If the issuer desired to recognize the conversion of the convertible debt as a significant transaction, the market value of the securities would be used to record the conversion. To illustrate the journal entries for the issuer using this reasoning, assume 100 bonds, face value $1,000, are exchanged for 2,000 shares of common stock, $40 par value, $55 market value. At the time of the conversion, there is an unamortized premium on the bond issue of $3,000. The conversion would be recorded as follows:

Bonds Payable	100,000	
Premium on Bonds Payable	3,000	
Loss on Conversion of Bonds	7,000	
Common Stock		80,000
Premium on Common Stock		30,000

Computation:

Market value of stock issued (2,000 shares at $55)		$110,000
Face value of bonds payable	$100,000	
Plus unamortized premium	3,000	103,000
Loss to company on conversion of bonds		$ 7,000

If the issuer did not consider the conversion as a culminating transaction, no gain or loss would be recognized. The bond carrying value would be transferred to the capital stock account on the theory that the company upon issuing the bonds is aware of the fact that bond proceeds may ultimately represent the consideration identified with stock. Thus, when bondholders exercise their conversion privileges, the value identified with the obligation is transferred to the security that replaces it. Under this assumption, the conversion would be recorded as follows:

Bonds Payable..	100,000	
Premium on Bonds Payable...	3,000	
Common Stock, $40 par		80,000
Premium on Common Stock		23,000

The profession has not resolved the accounting issues surrounding convertible debt. Although the practice of not recognizing gain or loss on either the issuer's or the investor's books is widespread, it seems inconsistent with the treatment of other items that are transferred by an entity. The economic reality of the transaction would seem to require a recognition of the change in value at least at the time conversion takes place. The movement toward the use of current values in the accounts would require recognition of gains or losses on these securities at even earlier dates if the market reflected a change in value.

TERMINATION OF BONDS

Bonds always include a specified termination or maturity date. At that time, the issuer must pay the current investor the maturity or face value of the bond. Bonds may be terminated earlier than the maturity date in one of two ways: (1) the issuer may **reacquire** individual bonds on the market and retire them, or (2) the issuer may utilize the call provision frequently included in bond indentures and **redeem** all or part of the issue prior to maturity. The following sections discuss the special accounting problems for both the issuer and the investor dealing with termination of bonds.

Bond Retirement at Maturity

Most bond issues are payable at the end of a specified period. When bond discount or premium and issue cost balances have been satisfactorily amortized over the life of the bonds, bond retirement simply calls for elimination of the liability or the investment by a cash transaction. Any bonds not presented for payment at their maturity date should be removed from the bonds payable balance on the issuer's books and reported separately as Matured Bonds Payable; these are reported as a current liability except when they are to be paid out of a sinking fund. Interest does not accrue on matured bonds not presented for payment.

If a bond fund is used to pay off a bond issue, any cash remaining in the fund may be returned to the cash account. Appropriations of retained earnings established during the life of the issue may be returned to retained earnings.

Bond Reacquisition Prior to Maturity

Corporations frequently reacquire their own bonds on the market when prices or other factors make such action desirable. Reacquisition of bonds prior to their maturity calls for the recognition of a gain or a loss for the difference between the bond carrying value and the amount paid.[5] This gain or loss is classified as an **early extinguishment of debt**, and according to FASB Statement No. 4, is reported as an extraordinary item on the income statement.[6] Payment of accrued interest on bond reacquisition is separately reported as a debit to Interest Expense.

When bonds are reacquired, amortization of bond premium, discount, and issue costs should be brought up to date. Reacquisition calls for the cancellation of the bond face value together with any related premium, discount, or issue costs as of the reacquisition date.

When bonds are reacquired and canceled, Bonds Payable is debited. When bonds are reacquired but are held for possible future reissue, Treasury Bonds instead of Bonds Payable may be debited. Treasury bonds are evidence of a liquidated liability. Although treasury bonds may represent a ready source of cash, their sale creates new creditors, a situation that is no different from the debt created by any other type of borrowing. Treasury bonds, then, should be recorded at their face value and subtracted from the bonds payable balance in reporting bonds issued and outstanding. If treasury bonds are sold at a price other than face value, Cash is debited, Treasury Bonds is credited, thus reinstating the bond liability, and a premium or a discount on the sale is recorded, the latter balance to be amortized over the remaining life of this specific bond group. While held, treasury bonds occupy the same legal status as unissued bonds. At the maturity of the bond issue, any balance in a treasury bonds account is applied against Bonds Payable.

To illustrate bond reacquisition, assume $100,000, 8% bonds of Atlas, Inc., are not held until maturity, but are sold back to the issuer on February 1, 1983, at 97 plus accrued interest. The book value of the bonds on both the issuer's and investor's books is $97,700 as of January 1. Discount amortization has been recorded at $50 a month using the straight-line method. Interest payment dates on the bonds are November 1 and May 1; accrued interest adjustments are reversed. Entries on both the issuer's and investor's books at the time of bond redemption would be as follows:

Issuer's Books

Feb. 1	Interest Expense	50	
	Discount on Bonds Payable		50
	To record discount amortization for January, 1983.		
1	Bonds Payable (*or* Treasury Bonds)	100,000	
	Interest Expense	2,000	
	Discount on Bonds Payable		2,250
	Cash		99,000
	Gain on Bond Reacquisition		750
	To record reacquisition of bonds and payment of three months' interest.		

[5]*Opinions of the Accounting Principles Board, No. 26*, "Early Extinguishment of Debt" (New York: American Institute of Certified Public Accountants, 1972), par. 20.

[6]*Statement of Financial Accounting Standards No. 4*, "Reporting Gains and Losses from Extinguishment of Debt" (Stamford: Financial Accounting Standards Board, 1975), par. 8.

Computation:

Book value of bonds, January 1, 1983	$97,700
Discount amortization for January	50
Book value of bonds, February 1, 1983	$97,750
Reacquisition Price	97,000
Gain on reacquisition	$ 750

Interest expense for 3 months:
$100,000 × .08 × ¼ = $2,000

Investor's Books

Feb. 1	Investment in Atlas, Inc., Bonds	50	
	Interest Revenue		50
	To record discount amortization for January, 1983.		
1	Cash	99,000	
	Loss on Call of Bonds	750	
	Investment in Atlas, Inc., Bonds		97,750
	Interest Revenue		2,000
	To record surrender of bonds and receipt of three month's interest.		

Bond Redemption Prior to Maturity

Provisions of a bond indenture frequently give the issuer the option of calling bonds for payment prior to maturity. Ordinarily the call must be made on an interest payment date, and no further interest accrues on the bonds not presented at this time. When only a part of an issue is to be retired, the bonds called may be determined by lot.

The inclusion of call provisions in a bond agreement is a feature favoring the issuer. The company is in a position to terminate the bond agreement and eliminate future interest charges whenever its financial position makes such action feasible. Furthermore, the company is protected in the event of a fall in the market interest rate by being able to retire the old issue from proceeds of a new issue paying a lower rate of interest. A bond contract normally requires payment of a premium if bonds are called. A bondholder is thus offered special compensation if the investment is terminated.

When bonds are called, the difference between the amount paid and the bond carrying value is reported as a gain or a loss on both the issuer's and investor's books. Any interest paid at the time of the call is recorded as a debit to Interest Expense on the issuer's books and a credit to Interest Revenue on the investor's books. The entries to be made are the same as illustrated previously for the sale and reacquisition of bonds.

When an investor acquires callable bonds at a premium, conservatism calls for an amortization policy that prevents the bonds from being reported at more than their redemption values at the various call dates. To illustrate, assume bonds of $10,000 are acquired for $10,800 on January 1, 1982. The bonds were originally issued on January 1, 1980, and have a maturity date of January 1, 2000. The following table of redemption values is included in the indenture.

Redeemable January 1, 1985, to December 31, 1989, at 105
Redeemable January 1, 1990, to December 31, 1994, at 102½
Redeemable January 1, 1995, to December 31, 1999, at 101

Regular premium amortization and accelerated amortization based upon bond redemption values of $10,500, $10,250 and $10,100, are compared below:

Regular Amortization	Accelerated Amortization
$800 ÷ 18 years = $44.44 per year (1982–2000)	($10,800 − $10,500) ÷ 3 years (1982–1984) = $100 per year ($10,500 − $10,250) ÷ 5 years (1985–1989) = $ 50 per year ($10,250 − $10,100) ÷ 5 years (1990–1994) = $ 30 per year ($10,100 − $10,000) ÷ 5 years (1995–1999) = $ 20 per year

If regular amortization procedures are followed on the books of the investor, bond redemption prior to maturity will result in a recovery of cash that is less than bond carrying value and will require recognition of a loss that nullifies in part the earnings recognized in the past. Accelerated amortization reduces the investment to its redemption value; bond redemption values are used for income measurement purposes and the need for recognition of a loss upon redemption is avoided. Obviously, bonds reported at a discount, or bonds reported at a premium reduced by normal amortization to an amount that is not greater than redemption value, require no special treatment.

VALUATION OF BONDS AND LONG-TERM NOTES

Thus far, no reference has been made in this chapter to adjusting investments and liabilities when the debt or investment valuation differs from cost. In Chapter 12, accounting for declines in value of long-term equity securities was presented. There it was noted that temporary declines in the market value of equity securities are recognized on the books of the investor by a debit to an equity offset account and by a credit to an allowance account. Permanent declines are recognized by a debit to a recognized loss account on the income statement and a credit to the Investment account. Debt instruments were not explicitly included in FASB Statement No. 12. However, if a market decline in debt securities is deemed to be permanent, and it is probable that the maturity value will not be paid when due, entries similar to those made for permanent declines in equity securities are normally made on the investor's books. If the market declines are considered temporary, no accounting entries are usually made, but the decline in value is recognized in a note to the financial statements. Entries likewise are not made to reflect increases in the market values of bond investments. Changes in the market value of the liability are ignored by the issuer.

REPORTING OF LONG-TERM DEBT ON THE BALANCE SHEET

Bond and long-term note accounts are frequently very significant items on the balance sheet of both the investor and the issuer. Generally, they are reported in the noncurrent section; however, under some circumstances they may be reported as current items. The valuation and reporting problems for the investor and issuer will be considered separately.

Reporting Bonds and Long-Term Notes as Investments

The market value of long-term debt varies with changes in the financial strength of the issuing company, changes in the level of interest rates, and shrinkage in the remaining life of the issue. In the absence of material price declines, bonds held as long-term investments are reported on the balance sheet at book value. This book value approaches par as the bonds move closer to maturity. To this extent, then, the accounting can be considered to follow a similar change that is taking place on the market as the bond life is reduced and a correspondingly lower valuation is attached to the difference between the actual rate and the market rate of remaining interest payments. Although investments are usually reported at book value, parenthetical disclosure of the aggregate market value of the securities makes the financial statements more informative.

Data relative to bond investments might be reported as follows:

Long-term investments:

Investment in Golden Corp. Long-Term Note, 11%, $50,000 face value, due July 1, 1985. (Market value, $48,500 at December 31, 1981).....................................	$ 50,000
Investment in Wilkins Co. Bonds; 10%, $1,000,000 face value, due July 1, 1992 (reported at cost as adjusted for amortized discount)...	982,500

Reporting Bonds and Long-Term Notes as Liabilities

In reporting long-term debt on the balance sheet, the nature of the liabilities, maturity dates, interest rates, methods of liquidation, conversion privileges, borrowing restrictions, and other significant matters should be indicated. For an example of a note describing long-term debt, see Note Five to General Mills Financial Statements, Appendix B.

Bond liabilities may be reported on a balance sheet as of December 31, 1981, as follows:

Current liabilities:

Serial 10% debenture bonds, installment due May 1, 1982		$ 10,000
Long-term liabilities:		
5-year, 12% notes outstanding, due January 1, 1984........		100,000
20-year 9% first-mortgage bonds outstanding, due January 1, 1993...	$210,000	
Less unamortized bond discount...................................	4,500	205,500
Serial 10% debenture bonds, due May 1, 1983 to May 1, 1992, inclusive		100,000

QUESTIONS

1. What factors should be considered in determining whether cash should be raised by the issue of bonds or by the sale of additional stock?

2. Distinguish between (a) secured and unsecured bonds, (b) collateral trust and debenture bonds, (c) guaranteed bonds and income bonds, (d) convertible bonds and callable bonds, (e) coupon bonds and registered bonds and (f) municipal bonds and corporate bonds.

3. What is meant by bond market rate, stated or contract rate, and effective rate? Which of these rates changes during the lifetime of the bond issue?

4. How should bond issuance costs be accounted for on the issuer's books?

5. An investor purchases bonds with a face value of $100,000. Payment for the bonds includes (a) a premium, (b) accrued interest, and (c) brokerage fees. How would each of these charges be recorded and what disposition would ultimately be made of each of these charges?

6. Distinguish between straight-line and interest methods of bond premium amortization. What arguments can be offered in support of each method?

7. The interest method of bond premium or discount amortization is not desirable for the issuer because it results in higher net income than would be found with straight-line amortization. Under what conditions would this be true?

8. The conversion of convertible bonds to common stock by an investor may be viewed as an exchange involving no gain or loss, or as a transaction for which market values should be recognized and a gain or loss reported. What arguments support each of these views for the investor and for the issuer?

9. What is the difference between bond reacquisition and bond redemption?

10. What purpose is served by using callable bonds? What effect does a call feature have upon the amortization of a bond premium?

11. How should bonds recorded as long-term investments be adjusted for price changes in periods subsequent to their purchase so that their valuation will be in accordance with GAAP?

EXERCISES

exercise 14-1

What is the market value of each of the following bond issues? Round to the nearest dollar.

(a) 10% bond of $50,000 sold on the bond issue date; 10-year life, interest payable semiannually, effective rate 12%.

(b) 9% bond of $200,000 sold on bond issue date; 20-year life, interest payable semiannually, effective rate 8%.

(c) 6% bond of $100,000 sold 30 months after bond issue date; 15-year life, interest payable semiannually, effective rate 10%.

exercise 14-2

The Aspen Co. has issued 10,000 shares of $100 par common stock. The company requires additional working capital and finds it can sell 6,000 additional shares of common at $70, or it can issue $420,000 of 9% bonds at par. Earnings of the company before income tax have been $100,000 annually, and it is expected that these will increase 20% (before additional interest charges) as a result of additional funds. Assuming that the income tax rate is estimated at 45%, which method of financing would you recommend as a common stockholder? Why? (Show calculations.)

exercise 14-3

The long-term debt section of Viking Company's balance sheet as of December 31, 1981, included 8% bonds payable of $100,000 less unamortized discount of $5,000. Further examination revealed that these bonds were issued to yield 10%. The amortization of the bond discount was recorded using the interest method. Interest was paid on January 1 and July 1 of each year. On July 1, 1982, Viking retired the bonds at 102 before maturity. Prepare the journal entries to record the July 1, 1982 payment of interest, the amortization of the discount since December 31, 1981, and the early retirement on the books of Viking Company.

exercise 14-4

Assume that $100,000 City School District 6% bonds are purchased on the bond issue date for $92,894. Interest is payable semiannually and the bonds mature in 10 years. The purchase price provides a return of 7% on the investment.

(1) What entries would be made on the investor's books for the receipt of the first two interest payments, assuming discount amortization on each interest date by (a) the straight-line method and (b) the interest method? Round to nearest dollar.
(2) What entries would be made on City School District's books to record the first two interest payments, assuming discount amortization on each interest date by (a) the straight-line method and (b) the interest method? Round to nearest dollar.

exercise 14-5

The ASA Corporation issued $100,000 of 8% debenture bonds on a basis to return 10%, receiving $92,278. Interest is payable semiannually and the bonds mature in 5 years.

(1) What entries would be made for the first two interest payments, assuming discount amortization on interest dates by (a) the straight-line method and (b) the interest method? Round to nearest dollar.
(2) If the sale is made on a 7% return, $104,158 being received, what entries would be made for the first two interest payments, assuming premium amortization on interest dates by (a) the straight-line method and (b) the interest method? Round to nearest dollar.
(3) What entries would be made on the books of the investor for the first two interest receipts assuming one party obtained all the bonds and the straight-line method of amortization was used? Round to nearest dollar.

exercise 14-6

L. Durfee acquired $80,000 of Bedrock Corp. 9% bonds on July 1, 1979. The bonds were acquired at 92; interest is paid semiannually on March 1 and September 1. The bonds mature September 1, 1986. Durfee's books are kept on a calendar year basis. On February 1, 1982, Durfee sold the bonds for 97 plus accrued interest. Assuming a straight-line discount amortization, give the entry to record the sale of the bonds on February 1. Round to the nearest dollar.

exercise 14-7

On December 1, 1979, the Taylor Company issues 10-year bonds of $200,000 at 104. Interest is payable on December 1 and June 1 at 10%. On April 1, 1981, the Taylor Company reacquires and retires 40 of its own $1,000 bonds at 98 plus accrued interest. The fiscal period for the Taylor Company is the calendar year. Prepare entries to record (a) the issuance of the bonds, (b) the interest payments and adjustments relating to the debt in 1980, (c) the reacquisition and retirement of bonds in 1981, and (d) the interest payments and adjustments relating to the debt in 1981. Round to the nearest dollar. Assume the premium is amortized on a straight-line basis.

exercise 14-8

On January 1, 1980, Tony Bell purchased $40,000 of Midwest Company 10% bonds at 108. Bonds are due on January 1, 1995, but can be redeemed by the company at earlier dates at premium values as follows:

January 1, 1988, to December 31, 1991, at 103
January 1, 1992, to December 31, 1994, at 101

(1) What alternatives does Bell have as to the method of recognizing the amortization of premium? Which is preferable? Why?
(2) What amortization amounts should Bell recognize over the life of the bond issue?

exercise 14-9

The December 31, 1981, balance sheet of Baylor Company includes the following items:

9% bonds payable due December 31, 1990..	$400,000
Premium on bonds payable..	10,800

The bonds were issued on December 31, 1980, at 103, with interest payable on June 30 and December 31 of each year. The straight-line method is used for premium amortization.

On March 1, 1982, Baylor retired $200,000 of these bonds at 98, plus accrued interest. Prepare the journal entries to record retirement of the bonds, including accrual of interest since the last payment and amortization of the premium.

exercise 14-10

For the Bectel Corporation, arrange the following information as you would present it on the balance sheet dated December 31, 1983.

(a) Investment in Holder Company 10% bonds, $100,000 face value, due July 1, 1987, (cost as adjusted for amortized premium $103,000) currently selling at 99.

(b) 20-year, 9% Bectel Corp., first-mortgage bonds, $500,000 face value, due January 1, 2000 (cost as adjusted for amortized discount $493,000).

(c) Investment in Stahman Corporation long-term notes, 12%, $60,000 face value, due September 1, 1989 (market value $63,000).

(d) Bectel Corporation, serial debenture bonds, 8%, last installment due July 1, 1984, $100,000 face value, carried on the books at par.

PROBLEMS

problem 14-1

Martin Products decided to issue $2,000,000 in 10-year bonds. The interest rate on the bonds is stated at 7%, payable semiannually. At the time the bonds were sold, the market rate had increased to 8%.

Instructions:

(1) Determine the maximum amount an investor should pay for these bonds. Round to the nearest dollar.

(2) Assuming that the amount in (1) is paid, compute the amount at which the bonds would be reported after being held for one year. Use two recognized methods of handling amortization of the difference in cost and maturity value of the bonds, and give support for the method you prefer. Round to the nearest dollar.

problem 14-2

Salter, Inc., was authorized to issue 8-year, 9% bonds of $500,000. The bonds are dated January 1, 1980, and interest is payble semiannually on January 1 and July 1. Checks for interest are mailed on June 30 and December 31. Bond sales were as follows:

April 1, 1980...$250,000 at 96 plus accrued interest.	
July 1, 1981..$150,000 at 102.	

On September 1, 1981, remaining unissued bonds were pledged as collateral on the issue of $84,000 of short-term notes.

Instructions:

(1) Give the journal entries relating to bonds that would appear on the corporation's books in 1980 and 1981. (Straight-line amortization is used. Adjustments are made annually.) Round to nearest dollar.

(2) Show how information relative to the bond issue will appear on the balance sheet prepared on December 31, 1981. (Give balance sheet section headings and accounts and account balances appearing within such sections.)

problem 14-3

The Young Co. acquired $20,000 of Mexico Sales Co. 7% bonds, interest payable semiannually, bonds maturing in 5 years. The bonds were acquired at $20,850, a price to return approximately 6%.

Instructions:
 (1) Prepare tables to show the periodic adjustments to the investment account and the annual bond earnings, assuming adjustment by each of the following methods: (a) the straight-line method, and (b) the interest method. Round to nearest dollar.
 (2) Assuming use of the interest method, give entries for the first year on the books of both companies.

problem 14-4

Bobco, Inc. issued $500,000 of 8-year, 12% notes payable dated April 1, 1981. Interest on the notes is payable semiannually on April 1 and October 1. The notes were sold on April 1, 1981, to an underwriter for $480,000 net of issuance costs. The notes were then offered for sale by the underwriter, and on July 1, 1981, Joan Farmer purchased the entire issue as a long-term investment. Farmer paid 101 plus accrued interest for the notes. On June 1, 1984, Farmer sold her investment in Bobco notes to Milo Barney as a short-term investment. Barney paid 96 plus accrued interest for the notes. He also paid $1,500 for brokerage fees. Farmer paid $1,000 broker's fees to sell the notes. Barney held his investment until April 1, 1985, when the notes were called at 102 by Bobco.

Instructions: Prepare all journal entries required on the books of Bobco, Inc. for 1981 and 1985; on the books of Farmer for 1981 and 1984; and on the books of Barney for 1984 and 1985. Assume each entity uses the calendar year for reporting purposes and that issue costs are netted against the note proceeds by Bobco. Any required amortization is made using the straight-line procedure at the end of each calendar year or when the bonds are transferred.

problem 14-5

In auditing the books for the Chemical Corporation as of December 31, 1981, before the accounts are closed, you find the following long-term investment account balance:

Account   Investment in Big Oil 9% Bonds (Maturity date, June 1, 1985)

Date		Item	Debit	Credit	Balance	
					Debit	Credit
1981						
Jan.	21	Bonds, $200,000 par, acquired at 102 plus accrued interest	206,550		206,550	
Mar.	1	Proceeds from sale of bonds, $100,000 par and accrued interest		106,000	100,550	
June	1	Interest received		4,500	96,050	
Nov.	1	Amount received on call of bonds, $40,000 par, at 101 and accrued interest		41,900	54,150	
Dec.	1	Interest received		2,700	51,450	

Instructions:
 (1) Give the entries that should have been made relative to the investment in bonds, including any adjusting entries that would be made on December 31, the end of the fiscal year. (Assume bond premium amortization by the straight-line method.)
 (2) Give the journal entries required at the end of 1981 to correct and bring the accounts up to date in view of the entries actually made.

problem 14-6

Johnson Company issued $1,000,000 of 10%, 10-year debentures on January 1, 1976. Interest is payable on January 1 and July 1. The entire issue was sold on April 1, 1976, at 102 plus accrued interest. On April 1, 1981, $500,000 of the bond issue was reacquired and retired at 99 plus accrued interest. On June 30, 1981, the remaining bonds were reacquired at 96 plus accrued interest and refunded with $400,000, 8% bonds issue sold at 100.

> **Instructions:** Give the journal entries for 1976 and 1981 (through June 30) on the Johnson Company books. The company's books are kept on a calendar year basis. Round to nearest dollar. Assume straight-line amortization of premium.

problem 14-7

On May 1, 1978, the Timp Co. acquired $40,000 of XYZ Corp. 9% bonds at 97 plus accrued interest. Interest on bonds is payable semiannually on March 1 and September 1, and bonds mature on September 1, 1981.

On May 1, 1979, the Timp Co. sold bonds of $12,000 for 103 plus accrued interest.

On July 1, 1980, bonds of $16,000 were exchanged for 2,250 shares of XYZ Corp. no-par common, quoted on the market on this date at $8. Interest was received on bonds to date of exchange.

On September 1, 1981, remaining bonds were redeemed.

> **Instructions:** Give journal entries for 1978–1981 to record the foregoing transactions on the books of the Timp Co., including any adjustments that are required at the end of each fiscal year ending on December 31. Assume bond discount amortization by the straight-line method. (Show all calculations.)

15

Accounting for Income Taxes

CHAPTER OBJECTIVES

Describe intraperiod income tax allocation assuming level rates.

Describe and illustrate interperiod income tax allocation assuming nonchanging income tax rates.

Describe alternate accounting methods for reporting investment tax credits, including the treatment of unused investment tax credits.

Describe and illustrate the disclosure of income taxes in the financial statements.

Accounting for federal and state income taxes has become an increasingly complex topic for the accounting profession. A direct tax based upon income has become a chief source of revenue for both federal and state governments. Although the first income tax was levied by the federal government during the Civil War, it was not until the Constitution was amended in 1913 by the 16th Amendment that the legality of such a tax was established. The tax rates were sufficiently low in the first years after the 16th Amendment that not too much attention was paid to this new tax outlay for individuals and businesses. However, as the services provided by governments have expanded, the rates have increased and the significance of income taxes on personal and business decision making has greatly expanded.

NATURE OF INCOME TAXES

Theoretically, income taxes could be viewed as either an expense of operating a business or as a distribution of profit between the governmental unit and the owners of the business. The private enterprise philosophy of the United States has led to an acceptance of the former view; income tax is a levy placed by a government on all businesses and thus it is a necessary expense of doing business within our society.

Although the federal income tax is the most significant income tax in most cases, state and local income taxes are also generally an important expense outlay. Many states and local governments pattern their income tax regulations after the federal government. This simplifies the preparation of income tax returns for businesses and permits more efficient tax planning. Although the emphasis in this chapter will be on the federal tax, accounting for state and local income taxes would be handled in a similar manner with variations depending upon the particular state laws involved.

Because income taxes affect almost every business entity, accounting for income taxes has widespread interest. The federal tax laws and regulations are complex, and specialists in income tax are usually employed to do the tax planning and tax return preparation. The purpose of this chapter is not to discuss the income tax laws specifically, except as they might have an impact upon the timing of tax payments. Most problems in accounting for income tax may be divided into three categories.

1. Accounting for intraperiod income tax allocation
2. Accounting for interperiod income tax allocation
3. Accounting for the investment tax credit

Each of these areas will be discussed in the remainder of this chapter.

INTRAPERIOD INCOME TAX ALLOCATION

Because income tax is related specifically to revenue and expense items, the reporting of the income tax should be directly related to the items involved. If all current revenues and expenses were directly related to continuing operations, the total income tax expense for the period would be reported as a single amount and deducted from "Income from continuing operations before income taxes." However, the income statement has several major divisions. These include income from continuing operations, income from discontinued operations, extraordinary items, and cumulative effects of accounting changes. Each of these items is usually included in taxable income, either as an addition or deduction. While the details of the special items are discussed in Chapter 18, the procedures for allocating total income tax expense for the period among the various components of income will be presented in this chapter. This allocation is referred to as **intraperiod tax allocation**.

To illustrate the concept of intraperiod tax allocation, assume that a firm has a $70,000 gain on the early retirement of long-term debt which must be reported as an extraordinary item according to generally accepted accounting principles. The gain would also be reported as income for income tax purposes, and a tax would be paid. The intraperiod tax allocation principle requires that the gain and the amount of income tax related to the gain on retirement be reported together in the income statement. If the tax rate were 40%, the disclosure might be shown as follows:

Extraordinary gain from early debt retirement	$70,000	
Less income tax on gain	28,000	$42,000

An alternative method of disclosure shows the amount of tax parenthetically as follows:

Extraordinary gain (net of $28,000 income tax)	$42,000

In either case, the income tax on ordinary operations would not include the tax on the extraordinary gain.

If the special item is a loss, such as a loss from discontinued operations that must be separately disclosed, the reduction in income tax arising from the loss is applied to reduce the loss in a similar way as the tax was applied to the gain to reduce its impact. Thus, if the loss on the sale of a discontinued division were $40,000, the special item might be disclosed as follows:

Loss from discontinued operations (net of $16,000 tax reduction on loss)	$24,000

When a prior period adjustment is reported as a direct adjustment to Retained Earnings, the related tax effect should be disclosed in the statement of retained earnings. To illustrate, assume that a company discovers in 1982 that depreciation for 1980 was overstated by $30,000 and the related increase in income tax is 40 percent or $12,000. The adjustment could be presented in the statement of retained earnings as follows:

Retained earnings, January 1, 1982, as previously reported	$210,000
Add:	
Prior period adjustment for overstatement of depreciation expense for 1980 (net of $12,000 increase in income tax payable)	18,000
Adjusted retained earnings, January 1, 1982	$228,000

Intraperiod Income Tax Allocation Assuming a Level Tax Rate

Income tax rates usually are graduated and increase as income increases. The federal corporate tax is currently a five-level tax as follows:

Income	Tax Rate	Income Tax
First $25,000	17%	$ 4,250
Second $25,000	20%	5,000
Third $25,000	30%	7,500
Fourth $25,000	40%	10,000
Income tax on first $100,000 of income		$26,750
Over $100,000	46%	

To simplify the following discussion, it will be assumed that the income tax rate is 40% and is constant over all income. Assume that examination of Springer Corporation's income tax return for 1981 revealed the following information before computation of the tax.

Income from continuing operations	$225,000
Income from discontinued operations	62,000
Loss on sale of segment of business	(100,000)
Extraordinary loss from earthquake	(50,000)
Taxable income	$137,000

Applying the 40% tax rate, the income tax of $54,800 ($137,000 × .40) would be allocated as follows:

Income tax on income from continuing operations ($225,000 × .40)	$90,000
Income tax on income from discontinued operations ($62,000 × .40)	24,800
Income tax reduction from loss on disposal of a business segment ($100,000 × .40)	(40,000)
Income tax reduction from extraordinary loss ($50,000 × .40)	(20,000)
Income taxes payable for current year	$54,800

The journal entry to record the computations on the books would be as follows:[1]

Income Tax on Income from Continuing Operations	90,000	
Income Tax on Income from Discontinued Operations	24,800	
Income Tax Reduction from Loss on Disposal of a Business Segment		40,000
Income Tax Reduction from Extraordinary Loss		20,000
Income Tax Payable		54,800

The abbreviated income statement below demonstrates how the amount of income tax applicable to each section might be disclosed.

Springer Corporation Income Statement For the Year Ended December 31, 1981		
Income from continuing operations before income tax		$225,000
Income tax expense on continuing operations		90,000
Income from continuing operations		$135,000
Discontinued operations:		
Income from operation of discontinued business segment (less applicable income tax expense of $24,800)	$37,200	
Loss on disposal of business segment (less applicable income tax reduction of $40,000)	(60,000)	(22,800)
Extraordinary loss from earthquake damage (less applicable income tax reduction of $20,000)		(30,000)
Net income		$ 82,200

The income statement of General Mills, Inc., reproduced in Appendix B, provides an additional illustration of intraperiod income tax allocation.

---

[1]In practice, the allocation detail is not always recorded in the accounts. When that is the case, the journal entry would be a debit to Income Tax Expense and a credit to Income Tax Payable for $54,800.

INTERPERIOD INCOME TAX ALLOCATION

Perhaps the most complex area involving accounting for income tax is the adjustment necessary to apply the accrual concept to income tax expense. Because the amount of tax expense is directly related to the income earned, control of the expense is limited to tax planning that will take advantage of income tax regulations to minimize the present value of tax outlays over the life of the business. Usually, this means taking advantage of provisions to minimize the tax payment for each year.

Application of these provisions often results in taxable income that differs from the pretax income reported in the financial statements, sometimes referred to as **pretax accounting or book income**. Taxable income is defined by Congress through laws enacted, and by regulations issued by the Internal Revenue Service. The objectives of Congress and the IRS are not the same as those of accounting bodies, such as the Financial Accounting Standards Board, who establish generally accepted accounting principles to determine book income. Income taxes are sometimes used to regulate the economy, to encourage additional investment, or to favor specific industries. Generally, the tax authorities are not as concerned about measuring income to determine whether a firm is better off, but are more interested in a firm's ability to pay the tax. Thus, most income is taxed when cash is received even though services are still to be rendered, and the income has not yet been recognized on the books.

Differences between tax and accounting or book income may be permanent or temporary. **Permanent differences** arise from: (1) items that are included in the computation of taxable income, but are never recognized for accounting purposes and (2) items that are recognized for accounting purposes, but are never included in the computation of taxable income. **Temporary** or **timing differences** arise from revenue and expense items which are recognized for accounting purposes in a period preceding or subsequent to the period in which they are included in the computation of taxable income. These temporary differences create the need for **interperiod tax allocation**.

This allocation and ramifications from it have created some of the greatest problems in accounting for income taxes.

Permanent Differences

As the name implies, permanent differences are defined as:

> Differences between taxable income and pretax accounting income arising from transactions that, under applicable tax laws and regulations, will not be offset by corresponding differences, or "turn around" in other periods.[2]

Most permanent differences can be classified as revenues exempt from income tax or expenses not deductible in determining taxable income. Examples of nontaxable revenues include:

---

[2]*Opinions of the Accounting Principles Board, No. 11*, "Accounting for Income Taxes" (New York: American Institute of Certified Public Accountants, 1967) par. 13.

1. Interest revenue on municipal bonds.
2. Life insurance proceeds on officers' lives.
3. 85% of dividends received from other corporations (100% of dividends from wholly owned subsidiaries).

Examples of nondeductible expenses include:

1. Fines and expenses arising from violation of laws.
2. Life insurance premiums paid on lives of a corporation's officers or employees if the corporation is the beneficiary.
3. Interest on indebtedness incurred to purchase tax-exempt municipal securities.
4. Goodwill amortization.

Expenses recognized for tax purposes but not recognized as expenses on the books are rarely encountered. An example of this type of permanent difference would be percentage depletion in excess of actual cost depletion. Although theoretically there could be revenue recognized on the tax return that is never recognized on the books, there are no common examples of such items.

Timing Differences

Most differences between accounting and taxable income are temporary in nature. An expense may be deducted for income tax purposes in the current year, but on the external financial statements in a subsequent year. A revenue item may be reported on the income tax return in the current year, but will be reported on the external financial statements when it is earned in a subsequent year. In order to match the tax expense with the related income, interperiod income tax allocation is necessary for timing differences. Essentially, it means that the income tax expense reported on the financial statements is the tax that would have been paid if the income on the financial statements had been used for income tax purposes. The difference between the amount reported as income tax expense and the amount currently payable is currently reported as a deferred charge or a deferred credit depending upon the nature of its balance. When the item *reverses* in subsequent periods, the deferred balance is eliminated.

Timing differences may be classified into the following categories. Examples of items fitting into each category are also included.

1. Reported book income before tax is less than taxable income.
   (a) Revenue is deferred for reporting purposes but is currently recognized for tax purposes.
      (1) Rent revenue received in advance of period earned and deferred for reporting purposes, but taxable in period of receipt.
      (2) Subscription revenue received in advance of period earned and deferred for reporting purposes but taxable in period of receipt.
   (b) Expense is currently recognized for reporting purposes but is deferred for tax purposes.
      (1) Warranty expense accrued in advance for reporting purposes but al-

lowed for tax purposes only when costs are incurred under the warranty.

(2) Reduction in market value of current marketable securities deducted for reporting purposes in the current period, but allowed for tax purposes only when securities are sold.

2. Reported book income before tax is more than taxable income.
   (a) Revenue is currently recognized for reporting purposes, but is deferred for tax purposes.
       (1) Installment sales method used for tax purposes but accrual method of sales used for reporting purposes.
       (2) Construction revenue recognized using the percentage-of-completion method for reporting purposes, but using the completed-contract method for tax purposes.
   (b) Expense is deferred for reporting purposes, but is currently recognized for tax purposes.
       (1) Straight-line depreciation used for reporting purposes, but accelerated depreciation used for tax purposes.
       (2) Intangible drilling costs for extractive industry capitalized and deferred for reporting purposes, but written off as incurred for tax purposes.

Partial versus Comprehensive Income Tax Allocation

The principle of interperiod income tax allocation was recognized by the Committee on Accounting Procedure in Bulletin No. 43, but the Committee recognized an exception to such allocation when it could be presumed that ". . . particular differences between the tax return and the income statement will recur regularly over a comparatively long period of time."[3] This led to varied interpretations and alternative procedures by different companies. For example, if a company uses an accelerated depreciation method for equipment on the income tax return but straight-line depreciation on the books, the amount of depreciation expense for tax purposes will exceed that for reporting purposes every year as long as the company is growing and adding new equipment faster than it is retiring the old equipment. This type of timing difference is defined as a **recurring timing difference** because, in total, the tax deferral will never reverse due to recurring purchase of new equipment. Some companies interpreted Bulletin No. 43 as applying to this type of item, and did not provide for interperiod income tax allocation for depreciation differences. This procedure is referred to as **partial allocation**. Other companies included these depreciation differences in their computation of interperiod income tax allocation balances. The Accounting Principles Board in Opinion No. 11 sought to extend the principle of income tax allocation, as well as to achieve uniformity in practice, by modifying the original position and concluding that ". . . comprehensive interperiod tax allocation is an integral part of the determination of income tax

---

[3]*Accounting Research and Terminology Bulletins — Final Edition*, "No. 43, Restatement and Revision of Accounting Research Bulletins" (New York: American Institute of Certified Public Accountants, 1961), Ch. 10, sect. B, par. 1.

expense."[4] **Comprehensive income tax allocation** requires allocation for all timing differences whether they are expected to recur in the future or not. The Board reasoned that although the total difference between accelerated depreciation and straight-line depreciation may increase each year, under the revolving account theory, depreciation on a specific asset does reverse itself in time so that in the latter part of an asset's life more depreciation is charged on the books than on the income tax return.

Computation of Income Tax Expense and Income Tax Payable

To illustrate the nature of interperiod tax allocation and the effect of permanent and temporary differences on the computation of income tax, assume that for the year ending December 31, 1981, the Barg Corporation reported pretax book income of $420,000. This amount includes $20,000 of tax-exempt income and $5,000 of nondeductible expenses. Depreciation expense for tax purposes exceeds that recognized for book purposes in the current year by $30,000. Assuming a tax rate of 40%, the income tax expense for accounting and reporting purposes and the income tax payable in the current period would be computed as follows:

	For Accounting Purposes	For Tax Purposes
Pretax book income...	$420,000	$420,000
Permanent differences:		
Nondeductible expenses............................. $ 5,000		
Tax-exempt income..................................... (20,000)		
Net permanent difference	(15,000)	(15,000)
Excess of tax depreciation over book depreciation.........		(30,000)
Income subject to income tax...	$405,000	$375,000
Income tax at 40%..	$162,000	$150,000

The $12,000 difference between the tax currently payable of $150,000 and the reported tax expense of $162,000 is attributable to the timing difference ($30,000 × .40 = $12,000). The $12,000 would be recorded on the books by a credit to Deferred Income Taxes. Net income reported on the income statement for 1981 would be $258,000 (pretax book income of $420,000 less income tax expense of $162,000).

This simplified example is intended to illustrate the manner in which permanent and timing differences affect the computation of income tax. Accounting for timing differences is discussed and illustrated in the following sections.

Interperiod Income Tax Allocation — No Change in Rates

To illustrate the accounting for interperiod income tax allocation when income tax rates are constant at 40%, assume the following:

---

[4]*Opinions of the Accounting Principles Board, No. 11, op. cit.,* par. 34.

Year	Reported Book Income Before Tax	Excess of Accelerated Depreciation Over Straight-Line	Excess of Rent Revenue Received In Advance Over Rent Revenue Earned	Taxable Income
1981	$100,000	$15,000	$10,000	$ 95,000
1982	130,000	25,000	(6,000)	99,000
1983	175,000	(5,000)	15,000	195,000

The excess of rent revenue received in advance over rent earned causes reported book income to be lower than taxable income. The excess of accelerated depreciation over straight-line depreciation causes the opposite effect: reported book income exceeds taxable income. If the item is reversed in a particular year, reported book and taxable income are affected in the opposite direction. Different kinds of timing differences should be maintained separately for computation purposes, although they may be combined for reporting purposes.

As previously illustrated, the income tax expense for the period is computed on the reported book income adjusted for any permanent differences. The current income tax liability for the period is computed on the taxable income for the period. The difference between the computed income tax expense and the computed income tax liability is recorded as a deferred charge or a deferred credit. To illustrate, the entries given would be recorded for the years 1981–83 for the preceding example:

```
1981:
Dec. 31  Income Tax Expense ...............................................  40,000
         Deferred Income Tax — Rent Revenue* ............................   4,000
             Deferred Income Tax — Depreciation* ..........................          6,000
             Income Tax Payable...............................................         38,000
```

Computation:
Income tax expense: 40% × $100,000 = $40,000
Deferred income tax — rent revenue: 40% × $10,000 = $4,000
Deferred income tax — depreciation: 40% × $15,000 = $6,000
Income tax payable: 40% × $95,000 = $38,000

    *These accounts may be combined and only the net effect reported as long as they are both current or both noncurrent items.

```
1982
Dec. 31  Income Tax Expense .............................................  52,000
             Deferred Income Tax — Rent Revenue ..........................          2,400
             Deferred Income Tax — Depreciation ...........................         10,000
             Income Tax Payable..............................................         39,600
```

Computation:
Income tax expense: 40% × $130,000 = $52,000
Deferred income tax — rent revenue: 40% × $6,000 = $ 2,400
Deferred income tax — depreciation: 40% × $25,000 = $10,000
Income tax payable: 40% × $99,000 = $39,600

```
1983
Dec. 31  Income Tax Expense .............................................  70,000
         Deferred Income Tax — Rent Revenue...............................   6,000
         Deferred Income Tax — Depreciation.................................   2,000
             Income Tax Payable..............................................         78,000
```

Computation:
Income tax expense: 40% × $175,000 = $70,000
Deferred income tax — rent revenue: 40% × $15,000 = $6,000
Deferred income tax — depreciation: 40% × $ 5,000 = $2,000
Income tax payable: 40% × $195,000 = $78,000

A comparison of reported results with and without interperiod income tax allocation is given below:

| | Reported Results Without Interperiod Income Tax Allocation | | | Reported Results With Interperiod Income Tax Allocation | | |
Year	*Reported Book Income Before Income Tax*	*Income Tax*	*Net Income*	*Reported Book Income Before Income Tax*	*Income Tax*	*Net Income*
1981	$100,000	$38,000	$62,000	$100,000	$40,000	$ 60,000
1982	130,000	39,600	90,400	130,000	52,000	78,000
1983	175,000	78,000	97,000	175,000	70,000	105,000

Examination of the table shows that without interperiod income tax allocation, the income tax expense in 1982 is almost the same as for 1981 even though reported income before taxes was $30,000 higher in 1982 than in 1981. The results using interperiod income tax allocation more accurately portray the accrual concept of matching expense against revenue and disclose a significant increase in income taxes when reported income is increased.

Balance Sheet Classification of Deferred Income Taxes

Debit balances in deferred income tax accounts are reported as deferred charges; credit balances are reported as deferred credits. The balances in the various accounts must be analyzed and classified as current or noncurrent. For reporting purposes, all current amounts are combined, and the net deferred charge or credit is presented with current assets or liabilities on the balance sheet. Likewise, all noncurrent balances are combined, and the net amount is reported. If the net noncurrent amount is a debit, it is usually reported after land, buildings, and equipment; if a credit, the amount is presented with noncurrent liabilities.

APB Opinion No. 11 states that the current or noncurrent classification of a deferred income tax charge or credit should be based on the classification of the asset or liability to which the timing difference relates.[5] For example, deferred income taxes arising from depreciation would be classified as noncurrent since the related depreciable assets are classified as noncurrent. Some timing differences, however, cannot be related to a specific asset or liability. The FASB issued Statement No. 37 to clarify the classification of deferred income taxes arising from these timing differences. The Board concluded that deferred income taxes that are not related to a specific asset or liability should be classified according to the expected reversal date of the timing difference.[6]

Problem Areas in Interperiod Income Tax Allocation

Several difficult questions have arisen concerning interperiod income tax allocation as it relates to specific industries and situations. For example, the equity method of accounting for investment revenue results in account-

---

[5]*Ibid.*, par. 57.

[6]*Statement of Financial Accounting Standards No. 37*, "Balance Sheet Classification of Deferred Income Taxes" (Stamford: Financial Accounting Standards Board, 1980.)

ing income in excess of taxable income. Income from investments is taxable only when distributed. If the distribution never occurs, the difference is really a permanent difference rather than a timing difference. The Accounting Principles Board considered this situation, and concluded that it should be presumed all undistributed earnings from an investment included in income should be accounted for as timing differences and a deferred tax credit recognized as if the earnings remittance had occurred in the current period.[7]

Similar reasoning was used to justify treating undistributed earnings of a subsidiary to its parent as timing differences unless "sufficient evidence shows that the subsidiary has invested or will invest the undistributed earnings indefinitely or that earnings will be remitted in a tax-free liquidation."[8]

The provisions of the Internal Revenue Code permit companies such as savings and loan associations and life insurance companies to exclude from taxable income amounts determined by formulas for bad debt reserves and policyholders' surplus. In both cases, the Board concluded that the entity involved controls the decision as to whether the item would or would not reverse. Therefore, no interperiod income tax allocation is required for these items.[9]

Another question that has been extensively discussed is whether the deferred tax credit should be discounted to report the amount at the present value of the expected future payments. In Accounting Principles Board Opinion No. 10, the Board concluded that because of the uncertainty of the reversal date, deferred income tax should not be accounted for on a discounted basis.[10]

THE INVESTMENT TAX CREDIT

In order to encourage investment in productive facilities, the Revenue Act of 1962 permitted taxpayers to reduce their federal income tax by an **investment credit** equal to a specified percentage of the cost of certain depreciable properties acquired after January 1, 1962. This act thus provided certain tax benefits as a stimulant to the economy. The investment credit has had a turbulent history both in politics and in accounting practice. The credit provisions were significantly amended in 1964; the credit was temporarily suspended in 1966 and suspended again in 1969 when the economy was in an inflationary period. The credit was reinstated in 1971, but the rate and coverage have changed through the years.

The investment tax credit applies to property defined by the tax regulations as "Section 38 Property." In general, such property is defined as property

1. on which depreciation is allowable to the taxpayer.

---

[7]*Opinions of the Accounting Principles Board, No. 24*, "Accounting for Income Taxes: Investments in Common Stock Accounted for by the Equity Method (Other than Subsidiaries and Corporate Joint Ventures)" (New York: American Institute of Certified Public Accountants, 1972), par. 7–9. Current tax regulations permit corporations to deduct an 85% dividends-received credit against dividend revenue.

[8]*Opinions of the Accounting Principles Board, No. 23*, "Accounting for Income Taxes — Special Areas" (New York: American Institute of Certified Public Accountants, 1972), par. 12.

[9]*Ibid.*, par. 23–28.

[10]*Opinions of the Accounting Principles Board, No. 10*, "Omnibus Opinion — 1966" (New York American Institute of Certified Public Accountants, 1967), par. 6.

2. which has a useful life of three years or more from the time the property is put into service.
3. which is tangible personal property, or other property (not including buildings and their components) used as an integral part of manufacturing, production, or extraction.

The credit percentage (10% in 1980) is applied to 100% of the property cost only if the remaining useful life is seven years or more. Only a portion of the property cost may be used for assets with remaining lives of less than seven years; ⅔ of cost if remaining life is at least five but less than seven years; and ⅓ of cost if the remaining life is at least three but less than five years.

The credit is directly applied against income tax otherwise due in the year the qualifying property is acquired, except that it is limited in any one year to $25,000 plus 80% of the liability for income tax in excess of $25,000.[11] Any unused investment credit can be carried back three years and forward seven years in the same way as was described for operating losses. If a company has an investment tax credit carryforward and has additional investment credit available for the current year, the carryforward credits are applied against the current income tax first. This permits a company to more fully utilize the carryforward provision.

In order to realize the full benefit of the investment tax credit, the property acquired must be held for at least seven years, or the life estimated when the assets were acquired, if shorter, before disposition is made. Disposition of an asset is defined to include its sale, sale and leaseback, or gift. If property is disposed of early, part or all of the credit must be **recaptured**, i.e., added to the tax liability in the year of disposition. The amount to be recaptured is the excess of the credit taken in the year of acquisition over the credit that would have been allowed based on the actual length of time the asset was held.

To illustrate, assume that Section 38 property is acquired at a cost of $120,000. The amount of investment tax credit available under varying estimates of the remaining life of the property can be summarized as follows:

Estimated Life at Acquisition	Investment Tax Credit
Less than 3 years	–0–
At least 3 but less than 5 years	($120,000 × 33⅓%) × 10% = $ 4,000
At least 5 but less than 7 years	($120,000 × 66⅔%) × 10% = $ 8,000
7 or more years	($120,000 × 100%) × 10% = $12,000

If the property was initially estimated to have a remaining life of 10 years, but was sold after only 6 years, the excess of the credit taken over the credit that would have been allowed based on a life of 6 years must be recaptured. Thus, $4,000 ($12,000 − $8,000) would be added to the tax otherwise due in the year of disposition. The possibility of recapture for overestimation of the asset life is probably preferred to the consequence of understatement. If the life is estimated to be 6 years, and the asset is actually used 10 years, the tax benefit for the difference would be lost due to the three year statute of limitations on amending prior year tax returns.

---

[11]To be raised to 90% for tax years ending in 1982 and thereafter.

Leased property is subject to special rules. A lessor of new property which qualifies as "Section 38 property" may either take the credit itself or elect to let the lessee take it. A lease by itself is not considered a disposition. If the lessor retains the right to the credit, it is deducted from the fair market value of the leased asset before computing the interest rate implicit in the lease.

Accounting for the Investment Tax Credit

Accounting for the investment tax credit has been the subject of much controversy and change. Essentially, there are two methods that can be used to record the tax reduction: (1) the credit can be used to reduce the income tax expense for the year in which it is received, commonly referred to as the **flow-through method**, or (2) the credit can be deferred and reflected as a reduction of tax expense over the period during which the asset is depreciated, commonly referred to as the **deferred method**.

Flow-Through Method. Accounting for the investment credit by the flow-through method is relatively uncomplicated. Income tax expense for the period of the credit is reduced by the amount allowed, and the income tax payable is also reduced by the credit. No adjustment is made to the assets whose purchase made it possible to receive the credit. The depreciation entry for the acquired assets is identical to what it would have been without the credit.

To illustrate this method, assume a business acquired machinery in 1981 for $100,000 when the investment credit was 10% on new assets. The asset had an estimated useful life of 10 years with no salvage value and is to be depreciated on a straight-line basis. Assume further that federal income tax for 1981 is $75,000 reduced by an investment credit of $10,000 (10% of $100,000). Entries in 1981 would be:

Machinery	100,000	
Cash		100,000
Purchase of machinery.		
Income Tax Expense	65,000	
Income Tax Payable		65,000
Recognition of income tax, $75,000 less investment credit, $10,000.		
Depreciation Expense	10,000	
Accumulated Depreciation — Machinery		10,000
Depreciation expense for year.		

Deferred Method. Accounting for the investment tax credit by the deferred method is complicated by the need to amortize the deferral over the life of the asset that gave rise to the credit. The entries to record the deferral and amortization of the deferred credit for the example above would be as follows:

Machinery	100,000	
Cash		100,000
Purchase of machinery.		

Income Tax Expense..	75,000	
Deferred Investment Tax Credit		10,000
Income Tax Payable		65,000
Recognition of income tax and amount payable.		
Deferred Investment Tax Credit..	1,000	
Income Tax Expense		1,000
Amortization of deferred tax credit over 10 years.		
Depreciation Expense...	10,000	
Accumulated Depreciation — Machinery.........................		10,000
Depreciation expense for the year.		

Investment Tax Credit Carryback and Carryforward. If in the example described on page 431 the new machinery had cost $1,150,000, the investment tax credit would have been $115,000. However, only $65,000 of the credit could be applied against the $75,000 income tax liability because of the $25,000, 80% limitation. The remaining $50,000 would be available for carryback and carryforward treatment. Assume the business had the following income tax liability for the preceding three years:

Year	Income Tax Paid
1978	$10,000
1979	$ 5,000
1980	$30,000

Applying the limitation to each year, the investment tax carryback would result in the following tax refund:

1978	$10,000	
1979	5,000	
1980	29,000	($25,000 + 80% of $5,000)
Total refund	$44,000	

The remaining $6,000 ($50,000 − $44,000) would be available as a carryforward.

The entry in 1981 to record the refund receivable from the investment tax credit carryback would depend upon whether the flow-through or deferred method were being used.

Flow-through method:

Income Tax Refund Receivable	44,000	
Adjustment of Prior Year's Income Tax Arising from Carryback		
of Investment Tax Credit*...		44,000

> *The first $10,000 could alternatively be used to reduce the 1981 income tax expense of $10,000 ($75,000 − $65,000 tax credit used for 1981). The balance could then be credited to this special revenue account.

Deferred method:

Income Tax Refund Receivable	44,000	
Deferred Investment Tax Credit		44,000
Deferred Investment Tax Credit..	4,400	
Income Tax Expense		4,400
Amortization of deferred investment tax credit over 10 years.		

Carryforwards of investment tax credits, frequently referred to as **unused investment tax credits**, are not to be recognized as assets even if the realization of them is assured because of future income projections.[12] When they are recognized, the credit may be used to reduce income tax expense of the period, or it may be reported as a separate revenue item. Investment tax credit carryforwards are not required to be recognized as extraordinary items as are operating loss carryforwards.

To illustrate the carryforward, if in 1982 the company in the preceding example had income tax payable of $30,000 before applying the investment tax credit carryforward, the $6,000 carryforward would be recorded as follows under the two common recording methods:

Flow-through method:

Income Tax Expense..	24,000	
Income Tax Payable		24,000
Tax liability, $30,000 − $6,000 = $24,000		

Deferred method:

Income Tax Expense..	30,000	
Deferred Investment Tax Credit		6,000
Income Tax Payable		24,000

The existence of deferred income tax charges or credits can greatly complicate carryforward computations. Because of the complexities of these relationships, further discussion of this area is considered to be beyond the scope of text coverage.

Evaluation of Accounting Treatment of Investment Tax Credit

The Accounting Principles Board favored the deferred method and approved it in Opinion No. 2. Lack of support for this view among many prominent accountants led to the issuance in 1964 of Opinion No. 4 in which the Board accepted both methods although still stating a preference for the deferred method. In 1968, a further attempt was made by the Accounting Principles Board to restore the deferred method as a single uniform method. Again, differences of opinion resulted in failure to adopt the original conclusions. In 1971, the Board once again made serious effort to restore the deferred method. However, they had to postpone such effort as a result of congressional action permitting the taxpayer to choose the method to be used in recognizing the benefit arising from the credit.

Good theoretical arguments can be presented for either of the methods. Those who advocate using the deferred method argue that the cost of the asset is effectively reduced by the investment credit, and the tax benefit should be spread over the acquired asset's useful life. This point of view is strengthened by the current tax requirement that a company must hold the asset for a specified period of time or return part of the allowed credit. Those who advocate using the flow-through method argue that the tax

---

[12]*Opinions of the Accounting Principles Board, No. 2,* "Accounting for the Investment Credit" (New York: American Institute of Certified Public Accountants, 1962) par. 21.

credit is in reality a tax reduction in the current period. They argue that tax regulations establish the tax liability each year, and that amount is the proper expense to match against current revenues. This latter treatment affects current income more and is favored by political leaders when the investment tax credit is being used to stimulate a sluggish economy.

It is unfortunate that this issue has become such a political item. It is an example of an area where there seems to be no justification for having two methods. It is difficult to see how different economic circumstances among companies would justify dual treatment. Uniformity in treatment of the investment tax credit is definitely preferable to the alternatives presently available under generally accepted accounting principles.

DISCLOSURE OF INCOME TAXES

As explained in the preceding sections, timing differences are reflected in balance sheet accounts as deferred charges and deferred credits. The net amount of these balance sheet accounts should be separated between current and noncurrent categories. The deferred charge or deferred credit should be classified in the same way as are the accounts to which they relate. A deferred item is related to an asset or liability if reduction of the asset or liability causes the timing difference to reverse. Thus, if installment receivables are classified as a current asset, the deferred credit related to these receivables should be classified as a current item. Similarly, if an estimated provision for warranties is classified as a current liability, the deferred charge relating to this liability should also be classified as a current item. If deferred items are not related to an asset or liability, they should be classified according to the expected reversal date of the timing difference.[13]

The refund receivable from an investment credit carryback should be classified according to the criteria presented in Chapter 5, i.e., current if collection is expected within one year or one operating cycle, whichever is longer; otherwise, noncurrent.

Income tax expense should be separated between tax on income before extraordinary or irregular items and the income tax related to these irregular items. The income tax expense on the income statement should clearly identify tax currently payable and the tax effects of timing differences. Normally, this information is contained in a note to the financial statements. In addition, the SEC requires a reconciliation of the differences between the statutory income tax rate and the effective rate actually paid by the company. Frequently, there is a considerable difference between the two because of such items as permanent differences, investment credit carrybacks and carryforwards, etc.

The following additional disclosure relating to income taxes is also required.

1. Amount of any unused investment tax credit, together with expiration dates.
2. Significant differences not already disclosed between pretax accounting income and taxable income.

---

[13]*Statement of Financial Accounting Standards No. 37, op. cit.*, par 4.

A good example of income tax disclosure is included in Note Eleven to the General Mills statements reproduced on page 675. This note separates the tax expense between federal taxes and the other taxes paid by the company to state, local, and foreign governments. It also discloses the effect of timing differences and identifies the principal causes of the differences. Finally, a reconciliation of the statutory rate and the actual rate paid is provided.

EVALUATION OF ACCOUNTING FOR INCOME TAXES

Accounting for income taxes is a very complex and challenging area. This chapter has been kept as simple as possible to permit students to focus on the principles involved. The introduction of interperiod income tax allocation into accounting has greatly complicated accounting for income taxes. Many accountants have questioned the wisdom of allocating income tax expense for timing differences that are expected to recur, such as for depreciation and installments receivable.

The interplay of tax regulations as they change to stimulate and repress the economy results in changes to the rates and changes in the tax rules that require making changes in the deferred amounts reported either immediately or at some future date when the deferred items reverse. Many foreign countries have recognized the morass of accounting rules that have accompanied deferred income tax accounting, and have rejected the comprehensive income tax allocation methods practiced in the United States and described in this chapter. The authors tend to agree with this position, and hope that the FASB will once again review carefully the entire conceptual rationale behind interperiod income tax allocation, with emphasis being placed on the qualitative characteristics of understandability and relevance to statement users.

QUESTIONS

1. What is meant by intraperiod income tax allocation?

2. Describe the entries that would be made in recognizing the income tax for the period in each case below:

   (a) There are earnings from ordinary operations and an extraordinary loss that is less than such earnings.

   (b) There are earnings of ordinary operations and a credit for a correction of an error recorded directly to Retained Earnings. An amended income tax return has been filed.

   (c) There is a loss from ordinary operations, an extraordinary gain that is greater than the loss, and a debit for a correction of an error recorded directly to Retained Earnings. A claim for an income tax refund has been filed.

3. Accounting methods used by a company to determine income for reporting purposes frequently differ from those used to determine taxable income. What is the justification for these differences?

4. Distinguish between a timing difference and a permanent difference when accounting for interperiod income tax allocation.

5. In adopting income tax allocation procedures for timing differences between reported book and taxable income, what adjustments are made when (a) reported book income before tax is less than taxable income, and (b) reported book income before tax is more than taxable income? What timing differences are most commonly found?

6. Under what circumstances will a Deferred Income Tax credit balance be reduced to zero? Why do most companies report an increasing balance in this account?

7. How should deferred income taxes be classified and reported on the balance sheet?

8. What type of property is eligible for investment tax credit benefits?

9. What is meant by investment tax credit recapture?

10. Two methods of accounting are available for reporting investment tax credits. What are they, and how does the accounting differ between them?

11. What is an unused investment tax credit? What benefit, if any, is it to a company?

EXERCISES

exercise 15-1

In 1981, the Berry Co. reported taxable operating income of $130,000 and a fully taxable extraordinary gain of $50,000. Assume an income tax rate for 1981 of 40% on all items. (1) Give the entry to record the income tax for 1981. (2) Assuming there was a fully deductible extraordinary loss of $50,000 rather than an extraordinary gain, give the entry to record the income tax for 1981.

exercise 15-2

The Theobold Corporation reported the following income items before tax for the year 1981.

Income from continuing operations before income tax	$175,000
Loss from operations of a discontinued business segment	15,000
Gain from disposal of a business segment	20,000
Extraordinary gain on retirement of debt	100,000

The income tax rate is 40% on all items. Prepare the portion of the income statement beginning with "Income from continuing operations before income tax" for the year ended December 31, 1981, after applying proper intraperiod income tax allocation procedures.

exercise 15-3

Indicate whether each of the items below is a timing difference or a permanent difference. For each timing difference, indicate whether it is a deferred credit or a deferred charge.

(a) Tax depreciation in excess of book depreciation, $200,000.
(b) Excess of income on installment sales over income reportable for tax purposes, $230,000.
(c) Premium payment for insurance policy on life of president, $50,000.
(d) Earnings of foreign subsidiary received in the current year but reported in a previous year, $150,000.
(e) Amortization of goodwill, $40,000.
(f) Rent collected in advance of period earned, $75,000.
(g) Actual expense for warranty repairs in excess of warranty provision for year, $50,000.
(h) Interest revenue received on municipal bonds, $20,000.

exercise 15-4

Using the information given in Exercise 3, and assuming a pretax reported book income of $1,680,000 and an income tax rate of 40%, calculate taxable income and give the entry to record income tax for the year. Your entry may "net" the various deferred income tax accounts into one account.

exercise 15-5

Billus Manufacturing Corporation reports income of $645,000 on its income tax return for the year ended December 31, 1981. Timing differences between pretax operating income and taxable income for the year are:

Book depreciation in excess of tax depreciation..	$125,000
Accrual for product liability claims in excess of actual claims...........................	105,000
Installment sales income in excess of taxable income..	265,000

Assuming an income tax rate of 40%, compute the book income tax expense, deferred income tax, and income tax payable. Give the necessary journal entry to record these amounts. Use one deferred income tax account.

exercise 15-6

The Ritzert Co. shows reported book income before income tax and taxable income for 1980 and 1981 as follows:

	Reported Book Income before Income Tax	Taxable Income
1980...	$140,600	$212,000
1981...	$257,000	240,200

The discrepancies arose because the company, organized on April 1, 1980, wrote off against revenue of that year organization costs totaling $84,000. For federal income tax purposes, however, the organization costs can be written off ratably over a period of not less than 60 months. For income tax purposes, then, the company deducted $9/60$ of the costs in 1980 and $12/60$ of the costs in 1981. Income tax is to be calculated at 40% of taxable income.

Give the entries that would be made on the books of the company at the end of 1980 and 1981 to recognize the income tax liability and to provide for a proper allocation of income tax in view of the differences in book and income tax reporting.

exercise 15-7

The Thunder Bay Mining Company reported book income before income tax of $945,000 for the calendar year 1981. Included in the "Other income" section of the income statement was $100,000 of interest revenue from municipal bonds held by the company. The income statement also included depreciation expense for a machine which cost $4,000,000. The machine, purchased January 2, 1981, has a useful life of eight years and an estimated salvage value of $400,000. Depreciation for book purposes is computed by the straight-line method and for tax purposes by the sum-of-the-years-digits method.

Prepare the journal entry necessary to record income tax for the year, assuming an income tax rate of 40%.

exercise 15-8

Damons Plumbing Company purchased a new machine on January 1, 1980, for $200,000. The machine had a ten-year life and was depreciated by the straight-line method. Assuming a 10% investment tax credit, give the entries to record the purchase of the machine and the recognition and payment of tax for the first two years under (a) the flow-through method and (b) the deferred method. (Income tax before the credit in 1980 and 1981 was $265,000 and $157,000 respectively.)

exercise 15-9

The Dela Torre Corporation purchased a stamping press for $125,000 on January 1, 1981. The press has an estimated useful life of ten years and no salvage value. The corporation uses the straight-line method of depreciation.

Assuming an income tax liability for the current year of $65,000 before the credit, and an investment tax credit rate of 10%, give the entries necessary to record the following:

(1) Using the flow through method, record
   (a) the income tax liability, reflecting the credit.
   (b) the entry to reflect depreciation on the press for 1981.
(2) Using the deferred method, record
   (a) the income tax liability, reflecting the credit.
   (b) the depreciation on the press, including amortization of the investment tax credit.

exercise 15-10

The Medicine Hat Company was formed on April 1, 1981. It purchased the following equipment on the dates indicated:

Date Purchased	Equipment	Cost	Est. Useful Life	Date Placed in Service
April 30, 1981	Hat Former	$200,000	10 years	May 10, 1981
Aug. 1, 1981	Stitcher #1	$150,000	7 years	Aug. 15, 1981
Nov. 1, 1981	Boxer	$100,000	7 years	Nov. 7, 1981
Dec. 1, 1981	Stitcher #2	$150,000	7 years	Jan. 3, 1982

The investment tax credit rate was 10%. What is the total investment tax credit which Medicine Hat may claim for its tax year ending December 31, 1981, assuming the tax liability for the year was $45,000?

exercise 15-11

The Avery Corporation purchased a machine on April 30, 1976. The machine cost $24,000 and had an estimated useful life of ten years. The corporation discontinued the operations in which the machine was used, effective May 1, 1981. The machine was taken out of service at that time and sold shortly thereafter.

Avery Corporation took the full amount of the investment tax credit in the year of the purchase. What amount of the credit must now be recaptured?

exercise 15-12

The Wabash Corporation's income tax liability for the year ended December 31, 1981, was $30,000. Investment tax credit available was $40,000. The income tax liability for the corporation for the past three years was: 1978 — $4,000; 1979 — $10,000; 1980 — $20,000. Give the entries necessary to record the carryback of the investment tax credit. What is the amount of investment tax credit available for a carryforward to 1982?

PROBLEMS

problem 15-1

Lethbridge Lithographing, Inc., reported taxable income for the fiscal year ended October 31, 1981, of $775,000. Ordinary income tax rates were 40%. Included in the $775,000 was a gain of $95,000 properly classified as extraordinary. The gain was taxed at 25%. Also included in taxable income was a loss from the disposal of a business segment of $100,000. The loss was deductible from ordinary income. The annual audit disclosed a $75,000 overstatement in income of the previous year. An amended income tax return will be filed. The income tax rate on the refund will be 40%.

Instructions:

(1) Prepare journal entries to record the income tax liability, including proper intra-period income tax allocation.
(2) Prepare the income statement for the fiscal year ending October 31, 1981, beginning with income from continuing operations before income tax.

problem 15-2

The Marathon Corporation accrued certain revenue on its books in 1979 and 1980 of $7,800 and $6,000 respectively, but such revenue was not subject to income tax until 1981. Reported book income before tax and taxable income for the three-year period are as follows:

	Reported Book Income Before Income Tax	Taxable Income
1979	$21,600	$13,800
1980	20,400	14,400
1981	14,400	28,200

Assume the income tax rate applicable to taxable income is 40% in each year.

> **Instructions:** Give the entries that would be made at the end of each year to recognize the income tax liability and to provide for a proper allocation of income tax in view of the differences between reported book income before income tax and taxable income.

problem 15-3

Income data of the Denny Company for the first five years of its operations are summarized below:

	1977	1978	1979	1980	1981
Sales	$1,000,000	$1,040,000	$1,120,000	$1,120,000	$1,200,000
Cost of goods sold	600,000	624,000	656,000	672,000	720,000
Gross profit on sales	$ 400,000	$ 416,000	$ 464,000	$ 448,000	$ 480,000
Operating expenses	160,000	168,000	184,000	176,000	192,000
Income before income tax	$ 240,000	$ 248,000	$ 280,000	$ 272,000	$ 288,000

Cost of goods sold includes depreciation on buildings and equipment items calculated by the straight-line method. However, for income tax purposes, the company employed the accelerated depreciation methods providing for higher charges in the early years of asset life and correspondingly lower charges in the later years. Depreciation charges on the books as compared with charges recognized for income tax purposes during the five-year period were as follows:

	1977	1978	1979	1980	1981
Depreciation per books	$132,000	$136,000	$136,000	$140,000	$140,000
Accelerated depreciation per tax return	216,000	180,800	144,000	124,000	100,000

All of the revenue of the company is taxable; all of the expenses are deductible for income tax purposes. Income tax rates in each year were 40% of taxable income.

> **Instructions:**
> (1) Give the entries that would be made by the company for the years 1977 through 1981 to record the accrual of income tax if income is debited with income tax allocable to such income.
> (2) Prepare comparative income statements for the Denny Company for the five-year period assuming the use of interperiod income tax allocation procedures.
> (3) Prepare comparative income statements for the Denny Company for the five-year period assuming the interperiod income tax allocation procedures were not used and charges for income tax were recognized at the amounts actually becoming payable each year.

problem 15-4

The Brandon Corporation has taxable income of $2,035,000 for the year ended December 31, 1981. The controller is unfamiliar with the treatment of timing and permanent differences in reconciling from taxable income to reported book income, and has requested your assistance. You are given the following list of differences.

Book depreciation in excess of tax depreciation	$300,000
Proceeds from life insurance policy upon death of officer	192,000
Unremitted earnings of foreign subsidiary, reported as income on the books. Remittance highly unlikely	140,000

> **Instructions:** Using the above information:
> (1) Compute reported book income before income tax.
> (2) Assuming an income tax rate of 40%, give the journal entry to record the income tax for the year.
> (3) Prepare a partial income statement beginning with "Income from continuing operations before income tax."

problem 15-5

The Selkirk Manufacturing Company prepared the following reconciliation between taxable and reported book income for 1981:

Income per tax return	$3,300,000
Add excess depreciation taken on the tax return as compared with books.....	240,000
	$3,540,000
Less: Extraordinary gain on early extinguishment of debt...............................	180,000
Estimated expenses of future warranties not allowable for tax purposes until expenses are actually incurred..	120,000
Advance rent revenue taxable in period of receipt	60,000
Reported book income before income tax and extraordinary items.................	$3,180,000

A prior period adjustment of $3,000 for the correction of an error was debited directly against Retained Earnings. An income tax refund claim has been filed for this adjustment. Ordinary income tax rates apply.

Instructions:

(1) Assuming an ordinary income tax rate of 40%, prepare required journal entries to record the income tax liability at December 31, 1981.

(2) Prepare the income statement for 1981 beginning with "Income from continuing operations before income tax."

problem 15-6

The Plowman Foundry is a large manufacturer of home gardening and farming implements. Its net taxable income for the year ended December 31, 1981 was $400,000. The tax rate was 40%.

Plowman made the following investments in machinery, equipment and fixed assets in 1981:

Item	Date Purchased	Cost	Estimated Useful Life	Date Placed in Service
Forge...	2/23/81	$400,000	10 years	2/25/81
Welder...	3/5/81	150,000	5 years	3/5/81
Metal Stamper #1	4/12/81	750,000	10 years	4/25/81
Storage Building.......................................	6/15/81	250,000	20 years	7/22/81
Delivery Trucks...	8/14/81	300,000	5 years	8/21/81
Metal Stamper #2	11/2/81	730,000	10 years	11/26/81
Lathe	12/20/81	150,000	5 years	1/5/82

Plowman took advantage of the investment tax credit provisions which were as described on page 430 of the text.

Plowman was begun in 1978. It paid income tax since the year of its inception as follows:

Year	Tax Paid
1978	$12,500
1979	30,000
1980	35,000

Instructions:

(1) Using the above information, give the entries necessary to record the following:
  a) The income tax liability for 1981, under the
    i) flow-through method of recording the investment tax credit.
    ii) deferred method of recording the investment tax credit.
  b) The amount of the refund of prior years' taxes due to the carryback of the investment tax credit.
  c) The amount of the carryforward available.

(2) Assuming Plowman's 1982 taxable income was $500,000 (40% rate), and Plowman made no new purchases of Section 38 property in 1982, compute its income tax liability for 1982.

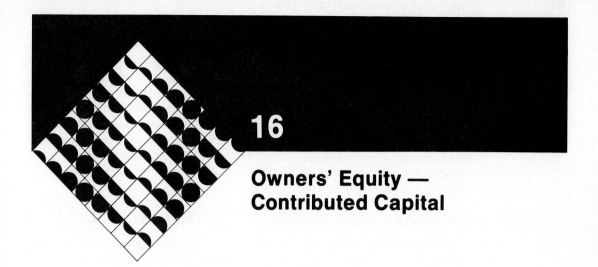

16

Owners' Equity — Contributed Capital

CHAPTER OBJECTIVES

Describe the nature and classifications of capital stock.

Explain and illustrate proper accounting for the issuance of capital stock.

Explain and illustrate proper accounting for the reacquisition and resale or retirement of capital stock.

Describe balance sheet disclosure of contributed capital.

The difference between assets and liabilities is owners' equity or capital. Assets represent entity resources while liabilities reflect the creditor claims against those resources. The owners' equity of an entity represents the residual interest of the owners in the net assets (total assets less total liabilities) of the business.

The capital of a business originates from two primary sources — investments by owners and business earnings. Reductions in capital result primarily from distributions to owners and business losses. In a proprietorship, the owner's entire equity resulting from investments, withdrawals, and earnings or losses is reflected in a single capital account. Similarly, in a partnership, a single capital account for each partner reports the partner's equity resulting from investments, withdrawals, and earnings or losses. In reporting corporate capital, however, a distinction is made between (1) investments by owners, called **contributed capital** or **paid-in capital** and (2) retention of net assets arising from earnings, designated as **retained earnings**. The issues surrounding contributed capital are discussed in this chapter, while those relating to retained earnings are considered in Chapter 17. Accounting for corporations is emphasized because they are the dominant form of organization in today's economy. Not only are corporations the major source of our national output, but they also provide the majority of employment opportunities. Millions of people hold equity securities in corporations throughout the world.

NATURE AND CLASSIFICATIONS OF CAPITAL STOCK

A corporation is an artificial entity created by law that has an existence separate from its owners and may engage in business within prescribed limits just as a natural person. Unless the life of the corporation is limited by law, it has perpetual existence. The modern corporation makes it possible for large amounts of resources to be assembled under one management. These resources are transferred to the corporation by individual owners because they believe they can earn a greater rate of return through the corporation's efficient use of the resources than would be possible from alternative investments. In exchange for these resources, the corporation issues **stock certificates** evidencing ownership interests. Directors elected by stockholders delegate to management responsibility for supervising the use, operation, and disposition of corporate resources.

Business corporations may be created under the corporation laws of any one of the fifty states or of the federal government. Since the states do not follow a uniform incorporating act, the conditions under which corporations may be created and under which they may operate are somewhat varied.

In most states at least three individuals must join in applying for a corporate charter. Application is made by submitting **articles of incorporation** to the secretary of state or other appropriate official. The articles must set forth the name of the corporation, its purpose and nature, the stock to be issued, those persons who are to act as first directors, and other data required by law. If the articles conform to the state's laws governing corporate formation, they are approved and are recognized as the **charter** for the new corporate entity. When stock of a corporation is to be offered or distributed outside the state in which it is incorporated, registration with the Securities and Exchange Commission may be required. The objective of such registration is to assure that all of the facts relative to the business and its securities will be adequately and honestly disclosed. A stockholders' meeting is called at which a code of rules or **bylaws** governing meetings, voting procedures, and other internal operations are adopted, a **board of directors** is elected, and the board appoints company administrative officers. Corporate activities may now proceed in conformance with laws of the state of incorporation and charter authorization. A complete record of the proceedings of both the stockholders' and the directors' meetings should be maintained in a minutes book.

In forming a corporation, most companies generally issue a single class of stock. However, corporations may later find there are advantages in issuing more than one kind of stock with varying rights and priorities. When a single class of stock is issued, shares are all alike and are known as **common stock**. When more than one class is issued, stock with certain preferences over the common stock issued is called **preferred stock**.

Unless restricted or withheld by terms of the stock contract, certain basic rights are held by each stockholder. These rights are as follows:

1. To share in distributions of corporate earnings.
2. To vote in the election of directors and in the determination of certain corporate policies.
3. To maintain one's proportional interest in the corporation through purchase of additonal capital stock if issued, known as the *preemptive right*.
4. To share in distributions of cash or other properies upon liquidation of the corporation.

If both preferred and common stocks are issued, the special features of each class of stock are stated in the articles of incorporation or in the corporation bylaws and become a part of the stock contract between the corporation and its stockholders. One must be familiar with the overall capital structure to understand fully the nature of the equity found in any single class of stock. Frequently, the stock certificate describes the rights and restrictions relative to the ownership interest it represents together with those pertaining to other securities issued. Shares of stock represent personal property and may be freely transferred by their owners in the absence of special restrictions.

Legal or Stated Value of Stock

As indicated, the capital of a corporation is divided between contributed capital and earned capital. This is an important distinction because readers of financial statements need to know the portion of equity derived from investments by owners as contrasted with the portion of equity that has been earned and retained by the business. The invested or contributed capital may be further classified into (a) an amount forming the corporate **legal or stated capital**, and (b) the balance not classified as legal capital. The amount of the investment representing the legal or stated capital is reported as **capital stock**. The balance is recognized as **additional paid-in capital** or **premium**. Contributions of properties by outsiders may also be included in the additonal paid-in capital grouping, although it would be possible to recognize these in a separate **donated capital** category.

The major components of owners' equity are shown on page 444. It should be recognized, however, that the definitions and classifications of legal and other capital categories may vary according to state statutes.

The significance of legal capital is that most state incorporation laws provide that dividends cannot reduce corporate capital below an amount

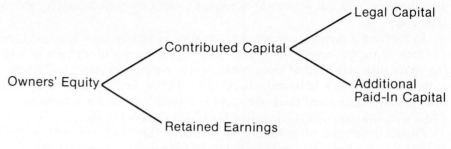

Elements of Owners' Equity

designated as legal capital. Modern corporation laws normally go beyond these limitations and add that legal capital cannot be impaired by the reacquisiton of capital stock. Creditors of a corporation cannot hold individual stockholders liable for claims against the company. But with a portion of the corporate capital restricted as to distribution, creditors can rely on the absorption by the ownership group of losses equal to the legal capital before losses are applied to the creditors' equity. As a practical matter, the legal capital of a corporation is generally small in comparison to total capital and does not strongly influence dividend policy nor provide significant creditor protection.

When a value is assigned to each share of stock, whether common or preferred, and is reported on the stock certificate, the stock is said to have a **par value**; stock without such an assigned value is called **no-par** stock. When shares have a par value, the legal or stated capital is normally the aggregate par value of all shares issued and subscribed. When a corporation is authorized to issue capital stock with a par value, the incorporation laws of most states permit such issue only for an amount equal to or in excess of par. Par value may be any amount, for example, $100, $5, or 25 cents. An amount received on the sale of capital stock in excess of its par value is recorded as a premium; the premium is added to capital stock at par in reporting total contributed capital.

When shares are no-par, laws of certain states require that the total consideration received for the shares, even when they are sold at different prices, be recognized as legal capital. Laws of a number of states, however, permit the corporate directors to establish legal capital by assigning an arbitrary value to each share regardless of issue price, although in some instances the value cannot be less than a certain minimum amount. The value fixed by the board of directors or the minimum value required by law is known as the share's **stated value**.

Prior to 1912, corporations were permitted to issue only stock with a par value. In 1912, however, New York state changed its corporation laws to permit the issuance of stock without a par value, and since that time all other states have followed with similar statutory provisions. Today many of the common stocks, as well as some of the preferred stocks, listed on the large securities exchanges are no-par. Usually, no-par stock must have a stated value for reporting purposes. This makes it very similar to par stock and defines a separation of the stock proceeds between stated value and additional paid-in capital.

Preferred Stock

When a corporation issues both preferred and common stock, the preference attaching to preferred stock normally consists of a prior claim to dividends. A dividend preference does not assure stockholders of dividends on the preferred issue but simply means that dividend requirements must be met on preferred stock before anything may be paid on common stock. Dividends do not legally accrue; a dividend on preferred stock, as on common stock, requires the legal ability on the part of the company to make such a distribution as well as appropriate action by the board of directors. When the board of directors fails to declare a dividend on preferred stock at the time such action would be called for, the dividend is said to be *passed*. Although preferred stockholders have a prior claim on dividends, such preference is usually accompanied by limitations on the amount of dividends they may receive.

Preferred stock is generally issued with a par value. When preferred stock has a par value, the dividend is stated in terms of a percentage of par value. When preferred stock is no-par, the dividend must be stated in terms of dollars and cents. Thus, holders of 5% preferred stock with a $50 par value are entitled to an annual dividend of $2.50 per share before any distribution is made to common stockholders; holders of $5 no-par preferred stock are entitled to an annual dividend of $5 per share before dividends are paid to common stockholders.

A corporation may issue more than one class of preferred stock. For example, preferred issues may be designated first preferred or second preferred with the first preferred issue having a first claim on earnings and the second preferred having a second claim on earnings. In other instances the claim to earnings on the part of several preferred issues may have equal priority, but dividend rates or other preferences may vary. Holders of the common stock may receive dividends only after the satisfaction of all preferred dividend requirements.

Other characteristics and conditions are frequently added to preferred stock in the extension of certain advantages or in the limitation of certain rights. Such factors may be expressed in adjectives modifying preferred stock, as *cumulative* preferred stock, *convertible* preferred stock, and *callable* preferred stock. More than one of these characteristics may be applicable to a specific issue of preferred stock.

Cumulative and Noncumulative Preferred Stock. Cumulative preferred stock provides that whenever the corporation fails to declare dividends on this class, such dividends accumulate and require payment in the future before any dividends may be paid to common stockholders. For example, assume a corporation has outstanding 100,000 shares of 9% cumulative preferred stock, $10 par. Dividends were last paid through December 31, 1978, and the company wishes to resume payments at the end of 1981.

The company will have to declare dividends on preferred for three years, or $270,000 before it may declare any dividends on common stock. Preferred dividends on cumulative preferred stock that are passed are referred to as **dividends in arrears**. Although these dividends are not a liability until declared by the board of directors, this information is of importance to stockholders and other users of the financial statements. Disclosure of the amount of the dividends in arrears is made by special note on the balance sheet.

If preferred stock is **noncumulative**, it is not necessary to provide for passed dividends. A dividend omission on preferred stock in any one year means it is irretrievably lost. Dividends may be declared on common stock as long as the preferred stock receives the preferred rate for the current period. Preferred stock contracts normally provide for cumulative dividends. Courts have generally held that dividend rights on preferred stock are cumulative in the absence of specific conditions to the contrary.

Convertible Preferred Stock. Preferred stock is **convertible** when terms of the issue provide that it can be exchanged by its owner for some other security of the issuing corporation. Conversion rights generally provide for the exchange of preferred stock into common stock. Since preferred stock normally has a prior but limited right to earnings, large earnings resulting from successful operations accrue to the common stockholders. The conversion privilege gives the preferred stockholders the opportunity to exchange their holdings for stock in which the rights to earnings are not limited. In some instances, preferred stock may be convertible into bonds. Here the investors have the option of changing their positions from stockholders to creditors. Convertible preferred issues have become increasingly popular in recent years.

The decision by a stockholder to convert preferred holdings into common stock is a difficult one and involves many factors including the time limitation, if any, on the conversion privilege, the relative dividend returns on common stock as compared with preferred stock, as well as other provisions related to the two classes of securities.

Callable Preferred Stock. Preferred stock is **callable** when it can be called or redeemed at the option of the corporation. Many preferred issues are callable. The **call price** is usually specified in the original agreement and provides for payment of dividends in arrears as part of the repurchase price. When convertible stock has a call provision, the holders of the stock frequently are given the option of converting their holdings into common stock. The decision made by the investor will be based on the market price of the common stock.

Redeemable Preferred Stock. Preferred stock is sometimes subject to mandatory redemption requirements or other redemption provisions which give the security overlapping debt and equity characteristics. This type of stock is referred to as **redeemable preferred stock** and is defined as preferred stock that is redeemable at the option of the holder, or at a fixed or determinable price on a specific date, or upon other conditions not solely within the control of the issuer (e.g., redemption upon reaching a certain level of earnings).[1] The FASB is currently considering whether redeemable preferred stock should be classified as a liability rather than an equity security. Pending resolution of that issue, the SEC now requires special disclosures with respect to redeemable preferred stock. Without specifying all the details, these disclosures include a separate and distinct heading on the balance sheet and a separate footnote captioned "Redeemable Preferred Stocks." The number of shares authorized, issued, and outstanding must be disclosed as well as a general description of each issue, its redemption features, the rights of holders, and the combined aggregate amount of the redemption requirements.[2]

Asset and Dividend Preferences upon Corporate Liquidation. Preferred stock is generally preferred as to assets distributed upon corporate liquidation. Such a preference, however, cannot be assumed but must be specifically stated in the preferred stock contract. The asset preference for stock with a par value is an amount equal to par, or par plus a premium; in the absence of a par value it is a stated amount. Terms of the preferred contract may also provide for the full payment of any dividends in arrears upon liquidation, regardless of the retained earnings balance reported by the company. When this is the case and there are insufficient retained earnings, i.e., a deficit, such dividend priorities must be met from paid-in capital of the common issue; common stockholders receive whatever assets remain after settlement with the preferred group.

Common Stock

Strictly speaking, there should be but one kind of common stock. Common stock represents the residual ownership equity and carries the greatest risk. In return for this risk, common stock ordinarily shares in earnings to the greatest extent if the corporation is successful. There is no inherent distinction in voting rights between preferred and common stocks; however, voting rights are frequently given exclusively to common stockholders as long as dividends are paid regularly on preferred stock. Upon failure to meet preferred dividend requirements, special voting rights may be granted to preferred stockholders, thus affording this group a more prominent role in the management. In some states, voting rights cannot be withheld on any class of stock.

ISSUANCE OF CAPITAL STOCK

The capital stock of a corporation may be authorized but unissued; it may be subscribed for and held for issuance pending receipt of cash on stock subscriptions; it may be outstanding in the hands of stockholders; it may be reacquired and held by the corporation for subsequent reissuance or bonus distribution; it may be canceled by appropriate corporate action. An accurate record of the position of the corporation as a result of the ex-

---

[1]Securities and Exchange Commission, *Accounting Series Release No. 268*, "Presentation in Financial Statements of 'Redeemable Preferred Stocks' " (Washington: U.S. Goverment Printing Office, July 1979).
[2]*Ibid.*

changes of property between stockholders and the corporation must be maintained in the accounts. Individual accounts should be maintained in the ledger for each source of capital including each class of stock.

A **stockholders ledger**, in which accounts are maintained for each stockholder, is controlled by the capital stock account. The issuance of stock by the corporation calls for a credit to a stockholder's account for the shares issued. A transfer of stock ownership is recorded by a debit to the account of the person making the transfer and a credit to the account of the person acquiring the stock; since the capital stock outstanding remains the same after transfer of individual holdings, general ledger accounts are not affected.

A **stock certificate book** also reports shares outstanding. Certificates in the book are usually serially numbered. As certificates are issued, the number of shares issued is reported on the certificate stubs. When ownership transfers, the original certificates submitted by the sellers are canceled and attached to the original stubs and new certificates are issued to the buyers. Frequently, a corporation will appoint banks or trust companies to serve as **registrars** and **transfer agents**. These parties are assigned various responsibilities, such as transferring stock certificates, maintaining the stockholders ledger, preparing lists of stockholders for meetings, and making dividend distributions.

Capital Stock Issued for Cash

The issuance of stock for cash is recorded by a debit to Cash and a credit to Capital Stock for the par or stated value.[3] When the amount of cash received from the sale of stock is greater than the par or stated value, the excess is recorded separately as a credit to a *premium* or special paid-in capital account. This account is carried on the books as long as the stock to which it relates is outstanding. When stock is retired, the capital stock balance as well as any related paid-in capital balance is generally cancelled.

To illustrate, assume the Whitni Corporation is authorized to issue 10,000 shares of $10 par common stock. On April 1, 1981, 4,000 shares are sold for $45,000 cash. The entry to record the transaction is:

```
1981
April 1  Cash .................................................................................  45,000
             Common Stock, $10 par.......................................................      40,000
             Premium on Common Stock.................................................       5,000
                 To record the issuance of 4,000 shares of $10 par com-
                 mon stock for $45,000.
```

If, in the above example, the common stock were no-par stock but with a $10 stated value, the entry would be the same except the description of the stock would be Common Stock, $10 stated value and the $5,000 excess designated Paid-In Capital from Sale of Common Stock at More Than Stated Value. Generally, stock is assigned a par or a stated value. However, if there is no such value assigned, the entire amount of cash received on the

---

[3]The term *Capital Stock* is used in account titles in the text when the class of stock is not specifically designated. When preferred and common designations are given, these are used in the account titles.

sale of stock is credited to the capital stock account and there is no premium account involved. Assuming Whitni Corporation's stock were no-par common without a stated value, the entry to record the sale of 4,000 shares for $45,000 would be:

```
1981
April 1  Cash.........................................................................................  45,000
              Common Stock...................................................................          45,000
                  To record the issuance of 4,000 shares of no-par, no
                  stated-value common stock for $45,000.
```

Capital stock is seldom sold at less than par or stated value, often because state laws preclude such a sale. If it were, however, a *discount* would be recorded. A discount on the sale of stock indicates a potential claim by creditors against stockholders in the event the company becomes insolvent; from a going-concern point of view, however, the discount should be recognized as a subtraction item in presenting the company's contributed capital rather than as a liability.

Capital Stock Sold on Subscription

Capital stock may be issued on a subscription basis. A **subscription** is a legally binding contract between the subscriber (purchaser of stock) and the corporation (issuer of stock). The document states the number of shares subscribed for, the subscription price, the terms of payment, and other conditions of the transaction. By express provisions, the contract may be binding only if the corporation receives subscriptions for a stated number of shares. A subscription, while giving the corporation a legal claim for the contract price, also gives the subscriber the legal status of a stockholder unless certain rights as a stockholder are specifically withheld by law or by terms of the contract. Ordinarily stock certificates evidencing share ownership are not issued until the full subscription price has been received by the corporation.

Upon receiving subscriptions, Capital Stock Subscriptions Receivable is debited for the subscription price, Capital Stock Subscribed is credited for the amount to be recognized as capital stock when subscriptions have been collected, and a paid-in capital account is credited for the amount of the subscription price in excess of par or stated value. A special *subscribers journal* may be used in recording capital stock subscriptions.

Capital Stock Subscriptions Receivable is a control account, individual subscriptions being reported in the subsidiary *subscribers ledger*. Subscriptions Receivable is regarded as a current asset when the corporation expects to collect the balance currently, which is the usual situation; remaining balances are regarded as noncurrent.

Subscriptions may be collected in cash or in other properties accepted by the corporation. When collections are made, the appropriate asset account is debited and the receivable account is credited. Credits are also made to subscribers' accounts in the subsidiary ledger.

The actual issuance of stock is recorded by a debit to Capital Stock Subscribed and a credit to Capital Stock. The following entries illustrate the recording and issuance of capital stock sold on subscription. It is assumed that the Bushman Corporation is authorized to issue 10,000 shares of $10 par value common stock.

Recording and Issuance of Capital Stock Sold on Subscription

November 1–30 Received subscriptions for 5,000 shares at 12½ with 50% down payment, balance payable in 60 days.	Common Stock Subscriptions Receivable	62,500	
	Common Stock Subscribed.........		50,000
	Premium on Common Stock		12,500
	Cash	31,250	
	Common Stock Subscriptions Receivable		31,250
December 1–31 Received balance due on one half of subscriptions and issued stock to the fully paid subscribers, 2,500 shares.	Cash	15,625	
	Common Stock Subscriptions Receivable		15,625
	Common Stock Subscribed	25,000	
	Common Stock		25,000
Stockholders' equity after the above transactions:	**Stockholders' Equity**		
	Contributed capital:		
	Common stock, $10 par, 10,000 shares authorized, 2,500 shares issued and outstanding		$25,000
	Common stock subscribed, 2,500 shares...		25,000
	Premium on common stock........................		12,500
	Total stockholders' equity		$62,500

Subscription Defaults

If a subscriber defaults on a subscription by failing to make a payment when it is due, the corporation may (1) return to the subscriber the amount paid, (2) return to the subscriber the amount paid less any reduction in price or expense incurred upon the resale of the stock, (3) declare the full amount paid as forfeited, or (4) issue to the subscriber shares equal to the number paid for in full. The practice followed will depend upon the policy adopted by the corporation within the legal limitations set by the state in which it is incorporated.

To illustrate the entries under these different circumstances, assume in the Bushman Corporation example described earlier (with subscriptions at 12½) that one subscriber for 100 shares defaults after making the 50% down payment. Defaulted shares are subsequently resold at 11. The entries to record the default by the subscriber and the subsequent resale of the defaulted shares would be as follows:

1. *Assuming the amount paid in is returned:*

Common Stock Subscribed	1,000	
Premium on Common Stock...	250	
Common Stock Subscriptions Receivable....................................		625
Cash...		625
Cash	1,100	
Common Stock..		1,000
Premium on Common Stock		100

2. *Assuming the amount paid in less the price reduction on the resale is returned:*

Common Stock Subscribed	1,000	
Premium on Common Stock	250	
Common Stock Subscriptions Receivable		625
Payable to Defaulting Subscriber (*payment withheld pending*		
stock resale)		625
Cash	1,100	
Payable to Defaulting Subscriber	150	
Common Stock		1,000
Premium on Common Stock		250
Payable to Defaulting Subscriber	475	
Cash		475

3. *Assuming the full amount paid in is declared to be forfeited:*

Common Stock Subscribed	1,000	
Premium on Common Stock	250	
Common Stock Subscriptions Receivable		625
Paid-In Capital from Forfeited Stock Subscriptions		625
Cash	1,100	
Common Stock		1,000
Premium on Common Stock		100

4. *Assuming shares equal to the number paid for in full are issued:*

Common Stock Subscribed	1,000	
Premium on Common Stock	125	
Common Stock		500
Common Stock Subscriptions Receivable		625
Cash	550	
Common Stock		500
Premium on Common Stock		50

Capital Stock Issued for Consideration Other Than Cash

When capital stock is issued for consideration in the form of property other than cash or for services, particular care is required in recording the transaction. When, at the time of the exchange, stock is sold by the company for cash or is quoted on the open market at a certain price, this price can be used in recording the consideration received and the capital increase. When means for arriving at the cash value of the securities are not available, it will be necessary to arrive at a value for the acquired consideration.

It may be possible to arrive at a satisfactory valuation of property received in exchange for stock through an appraisal by a competent outside authority. But this solution may not be available in arriving at a valuation for consideration in the form of certain services as, for example, promotional services in organizing the corporation.

Normally the board of directors is given the right by law to establish valuations for consideration other than cash received for stock. Such values will stand for all legal purposes in the absence of proof that fraud was involved in the action. The assignment of values by the board of directors should be subject to particularly careful scrutiny. There have been cases where directors have assigned excessive values to the consideration received for stock to improve the company's reported financial position. When the value of the consideration cannot be clearly established and the directors' valuations are used in reporting assets and invested capital, the source of the valuations should be disclosed on the balance sheet. When there is evidence that improper values have been assigned to the consideration received for stock, such values should be restated.

Stock is said to be **watered** when assets are overstated and capital items are correspondingly overstated. On the other hand, the balance sheet is said to contain **secret reserves** when there is an understatement of assets or an overstatement of liabilities accompanied by a corresponding understatement of capital. These misstatements may be intentional or unintentional. The accountant cannot condone either overstatement or understatement of net assets and capital. It should be observed once more that any failures in accounting for assets are not limited to the balance sheet: the overstatement of assets will result in understatements of net income as asset cost is assigned to revenue; the understatement of assets will result in overstatements of net income as asset cost is assigned to revenue.

Issuance of Capital Stock in Exchange for a Business

A corporation, upon its formation or at some later date, may be combined with another ongoing business, issuing capital stock in exchange for the net assets acquired. This is referred to as a **business combination**. In determining the amount of stock to be issued, the fair market value of the stock, as well as the values of the net assets acquired, must be considered.

Frequently the value of the stock transferred by a corporation will exceed the value of the identifiable assets acquired because of a favorable earnings record of the business acquired. If the exchange is accounted for as a *purchase*, the value of the stock in excess of the values assigned to identifiable assets is recognized as goodwill. Under this approach, the retained earnings of the company acquired *do not* become part of the combined retained earnings. On the other hand, if the exchange is treated as a *pooling of interests*, neither the revaluation of assets nor the recognition of goodwill is recorded. Assets are stated at the amounts previously reported; the retained earnings accounts of the two companies are added together and become the amount of retained earnings for the combined entity. The purchase method assumes that one of the companies is dominant and is acquiring the other company. The pooling of interests method assumes equal status and continuity of common ownership. The accounting for business combinations is dealt with in APB Opinion No. 16, and is discussed in detail in advanced accounting texts.

CAPITAL STOCK REACQUISITION AND RETIREMENT

A corporation may have the right to call certain classes of stock for redemption and may choose to exercise this right. In other cases, it may purchase stock on the open market and formally retire shares. Whether obtained through call for redemption or through purchase on the market, retirement of stock at a cost differing from the original issuance price presents special accounting problems.

The reacquisition and retirement of stock cannot be considered to give rise to income or loss. A company in issuing stock raises capital which it hopes to employ profitably; in reacquiring and retiring shares it reduces the capital to be employed in subsequent operations. Income or loss arises from the utilization of resources placed in the hands of the corporation, not from capital transactions between the company and its stockholders. Although there is general agreement on this matter, there are still certain problems in recording stock retirement.

If a class of stock is retired at the same amount originally recognized as capital stock, the capital stock account is debited and Cash is credited. All reference to the investment by the stockholders, then, is cancelled. However, when the purchase price of the stock retired exceeds the par or stated value of the stock, the excess must be assigned in some satisfactory manner to paid-in capital and retained earnings.

The Accounting Principles Board in Opinion No. 6 commented upon the procedure to be followed when stock of a corporation is retired:

    i. *an excess of purchase price over par or stated value* may be allocated between capital surplus [paid-in capital] and retained earnings. The portion of the excess allocated to capital surplus should be limited to the sum of (a) all capital surplus arising from previous retirements and net "gains" on sales of treasury stock of the same issue and (b) the prorata portion of capital surplus paid in, voluntary transfers of retained earnings, capitalization of stock dividends, etc., on the same issue. For this purpose, any remaining capital surplus applicable to issues fully retired (formal or constructive) is deemed to be applicable prorata to shares of common stock. Alternatively, the excess may be charged entirely to retained earnings in recognition of the fact that a corporation can always capitalize or allocate retained earnings for such purposes.

  ii. *an excess of par or stated value over purchase price* should be credited to capital surplus.[4]

The effects of these provisions are illustrated in the following examples. Assume that a corporation reports the following balances related to an issue of preferred stock:

Preferred stock outstanding, par $10, 10,000 shares	$100,000
Premium on preferred stock	10,000

1. Assume the corporation redeems and retires 2,000 shares, or 20%, of the preferred stock at $12.50 per share. Reductions are made in the preferred stock account for 2,000 shares, par $10, or $20,000, and in the premium on preferred stock for a pro rata share of the premium, 20% of $10,000, or $2,000, and the difference between the sum of these amounts and the amount paid is debited to Retained Earnings. The entry, then, is as follows:

Preferred Stock	20,000	
Premium on Preferred Stock	2,000	
Retained Earnings	3,000	
Cash		25,000

---

[4]*Opinions of the Accounting Principles Board, No. 6*, "Status of Accounting Research Bulletins" (New York: American Institute of Certified Public Accountants, 1965), par. 12a.

If the alternate method indicated by the Accounting Principles Board is followed, the entire amount paid over par or stated value of the retired shares would be debited to Retained Earnings. In the example, then, the entry would be:

Preferred Stock...	20,000	
Retained Earnings	5,000	
Cash		25,000

2. Assume the corporation redeems and retires the 2,000 shares of preferred stock at only $9 per share. The preferred stock account is reduced by the par value of the shares, $20,000, and the difference between the debit to Preferred Stock and the amount paid is credited to a paid-in capital account. The following entry is made:

Preferred Stock...	20,000	
Cash		18,000
Paid-In Capital from Preferred Stock Reacquisition..............		2,000

It would also be possible to reduce Premium on Preferred Stock for a pro rata share of the premium, $2,000, and report the Paid-In Capital from Preferred Stock Reacquisition at the difference between the amount at which the preferred shares were originally issued and the amount paid on their retirement. The following entry can be made:

Preferred Stock...	20,000	
Premium on Preferred Stock..	2,000	
Cash		18,000
Paid-In Capital from Preferred Stock Reacquisition..............		4,000

If additional shares of preferred stock are subsequently retired at amounts in excess of par, the differences between the amounts paid and the par value of the preferred stock retired can be debited to the paid-in capital from the earlier preferred stock acquisition.

When stock is formally retired, there is a reduction in the corporate legal or stated capital. State laws normally do not bar the reduction of legal or stated capital when stock is issued subject to redemption and redemption is made at the price provided by terms of the stock issue.

Treasury Stock

When a company's own stock, previously paid for and issued, is reacquired and held in the name of the company rather than formally retired, it is known as **treasury stock**. A company may acquire its own stock by purchase, by acceptance in satisfaction of a claim, or by donation from stockholders. Treasury shares may subsequently be sold or formally retired.

There are many reasons a company finds it desirable to repurchase its own stock. A survey by the Conference Board cited seven major reasons for repurchasing shares.[5]

1. To obtain shares for executive stock options and other compensation programs.
2. To obtain stock to be used in acquisitions.

[5]Francis J. Walsh, Jr., *Repurchasing Common Stock* (New York: The Conference Board, Inc., 1975), p. 5.

3. To improve per-share earnings by reducing the number of shares outstanding.
4. To obtain shares for conversion of other securities.
5. To invest surplus cash temporarily.
6. To support the market price of the stock.
7. To increase the ratio of debt to equity.

State laws vary widely in their regulations concerning treasury stock. In some states, accounting for treasury stock is governed largely by statute. In other states, only general restrictions are applied. The accounting for treasury stock requires careful review of the state laws. State laws normally provide that the reacquisition of stock must serve some legitimate corporate purpose and must be made without injury or prejudice to the creditors or to the remaining stockholders. In almost every state, it is provided that the legal or stated capital of the corporation may not be reduced by reacquisition.

Despite the fact that the legal capital remains the same after a company has reacquired shares of its own stock, treasury stock cannot normally be viewed as an asset but should be regarded as a reduction in corporate capital. A company cannot have an ownership interest in itself; treasury stock generally does not confer upon the corporation dividend, voting, or subscription rights.

Although treasury stock has a number of similarities to unissued stock, there are some significant differences. Among these differences are the following: (1) stockholders' preemptive rights do not apply to treasury stock; (2) treasury stock may be reissued without authorization by stockholders; (3) having already been issued in accordance with legal requirements governing legal or stated capital, treasury stock may be reissued without the conditions imposed upon its original issue, for example, the discount liability on the original issue; and (4) treasury stock remains a part of legal capital in most states.

The sale of treasury stock increases the number of shares outstanding. However, the legal capital, remaining unchanged upon its purchase, is not increased through its sale. If treasury stock is to be retired, such retirement is formalized by the preparation of a certificate or notice of reduction filed with appropriate state officials. Upon the formal retirement of shares, these revert to the status of unissued shares and there is a reduction in the corporate legal or stated capital. For federal income tax purposes, treasury stock transactions provide no taxable gain or loss; stock reacquisition, as well as stock reissue or retirement, is regarded as a transaction related to a company's invested capital.

Purchase and Sale or Retirement of Treasury Stock. Two primary methods for recording treasury stock transactions have been suggested: (1) the **cost method**, where the purchase of treasury stock is viewed as giving rise to a capital element whose ultimate disposition remains to be resolved; and (2) the **par or stated value method**, where the purchase of treasury stock is viewed as effective retirement of outstanding stock.

Cost Method. Under the cost method, the purchase of treasury stock is recorded by debiting a treasury stock account for the cost of the purchase and crediting Cash. The cost is determined by the current market price of the stock and is not necessarily tied to the original stock issue price. The balance in the treasury stock account is reported as a deduction from total stockholders' equity on the balance sheet. If treasury stock is subsequently retired, the debit balance in the treasury stock account is eliminated by allocating proportionate amounts to the appropriate capital stock, paid-in capital, and retained earnings accounts, as noted previously according to APB Opinion No. 6. If treasury stock is subsequently sold, the difference between the acquisition cost and the selling price is reported as an increase or decrease in stockholders' equity. If stockholders' equity is increased, the account credited is Paid-In Capital from Treasury Stock Transactions. If stockholders' equity is decreased, paid-in capital accounts previously established may be debited or the entire amount may be debited to Retained Earnings.

To illustrate the entries required for treasury stock transactions using the cost method, consider the following:

Cost Method of Accounting for Treasury Stock

1980
Issue of stock, 10,000 shares, $10 par, at $15.
Net income for year, $30,000.
	Cash 150,000
	    Capital Stock................................. 100,000
	    Premium on Capital Stock.......... 50,000
	Income Summary 30,000
	    Retained Earnings....................... 30,000

1981
Reacquisition of 1,000 shares at $16.
(1) Sale of treasury stock at $20.
	Treasury Stock 16,000
	    Cash... 16,000
	Cash 20,000
	    Treasury Stock............................. 16,000
	    Paid-In Capital from Sale of
	        Treasury Stock at More Than
	        Cost... 4,000

(2) Sale of treasury stock at $14.	Cash .... 14,000 Retained Earnings............................ 2,000 Treasury Stock.............................. 16,000
(3) Retirement of treasury stock (10% of original issue).	Capital Stock .... 10,000 Premium on Capital Stock .... 5,000* Retained Earnings........................... 1,000 Treasury Stock............................. 16,000 *As indicated earlier, the entire $6,000 difference between the debit to Capital Stock and the cost to acquire the treasury stock may be debited to Retained Earnings.

Illustration of stockholders' equity section of balance sheet assuming transaction (1) above.	Stockholders' Equity
	Contributed capital:
	    Capital stock.. $100,000
	    Premium on capital stock 50,000
	    Paid-in capital from sale of treasury
	        stock at more than cost....................... 4,000
	    Retained earnings 30,000
	    Total stockholders' equity $184,000

Par or Stated Value Method. If the par or stated value method (also known as the retirement method) is used, the purchase of treasury stock is regarded as a withdrawal of a group of stockholders calling for the cancellation of capital balances identified with this group. It follows that the sale of treasury stock, under this approach, represents the admission of a new group of stockholders calling for entries giving effect to the investment by this group. Thus, there are two separate transactions that must be recorded — the purchase and the sale.

Using the par or stated value method and the same basic data for 1980 as illustrated for the cost method, the following entries would be made in 1981:

Par Value Method of Accounting for Treasury Stock

1981 Reacquisition of 1,000 shares at $16 (assumed retirement of 10% of original issue).	Capital Stock .... Premium on Capital Stock............ Retained Earnings......................... Cash...................................... *Alternatively, the entire $6,000 may be debited to Retained Earnings.	10,000 5,000* 1,000 16,000

Sale of treasury stock at $20.	Cash...
	    Capital Stock.............................
	    Paid-In Capital from Sale of
	    Treasury Stock at More Than
	    Par ....
	**Alternatively, this amount may be appropriately credited to Premium on Capital Stock.
		20,000
		
		10,000
		
		10,000**

Illustration of stockholders' equity section of balance sheet after sale of treasury stock.	Stockholders' Equity
	Contributed capital:
	    Capital stock................................
	    Premium on capital stock ....
	    Paid-in capital from sale of treasury
	        stock at more than par.........................
	Retained earnings ....
	Total stockholders' equity ....
		
		$100,000
		45,000
		
		10,000
		29,000
		$184,000

Evaluating the Two Primary Methods of Accounting for Treasury Stock Transactions.

Neither the AICPA, through the Accounting Principles Board, nor the Financial Accounting Standards Board has expressed a preference between the two approaches of accounting for treasury stock transactions. Although there is theoretical support for each approach, in practice the cost method is generally followed.

In comparing the results of the two approaches, it should be noticed that the total stockholders' equity will be the same regardless of which method is used. There may be differences, however, in the amounts of contributed and earned capital reported. It also should be noted that Retained Earnings may be decreased with treasury stock transactions, but can never be increased by buying and selling treasury stock.

Retained earnings may be restricted for dividend purposes while treasury stock is held. There are several ways these restrictions may be shown on the balance sheet. The most common are (1) as an appropriation of retained earnings discussed in the next chapter, (2) as a parenthetical remark in the body of the statement, and (3) as a note to the financial statements. The restriction would be reported regardless of the method used to record the purchase of the stock.

The procedures illustrated in this chapter may be modified to meet existing legal requirements relative to the status of treasury stock and to the effects upon capital balances when treasury stock is sold or retired.

Conclusions Relative to Treasury Stock Transactions. From the discussion of treasury stock, several important conclusions may be summarized as follows:

1. Treasury stock is rarely includable as an asset on corporation books and does not qualify for dividends.
2. Neither gain nor loss can be recognized on the income statement relative to transactions in a company's own stock.
3. Retained earnings can be decreased as a result of treasury stock transactions; however, retained earnings cannot be increased through such transactions.
4. In most states, retained earnings equal to the cost of treasury stock is legally unavailable for dividends. This restriction on retained earnings is reported on the balance sheet by an appropriation of retained earnings, by parenthetical remark, or by a note to the financial statements.
5. The total stockholders' equity is not affected by the method used; however, the amounts reported for contributed capital and retained earnings can be affected by the accounting procedure followed.

Donated Treasury Stock

Treasury stock is occasionally acquired by donation from the stockholders. Shares may be donated to raise company working capital through their sale. In other instances, shares may be donated to eliminate a deficit. Ordinarily, all of the stockholders participate in the donation, each party donating a certain percentage of holdings so that relative interests in the corporation remain unchanged.

In the absence of any cost, the acquisition of treasury stock by donation may be reported on the corporation books by a memorandum entry. Assuming the assets of the company have been fairly valued, the sale of donated stock is then recorded by a debit to Cash and a credit to Donated Capital. If assets of the company have been overvalued, however, it would be improper to recognize an increase in capital arising from the sale of donated shares. Under these circumstances, the sale price for the stock should be employed as a basis for restating the company assets and contributed capital.

To illustrate this concept, assume the Bonanza Mining Co. is formed to take over the mining properties of partners Clark and Davis, and the corporation issues 10,000 shares of no-par stock to partners in exchange for the properties. A value of $250,000 is assigned to the properties and an entry is made for the acquisition as follows:

Mining Properties	250,000	
Capital Stock		250,000

Shortly after corporate formation, Clark and Davis donate 4,000 shares to the corporation, and the corporation sells these for $15 per share. If $15 can be regarded as a measure of the fair value of the stock exchanged for the properties, properties should be restated at $90,000, or $15 × 6,000, the number of shares actually exchanged for the properties. Upon the sale of the donated shares, then, entries should be made (1) to correct the property account and capital stock for both the stock overissue and the property overvaluation, and (2) to record the sale of the donated shares. These entries are:

Capital Stock	160,000	
Mining Properties		160,000
Cash	60,000	
Capital Stock		60,000

The balance sheet for the corporation would now show the following balances:

Cash	$60,000	Capital stock, no-par, 10,000	
Mining properties	90,000	shares outstanding	$150,000

When stock is donated so that a company may cancel a deficit, the company should take formal action to retire donated shares. Upon retirement, Capital Stock is debited for the decrease in legal capital and Additional Paid-In Capital is credited. The deficit can then be applied against the additional paid-in capital balance.

STOCK SPLITS AND REVERSE STOCK SPLITS

When the market price of shares is high and it is felt that a lower price will result in a better market and a wider distribution of ownership, a corporation may authorize the shares outstanding to be replaced by a larger number of shares. For example, 100,000 shares of stock, par value $100, are exchanged for 500,000 shares of stock, par value $20. Each stockholder receives 5 new shares for each share owned. The increase in shares outstanding in this manner is known as a **stock split** or **stock split-up**. The reverse procedure, replacement of shares outstanding by a smaller number of shares, may be desirable when the price of shares is low and it is felt there may be certain advantages in having a higher price for shares. The reduction of shares outstanding by combining shares is referred to as a **reverse stock split** or a **stock split-down**.

After a stock split or reverse stock split, the capital stock balance remains the same; however, the change in the number of shares of stock outstanding is accompanied by a change in the par or stated value of the stock. The change in the number of shares outstanding, as well as the change in the par or stated value, may be recorded by means of a memorandum entry. However, it would normally be desirable to establish a new account reporting the nature and the amount of the new issue. In any event, notations will be required in the subsidiary stockholders ledger to report the exchange of stock and the change in the number of shares held by each stockholder.

Stock splits are sometimes effected by issuing a large stock dividend. In this case, the par value of the stock is not changed and an amount equal to the par value of the newly issued shares is transferred to the capital account from either additional paid-in capital or from retained earnings. A further discussion of this type of stock split is included in Chapter 17.

BALANCE SHEET DISCLOSURE OF CONTRIBUTED CAPITAL

Contributed capital and its components should be disclosed separately from Retained Earnings in the balance sheet. Within the contributed capital section, it is important to identify the major classes of stock with their related additional paid-in capital accounts. Although it is common practice to report a single value for additional paid-in capital for each class of stock, separate accounts should be provided in the ledger to identify the individual sources of additional paid-in capital, e.g., premium on capital stock or paid-in capital in excess of stated value, paid-in capital from conversion of capital stock, from forfeited stock subscriptions, or from donations by stockholders.

A description of the major features should be disclosed for each class of stock such as par or stated value, dividend preference, or conversion option. The number of shares authorized, issued, and outstanding should also be disclosed. The balance sheet for General Mills, Inc. in Appendix B illustrates many of these points.

QUESTIONS

1. Mark Sears has been operating a small machine shop for several months. His business has grown, and he has given some thought to incorporating his business. What advantages and disadvantages would there be to such a change?

2. What are the four basic rights of stockholders?

3. (a) Define legal capital. (b) What limitations are placed upon the corporation by law to safeguard legal capital?

4. (a) What preferences are usually granted preferred stockholders? (b) What is callable preferred stock? Redeemable preferred stock? Convertible preferred stock? (c) Distinguish between cumulative and noncumulative preferred stock. (d) What limitations on stockholders' rights are generally found in preferred stock?

5. The controller for the Forsey Co. contends that the redemption of preferred stock at less than its issuance price should be reported as an increase in retained earnings since redemption at more than issuance price calls for a decrease in retained earnings. How would you answer this argument?

6. A new company decides to issue both preferred and common stock. The par value for both types is $100. An investor decides to purchase the preferred stock. Under what conditions would this be a wise decision?

7. The Carver Co. treats proceeds from capital stock subscription defaults as miscellaneous revenue. Would you approve of this practice?

8. (a) What alternatives may a company have when a subscriber defaults on a subscription? (b) What limits the choice between these alternatives?

9. The Jeffs Company acquires the assets of the Marino Company in exchange for 10,000 shares of its common stock, par value $10. (a) Assuming the appraised value of the property acquired exceeds the par value of the stock issued, how would you record the acquisition? (b) Assuming the par value of the stock issued exceeds the appraised value of the property acquired, suggest different methods for recording the acquisition. What factors will determine the method to be used?

10. Why might a company purchase its own stock?

11. Energy Resources, Inc., reports treasury stock as a current asset, explaining that it intends to sell the stock soon to acquire working capital. Do you approve of this reporting?

12. (a) Describe two approaches that may be taken in recording the reacquisition of treasury stock. (b) What are the entries in each case assuming: (1) the stock is purchased at more than its original issue price; (2) the stock is purchased at less than its original issue price?

13. There is frequently a difference between the purchase price and the sales price of treasury stock. Why isn't this difference properly shown as an income statement item, especially in view of accounting pronouncements that restrict entries to Retained Earnings?

14. The South West Co. issues 10,000,000 shares of no-par common stock in exchange for certain mineral lands. Property is established on the books at $5,000,000. Shortly thereafter, stockholders donate to the corporation 20% of their shares. The stock is resold by the company at 10¢ per share. What accounting problems arise as a result of the stock donation and resale?

EXERCISES

exercise 16-1

The Samuelson Company pays out dividends at the end of each year as follows: 1979, $150,000; 1980, $240,000; 1981, $560,000. Give the amount that will be paid per share on common and preferred stock for each year, assuming capital structures as follows:

    (a) 250,000 shares of no-par common; 20,000 shares of $100 par, 7%, noncumulative preferred.

    (b) 250,000 shares of no-par common; 20,000 shares of $100 par, 7%, cumulative preferred, dividends three years in arrears at the beginning of 1979.

    (c) 250,000 shares of $10 par common; 30,000 shares of $100 par, 7%, cumulative preferred, no dividends in arrears at the beginning of 1979.

exercise 16-2

The stockholders' equity for the Brandon Company on July 1, 1981, is as given below.

Contributed capital:

Preferred stock, cumulative, $10 stated value, 37,000 shares outstanding, entitled upon involuntary liquidation to $12 per share plus dividends in arrears amounting to $4 per share on July 1, 1981	$370,000
Common stock, $2 stated value, 90,000 shares oustanding	180,000
Paid-in capital from sale of common stock at more than stated value	200,000
Retained earnings	56,000
Total stockholders' equity	$806,000

Determine the amounts that would be paid to each class of stockholders if the company is liquidated on this date, assuming cash available for stockholders after meeting all of the creditors' claims is: (a) $300,000; (b) $500,000; (c) $640,000.

exercise 16-3

The Blackburn Corporation is organized with authorized capital as follows: 15,000 shares of no-par common and 2,000 shares of 8% preferred, par $200. Give the entries required for each of the following transactions:

(a) Assets formerly owned by G. Culligan are accepted as payment for 5,000 shares of common stock. Assets are recorded at values as follows: land, $20,000; buildings, $40,000; inventories, $80,000.

(b) Remaining common stock is sold at $15.

(c) Subscriptions are received for 1,250 shares of preferred stock at $206. A 50% down payment is made on preferred.

(d) One subscriber for 125 shares of preferred defaults and the down payment is retained pending sale of this lot. Remaining subscribers pay the balances due and the stock is issued.

(e) Lot of 125 shares of preferred is sold at $204. Loss on resale is charged against the account of the defaulting subscriber, and the down payment less the loss is returned to the subscriber.

exercise 16-4

On January 1, 1981, RSK Corporation received authorization to issue 100,000 shares of no-par common stock with a stated value of $10 per share. The stock was offered to subscribers at a subscription price of $40 per share. Subscriptions were recorded by a debit to Subscriptions Receivable and credits to Common Stock Subscribed and to a paid-in capital account. Subsequently, a subscriber who had contracted to purchase 500 shares defaulted after paying 20% of the subscription price. Give four methods of accounting for the default, and give the journal entry to record the default under each method.

exercise 16-5

The Giles Co. issues 10,000 shares of preferred stock and 45,000 shares of common stock, each with a par value of $10, in exchange for properties appraised at $600,000. Give the entry to record the exchange on the books of the corporation assuming:

(a) No price can be assigned at date of issuance to the preferred stock or common stock issues.

(b) Common stock is selling on the market at $10.50 per share; there was no preferred stock issued prior to this issue.

(c) Common stock is selling on the market at $10 per share, preferred stock is selling on the market at $15 per share.

exercise 16-6

The Cowart Company reported the following balances related to an issuance of common stock:

Common Stock, $10 par, 50,000 shares issued and outstanding $500,000
Premium on Common Stock 50,000

The company purchased and retired 5,000 shares at $13 on June 1, 1981, and 12,000 shares at $8 on December 31, 1981. Give the entries to record the acquisition and retirement of the common stock.

exercise 16-7

The capital accounts for the Crawford Co. were as follows on June 1, 1981:

Common Stock, $15 par, 240,00 shares	$3,600,000
Premium on Common Stock	480,000
Retained Earnings	900,000

On this date the company purchased 15,000 shares of stock at $16; and in December of the same year it reissued this stock at $19.

    (1) What entries should be made for the stock purchase and the reissuance if the par value method of recording treasury stock transactions is used? (If alternate treatments are possible, justify your selection.)

    (2) What entries should be made for the stock purchase and reissuance if the cost method is used?

    (3) After the reissuance of the treasury stock, how does the stockholders' equity differ under the two methods?

exercise 16-8

The Rojo Company issued 10,000 shares of no-par stock at $30 and 20,000 shares at $45. The state in which Rojo is incorporated does not require any stated capital. During 1981, 2,000 shares were reacquired at $42. Assume the treasury stock is to be carried at the weighted average price per share. Prepare the journal entry to record the reacquisition.

exercise 16-9

The assets of the Lumbard Company are properly valued at $5,000,000. The outstanding common stock of the company is no-par with a stated value of $30. The principal shareholders donated 10,000 shares of stock on June 30, 1981, when the market value was $46. The shares were then resold on September 15, 1981, at $50. Give the entries to record the donation and resale of the treasury stock.

exercise 16-10

In your first audit of a mining company, you note the following facts with respect to its capital stock transactions:

    Authorized capital consists of 2,500,000 shares of $1 par value common stock.

    All of the shares were issued initially in exchange for certain mineral properties. The properties were recorded on the company books at $5,000,000.

    One million shares were received by the company as a donation shortly after incorporation and were sold immediately for cash of $1,500,000. This amount was recorded as a credit to Donated Capital.

    (1) What values should be assigned to the mineral properties and the stockholders' equity? Discuss.

    (2) Prepare any required correcting entry.

exercise 16-11

From the following information, reconstruct the journal entries that were made by the Starlight Corporation during 1981.

	December 31, 1981		December 31, 1980	
	Amount	Shares	Amount	Shares
Common stock	$175,000	7,000	$150,000	6,000
Premium on common stock	54,250		36,000	
Paid-in capital from sale of treasury stock at more than cost	1,000	200	——	——
Retained earnings	76,500*	——	49,000	——
Treasury stock	15,000	300	——	——

    *Includes net income for 1981 of $40,000. There were no dividends.

Twenty-five hundred shares of common stock issued when the company was formed were purchased and retired during 1981. The cost method is used to record treasury stock transactions.

PROBLEMS

problem 16-1

Pulsipher Co. was organized on May 25, 1981, and was authorized to issue 250,000 shares of no-par common stock, stated value $20, and 10,000 shares of 9% preferred stock, par value $50.

The following were the company's capital stock transactions through September 15, 1981:

June   1   Issued 55,000 shares of common stock to an investment group at $25.

June 15   Assets were obtained from Lawler Co. in exchange for 75,000 shares of common stock. The assets were appraised as follows:

Merchandise inventory	$400,000
Furniture and fixtures	150,000
Machinery and equipment	575,000
Land	475,000

July   1   Subscriptions were received for 120,000 shares of common stock at $30 and for 5,000 shares of preferred 9% stock at $55; each class of stock is to be paid for in two installments, 25% on the date of subscription and 75% within 90 days.

Sept. 15   The second installments on the common stock and preferred stock were paid in full and the stock was issued.

Instructions:

   (1)   Give the journal entries to record the preceding transactions.

   (2)   Prepare a balance sheet based on the results of the preceding transactions.

problem 16-2

The Romero Company, organized on April 10, 1981, was authorized to issue stock as follows:

    250,000 shares of $10 par common stock
    10,250 shares of 8% preferred stock with a par value of $100

Capital stock transactions through September 15, 1981, were as follows:

May   15   Subscriptions were received for 100,000 shares of common stock at $16 on the following terms: 10% was paid in cash at the time of subscription, the balance being payable in three equal installments due on the fifteenth day of each succeeding month.

June   1   All of the preferred stock was issued to an investment company for cash at $102 and stock was issued.

June 15   The first installment on subscriptions to 95,000 shares was collected. Terms of the subscription contract provided that defaulting subscribers have 30 days in which to make payment and obtain reinstatement; failure to make payment within the specified period will result in the forfeiture of amounts already paid in.

July   15   The second installment on common subscriptions was collected. Collections included receipt of the first and second installment on 3,000 shares from subscribers who defaulted on their first installment; however, subscribers to 1,000 shares defaulted in addition to subscribers already in default.

Aug. 15   The third installment on common subscriptions was collected. Collections included receipt of the second and third installment from subscribers to 500 shares who defaulted on their second installment. Stock certificates were issued to fully paid subscribers.

Sept.   1   Stock in default was issued to an investment company at 14.

Instructions:

   (1)   Give the journal entries to record these transactions.

   (2)   Prepare the stockholders' equity section of the balance sheet on September 15, 1981.

problem 16-3

The Jorgensen Machine Co. was incorporated on January 31, 1981, with authorized common stock of $1,200,000 and 9% cumulative preferred stock of $240,000, each class with a par value of $60.

Subscriptions were received for 6,000 shares of common stock at $65 a share, to be paid in four equal installments on March 1, April 1, May 1, and June 1. The first installment was paid in full.

Subscribers for 400 shares defaulted on the second installment, and the amounts already received from these subscribers were returned. The second, third, and fourth installments were paid in full on their due dates by the remaining subscribers, and the stock was issued.

During March, preferred stock was offered for sale at $80, 1 share of common stock being offered with each subscription for 10 shares of preferred. During March, the market price for the common stock was $65 per share. On this basis subscriptions were received for all of the preferred stock. Subscriptions were payable in two equal installments: the first was payable by the end of March and the second was payable at any time prior to June 15. The first installment was paid in full. By June 1, $136,000 had been received on the second installment, and stock was issued to the fully paid subscribers.

Instructions:

(1) Journalize the above transactions.

(2) Prepare the stockholders' equity section of the balance sheet as of June 1 reflecting the foregoing.

problem 16-4

The capital accounts of the Malmrose Company were as follows on June 1, 1981.

Preferred 9% Stock, $100 par, 7,000 shares issued and outstanding..........	$ 700,000
Premium on Preferred Stock..	21,000
Common Stock, $20 par, 70,000 shares issued and outstanding.................	1,400,000
Premium on Common Stock..	350,000
Retained Earnings	190,000

During the remainder of 1981, the Malmrose Company called the preferred stock at $112 per share and then retired the stock. Also, the company reacquired 28,000 shares of common stock at $17, and 22,000 of the reacquired common shares were reissued at $24 per share.

Instructions:

(1) Give the entries to record the reacquisition and retirement of the preferred stock and the acquisition and reissue of the common stock assuming the par value method of recording treasury stock transactions is used.

(2) Give the entry to record the acquisition and resale of the common stock assuming the cost method of recording treasury stock transactions is used.

problem 16-5

The Monson Company has two classes of capital stock outstanding: 9%, $20 par preferred and $70 par common. During the fiscal year ending November 30, 1981, the company was active in transactions affecting the stockholders' equity. The following summarizes these transactions:

Type of Transaction	Number of Shares	Price per Share
(a) Issue of preferred stock..	10,000	$28
(b) Issue of common stock	35,000	70
(c) Retirement of preferred stock......................................	2,000	30
(d) Purchase of treasury stock — common (reported at cost)	5,000	80
(e) Stock split — common (par value reduced to $35)............	2 for 1	
(f) Reissue of treasury stock — common	5,000	52

Balances of the accounts in the stockholders' equity section of November 30, 1980, were:

Preferred Stock, 50,000 shares..	$1,000,000
Common Stock, 100,000 shares	7,000,000
Premium on Preferred Stock	400,000
Premium on Common Stock	1,200,000
Retained Earnings	550,000

Dividends were paid at the end of the fiscal year on the common stock at $1.20 per share, and on the preferred stock at the preferred rate. Net income for the year was $850,000.

Instructions: Based upon the above data, prepare the stockholders' equity section of the balance sheet as of November 30, 1981. (Note: A work sheet beginning with November 30, 1980 balances and providing for transactions for the current year will facilitate the preparation of this section of the balance sheet.)

problem 16-6

Transactions of the Tinker Company during 1981, the first year of operations, that affected its stockholders' equity are given below.

(a) Issued 30,000 shares of 9% preferred stock, $20 par, at $26.
(b) Issued 50,000 shares of $30 par common stock at $33.
(c) Purchased and retired 4,000 shares of preferred stock at $28.
(d) Purchased 6,000 shares of its own common stock at $35.
(e) Reissued 1,000 shares of treasury stock at $37.
(f) Stockholders donated to the company 4,000 shares of common when shares had a market price of $36. One half of these shares were issued for $38.

No dividends were declared in 1981 and net income for 1981 was $185,000.

Instructions:
(1) Record each of the transactions. Assume treasury stock acquisitions are recorded at cost.
(2) Give the entries for (d) and (e) assuming treasury stock acquisitions are reported as capital stock retirement.
(3) Prepare the stockholders' equity section of the balance sheet, assuming treasury stock is recorded at cost and assuming retained earnings restrictions are shown by parenthetical remarks.

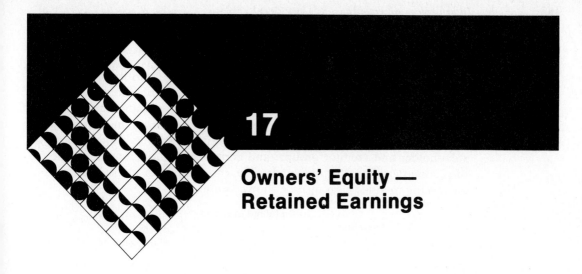

17

Owners' Equity —
Retained Earnings

CHAPTER OBJECTIVES

Describe the factors affecting retained earnings: prior period adjustments, earnings, dividends, and appropriations of retained earnings.

Identify other possible additions to or deductions from owners' equity.

Describe the measurement of book value per share.

Describe and illustrate the equity section in financial statements of corporations.

The nature of retained earnings is frequently misunderstood, and this misunderstanding may lead to seriously misleading inferences in reading and interpreting financial statements. Retained earnings is essentially the meeting place of the balance sheet accounts and the income statement accounts. In successive periods retained earnings are increased by income and decreased by losses and dividends. As a result, the retained earnings balance represents the net accumulated earnings of the corporation. If the retained earnings account were affected only by income (losses) and dividends, there would be little confusion in its interpretation. A number of other factors, however, can affect retained earnings. The purpose of this chapter is to identify and explain the different types of transactions that impact directly on retained earnings.

FACTORS AFFECTING RETAINED EARNINGS

One of the factors affecting retained earnings — treasury stock transactions — was discussed in Chapter 16. Other factors include: corrections of errors in prior periods; transactions between the corporation and its stockholders; stock dividends resulting in transfers from retained earnings to paid-in capital; legal restrictions upon retained earnings in protecting the stockholder and creditor groups; and contractual limitations upon the use of retained earnings for dividends. The most common items increasing or decreasing retained earnings are shown below.

Retained Earnings

Decreases	Increases
Prior period adjustments for decreases in past earnings	Prior period adjustments for increases in past earnings
Current net loss	Current net income
Cash dividends	
Stock dividends	
Treasury stock transactions	

Prior Period Adjustments

There are several types of errors that occur in measuring the results of operations and the financial status of an enterprise. Accounting errors can result from mathematical mistakes, a failure to apply appropriate accounting principles and procedures, or a misstatement or omission of certain information. In addition, a change from an accounting principle that is not generally accepted to one that is accepted is considered a correction of an error.[1]

Fortunately, most errors are discovered during the accounting period, prior to closing the books. When this is the case, corrections can be made by adjusting entries directly to the accounts. The proper balances are then shown on the balance sheet and an appropriate income measurement reported.

Sometimes errors go undetected during the current period, but they are affected by an equal misstatement in the subsequent period; that is, they are *counterbalanced*. When this happens, the under or overstatement of income in one period is counterbalanced by an equal under or overstatement of income in the next period, and after the closing process is completed for the second year, Retained Earnings is correctly stated. If a counterbalancing error is discovered during the second year, however, it should be corrected at that time.

When errors of past periods are not counterbalancing, Retained Earnings will be misstated until a correction is made in the accounting records. If the error is material, the Accounting Principles Board has specified it should be considered a **prior period adjustment** and the adjustment should

---

[1]*Opinions of the Accounting Principles Board, No. 20,* "Accounting Changes" (New York: American Institute of Certified Public Accountants, 1971) par. 13.

be made directly to the retained earnings account.[2] If an error resulted in an understatement of income in previous periods, a correcting entry would be needed to increase retained earnings; if an error overstated income in prior periods, then retained earnings would have to be decreased. These adjustments for corrections in net income of prior periods would typically be shown as a part of the total change in retained earnings as follows:

Retained Earnings, unadjusted beginning balance	$xxx
Add or subtract prior period adjustments	xx
Retained Earnings, adjusted beginning balance	$xxx
Add current year's net income or subtract current year's net loss	xx
Subtract dividends	(xx)
Retained Earnings, ending balance	$xxx

When errors are discovered, the accountant must be able to analyze the situation and determine what action is appropriate under the circumstances. This calls for an understanding of accounting standards as well as good judgment and skill in dealing with situations indicating a failure to meet such standards. The appendix to this chapter covers in detail the techniques for analyzing and correcting errors.

Earnings

The primary source of retained earnings is the net income generated by a business. The retained earnings account is increased by net income and is reduced by net losses from business activities. When operating losses or other debits to Retained Earnings produce a debit balance in this account, the debit balance is referred to as a **deficit**.

Corporate earnings transferred to retained earnings originate from revenue and expense transactions with individuals or businesses outside of the company. No increases in retained earnings are recognized on transactions with stockholders involving treasury stock; however, as indicated in Chapter 16, decreases may be recognized. The receipt of properties through donation is not recognized as earnings, but as paid-in capital. The earnings of a corporation may be distributed to the stockholders or retained to provide for expanding operations.

Dividends

Dividends are distributions to stockholders of a corporation in proportion to the number of shares held by the respective owners. Distributions may take the form of (1) cash, (2) other assets, (3) notes or other evidence of corporate indebtedness, in effect, deferred cash dividends, and (4) share of a company's own stock. Most dividends involve reductions in retained earnings. Exceptions include some stock dividends issued in the form of stock splits, which involve a transfer from additional paid-in capital to legal capi-

---

[2]*Ibid.*, par. 36.

tal, and dividends in corporate liquidation, which represent a return to stockholders of a portion or all of the corporate legal capital and call for reductions in invested capital.

Use of the term *dividend* without qualification normally implies the distribution of cash. Dividends in a form other than cash should be designated by their special form, and distributions from a capital source other than retained earnings should carry a description of their special origin. The terms *property dividend* and *stock dividend* suggest distributions of a special form; designations such as *liquidating dividend* and *dividend distribution of paid-in capital* identify the special origin of the distribution.

"Dividends paid out of retained earnings" is an expression frequently encountered. Accuracy, however, requires recognition that dividends are paid out of cash, which serves to reduce retained earnings. Earnings of the corporation increase net assets or stockholders' equity. Dividend distributions represent no more than asset withdrawals that reduce net assets.

Dividend Policy. Among the powers delegated by the stockholders to the board of directors is the power to control the dividend policy. Whether dividends shall or shall not be paid, as well as the nature and the amount of dividends, are matters the board determines. In declaring dividends, the board of directors must observe the legal requirements governing the maintenance of legal or stated capital. These requirements vary with the individual states. In addition, the board of directors must consider the financial aspect of dividend distributions — the company's asset position, the present asset requirements, and the future asset requirements. The board of directors must answer two questions: Do we have the legal right to declare a dividend? Is such a distribution financially advisable?

The laws of different states range from those making any part of capital other than legal capital available for dividends to those permitting dividends only from retained earnings and under specified conditions. In most states dividends cannot be declared in the event of a deficit; in a few states, however, dividends equal to current earnings may be distributed despite a previously accumulated deficit. The availability of capital as a basis for dividends is a determination to be made by the attorney and not by the accountant. The accountant must report accurately the sources of each capital increase; the attorney investigates the availability of such sources as bases for dividend distributions.

When a dividend is legally declared and announced, its revocation is not possible. In the event of corporate insolvency prior to payment of the dividend, stockholders have claims as a creditor group to the dividend, and as an ownership group to any assets remaining after all corporate liabilities have been paid. A dividend that was illegally declared, however, is revocable; in the event of insolvency at the time of declaration, such action is nullified and stockholders participate in asset distributions only after creditors have been paid in full.

The Formal Dividend Announcement. Three dates are essential in the formal dividend statement: (1) date of declaration, (2) date of stockholders of record, (3) date of payment. Dividends are made payable to stockholders of record as of a date following the date of declaration and preceding the date of payment. The liability for dividends payable is recorded on the declaration date and is canceled on the payment date. No entry is required on the record date, but a list of the stockholders is made as of the close of business on this date. These are the persons who receive dividends on the payment date. In practice, stock is said to sell ex-dividend three or four trading days prior to the date of record. A full record of the dividend action must be provided in the minutes book.

Cash Dividends. The most common type of dividend is a **cash dividend**. For a corporation, these dividends involve a reduction in retained earnings and in cash. A current liability for dividends payable is recognized on the declaration date; this is canceled when dividend checks are sent to stockholders. Entries to record the declaration and the payment of a cash dividend follow:

Retained Earnings	100,000	
Dividends Payable		100,000
Dividends Payable	100,000	
Cash		100,000

In declaring a dividend, the board of directors must consider the limitations set by the current financial position and the cash balance of the company. For example, a corporation may have retained earnings of $500,000. If it has cash of only $150,000, however, cash dividends must be limited to this amount unless it converts certain assets into cash or borrows cash. If the cash required for regular operations is $100,000, the cash available for dividends is only $50,000. Although legally able to declare dividends of $500,000, the company would be able to distribute no more than one tenth of that amount at this time. Generally, companies pay dividends which are significantly less than the legal amount allowed or the amount of cash on hand.

Property Dividends. A distribution to stockholders that is payable in some asset other than cash is generally referred to as a **property dividend**. Frequently the assets to be distributed are securities of other companies owned by the corporation. The corporation thus transfers to its stockholders its ownership interest in such securities. Property dividends usually occur in closely held corporations.

This transfer is sometimes referred to as a *nonreciprocal transfer to owners* inasmuch as nothing is received by the company in return for its distribution to the stockholders. This type of transfer should be recorded using the fair market value (as of the day of declaration) of the assets distributed, and a gain or loss recognized for the difference between the carrying value on the books of the issuing company and the fair market value of the assets.[3] Property dividends are valued at carrying value if the fair market value is not determinable.

To illustrate the entries for a property dividend, assume that the State Oil Corporation owns 100,000 shares in the Valley Oil Co., cost $2,000,000, fair market value $3,000,000, which it wishes to distribute to its stockholders. There are 1,000,000 shares of State Oil Corporation stock outstanding. Accordingly, a dividend of 1/10 of a share of Valley Oil Co. stock is declared on each share of State Oil Corporation stock outstanding. The entries for the dividend declaration and payment are:

Retained Earnings	3,000,000	
Property Dividends Payable		3,000,000
Property Dividends Payable	3,000,000	
Investment in Valley Oil Co. Stock		2,000,000
Gain on Distribution of Property Dividends		1,000,000

Stock Dividends. A corporation may distribute to stockholders additional shares of the company's own stock as a **stock dividend**. A stock dividend permits the corporation to retain within the business net assets produced by earnings while at the same time offering stockholders tangible evidence of the growth of their equity.

A stock dividend usually involves (1) the capitalization of retained earnings, and (2) a distribution of common stock to common stockholders. These distributions are sometimes referred to as *ordinary stock dividends*. In some states, stock dividends may be effected by the capitalization of certain paid-in capital balances. In other instances, common stock is issued to holders of preferred stock or preferred stock is issued to holders of common stock. These distributions are sometimes referred to as *special stock dividends*.

A stock dividend makes a portion of retained earnings no longer available for distribution while raising the legal capital of the corporation. In recording the dividend, a debit is made to Retained Earnings and credits are made to appropriate paid-in capital balances. A stock dividend has the same effect as the payment by the corporation of a cash dividend and a subsequent return of the cash to the corporation in exchange for capital stock.

In distributing stock as a dividend, the issuing corporation must meet legal requirements relative to the amounts to be capitalized. If stock has a par or a stated value, an amount equal to the par or stated value of the shares issued will have to be transferred to capital stock; if stock is no-par and without a stated value, the laws of the state of incorporation may provide specific requirements as to the amounts to be transferred, or they may leave such determinations to the corporate directors.

---

[3]*Opinions of the Accounting Principles Board, No. 29,* "Accounting for Nonmonetary Transactions" (New York: American Institute of Certified Public Accountants, 1973), par. 18.

Although the minimum amounts to be transferred to legal or stated capital balances upon the issuance of additional stock are set by law, the board of directors is not prevented from going beyond legal requirements and authorizing increases in both capital stock and paid-in capital balances. For example, assume that $100 par stock was originally issued at $120. Legal requirements may call for the capitalization of no more than the par value of the additional shares issued. The board of directors, however, in order to preserve the paid-in capital relationship, may authorize a transfer from retained earnings of $120 per share; for every share issued, capital stock would be increased $100 and a paid-in capital account would be increased $20; or the board of directors may decide that the retained earnings transfer shall be made in terms of the fair value of shares which exceeds the legal value. Here, too, the credit to capital stock is accompanied by a credit to a paid-in capital account.

Small vs. Large Stock Dividends. The amount of retained earnings to be capitalized depends upon the number of additional shares issued in proportion to the number of shares outstanding prior to the stock dividend. The Committee on Accounting Procedure of the AICPA has indicated that the majority of stock dividends ". . . are so small in comparison with the shares previously outstanding that they do not have any apparent effect upon the share market price and, consequently, the market value of the shares previously held remains substantially unchanged."[4] Thus, recipients of the stock dividend could sell the additional shares at market value, and the transaction would have the same effect as a cash dividend. The Committee stated that in these situations, an amount equal to the fair market value of the additional shares issued should be capitalized.

In contrast, when the number of additional shares issued is so large as to materially reduce the market value per share, retained earnings should be capitalized only to the extent necessary to meet legal requirements.[5] This type of transaction is more accurately termed a *stock split-up* than a stock dividend.

Although reluctant to specify a percentage rule for categorizing a particular stock dividend, the Committee did suggest that in stock distributions involving the issuance of less than 20% to 25% of the number of shares previously outstanding, referred to as a **small stock dividend**, the debits to Retained Earnings should normally be at the fair value of additional shares issued.

The following examples illustrate the entries for the declaration and the issue of a small stock dividend. Assume that the capital for the Hernandez Co. on July 1 is as follows:

Capital stock, $10 par, 100,000 shares outstanding	$1,000,000
Premium on capital stock	1,100,000
Retained earnings	750,000

---

[4]*Accounting Research and Terminology Bulletins – Final Edition*, "No. 43, Restatement and Revision of Accounting Research Bulletins" (New York: American Institute of Certified Public Accountants, 1961), Ch. 7, sec. B, par. 10.

[5]*Ibid*, par. 11.

The company declares a 10% stock dividend, or a dividend of 1 share for every 10 held. Shares are selling on the market on this date at $16 per share. The stock dividend is to be recorded at the market value of the shares issued, or $160,000 (10,000 shares at $16). The entries to record the declaration of the dividend and the issue of stock follow:

Retained Earnings..	160,000	
Stock Dividends Distributable...		100,000
Paid-In Capital from Stock Dividends...		60,000
Stock Dividends Distributable..	100,000	
Capital Stock, $10 par...		100,000

Assume, however, that the company declares a **large stock dividend** of 50%, or a dividend of 1 share for every 2 held. Legal requirements call for the transfer to capital stock of an amount equal to the par value of the shares issued. This transfer may be made from retained earnings or paid-in capital. When the transfer is made from paid-in capital, it is preferable to refer to the transaction as a stock split effected in the form of a dividend rather than as a stock dividend. Entries for the declaration of the dividend and the issue of stock follow:

Retained Earnings (*or* Premium on Capital Stock).............................	500,000	
Stock Dividends Distributable...		500,000
Stock Dividends Distributable..	500,000	
Capital Stock, $10 par...		500,000

Stock Dividends on the Balance Sheet. If a balance sheet is prepared after the declaration of a stock dividend but before issue of the shares, stock dividends distributable is reported in the stockholders' equity section as an addition to capital stock outstanding. Through stock dividends, the corporation reduces its retained earnings balance and increases its capital stock. The stock the corporation may still sell is limited to the difference between capital stock authorized and the sum of (1) capital stock issued, (2) capital stock subscribed, (3) stock reserved for the exercise of stock rights and stock options, and (4) stock dividends distributable.

Stock Dividends vs Stock Splits. Although a stock dividend can be compared to a stock split from the investors' point of view, its effects upon corporate capital differ from those of the stock split. A **stock dividend** results in an increase in the number of shares outstanding and in an increase in the capital stock balance, no change being made in the value assigned to each share of stock on the company records; the increase in capital stock outstanding is effected by a transfer from the retained earnings balance, retained earnings available for dividends being permanently reduced by this transfer. A **stock split** merely divides the existing capital stock balance into more parts with a reduction in the stated or legal value related to each share; there is no change in the retained earnings available for dividends, both the capital stock and the retained earnings balances remaining unchanged.

A stock split effected in the form of a large stock dividend is sometimes referred to simply as a stock split. This can be misleading because additional shares of stock are issued in this situation and the par value of the stock is not changed. A careful distinction should be made between a pure stock split as described in Chapter 16 and the large stock dividends discussed in this chapter.

There have been suggestions that special disclosure be provided on the balance sheet when retained earnings have been reclassified as paid-in capital as a result of stock dividends, recapitalizations, or other actions. Information concerning the amount of retained earnings transferred to paid-in capital will contribute to an understanding of the extent to which business growth has been financed through corporate earnings. For example, assume the information for the Hernandez Co. on pages 473–4 and the transfer to paid-in capital of $500,000 as a result of the 50% stock dividend. The stockholders' equity may be presented as illustrated below.

Contributed capital:		
Capital stock, $10 par, 150,000 shares	$1,500,000	
Premium on capital stock	1,100,000	$2,600,000
Retained earnings	$ 750,000	
Less amount transferred to paid-in capital by stock dividend	500,000	250,000
Total stockholders' equity		$2,850,000

Liquidating Dividends. A corporation will declare a **liquidating dividend** when the dividend is to be considered a return to stockholders of a portion of their original investments. These distributions by the corporation represent reductions of invested capital balances. Instead of actually debiting Capital Stock and Paid-In Capital balances, however, it is possible to debit a separate account for the reduction in invested capital. This balance is subtracted from the invested capital balances in presenting the stockholders' equity on the balance sheet.

Corporations owning wasting assets may regularly declare dividends that are in part a distribution of earnings and in part a distribution of the corporation's invested capital. Entries on the corporation books for such dividend declarations should reflect the decrease in the two capital elements. This information should be reported to stockholders so they may recognize dividends as representing in part income and in part a return of investment.

Dividends on Preferred Stock. When dividends on preferred stock are cumulative, the payment of a stipulated amount on these shares is necessary before any dividends may be paid on common. When the board of directors fails to declare dividends on cumulative preferred stock, information concerning the amount of dividends in arrears should be reported parenthetically or in note form on the balance sheet; or retained earnings may be divided on the balance sheet to show the amount required to meet dividends in arrears and the free balance for other purposes.

Appropriations of Retained Earnings

Sometimes the total amount of retained earnings is segregated into **appropriated retained earnings** and **unappropriated** or **free retained earnings**. Appropriations of retained earnings are recognized for a variety of purposes, which are explained in the next section. But whatever the purpose, retained earnings are always appropriated by the same entry: A debit to the regular unappropriated retained earnings account and a credit to a special appropriated retained earnings account. Once the purpose of an appropriation has been served, the entry to cancel it is always a reversal of the original entry.

To illustrate, assume that a corporation agrees to restrict retained earnings of $5,000,000 from dividend distribution during the full term of a bond issue. The entry to appropriate retained earnings when the bonds are issued would be:

Retained Earnings...	5,000,000	
Retained Earnings Appropriated for Redemption of Bonds		5,000,000

When the bond issue is liquidated, the entry to cancel the appropriation would be:

Retained Earnings Appropriated for Redemption of Bonds ...	5,000,000	
Retained Earnings		5,000,000

By itself, the appropriation of retained earnings does nothing more than disclose a restricted amount of retained earnings and an unrestricted amount from which dividends can be paid. There is no segregation of funds and no gains or losses are involved. Thus, in accounting for appropriations, only the two entries illustrated above are needed: one to establish the appropriation and one to cancel it. The appropriation of retained earnings has no effect upon individual assets and liabilities nor does it change total capital; amounts are merely transferred from regular retained earnings to special retained earnings accounts, and assets otherwise available for dividend distribution are kept within the business. The appropriation balance is no guarantee that cash or any other specific asset will be available to carry out the purpose of the appropriation.

However, the appropriation of retained earnings may be accompanied by the segregation of assets in a special fund, for example to retire the bond obligation at maturity in the illustration just mentioned. Such an appropriation is said to be **funded**. This practice results not only in the limitation of dividends but also in the accumulation of resources to meet the purpose for which the appropriation was made. However, it is the funding aspect — not the appropriation — that involves the segregation and/or accumulation of assets.

Purposes Served by Appropriations. Retained earnings may be appropriated for three main purposes: (1) To report legal restrictions on retained earnings. For example, the laws of the state of incorporation may require a company, upon reacquiring its own stock, to retain its earnings as a means of maintaining its legal capital. Such restrictions may be recognized in the accounts by the appropriation of retained earnings. (2) To report contractual restrictions on retained earnings. For example, agreements with creditors or stockholders may provide for the retention of earnings within the company to protect the interests of these parties and to assure redemption of the securities they hold. (3) To report discretionary action by the board of directors in the presentation of retained earnings. The board of directors may authorize that a portion or all of retained earnings be presented in a manner disclosing the actual use or the planned use in the future of the resources represented by this part of the stockholders' equity.

These types of restrictions on retained earnings may also be disclosed in notes to the financial statements, a practice more commonly followed than the use of appropriation accounts.

Other Additions to or Deductions from Owners' Equity

The previous sections have discussed the major items affecting retained earnings. The three most common items are prior period adjustments, earnings, and dividends. When retained earnings are combined with capital stock and other paid-in capital, the amount of total owners' equity is usually determined. Sometimes, however, there are other additions to or deductions from owners' equity.

As previously discussed, deductions from total stockholders' equity are made for the cost of treasury stock[6] and the accumulated changes in the valuation allowance for a marketable equity securities portfolio included in noncurrent assets.[7] These may be referred to as **contra-equity accounts**.

These deductions from total stockholders' equity are dissimilar in origin, but both have the result of reducing stockholders' equity. As an example, some loan agreements may require a company to maintain a certain amount of stockholders' equity in relation to its debt. The reduction of stockholders' equity due to the decline in value of long-term investments could cause a violation of these requirements. To illustrate, assume a company was required to maintain a debt-to-equity ratio of .66 or less, and that a market decline of $75,000 was incurred on long-term investments held by the company. Before the entry recognizing the market decline in long-term securi-

---

[6]Chapter 16, page 456.
[7]Chapter 12, page 345.

ties, the company had debt of $1,000,000 and stockholders' equity of $1,550,000, or a debt-to-equity ratio of .645 ($1,000,000 ÷ $1,550,000). This ratio thus meets the requirements. After the entry for the market decline, stockholders' equity would be reduced to $1,475,000 and the debt-to-equity ratio increased to .678, a figure that would be in violation of the loan agreement.

BOOK VALUE PER SHARE

Readers of corporate financial statements are interested in certain special measurements that can be developed from the data concerning stockholders' equity. One measurement of particular interest is **book value per share**. The book value per share measurement is the dollar equity in corporate capital of each share of stock. It is the amount that would be paid on each share assuming the company is liquidated and the amount available to stockholders is exactly the amount reported as the stockholders' equity.[8] The book value measurement is sometimes used as a factor in evaluating stock worth. However, care must be exercised because improper use may be misleading. Both single values and comparative values may be required, the latter to afford data relative to trends and growth in the stockholders' equity.

One Class of Outstanding Stock

When only one class of stock is outstanding, the calculation of book value is relatively simple; the total stockholders' equity is divided by the number of shares of stock outstanding at the close of the reporting period. When stock has been reacquired and treasury stock is reported, its cost should be recognized as a subtraction item in arriving at the stockholders' equity, and the shares represented by the treasury stock should be subtracted from the shares issued in arriving at the shares outstanding. When shares of stock have been subscribed for but are unissued, capital stock subscribed should be included in the total for the stockholders' equity and the shares subscribed should be added to the shares outstanding. To illustrate, assume a stockholders' equity for the Moore Corporation as shown below:

Contributed capital:	
Capital stock, $10 par, 100,000 shares issued, 5,000 shares reacquired and held as treasury stock (see below)	$1,000,000
Capital stock subscribed, 20,000 shares	200,000
Additional paid-in capital	350,000
Retained earnings	650,000
	$2,200,000
Less stock reacquired and held as treasury stock, at cost (5,000 shares)	75,000
Total stockholders' equity	$2,125,000

---

[8]Financial analysts frequently follow the practice of subtracting any amounts reported for intangible assets from the total reported for the stockholders' equity in calculating share book value.

The book value per share of stock is calculated as follows:

$2,125,000 (total capital) ÷ 115,000 (shares issued, 100,000, plus shares subscribed, 20,000, minus treasury shares, 5,000) = $18.48.

More than One Class of Outstanding Stock

When more than one class of stock has been issued, it is necessary to consider the rights of the different classes of stockholders. With preferred and common issues, for example, the prior rights of preferred stockholders must first be determined and the portion of the stockholders' equity related to preferred stockholders calculated. The preferred stockholders' equity when subtracted from the total stockholders' equity gives the equity related to the common stockholders, or the *residual equity*. The preferred equity divided by the number of preferred shares gives the book value of a preferred share; the common equity divided by the number of common shares gives the book value of a common share.

The portion of the stockholders' equity related to preferred would be that amount distributable to preferred stockholders in the event of corporate liquidation and calls for consideration of the liquidation value and also the special dividend rights of the preferred issue.

Liquidation Value. Preferred shares may have a liquidation value equal to par, to par plus a premium, or to a stated dollar amount. Capital equal to this value for the number of preferred shares outstanding should be assigned to preferred stock. A preferred call price differing from the amount to be paid to preferred stockholders upon liquidation would not be applicable for book value computations; the call of preferred stock is not obligatory, hence call prices are not relevant in the apportionment of values between preferred and common stockholders.

Dividend Rights. (1) Preferred stock may have certain rights in retained earnings as a result of special dividend privileges. For example, preferred shares may be entitled to dividends not yet declared for a portion of the current year, assuming liquidation; here a portion of retained earnings equal to the dividend requirements would be related to preferred shares. (2) Preferred stock may be cumulative with dividends in arrears. When terms of the preferred issue provide that dividends in arrears must be paid upon liquidation regardless of any retained earnings or deficit balance reported on the books, capital equivalent to the dividends in arrears must be assigned to preferred shares even though this impairs or eliminates the equity relating to common stockholders. When preferred stockholders are entitled to dividends in arrears only in the event of accumulated earnings, as much retained earnings as are available, but not in excess of such dividend requirements, are related to preferred stock.

The computation of book values for preferred and common shares is illustrated in the following series of examples. The examples are based upon the stockholders' equity reported by the Maxwell Corporation on December 31, 1981, which follows:

Preferred 6% stock, $50 par, 10,000 shares..	$ 500,000
Common stock, $10 par, 100,000 shares	1,000,000
Retained earnings..	250,000
Total stockholders' equity..	$1,750,000

Example 1 — Assume preferred dividends have been paid to July 1, 1981. Preferred stock has a liquidation value of $52 and is entitled to current unpaid dividends. Book values on December 31, 1981, are developed as follows:

Total stockholders' equity..		$1,750,000
Equity identified with preferred:		
Liquidation value, 10,000 shares @ $52..................................	$520,000	
Current dividends, 3% of $500,000	15,000	535,000
Balance — equity identified with common................................		$1,215,000
Book values per share:		
Preferred: $ 535,000 ÷ 10,000...		$53.50
Common: $1,215,000 ÷ 100,000		$12.15

Example 2 — Assume preferred stock has a liquidation value of $52. Preferred stock is cumulative with dividends 5 years in arrears that must be paid in the event of liquidation. Book values for common and preferred shares would be developed as follows:

Total stockholders' equity..		$1,750,000
Equity identified with preferred:		
Liquidation value, 10,000 shares @ $52...................................	$520,000	
Dividends in arrears, 30% of $500,000....................................	150,000	670,000
Balance — equity identified with common................................		$1,080,000
Book values per share:		
Preferred: $ 670,000 ÷ 10,000...		$67.00
Common: $1,080,000 ÷ 100,000..		$10.80

Example 3 — Assume preferred stock has a liquidation value equal to its par value. Preferred is cumulative with dividends 10 years in arrears payable in the event of liquidation even though impairing the invested capital of the common shareholders. Book values for common and preferred shares are developed as follows:

Total stockholders' equity..		$1,750,000
Equity identified with preferred:		
Liquidation value, 10,000 shares @ $50..................................	$500,000	
Dividends in arrears, 60% of $500,000....................................	300,000	800,000
Balance — equity identified with common...................................		$ 950,000
Book values per share:		
Preferred: $800,000 ÷ 10,000...		$80.00
Common: $950,000 ÷ 100,000..		$ 9.50

The nature and the limitations of the share book value measurements must be appreciated in using these data. Share book values are developed from the net asset values as reported on the books. Furthermore, calculations require the assumption of liquidation in the allocation of amounts to the several classes of stock. Book values of assets may vary materially from present fair values or immediate realizable values. Moreover, book values of property items are stated in terms of the "going concern"; the full implications of a "quitting concern" approach would call for many significant changes in the values as reported on the books.

STOCKHOLDERS' EQUITY IN THE FINANCIAL STATEMENTS

Transactions affecting the stockholders' equity have been described in this and the preceding chapter. The persons who refer to the financial statements of a corporation must be provided with a full explanation of the changes during the period in the individual balances comprising the stockholders' equity. In the remaining pages of this chapter, the financial statements for the Oslo Manufacturing Company are illustrated with special attention directed to the stockholders' equity section of the balance sheet. The statements are prepared as of December 31, 1981, and summarize the position of the company as of this date and operations for the year ending on this date. It should be noted that companies rarely show all the detail provided for illustrative purposes in the Oslo Manufacturing Company statements. Students are again referred to the actual financial statements for General Mills presented as Appendix B.

The Balance Sheet

The balance sheet for the Oslo Manufacturing Company as of December 31, 1981, is given on pages 482 and 483. Classifications and the presentation of financial data follow the standards developed in the preceding chapters. The following matters deserve special attention:

1. The stockholders' equity is reported in terms of its sources: (a) the amount paid in by stockholders; and (b) the amount representing earnings retained in the business.
2. The classes of capital stock are reported separately and are described in detail. Information is offered concerning the nature of the stock, the number of shares authorized, the number of shares issued, and the number of shares reacquired and held as treasury stock.
3. The capital items representing contributed capital and retained earnings are reported in detail; when paid-in capital and appropriated retained earnings are composed of a great many items, related balances are frequently combined and reported in total on the balance sheet.
4. In complying with legal requirements, the company has reported retained earnings equivalent to the cost of the treasury stock held as an appropriation of retained earnings.

Reference is made at the bottom of the balance sheet to the notes accompanying the financial statements. (These notes appear on page 486). This reference would also appear on the other financial statements prepared by the company.

		Oslo Balance December
Assets		
Current assets:		
Cash on hand and on deposit		$ 55,000
U.S. Government securities (reported at cost; market value, $87,500)..		86,000
Trade notes and accounts receivable....................................	$182,600	
Less allowance for doubtful accounts	2,600	180,000
Inventories (Note 1a):		
Finished goods..	$190,000	
Goods in process	200,000	
Raw materials and supplies	185,000	575,000
Loans, advances, and accrued income items		20,000
Prepayments including taxes, insurance, and sundry current items.....		14,500
Total current assets		$ 930,500
Long-term investments:		
Marketable equity securities (cost $124,000, less allowance to reduce valuation to market, $24,000)		$ 100,000
Fund consisting of U.S. Government securities to be used for prop- erty additions..		150,000
Land held for future expansion		110,000
Total long-term investments		360,000
Land, buildings, and equipment (Note 1b):		
Land, buildings, and equipment, at cost	$1,235,000	
Less accumulated depreciation on buildings and equipment............	580,000	
Total land, buildings, and equipment		655,000
Intangible assets (Note 1c):		
Patents, formulas, and goodwill — less amortization		120,000
Other assets:		
Advance payments on equipment purchase contracts		102,500
Total assets		$2,168,000

See accompanying notes to financial statements.

The Income Statement

The income statement for the Oslo Manufacturing Company is prepared in condensed single-step form. The income statement for the year ended December 31, 1981, is illustrated on page 484.

With single amounts reported for sales and for cost of goods sold, special supporting schedules may be provided to offer an analysis of these balances in terms of the major divisions of the business or of the different product

Manufacturing Company
Sheet
31, 1981

Liabilities

Current liabilities:

Notes and accounts payable		$ 52,500	
Income tax payable		12,000	
Payroll, interest, and taxes payable		23,500	
Serial debenture bonds due May 1, 1982		20,000	
Customers' deposits and sundry items		24,000	
Total current liabilities			$ 132,000

Long-term liabilities:

Twenty-year 7% first-mortgage bonds	$260,000		
Less unamortized discount on first-mortgage bonds	10,000	$ 250,000	
Serial 7½% debenture bonds due May 1, 1983, to May 1, 1991, inclusive		180,000	
Deferred leasehold revenue (Note 1d)		224,000	
Liability under pension plan (Note 2)		20,000	
Contingent liabilities (Note 3)			
Total long-term liabilities			674,000
Total liabilities			$ 806,000

Stockholders' Equity

Contributed capital:

Preferred 6% stock, $100 par, cumulative, callable, 5,000 shares authorized and issued (Note 4)		$500,000	
No-par common stock, $5 stated value, 100,000 shares authorized, 60,000 shares issued; treasury stock, 5,000 shares — deducted below		300,000	$ 800,000
Paid-in capital from sale of common stock at more than stated value		$260,000	
Paid-in capital from sale of treasury stock at more than cost		16,000	276,000
Total contributed capital			$1,076,000

Retained earnings:

Appropriated:

For purchase of treasury stock	$40,000		
For contingencies (Note 3)	85,000	$125,000	
Unappropriated		225,000	
Total retained earnings			350,000
Total contributed capital and retained earnings			$1,426,000
Deduct: Net treasury stock, at cost (5,000 shares acquired at $8)	$ 40,000		
Net unrealized loss on noncurrent marketable equity securities (Note 4)	24,000	64,000	
Total stockholders' equity			1,362,000
Total liabilities and stockholders' equity			$2,168,000

lines. With single amounts reported for selling, general and administrative, and other expenses, supporting schedules may be provided to indicate the individual items composing such totals.

The Statement of Changes in Owners' Equity

Those who wish to be fully informed on the financial position and results of operations of the corporation require full information explaining

Oslo Manufacturing Company
Income Statement
For Year Ended December 31, 1981

Revenues:		
Sales	$1,550,000	
Other revenue	100,000	$1,650,000
Expenses:		
Cost of goods sold	$ 940,000	
Selling expense	300,000	
General and administrative expense	125,000	
Other expense	80,000	
Income tax expense	92,500	1,537,500
Income before extraordinary items		$ 112,500
Extraordinary gain on early extinguishment of debt, net of tax		7,500
Net income		$ 120,000
Earnings per common share:*		
Income before extraordinary items		$1.50
Extraordinary income		.14
Net income		$1.64

*Preferred dividend requirements are subtracted from earnings to arrive at earnings related to common shares.

Condensed Single-Step Income Statement

Oslo
Statement of Changes
For the Year Ended

	Preferred Stock	Common Stock	Paid-In Capital
Balances, December 31, 1980	$300,000	$300,000	$260,000*
Prior period adjustment — correction of 1979 error, net of tax			
Adjusted balances, December 31, 1980	$300,000	$300,000	$260,000
Increase from sale of 1,000 shares of preferred stock in January, 1981, at par value	200,000		
Increase from sale of 25,000 shares of treasury stock, common, in January, 1981, cost $20,000, for $36,000			16,000
Net income for 1981			
Cash dividends:			
Preferred stock, $6 on 5,000 shares, $30,000			
Common stock, 50¢ on 55,000 shares, $27,500			
Return to retained earnings of amounts previously restricted through ownership of treasury stock			
Retained earnings appropriated for contingencies			
Purchase of 5,000 shares of common treasury stock @ cost, $8			
Net unrealized loss on noncurrent marketable equity securities			
Balances, December 31, 1981	$500,000	$300,000	$276,000

*From sale of common stock at more than stated value.

Statement of Changes

the change in the stockholders' equity. A **Statement of Changes in Owners' Equity** provides such information, and is illustrated on page 484 and below for the Oslo Manufacturing Company.

In some instances, it is necessary to recognize additional changes, such as those resulting from prior period adjustments, the acquisition of treasury stock, and transfers to paid-in capital. Sometimes, the statement is expanded to show changes in both unappropriated and appropriated balances. The statement then summarizes transfers from the unappropriated retained earnings account to accounts reporting appropriations, and also transfers from accounts reporting appropriations to the unappropriated retained earnings account.

The Statement of Changes in Financial Position

Reference was made in Chapter 5 to the statement of changes in financial position, which is required to offer a full reporting of a company's operations. As explained, this statement is prepared from comparative balance sheets as of the beginning and end of the period and summarizes the financing and investing activities that resulted in the change in financial position. The preparation of this statement is described and illustrated in Chapter 19.

Manufacturing Company
in Owners' Equity
December 31, 1981

Appropriated Retained Earnings for Purchase of Treasury Stock	Appropriated Retained Earnings for Contingencies	Unappropriated Retained Earnings	Contra- Equity Balances	Total
$60,000	$50,000	$202,500	–0–	$1,172,500
		(25,000)		(25,000)
$60,000	$50,000	$177,500	–0–	$1,147,500
				200,000
				16,000
		120,000		120,000
		(57,500)		(57,500)
(20,000)		20,000		
	35,000	(35,000)		
			$(40,000)	(40,000)
			(24,000)	(24,000)
$40,000	$85,000	$225,000	$(64,000)	$1,362,000

in Owners' Equity

Oslo Manufacturing Company
Notes to Financial Statements — Year Ended December 31, 1981

1. The following is a summary of significant accounting policies followed by Oslo Manufacturing Company.

    (a) Inventories are valued at cost or market, whichever is lower. Cost is calculated by the first-in, first-out method.

    (b) Depreciation is computed for both the books and the tax return by the double-declining balance method.

    (c) Intangible assets are being amortized over the period of their estimated useful lives: patents, 10 years; formulas, 8 years; and goodwill, 20 years.

    (d) The company leased Sinclair Street properties for a 15-year period ending January 1, 1993. Leasehold payment received in advance is being recognized as revenue over the life of the lease.

2. The company has accrued $20,000 more under the pension plan than it has paid. At December 31, 1981, the balance in the pension fund exceeds the vested benefits as of that date. No further accrual of past service cost is therefore considered necessary.

3. The company is contingently liable on guaranteed notes and accounts totaling $40,000. Also, various suits are pending on which the ultimate payment cannot be determined. In the opinion of counsel and management, such liability, if any, will not be material. Retained earnings have been appropriated in anticipation of possible losses.

4. Preferred stock may be redeemed at the option of the board of directors at 105 plus accrued dividends on or before December 31, 1983, and at gradually reduced amounts but at not less than 102½ plus accrued dividends after January 1, 1989.

The net ownership equity of a business is an important element. Analyses of the amounts and sources of contributed capital compared to those generated and retained by the company provide useful information for assessing the long-term profitability and solvency of a business. The techniques for analyzing financial statements are discussed in Chapter 21.

APPENDIX

ANALYSIS OF CORRECTION OF ERRORS

A number of special practices are usually adopted by a business unit to ensure accuracy in recording and summarizing business transactions. A prime requisite in achieving accuracy, of course, is the establishment of an accounting system providing safeguards against both carelessness and dishonesty. Despite the accounting system established and the verification procedures employed, some misstatements will enter into the financial statements. Misstatements may be minor ones having little effect on the financial presentations; others may be of a major character, resulting in material misrepresentations of financial position and the results of operations. Misstatements may arise from intentional falsifications by employees or officers as well as from unintentional errors and omissions by employees.

Kinds of Errors

There are a number of different kinds of errors. Some errors are discovered in the period in which they are made, and these are easily corrected. Others may not be discovered currently and are reflected on the financial statements until discovered. Some errors are never discovered; however, the effects of these errors are counterbalanced in subsequent periods and after this takes place, account balances are again accurately stated. Errors may be classified as follows.

1. *Errors discovered currently in the course of normal accounting procedures.* Examples of this type of error are clerical errors, such as an addition error, posting to the wrong account, or misstating or omitting an account from the trial balance. These types of errors usually are detected during the regular summarizing process of the accounting cycle and are readily corrected.

2. *Errors limited to balance sheet accounts.* Examples include debiting Marketable Securities instead of Notes Receivable, crediting Interest Payable instead of Notes Receivable, or crediting Interest Payable instead of Salaries Payable. Another example is not recording the exchange of convertible bonds for stock. Such errors are frequently discovered and corrected in the period in which they are made. When such errors are not found until a subsequent period, corrections must be made at that time and balance sheet data subsequently restated for comparative reporting purposes.

3. *Errors limited to income statement accounts.* The examples and correcting procedures for this type of error are similar to those in (2) above. For example, Office Salaries may be debited instead of Sales Salaries. This type of error should be corrected as soon as it is discovered. Even though the error would not affect net income, the misstated accounts should be restated for analysis purposes and comparative reporting.

4. *Errors affecting both income statement accounts and balance sheet accounts.* Certain errors, when not discovered currently, result in the misstatement of net income and thus affect both the income statement accounts and the balance sheet accounts. The balance sheet accounts are carried into the succeeding period; hence, an error made currently and not detected will affect earnings of the future. Such errors may be classified into two groups:

   a. *Errors in net income which, when not detected, are automatically counterbalanced in the following fiscal period.* Net income on the income statements for two successive periods are inaccurately stated; certain account balances on the balance sheet at the end of the first period are inaccurately stated, but the account balances in the balance sheet at the end of the succeeding period are accurately stated. In this class are errors such as the misstatement of inventories and the omission of adjustments for prepaid and accrued items at the end of the period.

   b. *Errors in net income which, when not detected, are not automatically counterbalanced in the following fiscal period.* Account balances on successive balance sheets are inaccurately stated until such time as entries are made compensating for or correcting the errors. In this class are errors such as the recognition of capital expenditures as revenue expenditures and the omission of charges for depreciation and amortization.

When these types of errors are discovered, careful analysis is required to determine the required action to correct the account balances. As indicated in the chapter, most of these errors will be caught and corrected prior to closing the books. Those that are not detected during the current period may be *counterbalancing*, i.e., affected by an equal misstatement in the subsequent period. The few material, noncounterbalancing errors not detected until subsequent periods must be treated as prior period adjustments according to APB Opinion No. 20.

The remaining sections of this appendix describe and illustrate the procedures to be applied when error corrections qualify as prior period adjustments. Accordingly, it is assumed each of the errors named is material and calls for correction directly to the retained earnings account summarizing past earnings. When errors are discovered, they usually affect the income tax liability for a prior period. Amended tax returns are usually prepared to either claim a refund or to pay any additional tax assessment. For simplicity, the extended example on the following pages and the exercises and problems ignore the income tax effect of errors.

Illustrative Example of Error Correction

The following example illustrates the analysis required upon the discovery of errors of prior periods and the entries to correct these errors.

Assume the R & G Wholesale Co. began operations at the beginning of 1980. An auditing firm is engaged for the first time in 1982. Before the accounts are adjusted and closed for 1982, the auditor reviews the books and accounts, and discovers the errors summarized on pages 490 and 491. Effects on the financial statements are listed before any correcting entries. A plus sign (+) indicates an overstatement; a minus sign (−) indicates an understatement. Each error correction is discussed in the following paragraphs.

(1) *Understatement of merchandise inventory.* It is discovered that the merchandise inventory as of December 31, 1980, was understated by $1,000. The effects of the misstatement were as shown below.

	Income Statement	Balance Sheet
For 1980:	Cost of goods sold overstated (ending inventory too low) Net income understated.	Assets understated (inventory too low) Retained earnings understated
For 1981:	Cost of goods sold understated (beginning inventory too low) Net income overstated	Balance sheet items not affected, retained earnings understatement for 1980 being corrected by net income overstatement for 1981.

Since this type of error counterbalances after two years, no correcting entry is required in 1982.

If the error had been discovered in 1981 instead of 1982, an entry could have been made to correct the account balances so that operations for 1981 might be reported accurately. The beginning inventory would have to be increased by $1,000, the asset understatement, and Retained Earnings would have to be credited for this amount representing the income understatement in 1980. The correcting entry in 1981 would have been:

Merchandise Inventory.. 1,000
    Retained Earnings 1,000

(2) *Failure to record merchandise purchases.* It is discovered that purchase invoices as of December 28, 1980, for $850 were not recorded until 1981. The goods were included in the inventory at the end of 1980. The effects of failure to record the purchases were as follows:

Income Statement	Balance Sheet
For 1980: Cost of goods sold understated (purchases too low)	Liabilities understated (accounts payable too low)
Net income overstated	Retained earnings overstated
For 1981: Cost of goods sold overstated (purchases too high)	Balance sheet items not affected, retained earnings overstatement for 1980 being corrected by net income understatement for 1981.
Net income understated	

Since this is a counterbalancing error, no correcting entry is required in 1982.

If the error had been discovered in 1981 instead of 1982, a correcting entry would have been necessary. In 1981, Purchases was debited and Accounts Payable credited for $850 for merchandise acquired in 1980 and included in the ending inventory of 1980. Retained Earnings would have to be debited for $850, representing the net income overstatement for 1980, and Purchases would have to be credited for a similar amount to reduce the Purchases balance in 1981. The correcting entry in 1981 would have been:

Retained Earnings 850
    Purchases 850

(3) *Failure to record merchandise sales.* It is discovered that sales on account for the last week of December, 1981, for $1,800 were not recorded until 1982. The goods sold were not included in the inventory at the end of 1981. The effects of the failure to report the revenue in 1981 were:

Income Statement	Balance Sheet
For 1981: Revenue understated (sales too low)	Assets understated (accounts receivable too low)
Net income understated	Retained earnings understated

When the error is discovered in 1982, Sales is debited for $1,800 and Retained Earnings is credited for this amount representing the net income understatement for 1981. The following entry is made:

Sales 1,800
    Retained Earnings 1,800

Analysis Sheet to Show Effects

	At End of 1980			
	Income Statement		Balance Sheet	
	Section	*Net Income*	*Section*	*Retained Earnings*
(1) Understatement of merchandise inventory of $1,000 on December 31, 1980.	Cost of Goods Sold +	—	Current Assets —	—
(2) Failure to record merchandise purchases on account of $850 in 1980, purchases were recorded in 1981.	Cost of Goods Sold —	+	Current Liabilities —	+
(3) Failure to record merchandise sales on account of $1,800 in 1981. (It is assumed that the sales for 1981 were recognized as revenue in 1982.)				
(4) Failure to record accrued sales salaries; expense was recognized when payment was made. On December 31, 1980, $450.	Selling Expense —	+	Current Liabilities —	+
On December 31, 1981, $300.				
(5) Failure to record prepaid taxes of $275 on December 31, 1980, amount was included as miscellaneous general expense.	General Expense +	—	Current Assets —	—
(6) Failure to record reduction in prepaid insurance balance of $350 on December 31, 1980, insurance for 1980 was charged to 1981.	General Expense —	+	Current Assets +	+
(7) Failure to record accrued interest on notes receivable of $150 on December 31, 1980, revenue was recognized on collection in 1981.	Other Revenue —	—	Current Assets —	—
(8) Failure to record unearned service fees; amounts received were included in Miscellaneous Revenue. On December 31, 1980, $175.	Other Revenue +	+	Current Liabilities —	+
On December 31, 1981, $225.				
(9) Failure to record reduction in unearned rent revenue balance on December 31, 1981, $125. (It is assumed that the rent revenue for 1981 was recognized as revenue in 1982.)				
(10) Failure to record depreciation of delivery equipment. On December 31, 1980, $1,200.	Selling Expense —	+	Non-current Assets +	+
On December 31, 1981, $1,200.				

of Errors on Financial Statements

At End of 1981				At End of 1982			
Income Statement		Balance Sheet		Income Statement		Balance Sheet	
Section	Net Income	Section	Retained Earnings	Section	Net Income	Section	Retained Earnings
Cost of Goods Sold −	+						
Cost of Goods Sold +	−						
Sales −	−	Accounts Receivable −	−	Sales +	+		
Selling Expense +	−						
Selling Expense −	+	Current Liabilities −	+	Selling Expense +	−		
General Expense −	+						
General Expense +	−						
Other Revenue +	+						
Other Revenue −	−						
Other Revenue +	+	Current Liabilities −	+	Other Revenue −	−		
Other Revenue −	−	Deferred Revenues +	−	Other Revenue +	+		
		Noncurrent Assets +	+			Noncurrent Assets +	+
Selling Expense −	+	Noncurrent Assets +	+			Noncurrent Assets +	+

(4) *Failure to record accrued expense.* Accrued sales salaries of $450 as of December 31, 1980, and $300 as of December 31, 1981, were overlooked in adjusting the accounts on each of these dates. Sales Salaries is debited for salary payments. The effects of the failure to record the accrued expense of $450 as of December 31, 1980, were as follows:

	Income Statement	Balance Sheet
For 1980:	Expenses understated (sales salaries too low)	Liabilities understated (accrued sales salaries not reported)
	Net income overstated	Retained earnings overstated
For 1981:	Expenses overstated (sales salaries too high) Net income understated	Balance sheet items not affected, retained earnings overstatement for 1980 being corrected by net income understatement for 1981.

The effects of failure to recognize the accrued expense of $300 on December 31, 1981, were as follows:

	Income Statement	Balance Sheet
For 1981:	Expenses understated (sales salaries too low)	Liabilities understated (accrued sales salaries not reported)
	Net income overstated	Retained earnings overstated

No entry is required in 1982 to correct the accounts for the failure to record the accrued expense at the end of 1980, the misstatement in 1980 having been counterbalanced by the misstatement in 1981. An entry is required, however, to correct the accounts for the failure to record the accrued expense at the end of 1981 if the net income for 1982 is not to be misstated. If accrued expenses were properly recorded at the end of 1982, Retained Earnings would be debited for $300, representing the net income overstatement for 1981, and Sales Salaries would be credited for a similar amount, representing the amount to be subtracted from salary payments in 1982. The correcting entry is:

Retained Earnings	300	
Sales Salaries		300

If the failure to adjust the accounts for the accrued expense of 1980 had been recognized in 1981 an entry similar to the one above would have been required in 1981 to correct the account balances. The entry in 1981 would have been:

Retained Earnings	450	
Sales Salaries		450

The accrued salaries of $300 as of the end of 1981 would be recorded at the end of that year by an appropriate adjustment.

(5) *Failure to record prepaid expense.* It is discovered that Miscellaneous General Expense for 1980 included taxes of $275 that should have been

deferred in adjusting the accounts on December 31, 1980. The effects of the failure to record the prepaid expense were as follows:

Income Statement	Balance Sheet
For 1980: Expenses overstated (miscellaneous general expense too high) Net income understated	Assets understated (prepaid taxes not reported) Retained earnings understated
For 1981: Expenses understated (miscellaneous general expense too low) Net income overstated	Balance sheet items not affected, retained earnings understatement for 1980 being corrected by net income overstatement for 1981.

Since this is a counterbalancing error, no entry to correct the accounts is required in 1982.

If the error had been discovered in 1981 instead of 1982, a correcting entry would have been necessary. If prepaid taxes were properly recorded at the end of 1981, Miscellaneous General Expense would have to be debited for $275, the expense relating to operations of 1981, and Retained Earnings would have to be credited for a similar amount representing the net income understatement for 1980. The correcting entry in 1981 would have been:

Miscellaneous General Expense	275	
Retained Earnings		275

(6) *Overstatement of prepaid expense.* On January 2, 1980, $1,050 representing insurance for a three-year period was paid. The charge was made to the asset account, Prepaid Insurance. No adjustment was made at the end of 1980. At the end of 1981, the prepaid insurance account was reduced to the prepaid balance on that date, $350, insurance for two years, or $700, being charged to operations of 1981. The effects of the misstatements were as follows:

Income Statement	Balance Sheet
For 1980: Expenses understated (insurance expense not reported) Net income overstated	Assets overstated (prepaid insurance too high) Retained earnings overstated
For 1981: Expenses overstated (insurance expense too high) Net income understated	Balance sheet items not affected, retained earnings overstatement for 1980 being corrected by net income understatement for 1981.

Since the balance sheet items at the end of 1981 were correctly stated, no entry to correct the accounts is required in 1982.

If the error had been discovered in 1981 instead of 1982, an entry would have been necessary to correct the account balances. Prepaid Insurance would have been decreased for the expired insurance of $350 and Retained Earnings would be debited for this amount representing the net income overstatement for 1980. The correcting entry in 1981 would have been:

Retained Earnings	350	
Prepaid Insurance		350

The expired insurance of $350 for 1981 would be recorded at the end of that year by an appropriate adjustment.

(7) *Failure to record accrued revenue.* Accrued interest on notes receivable of $150 was overlooked in adjusting the accounts on December 31, 1980. The revenue was recognized when the interest was collected in 1981. The effects of the failure to record the accrued revenue were:

Income Statement	Balance Sheet
For 1980: Revenue understated (interest revenue too low)	Assets understated (interest receivable not reported)
Net income understated	Retained earnings understated
For 1981: Revenue overstated (interest revenue too high)	Balance sheet items not affected, retained earnings understatement for 1980 being corrected by net income overstatement for 1981.
Net income overstated	

Since the balance sheet items at the end of 1981 were correctly stated, no entry to correct the accounts is required in 1982.

If the error had been discovered in 1981 instead of 1982, an entry would have been necessary to correct the account balances. If accrued interest on notes receivable had been properly recorded at the end of 1981, Interest Revenue would have to be debited for $150, the amount to be subtracted from receipts of 1981, and Retained Earnings would have to be credited for a similar amount representing the net income understatement for 1980. The correcting entry in 1981 would have been:

Interest Revenue..	150	
Retained Earnings		150

(8) *Failure to record unearned revenue.* Fees received in advance for miscellaneous services of $175 as of December 31, 1980, and $225 as of December 31, 1981, were overlooked in adjusting the accounts on each of these dates. Miscellaneous Revenue had been credited when fees were received. The effects of the failure to recognize the unearned revenue of $175 at the end of 1980 were as follows:

Income Statement	Balance Sheet
For 1980: Revenue overstated (miscellaneous revenue too high)	Liabilities understated (unearned service fees not reported)
Net income overstated	Retained earnings overstated
For 1981: Revenue understated (miscellaneous revenue too low)	Balance sheet items not affected, retained earnings overstatement for 1980 being corrected by net income understatement for 1981.
Net income understated	

The effects of the failure to recognize the unearned revenue of $225 at the end of 1981 were as follows:

Income Statement	Balance Sheet
For 1981: Revenue overstated (miscellaneous revenue too high)	Liabilities understated (unearned service fees not reported)
Net income overstated	Retained earnings overstated

No entry is required in 1982 to correct the accounts for the failure to record the unearned revenue at the end of 1980, the misstatement in 1980 having been counterbalanced by the misstatement in 1981. An entry is required, however, to correct the accounts for the failure to record the unearned revenue at the end of 1981 if the net income for 1982 is not to be misstated. If the unearned revenue were properly recorded at the end of 1982, Retained Earnings would be debited for $225, representing the net income overstatement for 1981, and Miscellaneous Revenue would be credited for the same amount, representing the revenue that is to be identified with 1982. The correcting entry is:

Retained Earnings	225	
Miscellaneous Revenue		225

If the failure to adjust the accounts for the unearned revenue of 1980 had been recognized in 1981 instead of 1982, an entry similar to the one above would have been required in 1981 to correct the account balances. The entry at that time would have been:

Retained Earnings	175	
Miscellaneous Revenue		175

The unearned service fees of $225 as of the end of 1981 would be recorded at the end of that year by an appropriate adjustment.

(9) *Overstatement of unearned revenue.* Unearned Rent Revenue was credited for $375 representing revenue for December, 1981, and for January and February, 1982. No adjustment was made on December 31, 1981. The effects of the failure to adjust the accounts to show revenue of $125 for 1981 were as follows:

Income Statement	Balance Sheet
For 1981: Revenue understated (rent revenue too low)	Liabilities overstated (unearned rent revenue too high)
Net income understated	Retained earnings understated

When the error is discovered in 1982, Unearned Rent Revenue is debited for $125 and Retained Earnings is credited for this amount representing the net income understatement in 1981. The following entry is made:

Unearned Rent Revenue	125	
Retained Earnings		125

(10) *Failure to record depreciation.* Delivery equipment was acquired at the beginning of 1980 at a cost of $6,000. The equipment has an estimated five-year life, and depreciation of $1,200 was overlooked at the end of 1980 and 1981. The effects of the failure to record depreciation for 1980 were as follows:

	Income Statement	Balance Sheet
For 1980:	Expenses understated (depreciation of delivery equipment too low)	Assets overstated (accumulated depreciation of delivery equipment too low)
	Net income overstated	Retained earnings overstated
For 1981:	Expenses not affected	Assets overstated (accumulated depreciation of delivery equipment too low)
	Net income not affected	Retained earnings overstated

It should be observed that the misstatements arising from the failure to record depreciation are not counterbalanced in the succeeding year.

Failure to record depreciation for 1981 affected the statements as shown below:

	Income Statement	Balance Sheet
For 1981:	Expenses understated (depreciation of delivery equipment too low)	Assets overstated (accumulated depreciation of delivery equipment understated)
	Net income overstated	Retained earnings overstated

When the omission is recognized, Retained Earnings must be decreased by the net income overstatements of prior years and accumulated depreciation must be increased by the depreciation that should have been recorded. The correcting entry in 1982 for depreciation that should have been recognized for 1980 and 1981 is as follows:

```
Retained Earnings......................................................................    2,400
        Accumulated Depreciation — Delivery Equipment..............................              2,400
```

Working Papers to Summarize Corrections

It is assumed in the following sections that the errors previously discussed are discovered in 1982 before the accounts for the year are adjusted and closed. Accounts are corrected so that revenue and expense accounts report the balances identified with the current period and asset, liability, and retained earnings accounts are accurately stated. Instead of preparing a separate entry for each correction, a single compound entry may be made for all of the errors discovered. The entry to correct earnings of prior years as well as to correct current earnings may be developed by the preparation of working papers. Assume the following retained earnings account for the R & G Wholesale Co.:

ACCOUNT Retained Earnings

Date		Item	Debit	Credit	Balance	
					Debit	Credit
1980 Dec.	31	Balance				12,000
1981 Dec.	20	Dividends declared	5,000			7,000
	31	Net income..............................		15,000		22,000

The working papers to determine the corrected retained earnings balance on December 31, 1980, and the corrected net income for 1981 are shown on page 498. As indicated earlier, no adjustment is made for income tax effects in this example.

The working papers indicate that Retained Earnings is to be decreased by $1,000 as of January 1, 1982. The reduction arises from:

Retained earnings overstatement as of December 31, 1980:
Retained earnings as originally reported	$12,000	
Retained earnings as corrected	10,400	$1,600

Retained earnings understatement in 1981:
Net income as corrected	$15,600	
Net income as originally reported	15,000	600
Retained earnings overstatement as of January 1, 1982		$1,000

The following entry is prepared from the working papers to correct the account balances in 1982:

Retained Earnings	1,000	
Sales	1,800	
Unearned Rent Revenue	125	
Sales Salaries		300
Miscellaneous Revenue		225
Accumulated Depreciation — Delivery Equipment		2,400

The retained earnings account after correction will appear with a balance of $21,000, as follows:

ACCOUNT Retained Earnings

Date		Item	Debit	Credit	Balance Debit	Balance Credit
1982 Jan.	1	Balance				22,000
Dec.	31	Corrections in net incomes of prior periods discovered during the course of the audit	1,000			21,000

The balance in Retained Earnings can be proved by reconstructing the account from the detail shown on the working papers. If the net incomes for 1980 and 1981 had been reported properly, Retained Earnings would have appeared as follows:

ACCOUNT Retained Earnings

Date		Item	Debit	Credit	Balance Debit	Balance Credit
1980 Dec.	31	Corrected balance per working papers				10,400
1981 Dec.	20	Dividends declared	5,000			5,400
	31	Corrected net income for 1981		15,600		21,000

R & G Wholesale Co.
Working Papers for Correction of Account Balances
December 31, 1982

	Explanation	Retained Earnings Dec. 31, 1980 Debit	Credit	Net Income Year Ended Dec. 31, 1981 Debit	Credit	Accounts Requiring Correction in 1982 Debit	Credit	Account	
1	Reported retained earnings balance,		12,000						1
2	Dec. 31, 1980								2
3	Reported net income for year ended								3
4	Dec. 31, 1981				15,000				4
5	Corrections:[1]								5
6	(1) Understatement of inventory on								6
7	Dec. 31, 1980, $1,000		1,000	1,000					7
8	(2) Failure to record merchandise								8
9	purchases in 1980, $850	850			850				9
10	(3) Failure to record merchandise								10
11	sales in 1981, $1,800				1,800	1,800		Sales	11
12	(4) Failure to record accrued sales								12
13	salaries:								13
14	(a) On Dec. 31, 1980, $450	450			450				14
15	(b) On Dec. 31, 1981, $300			300			300	Sales Salaries	15
16	(5) Failure to record prepaid taxes on								16
17	Dec. 31, 1980, $275		275	275					17
18	(6) Failure to record insurance ex-								18
19	pense on Dec. 31, 1980, $350, in-								19
20	surance of $700 for 1980 and 1981								20
21	being charged to 1981	350			350				21
22	(7) Failure to record accrued interest								22
23	on notes receivable on Dec. 31,								23
24	1980, $150		150	150					24
25	(8) Failure to record unearned ser-								25
26	vice fees:								26
27	(a) On Dec. 31, 1980, $175	175			175				27
28	(b) On Dec. 31, 1981, $225			225			225	Misc. Revenue	28
29	(9) Failure to record rent revenue on								29
30	Dec. 31, 1981, $125				125	125		Unearned Rent	30
31	(10) Failure to record depreciation of								31
32	delivery equipment:								32
33	(a) On Dec. 31, 1980, $1,200	1,200					1,200	Accumulated	33
34	(b) On Dec. 31, 1981, $1,200			1,200			1,200	Depr. — Delivery	34
35								Equipment	35
36	Corrected retained earnings balance,								36
37	Dec. 31, 1980	10,400							37
38		13,425	13,425						38
39	Corrected net income for 1981			15,600					39
40				18,750	18,750				40
41	Net correction to retained earnings as								41
42	of Jan. 1, 1982					1,000		Retained	42
43								Earnings	43
44						2,925	2,925		44

[1]For a more detailed description of the individual errors and their correction, refer to pages 488–496.

In the foregoing example, a corrected net income figure for only 1981 was required; hence any corrections in earnings for years prior to this date were shown as affecting the retained earnings balance as of December 31, 1980. Working papers on page 498 were constructed to summarize this information by providing a pair of columns for retained earnings as of December 31, 1980, and a pair of columns for earnings data for 1981. It may be desirable to determine corrected earnings for a number of years. When this is to be done, a pair of columns must be provided for retained earnings as of the beginning of the period under review and a separate pair of columns for each year for which corrected earnings are to be determined. For example, assume that corrected earnings for the years 1979, 1980, and 1981 are to be determined. Working papers for the correction of account balances would be constructed with headings as shown below. Corrections for the omission of accrued sales salaries for a four-year period would appear as follows:

Explanation	Retained Earnings Dec. 31, 1978		Net Income Year Ended Dec. 31, 1979		Net Income Year Ended Dec. 31, 1980		Net Income Year Ended Dec. 31, 1981		Accounts Requiring Correction in 1982		
	Debit	Credit	Debit	Credit	Debit	Credit	Debit	Credit	Debit	Credit	Account
Failure to record accrued sales salaries at end of:											
1978, $750.	750			750							
1979, $800.			800			800					
1980, $900.					900			900			
1981, $625.							625			625	Sales Salaries

QUESTIONS

1. Accumulated retained earnings are in general supported by a cross section of all of the assets. Directors are criticized by stockholders for failure to declare dividends when retained earnings are present. Are these two statements related? Explain.

2. Which of the following transactions are a source of stockholders' equity?

(a) Operating profits.

(b) Cancellation of a part of a liability upon prompt payment of the balance.

(c) Reduction of par value of stock outstanding.

(d) Discovery of an understatement of income in a previous period.

(e) Release of Retained Earnings Appropriated for Purchase of Treasury Stock upon the sale of treasury stock.

(f) Issue of bonds at a premium.

(g) Purchase of the corporation's own capital stock at a discount.

(h) Increase in the company's earning capacity, taken to be evidence of considerable goodwill.

(i) Donation to the corporation of its own stock.

(j) Sale of land, buildings, and equipment at a gain.

(k) Gain on bond retirement.

(l) Revaluation of land, buildings, and equipment resulting in an increase in asset book value as a result of increase in asset replacement value.

(m) Collection of stock assessments from stockholders.

(n) Discovery of valuable resources on company property.

(o) Conversion of bonds into common stock.

(p) Conversion of preferred stock into common stock.

3. The following announcement appeared on the financial page of a newspaper:

> The Board of Directors of the Benton Co., at their meeting on June 15, 1981, declared the regular quarterly dividend on outstanding common stock of 70 cents per share and an extra dividend of $1.40 per share, both payable on July 10, 1981, to the stockholders of record at the close of business June 30, 1981.

   (a) What is the purpose of each of the three dates given in the declaration?
   (b) When would the stock become "ex-dividend"?
   (c) Why is the $1.40 designated as an "extra" dividend?

4. The directors of The Fern Shoppe are considering issuance of a stock dividend. They have asked you to discuss the proposed action by answering questions below:

   (a) What is a stock dividend? How is a stock dividend distinguished from a stock split: (1) from a legal standpoint? (2) from an accounting standpoint?
   (b) For what reasons does a corporation usually declare (1) a stock dividend? (2) a stock split? (3) a stock split in the form of a stock dividend?

5. Eastern Supply, Inc., has 1,000,000 shares of no-par common outstanding. Dividends have been limited to approximately 20% of annual earnings, remaining earnings being used to finance expansion. With pressure from stockholders for an increase in dividends, the board of directors takes action to issue to stockholders an additional 1,000,000 shares of stock, and the president of the company informs stockholders that the company will pay a 100% stock dividend in view of the conservative dividend policy in the past. What is your comment on this statement?

6. It has been recommended that the balance sheet maintain a permanent distinction between contributed capital and retained earnings. How can such a distinction be maintained when action is taken to convert retained earnings into capital stock?

7. (a) What is a liquidating dividend? (b) Under what circumstances are such distributions made? (c) How would you recommend that liquidating dividends be recorded in the accounts of the corporation?

8. At the regular meeting of the board of directors of the Lawton Corporation, a dividend payable in the stock of the Colter Corporation is to be declared. The stock of the Colter Corporation is recorded on the books of the Lawton Corporation at $190,000; the market value of the stock is $230,000.

The question is raised whether the amount to be recorded for the dividend payable should be the book value or the market value. What is the proper accounting treatment?

9. Snow White Cleaners, acting within the law of the state of incorporation, paid a cash dividend to stockholders for which it debited Paid-In Capital from Sale of Stock at a Premium. A stockholder protested, saying that such a dividend was a partial liquidation of her holdings. Is this true?

10. What methods can be followed in reporting dividends in arrears on preferred stock on the balance sheet?

11. Why should Retained Earnings not be credited for gains arising from a company dealing in its own stock if losses for similar transactions are debited to the account?

12. A stockholder of Barker, Inc., does not understand the purpose of the Appropriation for Bond Redemption Fund that has been set up by periodic debits to Retained Earnings. He is told that this balance will not be used to redeem the bonds at their maturity. (a) What account will be reduced by the payment of the bonds? (b) What purpose is accomplished by the Appropriation for Bond Redemption Fund? (c) What dispositions may be made of the appropriation?

13. Strummin' Music Co. has appropriated retained earnings of $5,000,000 over a five-year period for plant expansion. In the sixth year the company completes an expansion program at a cost of $6,500,000; such expansion is financed through company funds of $4,500,000, and borrowed funds of $2,000,000. What disposition of the appropriation for plant expansion would you recommend?

14. Management of the Judd Construction Co., considering the possibility of a strike by employees, authorized the establishment of an appropriation for contingencies at the end of 1980 by a charge to revenue. The strike was called in 1981, and company losses incurred to the date of the strike settlement were charged against the appropriation. The company management points out that it exercised good judgment in anticipating strike losses and in providing a cushion for such losses. What criticism, if any, can you offer of the accounting procedures followed by the company?

15. What items are defined as contra-equity accounts and deducted from the total stockholders' equity?

16. Fujimoto, Inc., reports appropriations as a subtraction from net income at the bottom of the income statement. When an appropriation is canceled, it is reported as an addition to net income on the income statement. What objections would you raise to such a practice?

17. Which of the following transactions change total stockholders' equity? What is the nature of the change?

  (a) Declaration of a cash dividend.
  (b) Payment of a cash dividend.
  (c) Retirement of bonds payable for which both a redemption fund and an appropriation had been established.
  (d) Declaration of stock dividend.
  (e) Payment of a stock dividend.
  (f) Conversion of bonds payable into preferred stock.
  (g) The passing of a dividend on cumulative preferred stock.
  (h) Donation by the officers of shares of stock.
  (i) Operating loss for the period.

18. How would you report the following items on the balance sheet: (a) dividends in arrears on cumulative preferred stock, (b) unclaimed bond interest and unclaimed dividends. (c) stock that is callable at a premium at the option of the corporation?

19. Why is book value per share often a poor indicator of stock worth?

20. What adjustments are applied to the total stockholders' equity in computing book value per common share when there is more than one class of stock outstanding?

21. The liquidation value of preferred stock is 100 and the call price is 105. Which value should be used in computing book value for preferred stock? Why?

EXERCISES

exercise 17-1

The balance sheet of the Jenks Warehouse Supply Company shows the following on July 1:

Cash	$300,000
Capital stock, $10 par, 100,000 shares authorized, 75,000 shares issued and outstanding	750,000
Paid-in capital	150,000
Retained earnings	345,000

On July 1, Jenks declared a cash dividend of $2 per share payable on October 1. Then on November 1, the corporation declared a 15% stock dividend with the shares to be issued on December 31. Market value on November 1 was $15 per share. Give the necessary entries to record the declaration and payment or issuance of the dividends.

exercise 17-2

Lamoreaux Lumber Co. distributed the following dividends to its stockholders:

  (a) Investment of 400,000 shares of Accord Corporation stock, carrying value $1,200,000, fair market value $2,300,000.

     (b) Investment of 230,000 shares of Pfeifer Trailer Company stock, a closely held corpora-
tion. The shares were purchased three years ago at $5.60 per share, but no current
market price is available.

Give the journal entries to account for the declaration and the payment of the above dividends.

exercise 17-3

Thornton Excavating has been paying quarterly dividends of $.50 and wants to pay the same
amount in the third quarter. Given the following information, what is the total amount in dollars
that Thornton will have to pay in dividends in the third quarter in order to pay $.50 per share?

> 1981
> Jan.   1 Shares outstanding, 600,000; $10 par (1,000,000 shares authorized)
> Feb. 15 Issued 150,000 new shares at $16.50
> Mar. 31 Paid quarterly dividends of $.50 per share
> May 12 $1,600,000 of $1,000 bonds were converted to common stock at the rate of 80
>   shares of stock per $1,000 bond.
> June 30 Paid quarterly dividends of $.50 per share. Also issued a 5% stock dividend.

exercise 17-4

The balance sheet of the Far Valley Motors Co. shows the following:

Capital stock, $5 stated value, 80,000 shares issued and outstanding	$400,000
Paid-in capital	800,000
Retained earnings	350,000

A 25% stock dividend is declared, the board of directors authorizing a transfer from Retained
Earnings to Capital Stock at the stock stated value.

     (a) Give entries to record the declaration and payment of the dividend.
     (b) What was the effect of the issue of the stock dividend on the ownership equity of each
stockholder in the corporation?
     (c) Give entries to record the declaration and payment of the dividend if the board of direc-
tors had elected to transfer amounts from Retained Earnings to Capital Stock equal to
the market value of the stock ($10 per share).

exercise 17-5

The capital accounts for Kiddie Korner Furniture, Inc., on June 30, 1981, follow:

Capital Stock, $20 par, 60,000 shares	$1,200,000
Premium on Capital Stock	435,000
Retained Earnings	2,160,000

Shares of the company's stock are selling at this time at 36. What entries would you make in each
case below?

     (a) A stock dividend of 10% is declared and issued.
     (b) A stock dividend of 100% is declared and issued.
     (c) A 2-for-1 stock split is declared and issued.

exercise 17-6

The directors of Fairly Dry Cleaning, Inc., whose $80 par value common stock is currently selling at
$100 per share, have decided to issue a stock dividend. Fairly Dry has an authorization for 400,000
shares of common, has issued 220,000 shares of which 20,000 shares are now held as treasury
stock, and desires to capitalize $2,400,000 of the retained earnings account balance. What percent
stock dividend should be issued to accomplish this desire?

exercise 17-7

The dividend declarations and distributions by the Fenton Company over a three-year period are
as follows. Give the entry required in each case.

> 1980
> July   1 Declared a 30% stock dividend on 1,000,000 shares of stock, par value $15. The
>   stock was originally sold at $18, and Retained Earnings is to be debited for the
>   stock dividend for an amount equal to the original stock issuance price.

1982

July 1 Declared a dividend of 1 share of Eastern Co. common stock on every share of Fenton Company stock owned. Eastern Co. common stock is carried on the books of the Fenton Company at a cost of $1.60 per share, and the market price is $1.80 per share.

July 15 Distributed Eastern Co. common stock to shareholders.

exercise 17-8

On January 1, 1980, Pacific Manufacturing Corporation floated a $14,000,000 bond issue. The bond issue agreement with the underwriters required Pacific Manufacturing to appropriate earnings of $875,000 at the end of each year until the bonds are retired. During their 1982 board meeting, the directors decided to change the company's financing policy to just short-term debt and equity, and to drop their present insurance policy in favor of a self-insurance plan. On July 1, 1982, the company retired the bond issue and set up their first annual appropriation for self-insurance for $14,000.

(1) Give the entires to record the periodic appropriations under the bond issue agreement for 1980 and 1981 and their cancellation in 1982.

(2) How should the appropriation for self-insurance be recorded?

exercise 17-9

A physical inventory taken by the Eckles Storage Co. on December 31, 1981, discloses goods on hand with a cost of $2,580,000; the inventory is recorded at this figure less than an allowance of $108,000 to reduce it to the lower of cost or market. At the same time, the company authorizes that an appropriation for possible future inventory decline of $900,000 be established.

(1) Give the entries to be made at the end of 1981 in recording the inventory and establishing the accounts as indicated.

(2) Give the entries in 1982 to close the beginning inventory and balances established at the end of 1981, assuming that the estimated inventory decline does not materialize and that the inventory at the end of 1982 is properly reported at cost, which is lower than market.

(3) Give the entries in 1982 to close the inventory and other account balances established at the end of 1981 if a decline in the value of the December 31, 1981 inventory of $480,000 is to be recognized; the inventory at the end of 1982 is properly reported at cost, which is lower than its market value at this date.

exercise 17-10

For each of the following items, give the title of the account that would be credited and where it would be reported on financial statements.

(a) 15% stock dividend declared on common stock.

(b) Transfer to reserve for bond redemption fund.

(c) Profit-sharing bonus to employees.

(d) Gain on sale of treasury stock.

(e) Gain on sale of investment in securities.

(f) Premium on sale of bonds.

(g) Gain on sale of property originally acquired by exchange for capital stock.

exercise 17-11

As of December 31, the equity section of the Intermountain Tile Corp. balance sheet contained the following information: capital stock, 120,000 shares issued, $1,200,000; capital stock subscribed, 20,000 shares, $200,000; additional paid-in capital, $400,000; retained earnings, $1,800,000; treasury stock at cost, 20,000 shares, $120,000. Compute the book value per share of common stock.

exercise 17-12

The stockholders' equity of Greco, Inc., on December 31, 1981, follows:

Common stock, $15 par, 100,000 shares	$1,500,000
Preferred 6% stock, $25 par, 10,000 shares	250,000
Additional paid-in capital	150,000
Retained earnings	100,000
Total stockholders equity	$2,000,000

Compute the book values per share of preferred stock and common stock under each of the following assumptions:

(a) Preferred stock is noncumulative, callable at $30, and preferred as to assets at $27.50 upon corporate liquidation.
(b) Preferred stock is cumulative, with dividends in arrears for 6 years (including the current year). Upon corporate liquidation, shares are preferred as to assets up to par, and any dividends in arrears must be paid before distribution may be made to common shares.

*exercise 17-13

State the effect of each of the following errors made in 1980 upon the balance sheets and the income statements prepared in 1980 and 1981:

(a) The ending inventory is understated as a result of an error in the count of goods on hand.
(b) The ending inventory is overstated as a result of the inclusion of goods acquired and held on a consignment basis. No purchase was recorded on the books.
(c) A purchase of merchandise at the end of 1980 is not recorded until payment is made for the goods in 1981; the goods purchased were included in the inventory at the end of 1980.
(d) A sale of merchandise at the end of 1980 is not recorded until cash is received for the goods in 1981; the goods sold were excluded from the inventory at the end of 1980.
(e) Goods shipped to consignees in 1980 were reported as sales; goods in the hands of consignees at the end of 1980 were not recognized for inventory purposes; sale of such goods in 1981 and collections on such sales were recorded as credits to the receivables established with consignees in 1980.
(f) One week's sales total during 1980 was credited to Gain on Sales — Machinery.
(g) No depreciation is taken in 1980 for machinery sold in April, 1980. The company is on a calendar year and computes depreciation to the nearest month.
(h) No depreciation is taken in 1980 for machinery purchased in October, 1980. The company is on a calendar year and computes depreciation to the nearest month.
(i) Customers' notes receivable are debited to Accounts Receivable.

*exercise 17-14

The Nielson Co. reports net incomes for a three-year period as follows: 1979, $18,000; 1980, $10,500; 1981, $12,500.

In reviewing the accounts in 1982, after the books for the prior year have been closed, you find that the following errors have been made in summarizing activities:

	1979	1980	1981
Overstatement of ending inventories as a result of errors in count .	$1,600	$2,800	$1,800
Understatement of advertising expense payable	300	600	450
Overstatement of interest receivable..	250	——	200
Omission of depreciation on property items still in use	900	800	750

(a) Prepare working papers summarizing corrections and reporting corrected net incomes for 1979, 1980 and 1981.
(b) Give the entry to bring the books of the company up to date in 1982.

*exercise 17-15

The first audit of the books for the Warren Corporation was made for the year ended December 31, 1981. In reviewing the books, the auditor discovered that certain adjustments had been overlooked at the end of 1980 and 1981, and also that other items had been improperly recorded. Omissions and other failures for each year are summarized as follows:

*Exercises to appendix material.

	December 31	
	1980	1981
Sales salaries payable	$1,300	$1,100
Interest receivable	325	215
Prepaid insurance	450	300
Advances from customers	1,750	2,500

(Collections from customers had been included in sales but should have been recognized as advances from customers since goods were not shipped until the following year.)

Equipment	1,400	1,200

(Expenditures had been recognized as repairs but should have been recognized as cost of equipment; the depreciation rate on such equipment is 10% per year, but depreciation in the year of the expenditure is to be recognized at 5%).

Prepare journal entries to correct revenue and expense accounts for 1981 and record assets and liabilities that require recognition on the balance sheet as of December 31, 1981. Assume the nominal accounts for 1981 have not yet been closed into the income summary account.

PROBLEMS

problem 17-1

Ernst Photography Equipment was organized on June 30, 1979. After two and one-half years of profitable operations, the equity section of Ernst's balance sheet was as follows:

Contributed capital:
Common stock, $30 par, 500,000 shares authorized, 100,000 shares issued and outstanding	$3,000,000
Premium on common stock	500,000
Retained earnings	1,800,000
Total stockholders' equity	$5,300,000

During 1982, the following transactions affected the stockholders' equity:

Jan. 31 10,000 shares of common stock were reacquired at $33; treasury stock is reported at cost.

Apr. 1 The company declared a 35% stock dividend, (Applies to all issued stock.)

Apr. 30 The company declared a $.50 cash dividend. (Applies only to outstanding stock.)

June 1 The stock dividend was issued and the cash dividend was paid.

Aug. 31 The treasury stock was sold at $36.

Instructions: Give journal entries to record the above stock transactions.

problem 17-2

The stockholders' equity of the Ash Lumber Co. on June 30, 1981, was as follows:

Contributed capital:
Preferred 8% stock, $50 par, cumulative, 20,000 shares issued, dividends 5 years in arrears	$1,000,000
Common stock, $20 par, 160,000 shares issued	3,200,000
	$4,200,000
Less deficit from operations	600,000
Total stockholders' equity	$3,600,000

On this date the following action was taken:

(a) Common stockholders turned in their stock and received in exchange new common stock, 1 share of the new stock being exchanged for every 4 shares of the old. New stock was given a stated value of $40 per share.

(b) One-half share of the new common stock was issued on each share of preferred stock outstanding in liquidation of dividends in arrears on preferred stock.

(c) The deficit from operations was applied against the paid-in capital arising from the common stock restatement.

Transactions for the remainder of 1981 affecting the stockholders' equity were as follows:

Oct. 1 10,000 shares of preferred stock were called in at $55 plus dividends for 3 months at 8%. Stock was formally retired.

Nov. 10 60,000 shares of new common stock were sold at 42.

Dec. 31 Net income for the six months ended on this date was $170,000. (Debit Income Summary.) The semiannual dividend was declared on preferred shares and a $.50 dividend on common shares, dividends being payable January 20, 1982.

Instructions:

(1) Record in journal form the given transactions.

(2) Prepare the stockholders' equity section of the balance sheet as of December 31, 1981.

problem 17-3

Butler, Inc., was organized on January 2, 1980, with authorized stock consisting of 40,000 shares of 16%, nonparticipating, $200 par preferred, and 250,000 shares of no-par common. During the first two years of the company's existence, the following transactions took place:

1980

Jan. 2 Sold 10,600 shares of common stock at 16.

    2 Sold 2,600 shares of preferred stock at 216.

Mar. 2 Sold common stock as follows: 10,200 shares at 22; 2,400 shares at 24.

July 10 A nearby piece of land, appraised at $404,000 was acquired for 600 shares of preferred stock and 28,000 shares of common. (Preferred stock was recorded at 216, the balance being assigned to common.)

Dec. 16 The regular preferred and a $1.50 common dividend were declared.

    28 Dividends declared on December 16 were paid.

    31 The income summary account showed a credit balance of $408,000, which was transferred to retained earnings.

1981

Feb. 27 The corporation reacquired 12,000 shares of common stock at 18. The treasury stock is carried at cost. (State law requires that an appropriaton of retained earnings be made for the purchase price of treasury stock. Appropriations are to be returned to retained earnings upon resale of the stock.)

June 17 Resold 10,000 shares of the treasury stock at 20.

July 31 Resold all of the remaining treasury stock at 19.

Sept. 30 The corporation sold 12,000 additional shares of common stock at 21.

Dec. 16 The regular preferred dividend and a $.80 common dividend were declared.

    28 Dividends declared on December 16 were paid.

    31 The income summary account showed a credit balance of $356,000, which was transferred to retained earnings.

Instructions:

(1) Give the journal entries to record the foregoing transactions.

(2) Prepare the stockholders' equity section of the balance sheet as of December 31, 1981.

problem 17-4

A condensed balance sheet for Tax Trimmers, Inc., as of December 31, 1978, appears below:

Tax Trimmers, Inc.
Condensed Balance Sheet
December 31, 1978

Assets		Liabilities and Stockholders' Equity	
Assets..	$525,000	Liabilities	$120,000
		Preferred 8% stock, $100 par.....	75,000
		Common stock, $50 par	150,000
		Premium on common stock.......	30,000
		Retained earnings.......................	150,000
		Total liabilities and stock-	
Total assets	$525,000	holders' equity.........................	$525,000

Capital stock authorized consists of: 750 shares of 8%, cumulative, nonparticipating preferred stock with a prior claim on assets, and 15,000 shares of common stock.

Information relating to operations of the succeeding three years follows:

	1979	1980	1981
Dividends declared on Dec. 20, payable on Jan. 10 of following year:			
Preferred stock	8% cash	8% cash	8% cash
Common stock.......................................	{ $1.00 cash { 50% stock*	$1.25 cash	$1.00 cash
Net income for year.................................	$67,500	$39,000	$51,000

*Retained earnings is reduced by the par value of the stock dividend.

1980

Feb. 12 Accumulated depreciation was reduced by $72,000 following an income tax investigation. (Assume that this was an error that qualifies as a prior period adjustment.) Additional income tax of $22,500 for prior years was paid.

Mar. 3 300 shares of common stock were purchased by the corporation at $54 per share; treasury stock is recorded at cost and retained earnings are appropriated equal to such cost.

1981

Aug. 10 All of the treasury stock was resold at $59 per share and the retained earnings appropriation was canceled.

Sept. 12 By vote of the stockholders, each share of the common stock was exchanged by the corporation for 4 shares of no-par common stock with a stated value of $15.

Instructions:

    (1) Give the journal entries to record the foregoing transactions for the three-year period ended December 31, 1981.

    (2) Prepare the stockholders' equity section of the balance sheet as it would appear at the end of 1979, 1980 and 1981.

problem 17-5

On March 31, 1981, the retained earnings account of State-Wide Wrecking Service showed a balance of $19,000,000. The board of directors of State-Wide made the following decisions during the remainder of 1981 that possibly affect the retained earnings account.

Apr. 1 State-Wide decided to assume the risk for workers' compensation insurance. The estimated liability for 1981 is $120,000. Also, a fund was set up to cover the estimated liability.

Apr. 30 State-Wide has not experienced even a small fire since 1946; therefore, the board of directors decided to start a self-insurance plan. They decided to start with a $400,000 appropriation.

May 15 A fire did considerable damage to the outside warehouse. It cost $360,000 to repair the warehouse.

Aug. 20 The board of directors received a report from the plant engineer which indicated that the company is possibly in violation of pollution control standards. The fine for such a violation is $800,000. As a result of the engineer's report, the board decided to set up a general contingency reserve for $800,000.

Sept. 1 The company reacquired 80,000 shares of their own stock at $29; treasury stock is recorded at cost. Due to legal restrictions, State-Wide has to set up an appropriation to cover the cost of the treasury stock.

Dec. 31 The company had to pay a $800,000 fine for pollution control violations and the treasury stock was sold at $31. No workers' compensation was paid during the year.

Instructions: Prepare all of the necessary entries to record the above transactions.

problem 17-6

Accounts of Alpine Ranch on December 31, 1981, show the following balances:

Accumulated Depreciation — Buildings...		$ 272,000
Allowance for Purchase Discount	$ 2,400	
Bonds Payable		320,000
Bond Retirement Fund..	128,000	
Buildings	1,200,000	
Capital Stock (80,000 shares authorized)....................................		632,000
Capital Stock Subscribed (4,000 shares).....................................		40,000
Current Assets..	768,000	
Current Liabilities — Other...		260,000
Customers' Deposits		20,000
Dividends Payable — Cash		16,000
Income Tax Payable		40,000
Paid-In Capital from Sale of Treasury Stock at More Than Cost..		32,000
Premium on Capital Stock		24,000
Retained Earnings Appropriated for Contingencies		100,000
Retained Earnings Appropriated for Bond Retirement Fund		128,000
Retained Earnings Appropriated for Purchase of Treasury Stock		56,000
Stock Dividends Distributable		65,600
Treasury Stock, 4,800 shares at cost	56,000	
Unappropriated Retained Earnings		148,800
	$2,154,400	$2,154,400

Instructions: From this data prepare the stockholders' equity section as it would appear on the balance sheet.

problem 17-7

The stockholders' equity for the Kawakami Radio Corp. on December 31, 1981, follows:

Preferred 6% stock, $100 par, 20,000 shares	$2,000,000
Common stock, $25 par, 200,000 shares...	5,000,000
Additional paid-in capital...	500,000
Retained earnings	750,000
Total stockholders' equity	$8,250,000

Instructions: Calculate the book values of preferred shares and common shares as of December 31, 1981, under each of the following assumptions:

(1) Preferred dividends have been paid to October 1, 1981; preferred shares have a call value of $110, a liquidation value of $105, and are entitled to current unpaid quarterly dividends.

(2) Preferred shares have a liquidation value of $110; shares are cumulative, with dividends in arrears for 4 years including the current year and fully payable in the event of liquidation.

(3) Preferred shares have a liquidation value of par; shares are noncumulative, and no dividends have been paid for the past 5 years; however, the current year's dividend has been declared but not yet recorded on the books.

problem 17-8

The following accounts are taken from the ledger of Thompson Wholesale Co.

ACCOUNT   Retained Earnings Appropriated for Plant Expansion

Date		Item	Debit	Credit	Balance Debit	Balance Credit
1981 Jan.	1	Balance.........................				450,000
Dec.	31			75,000		525,000

ACCOUNT Retained Earnings Appropriated for Purchase of Treasury Stock

Date		Item	Debit	Credit	Balance	
					Debit	Credit
1981						
Jan.	1	Balance...............................				276,000
Apr.	1			93,000		369,000
July	1		126,000			243,000

ACCOUNT Unappropriated Retained Earnings

Date		Item	Debit	Credit	Balance	
					Debit	Credit
1981						
Jan.	1	Balance...				2,250,000
Apr.	1	Appropriated for purchase of treasury stock..........................	93,000			2,157,000
July	1	Appropriated for treasury stock acquisitions		126,000		2,283,000
Oct.	31	Preferred dividends....................	150,000			2,133,000
	31	Stock dividend on common stock..	600,000			1,533,000
Dec.	31	Appropriated for plant expansion...	75,000			1,458,000
	31	Net income for 1981		630,000		2,088,000

Instructions: Prepare a retained earnings statement for 1981 in support of the retained earnings balance to be reported on the company's balance sheet at the end of the year.

*problem 17-9

The auditors for the Hansen Co. in inspecting accounts on December 31, 1981, the end of the fiscal year, find that certain prepaid and accrued items had been overlooked in prior years and in the current year as follows:

	End of			
	1978	1979	1980	1981
Prepaid expenses	$700	$600	$750	$1,900
Expenses payable..	500	800	950	1,000
Prepaid revenues	140			420
Revenues receivable..		150	125	200

Retained earnings on December 31, 1978, had been reported at $25,600; and net income for 1979 and for 1980 were reported at $9,500 and $12,250 respectively. Revenue and expense balances for 1981 were transferred to the income summary account and the latter shows a credit balance of $12,500 prior to correction by the auditors. No dividends had been declared in the three-year period.

Instructions:

(1) Prepare working papers as illustrated on pages 686 and 687 to develop a corrected retained earnings balance as of December 31, 1978, and corrected earnings for 1979, 1980, and 1981. Disregard effects of corrections on income tax.

(2) Prepare a corrected statement of retained earnings for the three-year period ending December 31, 1981.

(3) Give the entry or entries required as of December 31, 1981, to correct the income summary account and retained earnings account and to establish the appropriate balance sheet accounts as of this date.

*Problems to appendix material

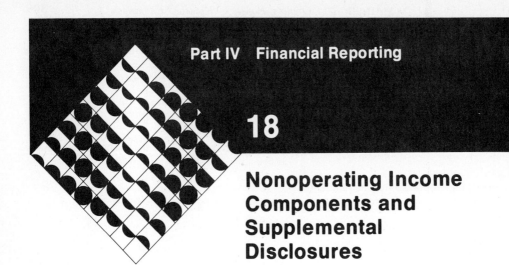

18

Nonoperating Income Components and Supplemental Disclosures

CHAPTER OBJECTIVES

Identify the major components of income.

Discuss the reporting problems associated with discontinued operations, extraordinary items, and accounting changes.

Provide a comprehensive illustration of reporting earnings components.

Discuss interim reporting, segment reporting, and forecasts.

The importance of measuring and reporting business income was established in Chapter 4. Information on past earnings as a measure of overall managerial performance and as an indicator of future earnings potential is useful to investors, creditors, and others. To be most beneficial, the major components of income should be clearly identified. Appropriate distinctions should be made between the results of activities or events which are normal to the business and can be expected to recur on a regular basis, and the results of activities or events which are unrelated to the normal operations of a particular business. This distinction between **regular** and **irregular earnings** was introduced in Chapter 4. As noted there, the irregular components of income are sometimes called **below-the-line** items, which include all material items listed as separate earnings components after income from continuing operations. In Chapter 4 the income statement was discussed primarily from the perspective of regular earnings. In this chapter the addi-

510

tional earnings components and supplementary disclosures associated with reporting income are discussed.

ADJUSTMENTS TO OPERATING INCOME

The reporting of income components may be categorized as shown below. The revenues and expenses relating to the normal, recurring activi-

Major Earnings Components

Normal Recurring Items	Operating revenues	$XXX
	Operating expenses..	XXX
	Operating income	**$XXX**
Peripheral Recurring Items	Other revenues..	XXX
	Other expenses	XXX
	Income from continuing operations before taxes	**$XXX**
	Income taxes	XXX
	Income from continuing operations	**$XXX**
	Below-the-line items:	
Irregular Items	Discontinued operations (net of tax)..	XXX
	Extraordinary items (net of tax)...	XXX
	Cumulative effect of change in accounting principle (net of tax)	XXX
	Net income	**$XXX**

ties of a business result in **operating income.** The results of transactions and events which are material in amount and occur on a regular basis but which are not related to the normal sales or service activities of the business (such as interest revenue for a manufacturing firm) are a separate category and are added or subtracted from operating income to derive **income from continuing operations before taxes.** After the provision for income taxes is deducted, the resulting amount is reported as **income from continuing operations.** Below-the-line items (reported net of tax) are then added or subtracted to derive the final **net income** figure. The main categories of below-the-line items are: (1) discontinued operations (2) extraordinary items, and (3) accounting changes. Each of these categories is discussed in the sections that follow.

Discontinued Operations

Occasionally, the management of a company will decide to discontinue or sell part of the business. The segment of the company to be disposed of may be a product line, a division, or a subsidiary company. Management may decide to dispose of the segment because it is unprofitable, it is too isolated geographically, it does not fit into future company plans, or any number of other reasons. Regardless of the reason, the discontinuance of a substantial portion of company operations is a significant event. Therefore, information about **discontinued operations** should be presented explicitly to readers of financial statements.

In APB Opinion No. 30, the Board indicated that the results of operating a business segment that has been or is expected to be discontinued should be reported as a separate component of income after income from continuing operations but before extraordinary items and cumulative effects of accounting changes. The Board further concluded "that any gain or loss from disposal of a segment of a business . . . should be reported in conjunction with the related results of discontinued operations and not as an extraordinary item."[1]

Note there are two aspects of the disclosure requirements for discontinued operations: (1) separate disclosure of the current year income or loss from operating the discontinued segment, and (2) disclosure of the gain or loss on the actual disposal of the business segment. To illustrate, assume the WhitCo Manufacturing Co. decides to discontinue its home furnishing division. During 1981, company income from continuing operations was $750,000, but the home furnishing division lost $40,000. The division was sold at the end of the year at a loss of $70,000. Assuming a tax rate of 40%, the partial income statement for WhitCo for 1981 should disclose the following:

Income from continuing operations		$750,000
Discontinued operations (Note X):		
Loss from operations of discontinued business segment (net of $16,000 tax reduction on loss)...........	$24,000	
Loss on disposal of business segment (net of $28,000 tax reduction on loss)................................	42,000	66,000
Net income...		$684,000

The income statement of General Mills, Inc., reproduced in Appendix B, provides an additional example of reporting for discontinued operations.

In accounting for discontinued operations, the disposal of a business segment should be distinguished from the disposal of assets which do not represent a major segment of the business. To qualify as a business segment, the assets and related activities must be clearly distinguishable, both physically and operationally as well as for financial reporting purposes, from the other assets, operating results, and activities of the company. For example, the disposal of assets incidental to the normal evolution of the entity's business would not qualify as a disposal of a business segment. Neither would the disposal of part but not all of a line of business, the shifting of the production or marketing functions from one location to another, the phasing out of a product line or loss of service, or other changes caused by technological advancements qualify as a disposal of a business segment.[2]

The reporting of discontinued operations can become complex. Only a summary of the guidelines provided by APB Opinion No. 30 are covered here. Application of the guidelines requires judgment. The goal should be to report information that will assist external users in assessing future cash flows by clearly distinguishing normal, recurring earnings patterns from those activities that are irregular yet significant in assessing the total company results of operations.

---

[1] *Opinions of the Accounting Principles Board, No. 30*, "Reporting The Results of Operations" (New York: American Institute of Certified Public Accountants, 1973), par. 8.

[2] *Ibid.*, par. 13.

Extraordinary Items

A second category of below-the-line items is extraordinary items. The Accounting Principles Board recognized that the distinction between ordinary operating items and extraordinary items will require the use of judgment by an accountant. To assist the accountant in making the distinction, the Board established certain criteria which must be met before an item should be classified as extraordinary. In Accounting Principles Board Opinion No. 30, the APB provided more definitive criteria for extraordinary items and clarified and modified to some extent the existing criteria originally established in APB Opinion No. 9.

Extraordinary items, according to APB Opinion No. 30, are events and transactions that are both **unusual** in nature and **infrequent** in occurrence. Thus, to qualify as extraordinary, an item must "possess a high degree of abnormality and be of a type clearly unrelated to, or only incidentally related to, the ordinary and typical activities of the entity . . . [and] be of a type that would not reasonably be expected to recur in the foreseeable future."[3] In addition, the item must be **material** in amount.

The overall effect of APB Opinion No. 30 is to severely restrict the items that can be classified as extraordinary. The Board offers certain examples of gains and losses that should *not* be reported as extraordinary items. They include: (1) the write-down or write-off of receivables, inventories, equipment leased to others, or intangible assets; (2) the gains or losses from exchanges or translation of foreign currencies, including those relating to major devaluations and revaluations; (3) the gains or losses on disposal of a segment of a business; (4) other gains or losses from sale or abandonment of property, plant, or equipment used in the business; (5) the effects of a strike; (6) the adjustment of accruals on long-term contracts.

On the other hand, according to the FASB, at least one item — a gain or loss from extinguishment of debt — is to be reported as an extraordinary item regardless of the criteria stated in APB Opinion 30.[4] This was discussed earlier in Chapter 14.

The reporting of extraordinary items will be rare due to the restrictive criteria of APB Opinion No. 30. However, when an extraordinary item is identified as such, it should be reported as a separate item below income from continuing operations. Generally, it should be shown after the information reporting the results of discontinued operations but before net income. Extraordinary items should always be shown net of tax, and, as will be explained in Chapter 21, should have a related earnings per share figure disclosed. The comprehensive illustration on page 522 shows a proper reporting format.

Items which are either unusual in nature or occur infrequently, but do not meet both criteria and, therefore, should not be classified as extraordinary items, should be reported as "Other revenues and expenses." However, if an item is material, separate disclosure should be made either in a note to

---

[3]*Ibid.*, par. 20.

[4]*Statement of Financial Accounting Standards No. 4.* "Reporting Gains and Losses from Extinguishment of Debt" (Stamford: Financial Accounting Standards Board, 1975).

the statements or by reporting it as a separate component of income from continuing operations.

Accounting Changes

As has been pointed out, a major objective of published financial statements is to provide users with information to help them predict, compare, and evaluate future earning power and cash flows to the reporting entity. When a reporting entity adjusts its past estimates of revenues earned or costs incurred, changes its accounting principles from one method to another, changes its nature as a reporting entity, or corrects past errors, it becomes more difficult for a user to predict the future from past historical statements. Is it better to record these changes and error corrections as adjustments of the prior periods' statements and thus increase their comparability with the current and future statements, or should the changes and error corrections affect only the current and future years?

At least four alternative procedures have been suggested as solutions for reporting accounting changes and correction of errors.

1. Adjust all prior periods' statements for the effect of the change or correction and adjust the beginning Retained Earnings balance for the cumulative amount of the change or correction.
2. Make no adjustment to prior periods' statements, but reflect all effects of the change only in current and future periods. Report the catch-up adjustment as it affects prior years in the current year
   a. as a special item in the income statement.
   b. as a direct entry to Retained Earnings in the current period.
3. Make an adjustment in the current period as in (2a), but also present limited pro forma statements for all prior years included in the financial statements reporting "what might have been" if the change or correction had been made in the prior years.
4. Make the change effective only for current and future periods with no catch-up adjustment. Correct errors only if they still affect the statements.

Each of these alternative methods for reporting an accounting change or correcting an error has been used by companies in the past, and arguments can be made for the various approaches. For example, some accountants argue that accounting principles should be applied consistently for all reported periods. Therefore, if a new accounting principle is used in the current period, the financial statements presented for prior periods should be restated so that the results shown for all reported periods are based on the same accounting principles. Other accountants contend that restating financial statements may dilute public confidence in those statements. Principles applied in earlier periods were presumably appropriate at that time and should be considered final. The only exceptions would be for changes in a reporting entity or for corrections of errors. In addition, restating financial statements is costly, requires considerable effort, and is sometimes impossible due to lack of data.

Because of the diversity of practice and the resulting difficulty in user understandability of the financial statements, the Accounting Principles

Board issued Opinion No. 20 to bring increased uniformity to reporting practice.[5] Only two-thirds of the Board approved the opinion, the minimum required. This indicates the degree of divergence in views concerning this matter. Evidence of compromise exists in the final opinion, as the Board attempted to reflect both its desire to increase comparability of financial statements and to improve user confidence in published financial statements.

The Accounting Principles Board defined three types of accounting changes: (1) change in an accounting estimate; (2) change in an accounting principle; and (3) change in the reporting entity. In addition, the Board made recommendations for reporting a correction of a past error, although they did not classify error corrections as accounting changes.

The proper accounting for a change in estimate has already been discussed in Chapter 4 and throughout the text in discussing areas where changes of estimates are common. By way of review, all changes in estimates should be reflected either in the current period or in the current and future periods. No retroactive adjustment or pro forma statements are to be prepared for a change in estimate. These adjustments are considered to be part of the normal accounting process and not changes of past periods.

In Chapter 17 it was noted that errors should be corrected as soon as they are discovered. If discovered in the current period, corrections should be made through adjustments to the current accounts. If errors are discovered in subsequent years and are material in amount, they must be corrected as prior period adjustments directly to Retained Earnings. Such adjustments occur infrequently.

Changes in accounting principles and a change in the reporting entity present additional problems as discussed in the following sections.

Change in Accounting Principles.[6] As indicated in previous chapters, companies may select among several alternative accounting principles to account for a business transaction. For example, a company may depreciate its buildings and equipment using the straight-line depreciation method, the double-declining-balance method, the sum-of-the-years-digits method, or any other consistent and rational allocation procedure. These and other alternative accounting methods are often equally available to a given company but in most instances criteria for selection among the methods is inadequate. As a result, companies have found it rather easy to justify changing from one method to another. The impact of a change on financial statements is frequently significant. For example, Union Carbide Corporation made several changes in accounting procedures that were expected to add over $300 million, approximately $5 per share, to 1980 earnings.

---

[5]*Opinions of the Accounting Principles Board, No. 20*, "Accounting Changes" (New York: American Institute of Certified Public Accountants, 1971).

[6]The classification "change in accounting principle" includes changes in methods used to account for transactions. No attempt was made by the Accounting Principles Board to distinguish between a principle and a method in Opinion No. 20. *Ibid.*

The Securities and Exchange Commission is concerned by the practice of changing accounting principles and is putting increased pressure on the independent auditor to insist that justification for a change be provided by a company and that the auditor agree with the change. They have even begun to question auditors who permit a client to use one accounting principle and then permit another client in similar circumstances to change to an alternative accounting principle.[7]

General Reporting Rule. The APB concluded that, in general, companies should not change their accounting principles from one period to the next. "Consistent use of accounting principles from one period to another enhances the utility of financial statements to users by facilitating analysis and understanding of comparative accounting data."[8] However, a company may change its accounting principles if it can justify a change because of a new accounting pronouncement by the authoritative accounting principle-making body, or because of a change in its economic circumstances. Just what constitutes an acceptable change in economic circumstances is not clear. However, it presumably could include such things as a change in the competitive structure of an industry, a change in the rate of inflation in the economy, a change resulting from government restrictions due to economic or political crisis, and so forth.

In general, the effect of a change from one accepted accounting principle to another is reflected by reporting the retroactive, cumulative effect of the change in the income statement in the period of the change. This cumulative adjustment is shown as a separate item on the income statement after extraordinary items and before net income. The financial statements for all prior periods reported for comparative purposes with the current year financial statements are to be presented as previously reported. However, to enhance trend analysis, pro forma income information is also required wherever possible to reflect the income before extraordinary items and net income that would have been reported if the new accounting principle had been in effect for the respective prior years. The pro forma information should include not only the direct effects of the change in method, but also the indirect effect of any nondiscretionary adjustment that would have been necessary if the new principle had been in effect for the prior periods. The indirect adjustments include items such as bonuses, profit sharing, or royalty agreements based upon income. Related tax effects should be recognized for both direct and indirect adjustments. Pro forma earnings per share figures should also be reported.

The **cumulative effect of a change in accounting principle** must usually be adjusted for the effect of interperiod tax allocation. The change is often from a method that was used for both tax and reporting purposes to a dif-

---

[7]Securities and Exchange Commission, *Accounting Series Release No. 177,* "Notice of Adoption of Amendments to Form 10-Q and Regulation S-X Regarding Interim Financial Reporting" (Washington, D.C.: U.S. Printing Office, 1975).

[8]*Opinions of the Accounting Principles Board, No. 20, op. cit.,* par. 15.

ferent method for reporting purposes. Retroactive changes in methods for tax purposes are generally not permitted. Thus, the current income tax payable is usually not affected by the change; however, an adjustment is usually necessary to the deferred income tax account. For example, if a company has been using the double-declining-balance method of depreciation for both reporting and tax purposes but changes to the straight-line method for reporting purposes, the tax effect should be reflected as a reduction in the cumulative change account and as a credit to Deferred Income Tax. If the change for reporting purposes is to a method used for tax purposes, the books and the tax return would be in agreement after the change; and previously recorded amounts in Deferred Income Tax would be reversed. An exception to the above situations arises when the change is made from lifo inventory to another method. This is because the income tax regulations do require consistency between the books and the tax return whenever lifo inventory is involved. Thus, a change on the books must also be made on the tax return. Any additional tax arising from the change must be paid, although the income tax regulations provide for some spreading of the liability over several future years.

To illustrate the general treatment of a change in accounting principle, assume Q & A Company elected in 1981 to change from the double-declining-balance method of depreciation used for both reporting and tax purposes to the straight-line method to bring its reporting practice in agreement with the majority of its competitors. The income tax rate is 40%, and the company pays a 20% management bonus on operating income before tax. The following information was gathered reflecting the impact of the change upon net income.

Year	Excess of Double-Declining-Balance Depreciation Over Straight-Line Depreciation	Effect of Change	
		Direct Effect Less Tax (40% Tax Rate)	Direct and Indirect Effect After 20% Management Bonus, Pro Forma Data
Prior to 1976	$ 80,000	$ 48,000 [.60($80,000)]*	$ 38,400 {.60 [$80,000 − .20($80,000)]}
1976	25,000	15,000 [.60($25,000)]	12,000 {.60 [$25,000 − .20($25,000)]}
1977	30,000	18,000 [.60($30,000)]	14,400 {.60 [$30,000 − .20($30,000)]}
1978	28,000	16,800 [.60($28,000)]	13,440 {.60 [$28,000 − .20($28,000)]}
1979	22,000	13,200 [.60($22,000)]	10,560 {.60 [$22,000 − .20($22,000)]}
1980	25,000	15,000 [.60($25,000)]	12,000 {.60 [$25,000 − .20($25,000)]}
	$210,000	$126,000	$100,800

*The direct effect could be computed as $80,000 − .40($80,000), or simply as the complement of the tax rate .60($80,000). The complement computation is used in this illustration.

The net income for prior years as originally reported was as listed below:

1976	$350,000	1979	$450,000
1977	400,000	1980	500,000
1978	410,000		

The partial income statement for 1981, the year of the change, would report the $126,000 after-tax, direct, retroactive adjustment as a separate item after any extraordinary items as follows:

Income from continuing operations	$560,000
Extraordinary gain on refunding of long-term debt (less applicable income tax of $60,000)...	90,000
Cumulative effect on prior years of changing from the double-declining-balance method of depreciation to the straight-line method (less applicable income tax of $84,000)	126,000
Net income..	$776,000

In addition to the above disclosure, pro forma income information would be disclosed by adding both direct and indirect effects to the net income as originally reported. These pro forma income amounts would be included on the face of the income statements reported.

	Pro Forma Income Data				
	1980	1979	1978	1977	1976
Net income as previously reported	$500,000	$450,000	$410,000	$400,000	$350,000
Effect of change in principle — direct and indirect	12,000	10,560	13,440	14,400	12,000
Pro forma net income	$512,000	$460,560	$423,440	$414,400	$362,000

Revised earnings per share figures would also be computed and disclosed reflecting the revised net income amounts. It is recognized that in rare instances, past records are inadequate to prepare the pro forma statements for individual years. This fact should be disclosed when applicable. For example, a change to the lifo method of inventory valuation is usually made effective with the beginning inventory in the year of change rather than with some prior year because of the difficulty in identifying prior year layers or dollar value pools. Thus, the beginning inventory in the year of change is the same as the previous inventory valued at cost, and this becomes the base lifo layer. No cumulative effect adjustment is required.

Exceptions to the General Reporting Rule. Although the general rule for recording changes in accounting principles provides for catch-up adjustments, three specific changes in accounting principles and one general condition change were identified by the Accounting Principles Board as being of such a nature that the "advantages of retroactive treatment in prior period reports outweigh the disadvantages."[9] The changes identified as exceptions to the general rule are given below.

1. Change from lifo method of inventory pricing to another method.
2. Change in the method of accounting for long-term construction contracts.
3. Change to or from the "full cost" method of accounting used in the extractive industries.
4. Changes made at the time of an initial distribution of company stock.[10]

In these cases, the cumulative effect of the change is recorded directly as an adjustment to the beginning Retained Earnings balance and all prior

---

[9]*Ibid.*, par. 27.

[10]This exception is available only once for a company, and may be used whenever a company first issues financial statements for (a) obtaining additional equity capital from investors, (b) effecting business combinations, or (c) registering securities, *Ibid.*, par. 29.

income statement data reported for comparative purposes are adjusted to reflect the new principle. No justification is given by the Board for selecting these items for special treatment; however, these items usually would be material and data would generally be available to adjust the prior years' statements.

To illustrate the exceptions, assume that the Weiss Company compiles the following information concerning its change in 1981 from the lifo method of inventory pricing to the fifo method. The assumed tax rate is 40%.

Year	Net Income — Lifo Method	Net Income — Fifo Method
1976	$ 20,000	$ 45,000
1977	60,000	70,000
1978	80,000	75,000
1979	75,000	110,000
1980	90,000	85,000
Total at beginning of 1981	$325,000	$385,000

The retained earnings statement for 1981 would reflect the effect of the change on prior years as follows:

Weiss Company Retained Earnings Statement For Year Ended December 31, 1981	
Retained earnings, January 1, 1981, as previously reported	$ 900,000
Add adjustment for the cumulative effect on prior years of applying retroactively the fifo method of inventory pricing as opposed to the lifo method (less applicable income tax of $40,000)	60,000
January 1, 1981, balance, as adjusted	$ 960,000
Add net income per income statement	660,000
	$1,620,000
Deduct dividends declared	400,000
Retained earnings, December 31, 1981	$1,220,000

All prior period income statements presented for comparative purposes would be adjusted to the amounts that would have been reported using the new principle. If the prior statements cannot be adjusted because of inadequate data, this fact should be disclosed and the cumulative impact would be reported only on the retained earnings statement. No pro forma information is required for these exceptions because the prior periods' statements are changed directly; however, full disclosure of the effect of the change should be made for all periods presented. The earnings per share data would be recomputed taking into consideration any impact the new income amount would have upon the computations.

If comparative retained earnings statements are prepared for 1980 and 1981, the cumulative adjustment to beginning retained earnings for each reported year would reflect only those years prior to that particular year. Thus, in the example, the 1980 beginning retained earnings balance would be adjusted by $65,000, the difference in net income under the two methods for the years 1976–1979 ($300,000 − $235,000).

If a change in accounting principle is caused by a new pronouncement of an accepted authoritative accounting body, the cumulative effect may be reported retroactively as a prior period adjustment or currently, depending upon the instructions contained in the pronouncement. In most cases, the Financial Accounting Standards Board has chosen to require retroactive adjustment for newly issued pronouncements. For example, such adjustment was required by the FASB in Statement No. 2 concerning the mandatory writing off of all deferred research and development costs.[11]

If an asset is affected by both a change in principle and a change in estimate during the same period, the APB requires that the change be treated as a change in estimate rather than a change in principle.[12]

Change in Reporting Entity. Companies sometimes change their nature or report their operations in such a way that the financial statements are in effect those of a different reporting entity. These changes include: (a) presenting consolidated or combined statements in place of statements of individual companies; (b) changing specific subsidiaries comprising the group of companies for which consolidated statements are presented; (c) changing the companies included in combined financial statements; and (d) a business combination accounted for as a pooling of interest.[13]

Because of the basic objective of preparing statements that assist in predicting future cash flows, the APB recommended that financial statements be adjusted retroactively to disclose what the statements would have looked like if the current entity had been in existence in the prior years. Of course, this requirement assumes that the companies acting as a unit would have made the same decisions as they did while acting alone. While this assumption is probably invalid, the retroactive adjustment will probably come closer to providing useful information for trend analysis than would statements clearly noncomparable because of the different components of the entity.

In the period of the change, the financial statements should describe the nature and reason for the change. They should also clearly show the effect of the change on income from continuing operations, net income, and the related earnings per share amounts for all periods presented. Subsequent years' statements do not need to repeat the disclosure.[14]

Summary of Accounting Changes and Correction of Errors. A summary of the appropriate accounting procedures applicable to each of the four main categories covered in APB Opinion No. 20 is presented on page 521. Naturally, accountants must apply these guidelines with judgment and should seek to provide the most relevant and reliable information possible.

---

[11]*Statement of Financial Accounting Standards No. 2*, "Accounting for Research and Development Costs" (Stamford: Financial Accounting Standards Board, 1974), par. 15.

[12]*Opinions of the Accounting Principles Board, No. 20, op. cit.*, par. 32.

[13]*Ibid.*, par. 12.

[14]*Ibid.*, par. 35.

**Summary of Procedures for Reporting Accounting Changes
and Corrections of Errors**

Category	*Accounting Procedures*
I. Change in estimate	1. Adjust only current period results or current and future periods.
	2. No separate, cumulative adjustment or restated financial statements.
	3. No pro forma disclosure needed.
II. Change in accounting principle	
a. General rule	1. Adjust for cumulative effect, i.e., a "catch-up" adjustment in current period as special item in income statement.
	2. No restated financial statements.
	3. Pro forma data required showing income and EPS information for all periods presented.
b. Exceptions to general rule	1. Direct cumulative adjustment to beginning Retained Earnings balance.
	2. Restate financial statements to reflect new principle for comparative purposes.
	3. No pro forma information required because prior period statements are changed directly.
III. Change in reporting entity	1. Restate financial statements as though new entity had been in existence for all periods presented.
IV. Error correction	1. If detected in period error occurred, correct accounts through normal accounting cycle adjustments.
	2. If detected in a subsequent period, adjust for effect of material errors by prior period adjustments directly to Retained Earnings.

Comprehensive Illustration

To summarize the reporting of earnings, a comprehensive illustration for the Tillson Company is presented on page 522. The sections shown relate to the regular earnings components and the below-the-line items discussed in this chapter and Chapter 4. It is unlikely that all the elements illustrated would be present in any one year for a company. They are shown here for completeness and illustrative purposes. The earnings per share amounts are also presented even though the EPS computations are not covered in detail until Chapter 21.

Tillson Company Income Statement For Year Ended December 31, 1981			
Sales			$1,000,000
Cost of goods sold			600,000
Gross profit on sales			$ 400,000
Operating expenses:			
Selling expenses		$120,000	
General and administrative expenses		191,000	311,000
Operating income			$ 89,000
Other revenue and expense items:			
Interest revenue	$ 6,000		
Dividend revenue	10,000		
Gain on sale of investment	10,000	$ 26,000	
Less interest expense		15,000	11,000
Income from continuing operations before income taxes			$ 100,000
Income taxes (Note X)			40,000
Income from continuing operations			$ 60,000
Discontinued operations:			
Income from operations of discontinued division (less applicable income tax of $8,360)		$ 12,540	
Gain on disposal of division (less applicable income tax of $5,820)		8,730	21,270
Extraordinary gain (less applicable income tax of $1,200)			1,800
Cumulative effect on prior years of a change in accounting principle (less applicable income tax of $2,480)			3,720
Net income			$ 86,790
Earnings per common share (50,000 shares outstanding):			
Income from continuing operations			$1.20
Income from discontinued operations			.43
Extraordinary gain			.04
Cumulative effect of change in accounting principle			.07
Net income			$1.74

INCOME-RELATED SUPPLEMENTAL DISCLOSURES

So far this chapter has emphasized the reporting of nonoperating income components. In addition to these items, there are several income-related disclosures that may assist readers of financial statements in assessing a company's operating results. The remaining sections of the chapter cover three topics: (1) interim reporting, (2) segment reporting, and (3) forecasting.

Interim Reporting

Statements showing financial position and operating results for intervals of less than a year are referred to as **interim financial statements**. Interim reports are considered essential in providing investors and others with more timely information as to the position and progress of an enterprise. This information is most useful in comparative form because of the relationship it shows to data for similar reporting intervals and to data in the annual report.

Notwithstanding the need for interim reports, there are significant difficulties associated with them. One problem is caused by the seasonal factors of certain businesses. For example, in some companies, revenues fluctuate widely among interim periods; in other businesses, significant fixed costs are incurred during a single period but are to benefit several periods. Not only must costs be allocated to appropriate periods of benefit, but they must be matched against the realized revenues for the interim period to determine a reasonable income measurement.

In preparing interim reports, adjustments for accrued items, generally required only at year end, have to be considered at the end of each interim period. Because of the additional time and extra costs involved to develop complete information, many estimates of expenses will have to be made for interim reports. The increased number of estimates adds an element of subjectivity to these reports.

Another problem is that extraordinary items or the disposal of a business segment will have a greater impact on an interim period's earnings than on the results of operations for an entire year. In analyzing interim financial statements, special attention should be given to these and similar considerations.

Partially because of some of the above problems and partially because of differing views as to the objective of interim reports, there has been a variety of practice in presenting interim financial information. Two prominent viewpoints exist. One viewpoint is that each reporting interval is to be recognized as a separate accounting period. Thus, the results of operations for each interim period are determined in essentially the same manner as for the annual accounting period. Under this approach, the same judgments, estimations, accruals, and deferrals are recognized at the end of each interim period as for the annual period.

The other viewpoint, and the one accepted by the APB in Opinion No. 28, is that the interim period is an integral part of the annual period.[15] Essentially, the revenues and expenses for the total period are allocated among interim periods on some reasonable basis, e.g., time, sales volume, or productive activity.

Under the **integral part of annual period concept**, the same general accounting principles and reporting practices employed for annual reports are to be utilized for interim statements, except modifications may be required so the interim results will better relate to the total results of operations for the annual period. As an example of the type of modification that may be required, assume a company uses the lifo method of inventory valuation and encounters a situation where liquidation of the base period inventory occurs at an interim date but the inventory is expected to be replaced by the end of

---

[15]*Opinions of the Accounting Principles Board, No. 28*, "Interim Financial Reporting" (New York: American Institute of Certified Public Accountants, 1973), par. 9.

the annual period. Under these circumstances, the inventory reported at the interim date should not reflect the lifo liquidation, and the cost of goods sold for the interim period should include the expected cost of replacing the liquidated lifo base.[16]

Another example of a required modification deals with a change in accounting principle during an interim period. In general, these changes should follow the provisions of APB Opinion No. 20.[17] However, the FASB has concluded in Statement No. 3 that for any cumulative effect-type change, other than a change to lifo, if the change is made "in other than the first interim period of an enterprise's fiscal year, the cumulative effect of the change on retained earnings at the beginning of that year shall be included in the determination of net income of the first interim period of the year of change."[18]

Applying generally accepted accounting practices to interim financial statements can become complex. This is an area which is developing to meet the perceived needs of users. For example, the SEC has adopted rules requiring significantly increased disclosure of interim financial information. Accounting Series Release No. 177 requires additional quarterly report data in Form 10-Q as well as summarized quarterly operating data in an "unaudited" note to the annual financial statements included in SEC filings.[19] Interpretations of old standards and the development of new standards will assist in presenting interim financial data that should help investors and others in analyzing and interpreting the financial picture and operating results of a company.

Segment Reporting

Many companies are large and complex organizations, usually engaging in a variety of activities. Sometimes these activities bear little relationship to each other. For example, a company might manufacture airplane engines, operate a real estate business, and manage a professional hockey team. Such companies are referred to as **conglomerates** or as **diversified companies**. The normal activities of other companies are more closely related, and they are sometimes called **unitary companies**.

When a company is diversified, the different segments of the company often operate in distinct and separate markets, involve different management teams, and experience different growth patterns, profit potentials, and degrees of risk. In effect, the segments of the company behave almost like, and in some cases are, separate companies within an overall corporate umbrella. Yet, if only total company information is presented for a highly diversified company, the differing degrees of risk, profitability, and growth potential for major segments of the company cannot be analyzed.

---

[16]*Ibid.*, par. 14.

[17]*Opinions of the Accounting Principles Board, No. 20, op. cit.*

[18]*Statement of Financial Accounting Standards No. 3*, "Reporting Accounting Changes in Interim Financial Statements" (Stamford: Financial Accounting Standards Board, 1974), par. 4.

[19]Securities and Exchange Commission, *Accounting Series Release No. 177, op. cit.*

Recognizing this problem, the accounting profession has taken steps to require supplemental disclosures of selected information for **segments of diversified companies**. In Statement No. 14 the FASB requires companies presenting financial statements to include information about operations in different industries, foreign operations and export sales, and major customers.[20] Information to be reported includes revenues, operating profit, and identifiable assets for each significant industry segment of a company. Essentially, a segment is considered significant if its sales, profit, or assets are 10 percent or more of the respective total company amounts. A practical limit of 10 segments is suggested, and at least 75 percent of total company sales must be accounted for. The segment profit data may be reported in the audited financial statements, notes to the financial statements, or in a separate schedule considered an integral part of the statements. Other provisions of Statement No. 14 require disclosure of revenues from major customers and provide guidelines for determining a company's foreign operations and export sales. Normally, the above requirements do not apply to interim financial reports, nor to financial statements that are presented in another enterprise's financial report.[21]

Reporting by lines of business presents several problems. For example, how does one determine which *business segments* should be reported upon? Certainly not all companies are organized in the same manner, even if they are engaged in similar business activities. Reporting on a particular division or profit-center in one company may not be comparable to another company. Another problem relates to *transfer pricing*. Not all companies use the same method of pricing goods or services that are "sold" among the different divisions or units of a company. This could lead to distorted segment profit data. Another related problem is the *allocation of common costs* among segments of a company. Certain costs, such as general and administrative expenses, are very difficult to assign to particular segments of a company on anything other than an arbitrary basis. This, again, could lead to misleading information.

In spite of these difficulties, the accounting profession has concluded that segment reporting is necessary to assist readers of financial statements in analyzing and understanding an enterprise's past performance and future prospects. The illustration on page 526 is an example of segment reporting by General Motors Corporation, which considers itself a highly vertically-integrated company. The disclosures made by General Mills in Appendix B provide another example of segment reporting by a more diversified company.

Forecasts

As noted throughout the book, financial reporting has traditionally been based on historical costs and has reported past transactions. Financial an-

---

[20]*Statement of Financial Accounting Standards No. 14*, "Financial Reporting for Segments of a Business Enterprise" (Stamford: Financial Accounting Standards Board, 1976).

[21]*Statement of Financial Accounting Standards No. 24*, "Reporting Segment Information in Financial Statements That Are Presented in Another Enterprise's Financial Report" (Stamford: Financial Accounting Standards Board, 1978.)

Supplementary Information

Lines of Business

General Motors is a highly vertically-integrated business operating primarily in the manufacture, assembly and sale of automobiles, trucks and related parts and accessories classified as automotive products. Substantially all of General Motors' products are marketed through retail dealers and through distributors and jobbers in the United States and Canada and through distributors and dealers overseas. To assist in the merchandising of General Motors' products, General Motors Acceptance Corporation and its subsidiaries offer financial services and certain types of automobile insurance to dealers and customers. The amount of net sales attributable to United States, Canadian and overseas operations, and by class of product is summarized for the five years ended December 31, 1979 as follows:

Net Sales Attributable to:	1979	1978	1977	1976	1975
	\(Dollars in Millions\)				
United States operations					
Automotive products	$51,093.5	$49,603.0	$44,317.0	$37,069.6	$26,137.3
Nonautomotive products	3,389.8	3,391.3	2,795.2	2,277.0	2,392.8
Defense and space	531.5	504.5	438.8	438.1	387.7
Total United States operations	55,014.8	53,498.8	47,551.0	39,784.7	28,917.8
Canadian operations	8,044.7	6,775.7	5,743.9	5,263.0	4,263.3
Overseas operations	12,394.4	10,975.0	8,399.1	7,495.2	7,227.3
Elimination of interarea sales	(9,142.7)	(8,028.4)	(6,732.7)	(5,361.9)	(4,683.5)
Total	$66,311.2	$63,221.1	$54,961.3	$47,181.0	$35,724.9
Worldwide automotive products	$62,006.6	$58,985.5	$51,429.5	$44,106.3	$32,536.0
Worldwide nonautomotive products	$ 4,304.6	$ 4,235.6	$ 3,531.8	$ 3,074.7	$ 3,188.9

Because of the high degree of integration, substantial interdivisional and intercompany transfers of materials and services are made. Consequently, any determination of income by areas of operations or class of products shown above is necessarily arbitrary because of the allocation and reallocation of costs, including corporate costs, benefiting more than one division or product. Within these limitations, the Corporation estimates that the percentage of net income attributable to the United States, Canadian and overseas operations, and by class of product for the five years ended December 31, 1979 is as follows:

Percentage of Net Income Attributable to:	1979	1978	1977	1976	1975
United States operations	79%	87%	89%	82%	85%
Canadian operations	8	5	3	6	9
Overseas operations	13	8	8	12	6
Total	100%	100%	100%	100%	100%
Automotive products	90%	96%	95%	·97%	90%
Nonautomotive products	10%	4%	5%	3%	10%

alysts and others have suggested for years that disclosure of future earnings **forecasts**, that is, predictions about corporate expectations, would be useful information. Prior to 1974 the SEC would not allow forecasted earnings in registration statements. However, the Commission has reversed that long-standing policy and now allows publication of forecasts, provided they meet guidelines established by the SEC. The AICPA has also given its support to the disclosure of financial forecasts, suggesting that appropriate care be exercised in providing the best information available and that assumptions be clearly stated and supported with adequate documentation.

The arguments *for* presenting forecasted supplemental information include:

1. Investors are trying to predict the future. Financial forecasts would provide relevant information for such investment decisions.
2. Forecasts are available to some individuals currently (key executives, selected analysts, etc.). Disclosing forecasts publicly would provide all investors access to the information.

3. Disclosing forecasts publicly, under specified guidelines, would likely improve the reliability of forecasts.
4. Management has long found it beneficial to make forecasts of future earnings and to compare forecasted and actual results. Investors should receive the benefits of similar information.

There are also seemingly valid arguments *against* presenting financial forecasts as a part of financial statements.

1. Forecasts are affected by many variables, many of which are not controllable by the company. Accordingly, there is no assurance that forecasted results will be achieved.
2. Forecasts are subjective and may be misunderstood by those unfamiliar with the assumptions upon which forecasts are made.
3. There may be serious economic and legal implications if forecasts are not met. Therefore, companies may seek to meet short-run forecasted results rather than take actions in the long-run best interest of the shareholders.
4. Required disclosure of forecasts may produce competitive disadvantages, especially with respect to foreign companies not required to disclose the same information.

So far the arguments against publicly disclosing forecasted earnings have prevailed, at least to the extent that neither the FASB nor the SEC currently *requires* forecasts. However, some U.S. companies are beginning to disclose forecasted earnings on a voluntary basis. One such company is Days Inns of America. Selected disclosures from their 1979 Annual Report are presented on pages 528 and 529. Forecasts are commonly reported in Great Britain, but it is significant to note that there are no class action suits in Great Britain. Therefore, the threat of legal liability is greatly reduced.

Concluding Comment

Investors are demanding more information upon which to base decisions. Supplemental disclosures, such as interim and segment reports and forecasts of future earnings, provide additional relevant information for external users. However, the presentation of such information is not without a cost. Users must be willing to pay for additional information as well as recognize appropriate uses and inherent limitations of the data. Such questions as legal liability, auditor involvement and responsibility, and optimum timing and manner of presentation have not yet been resolved.

QUESTIONS

1. Explain the distinctions between the major components of income: (a) operating income, (b) income from continuing operations, and (c) net income. Why are these distinctions important?
2. What are the major categories of below-the-line items?
3. The Pop-Up Company has decided to sell its lid manufacturing division even though the division is expected to show a small profit this year. The division's assets will be sold at a loss of $10,000 to another company. What information (if any) should Pop-Up disclose in its financial reports with respect to this division?

(continued on page 530)

COMPARISON OF ACTUAL TO FORECASTED INCOME AND STOCKHOLDERS' EQUITY

Days Inns of America, Inc.

	For the year ended September 30, 1979		
	Actual	Forecasted	Variance
Net revenue:			
Lodging.	$ 48,065,000	$ 46,185,000	$1,880,000
Food, gasoline and novelties.	44,024,000	40,362,000	3,662,000
Franchise fees — initial.	566,000	540,000	26,000
— recurring.	9,795,000	9,000,000	795,000
Rental income.	3,921,000	4,223,000	(302,000)
Other income.	2,192,000	2,525,000	(333,000)
Proceeds from officer's life insurance.	1,000,000	—	1,000,000
	109,563,000	102,835,000	6,728,000
Costs and expenses:			
Cost of food, gasoline and novelties.	31,434,000	27,342,000	4,092,000
Selling, general, administrative			
and operating expenses.	52,860,000	50,828,000	2,032,000
Rental expense.	10,411,000	10,258,000	153,000
Depreciation and amortization.	5,222,000	5,215,000	7,000
Interest expense net of			
interest income.	3,267,000	3,337,000	(70,000)
	103,194,000	96,980,000	6,214,000
Income before provision for			
income taxes.	6,369,000	5,855,000	514,000
Provision for income taxes.	2,028,000	2,251,000	(223,000)
Net income.	$ 4,341,000	$ 3,604,000	$ 737,000
Stockholders' equity.	$ 8,240,000	$ 8,261,000	$ (21,000)
Occupancy.	74.1%	76.0%	(1.9%)
Average room rate.	$17.83	$16.59	$1.24
Number of franchise motel openings.	16	20	(4)
Total rooms in chain.	42,790	44,900	(2,110)

Comments on 1979 Results of Operations

Overview

Gross revenue and net income for the year ended September 30, 1979, exceeded the forecast as set forth in the 1978 annual report. Although occupancy was down slightly, a higher average room rate for lodging and increased gasoline sales resulted in an overall increase in revenue. Comments on significant variances from the forecast are highlighted below.

Revenue

The increase in lodging revenue is attributable to a higher average room rate from rate increases during the year, offset partially by lower occupancy. Revenue, and the related cost of sales for food, gas, and novelties are summarized as follows:

(000's Omitted)

	Food		Gasoline		Novelties	
	Actual	Forecast	Actual	Forecast	Actual	Forecast
Revenue.	$15,184	$15,922	$25,152	$20,572	$3,688	$3,868
Cost of sales	5,457	5,826	23,230	18,720	2,747	2,796
Gross profit.	$ 9,727	$10,096	$ 1,922	$ 1,852	$ 941	$1,072
Cost of sales.	35.9%	36.6%	92.4%	91.0%	74.5%	72.3%
Revenues per rented room.	$5.73	$5.84	$9.49	$7.55	$1.39	$1.42

Gross profit from food and novelties was unfavorably affected by the reduced occupancy as well as lower volume from off the road customers. Gasoline operations was able to diminish the effect of this trend due to higher gasoline prices and proper scheduling of available supplies.

Franchise properties experienced the same trend in higher average room rates and increased gasoline sales and, in addition, the reservation formula was changed during the year, all of which resulted in recurring franchise fees exceeding forecast.

The decrease in other income resulted from a reduction in the size and frequency of September Days Club conventions and tours.

The proceeds from officer's life insurance was not included in the forecasted revenue.

Selling, general administrative and operating expenses

Key expense categories and major variances are noted below:

(000's Omitted)

	Actual	Forecast	Variance
Salaries and benefits.	$21,016	$20,844	$ 172
Utilities.	7,638	8,297	(659)
Advertising.	3,520	2,886	634
Repair and maintenance.	4,474	3,132	1,342
Travel and entertainment.	1,362	1,085	277
Professional fees.	1,334	1,179	155
Reservation fees.	2,821	3,437	(616)
Convention and tour costs.	287	804	(517)
Other.	10,408	9,164	1,244
	$52,860	$50,828	$2,032

The company experienced a favorable utility expense variance due to lower than expected rate increases. Also, energy conservation devices were effective in reducing overall utility costs.

Due to the effect of energy developments on summer travel, the national advertising program was expanded to enhance our competitive position. An aggressive campaign reflecting the value of our product and the availability of gasoline minimized the decrease in occupancy.

Expenditures for repair and maintenance were increased to insure that all properties were maintained at quality levels. Over $15,000,000 was committed to an extensive capital improvement and maintenance program.

The variance in travel and entertainment reflects the emphasis by management to insure quality control by a concentration of field and home office assistance for all properties. In addition, travel was expanded into new territories to promote the sale of new franchises.

The decrease in reservation fees resulted from lower call volume and the operation of a satellite center in Orlando, Florida which improved operating results and reduced the overall expense.

September Days Club sponsored fewer conventions which resulted in increased participation in a series of successful programs. As a result, the overall cost was less than projected and this reduction is offset by lower convention income.

The increase in other expenses resulted primarily from the costs incurred in the disposal of furniture, fixtures, and equipment.

General Comment on Forecasted Results of Operations 1980-1984

These forecasts are based on assumptions concerning future events and circumstances. The assumptions disclosed herein are those which management believes are significant to the forecasts or are key factors upon which financial results depend. Some assumptions inevitably will not materialize and unanticipated events and circumstances may occur subsequent to September 30, 1979. Therefore, the actual results achieved during the forecasted period may vary from the forecasts and the variations may be material.

It is expected that prices paid for goods and services and those charged to customers will continue to increase at an inflationary rate. It is also expected that volume increases will occur in room occupancy and food, gasoline and novelty sales.

The Days Inns chain expects to expand in its current market area as well as in new market areas. The bulk of this expansion is forecasted to be in franchised properties. Additionally, it is assumed the company will open and operate three motels each year beginning in 1981. The strategy will be to locate motels in two areas: 1) at selected sites within existing geographic areas where a void exists, and 2) in new geographic areas where motels will serve to form a base and further expand the franchise program.

Assumptions Utilized by Management in Preparation of These Forecasts

Lodging revenues are based upon a) an average occupancy of 73% in 1980 increasing one percent each year through 1984, b) an annual increase of approximately $.50 in the average room rate beginning in 1981, and c) the addition of three company operated sites per year from 1981 through 1984.

STATEMENTS OF FORECASTED INCOME AND STOCKHOLDERS' EQUITY

	For the years ending September 30,				
	1980	1981	1982	1983	1984
Net revenue:					
Lodging.	$ 50,756,000	$ 54,579,000	$ 58,712,000	$ 63,066,000	$67,585,000
Food, gasoline and novelties.	50,132,000	56,046,000	62,661,000	69,727,000	77,294,000
Franchise fees — initial.	538,000	665,000	792,000	929,000	1,046,000
— recurring.	10,907,000	12,506,000	14,230,000	16,247,000	18,758,000
Rental income.	4,187,000	3,505,000	1,263,000	1,318,000	1,372,000
Other income.	2,378,000	2,556,000	2,769,000	2,995,000	3,219,000
	118,898,000	129,857,000	140,427,000	154,282,000	169,274,000
Costs and expenses:					
Cost of food, gasoline and novelties.	36,875,000	41,416,000	46,318,000	51,582,000	57,182,000
Selling, general, administrative					
and operating expenses.	55,284,000	60,428,000	66,251,000	72,273,000	78,872,000
Rental expense.	9,584,000	9,113,000	—	—	—
Depreciation and amortization.	6,097,000	6,089,000	8,896,000	9,626,000	10,356,000
Interest expense net of					
interest income.	3,332,000	3,785,000	9,367,000	9,518,000	9,614,000
	111,172,000	120,831,000	130,832,000	142,999,000	156,024,000
Income before provision for					
income taxes.	7,726,000	9,026,000	9,595,000	11,283,000	13,250,000
Provision for income taxes.	3,327,000	3,711,000	3,947,000	4,732,000	5,656,000
Net income.	$ 4,399,000	$ 5,315,000	$ 5,648,000	$ 6,551,000	$ 7,594,000
Stockholders' equity.	$ 12,388,000	$ 17,703,000	$ 18,128,000	$ 24,679,000	$32,273,000
Occupancy.	73%	74%	75%	76%	77%
Average room rate.	$19.00	$19.50	$20.00	$20.50	$21.00
Number of franchise motel openings.	20	25	30	35	40
Total rooms in chain.	45,000	48,400	52,400	57,000	62,200

Food, gas, and novelty sales are forecasted on the basis of revenue per rented room. The average sale per rented room is expected to increase at 5% for food and novelties and 8% for gasoline. Although sales will increase, the cost of food and gasoline will remain constant at 35% and 93%, respectively. Novelty costs will decrease from 67% in 1980 to 60% in 1984, based on improved inventory controls and a modernized marketing concept.

Initial franchise fees from new openings are projected at $22,200 for each complete motel operation, as well as conversions of other motels, ownership transfers and site inspections. Recurring franchise fees were calculated using 1) an increase in total rooms, 2) approximately the same occupancy as company operated units, and 3) a slightly higher average room rate for 1981 through 1983. By 1984, the average room rate for franchise locations is expected to approximate the company average. Recurring franchise royalties from affiliates total $298,000, $306,000, $315,000, $323,000, and $332,000 for 1980 through 1984, respectively, and are estimated based on the terms of the amended agreements discussed in Note 2 to the consolidated financial statements.

Rental income includes revenue from leased motels and the operation of an apartment complex converted from a motel during 1978. Total rental income forecasted to be earned from the apartment complex during 1980 is based on an occupancy of approximately 95%. The apartment complex is expected to be sold by March 31, 1980 and therefore, no rental income or related expense is included in the projections for 1981 through 1984. No gain or loss on the sale of the property is included in the 1980 results.

Selling, general, administrative, and operating costs are forecasted to increase 5% to 10% per year. Salaries and wages have been adjusted for expected increases. Beginning in 1981, combined initial advertising and start-up costs of $300,000 a year are included for the expansion properties. Total operating expenses for the five year period are forecasted to increase by a total of approximately 43%.

Beginning in 1982, substantially all lease agreements will be required to be capitalized in accordance with Financial Accounting Standard No. 13 — Accounting for Leases (FAS 13). Accordingly, the forecasts for the years 1982, 1983, and 1984 reflect capitalizations of such leases in effect as of September 30, 1979, less any leases expected to be discontinued because of the sale of the property. Capitalization of such leases results in a decrease in net income of $284,000, $185,000, and $2,000 for 1982 through 1984, respectively. The cumulative effect on stockholders' equity at September 30, 1982 is a decrease of $5,223,000. Rental income and expense, depreciation, and interest expenses have been appropriately presented in accordance with FAS 13 for 1982 through 1984. If the provisions of FAS 13 had been adopted at September 30, 1979, the effect of capitalizing the company's leases would be to decrease forecasted net income by $318,000 and $251,000 in 1980 and 1981, respectively.

During 1980 and 1981, rental expense is based on lease agreements in existence at September 30, 1979, less any payment on properties expected to be sold, and net of income earned on sub-leases of $737,000 and $863,000, respectively. For the period from 1982 through 1984, rental expense has been restated in accordance with FAS 13 and the income earned on operating subleases of $924,000, $974,000, and $1,023,000, respectively, is shown in rental income.

Estimates of depreciation reflect a decrease in depreciable assets at leased properties, an increase in replacements and improvements at company operated sites, and the addition of three sites per year beginning in 1981. The estimated cost for replacements and additions is approximately $36,000,000 over the next five

years and for new sites is $22,000,000 for 1981 through 1984.

Interest expense is based on loans in effect at September 30, 1979, plus assumed financing at 12% per annum on the new properties. All other interest is based on a constant level of debt with repayments offset by additional financing of capital expenditures. Interest income will increase based on higher levels of cash available for investment.

Provisions for income taxes are calculated using the applicable tax rates, less investment tax credits from property and equipment additions and the construction of new motel properties.

Forecasted stockholders' equity assumes that the only changes arise from: 1) operations, 2) the restatement of lease agreements in accordance with FAS 13 in 1982, and 3) a cash dividend of $251,000 in 1980. No attempt has been made to forecast dividends for 1981 through 1984.

The accounting policies used in the forecasts are those applied in the financial statements for 1979. The consolidated financial statements and accompanying notes for the years ended September 30, 1979 and 1978 should be read in conjunction with the above forecasts.

Report of Independent Accountants

3700 FIRST NATIONAL BANK TOWER
ATLANTA,GEORGIA 30303
404·658·1800

November 16, 1979

To the Board of Directors
and Stockholders of
Days Inns of America, Inc.

We have reviewed the above Statements of Forecasted Income and Stockholders' Equity of Days Inns of America, Inc. for the five years ending September 30, 1984. These statements are based on assumptions and estimates of the Company's management which are described above. Our review included tests of the computations, investigation of methods of compiling the estimates and forecasts, discussions with officials of the Company, comparisons with the financial statements for 1979 which we examined and reported on under this same date and such other procedures as we considered necessary in the circumstances.

Since the Statements of Forecasted Income and Stockholders' Equity are based on assumptions and estimates, the reliability of which are dependent on future events and transactions, as independent accountants, we do not express an opinion on the fairness of these forecasts. However our review indicates that the aforementioned Statements of Forecasted Income and Stockholders' Equity were compiled on the basis of both the described assumptions of the Company's management and the accounting policies applied in the financial statements for the year 1979.

Price Waterhouse & Co.

4. Which of the following would *not* normally qualify as an extraordinary item?
- (a) The write-down or write-off of receivables.
- (b) Major devaluation of foreign currency.
- (c) Loss on sale of plant and equipment
- (d) Gain from early extinguishment of debt.
- (e) Loss due to extensive flood damage to asphalt company in Las Vegas, Nevada.
- (f) Loss due to extensive earthquake damage to furniture company in Los Angeles, California.
- (g) Farming loss due to unusually heavy spring rains in the Northwest.

5. Explain briefly the difference in treatments of (a) a change in an accounting principle, and (b) a change in an accounting estimate.

6. Why does the adoption of new and different accounting principles require justification, whereas the continuation of a principle already applied requires no such justification?

7. When should the effects of a change in accounting principle be shown as a restatement of prior periods? (Give examples.)

8. When should the effects of a change in accounting principles be shown as a cumulative effect on net income? (Give examples.)

9. Describe the effect on current net income, beginning retained earnings, deferred income tax, individual asset accounts and contra asset accounts when:
- (a) Depreciation is converted from the straight-line method to the double-declining-balance method.
- (b) Depreciation is converted from the sum-of-the-years-digits method to the straight-line method.
- (c) The valuation of inventories is changed from a fifo to a lifo basis. Records do not permit retroactive change in methods.
- (d) It is determined that the warranty expenses for sales in prior years should have been 5% instead of 4%.
- (e) The valuation of inventories is changed from a lifo to a fifo basis.
- (f) Your accounts receivable clerk reads that a major customer has declared bankruptcy.
- (g) Your patent lawyer informs you that your rival has perfected and patented a new invention making your product obsolete.

10. Distinguish between the two primary viewpoints concerning the preparation of interim financial statements.

11. Why must investors be careful in interpreting interim reports?

12. Why has the accounting profession chosen to require supplemental disclosures for diversified companies?

13. What information is required by FASB Statement No. 14 concerning segment reporting?

14. What are the major arguments *for* and *against* requiring forecasts as supplemental information?

EXERCISES

exercise 18-1

Clinton Manufacturing purchased a machine on January 1, 1977, for $50,000. At that time, it was determined that the machine had an estimated useful life of 20 years and an estimated residual value of $5,000. The company used the double-declining-balance method of depreciation. On January 1, 1981, the company decided to change its depreciation method from double-declining-balance to straight-line. The machine's remaining useful life was estimated to be six years with a residual value of $2,000.

- (1) Give the entry required to record Clinton's depreciation expense for 1981.
- (2) Give the entry, if any, to record the effect of the change in depreciation methods.

exercise 18-2

How would you report each of the following items on the financial statements?

(a) Plant shut-down and start-up costs due to a strike.
(b) Loss on sale of the fertilizer production division of a lawn supplies manufacturer.
(c) Material penalties arising from early payment of a mortgage.
(d) Gain resulting from changing asset balances to adjust for the effect of excessive depreciation charged in error in prior years.
(e) Loss resulting from excessive accrual in prior years of estimated revenues from long-term contracts.
(f) Costs incurred to purchase a valuable patent.
(g) Net income from the discontinued dune buggy operations of a custom car designer.
(h) Costs of rearranging plant machinery into a more efficient order.
(i) Error made in capitalizing advertising expense during the prior year.
(j) Gain on sale of land to the government.
(k) Loss from destruction of crops by a hail storm.
(l) Purchase and retirement of bonds outstanding at a price in excess of book value.
(m) Additional depreciation resulting from a change in the estimated useful life of an asset.
(n) Gain on sale of long-term investments.
(o) Loss from spring flooding.
(p) Sale of obsolete inventory at less than book value.
(q) Additional federal income tax assessment for prior years.
(r) Loss resulting from the sale of a portion of a line of business.
(s) Costs associated with moving an American business to Japan.
(t) Loss resulting from a patent which was recently determined to be worthless.

exercise 18-3

New Cosmetics, Inc., shows a retained earnings balance on January 1, 1981, of $460,000. For 1981, the income from continuing operations was $150,000 before income tax. Following is a list of special items:

Income from operations of a discontinued cosmetics division	$18,000
Loss on the sale of the cosmetics division	50,000
Gain on extinguishment of long-term debt	25,000
Correction of sales understatement in 1979	28,000
Omission of depreciation charges of prior years (A claim has been filed for an income tax refund of $8,000)	20,000

Income tax paid during 1981 was $40,400, which consisted of the tax on continuing operations, plus $8,000 resulting from operations of the discontinued cosmetics divisions and $12,000 from the gain from extinguishment of debt, less a $24,600 tax reduction for loss on the sale of the cosmetics division. Dividends of $30,000 were declared by the company during the year (50,000 shares of common stock are outstanding). Prepare the income statement for New Cosmetics, Inc., beginning with "Income from continuing operations before income tax." Include an accompanying retained earnings statement.

exercise 18-4

You have been asked to review the December 31, 1981 financial statements of Starback Company. The company has reported extraordinary losses totaling $926,000. Upon further investigation, you found that the $926,000 in losses was composed of the following items:

(a) Obsolete inventories recorded at $120,000 were written off.
(b) Loss on the translation of foreign currency received from foreign subsidiaries amounted to $65,000.
(c) Loss of $69,000 resulting from the abandonment of equipment which was no longer needed in the business.
(d) During 1981, buildings and equipment with a book value of $509,000 were destroyed when a dormant volcano suddenly erupted. Geologists believe that it is extremely unlikely that the volcano will be active again.
(e) During the winter of 1981, Starback's factories were shut down for several days due to unusually severe weather conditions. The costs resulting from this shutdown totaled $163,000.

Ignoring income taxes, what amount of extraordinary losses should Starback have reported for the year ended December 31, 1981? How should this be reported in the financial statements?

exercise 18-5

Taylor Manufacturing Company decides to change from the double-declining-balance method of depreciation it has used for both reporting and tax purposes to the straight-line method for reporting purposes. From the information which follows, prepare the income statement for 1981. Assume a 40% tax rate.

Year	Net Income As Reported	Excess of Double-Declining Balance Depreciation Over Straight-Line Depreciation	Direct Effect Less Tax (40%)
Prior to 1978		$12,500	$ 7,500
1978	$62,500	6,250	3,750
1979	54,500	7,500	4,500
1980	78,000	11,250	6,750
		$37,500	$22,500

In 1981, net sales were $190,000; cost of goods sold, $92,500; selling expenses, $47,500, and general and administrative expenses, $14,000. In addition, Taylor had a tax deductible extraordinary loss of $22,500. Assume the fiscal year ends on December 31.

exercise 18-6

Assume the change in net income as shown in Exercise 5 is the result of a change from the lifo method of inventory pricing to another method. During 1981, dividends of $17,500 were announced and distributed. Based upon this information, prepare the retained earnings statement for 1981. The December 31, 1980 retained earnings balance as reported was $260,000.

exercise 18-7

The Wicker Corporation purchased a patent on January 2, 1976, for $405,000. The original life of the patent was estimated to be 15 years. However, in December of 1981, the controller of Wicker received information proving conclusively that the product protected by the Wicker patent would be obsolete within two years. Accordingly, the company decided to write off the unamortized portion of the patent cost over three years beginning in 1981. How would the change in estimate be reflected in the accounts for 1981 and subsequent years?

exercise 18-8

The income statement for the year ended December 31, 1981, of Essex Technology, Inc., appears below. Using the yearly income statement and the supplemental information, reconstruct the third-quarter interim income statement for Essex.

Essex Technology, Inc.
Income Statement
For Year Ended December 31, 1981

Sales	$900,000
Cost of goods sold	560,000
Gross profit on sales	$340,000
Operating expenses	96,000
Operating income	$244,000
Other revenue:	
Gain on sale of equipment	28,000
Income from continuing operations before income taxes	$272,000
Income taxes	108,800
Income from continuing operations	$163,200
Extraordinary loss (less applicable income tax reduction of $40,000)	(60,000)
Net income	$103,200

Supplemental information:

(a) Assume a 40% tax rate.
(b) Third-quarter sales were 20% of total sales.
(c) For interim reporting purposes, a gross profit rate of 38% can be justified.
(d) Variable operating expenses are allocated in the same proportion as sales. Fixed operating expenses are allocated based on the expiration of time. Of the total operating expenses, $60,000 relate to variable expenses.
(e) The equipment was sold June 1, 1981.
(f) The extraordinary loss occurred September 1, 1981.

exercise 18-9

Lutz Industries operates in five different industries. From the information given below, determine which segments should be classified as reportable segments according to FASB Statement No. 14. Provide justification for your answer.

Lutz Industries
Information About Company Operations in Different Industries
For Year Ended December 31, 1981
(In Millions of Dollars)

	Industry 1	Industry 2	Industry 3	Industry 4	Industry 5	Total
Revenues	$ 577	$ 84	$ 93	$117	$ 96	$ 967
Operating profit	66	11	9	10	10	106
Identifiable assets	2,124	298	328	314	353	3,417

PROBLEMS

problem 18-1

Global Enterprises is a highly diversified company which operates in four separate industries — communications, computers, trucking, and petroleum exploration.

Financial data for the two years ended December 31, 1981 and 1980, are presented below:

	Net Sales	
	1981	1980
Trucking	$ 7,000,000	$ 6,000,000
Computers	4,000,000	2,540,000
Communications	3,160,000	2,800,000
Petroleum exploration	1,840,000	2,660,000
	$16,000,000	$14,000,000

	Cost of Sales	
	1981	1980
Trucking	$ 4,800,000	$ 3,600,000
Computers	2,200,000	1,400,000
Communications	1,000,000	1,800,000
Petroleum exploration	1,600,000	2,000,000
	$ 9,600,000	$ 8,800,000

	Operating Expenses	
	1981	1980
Trucking	$ 1,100,000	$ 550,000
Computers	600,000	250,000
Communications	400,000	300,000
Petroleum exploration	1,300,000	1,500,000
	$ 3,400,000	$ 2,600,000

On January 1, 1981, Global adopted a plan to sell the assets and product line of the petroleum exploration division and expected to realize a gain on the disposal. On August 31, 1981, the division's assets and product line were sold for $4,200,000 cash, resulting in a gain of $1,280,000 (exclusive of operations during the phase-out period).

The company's Communications Division had three manufacturing plants which produced a variety of communication equipment. In March 1981, the company sold one of these plants and realized a gain of $260,000. After the sale, the operations at the plant that was sold were transferred to the remaining two plants which the company continued to operate.

In July 1981, the main dock of the Trucking Division, located in Texas near the Gulf of Mexico, was severely damaged by a violent hurricane. The resulting loss of $840,000 is not included in the financial data given above. Historical records indicate that this particular area of Texas normally is hit by one or more hurricanes every five to six years, causing extensive damage to property.

For the two years ended December 31, 1981 and 1980, the company had interest revenue earned on investments of $140,000 and $80,000 respectively.

Assume an income tax rate of 40% for both years.

> **Instructions:** Prepare in proper form a comparative statement of income of Global Enterprises for the two years ended December 31, 1981, and December 31, 1980.
>
> (AICPA adapted)

problem 18-2

In 1981, Hutchison Shippers changed their method of depreciating equipment from the sum-of-the-years-digits method, used for both reporting and tax purposes, to the straight-line method. The following information shows the effect of this change on the amount of depreciation to be shown on the income statement.

Year	Net Income as Reported	Excess of Sum-of-the-Years-Digits Depreciation Over Straight-Line Depreciation
Prior to 1977		$40,000
1977	$200,000	15,000
1978	182,500	13,000
1979	190,000	14,000
1980	210,000	17,000
		$99,000

Assume the company has a tax rate of 40%. Employees have been given a 20% cash bonus on operating income during these years.

> **Instructions:**
> (1) Compute the effect of the change in accounting principle on income as follows: (a) the direct effect less the tax effect; (b) the direct and indirect effects.
> (2) Prepare (a) a partial income statement for 1981 if income before extraordinary items was $225,000 and an extraordinary loss of $36,000 before tax was incurred, and (b) pro forma income data for the years 1977–1980.

problem 18-3

On January 1, 1981, RX Drug Stores, Inc., decided to change from the lifo method of inventory pricing to the fifo method. The reported income for the four years RX Drug Stores had been in business was as follows:

1977	$250,000	1979	$310,000
1978	260,000	1980	330,000

Analysis of the inventory records disclosed that the following inventories were on hand at the end of each year as valued under both the lifo and fifo methods.

	Lifo Method	Fifo Method
January 1, 1977	0	0
December 31, 1977	$228,000	$256,000
December 31, 1978	240,000	238,000
December 31, 1979	270,000	302,000
December 31, 1980	288,000	352,000

The income tax rate is 40%.

Instructions:

(1) Compute the restated net income for the years 1977–1980.

(2) Prepare the retained earnings statement for RX Drug Stores, Inc., for 1981 if the 1980 ending balance had been previously reported at $600,000, 1981 net income using the fifo method is $360,000, and dividends of $200,000 were paid during 1981.

problem 18-4

Pentek Distributors has released the following condensed financial statements for 1979 and 1980 and has prepared the following proposed statements for 1981.

Pentek Distributors
Comparative Balance Sheet
December 31

Assets	1981	1980	1979
Current assets	$249,000	$219,000	$165,000
Land	60,000	45,000	30,000
Equipment	150,000	150,000	150,000
Accumulated depreciation — equipment	(45,000)	(30,000)	(15,000)
Total assets	$414,000	$384,000	$330,000
Liabilities and Stockholders' Equity			
Current liabilities	$177,000	$177,000	$147,000
Common stock	60,000	60,000	60,000
Retained earnings	177,000	147,000	123,000
Total liabilities and stockholders' equity	$414,000	$384,000	$330,000

Pentek Distributors
Comparative Income Statement
For Years Ended December 31

	1981	1980	1979
Sales	$315,000	$300,000	$255,000
Cost of goods sold	$240,000	$225,000	$189,000
Other expenses except depreciation	30,000	36,000	33,000
Depreciation expense — equipment	15,000	15,000	15,000
Total costs	$285,000	$276,000	$237,000
Net income	$ 30,000	$ 24,000	$ 18,000

Pentek Distributors acquired the equipment for $150,000 on January 1, 1979, and began depreciating the equipment over a 10-year estimated useful life with no salvage value, using the straight-line method of depreciation. The double-declining-balance method of depreciation, under the same assumptions, would have required the following depreciation expense:

1979	20% × $150,000 = $30,000
1980	20% × $120,000 = $24,000
1981	20% × $ 96,000 = $19,200

Instructions: In comparative format, prepare a balance sheet and a combined statement of income and retained earnings for 1981, giving effect to the following changes. Ignore any income tax effect. Pentek Distributors has 10,000 shares of common stock outstanding. The following situations are independent of each other.

(1) For justifiable reasons, Pentek Distributors changed to the double-declining-balance method of depreciation in 1981. The effect of the change should be included in the net income of the period in which the change was made.

(2) During 1981, Pentek Distributors found the equipment was fast becoming obsolete and decided to change the estimated useful life from 10 years to 5 years. The books for 1981 had not yet been closed.

(3) During 1981, Pentek Distributors found additional equipment, also acquired on January 1, 1979, costing $24,000, had been recorded in the land account and had not been depreciated. This error should be corrected using straight-line depreciation over a 10-year period.

problem 18-5

Abcom Industries operates in several different industries, some of which are appropriately regarded as reportable segments. Total sales for Abcom are $12,000,000 and total common costs are $6,000,000 for 1981. Abcom allocates common costs based on the ratio of a segment's sales to total sales, which is considered an appropriate method of allocation. Additional information regarding the different segments is contained in the following schedule:

	Segment 1	Segment 2	Segment 3	Segment 4	Other Segments
Contribution to total sales..........	23%	8%	31%	28%	10%
Identifiable assets as percent of total company assets...............	36%	9%	32%	8%	15%
Traceable costs	$800,000	$350,000	$1,200,000	$1,000,000	$650,000

Instructions: Prepare a schedule from which operating profit is derived for Abcom Industries which conforms to the reporting criteria set forth in FASB Statement No. 14.

19

Statement of Changes in Financial Position

CHAPTER OBJECTIVES

Explain the "all financial resources" concept of funds.

Identify the objectives and limitations of the funds statement.

Describe the steps to be followed in preparing a funds statement.

Illustrate the preparation of a funds statement on a working capital basis.

As noted in Chapters 4 and 5, the primary financial statements for a business unit consist of statements reporting the earnings or results of operations, the financial position, and the changes in financial position. The financial status of a business at a given time is reported on the balance sheet. The earnings for a given period are reported on the income statement and on the statement of changes in financial position — the funds statement. The income statement summarizes the revenues and expenses for the period and accounts for the major changes in retained earnings in successive periods. When there are further transactions that must be recognized in explaining the change in owners' equity, these would be reported in a separate statement accompanying the income statement. The funds statement, on the other hand, offers a summary not only of the operations of the business but also of any significant financing and investing activities for the period. Thus, it accounts for all of the changes in financial position as reported on successive balance sheets.

The funds statement has undergone several years of development in becoming one of the primary financial statements. In 1961 Accounting Research Study No. 2, sponsored by the AICPA, recommended that a funds statement be prepared and included with the income statement and balance sheet in annual reports to shareholders.[1] Two years later APB Opinion No. 3 was issued to provide guidelines for the preparation of the funds statement.[2] Even though Opinion No. 3 did not require a funds statement, most businesses sensed the value of the funds statement and included it in their annual reports. Thus, it was somewhat anticlimatic when the APB issued Opinion No. 19 in 1971 officially requiring that a funds statement be included as one of the three primary financial statements in annual reports to shareholders and be covered by the auditor's opinion.[3]

During this developmental period, the funds statement was referred to by a variety of titles including: *the statement of sources and uses of funds, the source and application of funds statement*, and *the statement of resources provided and applied*. In reporting funds flow, it is possible to adopt a funds concept that provides for limited recognition of financial changes or a funds concept broadened to cover all financial changes. However, the Accounting Principles Board in Opinion No. 19 recommended that the broadened concept of funds be adopted, and, in applying this concept that the funds statement be called the **statement of changes in financial position**. To simplify reference to the statement, the term "funds statement" is used in this chapter.

THE "ALL FINANCIAL RESOURCES" CONCEPT OF FUNDS

As explained in Chapter 5, funds may be defined in a variety of ways, and the definition used will determine the type of funds statement prepared. The two most common definitions of funds are working capital and cash. However, if these definitions were to be applied literally, a number of transactions involving highly significant information relative to financing and investing activities would be omitted from the funds statement and thus might not be recognized by the user. For example, debt and equity securities may be issued in exchange for land and buildings; long-term investments may be exchanged for machinery and equipment; shares of stock may be issued in payment of long-term debt; properties may be received as gifts.

The transactions carry significant implications in analyzing the change in financial position even though they are not factors in reconciling the

---

[1]Perry Mason, *Accounting Research Study No. 2*, " 'Cash Flow' Analysis and the Funds Statement" (New York: American Institute of Certified Public Accountants, 1961).

[2]*Opinions of the Accounting Principles Board, No. 3*, "The Statement of Source and Application of Funds" (New York: American Institute of Certified Public Accountants, 1963).

[3]*Opinions of the Accounting Principles Board, No. 19*, "Reporting Changes in Financial Position" (New York: American Institute of Certified Public Accountants, 1971).

change in funds defined either as working capital or cash. This suggests that in order to make the funds statement more useful, the funds interpretation should be broadened to recognize transactions such as those mentioned. The broadened view, for example, would recognize the issuance of capital stock for a plant asset as funds provided by the issuance of stock offset by funds applied to the acquisition of the asset. This treatment assumes that the transfer of an item in an exchange effectively provides the company with working capital or cash which is immediately applied to the acquisition of property, the liquidation of debt, or the retirement of capital stock. Because sources and applications from such transactions are equal in amount, the remaining items reported on the funds statement will serve to reconcile the change in funds for the period. This broadened interpretation of funds, often referred to as the **all financial resources concept**, is required by generally accepted accounting principles, and is assumed throughout this text.[4] It is important to recognize that the all financial resources concept can be applied on either the working capital or cash basis as illustrated in latter sections of this chapter.

OBJECTIVES AND LIMITATIONS OF THE FUNDS STATEMENT

As indicated in Chapter 5, the funds statement provides a summary of the sources from which funds became available during a period and the purposes to which funds were applied. Essentially, there are only two main sources of funds: (1) those provided internally from the operations of the business and (2) those provided from external sources through borrowing or the sale of stock. However, it is generally useful to show the amount of funds generated from the normal, ongoing operations of the business as distinct from those funds provided from unusual or irregular operations. Similarly, it is helpful to highlight those sources generated from long-term debt financing as a separate component from equity financing. The main uses of funds are for working capital purposes, purchasing plant and equipment, paying dividends, retiring debt, and acquiring stock. These primary inflows and outflows were illustrated in Chapter 5 in the diagram on page 125.

The funds statement is based on data taken from comparative balance sheets and the income statement. However, it is not intended to be a duplicate of or a substitute for those statements. Instead, the funds statement is intended to help investors, creditors, and other external users better understand the financing and investing activities of a company for a period of time. Thus, the funds statement highlights important relationships and helps answer questions such as: What was the total amount of funds used during the period? Where did they come from? How much was generated

---

[4]*Ibid.*, pars. 6 and 8.

from normal operations which can be expected to continue in the future? What amount of funds came from long-term debt which will have to be repaid in the future? Does the amount of dividends paid seem reasonable in light of other fund outlays and the total funds available? These questions and others require answers if the readers of the financial statements are to be fully informed and in the best position to evaluate the operations of a company and its management.

Notwithstanding its popular acceptance and potential usefulness, there are some accountants who feel the funds statement has some serious limitations.[5] One problem is that the term *funds* has not been specifically defined. The most common definitions are working capital and cash, but there are a variety of other possible definitions.

A more basic problem to some individuals is the confusion over the objectives of the statement. They argue that the objectives, as stated in Opinion No. 19, are unclear and that a single statement cannot do all that is expected of it. To solve this problem, they contend, requires more specific objectives and perhaps several different statements, each meeting a particular objective. For example, a statement of cash receipts and payments might better show the debt-paying ability of a company; a statement of financing activities might be presented to show the extent and nature of debt and equity financing; and a statement of investing activities showing the long-term investments of a company could highlight changes in noncurrent assets such as plant and equipment. Supporters of the funds statement feel it provides the information mentioned above in a single, concise statement.

Even if one were to agree with the criticisms of the funds statement, until the FASB clarifies or modifies the reporting requirements, the preparation of a statement of changes in financial position is required by generally accepted accounting principles. The steps to be followed in preparing a funds statement are introduced in the next section. The remainder of the chapter examines in more detail some of the complexities of funds statement analysis and preparation.

PREPARATION OF FUNDS STATEMENT

Regardless of how funds are defined, the funds statement is prepared from comparative balance sheets supplemented by operating income data from the income statement and by other explanatory data concerning individual account balance changes. The preparation of the statement calls for three specific steps:

1. Select a definition to be used for "funds."
2. Compute the total net change in funds by analyzing the fund accounts as listed on the comparative balance sheets. This amount should be the same as that determined in step (3).

---

[5]See, for example, Loyd C. Health, "Let's Scrap the 'Funds' Statement," *The Journal of Accountancy*, October 1978, pp. 94–103.

3. Analyze the changes in each nonfund account on the comparative balance sheets in conjunction with the other explanatory data available in order to classify the changes as sources or applications of funds. The resulting net increase or decrease arising from such changes should be the same amount as that computed in step (2). Through this analysis, the formal funds statement can be prepared. As explained earlier, application of the all financial resources concept may require certain transactions to be shown as both a source and an off-setting application of funds with the net result having no effect on funds.

To illustrate the process of analyzing accounts and preparing a funds statement, a simple example will be considered, first applying the working capital definition of funds and then the cash definition. Assume that a funds statement is to be prepared from the balance sheets and additional information for the Little Company as given below. To emphasize the nature of the account analysis required in preparing a funds statement, it is assumed that no other information is available. In practice, however, the data for preparation of the funds statement can be taken directly from the accounting records of the organization.

	1981	1980
Little Company		
Comparative Balance Sheet		
December 31, 1981 and 1980		
Assets	**1981**	**1980**
Cash	$ 8,200	$ 4,000
Receivables	18,000	15,000
Inventory	17,000	20,000
Equipment	20,000	14,000
Accumulated depreciation	(7,200)	(6,000)
	$56,000	$47,000
Liabilities and Stockholders' Equity		
Accounts payable	$10,000	$ 8,000
Long-term notes payable	10,000	5,000
Capital stock	25,000	25,000
Retained earnings	11,000	9,000
	$56,000	$47,000

Net income for the year as reported on the income statement was $9,000. Equipment which cost $3,000 and had a book value of $200 was sold during the year for $700.

Funds Defined as Working Capital

The first step in preparing a funds statement is to define the concept of funds to be used. In this case, it is working capital. The second step is to compute the net change in working capital. A schedule of changes in working capital, such as that shown on page 542, accomplishes this step and provides useful information that should be disclosed to the reader along with the formal statement of changes in financial position.

Schedule of Changes in Working Capital

Working Capital Items	December 31, 1981	December 31, 1980	Working Capital Increase (Decrease)
Current assets:			
Cash	$ 8,200	$ 4,000	$ 4,200
Receivables	18,000	15,000	3,000
Inventory	17,000	20,000	(3,000)
	$43,200	$39,000	$ 4,200
Current liabilities:			
Accounts payable	$10,000	$ 8,000	$ (2,000)
Working capital	$33,200	$31,000	$ 2,200

As shown in the schedule, the Little Company has experienced a net increase in working capital of $2,200 for the period. The objective of the funds statement is to explain how that change occurred. A funds statement can be prepared by analyzing all nonfund accounts (step 3) to see what financing and investing transactions took place and what effect they had on the sources and applications of funds. In this example, there are five nonfund accounts: Equipment, Accumulated Depreciation, Long-Term Notes Payable, Capital Stock, and Retained Earnings. To assist in the analysis of accounts, it is often helpful to use T accounts, especially for certain accounts such as Retained Earnings where the net change in the account balance does not clearly show the total picture of the inflows and outflows of funds.

To illustrate, the December 31, 1980 balance in Retained Earnings for the Little Company was $9,000. It has increased $2,000 during the period. Since net income was $9,000 for the year, there must have been a $7,000 reduction in Retained Earnings. The probable explanation for the $7,000 decrease is a declaration of dividends. A T account illustrates the situation as follows:

Retained Earnings

Dividends	7,000	Beginning balance	9,000
		Net income	9,000
		Ending balance	11,000

Based upon this analysis, the $9,000 of net income would be shown, prior to any adjustments, as a major source of funds (working capital) and the $7,000 of dividends as a major use of funds. These items would appear on the partially completed funds statement as shown below.

Working capital was provided by:
  Operations:
    Net income $9,000
Working capital was applied to:
  Dividends 7,000

Usually, the net income figure from the income statement must be adjusted to determine the working capital from operations. In the example,

Little Company's net income of $9,000 must be adjusted for two items. The $500 gain from the sale of equipment (selling price of $700 less book value of $200), which is included in net income, must be subtracted since gains on equipment sales do not measure working capital. It is the proceeds from the sale of equipment, $700 in this illustration, that provide working capital and are to be shown as a separate item on the funds statement. Therefore, the gain on the sale, which is included in the proceeds, must be subtracted from net income to avoid being counted twice. This adjustment to eliminate the gain on the sale and to recognize separately the increase in working capital from the total proceeds of the sale is illustrated in the partially completed funds statement that follows.

> Working capital was provided by:
>   Operations:
>   Net income $9,000
>   Less gain on sale of equipment .... (500) $8,500
>   Sale of equipment 700
> Working capital was applied to:
>   Dividends $7,000

The second adjustment is for depreciation. The entries for depreciation, amortization, and similar items have no effect on funds, whether defined as working capital or cash. However, they are valid expenses and have been deducted from revenues in arriving at net income. Therefore, such nonfund items must be added back to arrive at funds provided by operations.

The amount of depreciation expense for the period can be determined from the income statement. However, because of the limited information provided in this example, an analysis of Accumulated Depreciation and the related equipment account is necessary. The following T accounts facilitate the analysis of these nonfund accounts.

Equipment

Beginning balance	14,000	Sale of equipment	3,000
Purchase of equipment	9,000		
Ending balance	20,000		

Accumulated Depreciation

Sale of equipment	2,800	Beginning balance	6,000
		Depreciation expense	4,000
		Ending balance	7,200

When information is missing, assumptions must be made as to the logical reasons for increases or decreases in accounts. The $4,000 increase in Accumulated Depreciation presumably represents the amount of depreciation expense for the period. Because depreciation is a nonfund item, this amount must be added back to net income as an adjustment to derive the funds from operations figure. Similarly, the T-account analysis shows an increase in the equipment account of $9,000. The logical assumption is that additional equipment has been purchased and should be reflected on the funds statement as an application of funds. Now two more entries can be added to the developing funds statement:

Working capital was provided by:
  Operations:
    Net income.. $9,000
    Add depreciation expense............................ 4,000
    Less gain on sale of equipment................... (500) $12,500
    Sale of equipment... 700

Working capital was applied to:
  Dividends... $ 7,000
  Purchase of equipment................................... 9,000

At this point, all nonfund accounts have been analyzed and explained except for the Little Company's long-term notes and capital stock. There has been no change in the capital stock account, but the long-term notes payable balance has increased $5,000. Apparently, the Little Company borrowed an additional $5,000 which should be shown as a source of funds on the funds statement. Given this is the only change that occurred, it is probably not necessary to use a T account to see the relationship. Since there are no other nonfund accounts to be analyzed, the funds statement can now be completed as follows:

Little Company
Statement of Changes in Financial Position — Working Capital Basis
For Year Ended December 31, 1981

Working capital was provided by:
  Operations:
    Net income.. $9,000
    Add depreciation expense............................ 4,000
    Less gain on sale of equipment................... (500) $12,500
    Sale of equipment... 700
    Borrowing on long-term notes 5,000 $18,200

Working capital was applied to:
  Dividends... $ 7,000
  Purchase of equipment................................... 9,000 16,000

Increase in working capital*.............................. $ 2,200

*Schedule of Changes in Working Capital			Working Capital Increase (Decrease)
Working Capital Items	December 31, 1981	December 31, 1980	
Current assets:			
Cash....................	$ 8,200	$ 4,000	$ 4,200
Receivables...............	18,000	15,000	3,000
Inventory.................	17,000	20,000	(3,000)
	$43,200	$39,000	$ 4,200
Current liabilities:			
Accounts payable..............	$10,000	$ 8,000	$ (2,000)
Working capital	$33,200	$31,000	$ 2,200

The funds statement for the Little Company indicates that funds of $18,200 were provided by operations, by selling equipment, and by borrowing on long-term notes; funds of $16,000 were applied to the payment of dividends and to the purchase of equipment; and the difference, $2,200, was an increase in funds (working capital).

As illustrated, the funds statement reports working capital inflow and outflow and the change in working capital for the period. The supporting schedule reports the individual changes within the working capital pool, summarizing and reconciling the individual changes with the total net change in working capital reported in the statement.

Funds Defined as Cash

The preparation of a cash basis funds statement follows the same three basic steps used in preparing a working capital funds statement. First, funds are defined as cash. Normally, cash is used in the same sense as that employed for cash recognized as a current asset — cash on hand and unrestricted deposits in banks. The second step is to compute the net change in cash, which is the difference between beginning and ending balances. The Little Company's December 31, 1981 cash balance shows a $4,200 increase over its December 31, 1980 cash balance (see page 542).

Step 3 requires the analysis of all nonfund account changes in terms of their effects upon the flow of cash. Since cash is the only account included in the cash definition of funds, all balance sheet accounts (including working capital accounts), except cash, constitute the nonfund accounts. Each of these accounts will have to be analyzed in order to determine what effect each had on the sources and applications of cash. It should be noted that the cash basis funds statement might be developed by simply classifying and summarizing cash receipts and disbursements as reported in the cash account. However, the funds statement is prepared to point out the broad categories of sources and uses of cash, and such items as cash collected from customers, cash paid for merchandise, and cash paid for expenses are generally better disclosed in a "cash provided by operations" category.

In analyzing the nonfund (noncash) working capital accounts, changes in current assets and current liabilities are recognized by adjustments to net income in arriving at cash provided by operations. All increases in current assets other than cash and decreases in current liabilities are deducted from net income; all decreases in current assets other than cash and increases in current liabilities are added to net income. An exception to this adjusting process has to do with accounting for changes in marketable securities, which are recognized separately as a source or an application of cash.

In addition to the current asset and current liability adjustments, the net income figure is further adjusted by those items having no effect on cash but which represent valid expenses, revenues, gains, or losses already included in net income. For example, as is the case with the working capital statement, net income must be adjusted for depreciation, amortization, and gains and losses on disposal of business assets. All of these adjustments are required in order to convert the accrual net income measurement to the amount of cash provided by operations, a category on the funds statement which should be disclosed separately.

T accounts for the nonfund working capital accounts are presented below:

Receivables

Beginning balance	15,000		
Net increase	3,000		
Ending balance	18,000		

Accounts Payable

		Beginning balance	8,000
		Net increase	2,000
		Ending balance	10,000

Inventory

Beginning balance	20,000	Net decrease	3,000
Ending balance	17,000		

The $3,000 increase in receivables requires that net income be decreased by the same amount, since cash receipts for goods and services sold were less than the revenue recognized in arriving at net income. The $3,000 decrease in inventory is added to net income since purchases were less than the charge made against revenue for cost of sales in arriving at net income. The $2,000 increase in accounts payable requires an addition to net income since the cash disbursements for goods and services purchased were less than the charges made for these items in arriving at net income. These adjustments along with the reported net income figure for the year would appear on the partially completed cash funds statement as shown below:

Cash was provided by:
  Operations:
    Net income $9,000
    Items to be added to net income:
      Decrease in inventories $3,000
      Increase in accounts payable 2,000   5,000
    Items to be deducted from net income:
      Increase in receivables $3,000

Now that all of the noncash working capital accounts have been analyzed, attention should be directed toward analyzing the other nonfund accounts by following the same reasoning that was used in preparing the working capital funds statement. The adjustments for nonfund items such as depreciation and amortization are the same for cash as for working capital. Thus, the completed cash basis funds statement would appear as follows:

Little Company
Statement of Changes in Financial Position — Cash Basis
For Year Ended December 31, 1981

Cash was provided by:		
Operations:		
Net income...		$9,000
Items to be added to net income:		
Decrease in inventories...	$3,000	
Increase in accounts payable..	2,000	
Depreciation expense	4,000	9,000
		$18,000
Items to be deducted from net income:		
Increase in receivables...	$3,000	
Gain on sale of equipment...	500	3,500
Cash provided by operations...		$14,500
Sale of equipment...		700
Borrowing on long-term notes		5,000 $20,200
Cash was applied to:		
Dividends..		$ 7,000
Purchase of equipment		9,000 16,000
Increase in cash...		$ 4,200

The cash basis funds statement highlights the inflows and outflows of cash. Little Company generated $14,500 from its operations and an additional $5,700 by selling equipment and by borrowing on long-term notes. Cash was used to pay dividends, to purchase additional equipment, and to increase the cash account balance.

The cash-flow approach to the analysis of financial operations has received increased attention in recent years.[6] The statement is readily interpreted by the reader, and it can be a highly useful tool for the forecasting and planning of cash flow. However, a working capital analysis may still be required if questions are to be answered with respect to the effect of financial activities upon the working capital pool.

Analysis of Account Changes

As indicated earlier, analysis of account changes is required when preparing funds statements from comparative balance sheet data supplemented by additional information. Examples in the preceding sections were relatively simple. Ordinarily, however, more complex circumstances are encountered and it is not possible to rely on the net change in an account balance for a full explanation of the effect of that item on a company's funds flow. To illustrate, assume that comparative balance sheets report a $50,000 increase in bonds payable. Without further investigation, this might be in-

---

[6]See, for example, the emphasis placed on cash flows in the *Report of the Study Group on the Objectives of Financial Statements* (New York: American Institute of Certified Public Accountants, 1973).

terpreted as a source of funds of $50,000. However, reference to the liability account may disclose that bonds of $100,000 were retired during the period while new bonds of $150,000 were issued. A further analysis of the transactions affecting the liability account may reveal that a call premium of $2,000 was paid on bonds retired and a discount of $7,500 was identified with the new issue. The funds statement, then, should report that funds were provided by the new issue of $142,500 and that funds were applied to retirement of the old issue of $102,000.

Remaining pages of this chapter describe the nature of the analysis required as well as the procedures employed in developing a more complex funds statement.

Fund Sources. The following examples indicate fund sources and suggest the nature of the analysis required in determining the actual amounts provided.

1. *Decreases in noncurrent asset accounts.* Balances in land, equipment, long-term investments, and other noncurrent asset accounts may decrease as a result of assets sold, thus representing fund sources. However, an analysis of the transactions accounting for each change is necessary; sale of investments at a gain, for example, provides funds exceeding the decrease in the asset account.

2. *Increases in noncurrent liabilities.* Balances in long-term notes, bonds, and other noncurrent liability accounts may increase as a result of amounts borrowed, thus representing fund sources. An analysis of the transactions accounting for each change is necessary; issuance of bonds at a discount, for example, provides less funds than the increase in the bond account.

3. *Increases in owners' equity.* Capital stock balances may increase as a result of the sale of stock, thus representing fund sources. However, the amounts received for shares must be determined, for these may differ from the increases in the capital stock balances. When an increase in retained earnings cannot be explained solely by the net income for the period, an analysis of the retained earnings account is necessary. An increase in retained earnings resulting from profitable operations is recognized as a source of funds; a decrease in retained earnings resulting from cash dividends is separately recognized as an application of funds.

Fund Applications. The following examples indicate fund applications and suggest the nature of the analysis required in determining the actual amounts applied.

1. *Increases in noncurrent assets.* Balances in land, buildings, patents, and other noncurrent asset accounts may increase as a result of the acquisitions of such items, thus representing fund uses. An analysis of transactions accounting for the change is necessary; the amount paid for patents, for example, is greater than the increase in the patents account balance when the account is reduced during the period for patents cost amortization.

2. *Decreases in noncurrent liabilities.* The balance in mortgage, bond, and other noncurrent liability accounts may show decreases resulting from retirement of obligations, thus representing fund applications. An analysis of transactions accounting for each change is necessary; the amount paid bondholders, for example, exceeds the decrease in the bonds account when a call premium is paid upon bond retirement.

3. *Decreases in owners' equity.* Capital stock balances may show decreases as a result of the acquisition of shares previously issued, thus representing fund applications. However, the amounts paid for reacquired shares must be determined, for these may differ from the decreases in the capital stock balances. When a decrease in retained earnings cannot be explained solely by a net loss for the period, an analysis of the retained earnings account is necessary. A decrease in retained earnings resulting from operations at a loss is recognized as an application of funds; a further decrease resulting from cash dividends is separately recognized as an application of funds.

Changes in noncurrent asset and liability balances and in the owners' equity account balances must be analyzed and recognized as described regardless of the definition that is employed for funds. When the concept of funds is narrowed to cash, changes in certain current asset and current liability balances are also recognized in arriving at the amount of funds provided and applied.

Adjustments in Developing Amounts Provided and Applied. The preceding discussion has indicated that the changes in account balances require further analysis when they fail to report the amounts of funds actually provided or applied. When there are many adjustments to be made or when adjustments are complex, use of a work sheet such as that illustrated on pages 556 and 557 may facilitate the preparation of the funds statement. In employing a work sheet, a special adjustments column is used to explain the changes in account balances in terms of the actual amounts of funds provided and applied by such changes.

The adjustments that are required in developing funds data may be classified under three headings:

1. *Adjustments to explain account changes not representing fund sources or applications.* Certain account changes may carry no funds-flow implications. For example, fully depreciated assets may have been applied against accumulated depreciation balances. Errors of prior periods may have been discovered requiring changes in property and owners' equity balances. Stock dividends may have been issued and retained earnings transferred to paid-in capital accounts. The foregoing items result in changes in account balances but these changes should be disregarded in reporting the flow of funds. When a work sheet is prepared, the adjustments made to explain such account changes do not affect the amount of funds provided or applied.

2. *Adjustments to report the individual fund sources and applications when several transactions are summarized in a single account.* The change in the balance of an account may result from funds provided by several different sources or applied to several different purposes, or from a combination of funds provided and applied. For example, the change in land, buildings, and equipment bal-

ance may reflect funds applied to the construction of buildings and also to the purchase of equipment. The change in the bonds payable balance may reflect both funds applied to the retirement of an old bond issue and funds provided by a new issue. The change in the capital stock balance may reflect both funds provided by the issue of shares and funds applied to the reacquisition and retirement of shares. When a work sheet is prepared, adjustments are made to report separately the different fund sources and applications.

3. *Adjustments to report individual fund sources and applications when such information is reported in two or more accounts.* The amount of funds provided or applied as a result of a single transaction may be reflected in two or more accounts. For example, certain investments may have been sold for more than cost; the gain reported in net income and the decrease in the investment account must be combined in arriving at the actual amount provided by the sale. Bonds may have been issued at a discount; the increase in the discount account balance must be applied against the increase in the bond account in arriving at the actual amount provided by the issue. Stock may have been retired at a premium; the decreases in the paid-in capital and retained earnings account balances must be combined in arriving at the actual amount applied to the retirement. When a work sheet is prepared, adjustments are made to combine related changes.

Retained Earnings is an example of an account that may be affected by all three types of adjustments. To illustrate, assume that a retained earnings account shows an increase for a year of $10,000. Inspection of the account discloses the following:

ACCOUNT Retained Earnings

Date		Item	Debit	Credit	Balance	
					Debit	Credit
Jan.	1	Balance				200,000
Mar.	1	Appropriation for plant expansion	20,000			180,000
July	10	Cash dividends	30,000			150,000
Dec.	31	Net income for the year		60,000		210,000

Retained earnings was reduced by the appropriation for plant expansion. Although both retained earnings and the appropriated retained earnings balance show changes of $20,000, the changes do not affect funds. The decrease in retained earnings is explained by the increase in the appropriation for plant expansion; the account changes are thus explained and receive no recognition in the funds statement. Cash dividends of $30,000 are reported separately as funds applied. This leaves $60,000, the net income for the year, in the retained earnings account to be reported as funds provided by operations.

As illustrated previously, the net income figure must be adjusted for items such as depreciation which have no effect on funds. In calculating the funds provided by operations, net income must be increased by all charges that were recognized in arriving at net income from operations but involving no funds outflow. Net income is increased for such charges as depletion, depreciation of buildings and equipment, and amortization of patents, leaseholds, bond payable discounts, and bond investment premiums. Net income must be decreased by all credits recognized in arriving at net income but involving no funds inflow. Net income is decreased for such items as the amortization of bond payable premiums and bond investment discounts. Net income must also be adjusted for any gains or losses, and proceeds from the transactions should be identified as a separate source of funds. Any irregular or extraordinary items included in net income should be shown separately from funds provided by operations.

When a funds statement is prepared on a cash basis, additional adjustments to net income are necessary. Adjustments for changes in current asset and current liability accounts must be made to arrive at cash provided by operations.

The development of a working capital funds statement using a work sheet to facilitate the analysis of accounts is illustrated in the following sections.

COMPREHENSIVE ILLUSTRATION OF A FUNDS STATEMENT ON A WORKING CAPITAL BASIS

Assume for Atwood, Inc., the comparative balance sheet shown on page 552 and the supplementary data given below and on pages 552 and 553.

Supplementary data:

Changes in retained earnings during the year were as follows:

Balance, December 31, 1980		$125,500
Increases:		
Net income...	$ 44,000	
Appropriation for building expansion returned to retained earnings...	100,000	144,000
		$269,500
Decreases:		
Cash dividends..	$ 12,000	
50% stock dividend on common stock	80,000	
Prior period adjustment resulting from omission of charges for depreciation on certain office equipment items..............	3,500	
Acquisition of treasury stock for $15,000; par value of stock, $12,000, originally issued at premium of $2,000.....................	1,000	96,500
Balance, December 31, 1981		$173,000

The income statement for 1981 summarizes operations as follows:

Income from continuing operations...	$36,000
Add extraordinary gain on involuntary conversion of buildings........................	8,000
Net income...	$44,000

Atwood, Inc.
Comparative Balance Sheet
December 31, 1981 and 1980

	1981			1980		
Assets						
Current assets:						
Cash in banks and on hand...................		$ 59,350			$ 65,000	
Accounts receivable (net)......................		60,000			70,500	
Interest receivable................................		250			2,400	
Inventories...		75,000			76,500	
Prepaid operating expenses.................		16,500	$211,100		12,000	$226,400
Long-term investments in equity securities (at cost)			10,000			106,000
Land, buildings, and equipment:						
Land...		$183,500			$ 75,000	
Buildings..	$290,000			$225,000		
Less accumulated depreciation	122,600	167,400		155,000	70,000	
Machinery and equipment....................	$132,000			$120,000		
Less accumulated depreciation	32,800	99,200		43,500	76,500	
Delivery equipment	$ 40,000			$ 38,800		
Less accumulated depreciation	26,000	14,000		20,000	18,800	
Office equipment..................................	$ 34,000			$ 26,000		
Less accumulated depreciation	12,500	21,500	485,600	6,000	20,000	260,300
Patents...			35,000			40,000
Total assets...			$741,700			$632,700
Liabilities						
Current liabilities:						
Income tax payable..............................		$ 10,000			$ 9,500	
Accounts payable.................................		65,000			81,200	
Salaries payable		5,000			1,500	
Dividends payable		4,400	$ 84,400			$ 92,200
Bonds payable......................................		$ 60,000				
Less discount on bonds payable		2,700	57,300			
Deferred income tax			21,000			15,000
Total liabilities....................................			$162,700			$107,200
Stockholders' Equity						
Preferred stock.....................................		$140,000			$100,000	
Common stock......................................	$240,000				160,000	
Less treasury stock, common, at par.....	12,000	228,000				
Additional paid-in capital		38,000			40,000	
Retained earnings appropriated for building expansion................................					100,000	
Retained earnings................................		173,000	579,000		125,500	525,500
Total liabilities and stockholders' equity ..			$741,700			$632,700

Buildings costing $40,000 with a book value of $2,000 were completely destroyed in an extraordinary disaster. The insurance company paid $10,000 cash; new buildings were then constructed at a cost of $105,000.

Long-term investments in equity securities, cost $96,000, were sold for $102,500.

Delivery equipment was acquired at a cost of $6,000; $2,000 was allowed on the trade-in of dissimilar old delivery equipment with an original cost of $4,800 and a book value of $2,800; and $4,000 was paid in cash. The entire loss was recognized.

Land was acquired for $108,500, the seller accepting in payment preferred stock, par $40,000, and cash of $68,500.

New machinery was purchased for $12,000 cash. Additional machinery and equipment was overhauled which extended the useful life at a cost of $26,000, the cost being debited to the accumulated depreciation account.

The amortization of patent cost and depreciation expense on buildings and equipment were recorded as follows:

Buildings	$ 5,600
Machinery and equipment	15,300
Delivery equipment	8,000
Office equipment	3,000
Patents	5,000
Total	$36,900

Office equipment was acquired for $8,000 cash.

Ten-year bonds of $60,000 were issued at a discount of $3,000 at the beginning of the year; discount amortization for the year was $300.

The company recognizes depreciation on machines for tax purposes by the double-declining-balance method, and for accounting purposes by the straight-line method. This depreciation timing difference caused the income tax payable on 1981 taxable income to be $6,000 less than the income tax expense based on income per books.

In preparing a funds statement for Atwood, Inc., the first step is to define funds as working capital. The second step is to determine the change in fund balances, in this case the working capital account balances. A schedule of changes in working capital for Atwood, Inc., is given below:

	December 31 1981	December 31 1980	Working Capital Increase (Decrease)
Current assets:			
Cash in banks and on hand	$ 59,350	$ 65,000	$ (5,650)
Accounts receivable (net)	60,000	70,500	(10,500)
Interest receivable	250	2,400	(2,150)
Inventories	75,000	76,500	(1,500)
Prepaid operating expenses	16,500	12,000	4,500
Total	$211,100	$226,400	$ (15,300)
Current liabilities:			
Income tax payable	$ 10,000	$ 9,500	$ (500)
Accounts payable	65,000	81,200	16,200
Salaries payable	5,000	1,500	(3,500)
Dividends payable	4,400	0	(4,400)
Total	$ 84,400	$ 92,200	$ 7,800
Working capital	$126,700	$134,200	$ (7,500)

All nonfund accounts may now be analyzed using the work sheet illustrated on pages 556 and 557. The funds statement is taken directly from the work sheet and is illustrated on page 560.

It should be noted that the work sheet contains a summary working capital fund account and all the nonfund accounts, in this instance nonworking capital accounts. These are the accounts which must be analyzed to determine the sources, uses, and net change in the fund balance already determined and shown on page 553 in the schedule of changes in working capital. The format of the work sheet is straightforward. The first column contains the beginning balances, then there are two columns for analysis of transactions to arrive at the ending balances in the fourth column. The side headings added after the account titles are those to be used in preparing the formal funds statement.

In preparing work sheets, accumulated depreciation balances, instead of being reported as credit balances in the debit section, may be more conveniently listed with liability and owners' equity balances in the credit section. Similarly, contra liability accounts and contra owners' equity balances are separately recognized and more conveniently listed with assets in the debit section.

In developing a work sheet, it will normally prove most convenient to begin with an analysis of the change in retained earnings (see items (a) through (f) on the work sheet). In the process, the income from ordinary operations and any irregular components should be separately reported (item (a)). After the change in Retained Earnings has been accounted for, the remaining nonfund accounts should be reviewed in conjunction with the income statement and supplementary information to determine what additional adjustments are required. Operating income and any irregular or extraordinary income components should be adjusted (items (g), (i), (j), (o), (r), and (s)) to determine the actual amount of funds provided from each separately identified source; or, in the case of a loss, the amount of funds applied. Adjustments must also be made to determine all other sources and applications of funds (items (h), (k), (m), and (n)) and to reflect significant financing and investing activities which have no effect on funds (item (l)).

Explanations for individual adjustments recorded on the work sheet for Atwood, Inc., are given below and on pages 555–560. The letter preceding each explanation corresponds with that used on the work sheet.

(a) Net income included in the ending retained earnings balance is composed of income from continuing operations and an extraordinary gain. The operating income must be adjusted to arrive at the total funds provided by operations; the extraordinary item requires separate recognition as a source of funds and will also be adjusted to arrive at the full amount of funds provided. Net income, then, is analyzed and is reported by an adjustment as follows:[7]

Funds Provided by Income from Continuing Operations	36,000	
Funds Provided by Involuntary Conversion of Buildings	8,000	
Retained Earnings		44,000

---

[7]Entries presented in this section are for work sheet preparation purposes and are not recorded in the accounts.

"Income from continuing operations" is reported on a separate line as a primary element of working capital from operations. Since a number of adjustments may be required in arriving at the actual amount of funds provided by operations, adequate space should be allowed after this line for these adjustments. Adequate space should also be allowed after each irregular or extraordinary item for adjustments necessary to show the actual amount of funds provided or applied. Additional items requiring recognition are listed after any irregular and extraordinary items.

(b) The transfer of retained earnings appropriated for building expansion to retained earnings has no funds significance and the changes in the account balances are reconciled by the following entry:

Retained Earnings Appropriated for Building Expansion	100,000	
Retained Earnings		100,000

(c) The cash dividends reported in retained earnings are reported separately as an application of funds by the following entry:

Retained Earnings	12,000	
Funds Applied to Dividends		12,000

(d) The transfer of retained earnings to capital stock as a result of a common stock dividend has no funds significance and the changes in the account balances are reconciled by the following adjustment:

Retained Earnings	80,000	
Common Stock		80,000

(e) The recognition that depreciation had been omitted on certain office equipment items in prior periods is recorded by a debit to retained earnings and a credit to accumulated depreciation of office equipment. The correction of earnings of prior periods has no funds significance and the changes in the account balances may be reconciled as follows:

Retained Earnings	3,500	
Accumulated Depreciation — Office Equipment		3,500

(f) The acquisition of treasury stock, common, for $15,000 was recorded by a debit to Treasury Stock, Common at par, $12,000; a debit to Additional Paid-In Capital, $2,000; and a debit to Retained Earnings, $1,000. Funds applied to the acquisition of treasury stock are summarized by the following entry:

Treasury Stock, Common (at par)	12,000	
Additional Paid-In Capital	2,000	
Retained Earnings	1,000	
Funds Applied to Purchase Treasury Stock, Common		15,000

Debits to Retained Earnings of $96,500 and credits of $144,000 provide an ending balance of $173,000; fund sources and applications that were reflected in the retained earnings balance have been fully identified and given appropriate recognition.

(g) The destruction of the buildings and the subsequent insurance reimbursement produced an extraordinary gain of $8,000. This gain was recorded as "Funds Provided by Involuntary Conversion of Buildings," in entry (a), as the result of the earlier recognition of the individual component of net income. Since the effect of the destruction was to provide funds of $10,000, the proceeds from the insurance company, the funds of $8,000 recognized in entry (a) may now be adjusted to show the true amount of funds provided by relating the required adjustment to the appropriate asset accounts:

Accumulated Depreciation — Buildings...	38,000	
Funds Provided by Involuntary Conversion of Buildings...................	2,000	
Buildings		40,000

Atwood, Inc.
Work Sheet for Statement of Changes in Financial Position — Working Capital Basis
For Year Ended December 31, 1981

	Items	Beginning Balance Dec. 31 1980	Analysis of Transactions				Ending Balance Dec. 31 1981	
				Debit		Credit		
1	Debits							1
2	Working capital.....................................	134,200			(t)	7,500	126,700	2
3	Long-term investments in equity securi-							3
4	ties	106,000			(i)	96,000	10,000	4
5	Land	75,000	(k)	108,500			183,500	5
6	Buildings...	225,000	(h)	105,000	(g)	40,000	290,000	6
7	Machinery and equipment......................	120,000	(m)	12,000			132,000	7
8	Delivery equipment	38,800	(j)	6,000	(j)	4,800	40,000	8
9	Office equipment....................................	26,000	(p)	8,000			34,000	9
10	Patents	40,000			(o)	5,000	35,000	10
11	Discount on bonds payable....................		(q)	3,000	(r)	300	2,700	11
12	Treasury stock, common, at par		(f)	12,000			12,000	12
13	Totals...	765,000					865,900	13
14								14
15	Credits							15
16	Accumulated depreciation — buildings.	155,000	(g)	38,000	(o)	5,600	122,600	16
17	Accumulated depreciation —							17
18	machinery and equipment..................	43,500	(n)	26,000	(o)	15,300	32,800	18
19	Accumulated depreciation — delivery							19
20	equipment	20,000	(j)	2,000	(o)	8,000	26,000	20
21	Accumulated depreciation — office							21
22	equipment	6,000			(e)	3,500 ⎫		22
23					(o)	3,000 ⎭	12,500	23
24	Bonds payable.......................................				(q)	60,000	60,000	24
25	Deferred income tax	15,000			(s)	6,000	21,000	25
26	Preferred stock......................................	100,000			(l)	40,000	140,000	26
27	Common stock..	160,000			(d)	80,000	240,000	27
28	Additional paid-in capital	40,000	(f)	2,000			38,000	28
29	Retained earnings appropriated for							29
30	building expansion.............................	100,000	(b)	100,000				30
31	Retained earnings.................................	125,500	(c)	12,000 ⎫	(a)	44,000 ⎫		31
32			(d)	80,000 ⎬	(b)	100,000 ⎭		32
33			(e)	3,500 ⎬				33
34			(f)	1,000 ⎭			173,000	34
35	Total..	765,000		519,000		519,000	865,900	35
36								36

(Continued on next page.)

	Items	Beginning Balance Dec. 31 1980	Analysis of Transactions		Ending Balance Dec. 31 1981	
			Debit	Credit		
37	Working capital was provided by:					37
38	Operations:					38
39	Income from continuing operations		(a) 36,000			39
40	Add items not requiring working					40
41	capital:					41
42	Loss on trade of delivery					42
43	equipment		(j) 800			43
44	Amortization of patents		(o) 5,000			44
45	Depreciation expense		(o) 31,900			45
46	Amortization of bond discount		(r) 300			46
47	Increase in deferred income					47
48	tax		(s) 6,000			48
49	Deduct item not providing					49
50	working capital:					50
51	Gain on sale of investments			(i) 6,500		51
52	Involuntary conversion of					52
53	buildings		(a) 8,000⎫			53
54			(g) 2,000⎭			54
55	Sale of long-term investments					55
56	in equity securities...........................		(i) 102,500			56
57	Trade-in allowance on delivery equip.		(j) 2,000			57
58	Issuance of preferred stock					58
59	in part payment of land		(l) 40,000			59
60	Issuance of bonds at discount		(q) 57,000			60
61	Working capital was applied to:					61
62	Dividends..			(c) 12,000		62
63	Purchase treasury stock, common			(f) 15,000		63
64	Purchase land ($40,000 paid by					64
65	issuance of preferred stock)			(k) 108,500		65
66	Construct buildings............................			(h) 105,000		66
67	Purchase machinery and equipment..			(m) 12,000		67
68	Overhaul machinery and equipment...			(n) 26,000		68
69	Purchase delivery equipment			(j) 6,000		69
70	Purchase office equipment.................			(p) 8,000		70
71	Decrease in working capital..................		(t) 7,500			71
72	Total		299,000	299,000		72
73						73

(h) The buildings account was increased by the cost of constructing new buildings, $105,000. The cost of new buildings is reported separately as an application of funds by the following entry:

Buildings.. 105,000
    Funds Applied to Construction of Buildings..................................... 105,000

(i) The sale of long-term investments in equity securities was recorded by a credit to the asset account at cost $96,000, and a credit to a gain on sale of investment. At the end of the period, the gain account was closed into retained earnings as part of income from continuing operations. Since the effect of the sale was to provide funds of $102,500, this is reported on a separate line. The investments account balance is reduced and funds provided by operations are decreased by the amount of the gain. The following entry is made:

Funds Provided by Sale of Long-Term Investments in Equity Securities..	102,500	
Long-Term Investments in Equity Securities		96,000
Income from Continuing Operations — Gain on Sale of Investments		6,500

(j) New delivery equipment was purchased for $6,000; $2,000 was allowed on the trade-in of dissimilar old delivery equipment, cost $4,800, with a book value of $2,800; and $4,000 was paid in cash. The loss of $800 on the trade was closed to retained earnings as part of income from continuing operations.[8] This transaction resulted in a decrease in cash of $4,000, the amount of cash paid. Under the all financial resources concept, the $2,000 trade-in allowance is also disclosed as a source of funds and included in total funds of $6,000 applied to the purchase of delivery equipment. The changes in the delivery equipment balance and the balance for accumulated depreciation on delivery equipment are explained, while the funds provided by operations are increased by the loss that did not involve current funds outflow. The following entry is made:

Funds Provided from Trade-In of Dissimilar Delivery Equipment......	2,000	
Delivery Equipment..	6,000	
Accumulated Depreciation — Delivery Equipment	2,000	
Income before Extraordinary Items — Loss on Trade of Delivery Equipment..	800	
Delivery Equipment...		4,800
Funds Applied to Purchase Delivery Equipment..........................		6,000

(k) and (l) Land was acquired at a price of $108,500; payment was made in preferred stock valued at par, $40,000, and cash, $68,500. The analysis on the work sheet is as follows: (k) the increase in the land balance, $108,500, is reported separately as an application of funds; (l) the increase in the preferred stock balance, $40,000, is reported separately as a source of funds applied to the purchase of land. The entries are:

Land	108,500	
Funds Applied to Purchase Land..		108,500
Funds Provided by Issuance of Preferred Stock in Part Payment of Land..	40,000	
Preferred Stock...		40,000

Although the issuance of preferred stock for land has no effect on funds, it is a significant transaction that should be disclosed under the all financial resources concept.

---

[8]Since the trade-in was for dissimilar equipment, the loss is recognized for both accounting and income tax purposes. Thus, there is no effect on deferred income taxes. The treatment of gains and losses on exchanges is covered in Chapter 10.

(m) and (n) Machinery of $12,000 was acquired during the year. Payment was made in cash and is reported as funds applied to purchase machinery; the cost of overhauling other machinery and equipment also represents the application of funds and is reported separately. The cost was debited to the accumulated depreciation account. The entries are:

Machinery and Equipment	12,000	
Funds Applied to Purchase Machinery and Equipment		12,000
Accumulated Depreciation — Machinery and Equipment	26,000	
Funds Applied to Overhaul Machinery and Equipment		26,000

(o) The changes in the patents account and in the accumulated depreciation accounts result from the recognition of amortization of the patents and depreciation on the plant assets. Funds provided by operations are increased by the charges against earnings not involving current funds outflow by the following adjustment:

Income from Continuing Operations — Amortization of Patents	5,000	
Income from Continuing Operations — Depreciation Expense	31,900	
Patents		5,000
Accumulated Depreciation — Buildings		5,600
Accumulated Depreciation — Machinery and Equipment		15,300
Accumulated Depreciation — Delivery Equipment		8,000
Accumulated Depreciation — Office Equipment		3,000

(p) Office equipment of $8,000 was purchased during the year. The entry is as follows:

Office Equipment	8,000	
Funds Applied to Purchase Office Equipment		8,000

(q) and (r) During the year, bonds were issued at a discount. The result of this transaction was to credit Bonds Payable for $60,000 and debit Discount on Bonds Payable for $3,000. The funds provided by the bond issuance of $57,000 are recognized by entry (q). Subsequently, the bond discount was amortized by reducing the bond discount account. This decrease in the discount account is explained by increasing funds provided by operations by the amount of the charge against earnings not involving the use of funds — entry (r). The entries are as follows:

Discount on Bonds Payable	3,000	
Funds Provided by Issuance of Bonds	57,000	
Bonds Payable		60,000
Income from Continuing Operations — Amortization of Bond Discount	300	
Discount on Bonds Payable		300

(s) The depreciation timing difference was recognized by a debit to Income Tax Expense and credits to Income Tax Payable and Deferred Income Tax. The timing difference for 1981 is $6,000 and is shown on the work sheet by an increase in Deferred Income Tax and an increase in funds provided by operations. The extra $6,000 debit to Income Tax Expense is thus added back to income from operations because the extra charge against earnings did not involve current funds outflow. The following entry is made:

Income from Continuing Operations — Increase in Deferred Income Tax	6,000	
Deferred Income Tax		6,000

(t) The change in working capital is explained by the following entry:

Decrease in Working Capital.. 7,500
    Working Capital   7,500

This entry explains the net change occurring in all working capital accounts, and brings the work sheet into balance.

A funds statement for Atwood, Inc., may be prepared from the work sheet as follows:

Atwood, Inc.
Statement of Changes in Financial Position — Working Capital Basis
For Year Ended December 31, 1981

Working capital was provided by:			
Operations:			
Income from continuing operations...........................		$ 36,000	
Add items not requiring working capital:			
Loss on trade of delivery equipment	$ 800		
Amortization of patents	5,000		
Depreciation expense	31,900		
Amortization of bond discount	300		
Increase in deferred income tax	6,000		
	$44,000		
Deduct item not providing working capital:			
Gain on sale of investments	6,500	37,500	
Working capital provided by continuing operations		$ 73,500	
Involuntary conversion of buildings		10,000	
Sale of long-term investments in equity securities		102,500	
Trade-in allowance on delivery equipment		2,000	
Issuance of preferred stock in part payment of land			
(total cost of land, $108,500)		40,000	
Issuance of bonds at a discount		57,000	$285,000
Working capital was applied to:			
Dividends..		$ 12,000	
Purchase treasury stock, common		15,000	
Purchase land (cash paid, $68,500; preferred stock			
issued, $40,000)..		108,500	
Construct buildings...		105,000	
Purchase machinery and equipment.............................		12,000	
Overhaul machinery and equipment.............................		26,000	
Purchase delivery equipment		6,000	
Purchase office equipment..		8,000	292,500
Decrease in working capital..			$ 7,500*

*See Schedule of Changes in Working Capital, page 860.

The funds statement should begin with a summary of the funds related to normal operations. Income or loss from continuing operations is listed, and those items reflected in this balance not requiring funds are added back while those items not providing funds are subtracted. The adjusted balance, representing funds provided by or applied to operations, is followed by any irregular or extraordinary items not related to normal financial transactions, but representing direct sources or applications of funds from operations. Remaining sources and applications of funds are then listed in their respective sections in arriving at the net fund changes for the period.

The statements of General Mills, Inc., reproduced in Appendix B, provide an additional example of a funds statement on a working capital basis. Many variations in statement format are found in practice. Frequently, in published financial statements, much of the detail is omitted, e.g., a single amount may be shown for land, building and equipment additions, and a number of individual items may be combined and presented as "Other sources" or "Other uses."

Some persons object to the presentation of funds provided by operations in the form just illustrated. This form, they maintain, implies that the depreciation of assets generates funds. Actually, it is revenues that provide funds but the income from operations balance fails to report the full amount provided because of items such as depreciation. This objection is overcome by separately listing the individual revenues and expenses but excluding items and amounts not involving current fund inflows or outflows.

Special Problems

The analysis required in developing a working capital funds statement may be simple or complex. In each instance where a noncurrent asset, a noncurrent liability, or an owners' equity account balance has changed, the question should be asked: Does this indicate a change in working capital? Frequently the answer to this question is obvious, but in some cases careful analysis is required. The following items suggest special analysis that may be required.

1. In the previous example, charges for depreciation on the tax return exceeded those on the books. This resulted in an increase in the deferred income tax account. When charges for depreciation on the books later exceed those on the tax return, or when an asset with a related deferred tax liability is retired early, the deferred tax account will be decreased by a debit to Deferred Income Tax and a credit to Income Tax Expense. This decrease in Income Tax Expense does not increase the amount of funds provided by operations nor does the decrease in Deferred Income Tax indicate that funds have been applied; therefore, the decrease in Deferred Income Tax must be recorded and funds provided by operations must be decreased by the reduction in income tax expense that did not involve current funds inflow.

2. Assume that retained earnings are reduced upon the declaration of a cash dividend payable in the following period. Declaration of the dividend has increased current liabilities and, thus, reduced working capital. Subsequent payment of the dividend will have no effect upon the amount of working capital, simply reducing both cash and the current liability. Declaration of a dividend, then, should be reported as funds applied. The reduction in working capital is confirmed in the summary of net change in working capital.

3. Assume that a long-term obligation becomes payable within a year, and requires change to the current classification. This change calls for a recognition of funds applied. The change in classification has resulted in a shrinkage

of working capital; subsequent payment will have no effect upon the amount of working capital. The reduction in the long-term liability can be reported as "Funds applied to long-term obligations, maturing currently." The change in working capital balances will confirm the reduction in working capital.

4. In previous examples, prepaid expenses were classified as current assets and therefore treated as working capital items in the analysis of the change in working capital. Prepaid expenses are sometimes listed under a separate heading or reported with noncurrent assets. This treatment calls for the special analysis of the prepaid expenses just as for other items classified as noncurrent, since their exclusion from the current group makes them part of the explanation for the change that took place in the current classification.

SPECIAL OBSERVATIONS

Alternate methods may be used for the presentation of exchanges interpreted as both financing and investing activities. For example, the Atwood, Inc., acquisition of land for $68,500 cash and $40,000 of preferred stock may be presented as follows:

Purchase of land	$108,500	
Less preferred stock issued in part payment	40,000	$68,500

The difference represents the *net* amount of funds and would be shown in the application section. The financing and investing aspects of the transaction are related and the net effect on funds is reported. On the other hand, it may be maintained that the issuance of stock should be reported as funds provided and the acquisition of land at the full acquisition price as funds applied. This raises the totals for funds provided and applied but does not affect the increase or decrease in funds reported for the period. This is the approach used in the chapter illustrations and is consistent with APB Opinion No. 19.

The Accounting Principles Board in Opinion No. 19 recognized that the form, terminology, and content of the funds statement will not be the same for every company in meeting its objectives under different circumstances. Although recognizing the need for flexibility, the APB indicated that there is still a need for certain guides in the preparation of the statement and in its interpretation. At a minimum, disclosures should include the following:[9]

1. The amount of working capital or cash provided from operations;
2. The net changes in each element of working capital, either in the statement or a related tabulation;
3. Outlays for purchase of noncurrent assets;
4. Proceeds from sale of noncurrent assets not normally sold in the normal course of business;
5. Issuance, assumption, or redemption of long-term debt;
6. Issuance, redemption, or purchase of capital stock;
7. Conversion of long-term debt or preferred stock;
8. Dividends in cash or in kind, but not stock dividends or stock split-ups.

---

[9]*Opinions of the Accounting Principles Board, No. 19, op. cit.*, pars. 12–14.

The final recommendation of the board was that isolated statistics of working capital or cash provided from operations, especially per-share computations, should not be presented in annual reports to shareholders. The attempt has been made in this chapter to apply the above guidelines in funds-flow presentations.

The funds statement is now recognized as a primary statement, one which must be audited and which is considered essential for fully reporting the activities of a business unit. Even though not officially required for external reporting until APB Opinion No. 19 was issued in 1971, the funds statement has a long history of use. Many companies prepared the statement for management purposes long before actually presenting this information to external users. It is fortunate that this important statement is now readily available for all users of financial information.

QUESTIONS

1. Describe the statement of changes in financial position. What information does it offer that is not provided by the income statement? What information does it offer that is not provided by comparative balance sheets?

2. What is the "all financial resources" concept of funds? Why is use of this concept required by generally accepted accounting principles?

3. What are the major categories of funds flows for a business entity?

4. Why must all "nonfund" account balances be analyzed in preparing a funds statement?

5. In presenting a funds statement on a working capital basis, why is it important to also include a supporting schedule showing the changes in working capital?

6. Name a source of funds originating from a transaction involving (a) noncurrent assets, (b) noncurrent liabilities, (c) capital stock, (d) retained earnings. Name an application of funds identified with each group.

7. What three classes of adjustments are usually necessary in preparing the statement of changes in financial position?

8. (a) Why is it important to disclose separately the amount of working capital or cash provided from normal operations? (b) To compute "funds from operations" what adjustments are applied to the operating income figure when the funds statement is prepared on a working capital basis? (c) To compute "funds from operations" what adjustments are applied to operating income when the funds statement is prepared on a cash basis?

9. Brookshire Delivery Service had its worst year in 1981, operations resulting in a substantial loss. Nevertheless, without the sale of property items, borrowing, or the issue of additional stock, the company's working capital increased significantly. What possible explanation can you suggest for this increase?

10. Indicate how each of the following would be reported on a funds statement assuming that funds are regarded as working capital.

  (a) Land and buildings are acquired for cash equal to 40% of the purchase price and a long-term mortgage note for the balance.
  (b) Fully depreciated machinery is written off.
  (c) Long-term notes are due within the year and their classification is changed to current.
  (d) Capital stock is issued in exchange for land.

11. What alternatives exist to using work sheets in developing funds statements?

12. What uses might each of the following find for a cash-flow statement?

(a) Manager of a small laundry.
(b) Stockholder interested in regular dividends.
(c) Bank granting short-term loans.
(d) Officer of a labor union.

13. Should a funds statement be audited by public accountants? Give your conclusion and reasons for your conclusion.

EXERCISES

exercise 19-1

State how each of the following items will be reflected on the statement of changes in financial position if funds are defined as (1) working capital, and (2) cash.

(a) Marketable securities were purchased for $5,000.
(b) At the beginning of the year, equipment, book value $2,000, was traded for dissimilar equipment costing $3,500; a trade-in value of $700 was allowed on the old equipment, the balance of the purchase price to be paid in 12 monthly installments.
(c) Buildings were acquired for $187,500, the company paying $50,000 cash and signing a 12% mortgage note payable in 5 years for the balance.
(d) Uncollectible accounts of $225 were written off against the allowance for doubtful accounts.
(e) Cash of $62,500 was paid on the purchase of business assets consisting of: merchandise, $22,500; furniture and fixtures, $7,500; land and buildings, $23,750; and goodwill, $8,750.
(f) A cash dividend of $1,250 was declared in the current period, payable at the beginning of the next period.
(g) An adjustment was made increasing Deferred Income Tax by $5,000.
(h) Accounts payable shows a decrease for the period of $3,750.

exercise 19-2

The accountant for Alpine Hobby Stores prepared the following selected information for the year ending December 31, 1981.

	December 31, 1981	December 31, 1980
Equipment	$22,000	$20,000
Accumulated depreciation	9,000	8,000
Long-term debt	12,000	17,000
Common stock	16,000	11,500

A piece of equipment with a book value of $10,500 was sold for $11,000. The original cost of the equipment was $12,000.

What is the amount of working capital provided or applied for each of the items listed above?

exercise 19-3

Compute the working capital provided by operations from the following information:

Sales	$2,400,000
Cost of sales	1,400,000
Income tax expense	280,000
Depreciation expense	400,000
Amortization of bond discount	1,000
Amortization of bond premium	1,500
Gain on sale of land held for investment	35,000
Net income	500,000
Increase in deferred income tax	30,000
Amortization of patents	2,000
Loss on sale of equipment	3,500
Proceeds from sale of land	150,000
Issuance of bonds at a discount	490,000

exercise 19-4

Determine the major sources and uses of working capital for Sandpiper Golf Equipment, Inc., during 1981.

Net income	$850,000
Depreciation expense	220,000
Amortization of patents	200,000
Amortization of bond premium	10,000
Investment in Jensen Co. stock	250,000
Purchase of equipment	770,000
Issuance of long-term notes in satisfaction of trade accounts payable	160,000
Issuance of common stock to purchase production plant	600,000

exercise 19-5

Give the adjustments, in journal entry form, needed for a work sheet for a statement of changes in financial position upon analyzing the following account:

ACCOUNT Retained Earnings

Date		Item	Debit	Credit	Balance Debit	Balance Credit
1981						
Jan.	1	Balance				532,000
Mar.	20	Correction for error in inventory at end of 1980		10,500		542,500
June	1	Stock dividend	140,000			402,500
Aug.	5	Discount on sale of treasury stock, par $150,000 for $132,500	17,500			385,000
Dec.	5	Cash dividends	35,000			350,000
	31	Appropriation for loss contingencies	70,000			280,000
	31	Net income		52,500		332,500

exercise 19-6

From the following comparative balance sheet of the Carlton Bottle Company and the information provided on page 566, prepare a statement of changes in financial position on a working capital basis for the year ended December 31, 1982.

	December 31, 1982	December 31, 1981
Assets		
Cash	$ 8,500	$10,000
Accounts receivable	9,250	7,500
Inventories	5,780	13,100
Prepaid expenses	4,015	2,300
Machinery and equipment	50,100	57,600
Accumulated depreciation	(14,700)	(15,300)
Long-term investments	30,000	23,000
Total assets	$92,945	$98,200
Liabilities and Owners' Equity		
Accounts payable	$ 9,200	$12,300
Short-term notes payable	2,445	3,000
Salaries payable	2,300	1,150
Bonds payable	17,000	22,000
Common stock	22,000	24,750
Retained earnings	40,000	35,000
Total liabilities and equity	$92,945	$98,200

(a) Sold equipment during 1982 for $6,000; original cost of equipment, $12,000; accumulated depreciation totaled $5,600 on date of sale.

(b) Net income for 1982 was $11,000.

exercise 19-7

The Easy-Grow Seed Co. prepared for 1981 and 1980 the balance sheet data shown below.

Cash needed to purchase new equipment and to improve the company's working capital position was raised by selling marketable securities costing $351,000 for $360,000 and by issuing a mortgage. Equipment costing $75,000 with a book value of $15,000 was sold for $18,000; the gain on sale was included in net income. The company paid cash dividends of $90,000 during the year and reported earnings of $180,000 for 1981. There were no entries in the retained earnings account other than to record the dividend and the net income for the year. Marketable securities are carried at cost which is lower than market.

	December 31	
	1981	1980
Cash	$ 349,500	$ 255,000
Marketable securites	69,000	420,000
Accounts receivable (net)	360,000	345,000
Merchandise inventory	750,000	654,000
Prepaid insurance	4,500	6,000
Buildings and equipment	5,515,500	4,350,000
Accumulated depreciation — buildings and equipment	(2,235,000)	(1,995,000)
Total	$4,813,500	$4,035,000
Accounts payable	$ 613,500	$ 945,000
Salaries payable	75,000	105,000
Notes payable — bank (current)	150,000	600,000
Mortgage payable	1,500,000	0
Capital stock, $5 par	2,400,000	2,400,000
Retained earnings (deficit)	75,000	(15,000)
Total	$4,813,500	$4,035,000

Prepare funds statements without the use of a worksheet:

(a) On a working capital basis.

(b) On a cash basis.

exercise 19-8

Net income for Boman Industrial Supply for 1981 was $670,000. Compute the cash provided by operations, given the following information.

(a) Machinery costing $60,000 with a book value of $20,000 was stolen. The insurance company reimbursed Boman for $15,000, and new equipment was purchased for $85,000.

(b) Two delivery trucks were traded in for two new vans which are considered dissimilar from the trucks. Cost of the old trucks was $18,000 each and the corresponding accumulated depreciation was $13,000 each. Cash of $19,000 was paid for each new van and $6,000 was allowed on each trade-in. Market value of the new vans was $25,000 each.

(c) Boman used double-declining-balance depreciation for income tax purposes and straight-line depreciation for book purposes. This resulted in an increase in Deferred Income Taxes of $27,000.

(d) Book depreciation for the year was $220,000.

exercise 19-9

From the following information, give the necessary adjustments in journal entry form to explain the changes in accounts listed in preparing a work sheet for a statement of changes in financial position for 1981.

	December 31, 1981	December 31, 1980
Land	$ 50,000	$ 80,000
Buildings	200,000	200,000
Accumulated depreciation — buildings	137,000	125,000
Machinery	78,000	90,000
Accumulated depreciation — machinery	31,000	32,000
Delivery equipment	30,000	50,000
Accumulated depreciation — delivery equipment	13,000	25,000
Tools	28,000	24,000
Patents	7,000	9,000
Goodwill	0	80,000
Discount on bonds payable	0	12,000
Bonds payable	0	1,000,000
Capital stock	700,000	500,000
Treasury stock	44,000	0
Retained earnings appropriated for building expansion	0	200,000
Retained earnings	359,000	360,000

ACCOUNT Retained Earnings

Date		Item	Debit	Credit	Balance Debit	Balance Credit
1981 Jan.	1	Balance				360,000
		Stock dividend	200,000			160,000
		Retained earnings appropriated for building expansion		200,000		360,000
		Premium on purchase of treasury stock, par $44,000	16,000			344,000
		Cash dividends	20,000			324,000
Dec.	31	Net income		35,000		359,000

The income statement reports depreciation of buildings, $12,000; depreciation of machinery, $8,000; depreciation of delivery equipment, $4,000; tools amortization, $8,000; patents amortization, $2,000; and bond discount amortization, $2,000. The following additional information was taken from the income statement and accounting records:

Operating income			$ 80,000
Other revenue and expense items:			
Gain on sale of land, cost $30,000		$170,000	
Gain on sale of delivery equipment, cost $20,000, book value $4,000		10,000	180,000
			$260,000
Loss on scrapping machinery, cost $12,000, on which accumulated depreciation of $9,000 had been recognized		$ 3,000	
Goodwill written off		80,000	83,000
Income from continuing operations before income tax			$177,000
Income tax			72,000
Income from continuing operations			$105,000
Extraordinary loss on bond retirement (unamortized discount, $10,000, and call premium, $60,000)			70,000
Net income			$ 35,000

exercise 19-10

Determine how each of the following would be reported on a statement of changes in financial position — working capital basis.

(a) New equipment with a fair market value of $27,500 was acquired on August 1 with an issuance of common stock.

(b) Inventory showed a decrease of $7,200 during the period.

(c) Stock dividends were paid during the year. The fair market value of the dividends was $10,000.

(d) A machine with an original cost of $21,000 and a book value of $7,100 was sold for $5,900.

(e) A long-term investment in Timo Co. bonds was exchanged during the year for a long-term investment in Emo Co. common stock. The fair market value and the cost of each of the exchanged securities was $16,300.

PROBLEMS

problem 19-1

Blinton Shoe Company
Comparative Balance Sheet
December 31, 1982 and 1981

Assets	1982	1981
Cash..	$ 350,000	$ 265,000
Accounts receivable (net)..	275,000	237,000
Inventory	535,000	326,000
Interest receivable...	140,000	25,250
Prepaid expenses..	80,000	85,000
Land...	171,000	215,000
Building & equipment (net)	1,033,000	995,000
Investments..	459,000	673,250
Patents (net)...	57,000	63,500
Total assets	$3,100,000	$2,885,000

Liabilities and Stockholders' Equity	1982	1981
Accounts payable...	$ 565,000	$ 313,000
Income tax payable..	148,000	155,000
Salaries and wages payable...	207,000	57,250
Mortgage bonds (long-term)...	305,000	378,000
Bonds payable (long-term)..	63,000	51,000
Common stock	1,012,000	1,154,750
Retained earnings	800,000	776,000
Total liabilities and stockholders' equity.................................	$3,100,000	$2,885,000

(a) Net income for the year was $62,000.

(b) Land with a book value of $44,000 was exchanged for a building of similar value (no gain or loss).

(c) No new patents were issued during the year.

(d) Common stock was issued in exchange for equipment which had a fair market value of $21,500 (no gain or loss).

(e) A machine with a book value of $3,700 was sold for $5,100.

Instructions: From the comparative balance sheet of the Blinton Shoe Company and the information presented, prepare a schedule of changes in working capital and a statement of changes in financial position on a working capital basis for the year ended December 31, 1982.

problem 19-2

Comparative balance sheet data for the firm of Baker and Lewis are given below.

	December 31	
	1981	1980
Cash..	$ 13,500	$ 9,750
Accounts receivable...	22,000	25,500
Inventory	112,500	75,000
Prepaid expenses..	3,000	4,250
Furniture and fixtures	64,500	40,000
Accumulated depreciation	(33,875)	(25,125)
Total..	$181,625	$129,375
Accrued expenses..	$ 6,500	$ 4,750
Accounts payable...	19,125	24,875
Long-term note..	17,500	–0–
Charles Lewis, capital..	51,375	48,875
John Baker, capital	87,125	50,875
Total..	$181,625	$129,375

Income from operations for the year was $37,500 and this was transferred in equal amounts to the partners' capital accounts. Further changes in the capital accounts arose from additional investments and withdrawals by the partners. The change in the furniture and fixtures account arose from a purchase of additional furniture; part of the purchase price was paid in cash and a long-term note was issued for the balance.

> **Instructions:** Prepare a statement of changes in financial position applying the working capital concept of funds (work sheets are not required).

problem 19-3

Comparative balance sheet data for Abbie Lynne Sales, Inc., follow:

	December 31	
	1981	1980
Cash..	$ 45,000	$ 80,000
Accounts receivable...	120,000	100,000
Inventory	150,000	125,000
Prepaid expenses..	25,000	20,000
Land, buildings, and equipment.....................................	320,000	190,000
Accumulated depreciation	(90,000)	(70,000)
	$570,000	$445,000
Accrued expenses..	$ 15,000	$ 10,000
Accounts payable...	105,000	85,000
Bonds payable..	40,000	100,000
Capital stock, at par	250,000	200,000
Additional paid-in capital...	50,000	20,000
Retained earnings	110,000	30,000
	$570,000	$445,000

Land and buildings were acquired in exchange for capital stock; the assets were recorded at $80,000, their appraised value. Equipment was acquired for $50,000 cash. Net income for the year transferred to retained earnings was $110,000; cash dividends accounted for the remaining change in retained earnings.

> **Instructions:** Prepare a statement of changes in financial position applying the working capital concept of funds (work sheets are not required).

problem 19-4

Empire Bicycle Co. reported net income of $6,160 for 1981 but has been showing an overdraft in its bank account in recent months. The manager has contracted you as the auditor for an explanation. The information below was given to you for examination.

EMPIRE BICYCLE COMPANY
Comparative Balance Sheet
December 31, 1981 and 1980

	1981		1980	
Assets				
Current assets:				
Cash		$ (960)		$ 4,780
Accounts receivable.................................		4,000		1,000
Inventory..		2,350		750
Prepaid insurance....................................		70		195
Total current assets.............................		$ 5,460		$ 6,725
Land, buildings, and equipment:				
Land		$12,500		$12,500
Buildings..	$25,000		$25,000	
Less accumulated depreciation	15,000	10,000	14,000	11,000
Equipment	$37,250		$30,850	
Less accumulated depreciation	22,500	14,750	18,400	12,450
Total land, buildings, and equipment..................		37,250		35,950
Total assets		$42,710		$42,675
Liabilities and Stockholders' Equity				
Current liabilities:				
Accounts payable......................................		$ 4,250		$ 3,500
Taxes payable..		1,400		2,350
Wages payable		750		1,675
Notes payable — current portion.............		1,500		3,500
Total current liabilities		$ 7,900		$11,025
Long-term liabilities:				
Notes payable...		10,500		11,500
Capital stock		$17,500		$15,000
Retained earnings...		6,810		5,150
Total stockholders' equity		24,310		20,150
Total liabilities and stockholders' equity..................		$42,710		$42,675

You also determine the following:

    (a) Equipment was sold for $1,500, its cost was $2,500 and its book value was $500. The gain was reported as Other Revenue.

    (b) Cash dividends of $4,500 were paid.

    Instructions: Prepare a statement of changes in financial position applying the working capital concept of funds (work sheets are not required).

problem 19-5

Lowlands Dairy Products presented the following comparative information:

	1981	1980
Cash..	$174,000	$150,000
Accounts receivable...	95,000	80,000
Inventory (lower of cost or market)...	160,000	175,000
Land, buildings, and equipment (net)	315,000	350,000
Current liabilities...	(210,000)	(215,000)
Bonds payable	0	(200,000)

	1981	1980
Bond premium..	0	(6,000)
Common stock, $50 par..	(450,000)	(250,000)
Additional paid-in capital...	(35,000)	(15,000)
Retained earnings	(49,000)	(69,000)

ACCOUNT Retained Earnings

Date		Item	Debit	Credit	Balance Debit	Balance Credit
1981 Jan.	1	Balance...				69,000
		Cash dividends paid during the year	10,000			59,000
		Net loss (including $15,000 loss on bond conversion)	10,000			49,000

Buildings, with a book value of $80,000, were sold for $130,000 cash. Part of the proceeds were used to purchase land for $60,000. Depreciation recorded for the year was $15,000. The bonds payable were converted to common stock on December 31, 1981, after the annual bond premium amortization of $1,000 had been recorded. The conversion privilege provided for exchange of a $1,000 bond for 20 shares of stock. Market value of the stock on December 31, 1981, was $55 per share.

> **Instructions:** Prepare a funds statement applying the working capital concept of funds. (A work sheet is not required.)

problem 19-6

The following data were taken from the records of Alpine Enterprises.

	Balance Sheet December 31			
	1981		1980	
Current assets..		$185,200		$148,300
Land, buildings, and equipment	$100,500		$96,000	
Less accumulated depreciation	34,000	66,500	30,000	66,000
Investments in stocks and bonds....................................		32,000		35,000
Goodwill		0		25,000
Total assets...		$283,700		$274,300
Current liabilities..		$ 58,800		$ 43,300
Bonds payable...		0		50,000
Discount on bonds payable...		0		(1,250)
Preferred stock, $100 par		0		50,000
Common stock, $10 par...		165,000		105,000
Additional paid-in capital..		40,000		0
Retained earnings		19,900		27,250
Total liabilities and stockholders' equity........................		$283,700		$274,300

ACCOUNT Retained Earnings

Date		Item	Debit	Credit	Balance Debit	Balance Credit
1981 Jan.	1	Balance...				27,250
		Premium on retirement of preferred stock...	1,000			26,250
		Cash dividends..................................	17,500			8,750
		Net income		11,150		19,900

Income statement data for the year ended December 31, 1981, summarized operations as follows:

Income before extraordinary items	$14,650
Extraordinary loss on retirement of bonds	3,500
Net income	$11,150

Fully depreciated equipment, original cost $10,500, was traded in on similar new equipment costing $16,500; $1,500 was allowed by the vendor on the trade-in. One hundred shares of Byler Co. preferred stock, cost $20,000, held as a long-term investment, were sold at a loss of $2,500 at the beginning of the year. Additional changes in the investments account resulted from the purchase of Carbon Co. bonds. The company issued common stock in April, and part of the proceeds was used to retire preferred stock at 102 shortly thereafter. On July 1, the company called in its bonds outstanding, paying a premium of 5% on the call. Discount amortization on the bonds to the date of call was $250. Depreciation for the year on buildings and equipment was $14,500. Goodwill was judged worthless and was written off.

Instructions: Prepare a work sheet and a statement of changes in financial position applying the working capital concept of funds.

problem 19-7

The following information was assembled for Precious Pets, Inc.

Balance Sheet
December 31

	1981		1980	
Cash (overdraft in 1980)		$ 38,625		$ (5,625)
Accounts receivable		82,000		95,500
Inventories		73,250		50,000
Long-term investments		12,000		27,000
Land, buildings, and equipment	$130,000		$95,000	
Less accumulated depreciation	21,500	108,500	20,000	75,000
Patents		0		35,000
Total assets		$314,375		$276,875
Accounts payable		$ 55,875		$ 49,375
Bonds payable		50,000		20,000
Premium on bonds payable		2,375		0
Preferred stock, $100 par		0		50,000
Common stock, $10 par		160,000		100,000
Premium on common stock		24,000		0
Retained earnings		22,125		57,500
Total liabilities and stockholders' equity		$314,375		$276,875

ACCOUNT Retained Earnings

Date		Item	Debit	Credit	Balance	
					Debit	Credit
1981						
Jan.	1	Balance				57,500
Oct.	15	Cash dividends	25,000			32,500
Dec.	12	Premium on retirement of preferred				
		stock	5,000			27,500
Dec.	31	Net loss	5,375			22,125

Income statement data for the year ended December 31, 1981, summarized operations as follows:

Loss before extraordinary items	$4,375
Extraordinary loss on retirement of bonds	1,000
Net loss	$5,375

Equipment, cost $15,000, book value $3,000, was scrapped, salvage of $900 being recovered on the disposal. Additional equipment, cost $50,000, was acquired during the year. Long-term investments, cost $15,000, were sold for $18,250; 7% bonds, face value $20,000, were called in at 105, and new 10-year, 5% bonds of $50,000 were issued at 105 on July 1. Preferred stock was retired at a cost of $110 while 6,000 shares of common stock were issued at $14. Depreciation on buildings and equipment for the year was $13,500. Patents, costing $35,000, were written off.

Instructions: Prepare a work sheet and a statement of changes in financial position applying the working capital concept of funds.

20

Reporting the Impact of Changing Prices

CHAPTER OBJECTIVES

Discuss the underlying need and the alternatives for reporting the effects of changing prices on business enterprises.

Explain the basic concepts and procedures involved in constant dollar and current cost accounting.

Identify and illustrate the reporting requirements of FASB Statement No. 33.

FASB Statement No. 33, "Financial Reporting and Changing Prices," is one of the most important and complex pronouncements issued to date by the Financial Accounting Standards Board. In this chapter the major concepts relating to reporting price changes are presented, followed by a summary of the reporting and disclosure requirements of FASB Statement No. 33.

Traditionally, financial statements have reflected transactions in terms of the number of dollars exchanged. These statements are often referred to as **historical cost/nominal dollar** or simply **historical cost** statements, meaning statements reporting unadjusted original dollar amounts. The primary reason for reporting original dollar amounts is objectivity. Historical costs generally are based on arm's-length transactions and are considered to measure appropriate exchange values at a transaction date.

With the steady increase in prices over the past several years (see the price index below), there has been a growing awareness of the limitations of historical cost statements. Fluctuations in the general purchasing power of the dollar and significantly increased replacement costs of certain assets make it difficult to interpret the dollar amounts reported in conventional statements. Furthermore, there is growing concern that a substantial part of American industry is in a state of self-liquidation, i.e., distributing more than its real income in the form of taxes and dividends. A study of 1979 annual reports of 215 companies revealed that income from continuing operations declined 40% when adjusted for inflation and that the effective tax rate of these companies increased from 39% to 53%, which is in excess of the 46% maximum corporate tax rate imposed by the Internal Revenue Code.[1] Thus, many companies are currently paying dividends and taxes out of contributed capital rather than earnings.

Consumer Price Index for All Urban Consumers (CPI-U)
(1967 = 100)

Selected Years	Average for Year
1920	60.0
1930	50.0
1940	42.0
1950	72.1
1960	88.7
1965	94.5
1967*	100.0
1970	116.3
1971	121.3
1972	125.3
1973	133.1
1974	147.7
1975	161.2
1976	170.5
1977	181.5
1978	195.4
1979	217.4

*Currently the base year

Source: U.S. Department of Labor, Bureau of Labor Statistics

Thus, the validity of analytical data provided by historical cost statements has been challenged and has caused the FASB to require disclosure by most large companies of supplemental financial data reflecting price changes. The purpose of this chapter is to discuss the issues involved and illustrate the procedures for reporting the impact of changing prices.

---

[1]*Alexander Grant & Company Client Newsletter*, July 1980.

THE NEED FOR REPORTING THE EFFECTS OF CHANGING PRICES ON BUSINESS ENTERPRISES

As discussed in Chapter 3, the overall objective of financial reporting is to provide investors, creditors, and others with information that will assist them in making sound economic decisions. Specifically, external users need to assess the amounts, timing, and uncertainty of future cash flows. They also need to analyze the economic resources of an enterprise in a manner that provides direct and indirect evidence of cash flow potential. In fulfilling these objectives, preparers of financial statements have the responsibility to provide information that will help users evaluate the impact of changing prices on their companies.

With the effects of price changes disclosed, users of financial reports will be able to assess more realistically: (1) future cash flows, (2) enterprise performance, and (3) the erosion of operating capability and general purchasing power of enterprise capital. After careful consideration of these factors, the FASB has concluded that certain enterprises should report information about the effects of price changes on enterprise activity.[2]

General and Specific Price Changes

There are two kinds of price changes to account for. The first deals with changes in the general price level for all commodities and services. As mentioned in earlier chapters, in periods of rising prices this concept is referred to as **inflation**. The second kind of price change relates to changes in prices of particular items. Prices for individual items may fluctuate up or down and by differing magnitudes; the average of all specific price changes determines the change in the general price level. With respect to terminology, accounting for the first kind of price change is referred to as **constant dollar accounting** or general price-level adjusted accounting. Accounting for the second kind of price change is referred to as **current cost accounting** or current value accounting. This distinction is important in order to understand the reporting alternatives identified in the next section.

Reporting Alternatives

The major financial reporting alternatives, including the currently used historical cost/nominal dollar basis, may be classified as shown at the top of page 577.

The two distinct aspects of changing prices are highlighted by the matrix: the change in the unit of measurement (nominal and constant dollars) and the change in basis of valuation (historical and current costs). These distinctions are important since the accounting for and the effects on the financial statements are significantly different.

The first cell reflects financial statements which are currently reported in terms of nominal dollars using historical cost valuation. The dollar mea-

---

[2]*Statement of Financial Accounting Standards No. 33*, "Financial Reporting and Changing Prices" (Stamford: Financial Accounting Standards Board, September 1979), pars. 3 and 10.

	Historical Cost Valuation	Current Cost Valuation
Nominal Dollar Measurement	HC/ND Historical Cost/ Nominal Dollar	CC/ND Current Cost/ Nominal Dollar
Constant Dollar Measurement	HC/CD Historical Cost/ Constant Dollar	CC/CD Current Cost/ Constant Dollar

surement is not adjusted for changes in the general price level, and the valuation basis represents the historical exchange prices of transactions, not current costs or values of the items reported. This is contrasted to the cell labeled HC/CD. Reporting on this basis maintains historical cost valuation but measures the items in terms of constant dollars. This means that the original or nominal dollars are adjusted to constant dollars — dollars of equivalent purchasing power. Sometimes constant dollars are referred to as **general purchasing power dollars** because they represent quantities of goods or services that can be purchased given a general price level. This concept is explained in greater detail later in this chapter.

The cell identified as CC/ND does not adjust the dollar measurement; it reports nominal dollars. However, it changes the valuation basis from historical costs to current costs. This basis of reporting reflects changes in specific prices but does not account for changes in the general price level. The term **current cost** is used throughout this chapter in a general sense to mean the current value of an asset. It includes the FASB's technical definition — current replacement cost adjusted for the value of any operating advantages or disadvantages of the specific asset[3] — as well as other measures of current cost: reproduction cost, sales value, net realizable value, and net present value of expected cash flows. Current costs and current values are used interchangeably.

The cell identified as CC/CD combines current cost valuation with constant dollar measurement. Reporting on this basis reflects both specific price changes and general purchasing power changes.

In summary, reporting on the traditional basis (represented by HC/ND) does not reflect the impact of general price changes or specific price changes until assets are sold or otherwise disposed of. Reporting on the HC/CD basis considers general purchasing power changes but not specific price changes. The CC/ND basis is just the opposite. It reports the impact of specific price changes because of its current cost valuation but does not reflect changes in the general purchasing power of the dollar. Only by reporting on a CC/CD basis are both types of price changes accounted for.

The extent and manner of reporting the impact of changing prices is also an issue. One possibility is to choose one of the three nontraditional

---

[3]*Ibid.*, par. 99.

cells and require preparation of primary financial statements on the basis selected. Another alternative is to continue reporting the primary financial statements on the historical cost/nominal dollar basis, but to provide supplemental information adjusted to constant dollars and/or reflecting current costs. If the latter alternative were chosen, a remaining question is whether to restate all items or only selected items.

Historical Perspective: Reporting the Impact of Changing Prices

The issues involved and the proposed alternatives for reporting the effects of changing prices are not new. In the 1920s and 1930s Henry Sweeney and others advocated constant dollar accounting under the names of "stabilized" or price-level accounting.[4] However, only in recent years has the inflation rate accelerated in the United States at a rate high enough to encourage official action by accounting standard-setting bodies.

In 1963, the AICPA published Accounting Research Study No. 6, "Reporting the Financial Effects of Price-Level Changes." This study recommended that supplementary data be presented showing comprehensive restatement of all elements of financial statements using a general price index.[5] Later, in 1969, the APB issued Statement No. 3, which again recognized the potential benefits of general price-level adjusted information and suggested supplemental disclosure of such data.[6]

At the end of 1974, the FASB issued an exposure draft entitled "Financial Reporting in Units of General Purchasing Power." This proposed statement would have required constant dollar accounting, although still as supplemental information.[7] However, before the FASB adopted a final statement, the SEC issued ASR No. 190, which required many companies to disclose current replacement costs of selected assets.[8] Because this conflicted with the FASB's constant dollar exposure draft, the Board withdrew its proposal.

In 1979, after carefully evaluating this issue, the FASB decided to experiment with alternative ways of reporting the impact of changing prices by issuing Statement No. 33, "Financial Reporting and Changing Prices."[9] This statement requires certain companies to disclose supplemental information for selected items on *both* a constant dollar and a current cost basis, but is flexible in the manner in which the requirements may be met. Sub-

---

[4]See, for example, Henry W. Sweeney, *Stabilized Accounting*, (New York: Harper & Brothers, 1936).

[5]*Accounting Research Study No. 6*, "Reporting the Financial Effects of Price-Level Changes" (New York: American Institute of Certified Public Accountants, 1963).

[6]*Statement of the Accounting Principles Board, No. 3*, "Financial Statements Restated for General Price-Level Change" (New York: American Institute of Certified Public Accountants, 1969).

[7]*FASB Exposure Draft*, "Financial Reporting in Units of General Purchasing Power" (Stamford: Financial Accounting Standards Board, 1974).

[8]Securities and Exchange Commission, *Accounting Series Release No. 190*, "Disclosure of Certain Replacement Cost Data" (Washington: U.S. Government Printing Office, 1976).

[9]*Statement of Financial Accounting Standards No. 33, op. cit.* Also see, "FASB Statement No. 33 'The Great Experiment' " by Robert W. Berliner and Dale L. Gerboth, *Journal of Accountancy*, May 1980, pp. 48–54.

sequently, the SEC modified its requirements, as established in ASR No. 190, to comply with the more comprehensive FASB Statement No. 33. Thus, accounting practice for most large companies today requires elements of both constant dollar and current cost accounting.

CONSTANT DOLLAR ACCOUNTING

Recording transactions in terms of the number of nominal dollars exchanged ignores the fact that the dollar is *not* a stable monetary unit. As a unit of measurement, the dollar has significance only in reference to a particular price level. Thus, nominal dollar measurements represent diverse amounts of purchasing power. Unless statements are adjusted, readers are likely to regard dollars in terms of current general purchasing power rather than the general purchasing power at the time they were exchanged. The objective of constant dollar accounting is to convert all dollar measurements into **equivalent purchasing power units** so that a company's position and progress may be viewed in proper perspective.

To illustrate, it would not seem proper to add 100 U.S. dollars to 100 British pounds. It seems necessary to first convert one of the figures to its exchange equivalent before adding, subtracting, or comparing amounts. Similarly, it seems appropriate to convert the number of dollars spent years ago for land or buildings into equivalent purchasing power units expended currently to arrive at meaningful asset totals. This conversion of nominal dollar amounts to equivalent purchasing power units is the essence of constant dollar accounting. Historical costs, the original exchange values, are maintained as the valuation basis, but are adjusted for changes in the general price level. The basis of measurement changes from nominal dollar amounts to constant dollar amounts or equivalent purchasing power units. The conversion is accomplished using a general price index.

Price Indexes

The value or purchasing power of a monetary unit is inversely related to the price of goods or services for which it can be exchanged. Over a period of time, the prices of specific goods or services will move up or down depending on their relative scarcity and desirability. It would be possible to adjust for specific items, but those price changes may be different than changes in the general price level.

The general price level cannot be measured in absolute terms, but relative changes from period to period and the direction of change can be determined. To measure changes in the general price level, a sample of commodities and services is selected and the current prices of these items are compared with their prices during a base period. The prices during the base period are assigned a value of 100, and the prices of all other periods are expressed as percentages of this amount. The resulting series of numbers is called a **price index**.

Price indexes are valuable aids in measuring inflation or deflation.

There are, however, limitations in these measurements. In the first place, all price indexes are based on samples. Since all prices do not fluctuate in the same degree or direction, the selection of commodities to be included in the sample affects the computed amounts. In addition, improvements in products affect the general level of prices, but such qualitative changes are difficult to measure.

Although there is no perfect way to measure the changing value of the dollar, indexes have been developed which provide reasonable estimates of changes in the dollar's general purchasing power. Among these are the Consumer Price Index and the Wholesale Price Index, both provided by the Bureau of Labor Statistics, and the GNP (Gross National Product) Implicit Price Deflator provided by the Department of Commerce.

Each of these indexes exhibits a similar pattern of price-level change, but reports different values. This is because each index is based on a different sample. The index required by FASB Statement No. 33 is the Consumer Price Index for all Urban Consumers (CPI-U), which is published monthly.

Mechanics of Constant Dollar Restatement

Constant dollar accounting requires that nominal dollar amounts be restated to equivalent purchasing power units, i.e., constant dollars, usually for the current period. The general formula for restatement is:

$$\text{Nominal dollar amount} \times \frac{\text{Price index converting } to}{\text{Price index converting } from} = \text{Constant dollar amount}$$

To illustrate the conversion process, assume that a company issues capital stock worth \$50,000 in exchange for inventory valued at \$50,000. Further assume a current end-of-year price index of 105 and that the exchange took place when the general price index was 100. The company holds inventory during the year without engaging in any other activities. A conventional balance sheet prepared at the end of the year will show both inventory and invested capital at their nominal amounts, \$50,000. In preparing a constant-dollar balance sheet at the end of the year, however, inventory and capital stock will be reported as follows:

1. Inventory needs to be restated for the change in the general price level since its acquisition. Inventory, with a nominal acquisition cost of \$50,000, is expressed in constant dollars as \$50,000 $\times \dfrac{\text{Index converting to (105)}}{\text{Index converting from (100)}}$, or \$52,500.

2. Capital stock also requires restatement so that it expresses the stockholders' investment in terms of the current general price level. The capital stock balance is expressed in constant dollars as \$50,000 $\times \dfrac{\text{Index converting to (105)}}{\text{Index converting from (100)}}$, or \$52,500.

It is possible to use conversion ratios that express the relationship of one index to another. Thus, in the example cited, $\frac{105}{100}$ may be stated as a conversion ratio of 1.05.

In the example presented, the price index converted "to" was the end-of-year index. Alternatively, an average index for the current year could have been used. If such an approach were taken, the conversion factor would have been $\frac{102.5}{100}$ rather than $\frac{105}{100}$. Another approach would be to restate all amounts in terms of the price level of an earlier period, e.g., the year of purchase of an item or a base year. Then events occurring during the current year would be restated in terms of constant dollars of the earlier period selected. Nominal dollars can be restated to constant dollars of any period by modifying the indexes used for the conversion factor.

If current-year constant dollars are used to prepare comparative summaries, all past year data must be "rolled forward" to the current year. In this manner, data presented for several years will all be stated in terms of the same purchasing power units. To illustrate, assume land was purchased in 1975 for $100,000. Assume further that the general price level was 150 when the land was purchased, 200 at the end of 1980, and 215 at the end of 1981. In reporting the land on the balance sheet at the end of 1980, the land would be reported in current end-of-year constant dollars as follows:

$$\text{Land} \left(\$100,000 \times \frac{200}{150} \right) = \$133,333$$

However, in reporting comparative amounts at the end of 1981 in current end-of-year constant dollars, the 1980 amount would have to be rolled forward as follows:

$$\text{Land} \left(\$133,333 \times \frac{215}{200} \right) = \$143,333$$

Alternatively, the 1981 amount could be computed directly as follows:

$$\$100,000 \times \frac{215}{150} = \$143,333$$

Thus, the comparative balance sheet for December 31, 1981, would show the following:

	1980	1981
Land	$143,333	$143,333

This correctly shows no increase in the land account during 1980 and 1981 when amounts are all stated in terms of the same constant dollars. For comparative balance sheet purposes at the end of 1982, the $143,333 would again have to be rolled forward to reflect 1982 dollars.

As indicated earlier, all items may be reported in terms of constant dollars of an earlier base year. This would eliminate the need for a roll-forward adjustment because all items would be stated in terms of a base year's constant dollars. Even though restating amounts to current-year constant dollars requires a roll-forward procedure, it provides information that relates to the current general price level as opposed to some earlier price level. Current prices are usually more understandable and relevant for decision-making purposes.

To illustrate the application of constant dollar accounting to the balance sheet, consider a simple example — Mecham Auto Supply. All amounts are restated to current end-of-year constant dollars. Assume that the beginning-of-year index was 220; the end-of-year index was 260. The ending inventory was all purchased when the index was 225; the land was bought when the index was 125; all capital stock was issued when the index was 110.

Mecham Auto Supply
Balance Sheet
December 31, 1981
(Constant Dollar Basis)

Assets	HC/ND Amounts	Conversion Factor	HC/CD Amounts
Cash	$22,000		$22,000
Accounts receivable	14,000		14,000
Inventory	9,000	260/225	10,400
Land	20,000	260/125	41,600
Total assets	$65,000		$88,000
Liabilities and Stockholders' Equity			
Accounts payable	$ 4,000		$ 4,000
Mortgage payable	15,000		15,000
Capital stock	22,000	260/110	52,000
Retained earnings	24,000		17,000*
Total liabilities and stockholders' equity	$65,000		$88,000

*$88,000 − ($4,000 + $15,000 + $52,000)

Note that conversion is not made for cash, receivables, and payables. As explained fully in the next section, these *monetary items* are fixed in amount regardless of changes in the price level. It should also be observed that Retained Earnings cannot be converted directly, since it represents a composite of many different price levels.

Effects of General Price-Level Changes on Monetary Items

In recognizing the effects of general price-level changes, it is necessary to distinguish between monetary items and nonmonetary items. **Monetary items** are assets, liabilities, and equities whose balances are fixed in terms of numbers of dollars regardless of changes in the general price level. All items not representing a right to receive or an obligation to pay a fixed sum are **nonmonetary items**.

Monetary assets include cash and items such as accounts and notes receivable, loans to employees, and certain marketable securities, such as bonds that are expected to be held to maturity and redeemed at a fixed number of dollars. Regardless of changes in the general price level, these balances are fixed and provide for the recovery of neither more nor less than the stated amounts. Monetary liabilities include such items as accounts and notes payable, cash dividends payable, and bonds payable. Regardless of changes in the price level, these balances are fixed and call for the payment of neither more nor less than the stated amounts. Nonconvertible preferred stock is a monetary equity item while common stock is a nonmonetary item. (For a more extensive classification of monetary and nonmonetary items, see Appendix D of FASB Statement No. 33.) In periods of changing prices, **purchasing power gains or losses** result from holding monetary items. These gains or losses are not disclosed in conventional reporting.

For example, assume a person placed $1,000 cash under the mattress for "safekeeping" when the price index was 100. If the price index were to rise to 110 a year later, the individual would have suffered a purchasing-power loss because it would require $1,100 to purchase the same amount of goods that $1,000 would have bought a year ago. On the other hand, a debt of $1,000 payable a year later, again assuming an increase in the price index to 110 from 100, would result in a purchasing power gain. The equivalent purchasing power would be $1,100 yet the debt can be settled for the fixed amount of $1,000.

Nonmonetary assets include such items as inventories and supplies; land, buildings, and equipment; and intangible assets. These items are nonmonetary because with changes in the general price level, the nominal dollar amounts at which they are reported on the conventional financial statements will differ from the resources they actually represent. On the other hand, nonmonetary liabilities generally include such items as obligations to furnish goods or services, advances on sales contracts, and warranties on goods sold. These items are nonmonetary because with changes in the general price level, the dollar demands they actually make will differ from the dollar amounts reported on conventional financial statements.

The difference between a company's monetary assets and its monetary liabilities and equities is referred to as its **net monetary position**. With the number of dollars relating to monetary items remaining fixed, and reflecting current dollars regardless of the change in the price level, purchasing power gains and losses arise as prices change. In any given period, the gain or loss from holding monetary assets is offset by the loss or gain from maintaining monetary liabilities and equities. The net gain or loss for a period, then, depends upon whether a company's position in net monetary items is positive — monetary assets exceeding monetary liabilities and equities — or negative — monetary liabilities and equities exceeding monetary assets.

Gains and losses are associated with a company's net monetary position as follows:

	Rising Prices	Declining Prices
Positive Net Monetary Position	Loss	Gain
Negative Net Monetary Position	Gain	Loss

Constant dollar accounting requires that purchasing power gains and losses be determined. The steps to be followed in determining these gains and losses are explained and illustrated using the financial information for Mecham Auto Supply on page 582 and the following additional information.

Sales for the year were $90,000, purchases were $60,000, and other expenses were $24,000. These revenues and expenses were incurred evenly throughout the year.

The net monetary positions as of January 1, 1981, and December 31, 1981, are as follows:

	January 1, 1981	*December 31, 1981*
Cash	$19,000	$22,000
Accounts receivable	11,000	14,000
Accounts payable	(3,000)	(4,000)
Mortgage payable	(16,000)	(15,000)
Net monetary position	$11,000	$17,000

The purchasing power gain or loss is calculated as follows assuming conversion to end-of-year constant dollars:

1. The company's net monetary position at the beginning of the period is restated to end-of-year constant dollars. Mecham Auto Supply's net monetary position as of January 1, 1981, is $11,000. This amount can be restated to end-of-year dollars by multiplying it by the ratio of the year-end price index to the index at the beginning of the year: $11,000 \times \dfrac{260}{220} = \$13,000$.

2. Transactions involving monetary items during the year are expressed in terms of year-end constant dollars and are added to or subtracted from the beginning net monetary position. For Mecham Auto Supply, monetary items were increased by sales and decreased by purchases and other expenses. Because these items were incurred evenly during the year, the ratio of the year-end price index to the average index for 1981 can be used to restate them to end-of-year dollars.

	HC/ND	*Conversion Factor*	*HC/CD*
Sales	$90,000	260/240	$97,500
Purchases	(60,000)	260/240	(65,000)
Other expenses	(24,000)	260/240	(26,000)
Increase in net monetary position	$ 6,000	260/240	$ 6,500

If no gain or loss in purchasing power had occurred during the year, the ending net monetary position would be $19,500 computed as follows:

	HC/CD
Net monetary position, January 1, 1981	$13,000
Increase in net monetary position	6,500
Net monetary position, December 31, 1981	$19,500

3. The actual net monetary position at the end of the year is compared with the results from Step 2. If the actual net monetary position is less than the amount computed in Step 2, the company has sustained a loss in purchasing power. If it is greater, the company has experienced a gain. Mecham Auto Supply's actual net monetary position at the end of 1981 is $17,000. Since this amount is less than the $19,500 computed above, the company has sustained a $2,500 purchasing power loss. The foregoing calculations can be summarized in the following schedule:

Mecham Auto Supply
Schedule of Purchasing Power Loss
For the Year Ended December 31, 1981

	HC/ND	Conversion Factor	HC/CD
Net monetary position, January 1, 1981	$11,000	260/220	$13,000
Increase in net monetary position	6,000	260/240	6,500
			$19,500
Net monetary position, December 31, 1981	$17,000		17,000
Purchasing power loss			$ 2,500

This schedule shows several things. First, the beginning net monetary position plus the net increase (or less the net decrease) will always equal the ending net monetary position, all stated in nominal dollars. This amount can be computed directly from the balance sheet data. Second, the $19,500 represents the amount that the ending monetary position should be in terms of current end-of-year purchasing power units (constant dollars) if no gain or loss had occurred. However, the actual net monetary position is $17,000 because monetary items are fixed in amount. The result is a purchasing power loss of $2,500, the difference between what the monetary position would be if purchasing power had been maintained and the actual amount. On a constant dollar income statement, the purchasing power gain or loss is added to or subtracted from the constant dollar operating income and becomes a part of the ending retained earnings balance.

As indicated earlier, the objective of constant dollar accounting is to convert all nominal dollar amounts to dollars of equivalent purchasing power. Thus, nominal dollars may be converted to constant dollars of a prior period or to average dollars for the current year. The latter approach is frequently encountered in practice and is illustrated on page 586 for Mecham Auto Supply.

Mecham Auto Supply
Schedule of Purchasing Power Loss
For the Year Ended December 31, 1981

	HC/ND	Conversion Factor	HC/CD
Net monetary position, January 1, 1981...............	$11,000	240/220	$12,000
Increase in net monetary position........................	6,000		6,000
			$18,000
Net monetary position, December 31, 1981.........	$17,000	240/260	15,692
Purchasing power loss...			$ 2,308

When average-for-the-year constant dollars are used to determine purchasing power gain or loss, both beginning and ending amounts must be restated in terms of the average price index. No restatement was required for the ending balance in the previous example since this amount reflected end-of-year dollars. When using an average current-year index, the net increase or decrease is not converted when revenues and expenses are assumed to occur evenly throughout the period, because these amounts already reflect average price levels for the year. The purchasing power loss of $2,308 differs from the $2,500 loss in the previous example because it reflects a different price level. The $2,308 can be restated to end-of-year dollars as follows: $2,308 × 260/240 = $2,500.

Arguments For and Against Constant Dollar Accounting

Proponents of constant dollar accounting maintain that meaningful comparisons of accounting data are not possible unless the measuring units are comparable. They argue that the purchasing power of the dollar is not stable, fluctuating with changes in the general price level. Constant dollar accounting corrects this deficiency by measuring transactions in terms of equivalent purchasing power units, thus giving proper recognition to changes in the general price level. Those in favor of constant dollar accounting also point out that recognition of purchasing power gains and losses highlights the impact of inflation with respect to monetary assets, liabilities, and equities. They conclude that constant dollar information is relevant to decision makers and can be provided on a reliable basis without undue cost.

Those opposed to constant dollar accounting note that changes in specific prices of goods are not considered. Constant dollar accounting reflects only changes in the general price level. It ignores many underlying reasons for specific price changes, for example, those due to improvements in quality and specialized industry circumstances. In addition, the general price index used may not be relevant to particular industries. Constant dollar opponents also point out that price indexes are based on statistical averages and have many weaknesses. They question the reliability of the data, especially if used indiscriminately. Many accountants also question whether the benefits exceed the costs of providing constant dollar data. They fear companies will incur substantial costs, only to have users of the data be confused by or uninterested in the information.

CURRENT COST ACCOUNTING

The objective of **current cost accounting** is different from constant dollar accounting. Constant dollar accounting seeks to use comparable measuring units to reflect equivalent purchasing power for a specified general price level. Current cost accounting attempts to measure the current values of assets, liabilities, and equities. The current values may be measured in nominal dollars or in constant dollars, but they are intended to represent the current exchange prices of goods or services, not historical costs.

Current cost accounting measures changes in specific prices rather than changes in the general price level. While the general price level may have increased an average 12 percent during the past year, the current values of land may be up 22 percent, inventories may be up only 8 percent, and certain types of equipment, perhaps due to technological advancements, may have even decreased in value.

Concept of Well-Offness

From an income measurement perspective, current value accounting is based on a concept of *well-offness*. This concept is attributed to an economist, J. R. Hicks, and maintains that operating gain, often called economic income, is the amount a firm can spend during a period and be as well-off at the end of the period as at the beginning. Operationalized, economic income (loss) is the difference between the sales price of an item and the cost to replace that item. Alternatively, it may be viewed as the change in net assets during a period measured on a current value basis. For example, if an entity's net assets, in terms of current values, equaled $250,000 at the beginning of a period, and $300,000 at the end of the period, given no additional investments or withdrawals and holding the general price level constant, economic income would be $50,000.

Current values may be defined in several ways. Among the most common are: (1) input prices, i.e., replacement costs; (2) exit prices, i.e., sales values; (3) net realizable values, i.e., expected sales prices less costs to complete and sell; and (4) economic values, i.e., present values of future cash flows. These distinctions are technical refinements in implementing the general approach of reflecting current values in financial statements.

Different circumstances may require different approaches to presenting current value information. For example, the current value of inventory or plant assets is generally thought of as the cost to replace or reproduce those assets at the balance sheet date. However, assets such as timber can be replaced only over a long period of time; minerals and oil and gas reserves may not be renewable at all. In these circumstances, economic values probably offer better representations of current values than do replacement costs. This again points out the need for accountants to use judgment, within the guidelines established by the profession, in applying accounting principles.

Holding Gains or Losses

Current cost accounting not only emphasizes economic income but also makes it possible to isolate any gains or losses resulting from holding assets. Traditionally, accountants have recognized income at the point of sale, measuring the difference between the sales price and the historical cost of the item sold. Under current cost accounting, changes in asset values during a period would be recognized whether the assets were sold or not. The recognition of **holding gains or losses** is therefore an essential ingredient of current cost accounting.

Two types of gains and losses from holding assets need to be accounted for. **Realized holding gains and losses** are the difference between the current costs and the historical costs of assets sold during a period. **Unrealized holding gains and losses** are increases (or decreases) in the current values of assets held during a period, but not sold.

To illustrate, assume Current Cost Company had sales of $100,000, cost of goods sold of $65,000, and a cost of $80,000 to replace the inventory sold. The operating gross profit of $20,000 is the difference between the sales price and the current cost of the inventory. The realized holding gain of $15,000 represents the difference between the historical cost and replacement cost of the inventory sold. The total gross profit traditionally recognized is $35,000. However, that amount includes some inventory profits which will have to be reinvested if the firm is to be in an equally well-off position at the end of the period. Thus, the gross profit in an economic sense is the $20,000 operating gross profit.

Sales	$100,000	$20,000 Operating gross profit
Current cost of inventory	80,000	15,000 Realized holding gain
Cost of goods sold	65,000	
Total gross profit	$35,000	

If, in the example, Current Cost Company has additional inventory which was not sold but which had a change in value, it would have an unrealized holding gain or loss. Assume inventory that was not sold cost $50,000 and had a replacement cost of $75,000. There would be a $25,000 unrealized holding gain.

To show how these concepts would be applied over time, assume $10,000 of inventory was purchased by a company at the beginning of Year 1. At the end of Year 1 no inventory had been sold but its current cost was $12,000. At the end of Year 2, the inventory was sold for $18,000 and was replaced at a cost of $15,000. A comparison of the historical cost and current cost approaches over time is shown on page 589. For simplicity, assume that the only expense is cost of goods sold.

	Historical Cost			Current Cost		
	Year 1	*Year 2*	*Total*	*Year 1*	*Year 2*	*Total*
Sales revenue	–0–	$18,000	$18,000	–0–	$18,000	$18,000
Cost of goods sold	–0–	10,000	10,000	–0–	15,000	15,000
Operating income	–0–	$ 8,000	$ 8,000	–0–	$ 3,000	$ 3,000
Holding gain (loss)	–0–	–0–	–0–	$2,000	3,000	5,000
Net income	–0–	$ 8,000	$ 8,000	$2,000	$ 6,000	$ 8,000

Note that total income recognized is the same under either method. Under current cost accounting, however, changes in the values of inventory are recognized as they occur. The $2,000 increase in the value of the inventory during Year 1 was an unrealized holding gain, since the inventory had not been sold.

In Year 2, the difference between the current cost of the inventory and its historical cost, $5,000, is a realized holding gain. Note that this realized holding gain includes the $2,000 unrealized holding gain recognized in Year 1 as well as $3,000 realized in Year 2. There is no unrealized holding gain on the inventory in Year 2, since the ending inventory was acquired at the end of Year 2.

Current cost net income in this example consists of operating income and holding gains, both realized and unrealized. The total net income would be reflected in retained earnings and would offset changes in net asset values shown on the balance sheet. Some accountants argue, however, that holding gains and losses should be reported as a special account in the owners' equity section of the balance sheet and should not be included in the determination of net income. Another position is that only realized holding gains and losses should be reported as income, and unrealized gains or losses should be reported in an owners' equity account.

Mechanics of Current Cost Accounting

The major problem in current cost accounting is determining appropriate current values. There are two recommended approaches: (1) **Indexing** through internally or externally developed specific price indexes for the class of goods or services being measured, and (2) **direct pricing** from current invoice prices, vendors' price lists, or standard manufacturing costs that reflect current costs. If indexing is used, restatement is mechanically the same as for constant dollar accounting. The difference is that specific price indexes are used rather than a general price index. The direct pricing approach assigns current values, determined by analysis and estimate, to particular assets.

For example, assume that the land of Mecham Auto Supply had a current value of $60,000 at the end of 1981. On a December 31, 1981 current cost balance sheet, the land would be reported at its current value of $60,000 rather than its historical cost of $20,000 or its end-of-year constant dollar value of $41,600.

Arguments for and Against Current Cost Accounting

Many accountants were not in favor of the replacement cost reporting requirements of ASR 190. Some are opposed to FASB Statement No. 33, being especially critical of its complexity and the confusion it might cause. However, proponents of current cost accounting argue that historical cost financial statements, even if adjusted for general price-level changes, do not adequately reflect the economic circumstances of a business. The balance sheet is deficient because only historical costs are presented which do not reflect the current financial picture of an enterprise. The income statement is deficient because charges against revenues are based on historical costs which may differ from current costs. Also, increases in net asset values are not recognized at the time of a change in asset value but must await realization at time of sale. Under current cost accounting, assets are reported at their current values, thus more closely reflecting the actual financial position of a business. Expenses are based on the expiration of current costs of assets utilized, thus providing a more meaningful income measure, and changes in values of assets held are recognized as they occur.

Opponents of current cost accounting argue that determining current values is too subjective. For example, the current cost of a particular item may not be readily available at a reasonable cost, and may have to be determined by appraisal or estimation. It may be difficult or impossible to even find an identical replacement item to consider its replacement cost. If an identical asset is not used, a subjective adjustment for differences in the quality of a similar but not identical item would have to be made.

Another disadvantage is the increased subjectivity of the income measurement if changes in current values are recognized as income prior to transactions which confirm arms-length exchange values.

Additional arguments against current cost accounting include the lack of understanding of current cost financial statements; the question of whether the benefits are worth the extra costs involved; and the uncertainty of whether financial statement users will be better served by current cost accounting.

CURRENT COST/CONSTANT DOLLAR ACCOUNTING

A number of accountants argue against both constant dollar and current cost accounting, pointing out that each approach solves only one of the problems of accounting for changing prices. Constant dollar accounting adjusts for general price changes; current cost accounting recognizes the impact of specific price changes. Current cost/constant dollar accounting combines both approaches and reflects current cost valuation on a constant dollar basis. Such an approach recognizes that adjustments for specific and general price changes are neither mutually exclusive nor competing alternatives. Conceptually, this is the best reporting alternative if the objective is to give full effect to the impact of changing prices on business enterprises.

Its primary disadvantage, in addition to the shortcomings ascribed to the other approaches considered separately, is its complexity.

To a limited degree, accountants are beginning to experiment with the current cost/constant dollar approach by disclosing changes in the specific prices (current costs) of selected items, net of the impact of inflation (the change in general price level). Again referring to the Mecham Auto Supply example, on a December 31, 1981, current cost/constant dollar balance sheet, the land would be reported at its current cost stated in end-of-year constant dollars of $60,000. Note that this is the same amount as reported under the current cost/nominal dollar approach. For the $60,000 to be a current cost it would have to be a year-end amount. Conversion would be required, however, if average-year or base-year dollars were used.

In the example, the $60,000 current cost/constant dollar land amount is $40,000 higher than the $20,000 reported under the historical cost/nominal dollar approach. As explained earlier, this is a holding gain. However, only part of the $40,000 holding gain is real; a portion of it is an inflationary or fictitious holding gain due to changes in the general purchasing power of the dollar. The total increase in the asset value may be shown net of inflation as follows:

Increase in specific price (current cost) of land ($60,000 − $20,000) $40,000

Effect of increase in general price level ($20,000 $\times \frac{260}{125}$ = $41,600;

$41,600 − $20,000) 21,600

Excess of increase in specific price over increase in general price level . $18,400

This concept can be illustrated by the following diagram.

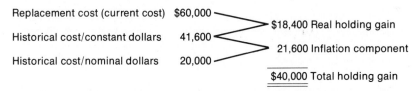

This example shows the impact of both general and specific price changes on only one balance sheet item. It is indeed a complex problem to determine and report such information for all items on a balance sheet as well as trace the impact of real and inflationary and realized and unrealized holding gains and losses through the income and retained earnings statements. It will be some time before guidelines are fully developed for this reporting alternative, but FASB Statement No. 33 is a first step in that direction. The next sections summarize the current FASB reporting requirements and illustrate the required disclosures.

FASB STATEMENT NO. 33 REPORTING REQUIREMENTS

FASB Statement No. 33 was published in September, 1979. The statement is a part of the measurement phase of the Board's Conceptual Frame-

work Study, and has been called the most significant FASB statement issued to date. The statement requires large public companies to disclose
supplemental accounting data in annual reports to shareholders showing
the effects of price changes on enterprise activity. The main points of Statement No. 33 are summarized in the following pages. It should be noted that
the FASB has tried to simplify its requirements by allowing various short
cuts and a variety of disclosure alternatives, all designed to help provide
experience and lead to a common solution to this important reporting issue.

Statement No. 33 applies to all public companies which, at the beginning of the year, have *either* total assets of more than $1 billion (net of
accumulated depreciation) *or* inventories and gross properties totaling more
than $125 million (before accumulated depreciation). Properties include
land, buildings, equipment, capitalized leasehold interests, and natural resources, but exclude goodwill and other intangible assets. All nonpublic
companies and public enterprises not meeting the size tests are encouraged,
but not required, to present the information called for by Statement No. 33.

FASB Statement No. 33 does not change the standards of financial accounting and reporting with respect to the primary financial statements. It
requires three types of supplemental disclosures: (1) information relating to
the latest fiscal year, (2) information for the most recent five years, and (3)
narrative information. The information must be included in any published
annual report that contains the primary financial statements but is not required to be included with interim financial reports. The information may
be presented in statement format, schedules, or as supplementary notes to
the financial statements. The minimum disclosure requirements are as follows:

1. For the **current year**, the supplemental information presented must disclose
    income from continuing operations on both a constant dollar basis *and* a cur-
    rent cost basis. The purchasing power gain or loss on net monetary items
    must also be disclosed in a supplemental schedule or note. The purchasing
    power gain or loss is *not* to be included in income from continuing operations
    but is to be shown as a separate item. In addition to the above disclosures
    companies must also report the current costs of inventory and property, plant,
    and equipment at the end of the year. Any increases or decreases in the cur-
    rent costs of these items, net of inflation, must also be shown. These holding
    gains or losses, are *not* to be included in income from continuing operations.

2. For its **five most recent fiscal years**, a company must report:[10]
    a. Net sales and other operating revenues, stated in constant dollars.
    b. Income from continuing operations on both a constant dollar basis *and*
        current cost basis.
    c. Income per common share from continuing operations on both a constant
        dollar basis *and* current cost basis.
    d. Net assets at fiscal year-end on both a constant dollar basis *and* current
        cost basis. (Net assets are defined as inventory and property, plant, and
        equipment unless comprehensive restatement is made.)

---

[10]*Ibid.*, par. 35.

e. Net increases or decreases in the current cost amounts of inventory and property, plant, and equipment, net of inflation.

f. Purchasing power gain or loss on net monetary items.

g. Cash dividends per common share.

h. Market price per common share at fiscal year-end.

In disclosing the five-year comparative data, companies may use the average CPI-U for the current year or the base-year index (1967 = 100). If the current-year average is used, the prior year amounts will have to be "rolled forward" each year to present comparable amounts in units of equivalent purchasing power. Also, the average level of the CPI-U must be disclosed for each of the five years. However, if the base-year index is used for the five-year summary, the current year data, being stated in terms of average current-year dollars, will have to be "rolled back" to the base year to be comparable with the other data in the summary.

3. In addition to this data, management is required to provide notes to the statements and narrative information explaining the bases of computations, the accounting principles employed, and the significance of the supplementary information with respect to the specific circumstances of the company.

Applying FASB Statement No. 33 Constant Dollar Requirements

Statement No. 33 does not require comprehensive constant dollar restatement of all nonmonetary items. It allows such restatement, but only requires constant dollar disclosures for inventory and property, plant, and equipment items and also for cost of goods sold and depreciation in reporting income from continuing operations. In addition, Statement No. 33 requires disclosures of the gain or loss on net monetary items due to general price-level changes.

Income from Continuing Operations. Statement No. 33 requires that only cost of goods sold and depreciation expense be adjusted to constant dollars in reporting income from continuing operations. The most difficult part in computing cost of goods sold and depreciation expense on a constant dollar basis is in determining when inventory and depreciable assets were acquired. This is referred to as "aging." Once the assets are aged, the process becomes mechanical, following the formula described earlier.

Conceptually, each item of inventory or depreciable asset should be adjusted for the impact of inflation since its acquisition. It is not difficult to age a single asset, but the problem becomes quite complex when many assets, which often are quite dissimilar, must be aged. Because of the magnitude of the problem, Statement No. 33 allows reasonable approximations and grouping of assets. For example, in aging inventory a turnover rate may be computed and an assumption made that the ending inventory was purchased or manufactured during the month (or quarter) indicated by that turnover rate. If the turnover rate is six times a year, it can be assumed that the ending inventory was purchased during the last two months of the year if the company values its inventory at fifo. Of course, major purchases of inventories or assets should be handled separately. An example follows, using arbitrary numbers and assumptions. The symbol C$ stands for constant dollars. In the example, the amounts are adjusted to the *average* current year index. The FASB requires the use of an average current year index unless a company elects to make comprehensive restatement; then either the average current year index or the end-of-year index may be used. Use of an average index simplifies restating certain items, which is presumably why the FASB selected that approach for noncomprehensive restatement.

Cost of goods sold		$450,000
Ending inventory, December 31, 1981	$52,000	
Major item purchased on September 1, 1981	14,500	$37,500
Turnover rate ($450,000 ÷ $37,500)		12 times

Constant dollar inventory, December 31, 1981:

$$\$37,500 \times \frac{258 \text{ (Average 1981)}}{265 \text{ (December 1981)}^*} \quad \text{.................................} \quad \text{C\$36,509}$$

$$\$14,500 \times \frac{258 \text{ (Average 1981)}}{260 \text{ (September 1981)}} \quad \text{.................................} \quad \underline{14,388}$$

$$\text{C\$50,897}$$

*Conversion factor for last month based on assumption that ending inventory purchased during last month due to inventory turnover rate.

To adjust lifo inventories, it is necessary to age and convert each lifo layer. An example is illustrated below:

	HC/ND Amounts	Conversion Factor	HC/CD Amounts
Inventory, January 1, 1981:			
1972	$30,000	$\dfrac{258 \text{ (Average 1981)}}{125 \text{ (Average 1972)}}$	C$ 61,920
1976	15,000	$\dfrac{258 \text{ (Average 1981)}}{170 \text{ (Average 1976)}}$	22,765
1980	10,000	$\dfrac{258 \text{ (Average 1981)}}{240 \text{ (Average 1980)}}$	10,750
	$55,000		C$ 95,435
1981 addition	5,000	$\dfrac{258 \text{ (Average 1981)}^*}{258 \text{ (Average 1981)}}$	5,000
Inventory, December 31, 1981 ...	$60,000		C$100,435

*Assumed purchased when index at average for the year.

A similar process is required to restate property, plant, and equipment items. Again reasonable assumptions and groupings of assets may be used. The restatement of these items is necessary to report net assets on a constant dollar basis in the five year supplementary summary and the impact of depreciation, depletion, and amortization on income from continuing operations. Once the age of the assets to be adjusted is determined, the conversion process is identical to that illustrated for inventory. The schedule on page 595 is reproduced from Appendix E of FASB Statement No. 33 to illustrate the conversion process.

Purchasing Power Gains and Losses. The second item required by Statement No. 33 with respect to constant dollar accounting is disclosure of the purchasing power gain or loss during the period. As explained earlier,

HISTORICAL COST OF PROPERTY, PLANT, AND EQUIPMENT IN AVERAGE 1980 DOLLARS

	(1)	*(2)*	*(3)* *(1) × (2)*	*(4)*	*(5)* *(3) × (4)*	*(6)* *(3) − (5)*
Date of Acquisition	*Historical Cost/ Nominal Dollars*	*Conversion Factor*	*Historical Cost/ Constant Dollars*	*Percent Depreciated*	*Accumulated Depreciation*	*Net*
	(000s)		(000s)		(000s)	
1973	$ 50,000	× 220.9 (Avg. 1980) / 133.1 (" 1973) =	C$ 82,983	80	C$66,386	
1974	5,000	× 220.9 (" 1980) / 147.7 (" 1974) =	7,478	70	5,235	
1975	5,000	× 220.9 (" 1980) / 161.2 (" 1975) =	6,852	60	4,111	
1976	5,000	× 220.9 (" 1980) / 170.5 (" 1976) =	6,478	50	3,239	
1977	5,000	× 220.9 (" 1980) / 181.5 (" 1977) =	6,085	40	2,434	
1978	5,000	× 220.9 (" 1980) / 195.4 (" 1978) =	5,652	30	1,696	
1979	10,000	× 220.9 (" 1980) / 205.0 (" 1979) =	10,776	20	2,155	
1980	15,000	× 220.9 (" 1980) / 220.9 (" 1980) =	15,000	10	1,500	
	$100,000		C$141,304		C$86,756	C$54,548

this gain or loss results from holding monetary items in periods of changing prices. The steps to be followed in computing the purchasing power gain or loss were illustrated earlier in this chapter. As noted previously, the gain or loss is computed in terms of the average-for-the-year index unless comprehensive restatement is elected.

Recoverable Amounts. It should be noted here that Statement No. 33 requires that both constant dollar and current cost measures be reported at the **net recoverable amount** when that amount is less than the constant dollar or current cost amounts. However, this adjustment is not required unless the net recoverable amount is materially and permanently less than the other measures. For inventories, the recoverable amount is the net realizable value defined as . . . "the amount of cash, or its equivalent, expected to be derived from sale of an asset net of costs required to be incurred as a result of the sale."[11] For property, plant and equipment, the recoverable amount is net realizable value if the asset is about to be sold. If the asset will not be sold, the recoverable amount is the net present value of future cash flows expected to be derived from future use and disposition of the asset discounted at a reasonable rate given the attendant risks.[12] Recoverable amounts, if used, replace the historical cost/constant dollar amounts and/or current costs in the calculations and supplemental disclosures.

Applying FASB No. 33 Current Cost Requirements

FASB No. 33 requires affected companies to disclose income from continuing operations after adjusting cost of goods sold and depreciation, de-

---

[11]*Ibid.*, p. 63.
[12]*Ibid.*

pletion, and amortization for current costs. In addition, the net change in
the current costs of inventories and property, plant, and equipment must be
disclosed both before and after the impact of general price-level changes.
This, in effect, discloses the holding gains or losses due to specific changes
in prices and the impact of general price-level changes. In meeting these
requirements, the major difficulty is determining the appropriate current
costs of affected assets. No single source for current cost information is
prescribed. Instead, experimentation is encouraged, but the bases of current
costs must be reasonable and well-documented.

The steps necessary to meet the required current cost disclosures of
FASB No. 33 are:

1. Determine the current cost amounts of inventory and property, plant, and
   equipment items.
2. Apply the "recoverable amount test" to the current cost amounts and select
   the lower amount.
3. Calculate cost of goods sold, depreciation, depletion, and amortization based
   on the results of Step 2.
4. Determine the change in current costs of inventory and property, plant, and
   equipment in terms of nominal amounts as well as constant dollars.

If an indexing method is used for Step 1, the process will be the same as
illustrated earlier for constant dollar accounting. It is important to select an
index that correlates closely with the price changes of the items included in
the index and the items being adjusted. If an indexing method is not used,
the amounts in Step 1 will have to be determined by direct pricing, appraisal, or estimation.

If a company determines that there is no significant difference between
income from continuing operations on a constant dollar basis and on a current cost basis, the supplemental current cost information is not required. If
omitted, however, the reasons for omission must be explained in a note to
the supplementary disclosures.

FASB STATEMENT NO. 33 DISCLOSURES ILLUSTRATED

The supplemental disclosures required by Statement No. 33 may be
shown in "reconciliation format" or in "statement format." Examples of
these formats are presented on page 597. The statement format, which ties
to the figures reported in the primary financial statements, might be less
confusing to readers.

An example of how the five-year comparative data might be presented is
shown on page 598. These examples are only illustrations, as the FASB has
not specified an exact format to be used.

PROSPECTS FOR THE FUTURE

In some respects the FASB has taken a middle-of-the-road approach in
dealing with changing prices. They have not yet determined which approach is better — constant dollar or current cost accounting — and therefore are experimenting with both. They require disclosure of only selected
items — essentially inventories and depreciable assets — instead of compre-

Statement of Income from Continuing Operations Adjusted for Changing Prices
For the Year Ended December 31, 1980
(In thousands of average 1980 dollars)

Income from continuing operations, as reported in the income statement		$ 9,000
Adjustments to restate costs for the effect of general inflation:		
Cost of goods sold	$ (7,384)	
Depreciation and amortization expense	(4,130)	(11,514)
Loss from continuing operations adjusted for general inflation		$ (2,514)
Adjustments to reflect the difference between general inflation and changes in specific prices (current costs):		
Cost of goods sold	$ (1,024)	
Depreciation and amortization expense	(5,370)	(6,394)
Loss from continuing operations adjusted for changes in specific prices		$ (8,908)
Gain from decline in purchasing power of net amounts owed		$ 7,729
Increase in specific prices (current cost) of inventories and property, plant, and equipment held during the year*		$24,608
Effect of increase in general price level		18,959
Excess of increase in specific prices over increase in the general price level		$ 5,649

Reconciliation Format

Statement of Income from Continuing Operations Adjusted for Changing Prices
For the Year Ended December 31, 1980
(In thousands of dollars)

	As Reported in the Primary Statements	Adjusted for General Inflation	Adjusted for Changes in Specific Prices (Current Costs)
Net sales and other operating revenues	$253,000	$253,000	$253,000
Cost of goods sold	$197,000	$204,384	$205,408
Depreciation and amortization expense	10,000	14,130	19,500
Other operating expense	20,835	20,835	20,835
Interest expense	7,165	7,165	7,165
Provision for income tax	9,000	9,000	9,000
	$244,000	$255,514	$261,908
Income (loss) from continuing operations	$ 9,000	$ (2,514)	$ (8,908)
Gain from decline in purchasing power of net amounts owed		$ 7,729	$ 7,729
Increase in specific prices (current cost) of inventories and property, plant, and equipment held during the year*			$ 24,608
Effect of increase in general price level			18,959
Excess of increase in specific prices over increase in the general price level			$ 5,649

Statement Format

*At December 31, 1980, current cost of inventory was $65,700 and current cost of property, plant, and equipment, net of accumulated depreciation was $85,100.

Source: FASB Statement No. 33, pp. 32–33.

Five-Year Comparison of Selected
Supplementary Financial Data Adjusted for Effects of Changing Prices
(In thousands of average 1980 dollars)

	Years Ended December 31,				
	1976	1977	1978	1979	1980
Net sales and other operating revenues ...	$265,000	$235,000	$240,000	$237,063	$253,000
Historical cost information adjusted for general inflation:					
Income (loss) from continuing operations				(2,761)	(2,514)
Income (loss) from continuing operations per common share				$ (1.91)	$ (1.68)
Net assets at year-end				55,518	57,733
Current cost information:					
Income (loss) from continuing operations				(4,125)	(8,908)
Income (loss) from continuing operations per common share				$ (2.75)	$ (5.94)
Excess of increase in specific prices over increase in the general price level				2,292	5,649
Net assets at year-end				79,996	81,466
Gain from decline in purchasing power of net amounts owed				7,027	7,729
Cash dividends declared per common share	$ 2.59	$ 2.43	$ 2.26	$ 2.16	$ 2.00
Market price per common share at year-end	$ 32	$ 31	$ 43	$ 39	$ 35
Average consumer price index	170.5	181.5	195.4	205.0	220.9

Source: FASB Statement No. 33, p. 34.

hensive restatement. The required disclosures will reflect much of the impact of general and specific price changes but will not show the total impact as comprehensive restatement would. On the other hand, there are significant problems with total restatement, and such an approach might be even more confusing to statement users.

Inflation and other economic environmental factors have already caused several countries to adopt accounting practices which reflect price changes. The Financial Accounting Standards Board has now taken a first step to make financial reporting in the United States more useful to statement users by reflecting the impact of changing prices. Continued developments in this area of financial reporting are expected over the next several years.

QUESTIONS

1. What has caused the increased interest in reporting financial statements adjusted for price changes?

2. Why have accountants traditionally preferred to report historical costs rather than current costs in conventional statements?

3. (1) Identify three alternatives to historical cost/nominal dollar financial statements. (2) Compare the concept of reporting current costs in financial statements with the concept of restating original dollar costs for general price-level changes.

4. How are general price indexes computed?

5. (1) Distinguish between monetary assets and nonmonetary assets. (2) Which of the following are monetary assets?

    (a) Cash
    (b) Investment in common stock
    (c) Investment in bonds
    (d) Merchandise on hand
    (e) Prepaid expenses
    (f) Buildings
    (g) Patents
    (h) Sinking fund — uninvested cash
    (i) Sinking fund — investments in real estate
    (j) Deferred developmental costs

6. Assume a company holds property or maintains the obligations listed below during a year in which there is an increase in the general price level. State in each case whether the position of the company at the end of the year is better, worse, or unchanged.

    (a) Cash
    (b) Cash surrender value of life insurance
    (c) Land
    (d) Unearned subscription revenue
    (e) Accounts receivable
    (f) Notes payable
    (g) Merchandise on hand
    (h) Long-term warranties on sales

7. Indicate whether a company sustains a gain or loss in purchasing power under each condition described below.

    (a) A company maintains an excess of monetary assets over monetary liabilities during a period of general price-level increase.
    (b) A company maintains an excess of monetary liabilities over monetary assets during a period of general price-level increase.
    (c) A company maintains an excess of monetary assets over monetary liabilities during a period of general price-level decrease.
    (d) A company maintains an excess of monetary liabilities over monetary assets during a period of general price-level decrease.

8. Some have suggested that accounting for the impact of changing prices should be limited to restatement of land, buildings, equipment, and related depreciation charges in terms of current purchasing power. Would you defend or reject such a proposal? Give your reasons.

9. Describe the restatement of inventories for general price-level changes when inventories are reported (a) on a first-in, first-out basis; (b) on a last-in, first-out basis.

10. The most time-consuming step in the restatement of accounts to report general price-level changes is the aging of the depreciable property and the corresponding restatement of the periodic depreciation. What is meant by aging as used here? Do you agree with this statement?

11. What are the advantages of current cost financial statements as compared to historical cost financial statements?

12. Distinguish between the current cost/constant dollar approach and the current cost/nominal dollar approach to financial reporting.

13. The Phares Company purchased land for $150,000 in 1980 when the price index was 150. At the end of 1981 when the price index was 175, the land had a fair market value of $180,000. How would the land be reported on the balance sheet under each of the following approaches?

    (a) Historical cost/nominal dollar
    (b) Historical cost/constant dollar
    (c) Current cost/nominal dollar
    (d) Current cost/constant dollar

EXERCISES

exercise 20-1

In each case below, compute the purchasing power gain or loss assuming that assets are held and liabilities are maintained during a period in which the general price level rises by 8%.

(a)	Cash	$ 50,000
	Accounts receivable	20,000
(b)	Cash	100,000
	Accounts payable	25,000
	Long-term payables	55,000
(c)	Cash	25,000
	Land	50,000
	Accounts payable	25,000
(d)	Cash	25,000
	Land and buildings	100,000
	Mortgage note payable	40,000

exercise 20-2

Assuming prices rise evenly by 9% during a year, compute the amount of the expense stated in terms of year-end constant dollars in each of the following independent cases:

(a) Expenses of $500,000 were paid at the beginning of the year for services received during the first half of the year.
(b) Expenses of $125,000 were paid at the end of each quarter for services received during the quarter.
(c) Expenses of $125,000 were paid at the beginning of each quarter for services received during the quarter.
(d) Expenses of $500,000 were paid at the end of the year for services received during the year.
(e) Expenses of $500,000 were paid evenly throughout the year for services received during the year.

In terms of year-end constant dollars, when is the best time to pay for services received in periods of rising prices?

exercise 20-3

Captain Ben's Seafood will prepare for the first time historical cost/constant dollar statements as of June 30, 1981. In connection with the restatement, an analysis of the equipment and related accumulated depreciation account was made before the 1981 adjustments for depreciation:

Year Acquired	Cost	Accumulated Depreciation June 30, 1980	Estimated Useful Life
1975	$100,000	$ 73,786	10 years
1977	250,000	147,600	10 years
1979	300,000	74,667	15 years
1980	50,000	33,333	3 years
1981	130,000	——	5 years

The double-declining balance method of depreciation is used with a full year's depreciation taken in the year of acquisition and none taken in the year of retirement. Adjust for general price-level changes the equipment and related accumulated depreciation account as of June 30, 1981. Round to the nearest dollar. Assume the general price index rose as follows:

June 30	Index
1975	100
1976	105
1977	110
1978	120
1979	130
1980	135
1981	145

exercise 20-4

A comparative income statement for the Benson Company for the first two years of operations appears below.

Results of Operations

	First Year		Second Year	
Sales		$750,000		$900,000
Cost of goods sold:				
Beginning inventory	—		$300,000	
Purchases	$750,000		500,000	
Goods available for sale	$750,000		$800,000	
Ending inventory	300,000	450,000	400,000	400,000
Gross profit on sales		$300,000		$500,000
Operating expenses:				
Depreciation	$ 30,000		$ 30,000	
Other	240,000	270,000	350,000	380,000
Net income		$ 30,000		$120,000
Dividends		15,000		30,000
Increase in retained earnings		$ 15,000		$ 90,000

Prepare a comparative income and retained earnings statement expressing items in constant dollars at the end of the second year, considering the following data:

(a) Prices rose evenly and index numbers expressing the general price-level changes were:
- Beginning of first year 100
- End of first year 110
- End of second year 140

(b) Sales and purchases were made and expenses were incurred evenly each year.

(c) Inventories were reported at cost using first-in, first-out pricing; average indexes for the year are applicable in restating inventories.

(d) Depreciation relates to equipment acquired at the beginning of the first year.

(e) Dividends were paid at the middle of each year.

(f) Assume no purchasing power gain or loss in either year.

exercise 20-5

Comparative balance sheet data for Forbes Industries, Inc., since its formation, appear below. The general price level during the two-year period went up steadily; index numbers expressing the general price-level changes are listed following the balance sheet. Restate the comparative balance sheet data in terms of constant dollars at the end of the second year.

	End of First Year	End of Second Year
Cash	$ 75,000	$ 62,500
Receivables	50,000	70,000
Land, buildings, and equipment (net)*	130,000	115,000
	$255,000	$247,500
Payables	$ 67,500	$ 45,000
Capital stock	160,000	160,000
Retained earnings	27,500	42,500
	$255,000	$247,500

*Acquired at the beginning of the first year.

Price Index

- At the beginning of the business 112
- At the end of the first year 125
- At the end of the second year 140

exercise 20-6

The income statement for Blaylock Oil Company is given below. Using the income statement, together with the additional data provided, prepare an income statement restated in terms of end-of-year constant dollars accompanied by a schedule summarizing the purchasing power gain or loss for the year.

Blaylock Oil Company
Income Statement
For Year Ended December 31, 19––

Sales			$990,000
Cost of goods sold:			
Beginning inventory		$ 150,000	
Purchases		900,000	
Goods available for sale		$1,050,000	
Ending inventory		450,000	600,000
Gross profit on sales			$390,000
Operating expenses			270,000
Income before income tax			$120,000
Income tax			60,000
Net income			$ 60,000

The general price level rose evenly from 140 to 160 in the preceding year and from 160 to 200 in the current year. Sales and purchases were made evenly and expenses were incurred evenly during the year. The average index is regarded as applicable in restating inventories. All of the company's assets and liabilities, both at the beginning and at the end of the period, were classified as current and, except for inventories, monetary. Current assets were $600,000 and current liabilities were $200,000 at the beginning of the year.

exercise 20-7

The historical cost/constant dollar income statement of the Hogan Corporation shows a purchasing power loss of $1,800 based on end-of-year constant dollars. Price indexes were as follows:

Beginning of year	220
Average	230
End of year	240

Calculate the purchasing power loss in average-year dollars as required by FASB Statement No. 33.

exercise 20-8

On September 1, 1981, Kaaren's Toy Store purchased 800 dolls at $2.50 per doll. As of December 31, 1981, Kaaren's had sold three fourths of the dolls at $6 per doll, and the doll manufacturer was selling to retailers at $3 per doll. With respect to the doll venture, how much should Kaaren's Toy Store recognize as (a) operating gain, (b) realized holding gain, and (c) unrealized holding gain under the current cost method of accounting?

PROBLEMS

problem 20-1

Classify the following accounts as either monetary or nonmonetary.

Assets	Liabilities and Stockholders' Equity
Current assets:	Current liabilities:
Cash	Accounts and notes payable
Marketable securities (stocks)	Dividends payable
Receivables (net of allowance)	Refundable deposits on returnable containers
Inventories	Advances on sales contracts
Prepaid rent	Long-term liabilities:
Discount on notes payable	Bonds payable
Deferred income tax expense	Premium on bonds payable
Long-term investments:	Stockholders' equity:
Affiliated companies, at cost	Preferred stock (at fixed liquidation price)
Cash surrender value of life insurance	Common stock
Bond sinking fund	Retained earnings
Investment in bonds	
Land, buildings, and equipment:	
Land	
Buildings	
Equipment	
Intangible assets:	
Patents	
Goodwill	
Advances paid on purchase contracts	

problem 20-2

The following information was taken from the books of the Fix-It Hardware Store during its first two years of operations:

	Useful Life	1980	1981
Beginning inventory		$150,000	$200,000
Purchases		550,000	500,000
Ending inventory		200,000	160,000
Building (acquired 1/1/80)	25 years	400,000	——
Office equipment (acquired 7/1/80)	12 years	30,000	——
Machinery (acquired 10/1/80)	8 years	16,000	——
Price index (1/1)		190	202
Price index (12/31)		202	214

Instructions:

(1) Calculate the cost of goods sold for 1980 and 1981 in terms of respective year-end dollars assuming a lifo inventory cost flow with average costs used for any increments. Assume the 1980 beginning inventory was purchased on January 1, 1980. Round to the nearest dollar amount.

(2) Restate depreciable assets and accumulated depreciation (straight-line, ignore salvage values) reporting the depreciation for 1980 and 1981 in terms of 1980 and 1981 year-end dollars respectively.

problem 20-3

The Camel Co. began operations in 1950. At the end of 1981 it was decided to furnish stockholders with a balance sheet restated in terms of uniform 1981 dollars as a supplement to the conventional financial statements. This is the first time such a statement was prepared. The balance sheet prepared in conventional form at the end of 1981 is shown on page 604.

All of the stock was issued in 1950. Land was purchased subject to a mortgage note of $1,000,000 at the time the company was formed. The present building is being depreciated on a straight-line basis with a 30-year life and no salvage value. The bonds were issued in 1960. The company uses the first-in, first-out method in pricing inventories.

Camel Co.
Balance Sheet
December 31, 1981

Cash	$ 187,600	Accounts payable	$ 379,900
Accounts receivable	342,400	Mortgage note payable	450,000
Inventory	742,300	Bonds payable	1,250,000
Land	1,720,000	Capital stock	1,000,000
Building	2,115,000	Premium on capital stock	200,000
Less accumulated depreciation	(705,000)	Retained earnings	1,122,400
		Total liabilities and	
Total assets	$4,402,300	stockholders' equity	$4,402,300

Instructions: Prepare a balance sheet for the Camel Co. restated in terms of 1981 dollars. Use the indexes below in making adjustments; assume the index for each year is regarded as representative of the price level for the entire year.

Year	Price Index	Year	Price Index
1950	54.9	1975	126.4
1960	70.7	1976	133.2
1965	75.9	1977	146.5
1970	93.0	1978	160.1
1971	96.8	1979	168.0
1972	100.0	1980	178.6
1973	105.9	1981	185.2
1974	116.2		

problem 20-4

The income statement prepared at the end of the year for the Phares Corporation follows:

Phares Corporation
Income Statement
For Year Ended December 31, 1981

Sales		$350,000
Less sales discount		15,000
Net sales		$335,000
Cost of goods sold:		
Inventory, January 1	$125,000	
Purchases	180,000	
Goods available for sale	$305,000	
Inventory, December 31	120,000	
Cost of goods sold		185,000
Gross profit on sales		$150,000
Operating expenses:		
Depreciation	$ 21,250	
Other operating expenses	50,000	
Total operating expenses		71,250
Income before income tax		$ 78,750
Income tax		31,300
Net income		$ 47,450

The following additional data are available:

(a) The price index rose evenly throughout the year from 120 on January 1 to 130 on December 31.

(b) Sales were made evenly throughout the year; expenses were incurred evenly throughout the year.

(c) The inventory was valued at cost using first-in, first-out pricing; average indexes for the year are used in restating inventories. The beginning inventory was acquired in the preceding period when the average index was 122.

(d) The depreciation charge related to the following items:

	Asset Cost	Index at Date of Acquisition	Depreciation Rate
Building	$75,000	95	3 %
Equipment	80,000	95	12½%
Equipment	20,000	98	12½%
Equipment*	39,000	120	16⅔%

*Acquired at the beginning of the current year.

(e) Semiannual dividends of $7,500 were declared and paid at the end of June and at the end of December.

(f) The balance sheet position for the company changed during the year as follows:

	January 1	December 31
Current assets	$180,000	$174,700
Building and equipment (net)	120,000	137,750
	$300,000	$312,450
Current liabilities	$ 55,000	$ 35,000
Capital stock	200,000	200,000
Retained earnings	45,000	77,450
	$300,000	$312,450

Instructions: Prepare a statement of income and retained earnings in which items are stated in end-of-year dollars accompanied by a schedule summarizing the purchasing power gain or loss for 1981.

problem 20-5

Financial statements are prepared for the Carver Co. at the end of each year in conventional form and also in general price-level adjusted form. Balance sheet data summarized in conventional and in general price-level form at the end of 1980 are given below.

	Conventional Form		General Price-Level Form (Reporting Purchasing Power at End of Year)	
Assets:				
Cash		$ 23,000		$ 23,000
Accounts receivable		70,000		70,000
Inventory		105,000		106,500
Buildings and equipment	$120,000		$153,600	
Less accumulated depreciation	48,000	72,000	61,440	92,160
Land		50,000		64,000
Total assets		$320,000		$355,660
Liabilities:				
Accounts payable		$ 48,000		$ 48,000
Long-term liabilities		40,000		40,000
Total liabilities		$ 88,000		$ 88,000
Stockholders' equity:				
Capital stock		$150,000		$192,000
Retained earnings		82,000		75,660
Total stockholders' equity		$232,000		$267,660
Total liabilities and stockholders' equity		$320,000		$355,660

Data from statements prepared in conventional form at the end of 1981 are given below:

Balance Sheet			Income Statement		
Assets			Sales		$1,100,000
Cash		$ 83,840	Cost of goods sold		600,000
Accounts receivable		72,500	Gross profit on sales		$ 500,000
Inventory		125,000	Operating expenses		308,000
Buildings and equipment		120,000			
Accumulated depreciation		(56,000)	Income before income tax		$ 192,000
Land		50,000	Income tax		85,660
		$395,340	Net income		$ 106,340
			Dividends		20,000
Liabilities and Stockholders' Equity			Increase in retained earnings		$ 86,340
Accounts payable		$ 37,000			
Long-term liabilities		40,000			
Capital stock		150,000			
Retained earnings		168,340			
		$395,340			

The following additional data are available at the end of 1981:

(a) Price indexes were as follows for the year:

January 1	150
December 31	153

The price level rose steadily during the year.

(b) Sales and purchases were made evenly and expenses were incurred evenly throughout the year.

(c) The first-in, first-out method was used to compute inventory cost; average indexes for the year are used in restating inventories.

(d) All of the land, buildings, and equipment were acquired when the company was formed.

(e) Dividends were declared and paid at the end of the year.

Instructions: Prepare in terms of end-of-year dollars: (1) an income and retained earnings statement accompanied by a schedule summarizing the purchasing power gain or loss for 1981; (2) a balance sheet as of December 31, 1981.

problem 20-6

Inventory information for the Charlotte Company is presented below.

	Historical Cost/ Nominal Dollar	Current Cost/ Nominal Dollar
Beginning inventory	$ 60,000	
Purchases	240,000	
Ending inventory	75,000	$90,000

The Charlotte Company uses the fifo inventory method.

The beginning inventory was purchased when the price index was 100. The ending inventory was purchased when the index was 120. Purchases were made evenly throughout the year. The current value of the goods sold was $270,000.

General price indexes were as follows:

Beginning of year	100
Average index	120
End of year	140

Instructions: Compute the cost of goods sold and ending inventory under each of the following accounting methods.
(a) Historical cost/nominal dollar
(b) Historical cost/end-of-year constant dollar
(c) Current cost/nominal dollar
(d) Current cost/end-of-year constant dollar

problem 20-7

The historical cost income statement for the Hawkeye Company is presented below.

Hawkeye Company
Income Statement
For the Year Ended December 31, 1981

Sales..		$180,000
Cost of goods sold:		
Beginning inventory...	$ 20,000	
Purchases...	140,000	
Goods available for sale..	$160,000	
Ending inventory	50,000	
Cost of goods sold		110,000
Gross profit..		$ 70,000
Operating expenses:		
Depreciation expense	$ 10,000	
Other expenses..	20,000	30,000
Net income..		$ 40,000

The following additional information is provided:

(a) Sales, purchases, and other expenses were incurred evenly over the year.
(b) The beginning inventory was purchased when the price index was 180. Assume the ending inventory was acquired when the price index was 220.
(c) Price indexes were as follows:

Beginning of year... 200
Average for the year..................................... 220
End of year... 240

(d) The equipment on which the depreciation expense is computed was purchased when the price index was 110.

Instructions: Prepare a statement showing income from continuing operations in average-year constant dollars as required by FASB Statement No. 33.

21

Financial Statement Analysis

CHAPTER OBJECTIVES

Describe the objectives of financial statement analysis.

Explain the major techniques used in analyzing financial statements.

Identify key company characteristics and related measurements.

Accounting provides information to assist various individuals in making economic decisions. A significant amount of information relevant to this purpose is presented in the primary financial statements of companies. Additional useful information is provided by reporting data in other than the financial statements. However, financial data are only part of the total information needed by decision makers. Nonfinancial data may also be relevant. Thus, the total information spectrum is broader than just financial reporting. It encompasses financial statements, financial reporting by means other than the financial statements, and additional nonfinancial information. The major categories of information are summarized on page 609 and classified according to whether the information is required by generally accepted accounting principles or is voluntary.

The Financial Accounting Standards Board has restricted its focus to general-purpose external financial reporting by business enterprises. This chapter concentrates on analysis of information in the primary financial statements. Notes are an integral part of financial statements. Significant accounting policies and other information included in notes to financial statements should be considered carefully in performing an analysis and in evaluating results. Supplementary information should also be considered in interpreting financial statement data.

INFORMATION SPECTRUM

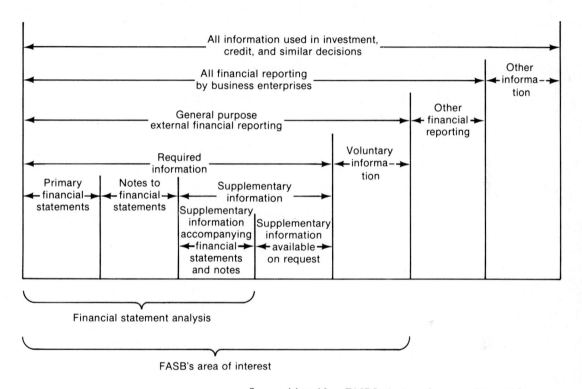

Source: Adapted from FASB *Invitation to Comment*, "Financial Statements and Other Means of Financial Reporting" (May 1980), p. 2.

OBJECTIVES OF FINANCIAL STATEMENT ANALYSIS

Nearly all businesses prepare financial statements of some type; the form and complexity of the statements vary according to the needs of those who prepare and use them. The owner of a small business might simply list the firm's cash receipts and disbursements and prepare an income tax return. On the other hand, a large corporation's accounting staff might work all year preparing its complex financial statements.

Whatever their form, financial statements serve to provide information about a business and its operations to interested users. For example, questions may be raised by external users concerning matters such as a company's sales, earnings, and trends for these items; the amount of working capital and changes in working capital; the relationship of earnings to sales, and of earnings to investments. These questions require analysis of data reported on the income statement, the balance sheet, and the statement of changes in financial position. Internal management is also concerned with analyzing the general-purpose financial statements, but requires additional special information in setting policies and making decisions. Questions may arise on matters such as the performance of various company divisions, the income from sales of individual products, and whether to make or buy product parts and equipment. These questions can be answered by establishing internal information systems to provide the necessary data. Thus, in analyzing financial data, keep in mind that the nature of analysis and the information needed depend on the requirements of users and the issues involved.

The analyses of financial data described in this chapter are directed primarily to the information needs of external users who must generally rely on the financial reports issued by a company. Many groups are interested in the data found in financial statements, including:

1. Owners — sole proprietor, partners, or stockholders.
2. Management, including board of directors.
3. Creditors.
4. Government — local, state, and federal (including regulatory, taxing, and statistical units).
5. Prospective owners and prospective creditors.
6. Stock exchanges, investment bankers, and stockbrokers.
7. Trade associations.
8. Employees of the business and their labor unions.
9. The general public (including students and researchers).

Questions raised by these groups can generally be answered by analyses that develop comparisons and measure relationships between components of financial statements. The analyses will form a basis for decisions made by the user.

Analysis is generally directed toward evaluating four aspects of a business: (1) liquidity, (2) stability, (3) profitability, and (4) growth potential.

To be liquid, a business must be able to meet its liabilities as they mature. The financial statements are analyzed to determine whether the business is currently liquid and whether it could retain its liquidity in a period of adversity. The analysis includes studies of the relationship of current assets to current liabilities, the size and nature of creditor and ownership interests, the protection afforded creditors and owners through sound asset values, and the amounts and trends of earnings.

Stability is measured by the ability of a business to make interest and principal payments on outstanding debt and to pay regular dividends to its stockholders. In judging stability, data concerning operations and financial position require study. For example, there must be a regular demand for the goods or services sold, and the margin on sales must be sufficient to cover operating expenses, interest, and dividends. There should be a satisfactory turnover of assets, and all business resources should be productivly employed.

Profitability is measured by the ability of a business to maintain a satisfactory dividend policy while at the same time steadily increasing ownership equity. The nature and amount of earnings, as well as their regularity and trend, are all significant factors affecting profitability.

The growth potential of a company is also of primary importance. This element, along with profitability, directly affects future cash flows, derived from increased earnings and/or appreciation in stock values. Growth potential is measured by the expansion and growth into new markets, the rate of growth in existing markets, the rate of growth in earnings per share, and the amount of expenditures for research and development.

An analysis must serve the needs of those for whom it is made. For example, owners are interested in a company's ability to obtain additional capital for current needs and possible expansion. Creditors are interested not only in the position of a business as a going concern but also in its position if it should be forced to liquidate.

ANALYTICAL PROCEDURES

Analytical procedures fall into two main categories: (1) comparisons and measurements based on financial data for two or more periods, and (2) comparisons and measurements based on financial data of only the current fiscal period. The first category includes comparative statements, ratios and trends for data on successive statements, and analyses of changes in the balance sheet, income statement, and statement of changes in financial position. The second category includes determining current balance sheet and income statement relationships and analyzing earnings and earning power. A review of financial data usually requires both types of analysis.

The analytical procedures commonly employed may be identified as: comparative statements, index-number trend series, common-size statements, and analysis of financial statement components. These techniques are described and illustrated in the following sections. It should be emphasized that the analyses illustrated herein are simply guides to the evaluation of financial data. Sound conclusions can be reached only through intelligent use and interpretation of such data.

Comparative Statements

Financial data become more meaningful when compared with similar data for preceding periods. Statements reflecting financial data for two or more periods are called **comparative statements**. Annual data can be compared with similar data for prior years. Monthly or quarterly data can be compared with similar data for previous months or quarters or with similar data for the same months or quarters of previous years.

Comparative data allow statement users to analyze trends in a company, thus enhancing the usefulness of information for decision making. The Accounting Principles Board stated that comparisons between financial statements are most informative and useful under the following conditions:

1. The presentations are in good form; that is, the arrangement within the statements is identical.
2. The content of the statements is identical; that is, the same items from the underlying accounting records are classified under the same captions.
3. Accounting principles are not changed or, if they are changed, the financial effects of the changes are disclosed.
4. Changes in circumstances or in the nature of the underlying transactions are disclosed.[1]

To the extent that the above criteria are not met, comparisons may be misleading. The factors of consistency in practices and procedures and reporting periods of equal and regular lengths are also important, especially when comparisons are made for a single enterprise.

Comparative financial statements may be even more useful to investors and others when the reporting format highlights absolute changes in dollar amounts as well as relative percentage changes. Statement users will benefit by considering both amounts as they make their analyses. For example, an investor may decide that any change in a financial statement amount of ten percent or more should be investigated further. A ten percent change in an amount of $1,000, however, is not as significant as a five percent change in an amount of $100,000. When absolute or relative amounts appear out of line, conclusions, favorable or unfavorable, are not justified until investigation has disclosed reasons for the changes.

The development of data measuring changes taking place over a number of periods is known as **horizontal analysis**. Using the Wycat Corporation's income statement as an example, and a reporting format that discloses both dollar and percentage changes, horizontal analysis is illustrated on page 613.

Index-Number Trend Series

When comparative financial statements present information for more than two or three years, they become cumbersome and potentially confusing. A technique used to overcome this problem is referred to as an **index-number trend series**.

To compute index numbers, the statement preparer must first choose a base year. This may be the earliest year presented or some other year considered particularly appropriate. Next, the base year amounts are all expressed as 100 percent. The amounts for all other years are then expressed as a percentage of the base year amounts. Index numbers can only be computed when amounts are positive. The set of percentages for several years may thus be interpreted as trend values or as a series of index numbers relating to a particular item. For example, Wycat Corporation had gross sales of $1,000,000 in 1979, $1,750,000 in 1980, and $1,500,000 in 1981. These amounts, expressed in an index-number trend series with 1979 as the base year, would be 100, 175, and 150, respectively.

---

[1] *Statements of the Accounting Principles Board, No. 4,* "Basic Concepts and Accounting Principles Underlying Financial Statements of Business Enterprises" (New York: American Institute of Certified Public Accountants, 1970), par. 95–99.

Wycat Corporation
Condensed Comparative Income Statement
For Years Ended December 31

| | 1981 | 1980 | 1979 | Increase (Decrease) | | | |
| | | | | 1980–1981 | | 1979–1980 | |
				Amount	Percent	Amount	Percent
Gross sales	$1,500,000	$1,750,000	$1,000,000	$(250,000)	(14%)	$750,000	75%
Sales returns	75,000	100,000	50,000	(25,000)	(25%)	50,000	100%
Net sales	$1,425,000	$1,650,000	$ 950,000	$(225,000)	(14%)	$700,000	74%
Cost of goods sold	1,000,000	1,200,000	630,000	(200,000)	(17%)	570,000	90%
Gross profit on sales	$ 425,000	$ 450,000	$ 320,000	$ (25,000)	(6%)	$130,000	41%
Selling expense	$ 280,000	$ 300,000	$ 240,000	$ (20,000)	(7%)	$ 60,000	25%
General expense	100,000	110,000	100,000	(10,000)	(9%)	10,000	10%
Total operating expenses	$ 380,000	$ 410,000	$ 340,000	$ (30,000)	(7%)	$ 70,000	21%
Operating income (loss)	$ 45,000	$ 40,000	$ (20,000)	$ 5,000	13%	$ 60,000	——
Other revenue items	85,000	75,000	50,000	10,000	13%	25,000	50%
	$ 130,000	$ 115,000	$ 30,000	$ 15,000	13%	$ 85,000	283%
Other expense items	30,000	30,000	10,000	——	——	20,000	200%
Income before income tax	$ 100,000	$ 85,000	$ 20,000	$ 15,000	18%	$ 65,000	325%
Income tax	30,000	25,000	5,000	5,000	20%	20,000	400%
Net income	$ 70,000	$ 60,000	$ 15,000	$ 10,000	17%	$ 45,000	300%

The index-number trend series technique is a type of horizontal analysis. It can give statement users a long-range view of a firm's financial position, earnings, and sources and uses of funds. The user needs to recognize, however, that long-range trend series are particularly sensitive to inflation.

Data expressed in terms of a base year are frequently useful for comparisons with similar data provided by business or industry sources or government agencies. When information used for making comparisons does not employ the same base period, it will have to be restated. Restatement of a base year calls for the expressing of each value as a percentage of the value for the base-year period.

To illustrate, assume the net sales data for the Wycat Corporation for 1979–1981 are to be compared with a sales index for its particular industry. The industry sales indexes are as follows:

	1981	1980	1979
(1972 − 1974 = 100)	146	157	124

Recognizing 1979 as the base year, industry sales are restated as follows:

1979	100
1980 (157 ÷ 124)	127
1981 (146 ÷ 124)	118

Industry sales and net sales for the Wycat Corporation can now be expressed in comparative form as follows:

	1981	1980	1979
Industry sales index	118	127	100
Wycat Corporation sales index*......................	150	174	100

*From comparative income statement on page 613.

Common-Size Financial Statements

Horizontal analysis measures changes over a number of accounting periods. Statement users also need data that express relationships within a single period, which is known as **vertical analysis**. Preparation of **common-size financial statements** is a widely used vertical analysis technique. The common-size relationships may be stated in terms of percentages or in terms of ratios. Common-size statements may be prepared for the same business as of different dates or periods, or for two or more business units as of the same date or for the same period.

Common-size financial statements are useful in analyzing the internal structure of a financial statement. For example, a common-size balance sheet expresses each amount as a percentage of total assets. A common-size income statement usually shows each revenue or expense item as a percentage of net sales. As an illustration, a comparative balance sheet for Wycat Corporation with each item expressed in both dollar amounts and percentages is shown on page 615. Other types of common-size financial statements, e.g., a common-size retained earnings statement or statement of changes in financial position, may be prepared. When a supporting schedule shows the detail for a group total, individual items may be expressed as percentages of either the base figure or the group total.

In preparing common-size statements for two companies, it is important that the financial data for each company reflect comparable price levels. Furthermore, the financial data should be developed using comparable accounting methods, classification procedures, and valuation bases. Comparisons should be limited to companies engaged in similar activities. When the financial policies of two companies are different, these differences should be recognized in evaluating comparative reports. For example, one company may lease its properties while the other may purchase such items; one company may finance its operations using long-term borrowing while the other may rely primarily on funds supplied by stockholders and by earnings. Operating results for two companies under these circumstances cannot be wholly comparable.

The above suggests that comparisons between different companies should be approached with care, and should be made with a full understanding of the inherent limitations. Reference was made earlier to the criteria that the Accounting Principles Board identified if comparisons are to be meaningful. Comparability between enterprises is more difficult to obtain than comparability within a single enterprise. Ideally, differences in companies' financial reports should arise from basic differences in the companies themselves or from the nature of their transactions and not from differences in accounting practices and procedures.

Wycat Corporation
Condensed Comparative Balance Sheet
December 31

	1981		1980		1979	
	Amount	Percent	Amount	Percent	Amount	Percent
Assets						
Current assets	$ 855,000	38%	$ 955,500	40%	$ 673,500	38%
Long-term investments	500,000	22	400,000	17	250,000	14
Land, buildings, and equipment (net)	775,000	34	875,000	37	675,000	38
Intangible assets	100,000	4	100,000	4	100,000	6
Other assets	48,000	2	60,500	2	61,500	4
Total assets	$2,278,000	100%	$2,391,000	100%	$1,760,000	100%
Liabilities						
Current liabilities	$ 410,000	18%	$ 546,000	23%	$ 130,000	7%
Long-term liabilities — 8% bonds	400,000	18	400,000	17	300,000	17
Total liabilities	$ 810,000	36%	$ 946,000	40%	$ 430,000	24%
Stockholders' Equity						
Preferred 6% stock	$ 350,000	15%	$ 350,000	15%	$ 250,000	14%
Common stock	750,000	33	750,000	31	750,000	43
Additional paid-in capital	100,000	4	100,000	4	100,000	6
Retained earnings	268,000	12	245,000	10	230,000	13
Total stockholders' equity	$1,468,000	64%	$1,445,000	60%	$1,330,000	76%
Total liabilities and stockholders' equity	$2,278,000	100%	$2,391,000	100%	$1,760,000	100%

Other Analytical Procedures

In addition to the financial statement analysis procedures described in the preceding sections, various measures may be developed with respect to specific components of financial statements. Some measurements are of general interest, while others have special significance to particular groups. Creditors, for example, are concerned with the ability of a company to pay its current obligations and seek information about the relationship of current assets to current liabilities. Stockholders are concerned with dividends and seek information relating to earnings that will form the basis for dividends. Managements are concerned with the activity of the merchandise stock and seek information relating to the number of times goods have turned over during the period. All users are vitally interested in profitability and wish to be informed about the relationship of earnings to both liabilities and owners' equity.

The computation of percentages, ratios, turnovers, and other measures of financial position and operating results for a period is a form of vertical analysis. Comparison with the same measures for other periods is a form of horizontal analysis. The measures described and illustrated in the following sections should not be considered all-inclusive; other measures may be useful to various groups, depending upon their particular needs. It should be emphasized again that sound conclusions cannot be reached from an individual measurement. But this information, together with adequate investigation and study, may lead to a satisfactory evaluation of financial data.

Liquidity Analysis

Generally, the first concern of a financial analyst is a firm's liquidity. Will the firm be able to meet its current obligations? If a firm cannot meet its obligations in the short run, it may not have a chance to be profitable or to experience growth in the long run. The two most commonly used measures of liquidity are the current ratio and the acid-test ratio.

Current Ratio. The comparison of current assets with current liabilities is regarded as a fundamental measurement of a company's liquidity. Known as the **current ratio** or **working capital ratio**, this measurement is computed by dividing total current assets by total current liabilities.

The current ratio is a measure of ability to meet current obligations. Since it measures liquidity, care must be taken to determine that proper items have been included in the current asset and current liability categories. A ratio of current assets to current liabilities of less than 2 to 1 for a trading or manufacturing unit has frequently been considered unsatisfactory. However, because liquidity needs are different for different industries and companies, any such arbitrary measure should not be viewed as meaningful or appropriate in all cases. A comfortable margin of current assets over current liabilities suggests that a company will be able to meet maturing obligations even in the event of unfavorable business conditions or losses on such assets as marketable securities, receivables, and inventories.

For the Wycat Corporation, current ratios for 1981 and 1980 are developed as follows:[2]

	1981	1980
Current assets	$855,000	$955,500
Current liabilities	$410,000	$546,000
Current ratio	**2.1:1**	**1.8:1**

A current ratio of 2.1 to 1 means that Wycat could liquidate its total current liabilities 2.1 times using only its current assets.

Ratio calculations are sometimes carried out to two or more decimal places; however, ratios do not need to be carried beyond one place unless some particularly significant interpretative value is afforded by the more refined measurement.

It is possible to overemphasize the importance of a high current ratio. Assume a company is normally able to carry on its operations with current assets of $200,000 and current liabilities of $100,000. If the company has current assets of $500,000 and current liabilities remain at $100,000, its current ratio has increased from 2:1 to 5:1. The company now has considerably more working capital than it requires. It should also be observed that

---

[2]Comparative data for more than two years are generally required in evaluating financial trends. Analyses for only two years are given in the examples in this chapter, since these are sufficient to illustrate the analytical procedures involved.

certain unfavorable conditions may be accompanied by an improving ratio. For example, with a slowdown in business and postponement of advertising and research programs and building and equipment repairs and replacements, a company's cash balance may rise. At the same time, slower customer collections may result in rising trade receivables, and reduced sales volume may result in rising inventories.

Acid-Test Ratio. A test of a company's immediate liquidity is made by comparing the sum of cash, marketable securities, notes receivable, and accounts receivable, commonly referred to as **quick assets**, with current liabilities. The total quick assets divided by current liabilities gives the **acid-test ratio** or **quick ratio**. Considerable time may be required to convert raw materials, goods in process, and finished goods into receivables and then into cash. A company with a satisfactory current ratio may be in a poor liquidity position when inventories form most of the total current assets. This is revealed by the acid-test ratio. In developing the ratio, the receivables and securities included in the total quick assets should be examined closely. In some cases these items may actually be less liquid than inventories.

Usually, a ratio of quick assets to current liabilities of at least 1 to 1 is considered desirable. Again, however, special conditions of the particular business must be evaluated. Questions such as the following should be considered: What is the composition of the quick assets? What special requirements are made by current activities upon these assets? How soon are current payables due?

Acid-test ratios for Wycat Corporation are computed as follows:

	1981	1980
Quick assets:		
Cash	$ 60,000	$100,500
Marketable securities	150,000	150,000
Receivables (net)	420,000	375,000
Total quick assets	$630,000	$625,500
Total current liabilities	$410,000	$546,000
Acid-test ratio	**1.5:1**	**1.1:1**

Other Measures of Liquidity. Other ratios may help to analyze a company's liquidity. For example, it may be useful to show the relationship of total current assets to total assets, and of individual current assets, such as receivables and inventories, to total current assets. In the case of liabilities, it may be useful to show the relationship of total current liabilities to total liabilities, and of individual current liabilities to total current liabilities.

The foregoing comparisons may provide information concerning the relative liquidity of total assets and the maturity of total obligations as well as the structure of working capital and shifts within the working capital group. The latter data are significant, since all items within the current classification are not equally current. What may be considered reasonable relationships in analyzing liquidity depends on the particular enterprise.

Activity Analysis

There are special tests that may be applied to measure how efficiently a firm is utilizing its assets. Several of these measures also relate to liquidity because they involve significant working capital elements, such as receivables, inventories, and accounts payable.

Accounts Receivable Turnover. The amount of receivables usually bears a close relationship to the volume of credit sales. The receivable position and approximate collection time may be evaluated by computing the **accounts receivable turnover**. This rate is determined by dividing net credit sales (or total net sales if credit sales are unknown) by the average trade notes and accounts receivable outstanding. In developing an average receivables amount, monthly balances should be used if available.

Assume in the case of Wycat Corporation that all sales are made on credit, that receivables arise only from sales, and that receivable totals for only the beginning and the end of the year are available. Receivable turnover rates are computed as follows:

	1981	1980
Net credit sales	$1,425,000	$1,650,000
Net receivables:		
Beginning of year	$ 375,000	$ 333,500
End of year	$ 420,000	$ 375,000
Average receivables	$ 397,500	$ 354,250
Receivables turnover for year	**3.6**	**4.7**

Number of Days' Sales in Receivables. Average receivables are sometimes expressed in terms of the **number of days' sales in receivables**, which shows the average time required to collect receivables. Assume for convenience that there are 360 days per year. Annual sales divided by 360 equals average daily sales. Average receivables divided by average daily sales then gives the number of days' sales in average receivables. This procedure for Wycat Corporation is illustrated below.

	1981	1980
Average receivables	$ 397,500	$ 354,250
Net credit sales	$1,425,000	$1,650,000
Average daily credit sales (net credit sales ÷ 360)	$ 3,958	$ 4,583
Number of days' sales in average receivables (average receivables ÷ average daily credit sales)	**100**	**77**

This same measurement can be obtained by dividing the number of days in the year by the receivable turnover. The same number of days for each year should be used in developing comparisons. Computations are generally based on the calendar year, consisting of 365 days, often rounded to 360 days, or a business year consisting of 300 days (365 days less Sundays and holidays). The calendar year basis, rounded to 360 days, is used here.

In some cases, instead of developing the number of days' sales in average receivables, it may be more useful to report the number of days' credit sales in receivables at the end of the period. This information would be significant in evaluating current position, and particularly the receivable position as of a given date. This information for Wycat Corporation is presented below:

	1981	1980
Receivables at end of year	$420,000	$375,000
Average daily credit sales...	$ 3,958	$ 4,583
Number of days' sales in receivables at end of year	**106**	**82**

What constitutes a reasonable number of days in receivables varies with individual businesses. For example, if merchandise is sold on terms of net 60 days, 40 days' sales in receivables would be reasonable; but if terms are net 30 days, a receivable balance equal to 40 days' sales would indicate slow collections.

Sales activity just before the close of a period should be considered when interpreting accounts receivable measurements. If sales are unusually light or heavy just before the end of the fiscal period, this affects total receivables as well as the related measurements. When such unevenness prevails, it may be better to analyze accounts receivable according to their due dates, as was illustrated in Chapter 7.

The problem of minimizing accounts receivable without losing desirable business is important. Receivables usually do not earn revenue, and the cost of carrying them must be covered by the profit margin. The longer accounts are carried, the smaller will be the percentage return realized on invested capital. In addition, heavier bookkeeping and collection charges and increased bad debts must be considered.

To attract business, credit is frequently granted for relatively long periods. The cost of granting long-term credit should be considered. Assume that a business has average daily credit sales of $5,000 and average accounts receivable of $250,000, which represents 50 days' credit sales. If collections and the credit period can be improved so that accounts receivable represent only 30 days' sales, then accounts receivable will be reduced to $150,000. Assuming a total cost of 10% to carry and service the accounts, the $100,000 decrease would yield annual savings of $10,000.

Inventory Turnover. The inventory carried frequently relates closely to sales volume. The inventory position and the appropriateness of its size may be evaluated by computing the **inventory turnover**. The inventory turnover is computed by dividing cost of goods sold by average inventory. Whenever possible, monthly figures should be used to develop the average inventory balance.

Assume that for Wycat Corporation the inventory balances for only the beginning and the end of the year are available. Inventory turnover rates are computed as follows:

	1981	1980
Cost of goods sold	$1,000,000	$1,200,000
Merchandise inventory:		
Beginning of year	$ 330,000	$ 125,000
End of year	$ 225,000	$ 330,000
Average merchandise inventory	$ 277,500	$ 227,500
Inventory turnover for year	**3.6**	**5.3**

Number of Days' Sales in Inventories. Average inventories are sometimes expressed as the **number of days' sales in inventories**. Information is thus afforded concerning the average time it takes to turn over the inventory. The number of days' sales in inventories is calculated by dividing average inventory by average daily cost of goods sold. The number of days' sales can also be obtained by dividing the number of days in the year by the inventory turnover rate. The latter procedure for Wycat Corporation is illustrated below:

	1981	1980
Inventory turnover for year	3.6	5.3
Number of days' sales in average inventory (assuming a year of 360 days)	**100**	**68**

As was the case with receivables, instead of developing the number of days' sales in average inventories, it may be more useful to report the number of days' sales in ending inventories. The latter measurement is determined by dividing ending inventory by average daily cost of goods sold. This information is helpful in evaluating the current asset position and particularly the inventory position as of a given date.

A company with departmental classifications for merchandise will find it desirable to support the company's inventory measurements with individual department measurements, since there may be considerable variation among departments. A manufacturing company may compute separate turnover rates for finished goods, goods in process, and raw materials. The finished goods turnover is computed by dividing cost of goods sold by average finished goods inventory. Goods in process turnover is computed by dividing cost of goods manufactured by average goods in process inventory. Raw materials turnover is computed by dividing the cost of raw materials used by average raw materials inventory.

The same valuation methods must be employed for inventories in successive periods if the inventory measurements are to be comparable. Maximum accuracy is possible if information relating to inventories and amount of goods sold is available in terms of physical units rather than dollar costs.

The effect of seasonal factors on the size of year-end inventories should be considered in inventory analyses. Inventories may be abnormally high or low at the end of a period. Many companies adopt a fiscal year ending when operations are at their lowest point. This is called a *natural business year*. Inventories will normally be lowest at the end of such a period, so that the organization can take inventory and complete year-end closing most conveniently. Under these circumstances, monthly inventory balances should be used to arrive at a representative average inventory figure. When a periodic inventory system is employed, monthly inventories may be estimated using the gross profit method as explained in Chapter 9.

With an increased inventory turnover, the investment necessary for a given volume of business is smaller, and consequently the return on invested capital is higher. This conclusion assumes an enterprise can acquire goods in smaller quantities sufficiently often at no price disadvantage. If merchandise must be bought in very large quantities in order to get favorable prices, then the savings on quantity purchases must be weighed against the additional investment, increased costs of storage, and other carrying charges.

The financial advantage of an increased turnover rate may be illustrated as follows. Assuming cost of goods sold of $1,000,000 and average inventory at cost of $250,000, inventory turnover is 4 times. Assume, further, that through careful buying the same business volume can be maintained with turnover of 5 times, or an average inventory of only $200,000. If interest on money invested in inventory is 10%, the savings on the $50,000 will be $5,000 annually. The above does not include advantages of decreased merchandise spoilage and obsolescence, savings in storage cost, taxes, and insurance, and reduction in risk of losses from price declines.

Inventory investments and turnover rates vary among different businesses. The facts of each business must be judged in terms of its financial structure and operations. Each business must plan an inventory policy that will avoid the extremes of a dangerously low stock, which may impair sales, and an overstocking of goods involving a heavy capital investment and risks of spoilage and obsolescence, price declines, and difficulties in meeting purchase obligations.

Total Asset Turnover. A measure of the overall efficiency of asset utilization is the ratio of net sales to total assets, sometimes called the **asset turnover rate**. This ratio is calculated by dividing net sales by total assets. The resulting figure indicates the contribution made by total assets to sales. With comparative data, judgments can be made concerning the relative effectiveness of asset utilization. A ratio increase may suggest more efficient asset utilization, although a point may be reached where there is a strain on assets and a company is unable to achieve its full sales potential. An increase in total assets accompanied by a ratio decrease may suggest overinvestment in assets or inefficient utilization.

In developing the ratio, long-term investments should be excluded from total assets when they make no contribution to sales. On the other hand, a valuation for leased property should be added to total assets to permit comparability between companies owning their properties and those that lease them. If monthly figures for assets are available, they may be used in developing a representative average for total assets employed. Often the year-end asset total is used for the computation. When sales can be expressed in terms of units sold, ratios of sales units to total assets offer more reliable interpretations than sales dollars, since unit sales are not affected by price changes.

Assume that for Wycat Corporation only asset totals for the beginning and end of the year are available, and that sales cannot be expressed in terms of units. Ratios of net sales to total assets are computed as follows:

	1981	1980
Net sales	$1,425,000	$1,650,000
Total assets (excluding long-term investments):		
Beginning of year	$1,991,000	$1,510,000
End of year	$1,778,000	$1,991,000
Average total assets	$1,884,500	$1,750,500
Ratio of net sales to average total assets	**0.8:1**	**0.9:1**

Other Measures of Activity. Turnover analysis, as illustrated for receivables, inventories, and total assets, can also be applied to other assets or groups of assets. For example, current asset turnover is calculated by dividing net sales by average current assets. This figure may be viewed as the number of times current assets are replenished, or as the number of sales dollars generated per dollar of current assets. Increases in turnover rates generally indicate more efficient utilization of assets.

Similar procedures may also be used to analyze specific liabilities. An accounts payable turnover, for example, may be computed by dividing purchases by average payables; the number of days' purchases in accounts payable may be computed by dividing accounts payable by average daily purchases. Assuming that all purchases are made on credit, all accounts payable arise from purchases, and that accounts payable totals are available only for the beginning and end of the year, the accounts payable turnover and the number of days' purchases in accounts payable for Wycat Corporation are computed as follows:

	1981	1980
Net purchases	$895,000	$1,405,000
Net accounts payable:		
Beginning of year	$546,000	$ 130,000
End of year	$410,000	$ 546,000
Average accounts payable	$478,000	$ 338,000
Accounts payable turnover for year	**1.9**	**4.2**

	1981	1980
Average payables	$478,000	$ 338,000
Net purchases	$895,000	$1,405,000
Average daily purchases (net purchases ÷ 360)	$ 2,486	$ 3,903
Number of days' purchases in accounts payable	**192**	**87**

Analysis of liabilities in terms of due dates may assist management in cash planning. Useful relationships may also be obtained by comparing specific assets or liabilities with other assets or liabilities, or with asset or liability totals. For example, data concerning the relationship of cash to accounts payable or of cash to total liabilities may be useful.

Profitability Analysis

Profitability analysis provides evidence concerning the earnings potential of a company and how effectively a firm is being managed. Since the reason most firms exist is to earn profits, the profitability ratios are among the most significant financial ratios. The adequacy of earnings may be measured in terms of (1) the rate earned on sales, (2) the rate earned on total assets, (3) the rate earned on stockholders' equity, and (4) the availability of earnings to common stockholders. Thus, the most popular profitability measurements are profit margin on sales, return on investment ratios, and earnings per share.

Profit Margin on Sales. The ratio of income to sales determines the **profit margin on sales**. This measurement represents the profit percentage per dollar of sales. The percentage is computed by dividing net income by net sales for a period. For Wycat Corporation, the profit margin on sales is:

	1981	1980
Net income	$ 70,000	$ 60,000
Net sales	$1,425,000	$1,650,000
Profit margin rate	**4.9%**	**3.6%**

This means that for 1981, Wycat generated almost five cents of profit per dollar of sales revenue. Because net income is used in the computation, any extraordinary or irregular items may distort the profit margin rate with respect to normal operating activities. Adjustments may be needed in the analysis to account for such items.

Rate Earned on Total Assets. Overall asset productivity may be expressed as the **rate earned on total assets**, also referred to as the **return on investment (ROI)** or the **asset productivity rate**. The rate is computed by dividing net income by the total assets used to produce net income. This rate measures the efficiency in using resources to generate net income. If total assets by months are available, they should be used to develop an average for the year. Frequently, however, the assets at the beginning of the year or the assets at the end of the year are used. In some cases it may be desirable to use net income from operations by excluding revenue from investments, such as interest, dividends, and rents. When this is the case, total assets should be reduced by the investments. Sometimes comparisons are developed for the rate of operating income to total assets or the rate of pretax income to total assets, so that results are not affected by financial management items or by changes in income tax rates.

Rates earned on total assets for Wycat Corporation are determined as follows:

	1981	1980
Net income	$ 70,000	$ 60,000
Total assets:		
Beginning of year	$2,391,000	$1,760,000
End of year	$2,278,000	$2,391,000
Average total assets	$2,334,500	$2,075,500
Rate earned on average total assets	**3.0%**	**2.9%**

Rate Earned on Stockholders' Equity. Net income may be expressed as the **rate earned on stockholders' equity** by dividing net income by stockholders' equity. In developing this rate, it is preferable to calculate the average stockholders' equity for a year from monthly data, particularly when significant changes have occurred during the year, such as the sale of additional stock, retirement of stock, and accumulation of earnings. Sometimes the beginning or the ending stockholders' equity is used.

For Wycat Corporation, rates earned on stockholders' equity are as follows:

	1981	1980
Net income	$ 70,000	$ 60,000
Stockholders' equity:		
Beginning of year..	$1,445,000	$1,330,000
End of year...	$1,468,000	$1,445,000
Average stockholders' equity	$1,456,500	$1,387,500
Rate earned on average stockholders' equity	**4.8%**	**4.3%**

As a company's liabilities increase in relationship to stockholders' equity, the spread between the rate earned on stockholders' equity and the rate earned on total assets rises. The rate earned on stockholders' equity is important to investors who must reconcile the risk of debt financing with the potentially greater profitability. The implications of debt and equity financing are further discussed on page 970.

Rate Earned on Common Stockholders' Equity. As a refinement to the rate earned on total stockholders' equity, earnings may be measured in terms of the residual common stockholders' equity. The **rate earned on common stockholders' equity** is computed by dividing net income after preferred dividend requirements by common stockholders' equity. The average equity for common stockholders should be determined, although the rate is frequently based on beginning or ending common equity.

In the case of Wycat Corporation, preferred dividend requirements are 6%. The rate earned on common stockholders' equity, then, is calculated as follows:

	1981	1980
Net income	$ 70,000	$ 60,000
Less dividend requirements on preferred stock	21,000	21,000
Net income related to common stockholders' equity.	$ 49,000	$ 39,000
Common stockholders' equity:		
Beginning of year..	$1,095,000	$1,080,000
End of year...	$1,118,000	$1,095,900
Average common stockholders' equity	$1,106,500	$1,087,500
Rate earned on average common stockholders' equity	**4.4%**	**3.6%**

Earnings per Share. Basic earnings per share calculations were described in Chapter 4. The Accounting Principles Board in Opinion No. 15 considers earnings per share data to be of such importance to investors and others that the Board prescribes that such data be prominently displayed on the income statement. APB Opinion No. 15 also requires the presentation of additional earnings per share information under certain specific conditions. Because the type of capital structure and the kinds of securities outstanding may have an effect on earnings per share data, a more detailed discussion of earnings per share calculations follows.

The term **earnings per share** generally refers to the amount earned during a given period on each share of common stock outstanding. It is a useful measurement for comparing net income across accounting periods that may have varying capital structures. As a successful company grows, net income will naturally increase. But an investor is interested in determining if net income is growing relative to the size of the company's capital structure. Investors use earnings per share figures to evaluate the results of operations of a business in order to make investment decisions. This measurement is frequently regarded as an important determinant of the market price of the common stock.

Evolution of Requirements for Earnings per Share Disclosure. Earnings per share figures were historically computed and used primarily by financial analysts. Sometimes the computation was disclosed in the unaudited section of the annual report along with a message from the company's president. However, because this measure was not audited, figures used to develop earnings per share were often different from those attested to by the auditor. The situation became more complex when some companies and analysts began computing earnings per share not only on the basis of common shares actually outstanding, but also on the basis of what shares would be outstanding if certain convertible securities were converted and if certain stock options were exercised. Usually, the conversion or exercise terms were very favorable to the holders of these securities, and earnings per share would decline if common stock were issued upon conversion or exercise. This result, a declining earnings per share, is referred to as a **dilution of earnings**. In some cases, however, the exercise of options or conversion of securities might result in an increasing earnings per share. This result is referred to as an **antidilution of earnings**. Securities that would lead to dilution are referred to as **dilutive securities**, and those that would lead to antidilution are referred to as **antidilutive securities**. Rational investors would not convert or exercise antidilutive securities because they could do better by purchasing common stock in the market place.

These forward-looking computations of earnings per share attempted to provide information as to what future earnings per share *might* be assuming conversions and exercises took place. Because these "as if" conditions were based on assumptions, they could be computed in several ways. The standard-setting bodies of the profession, principally the Accounting Principles Board, became involved in establishing guidelines for the computation of different earnings per share figures to be disclosed. The result was the issuance in 1969 of APB Opinion No. 15, "Earnings per Share," which concluded:

The Board believes that the significance attached by investors and others to earnings per share data, together with the importance of evaluating the data in conjunction with the financial statements, requires that such data be presented prominently in the financial statements. The Board has therefore concluded that earnings per share or net loss per share data should be shown on the face of the income statement. The extent of the data to be presented and the captions used will vary with the complexity of the company's capital structure. . . .[3]

For the first few years after Opinion No. 15 was issued, all business entities were required to include earnings per share data in their income statements. However, in 1978, the FASB removed this requirement for nonpublic entities by issuing Statement No. 21. A nonpublic company is defined as any enterprise other than "one (a) whose debt or equity securities trade in a public market on a foreign or domestic stock exchange or in the over-the-counter market, or (b) that is required to file financial statements with the Securities and Exchange Commission."[4]

In the process of establishing rules for computing earnings per share, the Accounting Principles Board felt it necessary to be very specific about how different future-oriented "as if" figures were to be computed. Many interpretations and amendments were issued with the intent to clarify the computations for a variety of securities and under varied circumstances. In some areas the rules became very arbitrary and complex, and the entire earnings per share computation has received much criticism as to its usefulness. Indeed, for companies with complex capital structures, the historical or simple earnings per share figure based upon actual shares of common stock outstanding may not even be reported. In its place the APB substituted two earnings per share amounts: (1) **primary earnings per share** based on the assumed conversion or exercise of certain securities identified as common stock equivalents and (2) **fully diluted earnings per share** based on the assumed conversion of all convertible securities or exercise of all stock options that would reduce or dilute primary earnings per share.

Although over ten years have passed since APB Opinion No. 15 was issued, there has been little evidence to support the usefulness of these forward-type earnings per share figures. Shortly after APB Opinion No. 15 was issued, in fact, the Canadian Institute of Chartered Accountants reviewed what the APB had done, and concluded that only a historical earnings per share and a fully diluted earnings per share had potential value. They rejected the attempt to define an intermediary figure that was intended to measure the probability of conversion or exercise.[5] A recent United States survey of investors indicated that various return on investment figures are becoming more popular than earnings per share as a measure of profitability.[6] Of those corporate, government, and accounting executives surveyed,

---

[3]*Opinions of the Accounting Principles Board, No. 15*, "Earnings per Share" (New York: American Institute of Certified Public Accountants, 1969), par. 12.

[4]*Statement of Financial Accounting Standards No. 21*, "Suspension of the Reporting of Earnings Per Share and Segment Information by Nonpublic Enterprises" (Stamford: Financial Accounting Standards Board, 1978), par. 13.

[5]*CICA Handbook, Section 3500*, "Earnings per Share" (Toronto: The Canadian Institute of Chartered Accountants, February 1970).

[6]As reported by a Lou Harris survey for the Financial Accounting Foundation in the Alexander Grant Newsletter, July 1980.

66% listed return on investment as highly important, while only 49% listed earnings per share as highly important. A majority of 3 to 1 felt that return on investment was a better or more desirable measure of corporate performance than earnings per share. However, because earnings per share figures are presently required for all public companies, accountants must understand how they are computed and the rationale for the computations. Only the basic recommendations can be presented here. When Opinion No. 15 fails to state the specific procedures to be followed under special circumstances, the accountant will have to exercise judgment in developing supportable presentations within the recommended framework.

Simple and Complex Capital Structures. The capital structure of a company may be classified as simple or complex. If a company has only common stock outstanding and there are no convertible securities, stock options, warrants, or other rights outstanding, it is classified as a company with a **simple capital structure**. Earnings per share is computed by dividing the net income for the period by the weighted average number of common shares outstanding for the period. If net income includes below-the-line items as discussed in Chapter 18, a separate earnings per share figure is required for each major component of income, as well as for net income. No future-oriented "as if" conditions need to be considered.

Even if convertible securities, stock options, warrants or other rights do exist, the company structure may be classified as simple if there is no potential material dilution to earnings per share from the conversion or exercise of these items. Potential earnings per share dilution exists if the earnings per share would decrease as a result of the conversion of securities or exercise of stock options, warrants, or other rights based upon the conditions existing at the financial statement date. The Accounting Principles Board defined **material dilution** as being a decrease of 3% or more in the aggregate earnings per share figure. If a company's capital structure does not qualify as simple, it is classified as a **complex capital structure**, and the two earnings per share figures identified previously are required. However, computation of earnings per share for companies with complex capital structures is beyond the scope of this text.

The Simple Capital Structure — Computational Guidelines. The earnings per share computation presents no problem when only common stock has been issued and the number of shares outstanding has remained the same for the entire period. The numerator is the income (loss), and the denominator is the number of shares outstanding for the entire period. Frequently, however, either the numerator, the denominator or both must be adjusted because of the following conditions:

(1) When common shares have been issued or have been reacquired by a company during a period, the resources available to the company have changed and this change should affect earnings. Under these circumstances, a weighted average for shares outstanding should be computed.

The weighted average number of shares may be computed by determining month-shares of outstanding stock and dividing by 12 to obtain the weighted average for the year. For example, if a company has 10,000 shares outstanding at the beginning of the year, issues 5,000 more shares on May 1, and retires 2,000 shares on November 1, the weighted average number of shares would be computed as illustrated below.

		Month-Shares
Jan. 1 to May 1..........10,000 × 4 months..........		40,000
May 1 to Nov. 1..........15,000 × 6 months..........		90,000
Nov. 1 to Dec. 31..........13,000 × 2 months..........		26,000
Total month-shares..........		156,000
Weighted average number of shares: 156,000 ÷ 12..........		13,000

The same answer could be obtained by applying a weight to each period equivalent to the portion of the year since the last change in shares outstanding, as follows:

Jan. 1 to May 1..........10,000 × 4/12 year..........	3,333
May 1 to Nov. 1..........15,000 × 6/12 year..........	7,500
Nov. 1 to Dec. 31..........13,000 × 2/12 year..........	2,167
Weighted average number of shares..........	13,000

(2) When the number of common shares outstanding has changed during a period as a result of a stock dividend, a stock split, or a reverse split, recognition of this change must be made in arriving at the amount of earnings per share. In developing comparative data, recognition of equivalent changes in the common stock of all prior periods included in the statements is necessary. To illustrate these changes, assume that in the above example a two-for-one stock split occurred on November 1 before the retirement of the 2,000 shares of stock. The computation of the weighted average number of shares would be changed as follows:

Jan. 1 to May 1 — 10,000 × 200% (two-for-one stock split) × 4/12 year..........	6,667
May 1 to Nov. 1 — 15,000 × 200% (two-for-one stock split) × 6/12 year..........	15,000
Nov. 1. to Dec. 31 — 28,000* × 2/12 year..........	4,667
Weighted average number of shares..........	26,334

*30,000 outstanding − 2,000 retired = 28,000 shares

Only with the retroactive recognition of changes in the number of shares can earnings per share presentations for prior periods be stated on a basis comparable with the earnings per share presentation for the current period. Similar retroactive adjustments must be made even if the stock dividend or stock split occurs after the end of the period but before the financial statements are prepared; disclosure of this situation should be made in a note to the financial statements.

(3) When a capital structure includes nonconvertible preferred stock, the claim of preferred stock should be deducted from net income and also from income before extraordinary or other special items when such items appear on the income statement, in arriving at the earnings related to common shares. If preferred dividends are not cumulative, only the dividends

declared on preferred stock during the period are deducted. If preferred dividends are cumulative, the full amount of dividends on preferred stock for the period, whether declared or not, should be deducted from income before extraordinary or other special items in arriving at the earnings or loss balance related to the common stock. If there is a loss for the period, preferred dividends for the period, including any undeclared dividends on cumulative preferred stock, are added to the loss in arriving at the full loss related to the common stock.

To illustrate the computation of earnings per share at December 31, 1981, for a company with a simple capital structure for a comparative two-year period, assume the following data:

Summary of changes in capital balances:

	8% Cumulative Preferred Stock $100 Par		Common Stock No Par		Retained Earnings
	Shares	Amount	Shares	Amount	
December 31, 1979 balances...................................	10,000	$1,000,000	200,000	$1,000,000	$4,000,000
June 30, 1980 issuance of 100,000 shares of common stock...			100,000	600,000	
June 30, 1980 dividend on preferred stock, 8%.........					(80,000)
June 30, 1980 dividend on common stock, 30¢..........					(90,000)
December 31, 1980 net income for year, including extraordinary gain of $75,000.................................					380,000
December 31, 1980 balances...................................	10,000	$1,000,000	300,000	$1,600,000	$4,210,000
May 1, 1981 50% stock dividend on common stock...			150,000	800,000	(800,000)
June 30, 1981 dividend on preferred stock, 8%..........					(80,000)
December 31, 1981 net loss for year...........................					(55,000)
	10,000	$1,000,000	450,000	$2,400,000	$3,275,000

Because comparative statements are desired, the denominator of weighted shares outstanding must be adjusted for the 50% stock dividend issued in 1981 as follows:

1980: January 1–June 30 — 200,000 × 150% (50% stock dividend in 1981) × 6/12 year 150,000
       July 1–December 31 — 200,000 + 100,000 (issuance of stock in 1980) × 150%
            (50% stock dividend in 1981) × 6/12 year......................... 225,000 375,000

1981: January 1–December 31 — 300,000 × 150% (50% stock dividend in 1981) × 12/12
          year.. 450,000

The numerator of the earnings per share in this example must be separated between income from continuing operations and net income. In addition, the preferred dividends must be deducted from both income figures. Since the preferred stock is cumulative, the 8% dividend would be deducted even if it had not been declared. The numerator for each year would be computed as follows:

1980: Net income	$380,000
Less extraordinary gain...	75,000
Income from continuing operations	$305,000
Less preferred dividends...	80,000
Income from continuing operations identified with common stock....	$225,000

1981: Net loss .... $ 55,000
       Less preferred dividends 80,000
       Loss identified with common stock $135,000

The earnings per share amounts can now be computed as follows:

1980: Earnings per common share from continuing operations ($225,000 ÷
       375,000) .... $.60
       Extraordinary gain ($75,000 ÷ 375,000) .... .20
       Net income per share ($300,000 ÷ 375,000) .... $.80
1981: Loss per share ($135,000 ÷ 450,000) .... $.30

It would be inappropriate to report earnings per share on preferred stock
in view of the limited dividend rights of such stock. In the case of preferred,
however, it may be informative to indicate the number of times or the extent
to which the dividend per share requirements were met. Such information
should be designated as *earnings coverage on preferred stock* and in the foregoing example would be computed as follows:

1980: Earnings coverage on preferred stock from net income: $380,000 ÷ $80,000 (cu-
       mulative preferred requirements) = 4.75 times.*
1981: Because there was a loss in 1981, no earnings coverage on preferred stock can
       be computed.
       *Earnings coverage on preferred stock from continuing operations, $305,000 ÷ $80,000 =
         3.81 times.

The Wycat Corporation financial statements (pages 613 and 615) which
are the basis of this financial analysis indicate that there are no potentially
dilutive securities. Therefore, earnings per share on common stock is calculated as follows:

	1981	1980
Net income	$70,000	$60,000
Less dividend requirements on preferred stock	21,000	21,000
Income related to common stockholders' equity	$49,000	$39,000
Number of shares of common stock outstanding	75,000	75,000
Earnings per share on common stock	**$ .65**	**$ .52**

Yield on Common Stock. A rate of return in terms of actual distributions
to common stockholders may be determined. Such a rate, referred to as the
yield on common stock, is found by dividing the annual dividends per common share by the latest market price per common share. For Wycat Corporation the yield on the common stock is computed as follows:

	1981	1980
Dividends for year per common share	$ .35	$ .32
Market value per common share at end of year	$10.00	$ 6.50
Yield on common stock	**3.5%**	**4.9%**

Price-Earnings Ratio. The market price of common stock may be expressed as a multiple of earnings to evaluate the attractiveness of common

stock as an investment. This measurement is referred to as the **price-earnings ratio** and is computed by dividing the market price per share of stock by the annual earnings per share. Instead of using the average market value of shares for the period covered by earnings, the latest market value is normally used. The lower the price-earnings ratio, the more attractive the investment. Assuming market values per common share of Wycat Corporation stock at the end of 1981 of $10 and at the end of 1980 of $6.50, price-earnings ratios would be computed as follows:

	1981	1980
Market value per common share at end of year	$10.00	$ 6.50
Earnings per share (calculated above)	$ .65	$ .52
Price-earnings ratio	**15.4**	**12.5**

As an alternative to the above, earnings per share can be presented as a percentage of the market price of the stock.

Capital Structure Analysis

The composition of a company's capital structure has significant implications for stockholders and creditors and potential investors and creditors. First, a company's creditors look to stockholders' equity as a margin of safety. To the extent that creditors supply the funds used in a business, they, rather than investors, bear the risks of the business. Second, when funds are obtained by borrowing, the stockholders retain control of the business; when funds are obtained by issuing additional stock, the existing shareholders must share the ownership rights with new investors. Third, as long as the return on investment of borrowed funds exceeds the cost of the debt (interest), the use of debt financing is advantageous. If, however, the return is less than the cost of borrowing, the use of debt is unfavorable. Fourth, there is a legal obligation to pay the interest on borrowed funds and to repay the principal. Dividends, however, are paid at the discretion of the board, and there is no obligation to return contributed capital to investors. Interest payments, unlike dividends, are deductible for tax purposes.

As stockholders' equity increases in relation to total liabilities, the margin of protection to the creditors also increases. From the stockholders' point of view, such an increase makes the organization less vulnerable to declines in business and an inability to meet obligations, and also serves to minimize the cost of carrying debt.

However, it is often advantageous to supplement funds invested by stockholders with borrowed capital. The effects of debt financing can be illustrated as follows. Assume that a company with 10,000 shares of stock outstanding is able to borrow $1,000,000 at 10% interest. The company estimates that pretax earnings will be $80,000 if it operates without the borrowed capital. Income tax is estimated at 40% of earnings. The following summary reports the effects upon net income and earnings per share, assuming a return on borrowed capital of (1) 20%, and (2) 8%.

	Results of Operations Without Borrowed Capital	Results of Operations If Borrowed Capital Earns 20%	Results of Operations If Borrowed Capital Earns 8%
Operating income..	$ 80,000	$280,000	$160,000
Interest expense		100,000	100,000
Income before income tax..............................	$ 80,000	$180,000	$ 60,000
Income tax at 40%...	32,000	72,000	24,000
Net income...	$ 48,000	$108,000	$ 36,000
Number of shares outstanding.......................	10,000	10,000	10,000
Earnings per share...	**$4.80**	**$10.80**	**$3.60**

The use of borrowed funds is known as **trading on the equity** or **applying leverage**. A company that relies heavily on debt financing is said to be "highly leveraged." Common leverage measurements include the equity to debt ratio, times interest earned, and fixed charge coverage.

Ratio of Stockholders' Equity to Total Liabilities. Stockholders' and creditors' equities may be expressed in terms of total assets or in terms of each other. For example, stockholders may have a 60% interest in total assets and creditors a 40% interest. This can be expressed as an **equity to debt ratio** of 1.5 to 1.

For Wycat Corporation, the relationships of stockholders' equity to total liabilities are calculated as follows:

	1981	1980
Stockholders' equity..	$1,468,000	$1,445,000
Total liabilities...	$ 810,000	$ 946,000
Ratio of stockholders' equity to total liabilities.........	**1.8:1**	**1.5:1**

Often the reciprocal of the equity to debt ratio is used. The **debt to equity rato** is computed by dividing total liabilities by total stockholders' equity. This shows the reciprocal relationship to that just described. It is still a measure of the amount of leverage used by a company. Investors generally prefer a higher debt to equity ratio while creditors favor a lower ratio.

Number of Times Interest Earned. A measure of the debt position of a company in relation to its earnings ability is the **number of times interest is earned**. The calculation is made by dividing income before any charges for interest or income tax by the interest requirements for the period. The resulting figure reflects the company's ability to meet interest payments and the degree of safety afforded the creditors. The number of times interest was earned by Wycat Corporation follows:

	1981	1980
Income before income tax....................................	$100,000	$ 85,000
Add bond interest (8% of $400,000).....................	32,000	32,000
Amount available in meeting bond interest requirements...	$132,000	$117,000
Number of times bond interest requirements were earned	**4.1**	**3.7**

Pretax income was used above since income tax applies only after interest is deducted, and it is pretax income that protects creditors. However, the calculation is frequently based on net income since it is consistent with other measures employing net income, and offers a more conservative approach in measuring ability to meet interest requirements. For Wycat Corporation, net income was $70,000 for 1981 and $60,000 for 1980. These amounts would be increased by interest requirements net of tax for each year and then divided by the bond interest expense to derive times interest earned.

A computation similar to times interest earned, but more inclusive, is the **fixed charge coverage**. Fixed charges include such obligations as interest on bonds and notes, lease obligations, and any other recurring financial commitments. The number of times fixed charges are covered is calculated by adding the fixed charges to pretax income and then dividing the total by the fixed charges.

Book Value per Share. Stockholders' equity can be measured by calculating the book value per share as discussed in Chapter 18. When there is only one class of stock outstanding, book value per share is calculated by dividing total stockholders' equity by the number of shares outstanding. When more than one class of stock is outstanding, total stockholders' equity must be allocated to the classes.

Summary of Analytical Measures

Financial ratios, percentages, and other measures are useful tools for analyzing financial statements. They enable statement users to make meaningful judgments about an enterprise's financial condition and operating results. These measures, like financial statements, are more meaningful when compared with similar data for more than one period and with industry averages or other available data. A summary of the major analytical measures discussed in this chapter is presented below and on page 973.

Summary of Major Analytical Measures

Liquidity Analysis

1. Current ratio	$\dfrac{\text{Current assets}}{\text{Current liabilities}}$	Measures ability to pay short-term debts.
2. Acid-test ratio	$\dfrac{\text{Quick assets}}{\text{Current liabilities}}$	Measures immediate ability to pay short-term debts.

Activity Analysis

3. Accounts receivable turnover	$\dfrac{\text{Net credit sales}}{\text{Average accounts receivable}}$	Measures receivable position and approximate average collection time.
4. Number of days' sales in receivables	$\dfrac{\text{Average accounts receivable}}{\text{Average daily credit sales}}$	Measures receivable position and approximate average collection time.

5. Inventory turnover	$$\frac{\text{Cost of goods sold}}{\text{Average inventory}}$$	Measures appropriateness of inventory levels in terms of time required to sell or "turn over" goods.
6. Number of days' sales in inventories	$$\frac{\text{Average inventory}}{\text{Average daily cost of goods sold}}$$	Measures appropriateness of inventory levels in terms of time required to sell or "turn over" goods.
7. Total asset turnover	$$\frac{\text{Net sales}}{\text{Average total assets}}$$	Measures effectiveness of asset utilization.

Profitability Analysis

8. Profit margin on sales	$$\frac{\text{Net income}}{\text{Net sales}}$$	Measures profit percentage per dollar of sales.
9. Rate earned on total assets	$$\frac{\text{Net income}}{\text{Average total assets}}$$	Measures overall asset productivity.
10. Rate earned on stockholders' equity	$$\frac{\text{Net income}}{\text{Average stockholders' equity}}$$	Measures rate of return on average stockholders' equity.
11. Rate earned on common stockholders' equity	$$\frac{\text{Net income}}{\text{Average common stockholders' equity}}$$	Measures rate of return on average common stockholders' equity.
12. Earnings per share	$$\frac{\text{Net income}}{\text{Number of shares of common stock outstanding}}$$	Measures net income per share of common stock.
13. Yield on common stock	$$\frac{\text{Dividends per share of common stock}}{\text{Market value per share of common stock}}$$	Measures rate of cash return to stockholders.
14. Price-earnings ratio	$$\frac{\text{Market price per share of common stock}}{\text{Earnings per share of common stock}}$$	Measures attractiveness of stock as an investment.

Capital Structure Analysis

15. Equity to debt ratio	$$\frac{\text{Stockholders' equity}}{\text{Total liabilities}}$$	Measures use of debt to finance operations.
16. Times interest earned	$$\frac{\text{Income before taxes and interest expense}}{\text{Interest expense}}$$	Measures ability to meet interest payments.

INTERPRETATION OF ANALYSES

The analyses discussed in this chapter are designed to help an analyst arrive at certain conclusions with regard to a business. As previously stated, these are merely guides to intelligent interpretation of financial data.

All ratios and measurements need not be used, but only those that will actually assist an analyst in arriving at informed conclusions with respect to questions raised. The measurements developed need to be interpreted in terms of the circumstances of a particular enterprise, the conditions of the particular industry in which the enterprise operates, and the general business and economic environment. If measurements are to be of maximum value, they need to be compared with similar data developed for the particular enterprise for past periods, with standard measurements for the industry as a whole, and with pertinent data relating to general business conditions and price fluctuations affecting the individual enterprise. Only through intelligent use and integration of the foregoing sources of data can financial weaknesses and strengths be identified and reliable opinions be developed concerning business structure, operations, and growth.

QUESTIONS

1. What groups may be interested in a company's financial statements?
2. What types of questions requiring financial statement analysis might be raised by external users, such as investors and creditors, as contrasted to internal management?
3. What are the factors that one would look for in judging a company's (a) liquidity, (b) stability, (c) profitability, (d) growth potential?
4. Why are comparative financial statements considered more meaningful than statements prepared for a single period? What conditions increase the usefulness of comparative statements?
5. Distinguish between horizontal and vertical analysis. What special purpose does each serve?
6. What information is provided by analysis of comparative changes in financial position that is not available from analysis of comparative balance sheets and income statements?
7. What is meant by a *common-size* statement? What are its advantages?
8. Mention some factors that may limit the comparability of financial statements of two companies in the same industry.
9. What factors may be responsible for a change in a company's net income from one year to the next?
10. The Black Co. develops the following measurements for 1980 as compared with the year 1979. What additional information would you require before arriving at favorable or unfavorable conclusions for each item?

   (a) Net income has increased $70,000.
   (b) Sales returns and allowances have increased by $25,000.
   (c) The gross profit rate has increased by 5%.
   (d) Purchase discounts have increased by $5,000.
   (e) Working capital has increased by $85,000.
   (f) Accounts receivable have increased by $150,000.
   (g) Inventories have decreased by $100,000.
   (h) Retained earnings have decreased by $300,000.

11. Define working capital and appraise its significance.

12. Distinguish between the current ratio and the acid-test ratio.

13. Balance sheets for the Rich Corporation and the Poor Corporation each show a working capital total of $500,000. Does this indicate that the short-term liquidity of the two corporations is approximately the same? Explain.

14. (a) How is the accounts receivable turnover computed? (b) How is the number of days' purchases in accounts payable computed?

15. (a) How is the merchandise inventory turnover computed? (b) What precautions are necessary in arriving at the basis for the turnover calculation? (c) How would you interpret a rising inventory turnover rate?

16. The ratio of stockholders' equity to total liabilities offers information about the long-term liquidity of a business. Explain.

17. Indicate how each of the following measurements is calculated and appraise its significance:

   (a) The number of times bond interest requirements were earned.
   (b) The number of times preferred dividend requirements were earned.
   (c) The rate of earnings on the common stockholders' equity.
   (d) The earnings per share on common stock.
   (e) The price-earnings ratio on common stock.
   (f) The yield on common stock.

EXERCISES

exercise 21-1

Indicate the dollar change, the percentage change, and also the ratio that would be reported for each case below, assuming horizontal analysis:

Gain (loss) on Sale of Investments

	1980	1979		1980	1979
(a)	$90,000	$40,000	(f)	$(30,000)	0
(b)	10,000	40,000	(g)	15,000	$ (5,000)
(c)	30,000	0	(h)	(20,000)	5,000
(d)	0	20,000	(i)	(10,000)	(10,000)
(e)	(15,000)	5,000	(j)	25,000	25,000

exercise 21-2

Sales for the Acme Company for a five-year period and an industry sales index for this period are listed below. Convert both series into indexes employing 1976 as the base year.

	1980	1979	1978	1977	1976
Sales of Acme Company (in thousands of dollars)	$8,400	$9,030	$8,710	$8,850	$8,530
Industry sales index (1966 − 1968 = 100)	190	212	210	170	158

exercise 21-3

Cost of goods sold data for The Ace Co., are presented below:

	1980	1979
Merchandise inventory, January 1	$ 40,000	$ 25,000
Purchases	100,000	90,000
Merchandise available for sale	$140,000	$115,000
Less merchandise inventory, December 31	35,000	40,000
Cost of goods sold	$105,000	$ 75,000

Prepare a comparative schedule of cost of goods sold showing dollar and percentage changes.

exercise 21-4

The financial position of the Anderson Co. at the end of 1980 and 1979 is presented on page 637.

	1980	1979
Assets		
Current assets	$ 40,000	$ 42,000
Long-term investments	15,000	14,000
Land, buildings, and equipment (net)	50,000	55,000
Intangible assets	10,000	10,000
Other assets	5,000	6,000
Total assets	$120,000	$127,000
Liabilities		
Current liabilities	$ 15,000	$ 20,000
Long-term liabilities	38,000	42,000
Total liabilities	$ 53,000	$ 62,000
Stockholders' Equity		
Preferred 6% stock	$ 10,000	$ 9,000
Common stock	39,000	39,000
Additional paid-in capital	5,000	5,000
Retained earnings	13,000	12,000
Total stockholders' equity	$ 67,000	$ 65,000
Total liabilities and stockholders' equity	$120,000	$127,000

Prepare a comparative balance sheet offering a percentage analysis of component items in terms of total assets and total liabilities and stockholders' equity for each year.

exercise 21-5

The following data are taken from the comparative balance sheet prepared for the Morton Company:

	1980	1979
Cash	$ 20,000	$ 10,000
Marketable securities (net)	9,000	35,000
Trade receivables (net)	43,000	30,000
Inventories	65,000	50,000
Prepaid expenses	3,000	2,000
Land, buildings, and equipment (net)	79,000	75,000
Intangible assets	10,000	15,000
Other assets	7,000	8,000
	$236,000	$225,000
Current liabilities	$ 80,000	$ 60,000

(1) From the data given, compute for 1980 and for 1979: (a) the working capital, (b) the current ratio, (c) the acid-test ratio, (d) the ratio of current assets to total assets, (e) the ratio of cash to current liabilities.

(2) Evaluate each of the above changes.

exercise 21-6

Income statements for the Parsons Sales Co. show the following:

	1981	1980	1979
Sales	$105,000	$100,000	$ 75,000
Cost of goods sold:			
Beginning inventory	$ 30,000	$ 25,000	$ 5,000
Purchases	95,000	80,000	85,000
	$125,000	$105,000	$ 90,000
Ending inventory	50,000	30,000	25,000
	$ 75,000	$ 75,000	$ 65,000
Gross profit on sales	$ 30,000	$ 25,000	$ 10,000

Give whatever measurements may be developed in analyzing the inventory position at the end of each year. What conclusions would you make concerning the inventory trend?

exercise 21-7

The following data are taken from the Thomas Corporation records for the years ending December 31, 1981, 1980, and 1979.

	1981	1980	1979
Finished goods inventory	$ 60,000	$ 40,000	$ 30,000
Goods in process inventory	60,000	65,000	60,000
Raw materials inventory	60,000	40,000	35,000
Sales	400,000	340,000	300,000
Cost of goods sold	225,000	230,000	210,000
Cost of goods manufactured	260,000	250,000	200,000
Raw materials used in production	150,000	130,000	120,000

Compute turnover rates for 1981 and for 1980 for (a) finished goods, (b) goods in process, and (c) raw materials.

exercise 21-8

The total purchases of goods by The Fast Sell Company during 1980 were $360,000. All purchases were on a 2/10, n/30 basis. The average balance in the vouchers payable account was $33,000. Was the company prompt, slow, or average in paying for goods? How many days' average purchases were there in accounts payable, assuming a 360-day year?

exercise 21-9

Compute the weighted average number of shares outstanding for Monson Tool Company, which has a simple capital structure, assuming the following transactions in common stock occurred during 1981:

Date	Transactions in Common Stock	Number of Shares $10 Par value
January 1, 1981	Shares outstanding	32,000
February 1, 1981	Issued for cash	6,400
April 1, 1981	Acquisition of treasury stock	(6,000)
July 1, 1981	Resold part of treasury stock shares	2,800
September 1, 1981	50% stock dividend	50% of shares outstanding
December 1, 1981	Issued in exchange for property	12,800

exercise 21-10

At December 31, 1981, the Meyers Corporation had 50,000 shares of common stock issued and outstanding, 40,000 of which had been issued and outstanding throughout the year and 10,000 of which had been issued on October 1, 1981. Operating income before income taxes for the year ended December 31, 1981, was $468,800. In 1981, a dividend of $32,000 was paid on 40,000 shares of 8% cumulative preferred stock, $10 par.

On April 1, 1982, 15,000 additional shares were issued. Total income before income taxes for 1982 was $477,000, which included an extraordinary gain before income taxes of $37,000. Assuming a 40% tax rate, what is Meyer's earnings per common share for 1981 and for 1982, rounded to the nearest cent? Show computations in good form.

exercise 21-11

The James Company estimates that pretax earnings for the year ended December 31, 1980, will be $70,000 if it operates without borrowed capital. Income tax is 40% of earnings. There are 15,000 shares of common stock outstanding for the entire year. Assuming that the company is able to borrow $800,000 at 10% interest, show the effects upon net income if borrowed capital earns (1) 20%, and (2) 8%.

exercise 21-12

The balance sheets for the Smith Corp. showed long-term liabilities and stockholders' equity balances at the end of each year as given below:

	1980	1979
8% Bonds payable	$ 600,000	$600,000
Preferred 6% stock, $100 par	600,000	400,000
Common stock, $25 par	1,200,000	900,000
Additional paid-in capital	150,000	100,000
Retained earnings	300,000	100,000

Net income after income tax was: 1980, $110,000; 1979, $80,000. Using the foregoing data, compute for each year:

(a) The rate of earnings on the total stockholders' equity at the end of the year.
(b) The number of times bond interest requirements were earned (income after tax).
(c) The number of times preferred dividend requirements were earned.
(d) The rate earned on the common stockholders' equity.
(e) The earnings per share on common stock.

exercise 21-13

The controller of the Pratt Manufacturing Co. wishes to analyze the activity of the finished goods, work in process, and raw materials inventories. Using the following information, compute the inventory turnovers.

Finished goods inventory, 12/31/79	$112,500
Finished goods inventory, 12/31/80	237,500
Work in process inventory, 12/31/79	211,000
Work in process inventory, 12/31/80	239,000
Raw materials inventory, 12/31/79	125,000
Raw materials inventory, 12/31/80	175,000
Cost of goods sold, 1980	245,000
Cost of goods manufactured, 1980	337,500
Cost of materials used, 1980	225,000

exercise 21-14

Donna Clark wishes to know which of two companies will yield the greatest rate of return on an investment in common stock. Financial information for 1980 for the Lopez Company and the Baker Company is presented below:

	Lopez Co.	Baker Co.
Net income	$ 140,000	$ 120,000
Preferred stock (7%)	600,000	600,000
Common stockholders' equity:		
January 1, 1980	1,450,000	1,100,000
December 31, 1980	1,350,000	980,000

Determine which company earned the greatest return on common stockholders' equity in 1980.

PROBLEMS

problem 21-1

Operations for the Hogwash Company for 1980 and 1979 are summarized below:

	1980	1979
Sales	$500,000	$450,000
Sales returns	20,000	10,000
Net sales	$480,000	$440,000
Cost of goods sold	350,000	240,000
Gross profit on sales	$130,000	$200,000
Selling and general expenses	100,000	120,000
Operating income	$ 30,000	$ 80,000
Other expenses	35,000	30,000
Income (loss) before income tax	$ (5,000)	$ 50,000
Income tax		22,500
Net income (loss)	$ (5,000)	$ 27,500

Instructions:

(1) Prepare a comparative income statement showing dollar changes and percentage changes for 1980 as compared with 1979.
(2) Prepare a comparative income statement offering a percentage analysis of component revenue and expense items in terms of net sales for each year.

problem 21-2

The financial position of Westgate Corp. at the end of 1980 and at the end of 1979 is summarized as follows.

Assets	1980	1979
Current assets:		
Cash	$ 70,000	$ 90,000
Marketable securities	90,000	100,000
Notes and accounts receivable, less allowance	400,000	300,000
Finished goods	400,000	350,000
Goods in process	200,000	160,000
Raw materials	350,000	300,000
Miscellaneous prepaid items	40,000	60,000
Total current assets	$1,550,000	$1,360,000
Long-term investments:		
Bond redemption fund	$ 400,000	$ 300,000
Investment in properties not in current use	250,000	250,000
Total long-term investments	$ 650,000	$ 550,000
Land, buildings, and equipment at cost, less accumulated depreciation	$ 920,000	$1,000,000
Intangible assets	$ 60,000	$ 70,000
Other assets:		
Unamortized bond issue costs	$ 34,000	$ 40,000
Machinery rearrangement costs	16,000	20,000
Total other assets	$ 50,000	$ 60,000
Total assets	$3,230,000	$3,040,000

Liabilities

Current liabilities:

Notes and accounts payable	$ 250,000	$ 240,000
Income tax payable	80,000	50,000
Payrolls, interest, and tax payable	50,000	40,000
Dividends payable	10,000	15,000
Miscellaneous payables	10,000	15,000
Total current liabilities	$ 400,000	$ 360,000
Long-term liabilities — 8%, 10-year first-mortgage bonds	300,000	350,000
Estimated employee pensions payable	110,000	150,000
Deferred revenues	20,000	30,000
Total liabilities	$ 830,000	$ 890,000

Stockholders' Equity

Contributed capital:

Preferred 6% stock, $25 par	$ 400,000	$ 400,000
No-par common stock, $10 stated value	600,000	600,000
Additional paid-in capital	700,000	700,000
Total contributed capital	$1,700,000	$1,700,000

Retained earnings:

Appropriated	$ 350,000	$ 300,000
Unappropriated	350,000	150,000
Total retained earnings	$ 700,000	$ 450,000
Total stockholders' equity	$2,400,000	$2,150,000
Total liabilities and stockholders' equity	$3,230,000	$3,040,000

Instructions:

(1) Prepare a comparative balance sheet showing dollar changes and changes in terms of ratios for 1980 as compared with 1979.

(2) Prepare a common-size balance sheet comparing financial structure ratios for 1980 with those for 1979.

problem 21-3

Balance sheet data for the Pen Company and the Ink Company are given as follows:

	Pen Company	Ink Company
Assets		
Current assets	$ 51,000	$ 24,000
Long-term investments	5,000	28,000
Land, buildings, and equipment (net)	48,000	52,000
Intangible assets	6,000	10,000
Other assets	5,000	6,000
Total assets	$115,000	$120,000
Liabilities		
Current liabilities	$ 15,000	$ 18,000
Long-term liabilities	25,000	30,000
Deferred revenues	5,000	7,000
Total liabilities	$ 45,000	$ 55,000
Stockholders' Equity		
Preferred stock	$ 5,000	$ 10,000
Common stock	30,000	20,000
Additional paid-in capital	25,000	18,500
Retained earnings	10,000	16,500
Total stockholders' equity	$ 70,000	$ 65,000
Total liabilities and stockholders' equity	$115,000	$120,000

Instructions:

(1) Prepare a common-size statement comparing balance sheet data for the year.

(2) What analytical conclusions can be drawn from this comparative common-size statement?

problem 21-4

Sales for Elton Mfg. Co. and its chief competitor, the Polk Company, and the sales index for the industry, are given below:

	1981	1980	1979	1978	1977
Sales of Elton Mfg. Co. (in thousands of dollars).........	$7,000	$7,280	$7,735	$8,450	$8,385
Sales of Polk Company (in thousands of dollars).........	$9,700	$9,690	$9,975	$9,785	$9,880
Industry sales index (1971 = 100)	140	154	161	147	133

Instructions:

(1) Convert the three series to index numbers using 1977 as the base year.

(2) Prepare a short report for the management of Elton Mfg. Co. summarizing your findings.

problem 21-5

Comparative data for Draper, Inc., for the three-year period 1978–1980 are presented below:

Income Statement Data

	1980	1979	1978
Net sales	$1,200,000	$ 900,000	$1,100,000
Cost of goods sold	760,000	600,000	650,000
Gross profit on sales	$ 440,000	$ 300,000	$ 450,000
Selling, general, and other expenses	350,000	280,000	290,000
Operating income..	$ 90,000	$ 20,000	$ 160,000
Income tax...	40,500	9,000	72,000
Net income..	$ 49,500	$ 11,000	$ 88,000
Dividends paid	35,000	30,000	30,000
Net increase (decrease) in retained earnings	$ 14,500	$ (19,000)	$ 58,000

Balance Sheet Data

Assets	1980	1979	1978
Cash..	$ 60,000	$ 40,000	$ 75,000
Trade notes and accounts receivable (net)....................	300,000	320,000	300,000
Inventory (at cost)...	380,000	420,000	350,000
Prepaid expenses	30,000	10,000	40,000
Land, buildings, and equipment (net)..........................	760,000	600,000	690,000
Intangible assets...	100,000	100,000	125,000
Other assets	70,000	10,000	20,000
	$1,700,000	$1,500,000	$1,600,000

Liabilities and Stockholders' Equity	1980	1979	1978
Trade notes and accounts payable.............................	$ 120,000	$ 180,000	$ 170,000
Wages, interest, dividends payable.............................	25,000	25,000	25,000
Income tax payable	39,500	10,000	80,000
Miscellaneous current liabilities	10,000	4,000	10,000
8% bonds payable	300,000	300,000	300,000
Deferred revenues	10,000	10,000	25,000
Preferred 6% stock, cumulative, $100 par and liquidating value ...	200,000	200,000	200,000
No-par common stock, $10 stated value	500,000	400,000	400,000
Additional paid-in capital.......................................	310,000	200,000	200,000
Retained earnings — appropriated...............................	80,000	60,000	60,000
Retained earnings — unappropriated	105,500	111,000	130,000
	$1,700,000	$1,500,000	$1,600,000

Instructions:

    (1) From the foregoing data, calculate comparative measurements for 1980 and 1979 as follows:

        (a) The amount of working capital.

        (b) The current ratio.

        (c) The acid-test ratio.

        (d) The trade receivables turnover rate for the year (all sales are on a credit basis).

        (e) The average days' sales in trade receivables at the end of the year (assume a 360-day year and all sales on a credit basis).

        (f) The trade payables turnover rate for the year.

        (g) The average days' purchases in trade payables at the end of the year.

        (h) The inventory turnover rate.

        (i) The number of days' sales in the inventory at the end of the year.

        (j) The ratio of stockholders' equity to total liabilities.

        (k) The ratio of land, buildings, and equipment to bonds payable.

        (l) The ratio of stockholders' equity to land, buildings, and equipment.

        (m) The book value per share of preferred stock (no dividends in arrears).

        (n) The book value per share of common stock.

    (2) Based upon the measurements made in (1), evaluate the liquidity position of Draper Inc., at the end of 1980 as compared with the end of 1979.

problem 21-6

Use the comparative data for Draper, Inc., as given in problem 21-5.

Instructions:

    (1) Compute comparative measurements for 1980 and 1979 as follows:

        (a) The ratio of net sales to average total assets.

        (b) The ratio of net sales to average land, buildings, and equipment.

        (c) The rate earned on net sales.

        (d) The gross profit rate on net sales.

        (e) The rate earned on average total assets.

        (f) The rate earned on average stockholders' equity.

        (g) The number of times bond interest requirements were earned (before income tax).

        (h) The number of times preferred dividend requirements were earned.

        (i) The rate earned on average common stockholders' equity.

        (j) The earnings per share on common stock.

    (2) Based upon the measurements made in (1), evaluate the profitability of Draper, Inc., for 1980 as compared with 1979.

problem 21-7

Inventory and receivable balances and also gross profit data for The Busy Baker Co. appear below:

	1980	1979	1978
Balance sheet data:			
Inventory, December 31	$100,000	$ 90,000	$ 80,000
Accounts receivable, December 31	60,000	40,000	20,000
Accounts payable, December 31	70,000	60,000	45,000
Net purchases	140,000	100,000	80,000
Income statement data:			
Net sales	$290,000	$270,000	$250,000
Cost of goods sold	210,000	200,000	180,000
Gross profit on sales	$ 80,000	$ 70,000	$ 70,000

Instructions: Assuming a 300-day business year and all sales on a credit basis, compute the following measurements for 1980 and 1979.

(1) The receivables turnover rate.
(2) The average days' sales in receivables at the end of the year.
(3) The inventory turnover rate.
(4) The number of days' sales in inventory at the end of the year.
(5) The accounts payable turnover rate.
(6) The number of days' purchases in accounts payable at the end of the year.

problem 21-8

Dan's Wholesale Products, Inc., had 50,000 shares of common stock outstanding at the end of 1979. During 1980 and 1981, the transactions shown below took place.

1980

March	31	Sold 10,000 shares at $27.
April	26	Paid cash dividend of 50¢ per share.
July	31	Paid cash dividend of 25¢ per share, and 5% stock dividend.
October	26	Paid cash dividend of 50¢ per share.

1981

February	28	Purchased 5,000 shares of treasury stock.
March	1	Paid cash dividend of 50¢ per share.
April	30	Issued 3-for-1 stock split.
November	1	Sold 6,000 shares of treasury stock.
November	3	Paid cash dividend of 50¢ per share.
December	20	Declared cash dividend of 25¢ per share.

Dan's Wholesale Products, Inc. has a simple capital structure.

Instructions: Compute the weighted average number of shares for 1980 and 1981 to be used in the earnings per share computation at the end of 1981.

problem 21-9

Stockholders' equities for the Strickling Corporation at the end of 1980 and 1979 were:

	1980	1979
Preferred 6% stock, $50 par and liquidating value	$100,000	$100,000
Common stock, $10 par	300,000	200,000
Additional paid-in capital	500,000	350,000
Retained earnings	90,000	150,000

Instructions: Compute the book value per share of both preferred stock and common stock at the end of 1980 and at the end of 1979, assuming the conditions stated in each case below. (Assume dividends may legally be paid from additional paid-in capital.)

(1) Preferred is cumulative; dividend requirements on preferred stock have been met annually.

(2) Preferred is cumulative; the last dividend on preferred stock was paid for the year 1977.

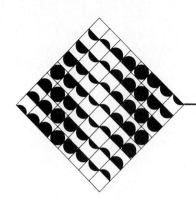

Appendix A

Future and Present Value: Concepts and Applications

Conceptual knowledge of future and present value techniques is becoming increasingly important for the accountant. To review these concepts, this appendix provides (1) a brief explanation of the basic concepts and applications of interest; and, (2) illustrations of business problems utilizing future and present value tables.

INTEREST DEFINED

Money, like other commodities, is a scarce resource, and a payment for its use is generally required. This payment (cost) for the use of money is **interest**. For example, if $100 is borrowed, whether from an individual, a business, or a bank, and $110 is paid back, $10 interest has been paid for the use of the $100. Thus, interest represents the excess cash paid or received over the amount of cash borrowed or loaned.

Generally interest is specified in terms of a percentage rate for a period of time, usually a year. For example, interest at 8% means the annual cost of borrowing an amount of money, called the **principal**, is equal to 8% of that amount. The interest rate and the time period are assumed to be stated in common units. If $100 is borrowed at 8% annual interest, the total to be repaid is $108 — the amount of the principal, $100, and the interest for a year, $8 ($100 × .08 × 1). Interest on a $1,000 note for 6 months at 8% is $40 ($1,000 × .08 × 6/12). Thus, the formula for computing **simple interest** is $i = p \times r \times t$, where:

i = Amount of simple interest
p = Principal amount
r = Interest rate (per period)
t = Time (number of periods)

The formula just presented relates to simple interest. Many transactions involve **compound interest**. This means that the amount of interest earned for a certain period is added to the principal for the next period. Interest for the subsequent period is computed on the new amount, which includes both principal and accumulated interest. As an example, assume $100 is deposited in a bank and left for two years at 6% annual interest. At the end of the first year, the $100 has earned $6 interest ($100 × .06 × 1). At the end of the second year, $6 has been earned for the first year, plus another $6.36 interest (6% on the $106 balance at the beginning of the second year). Thus, the total interest earned is $12.36 rather than $12 because of the compounding effect. The table below, based on the foregoing example, illustrates the computation of simple and compound interest for four years. Formulas relative to common compound interest situations are provided in the next section of this appendix.

Year	Simple Interest Computation	Interest	Total	Compound Interest Computation	Interest	Total
1	($100 × .06)	$6	106	($100.00 × .06)	$6.00	$106.00
2	(100 × .06)	6	112	(106.00 × .06)	6.36	112.36
3	(100 × .06)	6	118	(112.36 × .06)	6.74	119.10
4	(100 × .06)	6	124	(119.10 × .06)	7.15	126.25

Because of the compounding effect of interest, an adjustment of the stated annual rate of interest to its effective rate and for the appropriate number of interest periods often must be made. To illustrate, 6% annual interest for 10 years compounded semiannually would be converted to 3% for 20 periods; 12% for 6 years compounded quarterly would convert to 3% for 24 periods.

FUTURE AND PRESENT VALUE COMPUTATIONS

Since money earns interest, $100 received today is more valuable than $100 received one year from today. Future and present value analysis is a method of comparing the value of money received or expected to be received at different time periods.

Analyses requiring alternative computations in terms of present dollars relative to future dollars may be viewed from one of two perspectives, the future or the present. If a future time frame is chosen, all cash flows must be **accumulated** to that future point. In this instance, the effect of interest is to increase the amounts or values over time. Examples of questions which might be answered by future value computations include:

How much will $500 deposited today at 6% annual interest amount to in 20 years?

How long would it take to accumulate a $10,000 down payment on a home if one saved $100 a month and received 5% per year on those savings?

What rate of return on an investment must be received for money to double in 20 years?

If, on the other hand, the present is chosen as the point in time at which to evaluate alternatives, all cash flows must be **discounted** to the present. In this instance, the discounting effect reduces the amounts or values. Assuming a certain rate of interest, examples of questions using the present value approach include:

How much should be accepted today for an apartment house in lieu of rental income for the next 10 years?

How much is $5,000 due in 5 years worth today?

What lump-sum amount should be paid today for a series of equal payments of $100 a month, beginning now, for the next 5 years?

The future value and present value situations are essentially reciprocal relationships, and both are based on the concept of interest. Thus, if interest can be earned at 6% per year, the future worth of $100 one year from now is $106. Conversely, assuming the same rate of interest, the present value of a $106 payment due in one year is $100.

There are four common future and present value situations, each with a corresponding formula. Two of the situations deal with one-time, lump-sum payments or receipts[1] (either future or present values), and the other two involve annuities (either future or present values). An **annuity** consists of a series of equal payments over a specified number of periods.

Without going into the derivation of the formulas, these four situations are as follows:

1. *Future Value of a Lump-Sum Payment:* $FV = P(1 + i)^n$

   This may also be referred to as $FV = P(FVF_{\overline{n}|i})$ or simply $FV = P$(Table I value), where:

FV	= Future value
P	= Principal amount to be accumulated
i	= Interest rate per period
n	= Number of periods
$FVF_{\overline{n}|i}$	= Future value factor for a particular interest rate and for a certain number of periods from Table I

2. *Present Value of a Lump-Sum Payment:* $PV = A\left[\dfrac{1}{(1 + i)^n}\right]$

   This may also be referred to as $PV = A(PVF_{\overline{n}|i})$ or simply $PV = A$(Table II value), where:

PV	= Present value
A	= Accumulated amount to be discounted
i	= Interest rate per period
n	= Number of periods
$PVF_{\overline{n}|i}$	= Present value factor for a particular interest rate and for a certain number of periods from Table II

3. *Future Value of an Annuity:* $FV_n = R\left[\dfrac{(1 + i)^n - 1}{i}\right]$

   This may also be referred to as $FV_n = R(FVAF_{\overline{n}|i})$ or simply $FV_n = R$(Table III value), where:

FV_n	= Future value of an annuity
R	= Annuity payment or periodic rent to be accumulated
i	= Interest rate per period
n	= Number of periods
$FVAF_{\overline{n}|i}$	= Future value annuity factor for a particular interest rate and for a certain number of periods from Table III

---

[1] Hereafter in this appendix, the terms *payments* and *receipts* will be used interchangeably. A payment by one party in a transaction becomes a receipt to the other party and vice versa. The term *rent* is used to designate either a receipt or a payment.

4. ***Present Value of an Annuity:*** $PV_n = R\left[\dfrac{1 - \dfrac{1}{(1 + i)^n}}{i}\right]$

This may also be referred to as $PV_n = R(PVAF_{\overline{n}|i})$ or simply $PV_n = R(\text{Table IV value})$, where:

PV_n	= Present value of an annuity
R	= Annuity payment or periodic rent to be discounted
i	= Interest rate per period
n	= Number of periods
$PVAF_{\overline{n}|i}$	= Present value annuity factor for a particular interest rate and for a certain number of periods from Table IV

Because using the formulas may be time-consuming, tables have been developed for each of the four situations. Such tables are provided at the end of this appendix, beginning on page 1007. Each table is based on computing the value of $1 for various interest rates and periods of time. Future and present value computations can be made by multiplying the appropriate table value factor for $1 by the lump-sum or annuity payment (rent) involved in the problem. To illustrate, consider the question described earlier: How much will $500 deposited today at 6% annual interest amount to in 20 years? This is an example of the first situation, the future value of a lump-sum payment, and involves Table I. The table value for $n = 20$ and $i = 6\%$ is 3.2071. This value times $500, the principal amount to be accumulated, is approximately $1,604. Thus, the future value of $500 deposited now, accumulating at 6% per year for 20 years, is about $1,604.

The following examples demonstrate the application of future and present value tables in solving business problems. At least one example is provided for each of the four situations just described. Note that business problems sometimes require solving for the number of periods, the interest rate,[2] or the rental payment instead of the future or present value amounts. In each of the formulas there are four variables. If information is given about any three of the variables, the fourth (unknown value) can be determined.

Problem 1:

John Marsh loans Ann Brown $5,000 for a new car. Marsh accepts a note due in 4 years with interest at 8% compounded semiannually. After 1 year, Marsh needs cash and sells the note to Terry McKay who discounts the note at 12% compounded quarterly. How much cash did Marsh receive from McKay?

Solution to Problem 1:

This problem involves a lump-sum payment to be accumulated 4 years into the future at one interest rate, then discounted back 3 years at a different interest rate.

In many present and future value problems, a time line is helpful in visualizing the problem:

---

[2]When the interest rate is not known, it is properly called the *implicit rate of interest*, that is, the rate of interest implied by the terms of a contract or situation. (See Problems 7 and 9 in this appendix.)

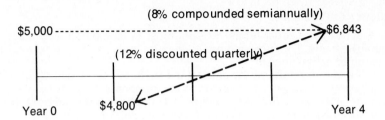

First, the $5,000 must be accumulated for 4 years at 8% compounded semiannually. Table I is used, and the applicable formula is:

$FV = P(FVF_{\overline{n}|i})$ where: FV = The future value of the lump sum
                                              P   = $5,000
                                              n   = 8 periods (4 years × 2)
                                              i   = 4% effective interest rate per period
                                                     (8% ÷ 2)

FV = $5,000 (Table I$_{\overline{8}|4\%}$)

FV = $5,000 (1.3686)

FV = $6,843

In 4 years, the holder of the note will receive $6,843. After Marsh sells the note, it will be worth $6,843 to McKay in 3 years. The opportunity cost of money to McKay is apparently 12% compounded quarterly. Therefore, the $6,843 must be discounted back 3 years at 12% to find the amount McKay is willing to pay Marsh. Table II is used, and the applicable formula is:

$PV = A(PVF_{\overline{n}|i})$ where: PV = The value of the future sum discounted
                                              back three years
                                              A   = $6,843
                                              n   = 12 periods (3 years × 4 quarters)
                                              i   = 3% effective interest rate per period
                                                     (12% ÷ 4 quarters)

PV = $6,843 (Table II$_{\overline{12}|3\%}$)

PV = $6,843 (.7014)

PV = $4,800

McKay will pay roughly $4,800. Thus, Marsh is willing to give up $2,043 ($6,843 − $4,800) in order to receive cash at the end of 1 year.

Problem 2:

Miller Sporting Goods Co. is considering an investment which will require $1,250,000 capital investment and which will provide the following expected net receipts:

Year	Estimated Net Receipts
1	$195,000
2	457,000
3	593,000
4	421,000
5	95,000
6	5,000

Miller will make the investment only if the rate of return is greater than 10%. Will Miller make the investment?

Solution to Problem 2:

A series of unequal future receipts must be compared with a present lump-sum investment. For such a comparison to be made, all future cash flows must be discounted to the present.

If the rate of return on the amount invested is greater than 10%, then the total of all yearly net receipts discounted to the present at 10% will be greater than the amount invested. Since the receipts are unequal, each amount must be discounted individually. Table II is used, and the applicable formula is:

$$PV = A(PVF_{\overline{n}|i})$$ where:

(1) Year = n	(2) A (Net Receipts)	(3) Table II$_{\overline{n}|\,10\%}$	(2) × (3) = (4) PV (Discounted Amount)
1	$195,000	.9091	$ 177,275
2	457,000	.8264	377,665
3	593,000	.7513	445,521
4	421,000	.6830	287,543
5	95,000	.6209	58,986
6	5,000	.5645	2,823
Total			$1,349,813

The total discounted receipts are greater than the investment; thus, the rate of return is more than 10%. Therefore, other things being equal, Miller will invest.

Problem 3:

Brothwell, Inc., owes an installment debt of $1,000 per quarter for 5 years. The creditor has indicated a willingness to accept an equivalent lump-sum payment at the end of the contract period instead of the series of payments. If money is worth 8% compounded quarterly and the first four payments have been made, what is the equivalent lump-sum payment?

Solution to Problem 3:

The equivalent lump-sum payment can be found by accumulating the quarterly $1,000 payments to the end of the contract period. Table III is used, and the applicable formula is:

$$FV_n = R(FVAF_{\overline{n}|i})$$ where: FV_n = The unknown equivalent lump-sum payment

R = $1,000 quarterly installment to be accumulated

n = 16 periods [(5 years × 4 quarters) − 4 quarters already paid]

i = 2% effective compound rate (8% ÷ 4 quarters)

FV_n = $1,000 (Table III$_{\overline{16}|\,2\%}$)

FV_n = $1,000(18.6393)

FV_n = $18,639

$18,639 paid at the end of the 5 years is equivalent to the remaining 16 payments.

Problem 4:

Neil Robinson, proprietor of Robinson Appliance, received two offers for his last deluxe-model refrigerator. Jane Butler will pay $650 in cash. Ed McBride will pay $700 consisting of a down payment of $100 and 12 monthly payments of $50. If the installment interest rate is 24% compounded monthly, which offer should Robinson accept?

Solution to Problem 4:

In order to compare the two alternative methods of payment, all cash flows must be accumulated or discounted to one point in time. As illustrated by the time line, the present is selected as the point of comparison.

McBride $100 $50 $50 $50 $50 $50 $50 $50 $50 $50 $50 $50 $50

0   1   2   3   4   5   6   7   8   9   10   11   12 months

Butler $650

Butler's offer is $650 today. The present value of $650 today is $650.

McBride's offer consists of an annuity of 12 payments, plus $100 paid today which is not part of the annuity. The annuity may be discounted to the present by using Table IV and the applicable formula:

$PV_n = R(PVAF_{\overline{n}|i})$ where: PV_n = Unknown present value of 12 payments
  R = $50 monthly payment to be discounted
  n = 12 periods (1 year × 12 months)
  i = 2% effective compound rate (24% ÷ 12 periods per year)

$PV_n = \$50$ (Table $IV_{\overline{12}|2\%}$)
$Pv_n = \$50(10.5753)$
$PV_n = \$529$

Present value of McBride's payments... $529
Present value of McBride's $100 down payment 100
Total present value of McBride's offer.. $629

Therefore, Butler's offer of $650 cash is more desirable than McBride's offer.

Problem 5:

The Angelo Company is investigating the purchase of a block of bonds. Each $1,000 bond has a stated interest rate of 12% paid semiannually and is due in 10 years. The prevailing market rate for comparable bonds is 8%, also paid semiannually. How much should Angelo Company pay for each bond?

Solution to Problem 5:

This problem involves finding the present value of the cash flows resulting from the purchase of a bond. A bond pays both a series of equal interest payments and the principal amount when the bond matures. To ascertain the fair market price of a bond, both the series of interest payments and the future payment of the principal must be discounted to the present at the going market rate of 8% compounded semiannually.

First the series of interest payments is discounted to the present using Table IV and the applicable formula:

$PV_n = R(PVAF_{\overline{n}|i})$ where: PV_n = Unknown present value
  R = $60 semiannual interest payment ($1,000 × .12 × ½ year)
  n = 20 periods (10 years × 2 periods per year)
  i = 4% effective compound rate (8% ÷ 2 periods per year)

$PV_n = \$60$ (Table $IV_{\overline{20}|\,4\%}$)

$PV_n = \$60(13.5903)$

$PV_n = \$815$

Second, the future payment of prinicipal is discounted to the present using Table II and the applicable formula:

$PV = A(PVF_{\overline{n}|\,i})$ where: PV = Unknown present value of the prinicpal payment

A = \$1,000, the principal payment

n = 20 periods

i = 4% effective compound rate

$PV = \$1,000$ (Table $II_{\overline{20}|\,4\%}$)

$PV = \$1,000\,(.4564)$

$PV = \$456$

Therefore, the price Angelo Company should pay for each bond is \$815 + \$456, or \$1,271.

INTERPOLATION

A difficulty in using future and present value tables arises when the exact factor does not appear in the table. One solution is to use the formula. **Interpolation** is another, often more practical, solution. Interpolation assumes the change between two values is linear. Although such an assumption is not correct, the margin of error is often insignificant, especially if the table value ranges are not too wide.

For example, determine the table value for the present value of \$1 due in 9 periods at 4½%. The appropriate factor does not appear in Table II. However, the two closest values are Table $II_{\overline{9}|\,4\%} = .7026$ and Table $II_{\overline{9}|\,5\%} = .6446$. Interpolation relates the unknown value to the change in the known values. This relationship may be shown as a proportion:

$$\frac{y}{Y} = \frac{x}{X}$$

$$\frac{5 - 4\frac{1}{2}}{5 - 4} = \frac{x}{.7026 - .6446}$$

$$\frac{\frac{1}{2}}{1} = \frac{x}{.0580}$$

$$X = .0290$$

The .0290 is the difference between the value for 5% and the value for 4½%. Therefore, the value needed is .0290 + .6446 = .6736. Using the mathematical formula for Table II $\left\{ PV = A\left[\dfrac{1}{(1 + i)^n}\right] \right\}$, the present value of \$1 at 4½% interest for 9 periods is .6729 $\left\{ PV = 1\left[\dfrac{1}{(1 + .045)^9}\right] \right\}$. The difference (.6736 − .6729 = .0007) is insignificant for many purposes.

Interpolation is useful in finding a particular unknown table value that lies between two given values. This procedure is also used in approximating the number of periods or unknown interest rates when the table value is known. The following problems illustrate the determination of these two variables.

Problem 6:

Joan Novella leaves $600,000 to a university for a new building on the condition that construction will not begin until the bequest, invested at 5% per year, amounts to $1,500,000. How long before construction may begin?

Solution to Problem 6:

This problem involves finding the time (number of periods) required for a lump-sum payment to accumulate to a specified future amount. Table I is used, and the applicable formula is:

$FV = P(FVF_{\overline{n}|i})$ where: FV = $1,500,000
                                        P = $600,000
                                        n = Unknown number of periods
                                        i = 5% effective interest rate per year

$1,500,000 = $600,000 \, (\text{Table } I_{\overline{n}|5\%})$

$\dfrac{\$1,500,000}{\$\ 600,000} = \text{Table } I_{\overline{n}|5\%}$

$2.5 = \text{Table } I_{\overline{n}|5\%}$

Referring to Table I, reading down the i = 5% column:

n	Table Factor
18 =	2.4066
19 =	2.5270

Interpolating:

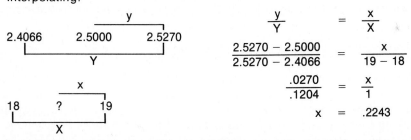

$$\frac{y}{Y} = \frac{x}{X}$$

$$\frac{2.5270 - 2.5000}{2.5270 - 2.4066} = \frac{x}{19 - 18}$$

$$\frac{.0270}{.1204} = \frac{x}{1}$$

$$x = .2243$$

The .2243 is the difference between the number of periods at table factor 2.5270 and the number of periods at table factor 2.5000. Therefore, the number of periods needed is 19.0000 − .2243 = 18.7757. In other words, about 18¾ periods (in this case, years) are required for $600,000 to amount to $1,500,000 at 5% annual interest.

Problem 7:

The Newports have entered into an automobile lease-purchase arrangement. The fair market value of the leased automobile is $5,814, and the contract calls for quarterly payments of $570 due at the end of each quarter for 3 years. What is the implicit rate of interest on the lease arrangement?

Solution to Problem 7:

The implicit interest rate must be computed for the present value of an annuity. The present value is the fair market value of the automobile, and the payment is the lease payment. Table IV is used, and the appropriate formula is given below.

$$PV_n = R(PVAF_{\overline{n}|\,i}) \quad \text{where:} \quad PV_n = \$5,814$$
$$R = \$570$$
$$n = 12(3 \text{ years} \times 4 \text{ payments per year})$$
$$i = \text{The unknown quarterly interest rate}$$

$$\$5,814 = \$570 \ (\text{Table IV}_{\overline{12}|\,i})$$

$$\frac{\$5,814}{\$570} = \text{Table IV}_{\overline{12}|\,i}$$

$$10.20 = \text{Table IV}_{\overline{12}|\,i}$$

Reading across the $n = 12$ row of Table IV:

i		Table Factor
2%	=	10.5753
3%	=	9.9540

Interpolating:

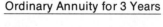

$$\frac{y}{Y} = \frac{x}{X}$$

$$\frac{10.2000 - 9.9540}{10.5753 - 9.9540} = \frac{x}{3.0 - 2.0}$$

$$\frac{.2460}{.6213} = \frac{x}{1.0}$$

$$x = .3959$$

The .3959 is the difference between the interest rate at the table factor 9.9540 and the interest rate at the table factor 10.2000. Therefore, the quarterly implicit interest rate is $3.0000 - .3959 = 2.6041\%$; and the annual implicit interest rate is 10.4164% ($2.6041\% \times 4$).

ORDINARY ANNUITY AND ANNUITY DUE

Annuities are of two types: ordinary annuities (annuities in arrears) and annuities due (annuities in advance). The periodic rents or payments for an **ordinary annuity** are made at the *end* of each period, and the last payment coincides with the end of the annuity term. The periodic rents or payments for an **annuity due** are made at the *beginning* of each period, and one period of the annuity term remains after the last payment. These differences are illustrated as follows:

Ordinary Annuity for 3 Years

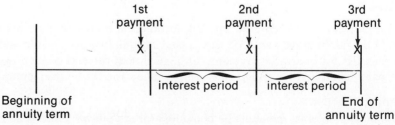

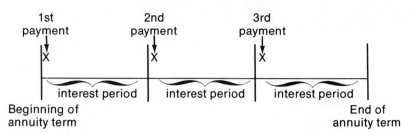

Annuity Due for 3 Years

Most future and present value tables are computed for ordinary annuities; however, with slight adjustment, these same tables may be used in solving annuity due problems. To illustrate the conversion of an ordinary annuity table value to an annuity due value, consider the future amount of an ordinary annuity for three years (see the diagram at the bottom of page 1000). This situation involves three payments (3p); but because the first payment is made at the end of the first period, interest is earned for only two periods (2i), or in total, 3p + 2i. On the other hand, the future amount of an annuity due for three years (the diagram above) involves three payments as well as interest for three periods because the first payment is made at the beginning of the first period (3p + 3i).

As shown below, an ordinary annuity involving four payments would earn interest for three periods (4p + 3i); thus, if the fourth payment were deducted, the value would be comparable to an annuity due of 3 periods [i.e., (4p + 3i) − 1p = 3p + 3i].

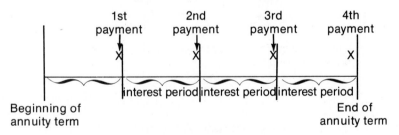

Ordinary Annuity for 4 Years

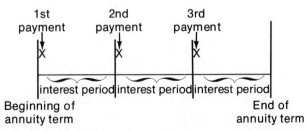

Annuity Due for 3 Years

Therefore, to find the future value of an annuity due using ordinary annuity table values, simply select the appropriate table value for an ordinary annuity for one additional period (n + 1) and subtract the extra payment (which is 1.0000 in terms of the table value because the tables are computed for rents of $1.0000). The formula is $FV_n = R(FVAF_{\overline{n+1}|i} - 1)$.

For example, the table value (Table III) for the future amount of an annuity due for 3 periods at 8% is:

(1) Factor for future value of an ordinary annuity of $1 for 4 periods (n + 1) at 8%..4.5061
(2) Less one payment 1.0000
(3) Factor for future value of an annuity due of $1 for 3 periods at 8%.................3.5061

The situation and the underlying reasoning are reversed in converting a present value factor of an ordinary annuity to the present value factor of an annuity due. As shown in the diagrams below, the present value of an annuity due for three years involves three payments; but interest (discount) is only earned for two periods (3p + 2i). To obtain comparable interest (discount) periods, an ordinary annuity for two years is required (2p + 2i). However, one additional payment must be added to make the situations equivalent; i.e., (2p + 2i) + 1p = 3p + 2i. Consequently, to convert the present value of an ordinary annuity to the present value of an annuity due, select the table factor for one less period (n − 1) and then add one payment (+1.0000). The formula is $PV_n = R(PVAF_{\overline{n-1}|i} + 1)$.

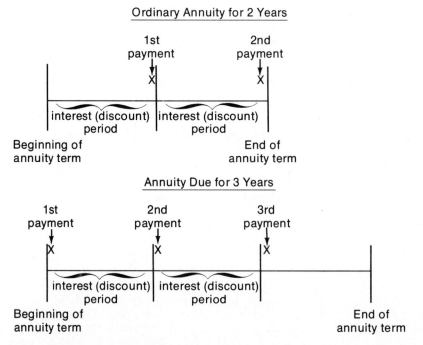

For example, the table value (Table IV) for the present value of an annuity due for three periods at 8% is:

(1) Factor for present value of an ordinary annuity of $1 for two periods (n − 1)
at 8%..1.7833
(2) Plus one payment...1.0000
(3) Factor for present value of an annuity due of $1 for 3 periods at 8% 2.7833

The following problems illustrate the application of converting from ordinary annuity table values to annuity due table values.

Problem 8:

The Sampson Corporation desires to accumulate funds to retire a $200,000 bond issue at the end of 15 years. Funds set aside for this purpose can be invested to yield 6%. What annual payment starting immediately would provide the needed funds?

Solution to Problem 8:

Annuity payments of an unknown amount are to be accumulated toward a specific dollar amount at a known interest rate. Therefore, Table III is used. Because the first payment is to be made immediately, all payments will fall due at the beginning of each period and an annuity due is used. The appropriate formula is:

$$FV_n = R(FVAF_{\overline{n+1}|i} - 1)$$ where: $FV_n = \$200,000$
R   = Unknown annual payment
n   = 15 periods
i   = 6% annual interest

$\$200,000 = R \text{ (Table III}_{\overline{16}|6\%} - 1)$

$\$200,000 = R(24.6725)$

$\dfrac{\$200,000}{24.6725} = R$

$\$8,106 = R$

Sampson Corporation must deposit $8,106 annually, starting immediately, to accumulate $200,000 in 15 years at 6% annual interest.

Problem 9:

Brigham Corporation has completed lease-purchase negotiations. The fair market value of the leased equipment is $45,897. The lease contract specifies semiannual payments of $3,775 for 10 years beginning immediately. At the end of the lease, Brigham Corporation may purchase the equipment for a nominal amount. What is the implicit annual rate of interest on the lease purchase?

Solution to Problem 9:

The implicit interest rate must be computed for the present value of an annuity due. The present value is the fair market value of the equipment, and the payment is the lease payment. Table IV is used, and the applicable formula is:

$$PV_n = R(PVAF_{\overline{n-1}|i} + 1)$$ where: $PV_n = \$45,897$
R   = $3,775
n   = 20 periods (10 years × 2 payments per year)
i   = The unknown semiannual interest rate

$45,897 = $3,775 (Table $IV_{\overline{19}|i}$ + 1)

$$\frac{\$45,897}{\$3,775} = 12.1581 = \text{Table IV}_{\overline{19}|i} + 1$$

$11.1581 = \text{Table IV}_{\overline{19}|i}$

Examination of Table IV for 19 periods and a factor of 11.1581 shows Table $IV_{\overline{19}|6\%} = 11.1581$. Therefore, $i = 6\%$. The implicit annual interest rate is twice the semiannual rate, or $2 \times 6\% = 12\%$.

Problem 10:

Three years remain on the lease of Nyland Food Service, Inc.'s building. The lease is noncancelable and requires payments of $5,000 on March 1 and September 1. During February, Nyland located a new store building and asked the lessor of the old store to accept $25,000 now in full payment of the old lease. The building is very old and will not be used again. If the value of money to the lessor is 16% compounded semiannually, should Nyland's offer be accepted?

Solution to Problem 10:

The lessor must compare the $25,000 now to the value of the six remaining lease payments. The lease payments must be discounted to the present for proper comparison. Because the next payment is due now, the lease payments are an annuity due. Table IV is adjusted to find the appropriate value. The formula is:

$$PV_n = R(\text{PVAF}_{\overline{n-1}|i} + 1)$$

where: PV_n = Unknown present value of lease payments

R = $5,000 per period (6 months)

n = 6 periods (3 years × 2 periods per year)

i = 8% (16% ÷ 2 periods per year)

PV_n = $5,000 (Table $IV_{\overline{5}|8\%}$ + 1)

PV_n = $5,000(3.9927 + 1)

PV_n = $24,964

The offer of $25,000 now is greater than $24,964, the present value of the remaining lease payments. Therefore, the lessor should accept the offer.

EXERCISES

1. John Foley borrowed $500 from a credit union at 8% simple interest. The loan is to be repaid in 6 months. How much will Foley have to pay to settle this obligation? How much of this payment will be interest? If Foley were to borrow the $500 from The Commercial Bank at 12% compounded quarterly, how much interest would he have to pay?

2. Indicate the rate per period and the number of periods for each of the following:

    (a) 10% per annum, for 3 years, compounded annually.
    (b) 10% per annum, for 3 years, compounded semiannually.
    (c) 10% per annum, for 3 years, compounded quarterly.
    (d) 10% per annum, for 3 years, compounded monthly.

3. What is the future amount for each of the following independent situations?

> (a) The amount of $1,000 for 4 years at 8% compounded annually.
> (b) The amount of $1,000 for 4 years at 8% compounded quarterly.
> (c) The amount of $500 for 1 year at 24% compounded monthly.

4. What is the present value for each of the following independent situations?

> (a) The present value of $1,000 due in 5 years at 10% compounded annually.
> (b) The present value of $1,000 due in 5 years at 10% compounded semiannually.
> (c) The present value of $25,000 due in 10 years at 8% compounded quarterly.

5. For each of the following, compute the future amount of an ordinary annuity (also known as an annuity in arrears).

> (a) 12 payments of $100 at 6%.
> (b) 8 payments of $500 at 10%.
> (c) 19 payments of $125 at 12%.

6. What are the future amounts in Exercise 5 if the annuities are annuities due (also known as annuities in advance)?

7. For each of the following, compute the present value of an ordinary annuity.

> (a) $1,000 for 10 years at 8%.
> (b) $350 for 7 years at 5%.
> (c) $250 for 20 years at 10%.

8. What are the present values in Exercise 7 if the annuities are annuities due?

9. Tim Baxter has $2,000 to invest. One alternative will yield 10% per year for 4 years. A second alternative is to deposit the $2,000 in a bank which will pay 8% per year, compounded quarterly. Which alternative should Baxter select?

10. RaNae Allen wishes to have $6,000 to buy a new car at the end of 5 years. How much must be invested today to accomplish this purpose if the interest rate on the investment is 6%?

11. The Nielsens plan to save $1,500 each year to apply as a down payment on a home. If their first deposit is made on January 1, 1982, and their last deposit is made on January 1, 1986, how much will the Nielsens have for their down payment by January 1, 1986? Assume an interest rate of 8%.

12. If Mike Knudsen invests $800 on July 1 of each year from 1979 to 1989, inclusive, how much will have accumulated on July 1, 1990, if the interest rate is 12%?

13. Professor Andersen has $55,000 accumulated in a retirement fund and plans to invest that amount in an annuity on September 1, 1983, when she retires. Assume that Andersen purchases an annuity of 20 annual payments, the first to be made on September 1, 1984, with an 8% rate of interest. What will be the amount of the yearly payments?

14. Jill Doakes borrowed $4,000 on a note due on August 1, 1980. On that date Doakes was unable to pay the obligation but was able to arrange for Western Loan Company to pay the holder of the note the $4,000. Doakes agreed to pay Western Loan Company a series of 5 equal annual payments beginning on August 1, 1980. Each payment is in part a payment on the unpaid principal and in part a payment of interest at 12% per annum. What is the amount of Doakes payment?

15. An accounting student bought a calculator for $250 to assist in homework assignments. The student bought the calculator on time, agreeing to pay $23.64 at the end of each month for 12 months. What annual interest rate did the student pay?

16. A new freezer may be purchased for $375 cash or for 8 monthly payments of $51.75 each. If you choose to buy the freezer over time, what approximate annual interest rate will you be paying?

17. The Johnsons are trying to accumulate $5,000 to buy some mountain property. They are able to deposit $1,200 a year into their savings account which earns 6% per year. In how many years can the Johnsons expect to buy their property?

18. K agrees to lease from L certain property for 10 years at the following annual rentals, payable in advance:

Years 1 and 2	$1,000 per annum
Years 3 to 6	$2,000 per annum
Years 7 to 10	$2,500 per annum

What single immediate sum will pay all of these rents if they are discounted at 6%? Prove by setting up a table showing the reduction of the leasehold.

19. Comment on the following statement issued by the president of a large corporation: "The directors have accepted a bid of $103.75 for $10,000,000, 20-year, first mortgage, 9½% bonds, thus securing $10,375,000 new capital. They gave serious consideration to a competing offer of par for 9% bonds. Although this would have meant an interest saving, the receipt of $375,000 additional capital at this time is of great advantage and offsets the interest saving under the lower coupon rate."

20. ABC Company is offered two alternative methods of purchasing a piece of equipment: (1) $20,000 cash or (2) $10,000 down plus $1,900 per year due at the end of each year for 6 years. Should the buyer accept the cash or the time-interest installment if money is worth 10% per annum?

21. An existing building is under consideration as an investment. Estimates of expected annual cash receipts for the next 20 years are $8,000 per year. Cash outlays will be $2,000 per year. (Assume cash flows at the end of the year.)

(a) How much is the building worth to the buyer if 10% per annum is an appropriate rate of return?

(b) If $30,000 is borrowed to finance purchase of the building and is to be repaid annually by means of 10 year-end payments at 6% interest, what will the annual payments be?

22. (a) Determine the price of a 5-year, $10,000, 9% bond, with semiannual coupons, bought to yield 12%. (b) What is the price if the above bond bears interest at 12% and is bought to yield 11%?

TABLE I

Amount of $1 Due in n Periods

$$FV = P(1 + i)^n = P(FVF_{\overline{n}|i})$$

n	2%	3%	4%	5%	6%	8%	10%	12%	16%	20%
1	1.0200	1.0300	1.0400	1.0500	1.0600	1.0800	1.1000	1.1200	1.1600	1.2000
2	1.0404	1.0609	1.0816	1.1025	1.1236	1.1664	1.1200	1.2544	1.3456	1.4400
3	1.0612	1.0927	1.1249	1.1576	1.1910	1.2597	1.3310	1.4049	1.5609	1.7280
4	1.0824	1.1255	1.1699	1.2155	1.2625	1.3605	1.4641	1.5735	1.8106	2.0736
5	1.1041	1.1593	1.2167	1.2763	1.3382	1.4693	1.6105	1.7623	2.1003	2.4883
6	1.1262	1.1941	1.2653	1.3401	1.4185	1.5869	1.7716	1.9738	2.4364	2.9860
7	1.1487	1.2299	1.3159	1.4071	1.5036	1.7138	1.9487	2.2107	2.8262	3.5832
8	1.1717	1.2668	1.3686	1.4775	1.5938	1.8509	2.1436	2.4760	3.2784	4.2998
9	1.1951	1.3048	1.4233	1.5513	1.6895	1.9990	2.3579	2.7731	3.8030	5.1598
10	1.2190	1.3439	1.4802	1.6289	1.7908	2.1589	2.5937	3.1058	4.4114	6.1917
11	1.2434	1.3842	1.5395	1.7103	1.8983	2.3316	2.8531	3.4785	5.1173	7.4301
12	1.2682	1.4258	1.6010	1.7959	2.0122	2.5182	3.1384	3.8960	5.9360	8.9161
13	1.2936	1.4685	1.6651	1.8856	2.1329	2.7196	3.4523	4.3635	6.8858	10.6993
14	1.3195	1.5126	1.7317	1.9799	2.2609	2.9372	3.7975	4.8871	7.9875	12.8392
15	1.3459	1.5580	1.8009	2.0789	2.3966	3.1722	4.1772	5.4736	9.2655	15.4070
16	1.3728	1.6047	1.8730	2.1829	2.5404	3.4259	4.5950	6.1304	10.7480	18.4884
17	1.4002	1.6528	1.9479	2.2920	2.6928	3.7000	5.0545	6.8660	12.4677	22.1861
18	1.4282	1.7024	2.0258	2.4066	2.8543	3.9960	5.5599	7.6900	14.4625	26.6233
19	1.4568	1.7535	2.1068	2.5270	3.0256	4.3157	6.1159	8.6128	16.7765	31.9480
20	1.4859	1.8061	2.1911	2.6533	3.2071	4.6610	6.7275	9.6463	19.4608	38.3376
25	1.6406	2.0938	2.6658	3.3864	4.2919	6.8485	10.8347	17.0001	40.8742	95.3962
30	1.8114	2.4273	3.2434	4.3219	5.7435	10.0627	17.4494	29.9599	85.8499	237.3763
40	2.2080	3.2620	4.8010	7.0400	10.2857	21.7245	45.2593	93.0509	378.7212	1469.7716
50	2.6916	4.3839	7.1067	11.4674	18.4202	46.9016	117.3909	289.0022	1670.7038	9100.4382

TABLE II

Present Value of $1 Due in n Periods

$$PV = A \left[\frac{1}{(1+i)^n} \right] = A(PVF_{\overline{n}|\,i})$$

n	2%	3%	4%	5%	6%	8%	10%	12%	16%	20%
1	0.9804	0.9709	0.9615	0.9524	0.9434	0.9259	0.9091	0.8929	0.8621	0.8333
2	0.9612	0.9426	0.9246	0.9070	0.8900	0.8573	0.8264	0.7972	0.7432	0.6944
3	0.9423	0.9151	0.8890	0.8638	0.8396	0.7938	0.7513	0.7118	0.6407	0.5787
4	0.9238	0.8885	0.8548	0.8227	0.7921	0.7350	0.6830	0.6355	0.5523	0.4823
5	0.9057	0.8626	0.8219	0.7835	0.7473	0.6806	0.6209	0.5674	0.4761	0.4019
6	0.8880	0.8375	0.7903	0.7462	0.7050	0.6302	0.5645	0.5066	0.4104	0.3349
7	0.8706	0.8131	0.7599	0.7107	0.6651	0.5835	0.5132	0.4523	0.3538	0.2791
8	0.8535	0.7894	0.7307	0.6768	0.6274	0.5403	0.4665	0.4039	0.3050	0.2326
9	0.8368	0.7664	0.7026	0.6446	0.5919	0.5002	0.4241	0.3606	0.2630	0.1938
10	0.8203	0.7441	0.6756	0.6139	0.5584	0.4632	0.3855	0.3220	0.2267	0.1615
11	0.8043	0.7224	0.6496	0.5847	0.5268	0.4289	0.3505	0.2875	0.1954	0.1346
12	0.7885	0.7014	0.6246	0.5568	0.4970	0.3971	0.3186	0.2567	0.1685	0.1122
13	0.7730	0.6810	0.6006	0.5303	0.4688	0.3677	0.2897	0.2292	0.1452	0.0935
14	0.7579	0.6611	0.5775	0.5051	0.4423	0.3405	0.2633	0.2046	0.1252	0.0779
15	0.7430	0.6419	0.5553	0.4810	0.4173	0.3152	0.2394	0.1827	0.1079	0.0649
16	0.7284	0.6232	0.5339	0.4581	0.3936	0.2919	0.2176	0.1631	0.0930	0.0541
17	0.7142	0.6050	0.5134	0.4363	0.3714	0.2703	0.1978	0.1456	0.0802	0.0451
18	0.7002	0.5874	0.4936	0.4155	0.3503	0.2502	0.1799	0.1300	0.0691	0.0376
19	0.6864	0.5703	0.4746	0.3957	0.3305	0.2317	0.1635	0.1161	0.0596	0.0313
20	0.6730	0.5537	0.4564	0.3769	0.3118	0.2145	0.1486	0.1037	0.0514	0.0261
25	0.6095	0.4776	0.3751	0.2953	0.2330	0.1460	0.0923	0.0588	0.0245	0.0105
30	0.5521	0.4120	0.3083	0.2314	0.1741	0.0994	0.0573	0.0334	0.0116	0.0042
40	0.4529	0.3066	0.2083	0.1420	0.0972	0.0460	0.0221	0.0107	0.0026	0.0007
50	0.3715	0.2281	0.1407	0.0872	0.0543	0.0213	0.0085	0.0035	0.0006	0.0001

TABLE III

Amount of an Annuity of $1 per Period

$$FV_n = R \left[\frac{(1 + i)^n - 1}{i} \right] = R(FVAF_{\overline{n}|i})$$

n	2%	3%	4%	5%	6%	8%	10%	12%	16%	20%
1	1.0000	1.0000	1.0000	1.0000	1.0000	1.0000	1.0000	1.0000	1.0000	1.0000
2	2.0200	2.0300	2.0400	2.0500	2.0600	2.0800	2.1000	2.1200	2.1600	2.2000
3	3.0604	3.0909	3.1216	3.1525	3.1836	3.2464	3.3100	3.3744	3.5056	3.6400
4	4.1216	4.1836	4.2465	4.3101	4.3746	4.5061	4.6410	4.7793	5.0665	5.3680
5	5.2040	5.3091	5.4163	5.5256	5.6371	5.8666	6.1051	6.3528	6.8771	7.4416
6	6.3081	6.4684	6.6330	6.8019	6.9753	7.3359	7.7156	8.1152	8.9775	9.9299
7	7.4343	7.6625	7.8983	8.1420	8.3938	8.9228	9.4872	10.0890	11.4139	12.9159
8	8.5830	8.8923	9.2142	9.5491	9.8975	10.6366	11.4359	12.2997	14.2401	16.4991
9	9.7546	10.1591	10.5828	11.0266	11.4913	12.4876	13.5795	14.7757	17.5185	20.7989
10	10.9497	11.4639	12.0061	12.5779	13.1808	14.4866	15.9374	17.5487	21.3215	25.9587
11	12.1687	12.8078	13.4864	14.2068	14.9716	16.6455	18.5312	20.6546	25.7329	32.1504
12	13.4121	14.1920	15.0258	15.9171	16.8699	18.9771	21.3843	24.1331	30.8502	39.5805
13	14.6803	15.6178	16.6268	17.7130	18.8821	21.4953	24.5227	28.0291	36.7862	48.4966
14	15.9739	17.0863	18.2919	19.5986	21.0151	24.2149	27.9750	32.3926	43.6720	59.1959
15	17.2934	18.5989	20.0236	21.5786	23.2760	27.1521	31.7725	37.2797	51.6595	72.0351
16	18.6393	20.1569	21.8245	23.6575	25.6725	30.3243	35.9497	42.7533	60.9250	87.4421
17	20.0121	21.7616	23.6975	25.8404	28.2129	33.7502	40.5447	48.8837	71.6730	105.9306
18	21.4123	23.4144	25.6454	28.1324	30.9057	37.4502	45.5992	55.7497	84.1407	128.1167
19	22.8406	25.1169	27.6712	30.5390	33.7600	41.4463	51.1591	63.4397	98.6032	154.7400
20	24.2974	26.8704	29.7781	33.0660	36.7856	45.7620	57.2750	72.0524	115.3797	186.6880
25	32.0303	36.4593	41.6459	47.7271	54.8645	73.1059	98.3471	133.3339	249.2140	471.9811
30	40.5681	47.5754	56.0849	66.4388	79.0582	113.2832	164.4940	241.3327	530.3117	1181.8816
40	60.4020	75.4013	95.0255	120.7998	154.7620	259.0565	442.5926	767.0914	2360.7572	7343.8578
50	84.5794	112.7969	152.6671	209.3480	290.3359	573.7702	1163.9085	2400.0182	10435.6488	45497.1908

TABLE IV

Present Value of an Annuity of $1 per Period

$$PV_n = R\left[\frac{1 - \frac{1}{(1+i)^n}}{i}\right] = R(PVAF_{\overline{n}|i})$$

n	2%	3%	4%	5%	6%	8%	10%	12%	16%	20%
1	0.9804	0.9709	0.9615	0.9524	0.9434	0.9259	0.9091	0.8929	0.8621	0.8333
2	1.9416	1.9135	1.8861	1.8594	1.8334	1.7833	1.7355	1.6901	1.6052	1.5278
3	2.8839	2.8286	2.7751	2.7232	2.6730	2.5771	2.4869	2.4018	2.2459	2.1065
4	3.8077	3.7171	3.6299	3.5460	3.4651	3.3121	3.1699	3.0373	2.7982	2.5887
5	4.7135	4.5797	4.4518	4.3295	4.2124	3.9927	3.7908	3.6048	3.2743	2.9906
6	5.6014	5.4172	5.2421	5.0757	4.9173	4.6229	4.3553	4.1114	3.6847	3.3255
7	6.4720	6.2303	6.0021	5.7864	5.5824	5.2064	4.8684	4.5638	4.0386	3.6016
8	7.3255	7.0197	6.7327	6.4632	6.2098	5.7466	5.3349	4.9676	4.3436	3.8372
9	8.1622	7.7861	7.4353	7.1078	6.8017	6.2469	5.7590	5.3282	4.6065	4.0310
10	8.9826	8.5302	8.1109	7.7217	7.3601	6.7101	6.1446	5.6502	4.8332	4.1925
11	9.7868	9.2526	8.7605	8.3064	7.8869	7.1390	6.4951	5.9377	5.0286	4.3271
12	10.5753	9.9540	9.3851	8.8633	8.3838	7.5361	6.8137	6.1944	5.1971	4.4392
13	11.3484	10.6350	9.9856	9.3936	8.8527	7.9038	7.1034	6.4235	5.3423	4.5327
14	12.1062	11.2961	10.5631	9.8986	9.2950	8.2442	7.3667	6.6282	5.4675	4.6106
15	12.8493	11.9379	11.1184	10.3797	9.7122	8.5595	7.6061	6.8109	5.5755	4.6755
16	13.5777	12.5611	11.6523	10.8378	10.1059	8.8514	7.8237	6.9740	5.6685	4.7296
17	14.2919	13.1661	12.1657	11.2741	10.4773	9.1216	8.0216	7.1196	5.7487	4.7746
18	14.9920	13.7535	12.6593	11.6896	10.8276	9.3719	8.2014	7.2497	5.8178	4.8122
19	15.6785	14.3238	13.1339	12.0853	11.1581	9.6036	8.3649	7.3658	5.8775	4.8435
20	16.3514	14.8775	13.5903	12.4622	11.4699	9.8181	8.5136	7.4694	5.9288	4.8696
25	19.5235	17.4131	15.6221	14.0939	12.7834	10.6748	9.0770	7.8431	6.0971	4.9476
30	22.3965	19.6004	17.2920	15.3725	13.7648	11.2578	9.4269	8.0552	6.1772	4.9789
40	27.3555	23.1148	19.7928	17.1591	15.0463	11.9246	9.7791	8.2438	6.2335	4.9966
50	31.4236	25.7298	21.4822	18.2559	15.7619	12.2335	9.9148	8.3045	6.2463	4.9995

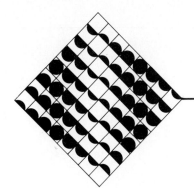

Appendix B

Illustrative Financial Statements

General Mills, Inc., and Subsidiaries
Consolidated Statements of Income and Retained Earnings

Consolidated Statements of Income

	Fiscal Year Ended	
(Amounts In Millions, Except Per Share Data)	May 27, 1979	May 28, 1978
Sales	$3,745.0	$3,243.0
Costs and Expenses:		
Costs of sales, exclusive of items shown below	2,336.3	2,015.3
Depreciation expense (Note 1-B)	70.5	56.1
Amortization expense (Note 1-D)	2.8	2.5
Interest expense	38.8	29.3
Contributions to employees' retirement plans (Notes 1-F and 8)	25.1	21.0
Selling, general and administrative expenses	1,007.6	873.6
Total Costs and Expenses	3,481.1	2,997.8
Earnings from Continuing Operations before Taxes on Income	263.9	245.2
Taxes on Income (Note 10)	(116.9)	(116.4)
Earnings from Continuing Operations	147.0	128.8
Results from Discontinued Specialty Chemicals Operations (Note 12):		
Earnings from operations, net of taxes of $1.5	—	1.8
Gain on disposal, net of taxes of $6.7	—	5.2
Net Earnings	$ 147.0	$ 135.8
Earnings per Common Share and Common Share Equivalent (Note 1-I):		
From continuing operations	$ 2.92	$ 2.58
Net earnings	$ 2.92	$ 2.72
Average Number of Common Shares and Common Share Equivalents (Notes 1-I and 6)	50.4	49.9

Consolidated Statements of Retained Earnings

	Fiscal Year Ended	
(In Millions)	May 27, 1979	May 28, 1978
Retained Earnings at Beginning of Year	$ 634.6	$ 547.0
Add net earnings for the year	147.0	135.8
Deduct dividends on common stock of $1.12 per share in 1979 and $0.97 per share in 1978	(56.1)	(48.2)
Retained Earnings at End of Year (Note 5)	$ 725.5	$ 634.6

See accompanying notes to consolidated financial statements.

General Mills, Inc., and Subsidiaries
Consolidated Balance Sheets

Assets

(In Millions)	May 27, 1979	May 28, 1978
Current Assets:		
Cash	$ 18.9	$ 4.8
Interest-bearing deposits	63.7	6.5
Marketable securities (at cost, which approximates market value)	14.4	8.6
Receivables:		
Customers	297.5	282.1
Miscellaneous	24.9	23.7
	322.4	305.8
Less allowance for possible losses	(9.0)	(8.2)
	313.4	297.6
Inventories (Notes 1-C and 3)	501.8	440.2
Prepaid expenses	24.2	30.7
Total Current Assets	**936.4**	**788.4**
Other Assets:		
Land, buildings and equipment, at cost (Note 1-B):		
Land	56.7	53.7
Buildings	347.6	317.5
Equipment	505.1	462.3
Construction in progress	65.6	53.2
	975.0	886.7
Less accumulated depreciation	(331.3)	(299.7)
	643.7	587.0
Miscellaneous assets:		
Investment in 20-50% owned companies (Note 1-A)	13.2	12.7
Other	62.4	50.4
	75.6	63.1
Intangible assets (Note 1-D):		
Excess of cost over net assets of acquired companies	168.1	163.5
Patents, copyrights and other intangibles	11.4	10.7
Total Other Assets	**898.8**	**824.3**
Total Assets	**$1,835.2**	**$1,612.7**

See accompanying notes to consolidated financial statements.

Liabilities and Stockholders' Equity

(In Millions)	May 27, 1979	May 28, 1978
Current Liabilities:		
Notes payable (Note 4)	$ 44.0	$ 59.0
Current portion of long-term debt	10.2	6.7
Accounts payable and accrued expenses:		
Accounts payable—trade	245.0	242.5
Accounts payable—miscellaneous	73.7	59.9
Accrued payroll	43.5	39.3
Accrued interest	6.5	4.9
	368.7	346.6
Accrued taxes	71.9	91.0
Total Current Liabilities	**494.8**	503.3
Other Liabilities:		
Long-term debt, excluding current portion (Note 5)	384.8	259.9
Deferred Federal income taxes (Note 1-H)	22.4	11.1
Deferred compensation	8.5	14.1
Other liabilities and deferred credits	5.7	3.6
Total Other Liabilities	**421.4**	288.7
Total Liabilities	**916.2**	792.0
Minority Interests	**2.8**	5.6
Stockholders' Equity:		
Common stock (Notes 6 and 7)	194.7	193.2
Retained earnings (Note 5)	725.5	634.6
Less common stock in treasury, at cost (Note 6)	(4.0)	(12.7)
Total Stockholders' Equity	**916.2**	815.1

Commitments, Litigation and Claims (Notes 2, 11, 13 and 14)

Total Liabilities and Stockholders' Equity	**$1,835.2**	$1,612.7

General Mills, Inc., and Subsidiaries
Consolidated Statements of Changes in Financial Position

	Fiscal Year Ended	
(In Millions)	May 27, 1979	May 28, 1978
Working Capital Provided by:		
Earnings from continuing operations	$147.0	$128.8
Add non-cash items:		
Depreciation and amortization	73.3	58.6
Deferred Federal income taxes	11.2	(2.9)
Other	6.0	10.1
Working capital provided from continuing operations	237.5	194.6
Earnings from discontinued operations	$ —	$ 1.8
Add non-cash items, principally depreciation	—	1.5
Working capital provided from discontinued operations	—	3.3
Total working capital provided from operations	237.5	197.9
Chemicals sale proceeds net of working capital sold and noncurrent note received (Note 12)	—	22.1
Proceeds from long-term debt issued	137.4	3.7
Common stock issued	10.2	2.6
Other sources	2.1	3.1
Total Working Capital Provided	**387.2**	**229.4**
Working Capital Used for:		
Gross additions to land, buildings and equipment	154.1	140.5
Less proceeds from sales	(30.9)	(7.3)
Net additions to land, buildings and equipment	123.2	133.2
Purchase price of businesses acquired	17.3	43.4
Less working capital acquired	(1.4)	(14.6)
Balance	15.9	28.8
Consisting of — Fixed assets	5.3	10.9
— Intangibles and miscellaneous assets	9.0	19.9
— Long-term debt	(1.2)	(2.1)
— Minority interests	3.0	.1
— Other	(.2)	—
Dividends	56.1	48.2
Reduction of long-term debt	15.8	22.6
Funding of deferred vacation liability	6.4	—
Other uses	13.3	9.7
Total Working Capital Used	**230.7**	**242.5**
Net Increase (Decrease) in Working Capital	**156.5**	**(13.1)**
Consisting of — Cash, deposits and marketable securities	77.1	(2.4)
— Receivables	15.8	66.0
— Inventories	61.6	14.4
— Prepaid expenses	(6.5)	(3.0)
— Current liabilities	8.5	(88.1)
Working Capital at Beginning of Year	**285.1**	**298.2**
Working Capital at End of Year	**$441.6**	**$285.1**

See accompanying notes to consolidated financial statements.

General Mills, Inc., and Subsidiaries
Notes to Consolidated Financial Statements
May 27, 1979, and May 28, 1978

Note One

Summary of Significant Accounting Policies

Significant accounting policies followed in preparing the consolidated financial statements are summarized below. These policies conform to generally accepted accounting principles and have been consistently applied. Certain 1978 amounts have been reclassified to conform to 1979's presentation.

A. Consolidation

The consolidated financial statements include the following domestic and foreign operations: (1) parent company and 100% owned subsidiaries; (2) majority-owned subsidiaries; and (3) General Mills' investment in and share of net earnings or losses of 20-50% owned companies.

All significant intercompany items have been eliminated from the consolidated financial statements.

The fiscal years of foreign operations generally end in April.

B. Land, Buildings, Equipment and Depreciation

Part of the cost of buildings and equipment is charged against earnings each year as depreciation expense. This amount is computed primarily by the straight-line method, which means that equal amounts of depreciation expense are charged against operations each year during the estimated useful life of an item. For tax purposes, accelerated methods of depreciation are used which provide more depreciation expense in the early years than in the later years of the estimated life of the item.

The useful lives employed for computing depreciation on principal classes of buildings and equipment are:

Buildings	20-50 years
Machinery and equipment	5-25 years
Office furniture and equipment	5-10 years
Transportation equipment	3-12 years

General Mills' policy is to charge maintenance, repair and minor renewal expenses to earnings in the year incurred. Major improvements to buildings and equipment are capitalized. When items are sold or retired, the accounts are relieved of cost and the related accumulated depreciation. Gains and losses on assets sold or retired are credited or charged to results of operations.

C. Inventories

Grain and flour inventories are valued at market. Grain inventories are adjusted to include unrealized gains and losses on open grain purchase and sale contracts.

Certain domestic inventories are valued at the lower of cost (determined by the LIFO method) or market. Other inventories are generally stated at the lower of cost (determined by the FIFO method) or market. See Note 3 for the amount of inventories valued by the LIFO and FIFO methods.

D. Amortization of Intangibles

The costs of patents and copyrights are amortized evenly over their lives by charges against earnings. Most of these costs were incurred through purchases of businesses.

"Excess of cost over net assets of acquired companies" (excess cost) is the difference between purchase prices and the values of assets of businesses acquired and accounted for by the purchase method of accounting. Any excess cost acquired after October, 1970, is amortized over not more than 40 years. Annually, the Audit Committee of the Board of Directors reviews these intangibles and writedowns thereof if the values have diminished. At its meeting on May 21, 1979, the Board of Directors determined that the unamortized amounts comprising the excess cost have continuing value.

E. Research and Development

All expenditures for research and development are charged against earnings in the year incurred. The charges for fiscal 1979 and 1978 were $37.3 million and $32.0 million, respectively.

General Mills, Inc., and Subsidiaries
Notes to Consolidated Financial Statements, Continued

Note One
Continued

F. Contributions to Employees' Retirement Plans

Contributions to defined-benefit plans are determined by enrolled actuaries using various methods and assumptions they consider appropriate in the circumstances of each plan. There were no significant changes in actuarial methods or assumptions during fiscal 1979. Contributions to defined-contribution plans are made in conformity with plan provisions. Contributions are funded with cash and are generally expensed by the company over the fiscal year in which the plan year associated with the contribution ends.

G. Foreign Exchange

Foreign balance sheet accounts are translated into U.S. dollars at year-end exchange rates except for accounts such as inventories, goodwill, land, buildings, equipment and capital stock, which are translated at the rates which were in effect when the items were acquired. Monthly income and expense amounts are translated at month-end rates, except that depreciation and cost of sales are translated at the same rate as the related assets. All gains and losses from translation procedures are credited or charged to income immediately.

H. Income Taxes

Investment tax credits are accounted for by the flow-through method which recognizes the benefit in the fiscal year the credit arises.

Deferred income taxes result from timing differences between income for financial reporting purposes and tax purposes.

The company accrues estimated income taxes payable on those earnings of foreign subsidiaries which are not expected to be permanently reinvested.

I. Earnings Per Share

Earnings per common share and common share equivalent is determined by dividing net earnings by the weighted average number of common shares and common share equivalents outstanding during the year. The common share equivalents consist of: (1) common stock which may be issuable upon exercise of outstanding stock options, (37,253 in 1979 and 34,678 in 1978); (2) treasury shares reserved for issuance under an incentive compensation plan (63,867 in 1979 and 60,641 in 1978); and (3) shares reserved for issuance to former owners of certain acquired companies, presently expected to be earned through profit performance contracts (252,024 in 1979 and 105,874 in 1978).

Note Two

Acquisitions

In fiscal 1978, General Mills purchased 100% of the common stock of Ship 'n Shore, Inc. for $35.1 million in cash. Following are the cash and common stock costs of this and other less significant acquisitions, plus increased ownership in partially-owned companies and additional payments under performance earnings agreements:

(Dollars in Millions)	Fiscal Year	
Acquisitions	1979	1978
— Cash	$ 4.8(a)	$ 41.4(b)
— Shares	189,478(a)	—
Increased ownership in partially-owned companies and performance earnings payments		
— Cash	$ 4.0(c)	$ 0.6
— Shares	275,126(c)	55,659

Note Two
Continued

(a) General Mills purchased the assets and operations of three companies (Chad Valley Company, Ltd., Lark Luggage Company and R & R Stamps, Inc.) for a total of $4.8 million in cash. In addition, the company acquired all the business of three companies (Casa Gallardo, Inc., in a purchase transaction, and Aroma Taste, Inc., and Louise's Home Style Ravioli Co., Inc., as pooling of interest transactions) in exchange for 189,478 shares of General Mills' common stock.

(b) In addition to the Ship 'n Shore purchase, the company also purchased the assets and operations of two other companies (Yoplait U.S.A. and Regal Toys Limited) for a total of $6.3 million in cash.

(c) General Mills purchased the remaining interests in three companies (Foot-Joy, Inc., Miro Company and Saluto Foods Corp.), two for cash totaling $4.0 million and one for 174,022 shares of General Mills' common stock. The company also issued 101,104 shares of common stock in satisfaction of performance earnings payments, primarily with respect to the acquisition of York Steak House Systems, Inc., in April of 1977.

As of May 27, 1979, General Mills was contingently liable for up to $9.0 million of additional performance earnings payments. The amount of payments will depend on actual earnings of the acquired company.

Sales, costs and earnings of businesses accounted for as purchases are included in results of operations from the dates of acquisition. Prior year financial statements have not been restated to reflect pooling transactions as the effect on operations would not be significant.

If the Ship 'n Shore acquisition had occurred at the beginning of fiscal 1978, pro-forma annual sales for Ship 'n Shore would have been $91 million. Related earnings were not significant to General Mills' consolidated earnings. Each of the other acquisitions in fiscal 1979 and 1978 affected consolidated sales and earnings by less than 1% in the year of acquisition.

Note Three

Inventories

Following is a comparison of year-end inventories:

(In Millions)	May 27, 1979	May 28, 1978
Grain, family flour and bakery flour	$ 38.0	$ 35.8
Raw materials, work in process, finished goods and supplies as follows:		
Valued at LIFO	208.0	187.0
Valued primarily at FIFO	255.8	217.4
Total inventories	$501.8	$440.2

If the FIFO method of inventory accounting had been used in place of LIFO, inventories (in millions) would have been $46.5 and $29.3 higher than reported at May 27, 1979, and May 28, 1978, respectively. See Note 1-C for a description of inventory valuation policies.

The total amounts of opening and closing inventories used in determining consolidated costs of sales (including discontinued operations at May 29, 1977) are as follows (in millions):

May 27, 1979	$501.8
May 28, 1978	$440.2
May 29, 1977	$425.8

General Mills, Inc., and Subsidiaries
Notes to Consolidated Financial Statements, Continued

Note Four

Short-Term Borrowings

The components of notes payable are as follows:

(Dollars in Millions)	May 27, 1979		May 28, 1978	
	Balance	Average Interest Rate	Balance	Average Interest Rate
Foreign banks	$41.7	10.2%	$34.8	9.1%
U.S. commercial paper	—	—	24.0	6.9
Miscellaneous	2.3	9.4	.2	5.7
Total	$44.0		$59.0	

The average balances outstanding, and the average interest rates incurred, were as follows:

(Dollars in Millions)	Fiscal 1979		Fiscal 1978	
	Average Balance Outstanding	Daily Average Interest Rate	Average Balance Outstanding	Daily Average Interest Rate
Foreign banks	$ 56.2	10.2%	$36.0	9.5%
U.S. commercial paper	96.0	9.0	48.6	6.2
Miscellaneous	.3	6.6	.9	8.9
Total	$152.5		$85.5	

The maximum amount of notes payable outstanding at any month end during fiscal 1979 and 1978 was $267.0 million on November 24, 1978 and $157.6 million on November 27, 1977, respectively. To ensure the availability of funds, the company during the year maintained bank credit lines sufficient to cover its outstanding commercial paper. At May 27, 1979, the Company had $48 million of such domestic lines available. These lines are on a fee-paid basis. As of May 27, 1979, foreign subsidiaries had $44 million of unused credit lines. The amount of the credit lines and the cost thereof are generally negotiated each year.

Note Five

Long-Term Debt

(In Millions)	May 27, 1979	May 28, 1978
7% sinking fund Eurodollar debentures, due November 1, 1980	$ 6.2	$ 11.1
Three 25-year 4¼% promissory notes of $10 million each, due May 1, 1982, May 1, 1983, and May 1, 1984	30.0	30.0
8% sinking fund Eurodollar debentures, due March 1, 1986	11.3	13.1
4⅝% sinking fund debentures, due August 1, 1990	18.3	20.2
8⅞% sinking fund debentures, due October 15, 1995	73.7	73.7
8% sinking fund debentures, due February 15, 1999	100.0	100.0
9⅜% sinking fund debentures, due March 1, 2009	125.0	—
Miscellaneous debt	35.3	21.1
Less unamortized bond discount	(4.8)	(2.6)
	395.0	266.6
Less amounts due within one year	(10.2)	(6.7)
	$384.8	$259.9

The sinking fund and principal payments due (in millions) on long-term debt are $10.2, $12.2, $23.0, $27.0 and $24.7 in fiscal years ending in 1980, 1981, 1982, 1983 and 1984, respectively.

Note Five
Continued

The terms of the promissory note agreements place restrictions on the payment of dividends, capital stock purchases and redemptions. At May 27, 1979, $486.5 million of retained earnings was free of such restrictions.

Note Six

Changes in Capital Stock

The following table describes changes in the $0.75 par value common stock from May 29, 1977, to May 27, 1979.

(Dollars in Millions)	Common Stock (70,000,000 Shares Authorized)			
	Issued		In Treasury	
	Shares	Amount	Shares	Cost
Balance at May 29, 1977	50,207,674	$192.5	543,811	$14.6
Stock option and profit sharing plans ...	27,553	.9	(19,374)	(.3)
Shares issued — other (Note 2)	—	(.2)	(55,659)	(1.6)
Balance at May 28, 1978	50,235,227	193.2	468,778	12.7
Stock option and profit sharing plans ...	14,263	1.3	(21,510)	(.5)
Shares issued — other (Note 2)	168,146	.2	(288,458)	(8.2)
Balance at May 27, 1979	50,417,636	$194.7	158,810	$ 4.0

The shareholders also have authorized 5,000,000 shares of cumulative preference stock, no par value. None of these shares was outstanding during either fiscal 1979 or 1978. If these shares are issued, the Directors may specify a dividend rate, convertibility rights, liquidating value and voting rights at the time of issuance.

Some of the unissued shares of common stock are potentially issuable for the following purposes:

	Number of Shares	
	May 27, 1979	May 28, 1978
Stock options outstanding (Note 7)	1,736,662	1,562,892
Stock options available for grant (Note 7)	47,050	243,200
Performance payments (Note 2)	344,498	340,000
Incentive plans	84,172	81,387
Purchase of minority interests (Note 13)	482,297	1,840,000

Note Seven

Stock Options

Under the company's 1975 stock option plan, options to purchase up to 1,200,000 shares of the company's common stock may be granted to officers and key employees. Options for a total of 47,050 shares are available for grant under this plan, which expires on August 31, 1980. The options may be granted subject to approval of the Compensation Committee of the Board of Directors, at a price of not less than 100% of the fair market value on the date the option is granted. Options now outstanding include some granted under a previous stock option plan which has expired and under which no further options may be granted. Both plans provide for termination of options at either five or ten years after date of grant.

The plan also permits the discretionary granting of stock appreciation rights (SAR's) in tandem with some options granted. Upon exercise of a SAR, the option is cancelled and the holder receives in stock or cash an amount equal to the appreciation between the option price and the market value of the stock on the date of exercise. This amount may not exceed the option price. On May 27, 1979, there were 390,760 stock options outstanding with associated SARs at an average option price of $28.30.

General Mills, Inc., and Subsidiaries
Notes to Consolidated Financial Statements, Continued

Note Seven
Continued

Information on stock options is shown in the following table:

	Shares	Average Per Share Option Price	Average Per Share Fair Market Value	Total Fair Market Value (In Millions)
Granted:				
1978	367,700	$27.87	$27.87	$10.2(a)
1979	223,600	26.30	26.30	5.9(a)
Became exercisable:				
1978	229,589	29.68	27.97	6.4(b)
1979	313,068	29.50	26.27	8.2(b)
Exercised:				
1978	27,553	26.90	29.58	0.8(c)
1979	14,263	24.87	30.56	0.4(c)
Expired:				
1978	134,350	28.87	—	—
1979	35,567	29.08	—	—
Outstanding at year-end:				
1978—to 425 officers and employees	1,562,892	28.74	28.74	44.9(a)
1979—to 411 officers and employees	1,736,662	28.45	28.45	49.4(a)

(a) At date of grant.   (b) At date exercisable.   (c) At date exercised.

Note Eight

Employees' Retirement Plans

The company and many of its subsidiaries have retirement plans covering most domestic and some foreign employees. Most plans provide for retirement with benefits based on length of service and the employee's earnings (defined-benefit plans). A few plans provide for benefits based on accumulated contributions and investment income (defined-contribution plans).

The following aggregated information on the company's pension plans is based on the latest actuarial estimates which are usually made as of the first day of the calendar year in which the fiscal year ends.

(In Millions)	1979	1978
Present value of participants' benefits:		
Vested	$270	$230
Non-vested	12	14
Total	$282	$244
Market value of assets in trust funds and balance sheet accruals	$248	$224
Unfunded vested benefits	$ 33	$ 21

Note Nine

Profit-sharing Plans

General Mills and certain of its subsidiaries have profit-sharing plans which function as incentives. These plans cover key individuals who have the greatest opportunity to contribute to current earnings and successful future operations.

The awards under these plans generally depend on profit performance in relation to pre-established goals, and are primarily available in cash shortly after year-end. These plans and payments are approved by the Board of Directors upon recommendation of the Compensation Committee. This committee consists of Directors who are not members of General Mills' management. The profit-sharing distribution was $5.1 million in fiscal 1979 and $4.9 million in fiscal 1978.

Note Ten

Taxes on Income

The provision for taxes on income from continuing operations is made up of the following:

(In Millions)	Fiscal Year	
	1979	1978
Federal taxes	$ 80.5	$103.3
U.S. investment tax credit ..	(7.1)	(6.8)
	73.4	96.5
State and local taxes	13.6	13.6
Foreign taxes	18.7	9.2
Deferred taxes	11.2	(2.9)
Total taxes on income..	$116.9	$116.4

The deferred taxes above result from timing differences in the recognition of revenue and expense for tax and financial statement purposes. The tax effects of these differences are as follows:

(In Millions)	Fiscal Year	
	1979	1978
Depreciation	$ 4.7	$ 3.8
Other	6.5	(6.7)
Total deferred taxes ..	$ 11.2	$ (2.9)

Effective as of January 1, 1979, the statutory U.S. Federal income tax rate was reduced from 48% to 46%. The portion of this reduction applicable to 1979 is included in the following table which reconciles the United States statutory tax rates with the effective rates:

	Fiscal Year	
	1979	1978
U.S. statutory rate..........	47.2%	48.0%
Investment tax credit	(2.7)	(2.8)
State and local income taxes, net of Federal tax benefits	2.7	2.9
Tax credit from termination of a business (note 15) ...	(3.8)	—
Other	.9	(.6)
Effective income tax rate	44.3%	47.5%

Unremitted earnings of foreign operations amounting to $77.2 million are expected by management to be permanently reinvested. Accordingly, no provision has been made for additional foreign or U.S. taxes which would be payable if such earnings were to be remitted to the parent company as dividends. Provision has been made for additional taxes on undistributed earnings in excess of this amount. These additional taxes were not material in either fiscal 1979 or 1978.

Note Eleven

Leases

Total rent expense was $33.9 million in fiscal 1979 and $28.9 million in fiscal 1978. Some leases require payment of property taxes, insurance and maintenance costs in addition to the rent payments. Contingent and escalation rent in excess of minimum rent payments totaled approximately $2.0 million in fiscal 1979 and $2.4 million in fiscal 1978. Sublease income netted in rent expense was insignificant.

An analysis of rent expense and non-cancellable future lease commitments, by type of property leased, follows:

(In Millions)	Rent Expense Fiscal Year 1979	Non-Cancellable Lease Commitments						
		1980	1981	1982	1983	1984	After 1984	Total
Retail and restaurant space	$10.5	$10.2	$10.0	$ 9.7	$ 9.2	$ 8.6	$54.1	$101.8
Office space	5.9	5.0	4.1	3.5	3.1	2.8	8.7	27.2
Computers	5.6	2.8	2.3	1.7	1.0	.1	—	7.9
Warehousing	4.5	2.3	1.8	1.2	.8	.5	1.0	7.6
All other	7.4	2.3	2.1	1.6	1.2	1.0	4.2	12.4
Total	$33.9	$22.6	$20.3	$17.7	$15.3	$13.0	$68.0	$156.9

The present value of future lease commitments, as of May 27, 1979, was approximately $100 million.

General Mills, Inc., and Subsidiaries
Notes to Consolidated Financial Statements, Continued

Note Twelve

Sale of Smiths Food Group (U.K.) and Specialty Chemicals Operations

Effective January 1, 1979, General Mills, Inc., sold the Smiths Food Group (U.K.) operations to Associated Biscuit Manufacturers (U.K.) for $30 million cash. A pretax gain of $4.4 million ($.05 per share) on the sale is included as a reduction of selling, general and administrative expenses in the consolidated statements of income. The Smiths Food Group (U.K.) operations reported sales through the date of disposition of $97 million in fiscal 1979; and

$118 million for 12 months in fiscal 1978.

On August 31, 1977, General Mills, Inc., sold its Specialty Chemicals operations to Henkel KGaA, a West German company. Sales proceeds were $71.8 million in cash plus a $22.9 million eight-year note in exchange for intercorporate debt. The $5.2 million after-tax gain on the sale is reflected in the consolidated statements of income as a part of results from discontinued Specialty Chemicals operations.

Note Thirteen

Other Commitments

At May 27, 1979, authorized but unexpended appropriations for property additions and improvements were $101.4 million.

In addition, there are options outstanding to purchase the remaining minority interests of some partially-owned companies. The options could have a maximum cost to General Mills of up to $16.1 million, the major portion of which would be payable with shares of common stock. In general, the option contracts provide for payments which are dependent up-

on average annual growth rates in after-tax earnings. The main option periods run from 1979 to 1985. In addition to these minority interests, which may be purchased at General Mills' option, some minority interests have the right during the same time period to require General Mills to purchase their interests, at an estimated cost of up to $17.1 million.

See Note 2 for additional performance earnings payments which may become due in the future.

Note Fourteen

Litigation and Claims

In management's opinion, all claims or litigation pending at May 27, 1979, which could have a significant effect on the consolidated financial position of General Mills, Inc., and its subsidiaries have been provided for in the accounts. The litigation with the Federal Trade Commission (FTC) is discussed below because of the significance of the company's cereal business.

In 1972, the FTC issued a complaint against General Mills, Inc., Kellogg Co., General Foods Corporation and the Quaker Oats Company, alleging that the four companies share an illegal monopoly of the ready-to-eat cereal industry. The FTC seeks relief in the forms of divestiture of certain cereal-producing assets, licensing of cereal brands and prohibitions of certain practices and future acquisitions in the cereal industry. The four companies have denied the allegations. An FTC administrative law judge started hearing testimony in April,

1976. On February 24, 1978, the administrative law judge issued an order dismissing the complaint as to the Quaker Oats Company. In the spring of 1978, the FTC completed its presentation, and the companies commenced their case. Before the completion of the defendants' case, the administrative law judge retired from government service. A new administrative law judge was appointed who ruled on May 24, 1979, that the case will be resumed without any prior testimony being reheard. The judge's ultimate findings will be subject to review by the FTC. Any adverse decision by the FTC will then be subject to further review in U.S. Federal courts. The company expects the matter to take several years and involve costly litigation. In the opinion of General Mills' General Counsel, the company's ready-to-eat cereal activities do not violate existing anti-trust laws. The company will continue to contest the complaint vigorously.

Note Fifteen

Quarterly Data (unaudited)

Summarized quarterly data for fiscal 1979 and 1978 are as follows:

(In millions, except per share and market price amounts.)	Three Months Ended			
	August	November	February	May
Fiscal 1979				
Sales	$906.6	1,094.6	846.9	896.9
Gross profit (a)	$344.5	424.3	315.1	324.8
Net earnings	$ 43.2	50.8	22.7	30.3
Net earnings per share	$ .86	1.01	.45	.60
Dividends per share	$ .25	.29	.29	.29
Market price of common stock:				
High	$ 34⅛	31⅞	30⅜	26⅞
Low	$ 29¼	28⅜	25¾	24
Fiscal 1978				
Sales	$764.2	928.9	742.9	807.0
Gross profit (a)	$300.7	361.6	276.7	288.7
Earnings from continuing operations .	$ 37.5	43.9	25.4	22.0
Net earnings	$ 39.3	49.1	25.4	22.0
Continuing operations,				
earnings per share	$ .75	.88	.51	.44
Net earnings per share	$ .79	.98	.51	.44
Dividends per share	$ .22	.25	.25	.25
Market price of common stock:				
High	$ 31	31¼	31⅜	31½
Low	$ 26¼	26⅞	27	26⅝

(a) Before charges for depreciation and retirement costs.

During the second quarter of fiscal 1979, the Parker Brothers Division voluntarily recalled all of its Riviton construction toys because of two accidental deaths associated with the misuse of the product. The pre-tax cost of the recall was $8.9 million, of which $8.3 was recorded in the second quarter and the balance in the fourth quarter.

During the third quarter of fiscal 1979, company results were adversely affected by a $17.5 million pre-tax loss at Ship 'n Shore, an apparel subsidiary acquired in September of 1977. The principal reasons were: (1) heavy returns of fall and holiday merchandise due to production problems with resultant late shipments to retailers and (2) major valuation adjustments revealed in an inventory taken in the third quarter. It is management's opinion that these problems at Ship 'n Shore, which were recorded in the third quarter, are of a non-recurring nature.

The fourth quarter of fiscal 1979 includes a $8.5 million after-tax benefit from the company's termination of its Kimberly Division women's apparel business. The business was acquired in fiscal 1973 in a pooling of interests transaction. The $3.2 million pre-tax loss with a normal tax benefit of $1.7 million is more than offset by a $10.0 million tax credit. The tax credit results from a difference between the book accounting and tax basis of the Kimberly investment, created in the pooling of interests transaction.

See Note 12 for a description of the impact of the sale of Smiths (U.K.) in the third quarter of fiscal 1979 and the sale of the company's Specialty Chemicals operations in the first quarter of fiscal 1978.

General Mills, Inc., and Subsidiaries
Notes to Consolidated Financial Statements, Continued

Note Sixteen

Segment Information

General Mills classifies its operations into five major product segments — Food Processing; Restaurant Activities; Creative Products; Fashion Activities; and Specialty Retailing and Other. These segments are similar to those which have been reported in prior years as "Major Product Groups" except that Fashion Activities was previously reported as part of Apparel, Accessories, Specialty Retailing and Other; and Crafts, Games and Toys has been renamed Creative Products.

Data for General Mills' product segments are shown below. Both transfers between segments and export sales are immaterial. Corporate expenses include interest expense, profit sharing and general corporate expenses. Corporate assets consist mainly of cash, time deposits, marketable securities and investments in unconsolidated companies.

(In Millions)	Food Processing	Restaurant Activities	Creative Products	Fashion Activities	Specialty Retailing and Other	General Corporate Items	Consolidated Total
Fiscal 1979							
Sales	$2,062.4	436.3	609.5	360.4	276.4	—	3,745.0
Operating profits	$ 193.2	42.6	59.7	20.3	15.7	(67.6)	263.9
Identifiable assets	$ 686.5	217.3	387.5	241.2	135.1	167.6	1,835.2
Capital expenditures . . .	$ 68.9	31.0	25.9	9.8	13.0	5.5	154.1
Depreciation expense . .	$ 31.9	11.9	18.8	3.7	3.2	1.0	70.5
Fiscal 1978							
Sales	$1,861.6	354.9	492.3	298.1	236.1	—	3,243.0
Operating profits	$ 169.0	35.9	62.7	39.5	8.5	(70.4)	245.2
Identifiable assets	$ 673.8	193.6	337.2	202.0	127.7	78.4	1,612.7
Capital expenditures	$ 58.2	34.5	26.0	10.2	5.0	6.6(a)	140.5
Depreciation expense . . .	$ 26.6	8.7	13.3	2.8	2.7	2.0	56.1

(a) Includes $1.8 relating to the discontinued Specialty Chemicals operations.

A summary of sales, profits and indentifiable assets, by geographic areas in which the company operates, is shown below. Transfers between areas are not material.

(In Millions)	U.S.A.	Other Western Hemisphere	Europe	Other	Unallocated Corporate Items	Consolidated Total
Fiscal 1979						
Sales	$3,187.5	161.8	377.8	17.9	—	3,745.0
Operating profits	$ 299.4	16.6	14.2(a)	1.3	(67.6)	263.9
Identifiable assets . . .	$1,384.2	97.6	172.6	13.2	167.6	1,835.2
Fiscal 1978						
Sales	$2,735.6	152.8	339.0	15.6	—	3,243.0
Operating profits	$ 286.5	11.7	16.1	1.3	(70.4)	245.2
Identifiable assets	$1,245.7	90.5	191.1	7.0	78.4	1,612.7

(a) Includes the $4.4 gain on the sale of Smiths U.K. (see Note 12).

Note Seventeen

Replacement Cost Information (unaudited)

Inflation in recent years has resulted in replacement costs of inventories, fixed assets and related depreciation expense that are generally greater than the historical costs of the assets reported in the financial statements. The Securities and Exchange Commission requires that Form 10-K annual reports contain replacement cost information for fixed assets, inventories, cost of sales and depreciation expenses. Replacement cost of cost of goods sold generally approximates the amounts shown in the financial statements. Stockholders wishing to obtain replacement cost information should request a copy of Form 10-K in accordance with the instructions on page 45.

Accountants' Report

PEAT, MARWICK, MITCHELL & CO.
CERTIFIED PUBLIC ACCOUNTANTS
1700 IDS CENTER
MINNEAPOLIS, MINNESOTA 55402

The Stockholders and the Board of Directors
General Mills, Inc.:

We have examined the consolidated balance sheets of General Mills, Inc. and subsidiaries as of May 27, 1979 and May 28, 1978 and the related consolidated statements of income, retained earnings and changes in financial position for the fiscal years then ended. Our examinations were made in accordance with generally accepted auditing standards, and accordingly included such tests of the accounting records and such other auditing procedures as we considered necessary in the circumstances.

In our opinion, the aforementioned consolidated financial statements present fairly the financial position of General Mills, Inc. and subsidiaries at May 27, 1979 and May 28, 1978 and the results of their operations and the changes in their financial position for the fiscal years then ended, in conformity with generally accepted accounting principles applied on a consistent basis.

July 20, 1979

Peat, Marwick, Mitchell & Co.

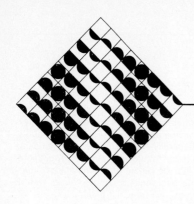

Appendix C

Index of References to APB and FASB Pronouncements

The following list of pronouncements by the Accounting Principles Board and the Financial Accounting Standards Board (as of December, 1980) is provided to give students an overview of the standards issued since 1962 and to reference these standards to the relevant chapters in this book. Earlier pronouncements by the Committee on Accounting Procedure of the AICPA have been largely superseded or amended. In those cases where no change has been made by subsequent standard-setting bodies, the earlier pronouncements are still accepted as official.

ACCOUNTING PRINCIPLES BOARD OPINIONS

Date Issued	Opinion Number	Title	Chapters to Which References Most Applicable
November, 1962	1	*New Depreciation Guidelines and Rules*	11
December, 1962	2	*Accounting for the "Investment Credit"; addendum to Opinion No. 2 — Accounting Principles for Regulated Industries*	15
October, 1963	3	*The Statement of Source and Application of Funds*	19
March, 1964	4	*Accounting for the "Investment Credit"*	15
September, 1964	5	*Reporting of Leases in Financial Statements of Lessee*	N/A
October, 1965	6	*Status of Accounting Research Bulletins*	7, 16
May, 1966	7	*Accounting for Leases in Financial Statements of Lessors*	N/A
November, 1966	8	*Accounting for the Cost of Pension Plans*	N/A
December, 1966	9	*Reporting the Results of Operations*	4
December, 1966	10	*Omnibus Opinion — 1966*	15
December, 1967	11	*Accounting for Income Taxes*	15
December, 1967	12	*Omnibus Opinion — 1967*	11
March, 1969	13	*Amending Paragraph 6 of APB Opinion No. 9, Application to Commercial Banks*	N/A
March, 1969	14	*Accounting for Convertible Debt and Debt Issued with Stock Purchase Warrants*	14, 16
May, 1969	15	*Earnings per Share*	21
August, 1970	16	*Business Combinations*	N/A
August, 1970	17	*Intangible Assets*	10, 11

APB OPINIONS (continued)

Date Issued	Opinion Number	Title	Chapters to Which References Most Applicable
March, 1971	18	*The Equity Method of Accounting for Investments in Common Stock*	12
March, 1971	19	*Reporting Changes in Financial Position*	19
July, 1971	20	*Accounting Changes*	18
August, 1971	21	*Interest on Receivables and Payables*	6, 13
April, 1972	22	*Disclosure of Accounting Policies*	5
April, 1972	23	*Accounting for Income Taxes — Special Areas*	15
April, 1972	24	*Accounting for Income Taxes — Investments in Common Stock Accounted for by the Equity Method (Other than Subsidiaries and Corporate Joint Ventures)*	15
October, 1972	25	*Accounting for Stock Issued to Employees*	16, 21
October, 1972	26	*Early Extinguishment of Debt*	14
November, 1972	27	*Accounting for Lease Transactions by Manufacturer or Dealer Lessors*	N/A
May, 1973	28	*Interim Financial Reporting*	18
May, 1973	29	*Accounting for Nonmonetary Transactions*	10, 12, 14
June, 1973	30	*Reporting the Results of Operations*	18
June, 1973	31	*Disclosure of Lease Commitments by Lessees*	N/A

ACCOUNTING PRINCIPLES BOARD STATEMENTS

Date Issued	Statement Number	Title	Chapters to Which References Most Applicable
April, 1962	1	*Statement by the Accounting Principles Board* (on Accounting Research Studies Nos. 1 and 3)	3
September, 1967	2	*Disclosure of Supplemental Financial Information by Diversified Companies*	18
June, 1969	3	*Financial Statements Restated for General Price-Level Changes*	20
October, 1970	4	*Basic Concepts and Accounting Principles Underlying Financial Statements of Business Enterprises*	3

FINANCIAL ACCOUNTING STANDARDS BOARD STATEMENTS OF FINANCIAL ACCOUNTING STANDARDS

Date Issued	Statement Number	Title	Chapters to Which References Most Applicable
December, 1973	1	*Disclosure of Foreign Currency Translation Information*	N/A
October, 1974	2	*Accounting for Research and Development Costs*	10
December, 1974	3	*Reporting Accounting Changes in Interim Financial Statements*	18

FASB STATEMENTS (continued)

Date Issued	Statement Number	Title	Chapters to Which References Most Applicable
March, 1975	4	*Reporting Gains and Losses from Extinguishment of Debt*	14, 18
March, 1975	5	*Accounting for Contingencies*	13
May, 1975	6	*Classification of Short-Term Obligations Expected to be Refinanced*	14
June, 1975	7	*Accounting and Reporting by Development Stage Enterprises*	10
October, 1975	8	*Accounting for the Translation of Foreign Currency Transactions and Foreign Currency Financial Statements*	N/A
October, 1975	9	*Accounting for Income Taxes — Oil and Gas Producing Companies*	N/A
October, 1975	10	*Extension of "Grandfather" Provisions for Business Combinations*	N/A
December, 1975	11	*Accounting for Contingencies — Transition Method*	13
December, 1975	12	*Accounting for Certain Marketable Securities*	6, 12
November, 1976	13	*Accounting for Leases*	N/A
December, 1976	14	*Financial Reporting for Segments of a Business Enterprise*	18
June, 1977	15	*Accounting by Debtors and Creditors for Troubled Debt Restructurings*	N/A
June, 1977	16	*Prior Period Adjustments*	17
November, 1977	17	*Accounting for Leases – Initial Direct Costs*	N/A
November, 1977	18	*Financial Reporting for Segments of a Business Enterprise — Interim Financial Statements*	18
December, 1977	19	*Financial Accounting and Reporting by Oil and Gas Producing Companies*	N/A
December, 1977	20	*Accounting for Forward Exchange Contracts*	N/A
April, 1978	21	*Suspension of the Reporting of Earnings per Share and Segment Information by Nonpublic Enterprises*	18, 21
June, 1978	22	*Changes in the Provisions of Lease Agreements Resulting from Refundings of Tax-Exempt Debt*	N/A
August, 1978	23	*Inception of the Lease*	N/A
December, 1978	24	*Reporting Segment Information in Financial Statements That Are Presented in Another Enterprise's Financial Report*	18
February, 1979	25	*Suspension of Certain Accounting Requirements for Oil and Gas Producing Companies*	N/A
April, 1979	26	*Profit Recognition on Sales-Type Leases of Real Estate*	N/A
May, 1979	27	*Classification of Renewals or Extensions of Existing Sales-Type or Direct Financing Leases*	N/A
May, 1979	28	*Accounting for Sales with Leasebacks*	N/A
June, 1979	29	*Determining Contingent Rentals*	N/A
August, 1979	30	*Disclosure of Information About Major Customers*	18
September, 1979	31	*Accounting for Tax Benefits Related to U.K. Tax Legislation Concerning Stock Relief*	N/A

FASB STATEMENTS (continued)

Date Issued	Statement Number	Title	Chapters to Which References Most Applicable
September, 1979	32	*Specialized Accounting and Reporting Principles and Practices in AICPA Statements of Position and Guides on Accounting and Auditing Matters*	N/A
September, 1979	33	*Financial Reporting and Changing Prices*	20
October, 1979	34	*Capitalization of Interest Cost*	10
March, 1980	35	*Accounting and Reporting by Defined Benefit Pension Plans*	N/A
May, 1980	36	*Disclosure of Pension Information*	N/A
July, 1980	37	*Balance Sheet Classification of Deferred Income Taxes*	15
September, 1980	38	*Accounting for Preacquisition Contingencies of Purchased Enterprises*	N/A
October, 1980	39	*Financial Reporting and Changing Prices: Specialized Assets — Mining and Oil and Gas*	20
November, 1980	40	*Financial Reporting and Changing Prices: Specialized Assets — Timberlands and Growing Timber*	20
November, 1980	41	*Financial Reporting and Changing Prices: Specialized Assets — Income-Producing Real Estate*	20
November, 1980	42	*Determining Materiality for Capitalization of Interest Cost*	10
November, 1980	43	*Accounting for Compensated Absences*	13

FINANCIAL ACCOUNTING STANDARDS BOARD STATEMENTS OF FINANCIAL ACCOUNTING CONCEPTS

Date Issued	Statement Number	Title	Chapters to Which References Most Applicable
November, 1978	1	*Objectives of Financial Reporting by Business Enterprises*	3
May, 1980	2	*Qualitative Characteristics of Accounting Information*	3
December, 1980	3	*Elements of Financial Statements of Business Enterprises*	3, 4, 5, 13
December, 1980	4	*Objectives of Financial Reporting by Nonbusiness Organizations*	3

FINANCIAL ACCOUNTING STANDARDS BOARD EXPOSURE DRAFTS (Proposed Statements of Standards)

Date Issued	Title	Chapters to Which References Most Applicable
August, 1980	*Foreign Currency Translation*	N/A
October, 1980	*Accounting for Intangible Assets of Motor Carriers*	N/A

(Proposed Statements of Standards, continued)

November, 1980	*Disclosure of Interest Rate Futures Contracts and Forward and Standby Contracts*	N/A
November, 1980	*Disclosure of Obligations*	13

FINANCIAL ACCOUNTING STANDARDS BOARD DISCUSSION MEMORANDUMS AND INVITATIONS TO COMMENT

Date Issued	Title	Chapters to Which References Most Applicable
July, 1979	*Reporting Earnings*	3
December, 1979	*Effect of Rate Regulation on Accounting for Regulated Enterprises*	N/A
May, 1980	*Financial Statements and Other Means of Financial Reporting*	3

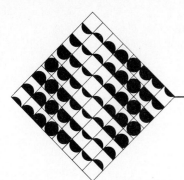

Index